Engaging Older Adults with Modern Technology:

Internet Use and Information Access Needs

Robert Z. Zheng
University of Utah, USA

Robert D. Hill
University of Utah, USA

Michael K. Gardner
University of Utah, USA

Information Science
REFERENCE

Managing Director:	Lindsay Johnston
Senior Editorial Director:	Heather A. Probst
Book Production Manager:	Sean Woznicki
Development Manager:	Joel Gamon
Development Editor:	Myla Merkel
Assistant Acquisitions Editor:	Kayla Wolfe
Typesetter:	Milan Vracarich, Jr.
Cover Design:	Nick Newcomer

Published in the United States of America by
Information Science Reference (an imprint of IGI Global)
701 E. Chocolate Avenue
Hershey PA 17033
Tel: 717-533-8845
Fax: 717-533-8661
E-mail: cust@igi-global.com
Web site: http://www.igi-global.com

Library of Congress Cataloging-in-Publication Data

Engaging older adults with modern technology : Internet use and information access needs / Robert Z. Zheng, Robert D. Hill and Michael K. Gardner,
editors.
    p. cm.
 Includes bibliographical references and index.
 Summary: "This book takes a structured approach to the research in aging and digital technology in which older adults' use of internet and other forms of digital technologies is studied through the lenses of cognitive functioning, motivation, and affordability of new technology"--Provided by publisher.
  ISBN 978-1-4666-1966-1 (hbk.) -- ISBN 978-1-4666-1967-8 (ebook) -- ISBN 978-1-4666-1968-5 (print & perpetual access) 1. Older people--Psychology. 2. Human-computer interaction. 3. Cognition--Age factors. 4. Internet and older people. 5. Technology and older people. 6. Adult learning. I. Zheng, Robert. II. Hill, Robert D. III. Gardner, Michael K.
 BF724.8.E54 2013
 155.6'713--dc23
                                            2012009819

British Cataloguing in Publication Data
A Cataloguing in Publication record for this book is available from the British Library.

All work contributed to this book is new, previously-unpublished material. The views expressed in this book are those of the authors, but not necessarily of the publisher.

Table of Contents

Section 1
Technology and Aging: Cognitive Perspectives

Section 2
Design and Develop Effective Technology for Older Adults

Section 3
Practical Application of Technology for Older Adults

Detailed Table of Contents

Section 1
Technology and Aging: Cognitive Perspectives

Chapter 1

    Christopher A. Was, Kent State University, USA
    Dan J. Woltz, University of Utah, USA

This chapter reviews the distinctions between explicit memory (i.e., effortful storage and retrieval of information) and implicit memory (i.e., learning and memory that does not require conscious effort) and presents the evidence that implicit memory does not decline at the same rate as explicit memory. The authors discuss the possibility of using implicit memory processes (e.g. procedural memory) to aid explicit memory processes (e.g., declarative memory). Finally, the authors discuss the need and the opportunity to incorporate information and communications technologies into the lives of older adults in order to support memory and learning.

Chapter 2

    Jason M. Watson, University of Utah, USA
    Ann E. Lambert, University of Utah, USA
    Joel M. Cooper, University of Utah, USA
    Istenya V. Boyle, University of Utah, USA
    David L. Strayer, University of Utah, USA

Theories of cognitive aging suggest diminished frontal lobe function and reduced attentional control could contribute to age-related changes in driving a motor vehicle. To address this possibility, the authors investigated the interrelationship among age, attentional control, and driving performance. Using a high-fidelity simulator, the authors measured individual differences in participants' abilities to maintain a prescribed following distance behind a lead vehicle, as well as their reaction time to press a brake pedal when this lead vehicle braked. Consistent with the literature on age-related changes in driving, following distance elongated with increased age, and brake reaction time slowed. Furthermore, regression analyses revealed the increase in following distance and the slowing in brake reaction time both co-varied with age deficits in attentional control. These results provide a novel demonstration of the inherent value of cognitive theory when applied to naturalistic settings, sharpening our understanding of the relevance of age-related deficits in attentional control for complex, real-world tasks like driving.

Kim Ouwehand, Erasmus University Rotterdam, The Netherlands
Tamara van Gog, Erasmus University Rotterdam, The Netherlands
Fred Paas, Erasmus University Rotterdam, The Netherlands & University of Wollongong, Australia

The present chapter describes the role of gestures in instructional design from a cognitive load theory perspective, addressing in particular how this might benefit aging adults. Healthy older adults have to cope with several cognitive changes related to their working memory, such as a decline in: 1) the ability to deal with interference, 2) cognitive speed in response to unimodal stimuli (e.g. visual information), and 3) the ability to associate and integrate information elements. Cognitive load theory, with its focus on adapting learning formats to the limitations of working memory, provides a promising framework to address learning in older adults. Research inspired by cognitive load theory has shown that attentional cueing can reduce interference during learning, presenting instructions in a multimodal format can make more efficient use of WM stores (both auditory and visual), and the manner of presentation of information can aid integrative learning. Interestingly, studies using gestures in instruction show that gestures accompanying verbal information improve learning in similar ways. In the present chapter, the authors discuss possibilities of gestures to improve multimedia learning in older adults using some important guidelines proposed by cognitive load theory.

Daniel Morrow, University of Illinois at Urbana-Champaign, USA
Jessie Chin, University of Illinois at Urbana-Champaign, USA

This chapter explores the role of technology in supporting collaboration between health care providers and older adults. The authors focus on two technologies that help link patients to their providers by giving them access to health information and services: 1) patient portals to Electronic Health Records, and 2) Personal Health Record systems. Theories of distributed cognition and common ground are used to frame a review of the small but growing body of research that investigates which older adults use or do not use these technologies, and why. The findings, while sparse, suggest that older adults with lower levels of health literacy stand to benefit the most from this technology, but they tend to have fewer cognitive, literacy, and other psychosocial resources needed to take advantage of the technology. This discrepancy is due in part to systems that are not designed with older adults' needs and abilities in mind. The authors conclude with recommendations for improving the use of these tools to support patient/ provider collaboration by making them easier to use, and by integrating them with other communication media to support the broader context of the patient/provider relationship.

Section 2
Design and Develop Effective Technology for Older Adults

Chapter 5

Renae Low, The University of New South Wales, Australia
Putai Jin, The University of New South Wales, Australia
John Sweller, The University of New South Wales, Australia

The purpose of this chapter is to consider the aged subpopulation's needs and their ability to use digital technology from the perspectives of human cognitive architecture and the principles of instructional design guided by cognitive load theory. The chapter focuses on the following critical issues: a) the evolution and formation of human cognitive architecture, b) cognitive functioning as influenced by aging, c) compatibility between elderly people's available mental resources and the cognitive requirements of digital equipment, and d) guidelines for human-computer multimedia interactions derived from the accumulated experimental evidence on effective instructional design and delivery.

Chapter 6

Marita A. O'Brien, University of Alabama in Huntsville, USA
Wendy A. Rogers, Georgia Institute of Technology, USA

This chapter describes best practices and challenges for enabling older adults to adopt everyday technologies transformed by technology innovations. First, the authors define everyday technologies and known factors influencing successful use including environmental support and context of use. Then, the authors discuss issues and challenges of design for everyday technologies and summarize the factors that influence everyday technology use in a conceptual diagram. The authors also present recommendations for specific constituents that may improve technology adoption by older adults. Lastly, the authors discuss future opportunities for enhancing everyday technology use with good design, useful support, and appropriate innovations.

Chapter 7

Yiwei Chen, Bowling Green State University, USA
Bob D. Lee, Bowling Green State University, USA
Robert M. Kirk, Bowling Green State University, USA

The primary purpose of this chapter is to use a Lifespan Developmental Perspective to examine both the constraints and the opportunities of Internet use among older adults. Given age-related changes in physical, cognitive, and socio-emotional processes, older adults may encounter different constraints in Internet use from younger adults. The Selective Optimization with Compensation Model is used to explore opportunities for older adults in using the Internet to improve quality of life. Future product designs and training programs should take into account older adults' physical and cognitive limitations, as well as their socio-emotional needs. It is also recommended that social policies should help older adults overcome these constraints in order to reduce the age-related digital divide and promote quality of life for older adults.

Chapter 8

This chapter examines the cognitive constraints related to older people in learning, particularly in e-learning and proposes a new design approach, which (1) assists instructional designers and Web development in identifying issues related to older people's involvement in e-learning, (2) helps reduce the mental load in designing and developing e-learning for older people, and (3) uses heuristics to systematically support the designers in making decisions about meeting the needs of the older people in their learning and searching for information online.

Section 3
Practical Application of Technology for Older Adults

Chapter 9

This chapter focuses on the impact of computer and internet use on several aspects of quality of life and autonomy of older adults. It is based on an intervention program that included concise computer training and the use of a computer and the Internet for twelve months. The results of this randomized controlled study showed no effects, neither positive nor negative, of computer and internet use on cognitive functioning, autonomy, well-being and social network, the use of everyday technological devices, and subjective physical functioning. Overall, it was concluded that computer and Internet usage by healthy older adults is a safe activity, albeit with no robust advantage for cognitive capacity in healthy older adults.

Chapter 10

This chapter reviews the episodic memory difficulties typically encountered by older adults. It presents data that demonstrates that mnemonic interventions can improve episodic memory in the elderly, though such improvements often do not transfer broadly and do not result in improvements in the area of subjective memory assessment. It then presents three approaches to improving episodic memory for numeric information, each based upon a different approach. These approaches demonstrate: (a) that a mnemonic targeted at numeric information can improve number recall; (b) that self-generated strategies can improve recall at nearly the same level as a targeted mnemonic; and (c) that episodic memory can be converted into procedural memory, though this approach did not demonstrate improved episodic memory performance. Future directions for memory remediation are discussed, based upon research findings to date.

Chapter 11

This chapter examines older adults' adoption and experience of using Information and Communication Technologies (ICT), in particular the Internet. The main arguments are based on the experiences of a group of older people, all already users of ICT, in a collaborative, relaxed, and self-managing environment—the virtual campus of the Universitat Oberta de Catalunya (an online university). Older adults adopt ICT in relation to a personal project, sometimes as a tool to achieve it, so ICT use has to be done on their own initiative, with a positive attitude, and under their control. Based on the Selective Optimization and Compensation (SOC) theory of adaptation processes, the authors believe that introducing ICT through selection and optimization strategies can be a successful means of assuring effective adoption of these technologies.

Chapter 12

e-Health has become a major focus for research in healthcare, with significant funding and political support at an international level. Older people stand to benefit more than others, as e-Health aims to facilitate provision of care at a distance and promote independent living for as long as possible. However, barriers remain, including an immature evidence-base, questions about risk and safety, and variable rates of uptake in this population. This chapter explores these issues and reviews the literature on e-Health for older adults. Successful clinical trials are identified, and the e-CAALYX project is described in detail as a case study. e-Health presents many exciting opportunities but needs further development and guidance.

Chapter 13

This chapter presents a guided framework for describing Remote Care Delivery Technologies (RCDT) in the processes of healthcare management among older patients diagnosed with chronic disease. To date, a process framework for the application of RCDT for chronic health conditions has not been systematically described, although much of the literature in RCDT, including telemedicine and telehealth, has focused on intervening with issues that involve monitoring of chronic disease symptoms and the coordination of ongoing care. To elucidate how this process framework operates in managing chronic health conditions examples are provided from the published literature to clarify and differentiate each of the steps of this framework. A final section describes guidelines informed by this framework for providing RCDT in the management of chronic disease.

Candice M. Daniel, VA Salt Lake City Health Care System, USA

Bret Hicken, VA Salt Lake City Health Care System, USA & University of Utah, USA

Marilyn Luptak, University of Utah, USA

Marren Grant, VA Salt Lake City Health Care System, USA

Randall Rupper, VA Salt Lake City Geriatric Research, Education, and Clinical Center, USA
   & University of Utah, USA

Caregivers of persons with dementia experience higher levels of anxiety, depressive symptoms, and other mental health problems, as well as increased rates of hypertension, cardiovascular disease, and premature mortality compared to their non-caregiving peers. They also face significant challenges in accessing support from local, state, and VA resources. Several empirically supported treatments have been developed to assist these caregivers. However, accessing these interventions can be difficult given the extent and demand of their caregiving duties. To address this problem, the authors developed a psycho-educational caregiver intervention for use with in-home digital technology that is currently underway at three Veteran's Health Affairs (VA) health care centers. The chapter provides: 1) a brief summary of the background and rationale for intervention development; 2) an overview of the project; and 3) the issues and lessons learned from developing interventions using digital technology for use with older adults.

Preface

Improvements in health care and life style choices, as well as changes in family reproductive patterns, have led to a dramatic increase in the world's older population (Grimes, Hough, Mazur, & Singorella, 2010). According to the World Health Organization (2010), over one billion people worldwide will reach the age of 60 or older by 2025. An earlier study by Humes (2005) indicates that 71.5 million Americans, which is about 20% of the U.S. population, consider themselves to be senior citizens. This burgeoning senior population has numerous special social, educational, and health needs. According to Dorin (2007), although large numbers of older adults in the United States will be productive in later life, many will be searching for new ways to contribute to the social good as well. Furlong (1997) refers to this extended period of active adulthood as the "Third Age," and Hough (2004) has characterized this stage of later adult development as an important period of learning and personal development.

The productivity and contributions of older adults can by significantly enhanced through the use of modern technology, but what is the current state of technology use among the elderly? Research suggests that seniors aged 65 and older are the fastest growing age group among online users, increasing by 25% yearly (Nielsen-NetRatings, 2003; cited from Bertera, et al., 2007). Evidence shows that engaging seniors in online activities enhances their life satisfaction (Dorin, 2007), self-efficacy (Bertera, et al., 2007), motivation (Hardt & Hollis-Sawyer, 2007), and knowledge and awareness of health-related prevention (Taha, Sharit, & Czaja, 2009). Clearly, technology use among older adults is a quickly growing phenomenon, with beneficial outcomes for those who choose to participate.

In the last ten years, the study of Internet use among older adult has emerged as a specific area of interest, and is gaining importance both in its contribution to theory and practice. Researchers have investigated: (1) the behaviors of seniors with regard to information search (Hardt & Hollis-Sawyer, 2007), (2) seniors attitudes toward the Internet (Trentin, 2004; Taha, et al., 2009), and (3) older individuals use of the Internet to obtain information on personal and health issues (Chen & Persson, 2002; Cresci, Yarandi, & Morrell, 2010). Beyond seniors' behavior, instructional designers have engaged in research related to issues of technology use and aging. For instance, cognitive load theory has exerted a strong influence on the design of multimedia instructional materials to be used with older populations (e.g., Paas, Van Gerven, & Tabbers, 2005; Van Gerven, Paas, Van Merriënboer, & Schmidt, 2000, 2002, 2004; Van Gerven, Pass, Van Merriënboer, Hendriks, & Schmidt, 2003). However, despite the rich research on aging individuals and the use of digital technology, there has been a failure to adequately integrate these many approaches and present an organized and coherent picture of the field. In this book, we hope to achieve this goal. In addition, we present an overarching theoretical framework that we hope will serve as an organizing scheme for adult educators, social workers, medical professionals, researchers, and policy makers.

Figure 1. Proposed theoretical framework for technology facilitated learning in older adults

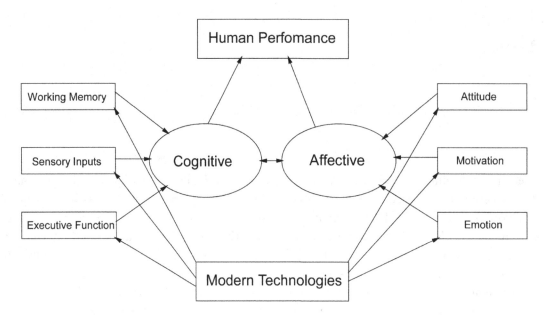

When considering older adults use of the Internet and other digital technologies, we must remember that they experience a predictable set of constraints that are the result of the aging process. Among these constraints are reduced sensory capabilities, a decrease in working memory, and a slowing of processing speed. One way to offset these constraints is to use the capabilities of modern technology to compensate for the deficits that occur as a natural result of aging. To the extent that this is possible, research suggests that improvements in cognitive performance are positively related to the affective aspect of learning (Avci, Yuksel, & Soyer, 2009; Hyland, 2010; Littledyke, 2008). Avci et al. (2009) demonstrated that cognitive and affective changes can be mediated by the learning environment. This was confirmed in an earlier study by Ke (2008), who identified the facilitation role of modern technology in cognitive and affective improvements. Although the aforementioned studies did not focus specifically on aging and technology, the theoretical and practical implications are clear: the human performance of older adults is a function of both cognitive and affective factors. These factors interact, but they can also be influenced by modern technology, which can serve to enhance cognitive capabilities and increase motivation. However, this enhancement requires a clear knowledge of the limitations of the cognitive system of older adults, the factors that serve to motivate older adults, and proven instructional design strategies that can scaffold these existing cognitive and affective systems. In Figure 1, we present our proposed model:

As can be seen from Figure 1, human performance (i.e., learning) is the result of cognitive and affective factors. Cognitive and affective factors themselves interact (e.g., if a person is seeking an important piece of health advice, they may persist even when cognitive limitations make the search difficult). However, these cognitive and affective factors may themselves be influenced by modern technologies. Technologies can help alleviate limitations that may exist in working memory capacity and the ability to receive sensory input. They may also enhance motivation and create positive emotional environments. However, the ability for modern technologies to enhance cognitive and affective factors is strongly influenced by instructional design. Good design results in enhanced cognitive and affective function. Bad design can simply make the limitations that older individuals face worse.

This text will present, for the first time, a structured approach to understanding the research on aging and digital technology. The use of the Internet and other forms of modern technology are studied through the lenses of cognitive function, motivation, and the affordances provided by new technologies. Good principles of instructional design, as well as new ideas on instructional design tailored to the needs older adults, will also be explored. There is a substantial need to integrate knowledge in this area within a single work. We hope that this book will serve that need, and that the preceding theoretical model will help provide an overarching organizing principle when reading the individual contributions presented in this volume.

THE CONTRIBUTION OF THIS BOOK

It has been demonstrated above that a unified theoretical framework in aging and Internet/digital technology use is lacking. This book will: (a) identify the role and function of the Internet and other forms of digital technology in older adult learning, (b) bring together studies in older adult Internet use with a focus on cognitive and affective domains in older adult learning and digital technologies, and (c) bridge the theories with practices in older adults' Internet/digital technology use by focusing on effective design and development of Internet and other digital technologies for older adults' learning. The book will target educators globally with an emphasis on diverse aspects in older adult and Internet learning that includes learner characteristics, cognition, design principles, and applications. Drawing on the authors' own expertise and research, the authors bring together researchers, practitioners, and theorists from institutions of higher education in the United States, Asia, and Europe, and from a variety of disciplines, including teaching and learning, instructional design, computer-human interaction, cognitive psychology, communication, and learning sciences. This book, thus, moves beyond traditional disciplinary and geographical boundaries. It accommodates issues in older adults' use of Internet/digital technologies across disciplines and at all levels.

THE ORGANIZATION OF THIS BOOK

The three sections of this book are organized to maximize the value for the readers as they move from the theoretical to the practical and from a focus on cognition to the design and application of the technology for older adults.

Section 1 presents a theoretical perspective on aging and technology. It contains four chapters that cover a wide range of topics on aging and technology, including cognitive architecture, working memory, gesture visualization, and social collaboration, in the use of technology for older adults.

In Chapter 1, Christopher A. Was of Kent State University and Dan J. Woltz of the University of Utah review the distinctions between explicit memory (i.e., effortful storage and retrieval of information) and implicit memory (i.e., learning and memory that does not require conscious effort) and present the evidence that implicit memory does not decline at the same rate as explicit memory. The authors discuss the possibility of using implicit memory processes (e.g. procedural memory) to aid explicit memory processes (e.g., declarative memory). Finally, the authors discuss the need and the opportunity to incorporate information and communications technologies into the lives of older adults in order to support memory and learning.

In Chapter 2, Jason M. Watson, Ann E. Lambert, Joel M. Cooper, Istenya V. Boyle, and David L. Strayer, all from the University of Utah, and Ann E. Lambert of the University of Virginia focus on attentional control and the behaviors of older adults. Using a high-fidelity simulator, the authors measure individual differences in participants' abilities to maintain a prescribed following distance behind a lead vehicle, as well as their reaction time to press a brake pedal when this lead vehicle brakes. Consistent with the literature on age-related changes in driving, following distance elongates with increased age, and brake reaction time slows. Furthermore, regression analyses reveal the increase in following distance and the slowing in brake reaction time both co-varied with age deficits in attentional control. These results provide a novel demonstration of the inherent value of cognitive theory when applied to naturalistic settings, sharpening our understanding of the relevance of age-related deficits in attentional control for complex, real-world tasks, like driving.

Chapter 3, by Kim Ouwehand, Tamara van Gog, and Fred Paas of Erasmus University Rotterdam, The Netherlands describes the role of gestures in instructional design from a cognitive load theory perspective, addressing, in particular, how this might benefit aging adults. Healthy older adults have to cope with several cognitive changes related to their working memory, such as a decline in: 1) the ability to deal with interference, 2) cognitive speed in response to unimodal stimuli (e.g. visual information), and 3) the ability to associate and integrate information elements. Cognitive load theory, with its focus on adapting learning formats to the limitations of working memory, provides a promising framework to address learning in older adults. Research inspired by cognitive load theory has shown that attentional cueing can reduce interference during learning, presenting instructions in a multimodal format can make more efficient use of WM stores (both auditory and visual), and the manner of presentation of information can aid integrative learning. Interestingly, studies using gestures in instruction show that gestures accompanying verbal information improve learning in similar ways. In the present chapter, the authors discuss the possibility of gestures improving multimedia learning in older adults using some important guidelines proposed by cognitive load theory.

Chapter 4 explores the role of technology in supporting collaboration between health care providers and older adults. Daniel Morrow and Jessie Chin of the University of Illinois discuss two technologies that help link patients to their providers by giving them access to health information and services: 1) patient portals to Electronic Health Records, and 2) Personal Health Record systems. Theories of distributed cognition and common ground are used to frame a review of the small but growing body of research that investigates which older adults use or do not use these technologies, and why. The findings, while sparse, suggest that older adults with lower levels of health literacy stand to benefit the most from this technology, but they tend to have fewer cognitive, literacy, and other psychosocial resources needed to take advantage of the technology. This discrepancy is due in part to systems that are not designed with older adults' needs and abilities in mind. The authors conclude with recommendations for improving the use of these tools to support patient/provider collaboration by making them easier to use and by integrating them with other communication media to support the broader context of the patient/provider relationship.

Section 2 deals with issues of instructional design in aging and technology. The section contains four chapters that introduce instructional design for older adults by considering the effects of cognitive architecture on learning. It explores everyday technologies and known factors influencing the successful use of technology and suggests ways to examine both the constraints and the opportunities of Internet use among older adults, which have significant implications in the design and development of technology for older adults. The section ends with a chapter on designing effective online learning for older people using a heuristic design approach.

Chapter 5 is authored by Renae Low and Putai Jin of the University of New South Wales, Australia, and John Sweller of University of New South Wales, who created the Cognitive Load Theory. The authors examine the aged subpopulation's needs and their ability to use digital technology from the perspectives of human cognitive architecture and the principles of instructional design guided by cognitive load theory. The chapter focuses on the following critical issues: a) the evolution and formation of human cognitive architecture, b) cognitive functioning as influenced by aging, c) compatibility between elderly people's available mental resources and the cognitive requirements of digital equipment, and d) guidelines for human-computer multimedia interactions derived from the accumulated experimental evidence on effective instructional design and delivery.

In Chapter 6, Marita A. O'Brien of the University of Alabama and Wendy A. Rogers of the Georgia Institute of Technology describe best practices and challenges for enabling older adults to adopt everyday technologies transformed by technology innovations. The authors first define everyday technologies and known factors influencing their successful use including environmental support and context of use. Then, the authors discuss issues and challenges of design for everyday technologies and summarize the factors that influence everyday technology use in a conceptual diagram. The authors also present recommendations for specific constituents that may improve technology adoption by older adults. Lastly, the authors discuss future opportunities for enhancing everyday technology use with good design, useful support, and appropriate innovations.

In Chapter 7, Yiwei Chen, Bob D. Lee, and Robert M. Kirk of Bowling Green State University use a Lifespan Developmental Perspective to examine both the constraints and the opportunities of Internet use among older adults. Given age-related changes in physical, cognitive, and socio-emotional processes, older adults may encounter different constraints in Internet use than younger adults. The Selective Optimization with Compensation model is used to explore opportunities for older adults in using the Internet to improve quality of life. The authors suggest that future product designs and training programs should take into account older adults' physical and cognitive limitations, as well as their socio-emotional needs. They also recommend that social policies should help older adults overcome these constraints in order to reduce age-related digital divide and promote quality of life for older adults.

Chapter 8 examines the cognitive constraints related to older people in learning, particularly in e-learning. Robert Zheng of the University of Utah proposes a new design approach, which (1) assists the instructional designer and Web development in identifying issues related to older people's involvement in e-learning, (2) helps reduce the mental load in designing and developing e-learning for older people, and (3) uses heuristics to systematically support the designers in making decisions about meeting the needs of older people in their learning and searching for information online.

Section 3 presents research studies and conceptual papers focusing on the practical aspects of applying technology for older adults. It entails chapters that focus on new perspectives pertaining to the use of technologies in various educational settings including e-learning for older adults.

This section opens with a theoretical investigation by Karin Slegers, Centre for User Experience Research, Belgium, and Martin P. van Boxtel, Maastricht University, The Netherlands. Chapter 9 focuses on the impact of computer and Internet use on several aspects of quality of life and the autonomy of older adults. It is based on an intervention program that included concise computer training and the use of a computer and the Internet for twelve months. The results of this randomized, controlled study showed no effects, neither positive nor negative, of computer and Internet use on cognitive functioning, autonomy, well-being and social network, the use of everyday technological devices, and subjective physical functioning. Overall, it was concluded that computer and Internet usage by healthy older adults is a safe activity, albeit with no robust advantage for cognitive capacity in healthy older adults.

In Chapter 10, Michael K. Gardner and Robert D. Hill of the University of Utah review the episodic memory difficulties typically encountered by older adults. Their study demonstrates that mnemonic interventions can improve episodic memory in the elderly, though such improvements often do not transfer broadly and do not result in improvements in the area of subjective memory assessment. The chapter then presents three approaches to improving episodic memory for numeric information, each based upon a different approach. These approaches demonstrate: (a) that a mnemonic targeted at numeric information can improve number recall; (b) that self-generated strategies can improve recall at nearly the same level as a targeted mnemonic; and (c) that episodic memory can be converted into procedural memory, though this approach did not demonstrate improved episodic memory performance. Future directions for memory remediation are discussed, based upon research findings to date.

In Chapter 11, Eulàlia Hernandez-Encuentra, Modesta P. Fernández, and Beni Gómez-Zúñiga of The Open University of Catalunya in Spain examine older adults' adoption and experience of using Information and Communication Technologies (ICT), in particular the Internet. The authors make their arguments based on the experiences of a group of older people, all already users of ICT, in a collaborative, relaxed, and self-managing environment—the virtual campus of the Universitat Oberta de Catalunya (an online university). Older adults adopt ICT in relation to a personal project, sometimes as a tool to achieve it, so ICT use has to be done on their own initiative, with a positive attitude, and under their control. Based on the Selective Optimization and Compensation (SOC) theory of adaptation processes, the authors believe that introducing ICT through selection and optimization strategies can be a successful means of assuring effective adoption of these technologies.

In Chapter 12, Shane O'Hanlon, Alan Bourke, and Valerie Power of the University of Limerick in Ireland examine the benefits of e-Health for older people. They point out that barriers concerning e-Health still remain, including an immature evidence-base, questions about risk and safety, and variable rates of uptake in this population. Their chapter explores these issues and reviews the literature on e-Health for older adults. Successful clinical trials are identified, and the e-CAALYX project is described in detail as a case study. e-Health presents many exciting opportunities but needs further development and guidance.

Chapter 13 features a conceptual paper by Robert D. Hill of the University of Utah. This chapter presents a guided framework for describing Remote Care Delivery Technologies (RCDT) in the processes of healthcare management among older patients diagnosed with chronic disease. To date, a process framework for the application of RCDT for chronic health conditions has not been systematically described, although much of the literature on RCDT, including telemedicine and telehealth, has focused on issues that involving the monitoring of chronic disease symptoms and the coordination of ongoing care. To elucidate how this process framework operates in managing chronic health conditions, examples are provided from the published literature to clarify and differentiate each of the steps of this framework. A final section describes guidelines informed by this framework for providing RCDT in the management of chronic disease.

Finally, in Chapter 14, Candice M. Daniel, Bret Hicken, Marren Grant, and Randall Rupper of the VA Salt Lake City Health Care Center, and Marilyn Luptak of the University of Utah present a case study for using tele-health technology to support caregiver training. The authors describe the barriers and challenges related to caregiver training. To address this problem, the authors develop a psycho-educational caregiver intervention for use with in-home digital technology that is currently underway at three Veteran's Health Affairs (VA) health care centers. The chapter provides: 1) a brief summary of the background and rationale for the intervention development; 2) an overview of the project; and 3) the issues and lessons learned from developing interventions using digital technology for use with older adults.

Robert Z. Zheng
University of Utah, USA

Robert D. Hill
University of Utah, USA

Mike K. Gardner
University of Utah, USA

REFERENCES

Avci, S., Yuksel, A., & Soyer, M. (2009). The cognitive and affective changes caused by the differentiated classroom environment designed for the subject of poetry. *Educational Sciences: Theory and Practice, 9*(3), 1069–1084.

Bertera, F., Bertera, R., Morgan, R., Wuertz, E., & Attey, A. (2007). Training older adults to access health information. *Educational Gerontology, 33*, 483–500. doi:10.1080/03601270701328250

Chen, Y. W., & Persson, A. (2002). Internet use among young and older adults: Relation to psychological well-being. *Educational Gerontology, 28*, 731–744. doi:10.1080/03601270290099921

Cresci, M., Yarandi, H., & Morrell, R. (2010). Pro-nets versus no-nets: Differences in urban older adults' predilections for internet use. *Educational Gerontology, 36*, 500–520. doi:10.1080/03601270903212476

Dorin, M. (2007). Online education of older adults and its relation to life satisfaction. *Educational Gerontology, 33*, 127–143. doi:10.1080/03601270600850776

Furlong, M. (1997). Creating online community for older adults. *Generations (San Francisco, Calif.), 21*(3), 33–35.

Grimes, G., Hough, M., Mazur, E., & Singorella, M. (2010). Older adults' knowledge of internet hazards. *Educational Gerontology, 36*, 173–192. doi:10.1080/03601270903183065

Hardt, J., & Hollis-Sawyer, L. (2007). Older adults seeking healthcare information on the internet. *Educational Gerontology, 33*, 561–572. doi:10.1080/03601270701364628

Hough, M. (2004). Exploring elder consumers' interactions with information technology. *Journal of Business & Economics Research, 2*(6), 61–66.

Humes, K. (2005). *The population 65 years and older: Aging in America*. Retrieved November 3, 2010 from http://www.csg.org/knowledgecenter/docs/BOS2005-AgingInAmerica.pdf

Hyland, T. (2010). Mindfulness, adult learning and therapeutic education: Integrating the cognitive and affective domains of learning. *International Journal of Lifelong Education, 29*(5), 517–532. doi:10.1 080/02601370.2010.512792

Ke, F. (2008). Computer games application within alternative classroom goal structures: Cognitive, metacognitive, and affective evaluation. *Educational Technology Research and Development, 56*(5-6), 539–556. doi:10.1007/s11423-008-9086-5

Littledyke, M. (2008). Science education for environmental awareness: Approaches to integrating cognitive and affective domains. *Environmental Education Research, 14*(1), 1–17. doi:10.1080/13504620701843301

Paas, F., Van Gerven, P. W. M., & Tabbers, H. K. (2005). The cognitive aging principle in multimedia learning . In Mayer, R. (Ed.), *Cambridge Handbook of Multimedia Learning* (pp. 339–354). Cambridge, UK: Cambridge University Press.

Taha, J., Sharit, J., & Czaja, S. (2009). Use of and satisfaction with sources of health information among older internet users and nonusers. *The Gerontologist, 49*, 663–673. doi:10.1093/geront/gnp058

Trentin, G. (2004). E-learning and the third age. *Journal of Computer Assisted Learning, 20*, 21–30. doi:10.1111/j.1365-2729.2004.00061.x

Van Gerven, P. W. M., Paas, F., Van Merriënboer, J. J. G., Hendriks, M., & Schmidt, H. G. (2003). The efficiency of multimedia learning into old age. *The British Journal of Educational Psychology, 73*, 489–505. doi:10.1348/000709903322591208

Van Gerven, P. W. M., Paas, F., Van Merriënboer, J. J. G., & Schmidt, H. G. (2000). Cognitive load theory and the acquisition of complex cognitive skills in the elderly: Towards an integrative framework. *Educational Gerontology, 26*, 503–521. doi:10.1080/03601270050133874

Van Gerven, P. W. M., Paas, F., Van Merriënboer, J. J. G., & Schmidt, H. G. (2002). Cognitive load theory and aging: Effects of worked examples on training efficiency. *Learning and Instruction, 38*, 87–107. doi:10.1016/S0959-4752(01)00017-2

Van Gerven, P. W. M., Paas, F., Van Merriënboer, J. J. G., & Schmidt, H. G. (2004). Memory load and task-evoked pupillary responses in aging. *Psychophysiology, 41*, 167–175. doi:10.1111/j.1469-8986.2003.00148.x

World Health Organization. (2010). *Our ageing world*. Retrieved November 3, 2010 from http://www.who.int/ageing/en/

Acknowledgment

This volume represents the collective wisdom of many who voluntarily spent hundreds of hours putting together a series of chapters that provide an excellent overview of the theories and practices in aging and technology. We would like to express our deepest gratitude and sincere appreciation to all these authors for their outstanding contribution.

Our appreciation also goes to our reviewers, who provided insightful input and suggestions. We thank all of our authors for their own expert assistance. We feel exceptionally fortunate to have worked with Myla Harty, editor at IGI Global, whose expertise and generous support made this project a great success. We would like to thank the publishing team at IGI Global, who have demonstrated the highest level of professionalism and integrity.

Finally, we would like to thank our families for their understanding and support, and for tolerating our erratic schedules as we worked on this project.

Robert Z. Zheng
University of Utah, USA

Robert D. Hill
University of Utah, USA

Mike K. Gardner
University of Utah, USA

January 2012

Section 1
Technology and Aging:
Cognitive Perspectives

Chapter 1
Implicit Memory and Aging:
Adapting Technology to Utilize Preserved Memory Functions

Christopher A. Was
Kent State University, USA

Dan J. Woltz
University of Utah, USA

ABSTRACT

There is clear evidence that aging has an effect on memory. However, not all memory processes suffer as one ages. In the current chapter, the authors review the distinctions between explicit memory (i.e., effortful storage and retrieval of information) and implicit memory (i.e., learning and memory that do not require conscious effort). They then review the evidence indicating that implicit memory does not decline at the same rate as explicit memory. They authors then discuss the possibility of using implicit memory processes (e.g. procedural memory), to aid explicit memory processes (e.g., declarative memory). Finally, they discuss the need and the opportunity to incorporate information and communications technologies into the lives of older adults in order to support memory and learning.

INTRODUCTION

Memory complaints among older adults are quite common. Not being able to recall where one left their keys, to take medication at 2:00 PM, learn the name of a new acquaintance, or commit to memory a new PIN or Internet password are the types of memory failures that are most common. Although many common failures of memory may be unavoidable, some memory processes appear to show less decline with age than others. If there are ways to tap the memory systems that have not degraded appreciably with age and take advantage of technologies that could support these intact memory systems, day to day functioning and enjoyment may improve. In the current chap-

DOI: 10.4018/978-1-4666-1966-1.ch001

ter, we hope to shed some light on how to take advantage of both.

The first goal of this chapter is to summarize literature regarding the impact of aging on implicit memory functions. Specifically, the chapter will describe and review representative evidence suggesting that implicit memory (i.e., non-declarative memory) does not suffer the same declines in older adults (or at least not the same rate of decline) as explicit (i.e., declarative) memory . The chapter will review this evidence from a dissociative perspective. Put differently, we will review selected literature that compares older adults' (age 60 or greater) and young adults' (often undergraduates, but typically less than 30 years of age) performance on explicit and implicit memory tasks. The second goal is to review principles of implicit memory function that may have implications for memory support.

This chapter is organized into three parts. In the first part of the chapter, we provide a brief explanation of the distinction between explicit and implicit memory processes. Then we provide a brief overview of the literature regarding differences between the two age groups in terms of their explicit and implicit memory performance. In the final section, we discuss the implications of adapting common technology applications to facilitate the use of implicit rather than explicit memory processes by older individuals in various learning activities.

Memory Distinctions

Long-term memory is commonly considered to consist of declarative memory (knowing that) and procedural memory (knowing how). For example, knowing that you spent the previous 4th of July at the beach is an example of declarative memory. More specifically, this is an example of episodic memory, or memory for an event that occurred in one's own life. Knowing how to tie your shoe is an example of procedural memory. Often when a skill has been well learned from extensive practice (i.e., performance is based on procedural memory), conscious awareness or control of the skill components is not necessary for effective performance. Proceduralization is the processes by which people go from relying on explicit use of declarative memory to accomplish a task to the direct application of procedural memory (Anderson, 1982). The latter type of memory function does not depend on conscious recall and is often described as a form of implicit memory. Put differently, implicit memory is a non-conscious form of memory that influences behavior. For example, one may be able to tie their shoe, but may not be able to recall the experience of learning to tie a shoe, and after deciding to perform the task, conscious awareness plays little role in successful completion of the task. This is in contrast to explicit memory that is often associated with a conscious and voluntary search such as in attempting to recall what you had for dinner the previous evening.

The division of memory into distinct systems such as declarative and non-declarative is not without controversy (Roediger, Rajaram, & Srinivas, 1990). Moreover, different theorists who advocate distinctions within memory processes often make different distinctions using diverse terminology. For example, explicit and implicit memory are often discussed in terms of different processes engaged by direct and indirect measures of memory respectively rather than different representation systems. Nevertheless, as we review the literature on aging and memory performance there will be an obvious need for a broad distinction between effortful, explicit memory processes and implicit memory processes that are not closely tied to conscious, effortful retrieval.

Explicit Memory

Explicit and effortful search of memory to retrieve specific information is typically defined as a search of declarative memory. Declarative memory is often subdivided into episodic and semantic memory (Squire & Knowlton, 1994; Wheeler, Stuss, & Tulving, 1997). Episodic memory is memory for life occurrences or events. There is a great deal of evidence to support the conclusion that older adults have more trouble with episodic memory tasks than younger adults and the declines in episodic memory are well documented (see Craik & Bosman, 1992, for a review).

Answering questions such as "What television program did you watch last evening?" is more problematic for older adults. Although the declines in episodic memory may not be as incapacitating as older adults might claim, based on the extant literature episodic memory seems to suffer the greatest decrements due to age as compared to procedural memory and other forms of declarative memory, such as semantic memory.

Semantic memory, such as knowing the capital of the state of Alaska, is often conceptualized as a highly interconnected network of nodes and associative links in long-term memory. Recall of information from semantic memory can involve deliberate, effortful retrieval processes. However, it is widely accepted that some semantic memory processes are implicit in nature. Spread of activation describes how the activation of one set of nodes, through retrieval for example, spreads to connected nodes involuntarily. Evidence based on the comparison of younger and older adults indicates that this non-voluntary spread of activation, often measured with priming tasks, does not show the impairment in older adults that is seen in many other memory measures (Laver & Burke, 1993). However, when retrieval tasks require attention or working memory processing in conjunction with semantic memory activation, older adults do demonstrate significant declines in performance (Luo & Craik, 2008). Therefore, the decrements demonstrated in some experimental tasks that tap semantic memory may in part be due to the working memory components of the experimental tasks.

A third type of declarative memory is prospective memory. Prospective memory refers to the retrieval of previously stored information about an intended action (Eysenck, 2009). Put differently, prospective memory is remembering to remember. For example, remembering to perform a task in the future, such as taking a pill in the afternoon. Evidence is clear that when prospective memory is time dependent there are serious declines in performance for older adults. When one must remember that something will occur in the future (e.g., one's favorite television program begins at 2 PM) older adults display greater impairment than young adults as compared to when retrieval is cue dependent (e.g., tell the doctor about your sore foot).

Implicit Memory

As previously described, implicit or non-declarative memory refers to a range of memory processes that affect thoughts and actions but do not depend on conscious awareness of the memory operations. The most predominant subcategories of implicit memory processes are procedural skills and priming effects. Procedural skills can range from performance on predominantly motor tasks such as riding a bicycle to predominantly cognitive tasks such as geometry proof generation. In both motor and cognitive skills, performance demands can range from relatively simple to multifaceted and complex. In all cases, with sufficient practice, performance is assumed to make the transition from slow, effortful execution based on declarative knowledge of task demands to fast, relatively effortless execution based on procedural memory representations.

The measurement of skill acquisition generally assesses performance following extensive practice. Priming effects general refer to facilitation in performance from a single or a small number of prior events. The priming events can be identical (or nearly so) to the target event in which case the facilitation is often large and relatively long lasting. For example, in a lexical decision task (deciding whether series of letters form a word or not) participants are faster at determining if the letters *n u r s e* form a word if they had recently read the same word. This is referred to as repetition or direct priming. Alternatively, the priming event can be semantically related to the target event in which case the facilitation is smaller and less persistent. For example, in the lexical decision task participants are faster at determining if the letters *n u r s e* form a word if the prior stimuli was *d o c t o r*, than if the prior stimuli was *b r e a d*. This is referred to as semantic or indirect priming. Most evidence suggests that younger and older adult performance is similar on repetition priming and semantic priming tasks that do not require effortful manipulation or storage of information (i.e., priming tasks that place little demand on working memory). For example, Java and Gardiner (1991) found that young adults performed significantly better at recalling words from a study list than older adults. However, priming measures (word stem completion) demonstrated little effect of aging. There have been numerous other studies over the past several decades that suggest preserved implicit memory processes in older adults, although this literature is not nearly as extensive the evidence demonstrating that older adults suffer from declines in explicit memory functions. An extensive review of the literature comparing younger and older adults on tasks that measure performance on all components of memory is beyond the scope of the proposed chapter. We will limit our review to selected studies that demonstrate a dissociation between implicit and explicit memory processes and age of participants. In describing this literature, we will rely on the distinction between declarative memory and non-declarative memory when discussing memory systems and explicit and implicit memory when discussing memory processes.

DISSOCIATION OF AGE AND TYPE OF MEMORY MEASURE

If two memory systems are functionally distinct, variables such as typical aging that influence one memory system should have no influence over the other. This is referred to as a single dissociation. A double dissociation occurs when one a variable that has a specific influence on one memory system (e.g., increases efficiency of that memory system) has an opposite effect on the other (e.g., decreases performance of that memory system). Dissociation effects have been used widely to investigate how a number of variables differentially influence distinct memory systems described as episodic vs. procedural memory, and episodic vs. semantic memory. Furthermore, results of investigations relying on dissociation effects have provided a great deal of evidence that explicit and implicit memory processes do not suffer the same rate of decline due to aging, with explicit memory processes being impacted to a much greater extent than implicit memory processes. As described earlier, implicit or non-declarative memory operations are demonstrated in both priming and skill learning experiments. We summarize representative experiments that demonstrate age dissociations in both. We place particular emphasis on the procedural skill literature, because this relates most closely to the issues of technology adaptation that we will propose. We also describe a method of error-less or error-free learning for memory impaired populations that capitalizes on preserved priming and skill learning processes.

Priming

Age effects on priming have been investigated within a variety of experimental tasks. Mitchell, Brown, and Murphy (1990) examined differences in older and younger adults' performance using a picture naming task to measure explicit memory (recognition of old vs. new pictures) and implicit memory (priming effects on picture naming of previously encountered stimuli). The performance of older and younger adults was similar on the measure of implicit memory, but the older adults performance was worse on the explicit memory task.

Another example of dissociation in priming effects was presented by Howard and Howard (1989). They found that older adults demonstrated just as much memory for a pattern as younger adults when indirect (implicit) tests of memory were used, but significantly less memory for patterns when direct (explicit) measures of memory were used. In order to understand these dissociations, it is important to provide a more detailed review of the literature describing the decline due to aging of both explicit and implicit memory.

Much of the evidence for implicit memory processes comes from priming experiments using the lexical decision word naming tasks, and most of this work has focused on short-term semantic rather than repetition priming effects. Laver and Burke (1993) completed a meta-analysis of studies using lexical decision and word pronunciation tasks to examine effect sizes of semantic priming effects on young and older adult participants. The meta-analysis indicated that priming effects were, in fact, larger for older adults.

Procedural Skills

Like the evidence for age differences in priming effects, the evidence regarding procedural skill acquisition is complicated to some degree by task demands that go beyond purely non-declarative memory functions (e.g., working memory demands and motor response demands). Nevertheless, there is evidence suggesting that the rate of skill acquisition is similar for older and younger individuals in some skill tasks. In this section, we will review the evidence from both skill acquisition studies that contrast performance of younger and older adults. This review is followed by discussion of the implications for aiding learning and memory function in older adults.

Increased performance of responding to a repeated sequence without explicit memory of the sequence is one measure of implicit learning or proceduralization. Howard and Howard (1989) investigated the learning and retention of a non-verbal sequence for both young and older adults using the Nissen, Knopman, and Schacter's (1987) Serial Reaction Time task (SRT). The task consisted of four squares spaced equally in a row at the bottom of a computer display. When an asterisk appeared in one of the squares participants were to respond as quickly and accurately as possible by pressing the designated key on the computer keyboard. The keys were spatially coordinated with the squares. Participants first responded to a 10-trial repeating sequence. After several blocks of 100 trails each (all containing the 10-trial repeating sequence), a new random sequence was presented. Nissen, et al. found that response time decreased over the blocks of the repeated sequences and then abruptly increased during the random sequence. The decrease in response time during the repeated sequence represented not only general practice effects, but quite likely, learning of the sequence. The increased response time that occurred during the random sequence represents an indirect measure of pattern learning, or implicit memory. Nissen and colleagues' work includes evidence of dissociation in that many participants who demonstrated severe impairment in a direct (explicit) measure of pattern learning (a generation task in which the goal was to predict the location of the next asterisk) demonstrated unimpaired learning as measured by the indirect (implicit) measure (Knopman & Nissen, 1987; Nissen & Bullemer, 1987).

Howard and Howard (1989) used the SRT task to investigate adult age differences in learning the sequence with 20 younger adults (M = 22.20) and 20 older adults (M = 71.25). The version of the SRT task used by Howard and Howard consisted of eight blocks of either of 100 or 160 (pattern lengths of 10 and 16 respectively). The pattern was repeated 10 times within a block of trials.

The first four blocks were repeated patterns and there was a 2 min break between blocks. The fifth block consisted of a random block of 100 or 160 trials for the 10 and 16 element trials respectively. Next, there was a 30 min interval during which participants completed a number of cognitive measures. Following the 30 min interval participants were exposed to three more blocks of repeated sequences and finally a generation task.

Howard and Howard subtracted the response time of Block 4 from that of Block 5 and used this as an indirect index of learning. This measure was significantly different from zero for all participants exposed to the shorter sequence, but only for older adults in the long sequence condition. As an indirect measure of retention, they compared response times to Block 6, which occurred after the 30 min retention interval to response times to Block 4. For all groups response on Block 6 was as fast as response times to Block 4. Howard and Howard therefore concluded that the older group demonstrated significant pattern learning and retention of the patterns was evident for both pattern lengths. The direct test of pattern learning did however provide striking evidence for a consistent age effect. Older adults scored more poorly than the younger adults when attempting to generate and report the patterns.

Howard and Howard's (1989) investigation demonstrated that when an indirect measure of pattern learning was used older adults performed as well or better than younger adults. However, when a direct measure was used, there appeared to be a lack of explicit learning by older adults. An important note is that Howard and Howard discussed participants' explicit recognition of patterns in the sequences. Although they did not collect data on participants' ability to recognize patterns in the sequence while completing the SRT task, participants of both age groups did spontaneously report recognizing patterns in the sequence.

Gaillard, Destrebecqz, Michiels, and Cleeremans (2009) also demonstrated that a when training adults using a deterministic repeating sequence older adults (59-90 years old) and middle-aged adults (39-51 years old) were able to implicitly acquire new information to the same degree as younger adults (18-29 years old). However, explicit measures of sequence learning did evidence age-related declines.

Gailard et al. (2009) presented the three age groups either 15 or 30 blocks of a Serial Reaction Time (SRT) task. Participants were presented, via computer screen, a display consisting of four dots on the screen in a horizontal orientation. A small black circle would appear on the screen below one of the four dots and participants were required to respond by pressing a respective key on the keyboard arranged in the same horizontal orientation. Participants were randomly assigned to the short condition (15 blocks) or a long condition (30 blocks). Two sequences of trails were created and counterbalanced across subjects. In each training length condition, participants were trained on the same sequence for all but one block and were trained on the other sequence for that block. In the short condition, the switch (transfer block) occurred at block 14 and for the long condition the transfer block occurred at block 29. After completing the training blocks participants then completed a generation task and a recognition task.

The generation task had two different instructions. First, participants were told to generate a series of 108 trials that were as close to the SRT training trials as possible (inclusion) and then asked to generate another 108 trials avoiding repetition of trials that occurred in the SRT training trials (exclusion).

Finally, participants completed a recognition task during which they were presented with 24 fragments of 3 trials and asked to judge on a 6-point scale how certain they were that these fragments were a part of the SRT training. Half of the stimuli were from SRT training trials experienced by the participants and half were fragments of the transfer block.

The main findings indicated that participants in all groups (three age levels and two practice levels) demonstrated learning of the patterns in the SRT task. As Gailard et al. (2009) stated, all participants "showed evidence of having become sensitive to the sequential regularities contained in the stimulus materials" (p. 24). Furthermore, participants in the short condition demonstrated less negative transfer effects during the transfer blocks, indicating more practice led to greater sensitivity or learning. These findings support previous evidence that aging does not interfere with implicit learning (Cherry & Stadler, 1995; Howard & Howard, 1989, 1992).

Unexpected findings included age related differences in the exclusion version of the generation task. Under the inclusion instruction, it was expected that all participants would perform equally as well because implicit learning is preserved, as demonstrated by learning in the SRT trials. However, in the exclusion version, participants are required to rely on controlled expression of acquired knowledge, which is often impaired in older adults (Cherry & Stadler, 1995; Howard & Howard, 1989, 1992).

Gailard et al. (2009) explained that the recognition task did provide results that revealed a decrement in performance due to aging. Although middle aged and older adults were able to discriminate between old and new fragments, the younger adults significantly out- performed both groups. In addition, the correlations between direct and indirect measures of learning were significant for the young adults, whereas this was not the case with the older adults. This suggests that the different measures of performance were not equally sensitive to forgetting or similarity between the tests. However, the dissociation between findings of explicit memory (recognition), implicit memory (generation) and implicit learning (SRT trials) supports the conclusion that implicit memory functions, remains in-tact and that perhaps it can be used to benefit the elderly.

Error-Free Learning

One way in which implicit memory can aid in learning is through the use of errorless learning procedures. Errorless learning procedures are learning conditions in which the possibility of making errors during the learning process have been eliminated or greatly reduced. Errorless learning conditions typically include the immediate correction of errors, eliminating the possibility of guessing, and fading cues. Clare and Jones (2008) reviewed the literature regarding the use of EL in memory rehabilitation concluding that some methods of errorless learning may be effective for those with explicit memory impairments by taping intact, implicit memory.

One early demonstration of errorless learning procedures improving learning was reported by Baddeley and Wilson (1994). Baddeley and Wilson used a word stem completion task in which participants were required to complete a five-letter word when provided with the first two letters. In the errorful condition, participants would be told by the experimenter that he was thinking of a five letter word that began with letters QU for example. If the target word was quote and the participant made any other guess (e.g., quick) the participant would be told that was not correct, the correct word was quote and the participant would write the correct response down. In the errorless condition, the participant would be told by the experimenter that he was thinking of a five-letter word beginning with the letters QU, that the word was quote, and would then be instructed to write the word down.

Participants in Baddeley and Wilson's (1994) investigation came from three groups: a group of amnesiac patients with severe memory impairment; a group of healthy older adults with ages ranging from 61 to 79 years of age; and a healthy younger adult group 20 - 58 years of age. The results of the investigation indicated that amnesiac patients clearly benefited from the errorless learning condition. Although the older adults did not demonstrate similar benefits of errorless learning, it is clear that those suffering from memory impairment did benefit from the errorless learning procedure in this study.

Baddeley and Wilson (1994) interpreted their findings in terms of the role of explicit memory in learning. Baddeley and Wilson proposed that explicit memory aids learning by supporting the elimination of response errors. Put differently, unimpaired explicit memory allows one to store and retrieve previous errors to prevent them from happening again. Errorless learning does not require the storage and retrieval of errors from explicit memory and therefore supports learning for those with impaired explicit memory.

One aspect of Baddeley and Wilson's (1994) investigation that must not be overlooked is the subject groups in the study. Recall that the group that benefitted from errorless learning were the amnesiac patients with severe explicit memory impairment. In a study conducted with healthy younger and healthy older adults, Anderson and Craik (2006) supported the explicit memory explanation proposed by Baddeley and Wilson (1994). Anderson and Craik used a design similar to that of Hay and Jacoby (1996) that allows for separate estimates of explicit recollection and implicit familiarity. In their experiment, Anderson and Craik presented two groups (older with an approximate mean age of 74 and younger adults with an approximate mean age of 21) with 16 nouns paired with two associates that complete that same word fragment (e.g., farm/yard for barn-_ar_). In the training phase of the standard learning condition, participants were presented with a stimulus word fragment pair and were instructed to guess the response word. Then the correct response was presented. In the errorless learning condition, training consisted of the complete word-pair being presented and in a third *errorless-speak* condition, participants were presented with the complete word-pair and were instructed to read the response words out loud. Response words from one of the two sets were the

correct response 75% of the time during training. For example, when the word barn was presented 75% of the time farm was the correct response (typical). The other 25% of the time yard was the correct response (atypical).

During the study-test phase, participants completed 16 study-test lists divided into two halves of eight. Each study list contained six typical and 2 atypical pairs. Study procedures were the same as those for the training procedures. Testing required participants to provide the correct response to the word fragment based on the study list just completed including the six typical, two atypical, and two unstudied pairs for which they were instructed to guess the answer. Based on Hay and Jacoby's (1999) work, it was presumed that participants would provide incorrect typical responses to atypical study items if they were unable to rely on recollection (i.e., explicit memory) of the study phase and instead relied on familiarity (i.e., implicit memory) to generate a response. Anderson and Craik found that the probability of providing correct typical responses for typical study pairs was higher in younger adults and higher in the standard learning condition, with no interaction. In addition, the probability of producing an incorrect typical response for atypical study pairs was higher in older adults and there was an interaction between age group and learning condition. Older adults produced more incorrect typical responses in the standard learning condition than in the two errorless learning conditions.

The results indicated that explicit memory processing (i.e., recollection) in the older adults was reduced in comparison to that younger adults, but there were no differences in implicit memory (i.e., familiarity). Furthermore, older adults with reduced explicit memory benefitted from the errorless learning because it bypasses the need to rely on explicit memory for monitoring of errors.

ADAPTING TECHNOLOGY TO PROMOTE SKILL ACQUISITION IN OLDER ADULTS

Can regular technology use by those experiencing normal aging effects reduce the impact of declining explicit and working memory capabilities and take advantage of implicit memory processes that by in large appear to be spared? Pop psychology and late night infomercials want us to believe that electronic mental games provide a simple way to improve memory. Even a simple search of research literature produces a number of peer-reviewed articles describing approaches to improving cognitive functioning in older adults by using technology. However, the answer to this question is not a simple one. In this section of the chapter, we present a brief review of this literature and relate it to the distinction between declarative and non-declarative memory declines in aging. We then turn to a discussion of how technology can be used to both exercise and capitalize on procedural learning and perhaps even maintain functional memory processes in healthy older adults.

At the onset of this discussion, it is worth noting that promoting the regular use of technology by older individuals who might have little prior experience with personal computers and related technologies is likely to present major challenges. No doubt there are large individual differences in this population as to relevant background, motivation and attitude toward acquiring new skills that appear to come naturally to younger generations. Despite the challenges and individual differences, we contend that there are potentially important benefits if computer applications are adapted for this population to promote the use of computers and the development of certain skills through this usage.

There are several general reasons why the regular use of technology could be a particularly effective tool to encourage skill acquisition and maintenance in older individuals. First, technology has become integral to many day-to-day tasks for most other generations. Lack of familiarity with computers and other personal electronic devices can limit older individuals' connection to modern culture and many conveniences therein. Due to the ubiquity of Information and Communications Technology (ICT), as well as the rapid changes in technology, it is important that older adults are educated and trained to use these technologies. ICT can be described as the integration of telecommunications, computers, software, and data storage that allows the individual to share and store information, remotely control electronic devices and to communicate both synchronously or asynchronously with others. Smart phones, laptops, notebook and tablet computers, are commonplace among professionals, students and anyone wanting to "stay connected." Selwyn (2004) provides an in-depth examination of older adults use of ICTs. Selwyn contends that older adults cannot be categorized simply as "users" and "non-users" of ICTs. Rather, we must view use of ICTs as an impermanent state. Selwyn provided the example of one who made regular use of computers during their career, but then only sporadic use of a computer after retiring. One can imagine how the rapid changes in technology may lead to even more sporadic, and less efficient, use of ICTs in later adulthood.

Is the use of ICTs necessary for a high quality or standard of living? Selwyn (2004) argues that there is a great deal of academic and political interest in older adults adapting and using technology because of the "implicit assumption that ICT use is an inherently useful and desirable activity throughout all sectors of society" (p. 381). Whether or not this assumption is correct, a move toward increasing older adults use of ICTs is occurring. As Czaja (2005) stated:

Use of automatic teller machines, interactive telephone-based menu systems, cellular telephones, and VCRs is also quite common. Furthermore, telephones, television, home security systems and other communication devices are becoming more integrated with computer network resources providing faster and more powerful interactive services (p. 7).

This statement was made only 7 years before this chapter was written and already some of the technology is outdated. VCRs have been replaced by DVD and Blu-ray players and cellular telephones by smart phones. Clearly, ICTs are even more ubiquitous now. Several investigations have demonstrated that although older adults can learn to use computer technology and ICTs, they also demonstrate the older adults have a great deal more difficulty than younger people in learning computer related skills (Czaja, 1996).

Second, and most relevant to the current topics of discussion, computer technology allows the control of instruction, practice event presentation and performance feedback that is essential for minimizing working memory and declarative memory demands and capitalizing on implicit memory functions central to procedural skill acquisition.

We organize our discussion of technology-based skill practice tailored to older populations around a broad distinction between two categories of skills that could be practiced for different purposes. First, there are skills that are domain-specific and related to real-world activities. This would include learning to use computer software to manage bank accounts, pay bills, conduct financial planning, and perform similar data management tasks. It could also include learning to use various communication applications in a computer, tablet, or smartphone. These skills generally are more complex than experimental tasks that have been used to demonstrate preserved implicit learning capabilities with aging. However, based on evidence of complex skill acquisition by individuals with severe memory impairment, we suggest moderately complex skills are well within the capabilities associated with normal aging. Many of these skills require a great deal of well-structured practice, and such practice often is best delivered by personal computers or related technology.

In contrast, to domain-specific skills, domain-general skills refer to performance improvements acquired from one set of practice tasks that may transfer broadly to many other tasks. We should expect some degree of transfer across closely related domain-specific skills such as the use of two different but similar word processing programs (Singley & Anderson, 1985). However, most procedural skills tend to be highly specific, so negative transfer is also possible (Fitts, 1947). For example, a keystroke sequence or icon can be linked to different functions in a new software program, and this can cause persistent interference and errors. Obviously, the concept of domain-general skills that transfer broadly is inherently attractive due to the potential impact on many cognitive activities. However, there is an extensive and disappointing history of research on attempts to develop skills that transfer broadly (see Singley & Anderson, 1989). Nevertheless, there is some recent research on computer delivered practice with a particular category of skills that has shown some promise and is worth discussing here.

Domain-specific skills. As noted, it is an ambitious goal for older individuals with little or no prior computer experience to acquire moderately complex computer-based skills in a reasonable amount of time. The complexity of this endeavor stems from the fact that learning novel performance tasks generally requires attention-based working memory and reasoning processes, and these are the very processes that are in decline. This is often exacerbated by attitudes of cautiousness and low self-efficacy for learning new technologies. For these reasons, we suggest that a special learning environment must be created that minimizes working memory demands and reduces performance failure that fuels the low self-efficacy. The principle of error-free practice described earlier is an ideal candidate for the acquisition of moderately complex procedural skills in elderly individuals, and use of technology is ideally suited for it application.

An extreme example of training a moderately complex procedural skill with this approach can be found in the work by Glisky and colleagues (Glisky & Schacter, 1987, 1989; Glisky, Schacter, & Tulving, 1986). They demonstrated that individuals suffering from various forms of amnesia could, with extensive practice, learn computer skills. In one case, a young woman with severe amnesia due to encephalitis was trained to perform a complex data entry task. She was trained in the skill in a laboratory setting and subsequently was able to perform successfully in the work environment of a large corporation. The job involved entering information from company documents into a computer spreadsheet: Specific information needed to be entered into different columns based on a set of rules, and the information to be entered was often mixed with irrelevant information that was to be ignored. The dissociation between this individual's ability to learn and perform a relatively complex computer skill and declarative memory related to the skill was described by Glisky and Schacter as follows.

Although H.D. learned to perform the task quickly and correctly both in the laboratory and in the workplace, she remained unable when asked to recount the specific details of the procedure. On a few occasions during laboratory training, the patient was queried by one of the experimenters as to the nature of her visits to the Unit. HD was able to say that she was learning a job that required typing on the computer but she could provide only a sketchy description of the procedures or materials. Similarly, the patient herself reported that when she left the laboratory, she was unable to remember exactly what she had been doing except that it had involved data entry from cards into a computer. Her husband noted that when friends or co-workers questioned her about the nature of the training, H.D. became somewhat embarrassed because she could say no more than she was doing something that involved the computer (p. 903).

The method of training used to train H.D. was referred to as the method of vanishing cues. In order to learn the data entry skill, a small vocabulary of computer commands needed to be learned. For example, the command *SAVE* needed to be associated with the action of storing information on a disk. This and other associations were practiced with presentation of the definition and instructions for the learner to type the command. The idea of vanishing cues was based on implicit memory research demonstrating that even severely amnesic individuals have a perceptually-based memory representation for recently presented words. Therefore, initial practice included several letters of the command, and the learner simply needed to complete the missing letters (S A V _). With practice, fewer letter cues were required for participants to type the correct command. Given the amnesia status of these learners, presumably they were acquiring a form of implicit knowledge of the commands. In the case of H. D., with extensive practice of this form of errorless training, she was eventually able to acquire a complex computer skill with little or no declarative or episodic memory of the task components.

Memory deficits from normal aging are obviously much less severe than that of amnesic patients. Declarative learning is clearly possible with normal aging, so the process of acquiring a skill such as data entry need not circumvent entirely those elements of the skill. However, the degree to which the working memory demands of declarative knowledge acquisition can be minimized can potentially speed skill learning and reduce the frustrations of a novel task. The method of vanishing cues, or other forms of error-free learning, could play a similar role in helping those with diminished declarative learning capacity acquire complex procedural skills.

The vanishing cues which could be easily incorporated into computer tutorials represent an application of priming, and the evidence reviewed earlier suggests that age has little if any effect on the magnitude of priming. If an individual with severe amnesia can learn a complex data entry skill, it seems very likely that older individuals with little or no computer background could readily acquire computer skills related to their personal finances.

The principle of error-free learning with vanishing cues minimizes demands on declarative learning, and capitalizes on preserved implicit memory processes. Nevertheless, care would be needed in design of computerized practice for this population. Lack of prior experience with computers or tablets can be intimidating and confusing. In addition, some individuals may have difficulty with mouse or keyboard responding and others may have vision or hearing difficulties that make computer interaction even more difficult. Clarity and simplicity of tutorials emphasizing error-free learning is essential, and voice recognition, touchscreens, animation, and repeatable auditory instruction could be required.

Improvements in recollection have been demonstrated in healthy older adults. Jennings and Jacoby (2003) tested a program where an incrementally-increasing learning strategy enhanced recognition memory in older person. Although this study did not employ a specific ICT per se, it does suggest that training employing procedural protocols exist for memory processes in healthy older adults. Jennings and Jacoby proposed that the incrementally-increasing learning strategy technique (i.e., increasing repetition lag) taps automatic influences of memory rather that controlled processes such as recollection.

Domain-general skills. There is common advice given to older individuals concerned with declining cognitive abilities to keep mentally active. Regular practice of completing crossword puzzles, recreational reading, playing bridge or other card games represent attempts to remain mentally engaged or even delay the onset of memory decline (Hall, Lipton, Sliwinski, Katz, Derby, & Vergese, 2009). If regular involvement in problem solving and other mental activity either slows or prevents effects of age on cognitive processes, this would represent the impact of acquiring domain general skills. Put differently, practice on these skills is

presumed to have a positive impact on a wide array of tasks beyond the domain practiced. As noted earlier, general transfer has been difficult to find over tasks that have limited overlap in processing demands. The doctrine of formal disciplines, once popular among educators in the early 20th century (e.g. Woodrow, 1927), held that the study of Latin, geometry and other demanding disciplines strengthened general mental faculties that benefited all other learning endeavors. There has been very little support for general transfer of learning of this form. In contrast, there has been extensive support for the notion that procedural skills tend to be specific rather than general, and transfer is found only when there is substantial overlap in the specific operations demanded by two or more tasks (e.g., Singley & Anderson, 1985; Thorndike & Woodworth, 1901). This also corresponds to the largely disappointing literature on attempts to increase general intellectual ability (Jensen, 1969; Detterman & Sternberg, 1982, 1993).

Despite the discouraging body of evidence regarding general transfer from acquiring cognitive skills, there is growing evidence for the potentially broad benefit of some forms of skill practice. Several researchers have reported broader than expected transfer from extensive practice on video games that appear to share several features. These games demand speeded encoding and decision-making, and they require, explicitly or implicitly, variable allocation of attention to various aspects of the game.

Gopher and colleagues (e.g., Gopher, Weil, & Bareket, 1994; Gopher, Weil, & Siegel, 1989) tested the idea that attention management was a skill that could be trained, and that performance improvements from such training would generalize across tasks. They modified an experimental game-like task named Space Fortress that was developed and used in prior research (Donchin, 1995; Mane & Donchin, 1989). Players of the game controlled a spacecraft with the goal of firing missiles to destroy a fortress. During practice performing this complex task, they instructed individuals to vary the relative emphasis placed on several task components. Gopher et al. (1989) demonstrated persistent and broad benefits of this in task performance compared to no-emphasis or emphasis on single task components, and the benefits were most dramatic for lower ability individuals. More intriguing was the finding reported by Gopher et al. (1994) that 10 hours of variable priority training on the modified Space Fortress game yielded improvements in subsequent flight training of Israeli Air Force pilots. The authors made every attempt to keep flight instructors who evaluated the flight performance blind to the purpose of the computer game, and the improvements were seen across multiple measures of pilot performance.

The transfer from 10 hours of computer game practice under variable priority instructions to flight training performance seems almost unimaginable given the long history of skill specificity. In fact, Boot et al (2010) reported an extensive examination of transfer from variable priority training in the Space Fortress game. They found that the varied distribution of attention on various skill components did in fact improve learning performance. Transfer was also better for some tasks, especially those with similarity to the training task. However, they failed to find broad transfer to performance on a variety of attention, memory, and reasoning tasks. Clearly, more evidence and finer scrutiny of the training-transfer overlap of processes is needed to feel confident about the possible transfer effects of this form of skill training. However, additional evidence that is consistent with findings of general transfer clearly justifies the importance of such research. Some of this evidence pertains to possible benefits to older individuals.

Kramer, Larish, and Strayer (1995) investigated the effects of variable priority training on a dual task skill other than Space Fortress. They also compared old and young participants on the impact of this training compared to a condition instructing participants to give equal priority

to task elements. Consistent with the previous evidence, they found that variable priority training led to faster learning and greater mastery of the training task. They also found evidence for improved transfer to a new, unrelated dual task. Of interest here, the older sample appeared to benefit as much or more from the variable priority training. This finding is of particular importance given previous evidence suggesting that age effects are most dramatic in dual task performance requiring a division of attention over different task components (e.g. Castel & Craik, 2003; Craik, Govoni, Naveh-Benjamin, & Anderson, 1996).

A distinct but related area of research has investigated the impact of extensive video game practice on general processing speed (Achtman, Green, & Bavelier, 2008; Dye, Green, & Bavelier, 2009a, 2009b). This research was not based on explicit variable priority attention training, but the similarity to priority training lies in the fact that action-based video games inherently require attention to be distributed over various task components. Evidence suggests that gaming practice results in improved visual attention processing speed in unrelated tasks including dual tasks (Green & Bavelier, 2006, 2007). Other findings suggest that the benefits of extensive video game training may extend beyond visual attention, and may also benefit executive functions (Basak, Boot, Voss, & Kramer, 2008). However, Goldstein et al. (1997) found that five hours a week for five weeks of the game Super Tetris improved reaction time and self-reported well-being, but had weak effects on cognitive performance measures. Indeed, participants in the study that did not play Super Tetris did not differ in their improvement on the Stroop Color Word Test as compared to participants in the extensive video game playing condition.

These lines of research have potentially important implications for maintaining or enhancing cognitive functioning in older individuals. Salthouse (1991) has suggested that declines in working memory performance by older individuals can be explained by the loss of processing speed. Because working memory performance is so closely linked to attention control (Baddeley, 1993), it raises the possibility that a form of skill practice that generally improves speed and efficiency of attention control could manifest itself in better working memory performance in general, and thereby affect a variety of cognitive activities.

How do we reconcile these findings with persistent findings over 100 years the general transfer across skills is minimal at best, and transfer requires substantial overlap of specific mental operations? It appears that the common set of mental operations found in the video games used in this research pertain to the control and engagement of attention. These mental operations, like most others, appear to benefit from extensive practice that emphasizes speed and flexible control. To the extent that efficient, rapid control of attention is important to other tasks beyond the video games, positive transfer seems plausible. Clearly, further research is needed to verify and understand this phenomenon, but the findings thus far warrant such effort.

As in the discussion of domain specific skill acquisition for aging populations, there are practical concerns about implementing videogames as domain general skill learning activities. First, as Dye et al. (2009b) noted, most current videogames might be inappropriate for some populations due to content (i.e., violent war games) and perceptual motor demands placed on the user. Most likely, the idea of action videogames that demand variable attention allocation would need to be adapted for an aging population. Nevertheless, if bingo and card games are popular, why could not attractive videogames be developed that better exercise the attention control mechanisms that could have broad benefits?

SUMMARY AND CONCLUSION

In this chapter, we discussed a range of topics from implicit memory research, practical computer skills and video games. They are all connected by the common theme that memory processes that are fundamental to each might be relatively preserved in older individuals who experience declines in other memory processes. Although there is clear evidence that non-declarative memory systems and implicit memory processes may not suffer the same declines associated with aging that declarative memory systems and explicit memory processes suffer, it is not yet clear how to take advantage of implicit memory processes to aid in day-to-day functioning of older adults. Our goal was to review research regarding dissociations between explicit and implicit memory processes and suggest possible ways in which technology might take advantage of preserved implicit memory processes. Learning to use applications on a smart phone through a procedural training application, prospective memory aids that use an incrementally increasing learning strategy and video games to improve processing speed are a few simple examples. A great deal of research is needed to investigate the proposed applications, but the future of technological support of older adults that capitalizes on preserved implicit learning and memory appears promising.

REFERENCES

Achtman, R. L., Green, C. S., & Bavelier, D. (2008). Video games as a tool to train visual skills. *Restorative Neurology and Neuroscience*, *26*(4-5), 435–446.

Anderson, J. R. (1982). Acquisition of cognitive skill. *Psychological Review*, *89*(4), 396–406. doi:10.1037/0033-295X.89.4.369

Anderson, N. D., & Craik, F. I. M. (2006). The mnemonic mechanisms of errorless learning. *Neuropsychologica, 44*, 2806–2813. doi:10.1016/j.neuropsychologia.2006.05.026

Baddeley, A. (1993). Working memory or working attention? In Baddeley, A., & Weiskrantz, L. (Eds.), *Attention: Selection, Awareness, and Control: A Tribute to Donald Broadbent* (pp. 152–170). Oxford, UK: Clarendon Press.

Baddeley, A., & Wilson, B. A. (1994). When implicit learning fails: Amnesia and the problem of error elimination. *Neuropsychologia, 32*(1), 53–68. doi:10.1016/0028-3932(94)90068-X

Basak, C., Boot, W. R., Voss, M. V., & Kramer, A. F. (2008). Can training in a real-time strategy video game attenuate cognitive decline in older adults? *Psychology and Aging, 23*(4), 765–777. doi:10.1037/a0013494

Boot, W. R., Basak, C., Erickson, K. I., Neider, M., Simons, D. J., & Fabiani, M. (2010). Transfer of skill engendered by complex task training under conditions of variable priority. *Acta Psychologica, 135*(3), 349–357. doi:10.1016/j.actpsy.2010.09.005

Castel, A. D., & Craik, F. I. M. (2003). The effects of aging and divided attention on memory for item and associative information. *Psychology and Aging, 18*(4), 873–885. doi:10.1037/0882-7974.18.4.873

Cherry, K. E., & Stadler, M. A. (1995). Implicit learning of a nonverbal sequence in younger and older adults. *Psychology and Aging, 10*(3), 379–394. doi:10.1037/0882-7974.10.3.379

Clare, L., & Jones, R. S. P. (2008). Errorless learning in the rehabilitation of memory impairment: A critical review. *Neuropsychology Review, 18*, 1–23. doi:10.1007/s11065-008-9051-4

Craik, F. I. M., & Bosman, E. A. (1992). Age-related changes in memory and learning. In Berman, H., & Graafmans, J. A. M. (Eds.), *Gerontechnology* (pp. 79–92). Burke, VA: IOS Press.

Craik, F. I. M., Govoni, R., Naveh-Benjamin, M., & Anderson, N. D. (1996). The effects of divided attention on encoding and retrieval processes in human memory. *Journal of Experimental Psychology. General, 125*(2), 159–180. doi:10.1037/0096-3445.125.2.159

Czaja, S. K. (1996). Aging and the acquisition of computer skills. In Rogers, W. A., Fisk, A. D., & Walker, N. (Eds.), *Aging and Skilled Performance: Advances in Theory and Applications* (pp. 201–220). Mahwah, NJ: Erlbaum.

Czaja, S. K. (2005). The impact of aging on access to technology. *Comput, 83*, 7–11.

Detterman, D. K., & Sternberg, R. (1982). *How and how much can intelligence be increased.* New York, NY: Ablex Publishing.

Detterman, D. K., & Sternberg, R. J. (1993). *Transfer on trial: Intelligence, cognition, and instruction.* Westport, CT: Ablex Publishing.

Donchin, E. (1995). Video games as research tools: The space fortress game. *Behavior Research Methods, Instruments, & Computers, 27*(2), 217–223. doi:10.3758/BF03204735

Dye, M. W. G., Green, C. S., & Bavelier, D. (2009a). The development of attention skills in action video game players. *Neuropsychologia, 47*(8-9), 1780–1789. doi:10.1016/j.neuropsychologia.2009.02.002

Dye, M. W. G., Green, S., & Bavelier, D. (2009b). Increasing speed of processing with action video games. *Current Directions in Psychological Science, 18*(6), 321–326. doi:10.1111/j.1467-8721.2009.01660.x

Eysenck, M. W. (2009). Prospective memory. In A. Baddeley, M. W. Eysenck, & M. C. Anderson (Eds.), *Memory,* (343-356). New York, NY: Psychology Press.

Fitts, P. M. (1947). *Psychological research on equipment design.* Washington, DC: US Government Printing Office.

Gaillard, V., Destrebecqz, A., Michiels, S., & Cleeremans, A. (2009). Effects of age and practice in sequence learning: A graded account of aging, learning and control. *The European Journal of Cognitive Psychology, 21,* 255–282. doi:10.1080/09541440802257423

Glisky, E. L., & Schacter, D. L. (1987). Acquisition of domain-specific knowledge in organic amnesia: Training for computer-related work. *Neuropsychologia, 25*(6), 893–906. doi:10.1016/0028-3932(87)90094-7

Glisky, E. L., & Schacter, D. L. (1989). Extending the limits of complex learning in organic amnesia: Computer training in a vocational domain. *Neuropsychologia, 27*(1), 107–120. doi:10.1016/0028-3932(89)90093-6

Glisky, E. L., Schacter, D. L., & Tulving, E. (1986). Computer learning by memory-impaired patients: Acquisition and retention of complex knowledge. *Neuropsychologia, 24*(3), 313–328. doi:10.1016/0028-3932(86)90017-5

Goldstein, J., Cajko, L., Oosterbroek, M., Michielsen, M., Van Houten, O., & Salverda, F. (1997). Video games and the elderly. *Social Behavior and Personality: An International Journal, 25*(4), 345–352. doi:10.2224/sbp.1997.25.4.345

Gopher, D., Weil, M., & Bareket, T. (1994). Transfer of skill from a computer game trainer to flight. *Human Factors, 36*(3), 387–405.

Gopher, D., Weil, M., & Siegel, D. (1989). Practice under changing priorities: An approach to the training of complex skills. *Acta Psychologica, 71*(1-3), 147–177. doi:10.1016/0001-6918(89)90007-3

Green, C. S., & Bavelier, D. (2006). Effect of action video games on the spatial distribution of visuospatial attention. *Journal of Experimental Psychology. Human Perception and Performance, 32*(6), 1465–1478. doi:10.1037/0096-1523.32.6.1465

Green, C. S., & Bavelier, D. (2007). Action-video-game experience alters the spatial resolution of vision. *Psychological Science, 18*(1), 88–94. doi:10.1111/j.1467-9280.2007.01853.x

Hall, C. B., Lipton, R. B., Sliwinski, M., Katz, M. J., Derby, C. A., & Vergese, J. (2009). Cognitive activities delay onset of memory decline in persons who develop dementia. *Neurology, 73*(5), 356–361. doi:10.1212/WNL.0b013e3181b04ae3

Hay, J. F., & Jacoby, L. L. (1996). Separating habit and recollection: Memory slips, process dissociations, and probability matching. *Journal of Experimental Psychology. Learning, Memory, and Cognition, 22*(6), 1323–1335. doi:10.1037/0278-7393.22.6.1323

Howard, D. V., & Howard, J. H. (1989). Ages differences in learning serial patterns: Direct versus indirect measures. *Psychology and Aging, 4,* 357–364. doi:10.1037/0882-7974.4.3.357

Howard, D. V., & Howard, J. H. (1992). Adult age differences in the rate of learning serial patterns: Evidence from direct and indirect tests. *Psychology and Aging, 7,* 232–241. doi:10.1037/0882-7974.7.2.232

Java, R. I., & Gardiner, J. M. (1991). Priming and aging: Further evidence of preserved memory function. *The American Journal of Psychology, 104*(1), 89–100. doi:10.2307/1422852

Jensen, A. R. (1969). How much can we boost IQ and scholastic achievement? *Harvard Educational Review, 39*(1), 1–123.

Knopman, D. S., & Nissen, M. J. (1987). Implicit learning in patients with probable Alzheimer's disease. *Neurology, 37*(5), 784–788. doi:10.1212/WNL.37.5.784

Kramer, A. F., Larish, J. F., & Strayer, D. L. (1995). Training for attentional control in dual task settings: A comparison of young and old adults. *Journal of Experimental Psychology. Applied*, *1*(1), 50–76. doi:10.1037/1076-898X.1.1.50

Laver, G. D., & Burke, D. M. (1993). Why do semantic priming effects increase in old age? A meta-analysis. *Psychology and Aging*, *8*, 34–43. doi:10.1037/0882-7974.8.1.34

Luo, L., & Craik, F. I. M. (2008). Aging and memory: A cognitive approach. *Canadian Journal of Psychiatry*, *53*(6), 346–353.

Mane, A. M., & Donchin, E. (1989). The space fortress game. *Acta Psychologica*, *71*(1-3), 17–22. doi:10.1016/0001-6918(89)90003-6

Mitchell, D. B., Brown, A. S., & Murphy, D. R. (1990). Dissociations between procedural and episodic memory: Effects of time and aging. *Psychology and Aging*, *5*(2), 264–276. doi:10.1037/0882-7974.5.2.264

Nissen, M. J., & Bullemer, P. (1987). Attentional requirements of learning: Evidence from performance measures. *Cognitive Psychology*, *19*, 1–32. doi:10.1016/0010-0285(87)90002-8

Nissen, M. J., Knopman, D. S., & Schacter, D. L. (1987). Neurochemical dissociation of memory systems. *Neurology*, *37*(5), 789–784. doi:10.1212/WNL.37.5.789

Roediger, H. L., Rajaram, S., & Srinivas, K. (1990). Specifying criteria for postulating memory systems. *Annals of the New York Academy of Sciences*, *608*, 572–595. doi:10.1111/j.1749-6632.1990.tb48910.x

Salthouse, T. A. (1991). Mediation of adult age differences in cognition by reductions in working memory and speed of processing. *Psychological Science*, *2*(3), 179–183. doi:10.1111/j.1467-9280.1991.tb00127.x

Selwyn, N. (2004). The information aged: A qualitative study of older adults' use of information and communications technology. *Journal of Aging Studies*, *18*, 369–384. doi:10.1016/j.jaging.2004.06.008

Singley, M. K., & Anderson, J. R. (1985). The transfer of text-editing skill. *International Journal of Man-Machine Studies*, *22*(4), 403–423. doi:10.1016/S0020-7373(85)80047-X

Singley, M. K., & Anderson, J. R. (1989). *The transfer of cognitive skill*. Cambridge, MA: Harvard University Press.

Squire, L. R., & Knowlton, B. J. (1994). The organization of memory. In Morowitz, H., & Singer, J. L. (Eds.), *The Mind, the Brain, and Complex Adaptive Systems* (pp. 63–97). Reading, MA: Addison Wesley/Addison Wesley Longman, Inc.

Thorndike, E. L., & Woodworth, R. S. (1901). The influence of improvement in one mental function upon the efficiency of other functions. *Psychological Review*, *8*, 247–261. doi:10.1037/h0074898

Wheeler, M. A., Stuss, D. T., & Tulving, E. (1997). Toward a theory of episodic memory: The frontal lobes and autonoetic consciousness. *Psychological Bulletin*, *121*, 331–354. doi:10.1037/0033-2909.121.3.331

Woodrow, H. (1927). The effect of type of training upon transference. *Journal of Educational Psychology*, *18*, 159–172. doi:10.1037/h0071868

ADDITIONAL READING

Balota, D., & Dolan, P. (2000). Memory changes in healthy older adults. In Tulving, E., & Craik, F. I. M. (Eds.), *Oxford Handbook of Memory* (pp. 395–410). Oxford, UK: Oxford University Press.

Berman, H., & Graafmans, J. A. M. (1992). *Gerontechnology*. Burke, VA: IOS Press.

Christensen, H., & Birrell, P. (1991). Explicit and implicit memory in dementia and normal ageing. *Psychological Research, 53*, 149–161. doi:10.1007/BF01371823

Churchill, J., Stanis, J., Press, C., & Kushelev, M. (2003). Is procedural memory relatively spared from age effects. *Neurobiology of Aging, 24*, 883–892. doi:10.1016/S0197-4580(02)00194-X

Craik, F. (1994). Memory changes in normal aging. *Current Directions in Psychological Science, 3*(5), 155–158. doi:10.1111/1467-8721.ep10770653

Gamberini, L., Alcaniz, M., Barresi, G., & Fabregat, M. (2006). Cognition, technology, and games for the elderly: An introduction to ELDERGAMES project. *Psychology Journal, 4*(3), 285–310.

Grady, C. L., & Craik, F. I. M. (2000). Changes in memory processing with age. *Current Opinion in Neurobiology, 10*, 224–231. doi:10.1016/S0959-4388(00)00073-8

Hess, T. (2005). Memory and aging in context. *Psychological Bulletin, 131*(3), 383–406. doi:10.1037/0033-2909.131.3.383

Kausler, D. H. (1994). *Learning and memory in normal aging*. San Diego, CA: Academic Press.

Lovelace, E. A. (1990). *Aging and cognition: Mental processes, self-awareness, and interventions*. Amsterdam, The Netherlands: North Holland.

Morowitz, H., & Singer, J. L. (1994). *The mind, the brain, and complex adaptive systems* (pp. 63–97). Reading, MA: Addison Wesley/Addison Wesley Longman, Inc.

Naveh-Benjamin, M., Moscovitch, M., & Roediger, H. L. (2001). *Perspectives on human memory and cognitive aging: Essays in honour of Fergus Craik*. New York, NY: Psychology Press.

Nilsson, L. (2003). Memory function in normal aging. *Acta Neurologica Scandinavica, 107*(79), 7–13. doi:10.1034/j.1600-0404.107.s179.5.x

Park, D., & Schwarz, N. (2000). *Cognitive aging: A primer*. Philadelphia, PA: Psychology Press.

Rebok, G., & Carlson, M. (2007). Training and maintaining memory abilities in healthy older adults: Traditional and novel approaches. *The Journals of Gerontology: Series B, 62*(1), 53–61. doi:10.1093/geronb/62.special_issue_1.53

Rogers, W. A., Fisk, A. D., & Walker, N. (1996). *Aging and skilled performance: Advances in theory and applications* (pp. 201–220). Mahwah, NJ: Erlbaum.

Russo, R., & Parkin, A. J. (1993). Age differences in implicit memory: More apparent than real. *Memory & Cognition, 21*(1), 73–80. doi:10.3758/BF03211166

KEY TERMS AND DEFINITIONS

Dissociation: Dissociation describes the relationship between a single variable's influence on two separate systems. If a single variable (e.g., age) impacts two memory systems (e.g., episodic memory and semantic memory) in different ways this is referred to as dissociation. For example, if it has a negative effect on episodic memory, but no effect on sematic memory, there is dissociation.

Errorless Learning: Errorless learning refers to experimental learning conditions in which the participant is provided with information or aids that greatly reduce or eliminate the possibility of making errors during the learning process.

Explicit Memory: Explicit memory is a range of memory processes often associated with a conscious and voluntary search of memory in an attempt to recall information.

Implicit Memory: Implicit memory is a range of memory processes in which previous experience affects thoughts and actions (e.g., improved task performance) but does not depend on conscious awareness of the previous experiences.

Information and Communications Technologies (ICT): Information and communication technologies refers to the integration digital and communications devices that allows individuals and organizations to share and store information, remotely control electronic devices, and to communicate both synchronously or asynchronously with others.

Variable Priority Training: Variable priority training is an experimental paradigm in which participants are trained to complete a task requiring two components (e.g., typing letters and categorizing numerals) to be completed at the same time. In contrast to fixed-priority training in which participants are instructed to give a certain priority to the task components throughout training, participants in variable priority training are instructed to change the task component to which they give priority across blocks of trials. Participants in variable priority training trials tend to outperform participants receiving fixed priority training on both components of the task.

Chapter 2
On Attentional Control and the Aging Driver

Jason M. Watson
University of Utah, USA

Ann E. Lambert
University of Utah, USA

Joel M. Cooper
University of Utah, USA

Istenya V. Boyle
University of Utah, USA

David L. Strayer
University of Utah, USA

ABSTRACT

Theories of cognitive aging suggest diminished frontal lobe function and reduced attentional control could contribute to age-related changes in driving a motor vehicle. To address this possibility, the authors investigated the interrelationship among age, attentional control, and driving performance. Using a high-fidelity simulator, they measured individual differences in participants' abilities to maintain a prescribed following distance behind a lead vehicle, as well as their reaction time to press a brake pedal when this lead vehicle braked. Consistent with the literature on age-related changes in driving, following distance elongated with increased age, and brake reaction time slowed. Furthermore, regression analyses revealed the increase in following distance and the slowing in brake reaction time both co-varied with age deficits in attentional control. These results provide a novel demonstration of the inherent value of cognitive theory when applied to naturalistic settings, sharpening our understanding of the relevance of age-related deficits in attentional control for complex, real-world tasks like driving.

DOI: 10.4018/978-1-4666-1966-1.ch002

INTRODUCTION

The term *attentional control* has been used to refer to cognitive processes that support one's ability to actively maintain task goals in the face of distraction (Kane & Engle, 2002) and are thought to be primarily mediated by Prefrontal Cortex (PFC). Further, evidence from neuropsychological studies implies the PFC is particularly susceptible to age-related decline (Chan & McDermott, 2007; West, 1996). As shown in Figure 1, the cognitive neuroscience literature reveals a striking symmetry between the biological development of frontal cortex across the life span and the corresponding rise and fall of goal-directed behavior (see Watson, Lambert, Miller, & Strayer, 2011, for a recent review). Hence, with advanced age, activities that require PFC-mediated attentional control and managing task goals to resist interference in information processing may become increasingly difficult to complete. Consistent with this argument, decades of laboratory research have reported age-related impairments on cognitive tasks thought to require attentional control such as Stroop color naming, where individuals are instructed to respond to the color of a stimulus like the word "RED" printed in green ink and to ignore conflicting words (Spieler, Balota, & Faust, 1996). While these findings contribute to a vast empirical literature on age-related deficits in controlled

Figure 1. The curvilinear development of frontal cortex across the life span. Developmental changes have been observed in a variety of dependent measures including myelination, dendritic branching, synaptogenesis, glucose metabolism, blood flow, dopamine neurotransmitter function, and brain volume. Adapted from Watson, Lambert, Miller, and Strayer (2011).

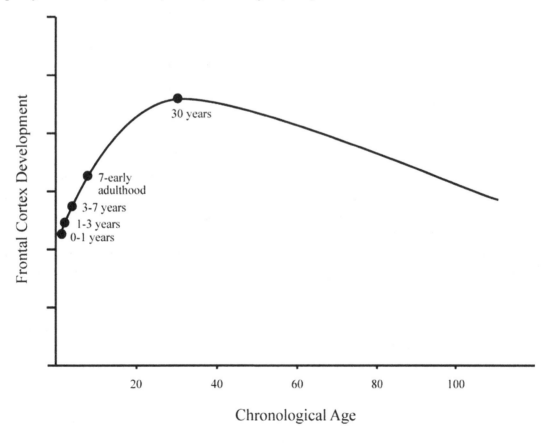

processing, an applied cognitive neuroscience perspective may provide a useful complement to traditional methods, enabling researchers to move beyond the examination of mental processes in lab tasks like Stroop to consider the implications of diminished PFC function and reduced attentional control in more naturalistic settings like driving a motor vehicle.

Though many aspects of driving become automated with practice, situations requiring drivers to exert attentional control often occur. Consider that turning left at a green light requires maintaining the goal of safe gap detection in the face of ongoing processing of the visual environment, where optimal functioning of attentional control may be the difference between a normal commute and a tragic accident. Older adults are six times more likely to be involved in an accident while attempting to turn left at a green light (National Highway and Traffic Safety Administration, 2009a). Moreover, when involvement in at-fault accidents are considered, there is a U-shaped function such that accidents decrease from teenage years, remain steady through middle age, and then increase for older adults (Allianz, 2006), particularly from age 75 onward. Factors such as lack of experience and increased risk-taking may account for the driving profile of teenagers (National Highway Traffic Safety Administration, 2009b). However, something else is necessary to explain the profile of older adults because they generally have more experience and are less likely to take risks (National Highway Traffic Safety Administration, 2009a). Again, diminished attentional control stemming from the declines in frontal cortex as shown in Figure 1 could partly explain these age-related changes in driving.

To quantify age-related changes in driving performance, using a high-fidelity simulator, Strayer and Drews (2004) compared young and older adults in a car-following paradigm where participants were instructed to maintain a prescribed following distance behind a lead vehicle and to press a brake pedal when the lead vehicle braked. Strayer and Drews found older adults not only had a greater following distance but also had a slower brake reaction time. They explained these age differences in terms of compensation. Specifically, in light of their slowed reaction time, to help avoid a rear-end collision with the lead vehicle, older adults may have purposefully increased their following distance. Alternatively, rather than strategic compensation, the increased following distance may indicate goal loss. That is, older adults may have failed to maintain the appropriate following distance as instructed by an experimenter, an explanation more consistent with deficits in attentional control or goal maintenance. Furthermore, older adults' slower brake reaction time may be partly explained by either general slowing of processing, the reduced speed that accompanies advanced age without regard to component processes (Salthouse, 1996), or slowing specific to a host of sensory/motor processes that may be necessary to press a brake pedal (Baltes & Lindenberger, 1997).

Aging, Driving, and Attentional Control: An Applied Cognitive Neuroscience Perspective

To test these hypotheses, we assessed the contribution of individual differences in attentional control to age-related changes in driving performance. We made several predictions on the interrelationship among these variables. First, if the age-related increase in following distance is due to individual differences in goal maintenance rather than strategic compensation, there will be a negative correlation such that participants with greater attentional control will better maintain a following distance defined by the experimenter. According to this prediction, individuals with reduced attentional control will be less likely to maintain the task goal, thereby increasing their distance from the lead vehicle. Second, if the age-related slowing in brake reaction time is largely due to individual differences in processing speed, there will be little if any correlation between individual differences in attentional control and brake reaction time. However, no task is process pure. Rather, tasks typically index multiple aspects of cognition. Thus, there may be a negative correlation such that participants with greater attentional control will better maintain the goal of pressing the brake pedal, thereby responding more quickly.

APPROACH

Participants

Sixty-three participants were tested. Thirty-one participants were recruited from a pool of community-dwelling older adults and were paid $30.00. Of these older adults, 16 were retained for subsequent analyses (M = 67.7 years; range = 61-80; 7 male). Thirty-two young adults were recruited from the Human Subjects Pool maintained by the Department of Psychology at the University of Utah and received course credit. Of these young adults, 20 were retained for subsequent analyses (M = 22.9 years; range = 18-30; 8 male).[1] These 36 participants had normal or corrected-to-normal vision, where acuity was assessed using a Snellen eye chart, and were not color blind. The Useful Field of View task (UFOV®), Visual Awareness, Inc.'s test of visual attention, was used to assess driver crash risk.[2] All participants had a valid driver's license at the time of testing.

Materials

Cognitive Measures. The operation span task assessed working memory capacity, a behavioral measure of individual differences in attentional control (Conway, et al., 2005). This computerized task requires participants to concurrently solve math problems while trying to memorize words. It consists of mathematical problems paired with to-be-remembered words (e.g., Is $(5 \times 2) - 3 = 6$? *DOG*). Participants received twelve trials in a random order, where the set size ranged from two to five math/word pairs. Participants read each equation aloud, solved it with a "yes" or "no" verbal response, and then spoke the word that followed. After each trial, they attempted to recall the entire set of words in the correct serial order. One point was awarded for each item recalled in the correct serial position (i.e., a partial scoring system, where the minimum possible score was 0 and the maximum 42). Importantly, participants were instructed to maintain 80% accuracy while solving math problems, receiving feedback on accuracy every three trials to insure compliance with task goals. These dual-task instructions revealed individual differences in attentional control, or goal maintenance of memorization in the face of ongoing math distraction.

PatrolSim driving simulator. A PatrolSim high-fidelity driving simulator was used, manufactured by L3 Communications/I-SIM, with high-resolution displays and 180-degree field of view. The simulator recreated a realistic driving environment through vehicle-dynamics, traffic-scenario, and road-surface software. Dashboard instrumentation, steering wheel, and gas and brake pedals were based on a Ford Crown Victoria with automatic transmission.

Procedure

Participants were tested individually. After assessing visual acuity and color blindness, the UFOV task and the operation span task were administered, where the order of the two tasks was counterbalanced. Participants were then taken to the driving simulator and trained to follow a lead vehicle on the highway at a two-second following distance, braking whenever they saw the lead vehicle's brake lights illuminate. If they fell too far behind the lead vehicle, a horn sounded, cueing them to shorten their following distance, with the horn stopping once participants were compliant with these instructions. Participants were told there would not be a horn in future driving scenarios;

Table 1. Bivariate correlations among age, working memory capacity, following distance, and brake reaction time

	Age	WMC	FD	BRT
Age	----------	-.35*	.48**	.40*
WMC		----------	-.49**	-.40*
FD			----------	.71**
BRT				----------

Note. * p<.05, **p<.01; WMC = working memory capacity; FD = following distance; BRT = brake reaction time.

however, they were instructed to use the practice sequence as a guide for maintaining an appropriate following distance in subsequent drives. Finally, during the experiment, participants drove two, 10-mile sections on a multilane highway, following a pace car programmed to drive in the right lane and to brake unexpectedly. To assess individual differences in driving performance, we measured each participant's following distance from the lead vehicle and their reaction time to press the brake pedal after the lead vehicle braked. Following distance has been found to discriminate between cases where drivers find themselves in dangerous situations from cases where drivers remain in control of their vehicle (Hirst & Graham, 1997). Moreover, sluggish brake reactions, such as the ones described herein, can increase the likelihood and severity of motor-vehicle collisions (Brown, Lee, & McGehee, 2001). Indeed, when considering the potential influence of distraction on driving performance, a meta-analysis conducted by Horrey and Wickens (2006) indicated reaction time is the most sensitive dependent measure (see Strayer, Watson, & Drews, 2011, for a recent review).

RESULTS

To assess the contribution of individual differences in working memory capacity to age-related changes in driving, we computed bivariate correlations among age expressed in years, partial score on the operation span test, mean following distance, and mean brake reaction time. See Table 1 for a complete correlation matrix for these four variables (Pearson's r).

There are three important points to note here. First, consistent with the literature on age-related decline in frontal development and function as illustrated on the right side of the curve depicted in Figure 1, increased age was associated with diminished attentional control. Specifically, as shown in Figure 2, as age increased, working memory capacity decreased ($r = -.35$). Second, with respect to age-related changes in driving, consistent with Strayer and Drews (2004), as shown in the top half of Figure 3, following distance increased with age ($r = .48$; Figure 3A), and brake reaction time slowed ($r = .40$; Figure 3B). Third and most importantly for the purposes of the present chapter, working memory capacity was indeed related to both aspects of driving performance. That is, as shown in the bottom half of Figure 3, as working memory capacity increased, following distance decreased ($r = -.49$; Figure 3C); similarly, as working memory capacity increased, brake reaction time quickened ($r = -.40$; Figure 3D).

Taken together, this pattern of correlations suggests age-related changes in driving may be partly due to individual differences in attentional control. Here, the logic is that the age variable offers little in explanatory value and thus must be considered in the context of underlying cognitive mechanisms known to change with and transcend age, such as attentional control or processing

Figure 2. Working memory capacity as a function of age. Consistent with age-related declines in both PFC development and attentional control, increased age was associated with diminished working memory capacity. The corresponding regression line is illustrated.

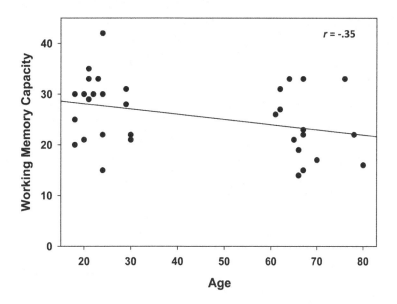

speed (see Watson, et al., 2011, for additional discussion of these possibilities). For example, if the relationship between age and driving performance is entirely due to reduced working memory capacity, the influence of age will no longer be statistically significant ($p<.05$) after accounting for individual differences in attentional control. To directly test this possibility, we conducted two hierarchical multiple regression analyses (see Chan & McDermott, 2007, for a similar analytic approach involving age, individual differences in frontal lobe functioning, and group differences in both accurate and false recall). In the first analysis, working memory capacity was entered in step one to predict following distance, yielding a statistically significant model reflecting the bivariate correlation reported above and shown in Figure 3C ($R^2=.24$, $F(1,34)=10.71$, $MSe=27.77$, $p<.01$). Critically, in the second step of this analysis, when age was entered as a second variable to further predict following distance, its unique contribution was still significant ($\beta=.35$, $\Delta R^2=.11$, $p<.05$), suggesting there is more to the predictive ability

of age than just deficits in attentional control. In the second regression analysis, working memory capacity was entered in step one to predict brake reaction time, yielding a statistically significant model reflecting the bivariate correlation reported above and shown in Figure 3D ($R^2=.16$, $F(1,34)=6.56$, $MSe=45,893$, $p<.05$). Moreover, in the second step of this analysis, when age was entered as a second variable to further predict brake reaction time, its unique contribution was only marginally significant ($\beta=.30$, $\Delta R^2=.08$, $p=.08$), suggesting it may not be necessary to appeal to individual differences in processing speed to explain age-related changes in driving, at least with respect to slower braking responses. Thus, as predicted, our hierarchical regression results are more generally consistent with the idea that the influence of age on two well-established measures of driving performance operates either partly (following distance) or almost entirely (brake reaction time) through individual differences in attentional control that co-vary with age.[3]

Figure 3. Following distance (A) and brake reaction time (B) as a function of age. Increased age was associated with both greater following distance (A) and slower brake reaction time (B). Following distance (C) and brake reaction time (D) as a function of individual differences in working memory capacity. Increased working memory capacity was associated with both shorter following distance (C) and faster brake reaction time (D). Corresponding regression lines are illustrated.

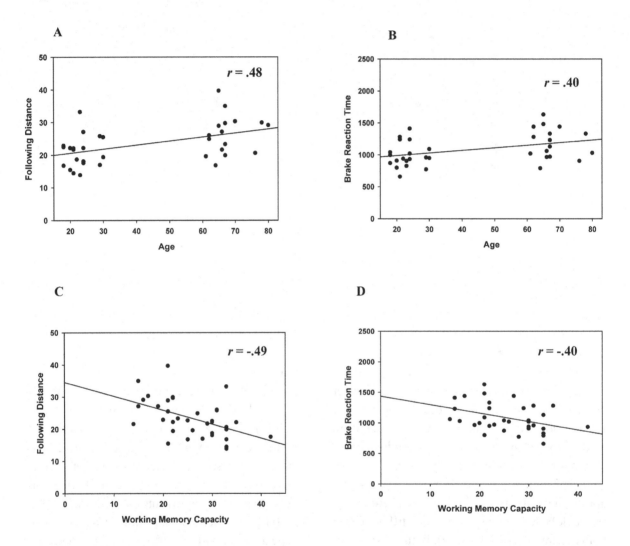

DISCUSSION

As predicted, regression analyses confirmed the increased following distance of older adults (Figure 3A) co-varied with age-related deficits in attentional control (Figure 2). That is, there was a negative correlation between individual differences in working memory capacity and driving performance such that participants with greater

attentional control maintained a following distance closer to what was established during training (Figure 3C). Had the opposite occurred, a positive correlation between working memory capacity and following distance, the results would have been more consistent with a strategic compensation account. In this case, one possible interpretation would have been that those with higher working memory capacity purposefully increased their following distance from the lead vehicle to cope with unexpected braking events in our car following paradigm. However, the present results are clearly more in line with a goal maintenance account where individuals higher in working memory capacity are less susceptible to goal loss while driving, and thus more closely followed the lead vehicle.

Furthermore, as predicted given the increased sensitivity of this dependent measure, the age-related slowing in brake reaction time (Figure 3B) is largely if not entirely explained by co-varying, age differences in attentional control. More specifically, there was a negative correlation between individual differences in working memory capacity and brake reaction time such that individuals with greater attentional control had a faster brake reaction time (Figure 3D). It may be that greater attentional control enabled participants to better maintain the goal of applying their brake when the lead vehicle braked. In this light, our results suggest an adaptive, flexible role for attentional control in simultaneously maintaining at least two different task goals while driving, including both maintaining an experimenter-prescribed following distance and pressing a brake pedal when a lead vehicle's brake lights illuminated. Hence, individuals with greater working memory capacity may be better at dividing attention and readily configuring attentional control to meet task demands and to avoid interference, whether on more traditional laboratory measures like the operation span task or real-world situations like driving.

CAVEATS AND FUTURE DIRECTIONS

We interpret variability in operation span task performance as due to individual differences in attentional control, or the ability to actively maintain task goals in interference-rich environments. However, while the present study was motivated by the resistance to interference hypothesis of Engle and colleagues, the source of individual differences in working memory capacity that arise out of this complex span task is still hotly debated. Indeed, attentional control is not a unitary construct; therefore, individual differences in performance could be due to other component processes including proficiency at selective attention, task switching, goal updating, or inhibition. Nevertheless, our study was not intended to be a referendum on the process purity of the operation span task (Jacoby, 1991). Rather, we relied on a common interpretation of operation span performance, where individual differences in working memory capacity have been shown to predict susceptibility to interference on traditional lab tasks thought to require goal maintenance including Stroop, antisaccade, and dichotic listening (see Kane & Engle, 2002, for a review). In keeping with this tradition, our study is the first to demonstrate age-related changes in driving can be explained in part by individual differences in top-down attentional control, defined as the frontally mediated ability to maintain task goals and avoid potential distractions.

Within this theoretical framework, we consider driving to be a complex, real-world example of multitasking that fundamentally requires a high level of attentional control. For example, driving often requires dividing attention among multiple task goals embedded in an ever-changing traffic environment where there is great potential for interference (e.g., maintaining a prescribed following distance behind a lead vehicle, while also being prepared to press the brake). Consistent with this argument, elsewhere we have shown that a hands-free cell phone conversation produces bidirectional cognitive impairments in measures of working memory capacity and driving performance (Watson & Strayer, 2010). Notably, these impairments include increased following distance and slower brake reaction time, as we report here for older adult drivers with reduced working memory capacity. One might wonder whether this pattern could be interpreted as an adaptive increase in following distance to overcome sluggish brake reaction time. If so, ironically, the present results suggest the older adults who are most likely to adopt this strategy may have insufficient working memory capacity to notice or compensate for the influence of their cognitive deficits on driving, experiencing a form of inattentional blindness to their own impairments. Thus, converging evidence from our lab suggests slower brake reaction time and elongated following distance are driving outcomes associated with breakdowns in goal maintenance and diminished attentional control.

However, it is noteworthy that individual differences in attentional control only explained a portion of the age-related changes observed in driving. For example, our results also indicated there may be an important role for other cognitive mechanisms influencing following distance, particularly with regard to a unique contribution for age above and beyond that associated with individual differences in working memory capacity. Future research may reveal that this age-related variance in driving will be attributable to a form of strategic compensation, or some other cognitive mechanism, that is evidently orthogonal to individual differences in working memory capacity. And while the unique contribution of age to brake reaction time was only marginally significant after statistically controlling for individual differences in working memory capacity via hierarchical multiple regression, it may be worthwhile to consider including independent measures of processing speed in future research on age-related changes in driving. In this way, one might be better able to more directly assess the relative contribution of individual differences in attentional control and processing speed to observed age differences in driving performance.

SUMMARY AND CONCLUSION

To summarize, this study demonstrated age-related changes in operating a motor vehicle can be explained, by and large, by diminished attentional control. In this way, our findings convincingly demonstrated the relevance of cognitive theory to naturalistic settings for a behavior many of us engage in daily regardless of our age, driving, where the ability to successfully maintain task goals and to avoid interference is likely critical. Furthermore, our study underscored the promise of adopting an applied cognitive neuroscience perspective to guide future research on age-related changes in cognition (Watson, et al., 2011). In conclusion, when evaluating driver safety in the elderly, it may be increasingly important to consider age in the context of cognitive mechanisms and potential breakdowns in frontally mediated attentional control (Carr, et al., 2006). Robust attentional control and successful goal maintenance may be essential when interacting with a myriad of complex technologies in the modern world including cars, cell phones, or other cognitively challenging devices (see Strayer & Watson, 2012, for more commentary on bottlenecks in human information processing and the multitasking brain).

REFERENCES

Allianz. (2006). *Who causes car accidents: Percent of at-fault accidents on all accidents with injuries.* Retrieved from http://knowledge.allianz.com/mobility/?807/Who-Causes-Car-Accidents

Ball, K., Owsley, C., Sloane, M. D., Roenker, D. L., & Bruni, J. R. (1993). Visual attention problems as a predictor of vehicle accidents in older drivers. *Investigative Ophthalmology & Visual Science, 34*, 3110–3123.

Baltes, P. B., & Lindenberger, U. (1997). Emergence of a powerful connection between sensory and cognitive function across the adult life span: A new window to the study of cognitive aging? *Psychology and Aging, 12*, 12–21. doi:10.1037/0882-7974.12.1.12

Brown, T. L., Lee, J. D., & McGehee, D. V. (2001). Human performance models and rear-end collision avoidance algorithms. *Human Factors, 43*, 462–482. doi:10.1518/001872001775898250

Carr, D. B., Duchek, J. M., Meuser, T. M., & Morris, J. C. (2006). Older adult drivers with cognitive impairment. *American Family Physician, 73*, 1029–1034.

Chan, J. C. K., & McDermott, K. B. (2007). Effects of frontal lobe functioning and age on veridical and false recall. *Psychonomic Bulletin & Review, 14*(4), 606–611. doi:10.3758/BF03196809

Conway, A. R. A., Kane, M. J., Bunting, M. F., Hambrick, D. Z., Wilhelm, O., & Engle, R. W. (2005). Working memory span tasks: A methodological review and user's guide. *Psychonomic Bulletin & Review, 12*, 769–786. doi:10.3758/BF03196772

Hirst, S., & Graham, R. (1997). The format and presentation of collision warnings. In Noy, Y. I. (Ed.), *Ergonomics and Safety of Intelligent Driver Interfaces* (pp. 203–319). Hillsdale, NJ: Lawrence Erlbaum.

Hoffman, L., McDowd, J. M., Atchley, P., & Dubinsky, R. (2005). The role of visual attention in predicting driver impairment in older adults. *Psychology and Aging, 20*, 610–622. doi:10.1037/0882-7974.20.4.610

Horrey, W. J., & Wickens, C. D. (2006). Examining the impact of cell phone conversations on driving using meta-analytic techniques. *Human Factors, 48*, 196–205. doi:10.1518/001872006776412135

Jacoby, L. (1991). A process dissociation framework: Separating automatic from intentional uses of memory. *Journal of Memory and Language, 30*, 513–541. doi:10.1016/0749-596X(91)90025-F

Kane, M. J., & Engle, R. W. (2002). The role of prefrontal cortex in working-memory capacity, executive attention, and general fluid intelligence: An individual-differences perspective. *Psychonomic Bulletin & Review, 9*, 637–671. doi:10.3758/BF03196323

National Highway and Traffic Safety Administration. (2007). *Traffic safety facts: Older population.* Retrieved from http://www.nhtsa.dot.gov/portal/site/nhtsa/menuitem.31176b9b03647a189ca8e410dba046a0/

National Highway and Traffic Safety Administration. (2009a). *Traffic safety facts: Identifying situations associated with older drivers' crashes.* Retrieved from http://www.nhtsa.gov/DOT/NHTSA/Communication%20&%20Consumer%20Information/Traffic%20Tech%20Publications/Associated%20Files/tt380.pdf

National Highway and Traffic Safety Administration. (2009b). *Traffic safety facts research note: Fatal crashes involving young drivers.* Retrieved from http://www-nrd.nhtsa.dot.gov/Pubs/811218.PDF

Owsley, C., Ball, K. K., Sloane, M. E., Roenker, D. L., & Bruni, J. R. (1991). Visual/cognitive correlates of vehicle accidents in older drivers. *Psychology and Aging, 6*, 403–415. doi:10.1037/0882-7974.6.3.403

Salthouse, T. A. (1996). The processing-speed theory of adult age differences in cognition. *Psychological Review, 103*, 403–428. doi:10.1037/0033-295X.103.3.403

Spieler, D. H., Balota, D. A., & Faust, M. E. (1996). Stroop performance in healthy younger and older adults and in individuals with dementia of the Alzheimer's type. *Journal of Experimental Psychology. Human Perception and Performance, 22*(2), 461–479. doi:10.1037/0096-1523.22.2.461

Strayer, D. L., & Drews, F. A. (2004). Profiles in driver distraction: Effects of cell phone conversations on younger and older drivers. *Human Factors, 46,* 640–649. doi:10.1518/hfes.46.4.640.56806

Strayer, D. L., & Watson, J. M. (2012, March/April). Supertaskers and the multitasking brain. *Scientific American Mind*.

Strayer, D. L., Watson, J. M., & Drews, F. A. (2011). Cognitive distraction while multitasking in the automobile. In Ross, B. (Ed.), *The Psychology of Learning and Motivation* (*Vol. 54*, pp. 29–58). Burlington, VT: Academic Press. doi:10.1016/B978-0-12-385527-5.00002-4

Watson, J. M., Lambert, A. E., Miller, A. E., & Strayer, D. L. (2011). The magical letters P, F, C, and sometimes U: The rise and fall of executive attention with the development of prefrontal cortex. In Fingerman, K., Berg, C., Antonucci, T., & Smith, J. (Eds.), *Handbook of Lifespan Psychology* (pp. 409–438). London, UK: Springer.

Watson, J. M., & Strayer, D. L. (2010). Supertaskers: Profiles in extraordinary multitasking ability. *Psychonomic Bulletin & Review, 17,* 479–485. doi:10.3758/PBR.17.4.479

West, R. (1996). An application of prefrontal cortex function theory to cognitive aging. *Psychological Bulletin, 120,* 272–292. doi:10.1037/0033-2909.120.2.272

ADDITIONAL READING

Braver, T., Gray, J., & Burgess, G. (2007). Explaining the many varieties of working memory variation: Dual mechanisms of cognitive control. In Conway, A. R. A., Jarrold, C., Kane, M. J., Miyake, A., & Towse, J. N. (Eds.), *Variation in Working Memory* (pp. 76–106). Oxford, UK: Oxford University Press. doi:10.1093/acprof:oso/9780195168648.003.0004

De Luca, C. R., & Leventer, R. L. (2008). Developmental trajectories of executive function across the lifespan. In Anderson, V., Jacobs, R., & Anderson, P. (Eds.), *Executive Functions and the Frontal Lobes: A Lifespan Perspective*. London, UK: Psychology Press.

Diamond, A. (2002). Normal development of prefrontal cortex from birth to young adulthood: Cognitive functions, anatomy, and biochemistry. In Stuss, D. T., & Knight, R. T. (Eds.), *Principles of Frontal Lobe Function* (pp. 466–503). Oxford, UK: Oxford University Press. doi:10.1093/acprof:oso/9780195134971.003.0029

Engle, R. (2002). Working memory capacity as executive attention. *Current Directions in Psychological Science, 11,* 19–23. doi:10.1111/1467-8721.00160

Engle, R. W., & Kane, M. (2004). Executive attention, working memory capacity, and a two-factor theory of cognitive control. In Ross, B. (Ed.), *The Psychology of Learning and Motivation* (*Vol. 44*, pp. 145–199). New York, NY: Elsevier. doi:10.1016/S0079-7421(03)44005-X

Kane, M., & Engle, R. (2003). Working memory capacity and the control of attention: The contributions of goal neglect, response competition, and task set to Stroop interference. *Journal of Experimental Psychology. General, 132,* 47–70. doi:10.1037/0096-3445.132.1.47

Kramer, A. F., & Madden, D. J. (2008). Attention. In Craik, F. I. M., & Salthouse, T. A. (Eds.), *Handbook of Aging and Cognition III* (pp. 189–249). New York, NY: Psychology Press.

McCabe, D. P., Roediger, H. L., McDaniel, M. A., Balota, D. A., & Hambrick, D. Z. (2010). The relationship between working memory capacity and executive functioning: Evidence for a common executive attention construct. *Neuropsychology, 24*, 222–243. doi:10.1037/a0017619

McDaniel, M., Einstein, G., & Jacoby, L. (2008). New considerations in aging and memory: The glass may be half full. In Craik, F. I. M., & Salthouse, T. A. (Eds.), *The Handbook of Aging and Cognition III* (pp. 251–310). New York, NY: Psychology Press.

Ophir, E., Nass, C. I., & Wagner, A. D. (2009). Cognitive control in media multitaskers. *Proceedings of the National Academy of Sciences of the United States of America, 106*, 15583–15587. doi:10.1073/pnas.0903620106

Raz, N. (2000). Aging of the brain and its impact on cognitive performance: Integration of structural and functional findings. In Craik, F. I. M., & Salthouse, T. A. (Eds.), *The Handbook of Aging and Cognition* (2nd ed., pp. 1–90). Mahwah, NJ: Erlbaum.

Schneider, B., & Pichora-Fuller, M. (2000). Implications of perceptual deterioration for cognitive aging research. In Craik, F. I. M., & Salthouse, T. A. (Eds.), *The Handbook of Aging and Cognition* (2nd ed., pp. 155–219). Mahwah, NJ: Erlbaum.

Strayer, D. L., & Drews, F. A. (2007). Attention. In Durso, F., Nickerson, R., Dumais, S., Lewandowsky, S., & Perfect, T. (Eds.), *Handbook of Applied Cognition II* (pp. 29–54). West Sussex, UK: John Wiley & Sons, Ltd. doi:10.1002/9780470713181.ch2

Underwood, G., Crundall, D., & Chapman, P. (2007). Driving. In Durso, F., Nickerson, R., Dumais, S., Lewandowsky, S., & Perfect, T. (Eds.), *Handbook of Applied Cognition II* (pp. 391–414). West Sussex, UK: John Wiley & Sons, Ltd. doi:10.1002/9780470713181.ch15

Wickens, C. D. (1984). Processing resources in attention. In Parasuraman, R., & Davies, R. (Eds.), *Varieties of Attention* (pp. 63–101). New York, NY: Academic Press.

KEY TERMS AND DEFINITIONS

Attentional Control: Attentional control is one's ability to maintain task goals and to avoid interference or distraction. It is thought to be mediated by the prefrontal cortex of the brain.

Frontal Lobe: The frontal lobe of the brain refers to the cortex anterior to the central sulcus and it contains several prominent areas including (1) the primary motor strip that supports gross motor movement, (2) premotor and supplementary motor areas that provide plans for guiding this gross motor movement, and (3) the prefrontal cortex with its various specialized sub-regions that support goal-directed behavior.

ENDNOTES

[1] Data was excluded from twelve young and fifteen older adults who were unable to complete the study due to motion sickness, failure to establish a reasonable following distance or brake reaction time (i.e., > 2.5 SDs from the mean of either of these two dependent measures of driving), vision problems, or epilepsy.

[2] We used the UFOV as a screening measure rather than a predictor. For the UFOV, scores can range from 1 (very low risk) to 5 (high risk) (Ball, et al., 1993). Not surprisingly,

given our participants' low risk scores (M = 1.17), collisions were rare (i.e., N = 3, with one occurring for an older adult, and one each for two different young adults). We refer the interested reader to additional empirical work addressing whether UFOV performance can explain age-related changes in driving (see Hoffman, McDowd, Atchley, & Dubinsky, 2005; Owsley, et al., 1991).

[3] Older adults' average following distance was also more variable than that of young adults (r = .26, p=.12), although this relationship was only marginally significant. With one notable exception, when the standard deviation of the mean following distance was substituted for the mean following distance in our analyses, the bivariate correlations and the regression results were qualitatively similar. Specifically, in the hierarchical regression analysis using the standard deviation of following distance, the unique contribution of age was no longer significant after accounting for individual differences in attentional control (β = .10, ΔR^2 = .01, p=.56).

Chapter 3
The Use of Gesturing to Facilitate Older Adults' Learning from Computer-Based Dynamic Visualizations

Kim Ouwehand
Erasmus University Rotterdam, The Netherlands

Tamara van Gog
Erasmus University Rotterdam, The Netherlands

Fred Paas
Erasmus University Rotterdam, The Netherlands & University of Wollongong, Australia

ABSTRACT

The present chapter describes the role of gestures in instructional design from a cognitive load theory perspective, addressing in particular how this might benefit aging adults. Healthy older adults have to cope with several cognitive changes related to their working memory, such as a decline in: 1) the ability to deal with interference, 2) cognitive speed in response to unimodal stimuli (e.g. visual information), and 3) the ability to associate and integrate information elements. Cognitive load theory, with its focus on adapting learning formats to the limitations of working memory, provides a promising framework to address learning in older adults. Research inspired by cognitive load theory has shown that attentional cueing can reduce interference during learning, presenting instructions in a multimodal format can make more efficient use of WM stores (both auditory and visual), and the manner of presentation of information can aid integrative learning. Interestingly, studies using gestures in instruction show that gestures accompanying verbal information improve learning in similar ways. However, not much research has been done in applying the instructional guidelines of cognitive load theory and the use of gestures to older adults' learning. In the present chapter, the authors will discuss possibilities of gestures to improve multimedia learning in older adults using some important guidelines proposed by cognitive load theory.

DOI: 10.4018/978-1-4666-1966-1.ch003

INTRODUCTION

In the present chapter, Cognitive Load Theory (CLT) (Paas, Renkl, & Sweller, 2003; Sweller, 1988, 2010; Sweller, Van Merriënboer, & Paas, 1998) and the cognitive architecture it describes is used as a framework to discuss the possibility of improving learning in older adults by using gestures in instructional design.

Normal aging has been associated with age-related changes in cognitive functioning, such as a decline in; WM functioning (Celnik, et al., 2005; Park, et al., 2002), the speed with which information is processed (Salthouse, 1996), and associative memory (for a review, see Old & Naveh-Benjamin, 2008). As will be discussed, a multimodal format of instruction (a format in which the information is simultaneously presented to two or more modalities, e.g. visual and auditory), has been found to speed up information processing in older adults (Laurenti, Burdette, Maldjian, & Wallace, 2006) and when the visual information contains a manual action, it can enhance associative memory in older adults (Kormi-Nouri & Nilsson, 2001). Because gestures are a form of manual actions, and provide an additional modality when combined with speech and/or pictorial information, we suggest that adding gestures to computer-based instructional dynamic visualizations can improve learning in older adults. Two types of gestures are of specific interest for this chapter: 1) deictic gestures, which are used to refer to something that is physically present in the environment (e.g., a pointing gesture; Iverson & Goldin-Meadow, 2005) and, 2) representational gestures, used to depict visual information, i.e. about an object or action.

First, we will discuss some main points of CLT with specific relevance for the present chapter. Within the context of this theory, age-related declines and changes in Working Memory (WM) of healthy older adults in relation to learning will be extensively discussed. We will then introduce research that has shown beneficial effects of producing or observing gestures on comprehension, learning, and cognitive load. We will then relate these findings to CLT-inspired instructional formats and guidelines for the design of computer-based dynamic visualizations that have proven successful. For example, instructional formats such as observational learning from modeling examples and worked examples (for reviews, see Atkinson, Derry, Renkl, & Wortham, 2000; Sweller, et al., 1998; Van Gog & Rummel, 2010), guidelines to use multiple modalities in instructional materials (Ginns, 2005; Tindall-Ford, Chandler, & Sweller, 1997; Van Gerven, Paas, Van Merriënboer, Hendriks, & Schmidt, 2003), and using cues to guide learners' attention to relevant elements of materials (for a review, see De Koning, Tabbers, Rikers, & Paas, 2009) have been found to reduce cognitive load and foster learning. However, the existing literature on the effects of gestures on learning has mainly focused on children or young adults, and to the best of our knowledge, it has not yet addressed learning in older adults. We will relate the beneficial effect of gestures on learning to the age-related declines and changes in WM and CLT-inspired guidelines for instructional design, and discuss how gestures might help optimize learning in older adults. Important shared features between CLT-inspired instructional designs and gesture-speech instructions discussed here, are: 1) gestures can function as attentional cues, guiding learners efficiently through dynamic visualizations such as animations and video-based examples, 2) gesture-speech instructions are a form of multimodal instruction, and 3) observational learning and gesture-speech instructions both make use of (human) models, which may provide a rich embodied representation of the study material. Based on this integration of research on gestures and CLT-inspired instructional formats and guidelines we will generate some hypotheses about how gestures can be implemented for multimedia learning in older adults, for example in the design of computer-based dynamic visualizations.

Cognitive Load Theory

The central tenet of CLT is that learning can be seriously inhibited if the capacity and duration limitations of WM are not taken into account in the design of instruction (Sweller, 2010). In short, CLT distinguishes three kinds of cognitive load in relation to learning: 1) intrinsic load, which is a fixed property of the study material, 2) extraneous load, which reflects how well the instructional design presents the learning material, and 3) germane cognitive load, which reflects the amount of WM resources that can be made available for learning. According to CLT, schema construction and automation are the most important processes for learning and transfer of knowledge. Schemata are stored in Long-Term Memory (LTM) and can be regarded as mental models in which all pieces of information, also called information elements, are categorized and organized (Sweller, et al., 1998; Van Merriënboer & Sweller, 2005). The amount of relationships between information elements is referred to as element interactivity, which is the main determinant of intrinsic load (Sweller, 2010; Sweller & Chandler, 1994; Tindall-Ford, et al., 1997). Learning materials with low element interactivity have a low intrinsic load because individual elements can be learned with minimal reference to other elements and therefore, put a low demand on WM. In contrast, in materials with high element interactivity, individual elements heavily interact and therefore cannot be learned in isolation. For successful learning of materials with high element interactivity, multiple elements need to be associated and integrated into the schema (Sweller, et al., 1998). Although schemata are stored in LTM, the construction of such schemata is an active process, which takes place in WM. Existing schemas, can be regarded as sophisticated rules that can be applied and eventually (after extensive practice) used automatically (Sweller, et al., 1998). According to Sweller (2010) total cognitive load stands for the total of intrinsic and extraneous load. Germane load and extraneous

load are negatively related, meaning that if extraneous load decreases, germane load increases and vice versa. To design effective instruction of complex cognitive tasks (high in intrinsic load), extraneous load should be reduced which can increase germane load, that is, WM capacity that can be allocated to schema construction and automation processes.

Mayer (2005) has proposed a Cognitive Theory of Multimedia Learning (CTML) which combines the principles of CLT and the view that auditory and visual information is processed by partly independent WM stores (Baddeley, 1992) and visual and verbal information corresponding to the same object, can have additive effects on memory (Clark & Paivio, 1991; Paivio, 1963, 1965). In CTML, learning is considered an active process in which the learner needs to select relevant information elements, organize these elements, and integrate them with existing knowledge (Mayer, 2001, 2005). In novices, who are expected to experience high cognitive load, because they do not possess the appropriate schema, several learning effects seem to support the principles of CLT and CTML, such as the worked example effect (e.g., Atkinson, et al., 2000; Paas & Van Gog, 2006; Paas & Van Merrienboer, 1994), the split-attention effect (e.g., Chandler & Sweller, 1992; Mayer & Moreno, 1998; Sweller, 2010; Sweller, Ayres, & Kalyuga, 2011), and the modality effect (e.g., Ginns, 2005; Tindall-Ford, et al., 1997; Van Gerven, et al., 2003), and the cueing/signaling effect (e.g., De Koning, Tabbers, Rikers, & Paas, 2009; Tabbers, Martens, & Van Merriënboer, 2004; Mautone & Mayer, 2001). The worked example effect reflects the superior learning from worked examples (problems with worked-out solutions and solution steps) compared to conventional problems (the initial problem state with the request to find the solution) when learners have low prior knowledge (e.g. Atkinson, et al., 2000). From a CLT perspective, learning is improved because extraneous load due to high element interactivity caused by considering alternative problem states and moves in conventional problem solving, is removed in worked examples, which frees up WM resources that can be dedicated to studying the procedure and constructing a schema of how the problem should be solved (Sweller, 2010).

The split-attention effect reflects the finding that for complex tasks with high element interactivity, an instructional format, which presents the study material an integrated manner, improves learning compared to a format in which learners have to integrate information elements themselves (Ayres & Sweller, 2005). This effect can be explained by the fact that in an integrative instructional format, the extraneous load imposed by the need to mentally integrate relations between information elements present in more segregated instructions, is removed, which frees up WM resources that can be dedicated to deal with the intrinsic load of the material (Sweller, 2010). For example, learning from worked examples consisting of a diagram and text is improved when the text is presented in the diagram in such a way that the solutions steps are presented in close physical proximity to the part of the diagram which they refer to, compared to presenting the picture and text separately (e.g. Sweller, Chandler, Tierney, & Cooper, 1990). Furthermore, Mayer and Moreno (2002) also emphasize temporal and spatial contiguity in multimedia design. Spatial contiguity refers to presenting mutually referring information sources in spatial proximity (cf. the integrated format just discussed), while temporal contiguity refers to presenting information in close temporal proximity. An instructional format that is very suitable for application of the temporal proximity principle (Mayer, 2001) is a multimedia format in which information is presented via different sensory modalities. Research has shown that example-based learning can be improved by using a multimodal instead of a unimodal format of instruction (e.g., Mousavi, Low, & Sweller, 1995; Tindall-Ford, et al., 1997). For example, Mousavi et al. (1995) showed that problem solving performance after studying worked examples in

geometry, was improved when worked examples were presented multimodally (pictures and spoken text, or written text and spoken text), compared to unimodally (pictures and written text). This finding has been replicated by Tindall-Ford et al. (1997) with worked examples about electricity. Furthermore, Tindall-Ford et al. (1997) manipulated intrinsic load and found that the multimodal instruction was only beneficial for learning materials with high element interactivity. Consistent with this finding, CLT also proposes that for instructions with high element interactivity, a multimodal format of instruction can reduce cognitive load by reducing visual search processes, information integration processes, and by distributing the load over different WM stores (Van Gerven, et al., 2003).

In summary, for complex learning, CLT-inspired research has shown that reducing the need to search, process and judge alternatives, to prevent processing of irrelevant information, and fostering the mental integration of information elements (i.e., presenting related information elements in close spatial or temporal proximity), can free up WM resources that can be dedicated to learning. In relation to the present chapter, these instructional formats and guidelines might be of specific importance for the design of instruction for older adults, because WM processes change with age.

Age-Related Changes in Active Processing and Interference Control

Normal aging has been found to be associated with a decrease in several memory functions (Hedden & Gabrieli, 2004; Kessels, Hobbel, & Postema, 2007; Spencer, & Raz, 1995) including WM functioning (Celnik, et al., 2005; Park, et al., 2002), which can seriously hamper learning. Within WM, a distinction between active and passive WM processes is proposed by Vecchi, Richardson, and Cavallini (2005). According to Vecchi et al. (2005), passive WM functions involve the (passive) storage of information and recall of this information in its presented format, while active WM functions involve more (active) processes, such as transformation, integration, and/ or manipulation of information. Evidence suggests that age-related differences in passive storage and maintenance of information are relatively small compared to differences in active processing (Bopp &Verhaeghen, 2005). As a result, older adults' performance maintains at a relatively high level for tasks in which information can be applied in the same format in which it was learned (e.g. remembering and typing a password for using an Internet website account). However, this passive WM system is not useful for complex learning, which often requires a more flexible understanding of underlying rules and their hierarchy. Moreover, existing knowledge might even interfere with retrieval of relevant information (Cansino, Guzzon, Martinelli, Barollo, & Casco, 2011). Research has shown that active compared to passive WM processes decline earlier in the process of aging (Vecchi, et al., 2005). Note that Mayer (2001, 2005) also emphasized that schema construction requires active control processes for selecting relevant information elements, discovering important element relations, and suppressing or ignoring irrelevant information. Therefore, the age-related decline in active WM functioning can be a major obstacle to learning for older adults, especially in learning tasks with high element interactivity.

Within these active WM functions, several researchers suggest that the mechanisms responsible for effective interference control decline with age (e.g., Hartman & Hasher, 1991; Hasher, Stolzfus, Zacks, & Rypma, 1991; Houx, Jolles, & Vreeling, 1993; McDown & Filion, 1995; Stolzfus, Hasher, Zacks, Ulivi, & Goldstein, 1993). This age-related decline in interference control means that older adults have difficulties with suppressing irrelevant information. This could cause an increase in ineffective (extraneous) cognitive load during learning, due to competition for resources between irrelevant and relevant information. However, studies investigating interference control in older adults are not conclusive.

A well-known paradigm to test interference control is the Stroop task (Stroop, 1935). In the classical Stroop task, participants are requested to name the ink color of color words presented in congruent (e.g., the word 'red' printed in red) or incongruent ink colors (e.g. the word 'red' printed in blue). The Stroop effect represents the robust finding that participants are slower to respond and make more errors in the incongruent condition. The dominant theoretical account for the Stroop effect is that in the incongruent condition, participants are slower, because it takes some time to resolve the conflict between the reading response and color naming (for a review, see McLeod, 1991). Consistent with the hypothesis that older adults are impaired in interference control, some studies showed a larger Stroop effect in older adults compared to younger adults (e.g., Cohn, Dustman, & Bradford, 1984; Houx, et al., 1993). However, Verhaegen and Meersman (1998) concluded from their meta-analysis of studies on the Stroop effect in older compared to younger adults that the differences between older and younger participants can be explained by general cognitive slowing and do not reflect an age-related decline in interference control functioning. However, more recent studies using ERP and fMRI found an age-related change in brain activation in areas that are believed to be involved in interference control in addition to an increase in the Stroop effect (Mathis, Schunck, Erb, Namer, & Luthringer, 2009; West & Alain, 2000). Another paradigm targeting interference control is the negative priming paradigm (Tipper, 1985). In this paradigm, the relevance of targets and distractor stimuli is manipulated in such a manner, that a stimulus that was irrelevant in previous trials becomes a target stimulus in subsequent trials. The negative priming effect reflects the increase in reaction time to the target stimulus that had to be ignored previously, because this target still activates inhibitory processes used in previous trials in which it had to be ignored. In support of the hypothesis that older adults have impaired functioning of their interference control mechanism, a number of studies have shown that the negative priming effect is absent in older adults (e.g., Hasher, et al., 1991; McDowd & Oseas-Kreger, 1991; Stolzfus, et al., 1993). However, other studies have failed to show absence of negative priming in older adults (e.g., Gamboz, Russo, & Fox, 2002; Kieley & Hartleyand, 1997). In further exploration of the mixed results from the Stroop interference and negative priming studies in older adults, Cansino et al. (2011) proposed that the ability to suppress irrelevant information in older adults might depend on which type of inhibitory function is needed. They used a new paradigm in which they were able to distinguish between two inhibitory processes originally proposed by Hasher et al. (1999), namely 'access' and 'deletion.' The first process, 'access,' is involved with preventing irrelevant information from accessing WM. The second process, 'deletion,' is involved with deleting information that has accessed WM, but is not relevant (anymore). In their experiment, each trial sequentially presented two test stimuli consisting of circles composed of Gabor elements, which looked like circles drawn by curved dashed lines, in which one dash is termed a Gabor element. In these circles, one, two, or three Gabor elements (dashes) were missing. After presentation of the two circles, a probe was presented, consisting of a circle with one Gabor element missing. Participants had to judge whether the gap in the probe (i.e., the position of the missing element) corresponded with the gap position of one of the two test stimuli. To distinguish between the two interference control functions ('access' and 'deletion'), the cue was presented *before* the presentation of the two test stimuli in the 'access' condition, and *after* the presentation of the two test stimuli in the 'deletion' condition. Both 'access' and 'deletion' conditions had a control condition, in which the cue that was presented consisted of two empty circles. The cues in the control

conditions signaled to participants that both test stimuli were relevant for judgment of the probe. The control conditions tapped into WM processes such as storage, maintenance, and matching. In addition to the WM processes required by the control conditions, the 'access' and 'deletion' conditions required interference control processes. The 'access' condition targeted selective attention in which participants had to filter out or prevent the encoding of the irrelevant test stimulus. The 'deletion' condition targeted processes in WM dedicated to deactivating the memory traces of the irrelevant test stimulus. The main finding was that older adults and younger adults performed better in the 'access' condition compared to the 'access' control condition. More specifically, in both age groups accuracy in the 'access' condition was 11% better compared to the 'access' control condition. However, performance of the older adults in the deletion condition was not superior to that in the deletion control condition, while the performance younger participants did improve with 9%. These results indicate that older adults have no trouble filtering out or ignoring irrelevant information before it accesses WM, but have problems in suppressing it after it accessed WM (Cansino, et al., 2011). This study can explain the mixed results of the previous studies investigating interference control in older adults, because the Stroop and negative priming paradigm might have elicited the use of 'access' and 'deletion' functions. In both paradigms, participants are cued beforehand (which may elicit the 'access' function). However, in the Stroop task, it is assumed that even if it is irrelevant, participants automatically read the color words (for a review, see McLeod, 1991), which allows the irrelevant information of the word meaning to enter WM. Furthermore, because in the negative priming paradigm, a to be ignored stimulus was a target previously, the memory trace of the previous task set ('respond to A') competes with the new task set ('not respond A, but respond to X') (for a review, see Tipper, 2001). Because a previously learned stimulus response association still gets activation in a new task set, it is possible that unlearning the old response requires the deletion function.

In summary, in older adults, the passive storage and maintenance of new information and the activation and use of existing knowledge seem to be relatively intact. However, the control processes needed to reduce interference from these internal representations decline with aging (Bopp & Verhaeghen, 2005). We suggest that this imbalance can seriously impair learning in older adults. Therefore, designing instructions so that relevance is signaled before or during encoding of information, which has proven effective for young adults (e.g., Grant & Spivey, 2003; Jamet, Gavota, & Quaireau, 2008; Mautone & Mayer, 2001; Thomas & Lleras, 2007) might be even more effective for older adults.

Age-Related Changes in Cognitive Speed and Multi-Modal Processing

Another obstacle for learning in older adults is that they become slower in the rate at which they process information (Salthouse, 1996). We suggest that this cognitive slowing might at least partially result from the decline in cognitive control functions discussed in the former paragraph. However, recent evidence suggests that the cognitive slowing of information processing in older adults might be dependent on how information is presented. More specifically, it seems that presenting information multimodally compared to unimodally can partly compensate for age-related cognitive slowing. The benefits of multi-modal over unimodal information presentation (also called bimodal or multimodal enhancement) are found in both older and younger adults, but this effect is more pronounced in older adults (Laurenti, Burdette, Maldjian, & Wallace, 2006).

As mentioned, CLT-research has also shown a beneficial role for multimodal compared to unimodal information presentation on learning (Mousavi, et al., 1995; Tindall-Ford, et al., 1997).

This multimodality effect is explained by the view that auditory and visual information is processed by partly independent WM stores (Baddeley, 1992) and visual and verbal information corresponding to the same object, can have additive effects on memory (Clark & Paivio, 1991; Paivio, 1963, 1965). Furthermore, neuroscience studies have shown that the brain is highly efficient in dealing with multimodal information. Several researchers have identified a specific brain area that is often associated with multimodal integration, namely the Superior Temporal Sulcus (STS) (Beauchamp, Argall, Bodurka, Duyn, & Martin, 2004; Beauchamp, Lee, Argall, & Martin, 2004). In the STS, neurons are identified that respond to auditory or visual stimuli in isolation (Beauchamp, et al., 2004). An important finding has been that some of these neurons are especially sensitive to multimodal stimulation (visual and auditory) reflected in a response that surpasses the sum of activations elicited by visual or auditory stimuli in isolation.

Interestingly, recent evidence suggests that multimodal compared to unimodal information presentation can also speed up reaction times, and that this effect is larger in older compared to young adults (Laurenti, et al., 2006). As mentioned earlier, Verhaeghen and Cerella (2002) suggested that the age-related differences on the Stroop interference task and negative priming paradigm could be explained by general cognitive slowing. Although general cognitive slowing, reflected in larger reaction times in older adults compared to young adults, is a well-known finding, most of these results are from experiments using unimodal stimuli. Interestingly, there is some recent evidence that suggests a facilitating effect of multimodal stimuli on the reaction time of older adults. Laurenti et al. (2006) used a discrimination task in which the targets were presented in a unimodal or multimodal format, and asked participants to respond to color information. When the information concerned the color red, they had to respond with their index finger as fast as possible and when it concerned blue, they had to respond with their middle finger. In this discrimination task, visual stimuli in the form of red or blue colored disks, auditory stimuli presenting the words 'red' and 'blue' and multisensory stimuli (the blue disk paired with the spoken word 'blue' or the red disc paired with the spoken word 'red') were presented. It was found that compared to young adults, older adults were slower to respond to both unimodal (visual or auditory) and multimodal stimuli (visual paired with auditory). Secondly, both groups responded faster to multimodal stimuli compared to unimodal stimuli. Interestingly, however, this decrease was significantly more pronounced in older adults compared to young adults. This finding suggests that information processing can be accelerated by multisensory presentation and that this especially benefits older adults.

However, from these results, it is not clear whether an age-related change in multisensory processing or a more general attentional mechanism underlies this effect. This question was addressed by Hugenschmidt, Mozolic, and Laurenti (2009), who used a similar discrimination task as Laurenti et al. (2006) but added a cue preceding the target presentation that directed attention unimodally to either the auditory or visual modality, or multimodally. Participants were told that the auditory cue predicted an auditory unimodal or visual-auditory multimodal target stimulus, that a visual cue predicted a visual unimodal or visual-auditory multimodal target stimulus and that a multimodal cue could be followed by unimodal (auditory or visual) or multimodal targets. Cues always correctly predicted the target stimulus. The results showed that when attention was unimodally cued but the target was multimodal, the reaction time of the young adults was similar, and the reaction time of the older adults also became more similar to their reaction time to unimodally cued unimodal targets. And older adults were a little bit faster in responding to all multimodal targets, compared to unimodal targets. Thus although older adults were faster to respond to all multimodal compared to unimodal stimuli, the same pattern

as in the young adults emerged in that the modality effect decreased when they were unimodally cued, compared to multimodally. From these results, Hugenschmidt et al. (2009) concluded that modality specific attention can be effectively cued in older adults, but that the baseline level of sensory processing is different in older compared to young adults, in that they become more sensitive to multimodal compared to unimodal stimuli. These results are consistent with the findings by Cansino et al. (2011) and Verhaeghen and Cerella (2002) who also concluded that when cued prior to stimulus presentation, older adults compared to younger adults are equally able to focus attention on relevant information and filter out irrelevant information.

The effect of multimodal enhancement in older adults was also found with more educationally relevant materials: acquiring knowledge of a problem-solving procedure from worked examples (Van Gerven, et al., 2003). A problem-solving task, based on Luchin's (1942) water jug task was used. In the classic water jug task participants are required to determine a series of moves to acquire a certain amount of water in a target jug by pouring jugs of different sizes and containing different amounts of water into each other. Participants were presented with worked examples in which the problem solution procedure was demonstrated. In the unimodal condition, the worked example was presented only visually: a sequence of pictures accompanied with explanatory written text presented the initial problem state, intermediate states, and the goal state. In the multimodal condition, the text accompanying the pictures was spoken. In a third condition, conventional problems were presented. The results showed that in both age groups, the participants who studied the worked examples invested less mental effort (a measure of cognitive load) (Paas, et al., 2003) during subsequent problem solving, than the participants in the conventional problem condition. Training efficiency (the ratio between cognitive load and performance) was significantly higher in participants who received the multimodal training compared to the participants who studied conventional problems in both age groups. Moreover, compared to younger adults, the older adults reported significantly lower mental effort in the multimodal condition and older adults needed significantly less study time for the multimodal training condition compared to the conventional problems condition, while for younger participants this was reversed.

In sum, both for processing simple perceptual stimuli and for training complex tasks, a multimodal format of instruction presenting information in the visual and auditory modality, seems beneficial for both older and younger adults, but seems to be especially effective for older adults.

Age-Related Changes in the Ability to Associate and Integrate Information Elements

A third age-related change in memory is a decline in episodic memory functioning. Episodic memory involves the formation of associations between different elements of an event (Mangels & Heinberg, 2006). Episodic memory supports learning and binding of several aspects of learning materials: perceptual (e.g. visual and/or auditory instructions), conceptual (i.e. semantics of the learning materials), spatial (i.e. location of presented information elements), and temporal aspects (i.e. order in which the information is presented). The main finding in research on aging and episodic memory is that older adults have more problems with memory for associations than for single items (for a review, see Old & Naveh-Benjamin, 2008). For example, Chalfonte and Johnson (1996) found that older and young adults performed equally well on remembering colors and objects. However, older adults performed worse when they were asked to remember the color of an object, that is, when they had to bind color and object. Another study of Kessels et al. (2007) showed that older participants had more problems overall with

memory for 'where' (spatial aspects) and 'when' (temporal aspects) a certain target was presented, compared to the recollection that a specific target was presented. This dichotomy between memory for separate items and associations between items and contextual information (i.e. spatial, temporal) implies that there are different mechanisms underlying memory for associations and item memory.

Consistent with this idea, Naveh-Benjamin (2000) proposed the Associative Deficit Hypothesis (ADH). According to the ADH, the relatively impaired memory for associations is a dominant factor in the age-related decline in episodic memory functioning. The ADH has received support from several experiments using different kinds of stimuli, such as word-non-word pairs, word-word pairs and words presented in different font (Naveh-Benjamin, 2000), name face pairs (Naveh-Benjamin, Guez, Kilb, & Reedy, 2004), picture pairs (Naveh-Benjamin, Hussain, Guez, & Bar-On, 2003), and face-spatial location pairs (Bastin & Van der Linden, 2006). More generally, the impaired associative memory can be regarded as a difficulty to bind or integrate information elements into complex memories (Chalfonte & Johnson, 1996). Alternatively, in terms of CLT, this impairment in associative memory, can inhibit or slow down schema construction. For example, in learning the solution steps to solve the water jug problem described earlier, participants need to associate between a specific action and a specific jug for each step, and remember the correct order in which the steps must be conducted.

Interestingly, evidence from enactment studies suggests that producing and/ or observing actions, can facilitate episodic integration (Kormi-Nouri & Nilsson, 2001). In a typical enactment experiment, participants are presented with lists of action phrases, followed by a memory test in the form of free recall. In the passive condition (Verbal Task [VT]), participants only listen to the action phrases and in the enactment condition (Subject-Performed Task [SPT]), participants had to enact the phrases, either using the actual objects or pantomiming the action. The enactment effect represents the robust finding that memory for action phrases that were enacted is superior to memory for action phrases only read or heard (Engelkamp, 1998; Feyereisen, 2009; Nilsson, 2000; Zimmer, 2001). Furthermore, similar enactment effects are found for well-Integrated Phrases (IPs), describing objects and actions that are semantically related (e.g., put money in the wallet) and Poor Integrated Phrases (PIs) (e.g., put candy in the wallet), and in young and older adults. The underlying mechanism driving the enactment effect has been explained by the multimodal memory theory (Engelkamp, 2001a), which proposes that performing the action in enactment conditions provides an extra memory code for retrieval and therefore plays an important role in the effect on memory. An alternative explanation is provided by Kormi-Nouri and Nilsson (2001) who stated that enactment promotes episodic integration, because the action and object that is acted upon are encoded and stored as a single event, and therefore results in better memory performance. A recent study of Feyereisen (2009) tested both explanations in younger and older adults by investigating memory performance in three encoding conditions, an SPT condition, a VT condition, and a condition in which participants, watched an experimenter perform the task (Experimenter Performed Task [EPT]). The design also included levels of task difficulty: action phrases consisting of WI items represented 'easy to remember' phrases while action phrases consisting of PI items represented 'difficult to remember' phrases. For example, in WI's, the noun and action verb were semantically related, and in PI's the nouns and action verbs were semantically unrelated. Memory performance was measured by a recognition test and a cued recall test. This experimental set-up allows for distinguishing predictions following from the multimodal theory of Engelkamp (2001a) and the semantic integration hypothesis of Kormi-Nouri and Nilsson (2001). First, because the multimodal theory of memory (Engelkamp, 2001a) emphasizes the importance

of a motor memory induced by subject enactment, this theory predicts that memory for SPTs would be superior to that of EPTs and VTs. However, because according to Kormi-Nouri and Nilsson (2001) the main benefit for memory of enacted phrases is that the nouns and objects are integrated in a single episode, superior memory performance in both the SPT and EPT compared to the VT conditions is expected. Moreover, no difference in memory performance is expected between the SPT and EPT condition, because both incorporate episodic integration. Moreover, if a similar mechanism underlies the enactment effect in EPTs and SPTs, on both older and young adults, then memory performance in both groups for PIs and WIs should show similar patterns. Results were in support of an 'episodic integration' account (Kormi-Nouri & Nilsson, 2001) in that both SPT and EPT compared to VT improved memory performance in both older and younger adults. Furthermore, no difference in memory performance was found between items encoded in the SPT and EPT conditions. Moreover, the effect of SPT and EPT over VT was found for WIs and PIs and on both age groups. It was concluded that enactment, either performed or observed, enhanced integrative processes in WIs and PIs. In relation to the age-related decline in the ability to associate and integrate information, embedding information elements in an action helps, because it presents the information in an already integrated episode. Therefore, we suggest that the integrative effect of action, either produced or observed, might be especially helpful for older adults in learning.

In summary, three main conclusions can be drawn related to age-related changes in memory functioning. First, older adults are capable to direct attention to relevant information when they are cued previously; however, they are impaired in suppressing irrelevant information that has accessed WM. Secondly, older adults show a relatively smaller decrease in cognitive speed for processing multimodal compared to unimodal stimuli. Third, older adults show a decline in the ability to integrate information elements in order to form complex memories. Some promising inferences about improving learning in older adults can be drawn from these conclusions. Concerning the first point, it has been found that older adults are capable to allocate attention when cued before information presentation has accessed WM, but have problems in deleting irrelevant information after it accessed WM. Therefore, learning effectiveness in older adults might be significantly improved when relevance is signaled at the right time (i.e. before or during information presentation and not afterwards). On the second point, in relation to younger adults, older adults show a larger benefit in reaction time from a multimodal compared to a unimodal information presentation. Therefore, presentation in a multimodal format might partly compensate for age-related cognitive slowing. Finally, adding an action component in the information presented, can improve memory, by enhancing episodic integration, a memory function that declines with aging. In the next paragraphs, we will propose how education can use gestures in multimedia instructions, to take important age-related changes related to learning into account.

Gestures Can Act as Attentional Cues in Computer-Based Dynamic Visualisations

In multimedia learning, Dynamic Visualisations (DVs), such as animations, animated modelling examples, or video-based modelling examples, can play an important role in instruction (Höffler & Leutner, 2007; Paas & Sweller, 2011), especially in interactive learning environments (for a review, see Wouters, Tabbers, & Paas, 2007). However, a challenge in the design of computer-based DV's is to deal with their transient nature (Höffler & Leutner, 2007). That is, the information is not permanent, but changes throughout the instruction and therefore earlier episodes are no longer available for the learner. To discover important

element relations, the learner must actively hold information elements in WM while simultaneously processing new incoming information, and this imposes a high cognitive load (Chandler & Sweller, 1994). However, when learner's attention is cued to relevant information and element relations are signaled throughout DVs, these instructions could improve the effectiveness of computer-based DVs. Indeed, several studies in learning from animations found a beneficial effect of attentional cueing. For example, De Koning, Tabbers, Rikers, and Paas (2007) investigated the effect of cueing on learning from an animation showing the functioning of the cardiovascular system. Cueing was done by darkening irrelevant areas in the animation, so that the relevant areas became more salient. It was found that learning from the cued animation, was superior compared to that from the uncued animation. In a study investigating learning from an animation about long-term potentiation (a chemical and electrical process in the synapse), attention was guided by sequentially zooming in to each phase of the long-term potentiation process, thereby occluding the rest of the animation (Amadieu, Mariné, & Laimay, 2011). Again, learning was improved in the cued compared to the uncued condition. It is suggested that perceptually cueing information enhances selection processes needed to extract relevant aspects for the task and that this improves subsequent learning effectiveness (De Koning, et al., 2009).

Research on the use of gestures in learning suggests that gestures can also improve learning, by cueing relevance (McNeill, Alibali, & Evans, 2000; Ping & Goldin-Meadow, 2008; Valenzeno, Alibali, & Klatzky, 2003). In a study with pre-schoolers, it was found that learning was improved when the instruction consisted of a speech-gesture format, compared to a speech-only format (Valenzeno, et al., 2003). In this experiment, children watched a video in which a teacher explained the concept of symmetry, in 5 shapes (2 symmetrical and three asymmetrical).

In the verbal-only condition, the teacher stood next to the shapes and verbally explained about symmetry, and in the speech-gesture condition, the teacher used the same verbal script, but used gestures to index the whole shape, the centre of the shape, and in comparing the two halves. The results showed that children in the speech-gesture condition performed better on a post-test than children in the speech-only condition, which suggest that cueing relevant task features (the violations of the principle of symmetry) by gestures, improved learning. Another study of Ping and Goldin-Meadow (2008) investigated kindergarten and first graders' learning about the concept of conservation (i.e. that the amount of water from a flat wide glass, does not change when it is poured into a tall small glass). This was tested in a 2 x 2 design (speech-gesture or speech only instruction x objects present or objects absent). In all conditions, the verbal explanation was the same, but in the speech-gesture condition, the instructor made iconic gestures, indexing the height and width of the differently shaped glasses. Results of this study showed that learning was improved in the speech-gesture compared to the speech only condition, regardless of whether the objects were present or absent. The researchers concluded that the finding that gestures improve learning even when objects referred to are not physically present indicates that gestures might also help to construct a more abstract representation of the problem, which can promote transfer of learning (Ping & Goldin-Meadow, 2008). Although these results look very promising for the use of gesture in instruction, some issues need to be addressed. On the one hand, gestures can serve as cues, on the other hand, they are another, additional information source that needs to be processed, which might increase cognitive load. Concerning this issue, Kelly, Creigh, and Bartolotti (2009) showed in an ERP study that observing gestures that are semantically congruent with the verbal message they accompany (e.g., hearing the word 'chop' and see the gesture for 'chop') are processed and integrated automatically, but that effortful semantic integration is needed when the gestures are not congruent (e.g. hearing the word 'chop' and see the gesture for 'stir'). A similar result has been found for the temporal alignment of speech and gestures (Obermeier, Holle, & Gunter, 2011). In this ERP study, the researchers found evidence for automatic integration of speech and gestures when they were presented simultaneously, but found that integration became effortful when speech and gesture onset were asynchronous. From these results, it can be concluded that gestures that are semantically related, and synchronized to the speech they accompany, do not increase WM load. Another point of discussion is that, the studies discussed here, that show a beneficial effect of gestures in instruction on learning, were not conducted in children. Concerning the second issue, a large body of evidence has shown that children, just as older adults, are less able to efficiently control interference of irrelevant information, compared to young adults (e.g., Brainerd & Reyna, 1993; Durston, et al., 2002). For example, children show a similar effect as older adults in the Stroop paradigm in that they show a larger interference effect than young adults and this interference effect declines with age (Bub, Masson, & Lalonde, 2006; Schroeter, Zysset, Wahl, & Von Cramon, 2004). Therefore, we suggest that decreasing interference from irrelevant information by means of attentional cueing with gestures might also improve learning from computer-based DVs in older adults.

The Multimodality of Gesture-Speech Instruction

As discussed, the studies of Laurenti et al. (2006) and Hugenschmidt et al. (2009) show that multimodal presentation of information can speed up reaction time in a discrimination task and that this benefit is more pronounced in older compared to younger adults. Interestingly, Holle et al. (2010) found a similar enhanced response to multimodal speech-gesture stimuli in the superior temporal areas of the brain that were identified by Beauchamp et al. (2004) as integration areas for multimodal stimuli. In support of the multimodal enhancement theory, Holle et al. (2010) suggested that gestures boost speech comprehension under adverse listening conditions, with a crucial role of the left superior temporal areas in this process. This was confirmed by behavioral measures showing that participants understood significantly more under the speech-gesture condition compared to the speech only condition. When a gesture accompanied an action phrase that was hard to comprehend, participants understood 57% of all stimuli, but without a gesture, they only understood 25%. These findings suggest that the human brain deals quite efficiently with information presented in a multimodal format, including a speech- gesture format. Despite the fact that this study was done with young adult participants, the findings of Laurenti et al. (2006) and Hugenschmidt et al. (2009) suggest that similar or even stronger multimodal enhancement effects may be found in older adults.

Gesture-Speech Instructions integrate Information Elements into an Embodied Representation of the Study Material

In addition to visual and auditory information, we have discussed evidence showing that action information can facilitate learning in young and older adults (Feyereisen, 2009). Evidence for the role of actions in learning comes from research on the enactment effect (e.g. Engelkamp, 1998), which showed that episodic memory, which declines with age (e.g., Naveh-Benjamin, 2000), can be improved in young and older adults by adding an action component in the instructional format (Feyereisen, 2009). Because the gesturing itself is an action, we suggest that gestures (either performed or observed) could facilitate episodic integration and add action information

to the learners' representational format (Beilock & Goldin-Meadow, 2010).

To explain the way gestures in instruction can help integrative processes; we will use the embodied view of cognition as a framework. This view states that cognition is grounded in perception and action (Gibbs, 2006; Shapiro, 2007), and that language is grounded in sensorimotor experiences (Glenberg & Robertson, 2000; Zwaan & Madden, 2005). According to the embodied cognition view of language, words are mentally represented in the brain by their perceptual properties. Important evidence for this bidirectional relationship between bodily experiences and perception comes from studies showing the existence of a Mirror Neuron System (MNS) also in humans. The MNS was discovered by studies in monkeys that defined regions in the Inferior Parietal (IPC) and Inferior Frontal Cortex (IFC) that respond to the execution of an action and in a 'mirror' fashion to observation of that action (Di Pellegrino, Fadiga, Fogassi, Gallese, & Rizzolatti, 1992; Gallese, Fadiga, Fogassi, & Rizzolatti, 1996; Rizzolatti, et al., 1996). A similar system seems to exist in humans in the IPC and IFC and additionally in the dorsal premotor, somatosensory, cerebellar, and posterior temporal cortex (Chong, Cunnington, Williams, Kanwisher, & Mattingley, 2008; Gazzola & Keysers, 2008). Because the MNS simulates bodily experiences, we suggest that it might play a role in the beneficial effects of observing gestures on comprehension and learning. Further research on the role of the MNS in embodied cognition has shown that processing of action word meaning is somatopically represented in the sensory-motor areas (Hauk, Johnsrude, & Pulvermüller, 2004). This means that action words related to arm movements activate pre-motor areas representing hand motor actions and action words related to leg movements activate motor areas representing the leg. Another study found that with perception of manageable objects, irrespective of the intention of the participants, there is partial involvement of the motor areas that activate when participants actually use the object (Grèzes & Decety, 2002).

As the embodied view of cognition assumes a bidirectional relationship between action and perception, the effect of actions in instructions should produce similar results for observing and performing actions during learning. Indeed, evidence from enactment studies has shown that either performing or observing actions has beneficial effects on learning (Feyereisen, 2009). Importantly, although less clear-cut, both observing and performing gestures during learning and instruction, have been proven to be beneficial for learning. As earlier discussed, we suggest that observing gestures in instruction in the form of attentional cues reduce cognitive load. In addition, several researchers have found that producing gestures during learning can also lighten cognitive load (Goldin-Meadow, Nusbaum, Kelly, & Wagner, 2001; Ping & Goldin-Meadow, 2010). Using a dual-task paradigm for cognitive load measurement (for a review, see Brunken, Plass, & Leutner, 2003) Goldin-Meadow et al. (2001) asked participants to solve a math problem, after which they were presented with a list of words they had to remember while verbally explaining how they came to their solution. Half of the participants was permitted to gesture, and the other half was not. The main finding was that participants who were allowed to gesture compared to those who were not allowed to gesture, remembered more words from the word list. This finding suggests that gestures lower the WM load imposed by explaining the solution procedure (i.e., the primary task), freeing up resources that could be successfully dedicated to remembering the word list (i.e., the secondary task). Another study found that requesting children to produce gestures during learning about mathematical equations enhanced the retention of the learned material relative to when they were not requested to gesture (Wagner, Cook, Mitchell, & Goldin-Meadow, 2008). Furthermore, a series of experiments of Chu and Kita (2011) showed that gestures enhance learning spatial problem solving

tasks. In the first experiment, it was found that participants produced more spontaneous gestures when they found it difficult to solve the problems. Secondly, it was found that participants that were encouraged to gesture, solved more problems in a mental rotation task, compared to participants that were prohibited to gesture and that gesture rates in the first group decreased as they solved more problems. According to the researchers, gesture production with experience in the task decreases because the spatial computation processes initially supported by gestures, become internalized. Gesture production has also been found to enhance the verbalisation of pictures that are difficult to conceptualize (Hostetter, Alibali, & Kita, 2007; Melinger & Kita, 2007). This finding can be explained by the information-packaging hypothesis (Kita, 2000), which states that gestures help speakers to translate images consisting of spatial and motoric components, into units of language. In sum, these findings suggest that gesture production is especially beneficial for learning when cognitive load is high, such as in novel problem solving (Chu & Kita, 2011) and in describing pictures that are hard to verbalize ((Hostetter, Alibali, & Kita, 2007; Melinger & Kita, 2007).

From an embodied view, we suggest that besides producing gestures (action), observing gestures (perception) can also lighten cognitive load in a similar manner. In a study of McNeill et al. (2000) with children showed that observing gestures also facilitated language comprehension when the verbal message was complex. In this experiment children got a description of a picture, either just verbally or verbally with a corresponding gesture. However, the verbal description was easy or difficult to understand in terms of how many pieces of information it contained and syntax. It was found that gestures improved task performance when they accompanied a complex verbal description. These results suggest that observing gestures help speech comprehension when facing high element interactivity. Although this is very tentative, we suggest that observing gestures accompanying complex speech can also help the translation from a verbal message to a more integrated imagery representation of the information presented. In other words, in speech production and perception, gestures bind information elements, which in turn facilitate the processing of these element relations.

In educational research, it has also been suggested that the MNS might play an important role in learning from computer-based dynamic visualizations that incorporate human movement (Van Gog, Paas, Marcus, Ayres, & Sweller, 2009). Dynamic visualizations about non-human movement procedures or processes (e.g., demonstrating cell division, how lightning develops, how brakes or engines work) are often less effective for learning than a series of static visualizations, because of the high perceptual and cognitive load imposed by transience of information in the dynamic visualizations (Ayres & Paas, 2007). However, this is not the case for dynamic visualizations about procedures involving human movement (Höffler & Leutner, 2007; Van Gog, et al., 2009; Wong, et al., 2009). Van Gog et al. (2009) propose that the high load imposed by transience is not a problem in dynamic visualizations on human movement procedures due to the automatic processing in the MNS of (or part of) the information.

However, some researchers suggest that the embodied view of cognition is also applicable for more abstract concepts, for example, metaphors used in language, can situate abstract concepts in space (e.g., Lakoff & Johnson, 1999). Think of utterances that express hierarchy on a vertical continuum. This space can for example be used by history teachers in explaining the feudal system by talking about populations in 'higher ranks' in relation to 'lower ranks.' It is clear that these expressions should not be taken literally in the sense that the people from the higher ranks are taller than those of the lower ranks. Cassanto (2009) points out that a vertical continuum is metaphorically used for affective valence, in that

'feeling high' refers to a positive feeling while 'feeling down' is refers to a negative feeling, and that this influences the way these affections are represented. Other studies have shown similar results for other mental concepts, such as time (Boroditsky, 2000, 2001; Casasanto & Boroditsky, 2008), number (Dehaene, Bossini, & Giraux, 1993), power (Schubert, 2005), and similarity (Casasanto, 2008b). Because vertical and horizontal organisation often tends to accompany and clarify abstract concepts, these spatial structures get associated with the meaning of these abstract concepts. We suggest that learners can use gestures to depict these spatial representations and that this helps to organize information. For instance, in the example of the history teacher explaining the feudal system, it is possible to position a hand above their head while discussing characteristics of the highest rank, and point somewhat lower when talking about the second highest, etc.

Indeed, gestures can be used in all kinds of forms and functions, including metaphorically for more abstract concepts as well (for a review see Roth, 2001) and it has been found that these metaphoric gestures also improve memory (Straube, Green, Weis, Chatterjee, & Kircher, 2009). In sum, we suggest that if spatially and temporally aligned, gesture-speech instructions already present some information elements in relation to each other, which decreases the cognitive load otherwise spent on these integrative processes. Furthermore, besides the fact that gestures are visually perceived, they present information in action, which provides an embodied representation of this information. In short, gestures might decrease element interactivity in complex tasks by providing information in a more integrated format, and rich representational format.

CONCLUSION

In this chapter, we have discussed how gestures in multimedia instruction can improve learning in older adults. When engaging older adults in multimedia learning, it is important to take both functions that decline and functions that seem be relatively unaffected by age into account. CLT-inspired research can provide for useful guidelines of how to optimize instructional design for older adults. For example, we have discussed that older adults are well able to filter out irrelevant information when they are cued prior to the presentation, but that they are impaired in suppressing irrelevant information when it has accessed WM (Cansino et al., 2011). CLT-inspired research has shown that attentional cueing can help to avoid irrelevant information to access WM (for a review, see De Koning, et al., 2009). Secondly, older adults become slower to respond to unimodal information compared to multimodal information presentation (Hugenschmidt, et al., 2009; Laurenti, et al., 2006). CLT-inspired research has found beneficial effect on learning of multimodal compared to unimodal instruction. Finally, older adults have more trouble integrating separate information elements (e.g., Naveh-Benjamin, 2000). However, adding an action component in instruction can facilitate integrative processes (Feyereisen, 2009), presumably by binding the information elements into one event.

Importantly, we have discussed that gesture-speech instructions can reduce extraneous cognitive load for older adults by alleviating WM functions that are found to decline with age. Importantly, gestures in instruction can serve functions simultaneously, which might even increase the effect for learning. For example, by pointing and tracing, gestures can act as attentional cues, by representing iconic information, such as shape or size, as the gestures mentioned in this chapter accompany speech, they provide for a multimodal format of instruction and as gestures can convey information not expressed in speech, it can present information in a more integrative manner. For example, one can verbally say: "I removed the screw by twitching it clockwise towards my body." Or one can say "I removed the screw," while simultaneously making a clockwise twitch-

ing movement with the wrist towards the body. Whereas in the first sentence, the listener must integrate important information elements, in the second, this is partly done for the learner, and this can be especially beneficial for older adults, who are relatively impaired compared to younger adults in the ability to integrate information.

Future studies are needed to investigate the possible effect of gestures in multi-media instructions for older adults. Besides video-based instructions, we also suggest that gestures can be uses in animated DV's in animated pedagogical agents, which are increasingly used in multimedia learning (Craig, Gholson, & Driscoll, 2002). In studies with younger adults, a beneficial effect has been found of adding gestures to animated agents (e.g. Buisine & Martin, 2007; Dunsworth & Atkinson, 2007; Lusk & Atkinson, 2007). For example, in a study by Buisine and Martin (2007), participants learned from an animation about the functions of a remote control. The animations consisted of a simultaneous presentation of a picture of the remote control and an animated agent explaining the button functions of this remote control in three conditions. In the first condition, the agent made gestures that were redundant to its verbal explanation (i.e. saying 'You have to use the large button in the centre to…' while simultaneously pointing at this button). In the second condition, the animated agent made gestures that were complementary to its verbal explanation (i.e. 'You have to use this button to…' while simultaneously pointing at the large button in the centre). In the third condition, the verbal explanation was similar to the first condition, but the animated agent did not gesture. Some important results were that participants in the redundant condition as compared to the 'complementary' and 'no gesture' condition recalled more verbal information, and gave higher ratings about the quality of the instruction. As discussed earlier in the chapter, redundancy in multi-modal information presentation has also been found to benefit information processing (Laurenti, et al., 2006) and associative memory in older adults (Kormi-Nouri & Nilsson, 2001). Therefore, we suggest that when studying instructions about modern technological concepts (i.e. managing a remote control, computer, and Internet use), gestures (made either by a human or an animated agent) that refer to information elements that are verbally explained, can enhance older adults' learning. Although gesturing is a very old communicative tool, its potential as a vital instructional tool remains. In the future, the potentials for learning, especially for older adults, should be further exploited in research and instructional design.

REFERENCES

Amadieu, F., Mariné, C., & Laimay, C. (2011). The attention-guiding effect and cognitive load in the comprehension of animations. *Computers in Human Behavior*, *27*, 36–40. doi:10.1016/j.chb.2010.05.009

Atkinson, R. K., Derry, S. J., Renkl, A., & Wortham, D. (2000). Learning from examples: Instructional principles from the worked examples research. *Review of Educational Research*, *70*, 181–214. doi:10.3102/00346543070002181

Ayres, P., & Sweller, J. (2005). The split-attention principle in multimedia learning. In R.E. Mayer, (Ed.), *The Cambridge handbook of multimedia learning* (pp. 135–146). Cambridge, UK: Cambridge University Press.

Ayres, P., & Paas, F. (2007). Can the cognitive load approach make instructional animations more effective? *Applied Cognitive Psychology*, *21*, 811–820. doi:10.1002/acp.1351

Baddeley, A. D. (1992). Working memory. *Science*, *255*, 556–559. doi:10.1126/science.1736359

Bastin, C., & Van der Linden, M. (2006). The effects of aging on the recognition of different types of associations. *Experimental Aging Research*, *32*, 61–77. doi:10.1080/03610730500326291

Beauchamp, M. S., Argall, B. D., Bodurka, J., Duyn, J. H., & Martin, A. (2004). Unraveling multisensory integration: Patchy organization within human STS multisensory cortex. *Nature Neuroscience*, *7*, 1190–1192. doi:10.1038/nn1333

Beauchamp, M. S., Lee, K. E., Argall, B. D., & Martin, A. (2004). Integration of auditory and visual information about objects in superior temporal sulcus. *Neuron*, *41*, 809–823. doi:10.1016/S0896-6273(04)00070-4

Beilock, S. L., & Goldin-Meadow, S. (2010). Gesture changes thought by grounding it in action. *Psychological Science*, *21*, 1605–1610. doi:10.1177/0956797610385353

Bopp, K. L., & Verhaeghen, P. (2005). Aging and verbal memory span: A meta-analysis. The Journals of Gerontology: Series B: Psychological Sciences and Social Sciences, 60, 223–233. doi:10.1093/geronb/60.5.P223

Boroditsky, L. (2000). Metaphoric structuring: Understanding time through spatial metaphors. *Cognition*, *75*, 1–28. doi:10.1016/S0010-0277(99)00073-6

Boroditsky, L. (2001). Does language shape thought? Mandarin and English speakers' conceptions of time. *Cognitive Psychology*, *43*, 1–22. doi:10.1006/cogp.2001.0748

Brainerd, C. J., & Reyna, V. F. (1993). Memory independence and memory interference in cognitive development. *Psychological Review*, *100*, 42–67. doi:10.1037/0033-295X.100.1.42

Brunken, R., Plass, J. L., & Leutner, D. (2003). Direct measurement of cognitive load in multimedia learning. *Educational Psychologist*, *38*, 53–61. doi:10.1207/S15326985EP3801_7

Bub, D. N., Masson, M. E. J., & Lalonde, C. E. (2006). Cognitive control in children: Stroop interference and suppression of word reading. *Psychological Science*, *17*, 351–357. doi:10.1111/j.1467-9280.2006.01710.x

Buisine, S., & Martin, J. C. (2007). The effects of speech–gesture cooperation in animated agents' behavior in multimedia presentations. *Interacting with Computers, 19*, 484–493. doi:10.1016/j.intcom.2007.04.002

Cansino, S., Guzzon, D., Martinelli, M., Barollo, M., & Casco, C. (2011). Effects of aging on interference control in selective attention and working memory. *Memory and Cognition. 39*, 1409-1422. doi:10.3758/s13421-011-0109-9

Casasanto, D. (2008). Similarity and proximity: When does close in space mean close in mind? *Memory & Cognition, 36*, 1047–1056. doi:10.3758/MC.36.6.1047

Casasanto, D. (2009). Embodiment of abstract concepts: Good and bad in right- and left-handers. *Journal of Experimental Psychology. General*, 138, 351–367. doi:10.1037/a0015854

Casasanto, D., & Boroditsky, L. (2008). Time in the mind: Using space to think about time. *Cognition, 106*, 579–593. doi:10.1016/j.cognition.2007.03.004

Celnik, P., Stefan, K., Hummel, F., Duque, J., Classen, J., & Cogen, L. G. (2005). Encoding a motor memory in the older adult by action observation. *NeuroImage, 29*, 677–684. doi:10.1016/j.neuroimage.2005.07.039

Chalfonte, B. L., & Johnson, M. K. (1996). Feature memory and binding in young and older adults. *Memory & Cognition, 24*, 403–416. doi:10.3758/BF03200930

Chandler, P., & Sweller, J. (1992). The split-attention effect as a factor in the design of instruction. *British Journal of Educational Psychology, 62*, 233–246. doi:10.1111/j.2044-8279.1992.tb01017.x

Chandler, P., & Sweller, J. (1994). Why some material is difficult to learn. *Cognition and Instruction, 12*, 185–233. doi:10.1207/s1532690xci1203_1

Chong, T. T., Cunnington, R., Williams, M. A., & Mattingley, J. B. (2009). The role of selective attention in matching observed and executed actions. *Neuropsychologia, 47*, 786–795. doi:10.1016/j.neuropsychologia.2008.12.008

Chu, M., & Kita, S. (2011). The nature of gestures' beneficial role in spatial problem solving. *Journal of Experimental Psychology: General, 140*, 102–116. doi:10.1037/a0021790

Clark, J. M., & Paivio, A. (1991). Dual coding and education. *Educational Psychology Review, 3*, 149–210. doi:10.1007/BF01320076

Cohn, N. B., Dustman, R. E., & Bradford, D. C. (1984). Age-related decrements in Stroop color test performance. *Journal of Clinical Psychology, 40*, 1244–1250. doi:10.1002/10974679(198409)40:5<1244::AID-JCLP2270400521>3.0.CO;2-D

Craig, S. D., Gholson, B., & Driscoll, D. M. (2002). Animated pedagogical agents in multimedia educational environments: Effects of agent properties, picture features and redundancy. *Journal of Educational Psychology, 94*, 428–434. doi:10.1037/0022-0663.94.2.428

De Koning, B. B., Tabbers, H. K., Rikers, R. M. J. P., & Paas, F. (2007). Attention cueing as a means to enhance learning from an animation. *Applied Cognitive Psychology, 21*, 731–746. doi:10.1002/acp.1346

De Koning, B. B., Tabbers, H. K., Rikers, R. M. J. P., & Paas, F. (2009). Towards a framework for attention cueing in instructional animations: Guidelines for research and design. *Educational Psychology Review, 21*, 113–140. doi:10.1007/s10648-009-9098-7

Dehaene, S., Bossini, S., & Giraux, P. (1993). The mental representation of parity and number magnitude. *Journal of Experimental Psychology: General, 122*, 371–396. doi:10.1037/0096-3445.122.3.371

Di Pellegrino, G., Fadiga, L., Fogassi, L., Gallese,V., & Rizzolatti, G. (1992). Understanding motor events: A neurophysiological study. *Experimental Brain Research, 91,* 176–180. doi: 10.1007/BF00230027

Dunsworth, Q., & Atkinson, R. K. (2007). Fostering multimedia learning of science: Exploring the role of an animated agent's image. *Computers & Education, 49,* 677–690. doi:10.1016/j.compedu.2005.11.010

Durston, S., Thomas, K. M., Yang, Y., Ulŭg, A. M., Zimmerman, R. D., & Casey, B. J. (2002). A neural basis for the development of inhibitory control. *Developmental Science, 5,* 9–16. doi:10.1111/1467-7687.00235

Engelkamp, J. (1998). *Memory for action.* Hove, UK: Psychology Press/Taylor & Francis.

Engelkamp, J. (2001a). Action memory: A systems-oriented approach . In H. D. Zimmer, R. L. Cohen, M. J. Guynn, J. Engelkamp, R. Kormi-Nouri, & M. A. Foley, (Eds.), *Memory for action: A distinct form of episodic memory?* (pp. 49–96). Oxford, UK: Oxford University Press.

Feyereisen, P. (2009). Enactment effects and integration processes in younger and older adults' memory for actions. *Memory, 17,* 374–385. doi:10.1080/09658210902731851

Gallese,V., Fadiga, L., Fogassi, L., & Rizzolatti, G. (1996). Action recognition in the premotor cortex. *Brain, 119,* 593–609. doi:10.1093/brain/119.2.593

Gamboz, N., Russo, R., & Fox, E. (2002). Age differences and the identity negative priming *effect: An updated meta-analysis. Psychology* and Aging, *17,* 525–531. doi:10.1037/0882-7974.17.3.525

Gazzola, V., & Keysers, C. (2008). The observation and execution of actions share motor and somatosensory voxels in all tested subjects: Single-subject analyses of unsmoothed fMRI data. *Cerebral Cortex, 19,* 1239–1255. doi:10.1093/cercor/bhn181

Gibbs, R. W. Jr. (2006). *Embodiment and cognitive science.* Cambridge, UK: Cambridge University Press.

Glenberg, A. M., & Robertson, D. A. (2000). Symbol grounding and meaning: A comparison of high-dimensional and embodied theories of meaning. *Journal of Memory and Language, 43,* 379–401. doi:10.1006/jmla.2000.2714

Goldin-Meadow, S., Nusbaum, H., Kelly, S. D., & Wagner, S. (2001). Explaining math: Gesturing lightens the load. *Psychological Science, 12,* 516–522. doi:10.1111/1467-9280.00395

Grant, E. R., & Spivey, M. J. (2003). Eye movements and problem solving: Guiding attention guides thought. *Psychological Science, 14,* 462–466. doi:10.1111/1467-9280.02454

Grèzes, J., & Decety, J. (2002). Does visual perception of object afford action? Evidence from a neuroimaging study. *Neuropsychologia, 40,* 212–222. doi:10.1016/S0028-3932(01)00089-6

Hartman, M., & Hasher, L. (1991). Aging and suppression: Memory for previously relevant information. *Psychology and Aging, 6,* 587–594. doi:10.1037/0882-7974.6.4.587

Hasher, L., Stoltzfus, E. R., Zacks, R. T., & Rypma, B. (1991). Age and inhibition. *Journal of Experimental Psychology: Learning, Memory, and Cognition, 17,* 163–169. doi:10.1037/0278-7393.17.1.163

Hauk, O., Johnsrude, I., & Pulvermüller, F. (2004). Somatotopic representation of action words in human motor and premotor cortex. *Neuron, 41,* 310–307. doi:10.1016/S0896-6273(03)00838-9

Hedden, T., & Gabrieli, J. D. (2004). Insights into the ageing mind: A view from cognitive neuroscience. Nature Reviews. *Neuroscience, 5,* 87–96. doi:10.1038/nrn1323

Höffler, T. N., & Leutner, D. (2007). Instructional animation versus static pictures: A meta-analysis. *Learning and Instruction, 17,* 722–738. doi:10.1016/j.learninstruc.2007.09.013

Hostetter, A. B., Alibali, M. W., & Kita, S. (2007). I see it in my hands' eye: Representational gestures reflect conceptual demands. *Language and Cognitive Processes, 22,* 313–336. doi:10.1080/01690960600632812

Houx, P. J., Jolles, J., & Vreeling, F. W. (1993). Stroop interference: Aging effects assessed with the Stroop color-word test. *Experimental Aging Research, 19,* 209–224. doi:10.1080/03610739308253934

Hugenschmidt, C. E., Mozolic, J. L., & Laurienti, P. J. (2009). Suppression of multisensory integration by modality-specific attention in aging. *Neuroreport, 20,* 349–353. doi:10.1097/WNR.0b013e328323ab07

Iverson, J. M., & Goldin-Meadow, S. (2005). Gestures pave the way for language development. *Psychological Science, 16,* 367–371. doi:10.1111/j.0956-7976.2005.01542.x

Jamet, E., Gavota, M., & Quaireau, C. (2008). Attention guiding in multimedia learning. *Learning and Instruction, 18,* 135–145. doi:10.1016/j.learninstruc.2007.01.011

Kelly, S. D., Creigh, P., & Bartolotti, J. (2009). Integrating speech and iconic gestures in a Stroop-like task: Evidence for automatic processing. *Journal of Cognitive Neuroscience, 22,* 683–694. doi:10.1162/jocn.2009.21254

Kessels, R. P. C., Hobbel, D., & Postema, A. (2007). Ageing, context memory and binding: A comparison of "what, where and when" in young and older adults. *The International Journal of Neuroscience, 117,* 795–810. doi:10.1080/00207450600910218

Kieley, J. M., & Hartley, A. A. (1997). Age-related equivalence of identity suppression in the Stroop color-word task. *Psychology and Aging, 12,* 22–29. doi:10.1037/0882-7974.12.1.22

Kormi-Nouri, R., & Nilsson, L.-G. (2001). The motor component is not crucial! In H. D. Zimmer, R. L. Cohen, M. J. Guynn, J. Engelkamp, R. Kormi-Nouri, & M. A. Foley, M. A. (Eds.), *Memory for Action: A Distinct from Episodic Memory?* (pp. 97–111). Oxford, UK: Oxford University Press.

Lakoff, G., & Johnson, M. (1999). *Philosophy in the flesh.* New York, NY: Basic Books.

Laurenti, P. J., Burdette, J. H., Maldjian, J. A., & Wallace, M. T. (2006). Enhanced multisensory integration in older adults. *Neurobiology of Aging, 27,* 1155–1163. doi:10.1016/j.neurobiolaging.2005.05.024

Luchins, A. S. (1942). Mechanization in problem solving. *Psychological Monographs, 54.* (Whole No. 248).

Lusk, M. M., & Atkinson, R. K. (2007). Animated pedagogical agents: Does their degree of embodiment impact learning from static or animated worked examples? *Applied Cognitive Psychology, 21,* 747–764. doi:10.1002/acp.1347

Mangels, J. A., & Heinberg, A. (2006). Improved episodic integration through enactment: Implications for aging. *The Journal of General Psychology, 26,* 1170–1187.

Mathis, A., Schunk, T., Erb, G., Namer, I. J., & Luthringer, R. (2009). The effect of aging on the inhibitory function in middle-aged subjects: A functional MRI study coupled with a color-matched Stroop task. *International Journal of Geriatric Psychiatry, 24,* 1062–1071. doi:10.1002/gps.2222

Mautone, P. D., & Mayer, R. E. (2001). Signaling as a cognitive guide in multimedia learning. *Journal of Educational Psychology, 93,* 377–389. doi:10.1037/0022-0663.93.2.377

Mayer, R. E. (2001). *Multimedia learning*. New York: Cambridge University Press.

Mayer, R. E. (2005). Cognitive theory of multimedia learning. In Mayer, R. E. (Ed.), *The Cambridge handbook of multimedia learning* (pp. 31–48). Cambridge, UK: Cambridge University Press.

Mayer, R. E., & Moreno, R. (1998). A split-attention effect in multimedia learning: Evidence for dual processing systems in working memory. *Journal of Educational Psychology, 90,* 312–320. doi:10.1037/0022-0663.90.2.312

Mayer, R. E., & Moreno, R. (2002). Aids to computer-based multimedia learning. *Learning and Instruction, 12,* 107–119. doi:10.1016/S0959-4752(01)00018-4

McDowd, J. M., & Filion, D. L. (1995). Aging and negative priming in a location suppression task: The long and the short of it. *Psychology and Aging, 10,* 34–47. doi:10.1037//0882-7974.10.1.34

McDowd, J. M., & Oseas-Kreger, D. M. (1991). Aging, inhibitory processes, and negative priming. Journal of Gerontology: *Psychological Sciences, 46,* 340–345.

McLeod, C. M. (1991). Half a century of research on the Stroop effect: An integrative review. *Psychological Bulletin, 109,* 163–203. doi:10.1037/0033-2909.109.2.163

McNeill, N. M., Alibali, M. W., & Evans, J. L. (2000). The role of gesture in children's comprehension of spoken language: Now they need it, now they don't. *Journal of Nonverbal Behavior, 24,* 131–150. doi:10.1023/A:1006657929803

Melinger, A., & Kita, S. (2007). Conceptualization load triggers gesture production. *Language and Cognitive Processes, 22,* 473–500. doi:10.1080/01690960600696916

Mousavi, S. Y., Low, R., & Sweller, J. (1995). Reducing cognitive load by mixing auditory and visual presentation modes. *Journal of Educational Psychology, 87,* 319–334. doi:10.1037/0022-0663.87.2.319

Naveh- Benjamin, M. (2000). Adult age differences in memory performance: Tests of an associative deficit hypothesis. *Journal of Experimental Psychology: Learning, Memory, and Cognition, 25,* 1179–1187. doi:10.1037/0278-7393.26.5.1170

Naveh-Benjamin, M., Guez, J., Kilb, A., & Reedy, S. (2004). The associative memory deficit of older adults: Further support using face-name associations. *Psychology and Aging, 19,* 541–546. doi:10.1037/0882-7974.19.3.541

Naveh-Benjamin, M., Hussain, Z., Guez, J., & Bar-On, M. (2003). Adult age differences in episodic memory: Further support for an associative-deficit hypothesis. *Journal of Experimental Psychology: Learning, Memory, and Cognition, 29,* 826–837. doi:10.1037/0278-7393.29.5.826

Nilsson, L. G. (2000). Remembering actions and words . In E. Tulving, & F. I. M. Craik, (Eds.), *The Oxford handbook of memory* (pp. 137–148). Oxford, UK: Oxford University Press.

Obermeier, C., Holle, H., & Gunter, T. C. (2011). What iconic gesture fragments reveal about gesture–speech integration: When synchrony is lost, memory can help. *Journal of Cognitive Neuroscience, 23,* 1648–1663. doi:10.1162/jocn.2010.21498

Old, S. R., & Naveh-Benjamin, M. (2008). Differential effects of age on item and associative measures of memory: A meta-analysis. *Psychology and Aging, 23,* 104–118. doi:10.1037/0882-7974.23.1.104

Paas, F., Renkl, A., & Sweller, J. (2003). Cognitive load theory and instructional design: Recent developments. *Educational Psychologist, 38,* 1–4. doi:10.1207/S15326985EP3801_1

Paas, F., & Sweller, J. (2011). An evolutionary upgrade of cognitive load theory: Using the human motor system and collaboration to support the learning of complex cognitive tasks. *Educational Psychology Review*, *24*, 1–19. doi:10.1007/s10648-011-9179-2

Paas, F., & Van Gog, T. (2006). Optimizing worked example instruction: Different ways to increase germane cognitive load. *Learning and Instruction*, *16*, 87–91. doi:10.1016/j.learninstruc.2006.02.004

Paas, F., & Van Merriënboer, J. J. G. (1994). Variability of worked examples and transfer of geometrical problem-solving skills: A cognitive-load approach. *Journal of Educational Psychology*, *86*, 122–133. doi:10.1037/0022-0663.86.1.122

Paivio, A. (1963). Learning of adjective-noun paired associates as a function of adjective-noun order and noun abstractness. *Canadian Journal of Psychology*, *17*, 370–379. doi:10.1037/h0083277

Paivio, A. (1965). Abstractness, imagery and meaningfulness in paired associate learning. *Journal of Verbal Learning and Verbal Behavior*, *4*, 32–38. doi:10.1016/S0022-5371(65)80064-0

Park, D. C., Lautenschlager, G., Hedden, T., Davidson, N. S., Smith, A. D., & Smith, P. K. (2002). Models of visuospatial and verbal memory across the adult life span. *Psychology and Aging*, *17*, 299–320. doi:10.1037/0882-7974.17.2.299

Ping, R., & Goldin-Meadow, S. (2008). Hands in the air: Using ungrounded iconic gestures to teach children conservation of quantity. Developmental *Psychology*, *44*, 1277–1287. doi:10.1037/0012-1649.44.5.1277

Ping, R., & Goldin-Meadow, S. (2010). Gesturing saves cognitive resources when talking about non-present objects. *Cognitive Science*, *34*, 602–619. doi:10.1111/j.1551-6709.2010.01102.x

Rizolatti, G., Fadiga, L., Matelli, M., Bettinardi, V., Paulesu, E., & Perani, D. (1996). Localization of grasp representations in humans by PET: 1. Observation versus execution. *Experimental Brain Research*, *111*, 246–252. doi:10.1007/BF00227301

Roth, W. M. (2001). Gestures: Their role in teaching and learning. *Review of Educational Research*, *71*, 365–392. doi:10.3102/00346543071003365

Salthouse, T. A. (1996). The processing-speed theory of adult age differences in cognition. *Psychological Review*, *103*, 403–428. doi:10.1037/0033-295X.103.3.403

Schroeter, M. L., Zysset, S., Wahl, M., & Von Cramon, D. Y. (2004). Prefrontal activation due to Stroop interference increases during development: An event-related fNIRS study. *NeuroImage*, *23*, 1317–1325. doi:10.1016/j.neuroimage.2004.08.001

Shapiro, L. (2007). The embodied cognition research programme. *Philosophy Compass*, *2*, 338–346. doi:10.1111/j.1747-9991.2007.00064.x

Spencer, W. D., & Raz, N. (1995). Differential effects of aging on memory for content and context: A meta-analysis. *Psychology and Aging*, *10*, 527–539. doi:10.1037/0882-7974.10.4.527

Stolzfus, E. R., Hasher, L., Zacks, R. T., Ulivi, S., & Goldstein, D. (1993). Investigations of inhibition and interference in younger and older adults. *Journal of Gerontology: Psychological Sciences*, *48*, 179–188. doi: 10.1093/geronj/48.4.P179

Straube, B., Green, A., Weis, S., Chatterjee, A., & Kircher, T. (2009). Memory effects of speech and gesture binding: cortical and hippocampal activation in relation to subsequent memory performance. *Journal of Cognitive Neuroscience*, *21*, 821–836. doi:10.1162/jocn.2009.21053

Stroop, J. R. (1935). Studies of interference in serial verbal reactions. *Journal of Experimental Psychology*, *18*, 643–662. doi:10.1037/h0054651

Sweller, J. (1988). Cognitive load during problem solving: Effects on learning. *Cognitive Science*, *12*, 257–285. doi:10.1207/s15516709cog1202_4

Sweller, J. (2010). Element interactivity and intrinsic, extraneous, and germane cognitive load. *Educational Psychology Review*, *22*, 123–138. doi:10.1007/s10648-010-9128-5

Sweller, J., Ayres, P., & Kalyuga, S. (2011). The split-attention effect. In J. Sweller, P. Ayres, & S. Kalyuga, (Eds.), *Cognitive Load Theory* (pp. 111–128). Berlin, Germany: Springer. doi:10.1007/978-1-4419-8126-4_9

Sweller, J., & Chandler, P. (1994). Why some material is difficult to learn. *Cognition and Instruction*, *12*, 185–233. doi:10.1207/s1532690xci1203_1

Sweller, J., Chandler, P., Tierney, P., & Cooper, M. (1990). Cognitive load as a factor in the structuring of technical material. *Journal of Experimental Psychology: General*, *119*, 176–192. doi:10.1037/0096-3445.119.2.176

Sweller, J., Van Merriënboer, J. J. G., & Paas, F. (1998). Cognitive architecture and instructional design. *Educational Psychology Review*, *10*, 251–296. doi:10.1023/A:1022193728205

Tabbers, H. K., Martens, R. L., & Van Merriënboer, J. J. G. (2004). Multimedia instructions and cognitive load theory: Effects of modality and cueing. *The British Journal of Educational Psychology*, *74*, 71–81. doi:10.1348/000709904322848824

Thomas, L. E., & Lleras, A. (2007). Moving eyes and moving thought: On the spatial compatibility between eye movements and cognition. *Psychonomic Bulletin & Review*, *14*, 663–668. doi:10.3758/BF03196818

Tindall-Ford, S., Chandler, P., & Sweller, J. (1997). When two sensory modes are better than one. *Journal of Experimental Psychology: Applied*, *3*, 257–287. doi:10.1037/1076-898X.3.4.257

Tipper, S. P. (1985). The negative priming effect: Inhibitory priming by ignored objects. Quarterly *Journal of Experimental Psychology*, *37*, 571–590. doi:10.1080/14640748508400920

Valenzeno, L., Alibali, M. W., & Klatzky, R. (2003). Teachers' gestures facilitate students' learning: A lesson in symmetry. *Contemporary Educational Psychology*, *28*, 187–204. doi:10.1016/S0361-476X(02)00007-3

Van Gerven, P. W. M., Paas, F., Van Merriënboer, J. J. G., Hendriks, M., & Schmidt, H. G. (2003). The efficiency of multimedia learning into old age. *British Journal of Educational Psychology*, *73*, 489–505. doi:10.1348/000709903322591208

Van Gog, T., Paas, F., Marcus, N., Ayres, P., & Sweller, J. (2009). The mirror neuron system and observational learning: Implications for the effectiveness of dynamic visualizations. *Educational Psychology Review*, *21*, 21–30. doi:10.1007/s10648-008-9094-3

Van Gog, T., & Rummel, N. (2010). Example-based learning: Integrating cognitive and social-cognitive research perspectives. *Educational Psychology Review*, *22*, 155–174. doi:10.1007/s10648-010-9134-7

Van Merriënboer, J. G., & Sweller, J. (2005). Cognitive load theory and complex learning: Recent developments and future directions. *Educational Psychology Review*, *17*, 147–177. doi:10.1007/s10648-005-3951-0

Vecchi, T., Richardson, J., & Cavallini, E. (2005). Passive storage versus active processing in working memory: Evidence from age-related variations in performance. *Journal of Cognitive Psychology*, *17*, 521–539. doi:10.1080/09541440440000140

Verhaeghen, P., & Cerella, J. (2002). Aging, executive control, and attention: a review of meta-analyses. *Neuroscience and Biobehavioral Reviews, 26*, 849–857. doi:10.1016/S0149-7634(02)00071-4

Verhaeghen, P., & De Meersman, L. (1998). Aging and the Stroop effect: A meta-analysis. *Psychology and Aging, 13*, 120–126. doi:10.1037/0882-7974.13.1.120

Wagner-Cook, S., Mitchell, Z., & Goldin-Meadow, S. (2008). Gesturing makes learning last. *Cognition, 106*, 1047-1058. doi:10.1016/j.cognition.2007.04.010

West, R., & Alain, C. (2000). Age-related decline in inhibitory control contributes to the increased Stroop effect observed in older adults. *Psychophysiology, 37*, 179–189. doi:10.1111/14698986.3720179

Wong, A., Marcus, N., Ayres, P., Smith, L., Cooper, G. A., Paas, F., & Sweller, J. (2009). Instructional animations can be superior to statics when learning human motor skills. *Computers in Human Behavior, 25*, 339–347. doi:10.1016/j.chb.2008.12.012

Wouters, P., Tabbers, H. K., & Paas, F. (2007). Interactivity in video-based models. *Educational Psychology Review, 19*, 327–342. doi:10.1007/s10648-007-9045-4

Zimmer, H. D. (2001). Why do actions speak louder than words: Action memory as a variant of encoding manipulations or the result of a specific memory system? In H. D. Zimmer, R. L. & Cohen, (Eds.), *Memory for Action: A Distinct Form of Episodic Memory?* (pp. 151–198). Oxford, UK: Oxford University Press.

Zwaan, R. A., & Madden, C. J. (2005). Embodied sentence comprehension . In D. Pecher, & R. A. Zwaan, (Eds.), *Grounding Cognition: The Role of Perception and Action in Memory, Language, and Thinking* (pp. 224–246). Cambridge, UK: Cambridge University Press. doi:10.1017/CBO9780511499968.010

ADDITIONAL READING

Alibali, W. M., Spencer, R. C., Knox, L., & Kita, S. (2011). Spontaneous gestures influence strategy choices in problem solving. *Psychological Science, 22*, 1138-1144. doi:10.1177/0956797611417722

Barsalou, L. W. (2008). Grounded cognition. *Annual Review of Psychology, 59*, 617-645. doi:10.1146/annurev.psych.59.103006.093639

Braver, T. S., & Barch, D. M. (2002). A theory of cognitive control, aging cognition and neuromodulation. *Neuroscience and Biobehavioral Reviews, 26*, 809-817. doi:10.1016/S0149-7634(02)00067-2

Diederich, A., Colonius, H., & Schomburg, A. (2008). Assessing age-related multisensory enhancement with the time-window-of-integration-model. *Neuropsychologia, 46*, 2556-2562. doi:10.1016/j.neuropsychologia.2008.03.026

Feyereisen, P., & Havard, I. (1999). Mental imagery and production of hand gestures while speaking in younger and older adults. *Journal of Non-verbal Behavior, 23*, 153-171. doi:10.1023/A:1021487510204

Guerreiro, M. J. S., & Van Gerven, P. W. M. (2011). Now you see it, now you don't: Evidence for age-dependent and age-independent cross-modal distraction. *Psychology and Aging, 26*, 415-426. doi:10.1037/a0021507

Hawthhorn, D. (2000). Possible implications of aging for interface designers. *Interacting with Computers, 12*, 507-528. doi:10.1016/S0953-5438(99)00021-1

Hostetter, A. B., & Alibali, M. W. (2008). Visible embodiment: Gestures as simulated action. *Psychonomic Bulletin & Review, 15*, 495-514. doi:10.3758.PBR.15.3.495

Kendon, A. (1997). Gesture. Annual Review of *Anthropology, 26*, 109-128. doi:10.1146/annurev.anthro.26.1.109

Kukolja, J., Thiel, C. M., Wilms, M., Mirzazade, S., & Fink, G. R. (2009). Ageing-related changes of neural activity associated with spatial contextual memory. *Neurobiology of Aging*, *30*, 630-645. doi:10.1016/j.neurobiolaging.2007.08.015

Manzi, A., & Nigro, G. (2008). Long-term memory for performed and observed actions: Retrieval awareness and source monitoring. *Memory*, *16*, 595-603. doi:10.1080/09658210802070749

McNeill, D. (2006). *Gesture and thought*. Chicago: University of Chicago Press.

Morris, J. M. (1994). User interface design for older adults. *Interacting with Computers*, *6*, 373-393. doi:10.1145/564526.564543

Mulligan N. W., & Hornstein, S. L. (2003). Memory for actions: Self-performed tasks and the reenactment effect. *Memory & Cognition*, *31*, 412-421. doi:10.3758/BF03194399

Nissen, M. J., & Corkin, S. (1985). Effectiveness of attentional cueing in older and younger adults. *Journal of Gerontology*, *40*, 185-191. doi:10.1093/geronj/40.2.185

Reed, S. K. (2010). Cognitive architectures for multimedia learning. *Educational Psychologist*, *41*, 87-98. doi:10.1207.s15326985ep4102_2

Schippers, M. B., Gazzola, V., Goebel, R., & Keysers, C. (2009). Playing the charades in the fMRI: Are mirror and/ or mentalizing areas involved in gestural communication? *Public Library of Science One*, *4*, 1-12. doi:10.1371/journal.pone.0006801

Sharps, M. J., & Antonelli, R. S. (2010). Visual and semantic support for paired-associates recall in young and older adults. *The Journal of Genetic Psychology*, *158*, 347-355. doi:10.1080/00221329709596673

Tversky, B., & Morrison, J. B. (2002). Animation: can It facilitate? *International Journal of Human-Computer Studies*, *57*, 247-262. doi:10.1006/ijhc.1017

KEY TERMS AND DEFINITIONS

Attentional Cueing: Attentional cueing is a technique that guides learners' attention to relevant parts of information throughout an instruction, i.e. by temporarily highlighting important information.

Baddeley's Model of Working Memory: In working memory information is simultaneously processed and temporarily stored. `Working memory consists of the central executive and two slave systems, called the visuospatial sketch pad and the phonological loop. The visuospatial sketchpad is concerned with the processing and storage of visual images, and the phonological loop with speech-related information. The central executive controls the distribution and allocation of attention during the processing and storage of information in the two slave systems.

Cognitive Load Theory: Cognitive Load Theory proposes that in instructional designers need to take the limitations of working memory into account. CLT distinguishes three kinds of cognitive load in relation to learning: 1) intrinsic load, which is a fixed property of the study material, 2) extraneous load, which reflects how well the instructional design presents the learning material, and 3) germane cognitive load, which reflects the amount of WM resources that can be made available for learning.

Computer-Based Dynamic Visualisations: Computer-based dynamic visualisations refer to computer controlled information presentation in which the information is dynamically presented and transient in nature, e.g. a video or an animation.

Gestures: Gestures are hand movements made in combination with speech. There are different types of gestures, e.g 1) deictic gestures, which are used to refer to something that is physically present in the environment, and 2) representational gestures, used to depict visual information, i.e. about an object or action that is not necessarily present in the environment.

Interference Control: Interference control refers to the ability to inhibit the processing of irrelevant information.

Multimodal Instruction: Multimodal instruction is a form of instruction in which information is simultaneously presented to more than one modality, i.e. an instruction in which pictures are visually shown and verbal information is presented auditorally.

Chapter 4
Technology as a Bridge between Health Care Systems and Older Adults

Daniel Morrow
University of Illinois at Urbana-Champaign, USA

Jessie Chin
University of Illinois at Urbana-Champaign, USA

ABSTRACT

The authors explore the role of technology in supporting collaboration between health care providers and older adults. They focus on two technologies that help link patients to their providers by giving them access to health information and services: 1) patient portals to Electronic Health Records, and 2) Personal Health Record systems. Theories of distributed cognition and common ground are used to frame a review of the small but growing body of research that investigates which older adults use or do not use these technologies, and why. The findings, while sparse, suggest that older adults with lower levels of health literacy stand to benefit the most from this technology, but they tend to have fewer cognitive, literacy, and other psychosocial resources needed to take advantage of the technology. This discrepancy is due in part to systems that are not designed with older adults' needs and abilities in mind. The authors conclude with recommendations for improving the use of these tools to support patient/provider collaboration by making them easier to use, and by integrating them with other communication media to support the broader context of the patient/provider relationship.

DOI: 10.4018/978-1-4666-1966-1.ch004

INTRODUCTION

This chapter explores the role of technology in supporting collaboration between health care providers and older adults, focusing on recent types of technology that help link patients to their providers by giving patients access to their health records and other health information. We draw on theories of distributed cognition as they relate to aging in order to inform our review of recent research related to patient portals and personal health records. We consider who tends to use these technologies, what factors predict their use, and the implications of such findings for making the technology easier to use and more useful for supporting collaboration between older adults and their providers.

Health springs from many sources, especially patient-centered care that supports prevention and treatment goals (Bodenheimer, Lorig, Holman, & Grumbach, 2002; Wagner, Bennett, Austin, Greene, Schaefer, & Vonkorff, 2005). Patient-centered care in turn requires the free flow of health information to patients, who have some degree of control over this information (IOM, 2003). Because health care providers remain the most frequent source of health information, patient-centered care ultimately depends on effective patient/provider collaboration that support patient decision making and self-care (Aspden, et al., 2007; Bodenheimer, et al., 2002; Stewart, et al., 1995). For example, measures of patient/provider collaboration are associated with patient satisfaction, health behaviors, and outcomes (e.g., Greene, Adelman, Friedmann, & Charon, 1994; Hall, Roter, & Katz, 1988; Stewart, et al., 1995).

Patient-centered care may have drawbacks as well as benefits, depending on how it is implemented. Greater scope of responsibility for patients' own care (e.g., more information to be understood; more decision making required) may undermine health if it is not accompanied by effective support (e.g., McNutt, 2004). This may be especially true for patients with lower levels of health literacy, who struggle with health care tasks that requires comprehension, decision making and other cognitively demanding activities (Aspden, et al., 2007; Nielson-Bohlman, Panzer, & Kindig, 2004).

Health Information Technology (IT) is a key to effectively implementing patient-centered care. Robust health care delivery systems generally depend on IT infrastructure that supports ready access to large amounts of information integrated from multiple sources (e.g., electronic health records) (IOM, 2003). While health IT adoption is driven by many factors (e.g., reduce cost, improve safety, document quality of care), an important goal related to federal requirements for 'meaningful use' of IT in health care is to support patient-centered care by helping patients access information and services, so that care is more continuous between face-to-face encounters (IOM, 2003; Federal Health IT Initiative, 2011; Stead & Linn, 2009). Benefits of IT-supported patient care may include: a) improved patient education and decision making; b) integrated and updated health information and services provided to patients, which reduces fragmented care; c) tailored information and services to individual patient needs (Kreider & Haselton, 1997); d) improved provider/patient communication; e) support for self-care activities (symptom monitoring, adherence; Wald, et al., 2007); and f) social support. An example, described in detail later in the chapter, are well-designed patient portals to Patient Health Records (PHR) systems in integrated health care organizations, which allow patients to access general health information through the Web as well as patient-specific information about treatment and diagnoses from multiple providers (e.g., test results; medication list), allow patients to communicate and make appointments with their providers through Web-based email, and perhaps to chat with other patients who have similar conditions and concerns.

Older adults may especially benefit from health IT. As the most frequent consumers of health care (they are more likely to have chronic illness with high self-care demands; see Morrow & Wilson, 2010, for review), older adults have more need for IT-based care. There is some evidence that they also recognize the potential benefit of this resource. Older adults with chronic illness report wanting to access health information from the Web (Flynn, et al., 2006; Fox, 2007), and they think this access would help them manage illness at home (Leonard, 2004). However, they may be more interested in using the Web to find information that helps them make sense of their illness than to make health decisions independently of their providers (e.g., Xie, 2009). In short, older adults may see the value of the Internet and other forms of IT that is integrated with their ongoing health care.

Older adults with lower health literacy especially stand to benefit because they are most likely to have chronic illness and complex self-care needs (e.g., Nielson-Bohlman, et al., 2004). Patients with lower health literacy are more likely to report that physicians are their major source of health information, yet they are less likely to actively provide information, request information, or ask for clarification during medical visits with their physicians (Makoul, Arntson, Scholfield, 1995; Rollins, 2003). If patients with inadequate health literacy rely on their health care providers, but do not receive adequate support from them, there is a potential for these patients to benefit from IT-based support. Indeed, patients in one study who were more dissatisfied with their provider relationship tended to view IT-based communication more positively (Zickmund, Hess, Bryce, McTigue, Olshansky, Fitzgerald, et al., 2008). However, while older adults with lower health literacy have the most need, they also tend to have fewer cognitive, literacy, and other psychosocial resources to take advantage of technology support for self-care, especially if this technology is not designed with their needs and abilities in mind (Aspden, et al., 2007; Paasche-Orlow, Schillinger, Greene, & Wagner, 2006).

Health IT must be easy to use and provide ready access to clear, accurate information, otherwise it will only increase rather than decrease disparities in access to health care (Stead & Linn, 2009; Tang, et al., 2006). In the present chapter, we address the following issues related to how well IT supports older adults' collaboration with providers:

a. How well do different forms of IT support collaboration between providers and older adults?
b. What are the barriers to effective IT use by older adults? We focus on barriers related to older adults' cognitive resources that may constrain use of technology in the context of the provider/patient relationship. Clues to these barriers are provided by considering which patients tend to use technology to access health information and decision support.
c. How can technology be designed to suit older adults' needs, wants, and abilities and to support robust connections between older adults and health providers?

BACKGROUND

In this section, we describe several theoretical frameworks that help organize the literature on IT-based collaboration between providers and older adults.

Collaboration as Distributed Cognition

IT-based collaboration between patients and providers can be analyzed as a form of distributed cognition, with cognitive activity (e.g., information search, decision making) distributed across individuals and external representations such as computers and paper documents (Hazelhurst, Gorman, & McMullen, 2007; Hutchins, 1995). In general, patient/provider collaboration depends on establishing and managing common ground between conversational partners, which requires coordinating communication process (e.g., speakers need to ensure that addressees are attentive, and addressees must signal that they pay attention) and content—what can be presupposed as known, what needs to be stated. Both speakers and addresses are responsible for grounding information—ensuring that it is mutually understood and accepted as accurate and relevant to shared goals (Clark, 1996). This is especially critical in health care—information must be viewed as credible as well as understood in order to be acted on.

Grounding relies on many processes involved in producing, understanding, and evaluating messages (at the word, sentence and discourse level), such as updating shared mental models of the described events (*situation models*) in response to linguistic, nonlinguistic (e.g., pictorial), or perceptual information (Durso, Rawson, & Girotto, 2007; Morrow & Fischer, 2012). Thus, situation models are co-created by communication partners by coordinating attention to relevant information (Clark, 1996). For example, listeners better understand a speaker's description of a situation (e.g., a painting) when they synchronize their eye movements with the speaker's gaze on the shared situation (Richardson, Dale, & Kirkham, 2007). Grounding processes are constrained by a variety of resources, such as the communication media and speaker and listener cognition.

Communication media. Different media influence how easily communication partners establish common ground (Clark & Brennan, 1991; Monk, 2009). Face-to-face communication provides many options for grounding: gesture and facial expressions are used to offer and accept proposed messages, so that partners' attention is coordinated by nonverbal as well as verbal means. Rapid turn taking allows for quick detection and repair of misunderstanding. In this way, communication is streamlined, with less need for verbalization. Face-to-face communication may be especially suited

for conveying emotional information, which may be important for evaluating message credibility.

Remote communication is more constrained, offering fewer resources for grounding. Remote communication with partners temporally co-present (telephone or other synchronous communication) still allows rapid turn taking and simultaneity that support grounding, but eliminates visual cues. Therefore, the costs of producing and accepting contributions to conversation may be higher (Clark & Brennan, 1991). Grounding may be even more challenging for asynchronous remote communication such as email, which lacks simultaneity, and sometimes sequentiality (the order of turns may not be preserved). More effort may be involved in producing messages (typing vs. speaking). On the other hand, media such as email support message reviewability compared to face-to-face communication, where partners may lose the thread of multiple topics during rapid turn-taking (Olson & Olson, 2008). Communication media may also influence message acceptability. For example, the distance between communication partners may be perceived as greater for remote communication, which can make messages less persuasive (Moon, 1999). This might undermine the impact of remote communication on self-care. For example, a recommendation about exercise might have more impact if conveyed face-to-face than by email.

Participant resources. Grounding messages in order to build a shared situation model may impose variable demands on processing capacity (e.g., working memory) and knowledge (e.g., related to language or health) (Morrow & Fischer, 2012). On the other hand, knowledge arising from partner familiarity (shared history of interaction) or joint membership in linguistic/cultural communities (Clark, 1996) may make communication more efficient. For example, partners who share knowledge about the discourse topic can more quickly establish co-reference (Isaacs & Clark, 1987), in part by coordinating attention to key information (Richardson, et al., 2007).

From the perspective of distributed cognition theory, critical features of patient-provider collaboration include the free flow of information tailored to patient needs so that it is accurate and relevant, with interactive communication that enables patients and providers to easily ground this information in the context of a patient/provider partnership that supports self-care (e.g., Wagner, et al., 2005).

Aging and Distributed Cognition

The cognitive resources underlying collaboration have different lifespan-related trajectories (Beier & Ackerman, 2005). Processing capacity tends to decline, which helps explain why older adults are generally less successful than younger adults at understanding demanding communication (e.g., rapidly presented, conceptually dense messages). These declines may also explain age-related problems understanding numeric information (about risk, probabilistic outcomes) or using tables and similar formats to support decision-making (Finucane, Mertz, Slovic, & Scholze Schmidt, 2005; Peters Dieckmann, Västfjäll, Mertz, Slovic, & Hibbard, 2009).

More positively, general knowledge (Stanovich, West, & Harrison 1995) and domain knowledge (Morrow, Menard, et al., 2001) tend to increase with age, reflecting experience in work or other domains. Knowledge-related gains may improve processing efficiency and especially benefit older adults. For example, older domain experts effectively deploy their knowledge despite processing capacity limits to support comprehension (Miller, Stine-Morrow, Kirkorian, & Conroy, 2004; Morrow, et al., 2001). Similarly, older adults are adept at creating situation models despite processing limits, in part because of age-related accumulation of knowledge (Radvansky & Dykstra, 2007). Their communication may also be supported by increasing socio-emotional selectivity that results in more attention to emotionally relevant information, which can improve

comprehension and decision-making (Mikels, Lockenhoff, Maglio, Carstensen, Goldstein, & Garber, 2010).

In the health domain, aging is associated with health-related knowledge gains resulting from illness experience (Beier & Ackerman, 2005; Chin, et al., 2009a). These gains may offset processing capacity declines to support search for (Chin, Fu, & Kannampallil, 2009b) and learning about (Beier & Ackerman, 2005; Chin, et al., 2011) health information. Older adults with low health literacy may leverage their knowledge to support self-care despite inadequate processing capacity to the extent knowledge use is supported by well designed technology (Chin, et al., 2011). For example, as described below, the information provided through patient portals or other provider-based technology can serve as a context that activates patient knowledge about illness and treatment, which helps them plan for taking medication.

Older adults may especially benefit from face-to-face communication because they rely on pausing, intonation, and other voice-based cues (e.g., Wingfield & Tun, 2007) and facial cues (Brault, Gilbert, Lansing, McCarley, & Kramer, 2010) to support comprehension. These cues are also important for conveying emotional information, particularly for older adults (Thompson, Aidinejad, & Ponte, 2001).

Health IT may serve as a form of environmental support that enhances benefits of patient-provider collaboration for self-care, especially for older adults with low health literacy. It can serve as an external resource reducing older adults' reliance on limited processing capacity to accomplish health-related tasks because older adults can offload cognitively demanding processes to these tools. Computer displays of patient information can be used as a shared reference to support discussion, reducing the need for verbally presenting information and coordinating attention to key information during office visits. Patients may more easily convey what they do or do not understand by using the tools, which supports grounding of the information. To sum up, well designed IT may help providers and patients present and ground health information, which is required to develop a shared mental model. This in turn may support medication adherence and other self-care tasks—patient/provider agreement about medication goals and plans is associated with adherence (Machtinger, Wang, Chen, Rodríguez, Wu, & Schillinger, 2007).

IT may also support remote forms of collaboration, where patient and provider cannot rely on face-to-face resources such as gesture and rapid turn-taking (Morrow & Fischer, 2012). However, older adults' ability to take advantage of such IT-based support hinges on many factors related to patient resources, the communication medium, and other characteristics of the technology, as well as the task and environment (Fisk, Rogers, Charness, Czaja, & Sharit, 2009).

TECHNOLOGY AS A BRIDGE FOR PATIENT/PROVIDER COLLABORATION: SUCCESSES AND CHALLENGES

The previous section identifies potential barriers to technology-based collaboration between patients and providers, as well as strategies that may help mitigate these barriers. We next review the literature on older adults' use of technology as it relates to patient/provider collaboration. We first consider technology that is largely controlled by providers and integrated with clinic-based systems (patient portals) and then focus on technology that is more controlled by patients/less integrated with clinic systems (e.g., personal health records) (Tang, et al., 2006).

Patient Portals

Systems such as patient portals tether patients' access to health information and services to their providers' IT systems. Internet-based portals provide patient access to an account on the provider's

EHR or other IT system, so that patients can view results of clinical tests, order prescription refills, arrange appointments, and communicate with providers (Detmer, Bloomrosen, Raymond, & Tang, 2008; Grant, et al., 2006; Hess, et al., 2006). Portals have the potential to improve health outcomes by supporting older adults' management of their chronic illness (Grant, et al., 2006; Zhou, et al., 2010), and may address issues related to variable quality of health information on the Internet by supporting access to credible health information (Rockoff, Czaja, Kahn, Miller, & Szerencsy, 2010). Of course, such benefits will occur only if portals are perceived as useful and as easy to use. Usability in turn may require processing capacity as well as knowledge related to logging on the system, finding system functions (e.g., navigating menu-based systems), and understanding and reasoning about test results or other information.

Who uses patient portals? In general, adults who are older, less educated, and from minority ethnic/racial groups are less likely to use the Internet and other forms of computer technology (e.g., Fox, 2007). This 'digital divide' not only reflects differences in access to technology (e.g., broadband connection to Internet), but differences in willingness and ability to use the technology on an ongoing basis, which depends on understanding the tool's functions, ease of use, and other factors related to design and training (Alpay, et al., 2009; Fisk, et al., 2009). Research focused on patient portals, while sparse, reveals a similar picture. Weingert et al. (2006) examined factors predicting who used a patient portal for a family medicine practice. Early adopting patients tended to be younger, better educated, and healthier. Similarly, a more recent study of portal use among diabetic patients found that more educated, younger, and non-Hispanic White patients were more likely to request a system password (Sarkar, et al., 2011; Goel, et al., 2011), and these differences in accessing the portal extended to the frequency of using the system (although the educational differences were smaller among this subgroup). For those patients who logged on at least once, older patients logged on more frequently, perhaps reflecting age differences in need for health services and thus for using the portal (also see Goel, et al., 2011). In another study with the same sample, patients who scored lower on a measure of health literacy were less likely to access and use the portal (Sarkar, et al., 2010). These findings suggest that those patients most in need of portal-based services (chronically ill patients) may be less likely to use these tools to support self-care.

Why are portals (not) used? Barriers may differ for accessing portals and for using them on an ongoing basis. Like other technology, accessing portals may require financial resources, as well as beliefs compatible with technology use (e.g., value of portal, concerns about privacy of health information). Both financial resources and compatible beliefs may in turn relate to patient education. Interestingly, concerns about privacy and security of health-related information, an often noted concern about the Internet among older adults, may not be the key barrier among older adult users of portals (Hassol, et al., 2004; Rockoff, et al., 2010; Zickmund, et al., 2008), although there are few studies investigating this issue. A more important factor for predicting portal access may be knowledge about technology based on prior experience (Sarkar, et al., 2011).

Once accessed, using portals may depend heavily on cognitive and literacy abilities that are needed to learn to use portals to accomplish specific health goals, such as ordering prescription refills or understanding test results. In general, measures of processing capacity predict ease of learning to use computer applications such as word processing (Fisk, et al., 2009), and to search for and understand health-related information obtained from the Internet (Sharit, Hernandez, Czaja, Pirolli, 2008). Age differences in processing capacity also help explain differences in numeracy skills needed to interpret quantitative clinical test results (Finucane, et al., 2005). The small literature on older adults' use of patient portals suggests the same cognitive barriers exist for this technology. Older adults in focus groups express concern about their ability to understand information provided through portals (Rockoff, et al., 2010; Zickmund, et al., 2008). Difficulty using portals to accomplish health tasks reflects a variety of problems, including understanding technical language and health concepts, as well as using the interface (e.g., navigation, search) (Rockoff, et al., 2010). However, any conclusions must be tentative because there are few experimental studies that systematically investigate effects of portal characteristics (e.g., input control, menu organization, information format) on how patients perform tasks. Such studies are needed to evaluate theories of how interfaces influence older adults' portal use.

As discussed in Section 2, older adults' knowledge about IT (reflecting computer experience) and health concepts (reflecting illness-related and literacy experience) may support portal use. More general research on aging and technology use suggests that both types of knowledge can mitigate age-related differences in computer use, presumably by offsetting the impact of processing capacity limits (Chin, et al., 2009b; Sharit, et al., 2008). Less positively, this also suggests older adults with limited knowledge and experience related to technology are the most disadvantaged. For example, patients in one study reported having trouble reviewing their own records on portal systems because of inadequate knowledge about health concepts and terminology, and more generally about quantitative concepts (e.g., probability, risk) (Keselman, et al., 2007).

Knowledge-related problems can partly be addressed by using less technical language in portals (Friedman, Hoffman-Goetz, & Arocha, 2006) as well as graphic formats that reduce the need for computationally demanding or knowledge-based strategies for evaluating risk or numeric concepts such as proportions (e.g., Peters, et al., 2009). However, these kinds of formats are rarely used in patient portals.

It is also important to consider older adults' use of patient portals within the broader context of the patient/provider relationship as supported by different communication media. Age differences in cognitive/literacy abilities may interact with different media to influence the success of communication, and ultimately self-care. As described in Section II, remote compared to face-to-face communication can challenge critical processes such as how well patients and providers ground messages as mutually understood and accepted as relevant to self-care because remote communication tends to provide fewer resources for grounding (e.g., absence of visual cues such as gesture and facial expressions, limited turn-taking). Therefore, remote communication may impose heavier demands on participants' cognitive resources (Morrow & Fischer, 2012). However, there are no studies systematically comparing the success of portals (as a form of remote, asynchronous communication) with face-to-face, telephone, or other communication media for supporting patient comprehension, decision-making, and health behaviors. Nonetheless, some research suggests that older adults evaluate the benefits of patient portals relative to other media that they use to collaborate with providers. Several focus group studies comparing patients who do or do not use portals suggest that patients consider the value of portals in the context of the relationship with their provider. Diabetic patients in one study who were less satisfied with their provider visits were also more positive about using a new patient portal, while those patients more satisfied with their provider were less open to the portal (Zickmund, et al., 2008). Although it is difficult to generalize from this study because the participants were relatively young and well educated, the findings suggest patients are concerned that Internet-based communication will replace rather than enhance face-to-face patient/provider collaboration. Older adults in another study expressed interest in receiving information through a portal, but wanted providers to help them interpret emotionally

charged information such as test results (Rockoff, et al., 2010). Patients may also prefer face-to-face rather than remote communication for receiving directions for self-care tasks such as taking medication (Hassol, et al., 2004). Similarly, Xie (2009) found that older adults value the Internet for finding health-related information, but want to collaborate with their providers to make important health decisions (also see Wald, et al., 2007).

Collectively, these findings suggest that older adults consider the value of portals within the context of the provider relationship. They may view portals as important for receiving health information and services (especially if the providers help ensure the quality of portal-based information), but they want to directly collaborate with their providers in order to interpret and use this information. Younger, more educated, and more technology-experienced patients, on the other hand, may be more comfortable using remote forms of communication with their providers to accomplish a broader range of goals, especially if such communication increases the amount of information and services provided. Young adults in several studies expressed more satisfaction using Web email than the telephone because of greater access to providers and a broader range of health information (Hassol, et al., 2004; Lin, Wittevrongel, Moore, Beaty, & Ross, 2005).

Personal Health Records

Provider/patient collaboration can also be supported by more patient-driven forms of technology that are intended to support patient health by harnessing the large amount of health information available on the Internet and other digital information sources (e.g., Bass, 2003; Gustafson, et al., 1999; Neuhauser & Kreps, 2003; O'Connor & Johanson, 2000). The concept of Personal Health Records (PHRs) refers to a variety of integrated digital tools for patients to manage their medical knowledge and track their personal health history. PHRs combine patient data, software tools, and medical knowledge repositories to support self-care activities. They were first introduced to serve as a patient-oriented version of Electronic Medical Records (EMR) tailored to patients' needs and managed by patients themselves (e.g., Kaelber, Jha, Johnston, Middleton, & Bates, 2008; Keselman, et al., 2007; Mitchell & Begroay, 2010; Tang, et al., 2006). Currently, there are more than 60 PHRs available (AHIMA, 2009). Some are hosted in clinics, and some developed and offered to patients by IT manufactures such as Google Health and Microsoft HealthVault (Halamka, Mandl, & Tang, 2008; Tang, et al., 2006). These systems vary from basic patient-entry stand-alone electronic records to more integrated Web-based PHRs that include information from multiple resources such as patient-entered data, pharmacy records, medical knowledge databases and home diagnostic equipment, as well as EMR-embedded tethered PHR systems (Detmer, et al., 2008). While PHRs can be linked to provider EMRs, they generally require more patient management than patient portals (Tang, et al., 2006).

Some studies suggest that PHRs benefit patients with chronic illness, including strengthening the relationship between physicians and patients and empowering illness self-management among patients (Mitchell & Begoray, 2010; Tang, et al., 2006; Tenforde, Jain, & Hickner, 2011). However, the effects of using PHR on health outcomes (e.g., better control in blood pressure, cholesterol, and glucose) are inconsistent (Tenforde, et al., 2011).

Who uses PHRs? A 2009-2010 national survey found that only 7% of the US population has used PHR systems (Undem, 2010). Similar to portals, PHR users tend to be younger, better educated, have more income, and from white nonhispanic groups (racial-ethnic differences are not explained by differences in education or access to Internet). However, lower-income adults with chronic illness are still more likely to use PHRs. More interestingly, patients with two or more chronic conditions tend to use PHRs more often than those with fewer than two chronic conditions. Furthermore,

9% of the patients with more than three chronic conditions in the survey used PHRs, suggesting those with greater need may in fact be more likely to use these tools.

Although PHRs have the potential to help patients to manage their chronic illness, the development and use of PHRs have lagged behind other types of health IT. More than 80% of Internet users go online for health information (Pew Internet and American Life Report, 2011). Among older users (age 65 and more), a large proportion (76%) search for health information on the Internet. In contrast, as mentioned above, only about 7% of consumers have tried PHRs, and fewer than half of this group continued to use the tools (Undem, 2010). In fact, Google Health recently announced plans to shut down their online PHR service in 2011 because it did not reach the expected user engagement since it was introduced in 2008. This development suggests that even though patients are interested in using such tools, they may not do so because of poor usability, limited technology literacy, and health literacy.

Why are PHRs (not) used? The finding that PHRs may be used more by chronically ill patients, that is, those most in need of support (Mitchell & Begoray, 2010; Tang, et al., 2006; Tenforde, et al., 2011), suggests that the tools can help offload the heavy demands of self-care by helping patients track their health data constantly and regularly, especially if the system is integrated with home diagnostic equipment data (such as blood pressure, glucose levels, or peak flow). PHRs may also increase patients' interest and engagement in self-care (Tang, et al., 2006), perhaps by supporting collaborative monitoring of chronic illness by patients and providers, such that both parties can access patient-entered health data (e.g., blood pressure readings), which can increase patient satisfaction (Tang, et al., 2006). Thus, as with patient portals, use of PHRs needs to be considered within the context of the patient/provider relationship.

Nonetheless, despite some evidence that PHRs are used by chronically ill patients, overall adoption rates are low (Undem, 2010). This appears to reflect the demands of using the tools on patients' cognitive and literacy skills as well as knowledge. Using PHRs requires accessing the system, connecting the PHR to computers, mobile devices, or other systems, and then entering and editing patient information. Perhaps most important, users must monitor and update the information over time as their health status and treatment changes (Mitchell & Begroay, 2010; Lober, et al., 2006). Therefore, PHRs heavily rely on patients' effort and motivation (Detmer, et al., 2008), and perceived PHR usefulness and usability influence user attitudes, preferences, and adoption (Or, et al., 2010; Peters, et al., 2009).

While older adults with chronic illness may have the most need for these tools, many also find these tools very challenging. Because they have more illnesses that require complex treatment and self-care (e.g., medications, clinical tests), they need to enter and update more health information than other patients do in order to use the tool. Yet, as reviewed in Section 2, they experience age-related declines in processing capacity (e.g., psychomotor speed, working memory capacity), and the design of these tools tends to impose heavy demands on these limited cognitive resources (as well as on physical and other patient resources). For example, a usability study comparing two PHRs (Google Health and Microsoft HealthVault) found that entering medication information was a click-intensive task for both system interfaces, even though the tools allowed use of pop-up windows or scroll-down menus to add information (Peters, et al., 2009). While there was a narrow age range among participants in this study, more general research on age-related differences in searching for health information on the Internet suggests that older computer users tend to spend more time and click on fewer items to search online information (e.g., Chin, et al., 2009b; Sharit, et al., 2008). The high search/click costs of older

users may lead to inadequate exploration and management of health information. This suggests that complex PHR interfaces will pose greater challenges for older adults because of age-related declines in cognitive resources, which may help explain the low rates of adoption of PHRs (because older adults are likely to be the most likely users of these tools). Perhaps most concerning, older adults may be at greater risk for creating partial or even inaccurate health records through PHRs because of difficulties using the system on an ongoing basis. Converging evidence comes from a study in which low-income older adults were given access to a PHR. Difficulties using the tool related to cognitive ability (e.g., forgetting information needed to log on to the system), as well as limited basic computer knowledge and health literacy (Lober, et al., 2006).

Another barrier relates to how information is presented in PHRs. These tools provide patients with a wide range of information related to patient-entered data from sources such as home diagnostic equipment and patient medical records from their providers. Older adults with limited health literacy are likely to have difficulty understanding and making decisions about this information (Tang, et al., 2006), perhaps because of age-related declines in processing capacity coupled with inadequate knowledge about language and health (Chin, et al., 2011; Peters, et al., 2009). The design of PHR systems tends to exacerbate these problems because unfamiliar medical terminology is pervasive. For example, variable use of medical terms by physicians poses a translation problem for patients (Ball, Smith, & Bakalar, 2007).

SUMMING UP: CAN WE BUILD BETTER TECHNOLOGY-BASED BRIDGES FOR PATIENT/PROVIDER COLLABORATION?

The research on patient portals and PHRs, while sparse, suggests that older adults are interested in using these tools to support health-related goals. Consistent with distributed cognition theory (e.g., Hutchins, 1995), older adults see the value of these tools for offloading cognitively demanding self-care activities such as managing information. Nonetheless, older adults with chronic illness, who stand to gain the most from using these tools, may use them the least. Although PHR users tend to be patients with chronic illness, few patients use them in the first place. The limited research in this area suggests that barriers to using both patient portals and PHRs include age-related limitations in cognitive and other resources (although for those who access these tools in the first place, older adults may be more likely to continue using them). PHRs in particular are rarely used by older adults because they require more effort (e.g., to enter and update data). More speculatively, older adults may prefer tools that are more integrated with provider systems and that support communication with providers, compared to stand-alone versions of PHRs.

Improving IT-Based Tools

Our review suggests recommendations for improving the use of these tools to support patient/provider collaboration including making them easier to use through interface redesign, and making them more useful within the broader context of the patient/provider relationship.

To better support patient/provider collaboration, tool interfaces can be improved in several ways by reducing demands on processing capacity and leveraging user knowledge.

- Inputting data (especially for PHRs) currently requires substantial psychomotor and cognitive effort (e.g., many clicks). Data entry and user interaction with the systems more generally, can be improved by using multiple data-entry methods, such as keyboard entry, writing pads, or voice

control, as well as more efficient organization of input screens.

- The information can be more effectively presented in portals and PHRs in order to improve comprehension among older users. For example, use of simple, consistent, and familiar language will especially benefit older adults with low health literacy (Nielson-Bohlman, et al., 2004). Information can also be organized to be consistent with older adults' expectations (Morrow & Leirer, 1999). Presentation of quantitative information (e.g., test results) may be improved by graphical formats that reduce the need for quantitative reasoning or knowledge (e.g., Peters, et al., 2009).

- User navigation through the system can be improved by using simple and meaningful labels for links, shallow menus with limited options at each level, and other strategies recommended for supporting older adults' Internet use (e.g., Mead, Lamson, & Rogers, 2002; Fisk, et al., 2009). Such improvements may increase adoption of portals, PHRs, and similar tools because older adults are more likely to think the benefits of using them will outweigh the effort involved in using them.

More broadly, the value of these tools for patient-centered care should be analyzed within the context of older adults' relationship with their providers in order to make the tools more useful to older adults. This can be done by drawing on research and theories in human-technology interaction, such as theories of distributed cognition and common ground. This approach helps identify costs and benefits of using these tools compared to alternative communication media, which may address barriers to tool use related to patients' concern that the tools will replace rather than enhance their connection to their providers.

Potential costs of IT-based tools. Face-to-face communication (e.g., during office visits) may effectively support patient and provider exchange of health information because it provides a range of resources for grounding the information as mutually understood (e.g., visual cues such as gestures and facial expressions and rapid turn taking) (Clark & Brennan, 1991). These resources may be especially important for conveying emotionally related information that may be critical for accepting information as credible and personally relevant to self-care. Research on patient portals suggests that older adults consider face-to-face communication with providers as critical for helping them interpret some types of health information (e.g., test results) within the context of their illness, for making health decisions, and for providing emotional support. This finding is consistent with patient-centered models of health care that focus on the patient/provider relationship (Bodenheimer, et al., 2002; Stewart, et al., 1995), and with lifespan development theories that highlight the increasing importance of social relationships as we age (Mikels, et al., 2010). However, face-to-face communication also has drawbacks, such as imposing heavy demands on memory because it tends to lack reviewability. Perhaps more concerning, patient-provider collaboration during office visits may fall short of the potential of this medium because providers do not provide critical information or do not check patients' comprehension of the information that is provided (for review, see Morrow & Wilson, 2010).

Patient portals, as a form of remote asynchronous communication, provide fewer resources for patients and providers to ground their communication, making it vulnerable to patient misunderstanding that is not clarified by providers. This is a particular concern for PHRs that are not integrated with provider systems because there is no check on patient-entered information, which increases the chance of inaccurate information in these tools.

Potential benefits of IT-based tools. More positively, portals and PHRs are a more permanent medium than face-to-face communication. Therefore, communication may be less constrained by memory limitations, which may especially benefit older adults. Moreover, the fact that portals are tethered to provider EMRs allows providers an opportunity to support patient comprehension (e.g., Rockoff, et al., 2010). For example, Web-based email (as part of a portal) is valuable for follow-up communication to clarify issues or to provide additional information. This form of asynchronous communication is sometimes preferred to remote synchronous communication such as the telephone because the latter transient voice medium limits amount of information that can be easily exchanged. An important open question is whether remote forms of communication can effectively supplement, or perhaps even replace, face-to-face communication as a bridge between older adults and their providers if this communication can better support provider/patient interaction by providing resources typically available in face-to-face communication, such as rapid turn-taking (e.g., chat, texting) or nonverbal cues (e.g., video-based telemedicine) (Monk, 2009).

Integrating communication media. Technology may support communication, planning, and decision making during face-to-face encounters by reducing the demands of communication and problem solving on memory and other limited cognitive resources. For example, a computer-based tool designed to support collaborative medication scheduling between patients and providers during routine office visits may improve planning compared to less structured tools used for medication review and reconciliation (Kannampallil, et al., 2011). The impact of an EMR-based version of the tool on patients' medication knowledge and adherence is now being tested (Liao, et al., 2011). Such IT-based support for face-to-face patient/provider collaboration may be enhanced if integrated with home-based systems such as PHRs.

Finally, there is a need to consider how patient portals and other technologies that support patient/provider collaboration also relate to patients' use of the Internet and social media to support their health goals. Patients are increasingly accessing health information from the Internet in addition to, or rather than, traditional sources such as providers (Estabrook, et al., 2007). Older adults, the major health information consumers, in particular search for and use online health information (Chin, et al., 2009b; Flynn, et al., 2006; Sharit, et al., 2008). For example, more than 70% of Internet users over age sixty-five have used online health information to assist their medical decision-making (Pew Internet and American Life Report, 2011), and more than half of adults in one survey were interested in using online applications to track their health data (Undem, 2010). Integrating portals and PHRs with the Internet may capitalize on this trend, making them more useful to older adults for managing their health conditions. To respond to the increasing information needs of online patients:

- Web-based PHRs might be more likely to engage older users in their self-care activities if these tools easily integrate with provider IT systems. Web-based PHRs allow connections with providers though integration with patient portals or EMR systems. Therefore, patients and providers can collaboratively monitor their disease and self-care activities through patient-entered symptom reporting or health data records (such as their blood pressure readings or glucose levels).

- Patients are also increasingly turning to social network media to obtain socially based health information, such as medication or treatment reviews (Pew Internet and American Life, 2011). Online social support and shared personal experiences among patients that are enabled by social network sites are also increasingly important. Some PHRs such as PatientLikeMe have networking functions for patients to educate or support each other in terms of "peer-to-peer healthcare." Peer-to-peer

healthcare supported by this social-network-based PHR empowered patients to manage and share their health data and obtain the advice for the treatment decisions (Frost & Massagli, 2009). Integrating social network sites with PHR systems to encourage the engagement of patients might be a future direction for PHRs.

Future Research Directions

These recommendations for improving the usability and usefulness of technology to support patient/provider collaboration in turn help define an agenda for future research in this area. First, more analytic and systematic studies are needed to evaluate how current portal and PHR systems do or do not support specific patient task goals. As in other areas of health care research (e.g., Morrow & Durso, 2011), such research might begin with more controlled studies with simulated tasks that systematically vary properties of the interface (e.g., different menu structures, information formats) to investigate their impact on important measures of tool use (e.g., navigation or comprehension errors). This would provide the foundation for investigating the impact of portal characteristics on communication and self-care in complex and realistic settings such as clinic and home.

Second, an important research question is which tools or communication media are best suited for different patient goals and health care tasks. Answering this question will require analysis of how specific features of these media satisfy goal/task requirements. This in turn depends on analysis of how provider/patient collaboration is accomplished through the interaction of different communication media in the context of the health care system. Such research may help identify optimal blends of technologies for supporting different facets of patient/provider collaboration.

ACKNOWLEDGMENT

Preparation of this chapter was supported by the National Institute of Aging (Grant R01 AG31718) and the National Institute of Nursing Research (Grant R01 NR011300). Any opinions, findings, and conclusions or recommendations expressed in this publication are those of the authors and do not necessarily reflect the views of the NIH.

REFERENCES

AHIMA. (2009). *How to choose a PHR supplier.* Retrieved on January 26, 2009, from http://myphr.com/resources/phr_search.asp

Alpay, L., Verhoef, J., Xie, B., Te'eni, D., & Zwetsloot-Schonk, J. H. M. (2009). Current challenge in consumer health informatics: Bridging the gap between access to information and information understanding. *Biomedical Informatics Insights, 2*, 1–10.

Aspden, P. Wolcott. J. A., Bootman, J. L., & Croenwett. L. R. (2007). *Preventing medication errors.* Washington, DC: The National Academies Press.

Ball, M., Smith, C., & Bakalar, R. (2007). Personal health records: Empowering consumers. *Journal of Healthcare Information Management, 21*, 76–86.

Bass, S. B. (2003). How will internet use affect the patient? A review of computer network and closed internet-based system studies and the implications in understanding how the use of the internet affects patient populations. *Journal of Health Psychology, 8*, 25–38. doi:10.1177/1359105303008001427

Beier, M. E., & Ackerman, P. L. (2005). Age, ability and the role of prior knowledge on the acquisition of new domain knowledge. *Psychology and Aging, 20*, 341–355. doi:10.1037/0882-7974.20.2.341

Bodenheimer, T., Lorig, K., Holman, H., & Grumbach, K. (2002). Patient self-management of chronic illness in primary care. *Journal of the American Medical Association, 288*, 2469–2475. doi:10.1001/jama.288.19.2469

Brault, L. M., Gilbert, J. R., Lansing, C. R., McCarley, J. S., & Kramer, A. F. (2010). Bimodal stimulus presentation and expanded auditory bandwidth improve older adults' speech perception. *Human Factors, 52*, 479–491. doi:10.1177/0018720810380404

Chin, J., D'Andrea, L., Morrow, D. G., Stine-Morrow, E. A. L., Conner-Gercia, T., Graumlich, J. F., & Murray, M. D. (2009a). Cognition and illness experience are associated with illness knowledge among older adults with hypertension. In *Proceedings of the 53rd Annual Meeting of the Human Factors and Ergonomics Society 2009.* Santa Monica, CA: Human Factors and Ergonomics Society.

Chin, J., Fu, W.-T., & Kannampallil, T. (2009b). Adaptive information search: Age-dependent interactions between cognitive profiles and strategies. In *Proceedings of the 27th ACM Conference on Human Factors in Computing Systems CHI 2009.* Boston, MA: ACM Press.

Chin, J., Morrow, D., Stine-Morrow, E. A. L., Conner-Garcia, T., Graumlich, J. F., & Murray, M. D. (2011). The process-knowledge model of health literacy: Evidence from a componential analysis of two commonly used measures. *Journal of Health Communication, 16*, 222–241. doi:10.1080/10810730.2011.604702

Clark, H. H. (1996). *Using language.* Cambridge, UK: Cambridge University Press.

Clark, H. H., & Brennan, S. E. (1991). Grounding in communication. In Resnick, L. B., Levine, J., & Teasley, S. D. (Eds.), *Perspectives on Socially Shared Cognition* (pp. 127–149). Washington, DC: American Psychological Association. doi:10.1037/10096-006

Detmer, D., Bloomrosen, M., Raymond, B., & Tang, P. (2008). Integrated personal health records: Transformative tools for consumer-centric care. *BMC Medical Informatics and Decision Making*, *8*, 45. doi:10.1186/1472-6947-8-45

Durso, F. T., Rawson, K. A., & Girotto, S. (2007). Comprehension and situation awareness. In F. T. Durso, R. S. Nickerson, S. T., Dumais, S. Lewandowsky, & T. J. Perfect (Eds.), *Handbook of Applied Cognition,* (pp. 163-194). Chichester, UK: Wiley.

Estabrook, L., Witt, E., & Rainie, L. (2007). *Information searches that solve problems: How people use the internet, libraries, and government agencies when they need help.* Washington, DC: Pew Internet & American Life Project. Retrieved on August 10, 2008 from http://www.pewinternet. org/pdfs/Pew_UI_LibrariesReport.pdf

Finucane, M. L., Mertz, C. K., Slovic, P., & Scholze Schmidt, E. S. (2005). Task complexity and older adults' decision-making competence. *Psychology and Aging*, *20*, 71–84. doi:10.1037/0882-7974.20.1.71

Fisk, A. D., Rogers, W., Charness, N., Czaja, S. J., & Sharit, J. (2009). *Designing for older adults: Principles and creative human factors approach* (2nd ed.). London, UK: CRC Associates.

Flynn, K. E., Smith, M. A., & Freese, J. (2006). When do older adults turn to the Internet for health information? Findings from the Wisconsin longitudinal study. *Journal of General Internal Medicine*, *21*, 1295–1301. doi:10.1111/j.1525-1497.2006.00622.x

Fox, S. (2007). *E-patients with a disability or chronic disease.* Washington, DC: PEW Internet & American Life. Retrieved on August 20, 2009 from http://www.pewinternet.org/~/media// Files/Reports/2007/EPatients_Chronic_Conditions_2007.pdf

Friedman, D. B., Hoffman-Goetz, L., & Arocha, J. F. (2006). Health literacy and the world wide web: Comparing the readability of leading incident cancers on the internet. *Medical Informatics and the Internet in Medicine*, *31*, 67–87. doi:10.1080/14639230600628427

Frost, J., & Massagli, M. (2009). PatientsLikeMe the case for a data-centered patient community and how ALS patients use the community to inform treatment decisions and manage pulmonary health. *Chronic Respiratory Disease*, *6*, 225–229.

Goel, M. S., Brown, T. L., Williams, A., Hasnain-Wynia, R., Thompson, J. A., & Baker, D. W. (2011). Disparities in enrollment and use of an electronic patient portal. *Journal of General Internal Medicine*, *26*, 1112–1116. doi:10.1007/s11606-011-1728-3

Grant, R. W., Wald, J. S., Poon, E. G., Schnipper, J. L., & Gandhi, T. K. (2006). Design and implementation of a web-based patient portal linked to an ambulatory care electronic health record: Patient gateway for diabetes collaborative care. *Diabetes Technology & Therapeutics*, *8*, 576–586. doi:10.1089/dia.2006.8.576

Greene, M. G., Adelman, R. D., Friedmann, E., & Charon, R. (1994). Older patient satisfaction with communication during an initial medical encounter. *Social Science & Medicine*, *38*, 1279–1288. doi:10.1016/0277-9536(94)90191-0

Gustafson, D., Hawkins, R., Boberg, E., Pingree, S., Serlin, R., & Graziano, F. (1999). Impact of a patient-centered, computer-based health information/support system. *American Journal of Preventive Medicine*, *16*, 1–9. doi:10.1016/S0749-3797(98)00108-1

Halamka, J. D., Mandl, K. D., & Tang, P. C. (2008). Early experiences with personal health records. *Journal of the American Medical Informatics Association*, *15*, 1–7. doi:10.1197/jamia.M2562

Hall, J. A., Roter, D. L., & Katz, N. R. (1988). Meta-analysis of correlates of provider behaviors in medical encounters. *Medical Care, 26,* 657–675. doi:10.1097/00005650-198807000-00002

Hassol, A., Walker, J. M., Kidder, D., Rokita, K., Young, D., & Pierdon, S. (2004). Patient experiences and attitudes about access to a patient electronic health care record and linked web messaging. *Journal of the American Medical Informatics Association, 11,* 505–513. doi:10.1197/jamia.M1593

Hazlehurst, B., Gorman, P. N., & McMullen, C. K. (2008). Distributed cognition: an alternative model of cognition for medical informatics. *International Journal of Medical Informatics, 77,* 226–234. doi:10.1016/j.ijmedinf.2007.04.008

Healthit. (2011). *Federal health IT strategic plan.* Retrieved on June 27, 2011, from http://healthit.hhs.gov/portal/server.pt/document/954074/federal_hit_strategic_plan_public_comment_period

Hess, R., Bryce, C. L., & McTigue, K. (2006). The diabetes patient portal: Patient perspectives on structure and delivery. *Diabetes Spectrum, 92,* 106–110. doi:10.2337/diaspect.19.2.106

Hutchins, E. (1995). How a cockpit remembers its speeds. *Cognitive Science, 19,* 265–288. doi:10.1207/s15516709cog1903_1

Institute of Medicine. (2003). *Key capabilities of an electronic health record system: Letter report.* Washington, DC: Institute of Medicine, Board on Health Care Services, Committee on Data Standards for Patient Safety.

Isaacs, E., & Clark, H. H. (1987). References in conversation between experts and novices. *Journal of Experimental Psychology. General, 116,* 26–37. doi:10.1037/0096-3445.116.1.26

Kaelber, D. C., Jha, A. K., Johnston, D., Middleton, B., & Bates, D. W. (2008). A research agenda for personal health records (PHRs). *Journal of the American Medical Informatics Association, 15,* 729–736. doi:10.1197/jamia.M2547

Kannampallil, T., Waicekauskas, K., Morrow, D., Kopren, K., & Fu, W.-T. (2011). *Collaborative tools for a simulated patient-provider medication scheduling task.* Paper presented at the 54th Conference of the Human Factors and Ergonomics Society. San Francisco, CA.

Keselman, A., Slaughter, L., Smith, C. A., Kim, H., Divita, G., Browne, A., et al. (2007). Towards consumer-friendly PHRs: Patients' experience with reviewing their health records. In *Proceedings of the AIMA 2007 Symposium,* (pp. 399-403). AIMA.

Kreider, A., & Haselton, N. (1997). *The systems challenge.* Chicago, IL: American Hospital Publishing.

Leonard, K. J. (2004). The role of patients in designing health information systems: The case of applying simulation techniques to design an electronic patient record (EPR) interface. *Health Care Management Science, 7,* 275–284. doi:10.1007/s10729-004-7536-0

Liao, Q., Chin, C., McKeever, S., Kopren, K., Morrow, D., & Davis, K. … Graumlich, J. (2011). Medtable: An EMR-based tool to support collaborative planning for medication use. In *Proceedings of the Human Factors and Ergonomics Society 55th Annual Meeting.* Santa Monica, CA: Human Factors & Ergonomics Society.

Lin, C., Wittevrongel, L., Moore, L., Beaty, B., & Ross, S. (2005). An internet-based patient-provider communication system: Randomized controlled trial. *Journal of Medical Internet Research, 7*(4), e47. doi:10.2196/jmir.7.4.e47

Lober, W. B., Zierler, A., Herbaugh, S. E., Shin-strom, A., & Stolyar, E. H. Kim, et al. (2006). Barriers to the use of a personal health record by an elderly population. In *Proceedings of the American Medical Informatics Association Annual Meeting*, (pp. 514-518). Washington, DC: AMIA.

Machtinger, E., Wang, F., Chen, L., Rodríguez, M., Wu, S., & Schillinger, D. (2007). A visual medication schedule to improve anticoagulant care: A randomized controlled trial. *Joint Commission Journal on Quality and Patient Safety*, *13*, 263–268.

Makoul, G., Arntson, P., & Schofield, T. (1995). Health promotion in primary care: Physician-patient communication and decision making about prescription medications. *Social Science & Medicine*, *41*, 1241–1254. doi:10.1016/0277-9536(95)00061-B

McNutt, R. A. (2004). Shared medical decision making: Problems, process, progress. *Journal of the American Medical Association*, *292*, 2516–2518. doi:10.1001/jama.292.20.2516

Mead, S., Lamson, N., & Rogers, W. A. (2002). Human factors guidelines for web site usability: Health-oriented websites for older adults. In Morrell, R. W. (Ed.), *Older Adults, Health Information, and the World Wide Web* (pp. 89–107). Hillsdale, NJ: Erlbaum.

Mikels, J. A., Löckenhoff, C. E., Maglio, S. J., Carstensen, L. L., Goldstein, M. K., & Garber, A. (2010). Following your heart or your head: Focusing on emotions versus information differentially influences the decisions of younger and older adults. *Journal of Experimental Psychology. Applied*, *16*, 87–95. doi:10.1037/a0018500

Miller, L. M. S., Stine-Morrow, E. A. L., Kirkorian, H. L., & Conroy, M. L. (2004). Adult age differences in knowledge-driven reading. *Journal of Educational Psychology*, *96*(4), 811–821. doi:10.1037/0022-0663.96.4.811

Mitchell, B., & Begoray, D. (2010). Electronic personal health records that promote self-management in chronic illness. *Online Journal of Issues in Nursing*, *15*(3).

Monk, A. F. (2009). Common ground in electronically mediated conversation. In Carroll, J. M. (Ed.), *Synthesis Lectures on Human-Centered Informatics* (pp. 1–50). New York, NY: Morgan & Claypool.

Moon, Y. (1999). The effects of physical distance and response latency on persuasion in computer-mediated communication and human-computer communication. *Journal of Experimental Psychology. Applied*, *5*, 379–392. doi:10.1037/1076-898X.5.4.379

Morrow, D. G., & Durso, F. T. (2011). Patient safety research that works: Introduction to the special issue on human performance and health care. *Journal of Experimental Psychology. Applied*, *17*, 191–194. doi:10.1037/a0025244

Morrow, D. G., & Fischer, U. M. (2012). Communication in socio-technical systems. In Lee, J. D., & Kirlik, A. (Eds.), *Oxford Handbook of Cognitive Engineering*. Oxford, UK: Oxford University Press.

Morrow, D. G., & Leirer, V. (1999). Designing medication instructions for older adults. In Park, D., Morrell, R., & Shifren, K. (Eds.), *Aging Patients and Medical Treatment: An Information-Processing Perspective* (pp. 249–265). Mahwah, NJ: Erlbaum.

Morrow, D. G., Menard, W. E., Stine-Morrow, E. A. L., Teller, T., & Bryant, D. (2001). The influence of task factors and expertise on age differences in pilot communication. *Psychology and Aging*, *16*, 31–46. doi:10.1037/0882-7974.16.1.31

Morrow, D. G., & Wilson, E. A. H. (2010). Medication adherence among older adults: A systems perspective. In Cavanaugh, J. C., & Cavanaugh, C. K. (Eds.), *Aging in America: Psychological, Physical, and Social Issues* (*Vol. 2*). Westport, CT: Greenwood.

Neuhauser, L., & Kreps, G. L. (2003). Rethinking communication in the e-health era. *Journal of Health Psychology*, *8*, 7–23. doi:10.1177/1359105303008001426

Nielsen-Bohlman, L., Panzer, A. M., & Kindig, D. A. (2004). *Health literacy: A prescription to end confusion*. Washington, DC: The National Academies Press.

O'Connor, J., & Johanson, J. (2000). Use of the web for medical information by a gastroenterology clinic population. *Journal of the American Medical Association*, *284*, 1962–1964. doi:10.1001/jama.284.15.1962

Olson, G. M., & Olson, J. S. (2008). Computer-support cooperative work. In Durso, F. T., Nickerson, R. S., Dumais, S. T., Lewandowsky, S., & Perfect, T. J. (Eds.), *Handbook of Applied Cognition* (pp. 497–526). Chichester, UK: Wiley.

Or, C. K. L., Karsh, B.-T., Severtson, D. J., Burke, L. J., Brown, R. L., & Brennan, P. F. (2010). Factors affecting home care pateints' acceptance of a web-based interactive self-management technology. *Journal of the American Medical Informatics Association*, *18*, 51–59. doi:10.1136/jamia.2010.007336

Paasche-Orlow, M. K., Schillinger, D., Greene, S. M., & Wagner, E. H. (2006). How health care systems can begin to address the challenge of limited literacy. *Journal of General Internal Medicine*, *21*, 884–887. doi:10.1111/j.1525-1497.2006.00544.x

Peters, E., Dieckmann, N. F., Västfjäll, D., Mertz, C. K., Slovic, P., & Hibbard, J. H. (2009). Bringing meaning to numbers: The impact of evaluative categories on decisions. *Journal of Experimental Psychology. Applied*, *15*, 213–227. doi:10.1037/a0016978

Peters, K., Niebling, M., Green, T., Slimmer, C., & Schumacher, R. (2009). *Consumers compare online personal health record (PHR) applications*. Retrieved on August 10, 2010 from http://www.usercentric.com/publications/2009/02/02/google-health-vs-microsoft-healthvault-consumers-compare-online-personal-hea

Pew Internet and American Life Project. (2011). *Mind the gap: Peer-to-peer healthcare*. Retrieved on August 25, 2011 from http://pewinternet.org/Reports/2011/20-Mind-the-Gap.aspx

Radvansky, G. A., & Dijkstra, K. (2007). Aging and situation model processing. *Psychonomic Bulletin & Review*, *14*, 1027–1042. doi:10.3758/BF03193088

Richardson, D. C., Dale, R., & Kirkham, N. Z. (2007). The art of conversation is coordination: Common ground and the coupling of eye movements during dialogue. *Psychological Science*, *18*(5), 407–413. doi:10.1111/j.1467-9280.2007.01914.x

Rockoff, M. L., Czaja, S., Kahn, J. S., Miller, N., & Szerencsy, A. (2010). Spanning the digital divide: Personal health records and patient portals for the underserved. In *Proceedings of the American Medical Informatics Association Annual Meeting*, (pp. 1400-1402). Washington, DC: AMIA.

Rollins, G. (2003). Adverse drug events among elderly outpatients are common and preventable. *Report on Medical Guidelines & Outcomes Research*, *14*, 6–7.

Sarkar, U., Karter, A. J., Liu, J. Y., Adler, N. E., Nguyen, R., López, A., & Schillinger, D. (2010). The literacy divide: Health literacy and the use of an internet-based patient portal in an integrated health system—Results from the diabetes study of Northern California (DISTANCE). *Journal of Health Communication*, *15*(2), 183–196. doi:10.1080/10810730.2010.499988

Sarkar, U., Karter, A. J., Liu, J. Y., Adler, N. E., Nguyen, R., López, A., & Schillinger, D. (2011). Social disparities in internet patient portal use in diabetes: Evidence that the digital divide extends beyond access. *Journal of the American Informatics Association*, *18*, 318–321. doi:10.1136/jamia.2010.006015

Sharit, J., Hernandez, M., Czaja, S. J., & Pirolli, P. (2008). Investigating the roles of knowledge and cognitive abilities in older adult information seeking on the web. *ACM Transactions on Computer-Human Interaction*, *15*, 1–25. doi:10.1145/1352782.1352785

Stanovich, K. E., West, R. F., & Harrison, M. R. (1995). Knowledge growth and maintenance across the life span: The role of print exposure. *Developmental Psychology*, *31*, 811–826. doi:10.1037/0012-1649.31.5.811

Stead, W. W., & Linn, H. S. (2009). *Computational technology for effective health care: Immediate steps and strategic directions*. Washington, DC: National Academies Press.

Stewart, M. (1995). Effective physician-patient communication and health outcomes: A review. *Journal of the Canadian Medical Association*, *152*, 1423–1433.

Tang, P. C., Ash, J. S., Bates, D. W., Overhage, M., & Sands, D. Z. (2006). Personal health records: Definitions, benefits, and strategies for overcoming barriers to adoption. *Journal of the American Medical Informatics Association*, *13*, 121–126. doi:10.1197/jamia.M2025

Tenforde, M., Jain, A., & Hickner, J. (2011). The value of personal health records for chronic disease management: What do we know? *Family Medicine*, *43*, 351–354.

Thompson, L. A., Aidinejad, M. R., & Ponte, J. (2001). Aging and the effects of facial and prosodic cues on emotional intensity ratings and memory reconstructions. *Journal of Nonverbal Behavior*, *25*, 101–125. doi:10.1023/A:1010749711863

Undem, T. (2010). *Consumers and health information technology: A national survey*. Retrieved on July 31, 2011, from http://www.chcf.org/publications/2010/04/consumers-and-health-information-technology-a-national-survey

Wagner, E. H., Bennett, S. M., Austin, B. T., Greene, S. M., Schaefer, J. K., & Vonkorff, M. (2005). Finding common ground: Patient-centeredness and evidence-based chronic illness care. *Journal of Alternative and Complementary Medicine (New York, N.Y.)*, *11*, S7–S15. doi:10.1089/acm.2005.11.s-7

Wald, H. S., Dube, C. E., & Anthony, D. C. (2007). Untangling the web—The impact of internet use on health care and the physician-patient relationship. *Patient Education &. Counseling*, *68*, 218–224.

Weingart, S. N., Rind, D., Tofias, Z., & Sands, D. Z. (2006). Who uses the patient portal internet? The PatientSite experience. *Journal of the American Medical Informatics Association*, *13*, 91–95. doi:10.1197/jamia.M1833

Wingfield, A., & Tun, P. A. (2007). Cognitive supports and cognitive constraints on comprehension of spoken language. *Journal of the American Academy of Audiology*, *18*, 548–558. doi:10.3766/jaaa.18.7.3

Xie, B. (2009). Older adults' health information wants in the internet age: Implications for patient-provider relationships. *Journal of Health Communication*, *14*(6), 510–524. doi:10.1080/10810730903089614

Zhou, Y. Y., Kanter, M. H., & Wang, J. J. (2010). Improve quality at Kaiser Permanente through email between physicians and patients. *Health Affairs*, *29*, 1370–1375. doi:10.1377/hlthaff.2010.0048

Zickmund, S. L., Hess, R., Bryce, C. L., McTigue, K., Olshansky, E., Fitzgerald, K., & Fischer, G. S. (2008). Interest in the use of computerized patient portals: Role of the provider–patient relationship. *Journal of General Internal Medicine*, *23*(1), 20–26. doi:10.1007/s11606-007-0273-6

ADDITIONAL READING

Beier, M. E., & Ackerman, P. L. (2005). Age, ability and the role of prior knowledge on the acquisition of new domain knowledge. *Psychology and Aging*, *20*, 341–355. doi:10.1037/0882-7974.20.2.341

Chin, J., Morrow, D., Stine-Morrow, E. A. L., Conner-Garcia, T., Graumlich, J. F., & Murray, M. D. (2011). The process-knowledge model of health literacy: Evidence from a componential analysis of two commonly used measures. *Journal of Health Communication*, *16*, 222–241. doi:10.1080/10810730.2011.604702

Fisk, A. D., Rogers, W., Charness, N., Czaja, S. J., & Sharit, J. (2009). *Designing for older adults: Principles and creative human factors approach* (2nd ed.). London, UK: CRC Associates.

Hazlehurst, B., Gorman, P. N., & McMullen, C. K. (2008). Distributed cognition: an alternative model of cognition for medical informatics. *International Journal of Medical Informatics*, *77*, 226–234. doi:10.1016/j.ijmedinf.2007.04.008

Masys, D., Baker, D., Butros, A., & Cowles, K. E. (2002). Giving patients access to their medical records via the Internet: The PCASSO experience. *Journal of the American Medical Informatics Association*, *9*, 181–191. doi:10.1197/jamia.M1005

Monk, A. F. (2009). Common ground in electronically mediated conversation. In Carroll, J. M. (Ed.), *Synthesis Lectures on Human-Centered Informatics* (pp. 1–50). New York, NY: Morgan & Claypool.

Morrow, D. G., & Wilson, E. A. H. (2010). Medication adherence among older adults: A systems perspective. In Cavanaugh, J. C., & Cavanaugh, C. K. (Eds.), *Aging in America: Psychological, Physical, and Social Issues* (*Vol. 2*). Westport, CT: Greenwood.

Nielsen-Bohlman, L., Panzer, A. M., & Kindig, D. A. (2004). *Health literacy: A prescription to end confusion*. Washington, DC: The National Academies Press.

Paasche-Orlow, M. K., Schillinger, D., Greene, S. M., & Wagner, E. H. (2006). How health care systems can begin to address the challenge of limited literacy. *Journal of General Internal Medicine*, *21*, 884–887. doi:10.1111/j.1525-1497.2006.00544.x

Pew Internet and American Life Project. (2011). *Mind the gap: Peer-to-peer healthcare*. Retrieved on August 25, 2011 from http://pewinternet.org/Reports/2011/20-Mind-the-Gap.aspx

Tang, P. C., Ash, J. S., Bates, D. W., Overhage, M., & Sands, D. Z. (2006). Personal health records: Definitions, benefits, and strategies for overcoming barriers to adoption. *Journal of the American Medical Informatics Association*, *13*, 121–126. doi:10.1197/jamia.M2025

Weingart, S. N., Rind, D., Tofias, Z., & Sands, D. Z. (2006). Who uses the patient portal internet? The PatientSite experience. *Journal of the American Medical Informatics Association*, *13*, 91–95. doi:10.1197/jamia.M1833

KEY TERMS AND DEFINITIONS

Cognitive Aging: Cognitive development has distinctive trajectories across the life span. Processing capacity tends to decline, while knowledge tends to sustain with age.

Distributed Cognition: Cognitive activity that is distributed across individuals and external representations such as computers and paper documents in order to achieve task goals.

Health Literacy: The capacity to obtain, understand and use health information to make health decisions.

Patient Portals: Information technology systems that provide patients access to health information and services, often by being integrated with their providers' IT systems.

Patient Health Records: A variety of integrated digital tools for patients to manage their medical knowledge and track their personal health history. PHRs combine patient data, software tools, and medical knowledge repositories to support self-care activities.

Processing Capacity: The ability to process (often novel) information; it includes several processing speed, working memory, attention, and other general cognitive abilities.

Situation Model: A mental representation of the events and situations described by text, which is created during comprehension by elaborating information that is directly stated in the text with knowledge about the described situation.

Section 2
Design and Develop Effective Technology for Older Adults

Chapter 5

Instructional Design in Digital Environments and Availability of Mental Resources for the Aged Subpopulation

Renae Low
The University of New South Wales, Australia

Putai Jin
The University of New South Wales, Australia

John Sweller
The University of New South Wales, Australia

ABSTRACT

In this digital era, the gap between the elderly and younger generations in their use of computer-based technology is wide, and many researchers in behavioural and social sciences, along with educators, welfare workers, and policy makers, are concerned about this disturbing phenomenon. However, it is not clear whether this discrepancy is due to a lack of previous access to information technology or declining mental ability in the course of aging. The purpose of this chapter is to consider the aged subpopulation's needs and their ability to use digital technology from the perspectives of human cognitive architecture and the principles of instructional design guided by cognitive load theory. The authors focus on the following critical issues: a) the evolution and formation of human cognitive architecture, b) cognitive functioning as influenced by aging, c) compatibility between elderly people's available mental resources and the cognitive requirements of digital equipment, and d) guidelines for human-computer multimedia interactions derived from the accumulated experimental evidence on effective instructional design and delivery.

DOI: 10.4018/978-1-4666-1966-1.ch005

INTRODUCTION

Two significant phenomena, rapid population aging and proliferation of the Internet and other digital technologies, have coincidently occurred during the recent two decades. This trend, according to researchers in multiple disciplines, such as gerontologists, psychologists, sociologists, and information technology experts, will continue and have a profound impact on society as a whole (e.g., Crimmins, Kim, Langa, & Weir, 2011; Eastman & Iyer, 2005; Henke, 1999; Oerlemans, Bakker, & Veenhoven, 2011; Kaye, et al., 2011; Opalinski, 2001; Payette, Gueye, Gaudreau, Morais, Shatenstein, & Gray-Donald, 2011; Reisenwitz, et al., 2007; Seeman, Miller-Martinez, Stein Merkin, Lachman, Tun, & Karlamangla, 2011; Zaphiris & Rifaht, 2006). The first phenomenon, rapid population aging, was initially evident in developed countries such as the United States, France, and Japan due to increased life expectancy and lowered birth rate; now even a proportion of developing countries such as China are faced with a number of challenging issues associated with their aging populations. Research in gerontology and psychology has in general indicated the importance for seniors to be engaged in social, physical, and cognitive activities to improve their quality of life. For instance, in a large-scale, two-year daily reconstruction study, seniors ranging from 55 to 88 years reported that their feeling of happiness increased when they combined effortful activities in social, physical, cognitive, and household-related aspects with restful routines; notably, this study was completed by seniors using a hyperlink highlighted in a received e-mail to fill in an electronic diary (Oerlemans, et al., 2011). Social policies and community programs have been developed and implemented to promote the elderly's general wellbeing and to accommodate their special needs. One of the significant changes in recent years due to the improvement of health services and raised living standards is that a growing proportion of seniors are relatively independent, active, and eager to learn. Hence, life-long learning becomes a real, challenging issue on the agenda in education. Policy makers can no longer afford just to pay lip service to the issue and educators must find effective, efficient, and economical ways to deliver various useful programs to the elderly.

Not long after the Internet first came into popular use in 1994, there appeared accumulated anecdotal evidence about the potentiality of this new technology to be used by the elderly to overcome their social isolation and to the facilitate their daily activities including self-organized learning. As pointed out by a number of researchers (e.g., Henke, 1999; Opalinski, 2001; Reisenwitz, Iyer, Kuhlmeier, & Eastman, 2007), the growth in the use of the Internet by the elderly in the following aspects can make their life easier and more colourful: trip-making, shopping, financial management, health education, government information, learning material, career reorientation, volunteer engagement, hobby development, pastime planning, social connection, political participation, and religious involvement. All those activities via the Internet can be helpful to overcome older adults' feelings of loneliness, boredom, helplessness, and a decline of mental skills that are known as the four plagues in elderly people's life, and may even be useful for them to re-define careers and/or re-set future life goals. However, despite the fact that seniors comprise a fast growing segment of Internet users, relative to other consumer groups, they are still much under-represented (Eastman & Iyer, 2005; Reisenwitz, Iyer, Kuhlmeier, & Eastman, 2007). Research indicates that seniors with higher levels of nostalgia proneness tend not to access the Internet frequently, have an inadequate online experience, with a proportion of seniors feeling uncomfortable using the Internet. Even elderly people who are willing to use the Internet as a source of general information use it less than young adults. To reduce this "digital divide" between information technologies and our population of older adults, it is vital to form appropriate

IT policies and provide suitable services for this targeted subpopulation. Both policies and services should be based on insights into 1) demographic distribution, 2) economic sustainability, and 3) older adults' cognitive functioning. The third aspect frames the focus of this chapter.

We aim to discuss evidence-based principles of instructional design in digital environments and analyse the availability of mental resources for the aged subpopulation. In the following sections, we attempt to 1) present contemporary understanding of human cognitive architecture, 2) evaluate cognitive functioning as influenced by aging, 3) examine the compatibility between older adults' available mental resources and digital means, and 4) provide guidelines for instructional design and delivery in general and some suggestions for research and applications related to human-computer interactivities for the aged subpopulation in particular.

CONTEMPORARY UNDERSTANDING OF HUMAN COGNITIVE ARCHITECTURE

As a general term, cognition refers to mental processes by which an individual accomplishes the acquisition, storage, transformation, refinement, elaboration, development, synthesis, and use of knowledge. Cognitive activity involves the perception of sensory input, capability to learn and manipulate new information, recognition of familiar objects, recollection of past experiences, retrieval of established schemata from long-term memory, problem solving, abstract thinking, reasoning, judgement, and decision making.

Cognition has been studied and interpreted through various models proposed by researchers who have attempted to depict the human cognitive architecture and its functioning. Basically, humans are considered to possess an innate capacity to mentally construct the external world, and complex ideas are derived from perceptual abstractions of

sensory experience and acquired knowledge. Since the mid-1950s, significant research progress in the areas of problem solving, memory, psycholinguistics, and developmental/educational psychology has enabled cognitive approaches as one of the most productive areas. Among those cognitive approaches, the information processing approach stands as the main stream. Using this approach, mental activities can be interpreted as information progressing through the human cognitive system in a series of stages. It is basically an abstract model of human cognitive architecture that is formed by sensory memory, working memory, and long-term memory components (Atkinson & Shiffrin, 1968). Sensory memory is the temporary storage of information that is brought into the central nervous system through the senses and typically only lasts a very brief period of time. Working memory is in general regarded as "a processing resource of limited capacity involved in the preservation of information while simultaneously processing the same or other information" (Swanson, 1999, p. 986). In contrast, long-term memory can store immeasurably large amounts of information for a potentially unlimited duration (for example, an old master of *go* or chess can remember thousands of configurations through decades of intensive practice and continuing research).

According to accumulated evidence from research using the information processing model, the fundamental limits of the human cognitive system are that a) working memory can hold five to seven chunks or even much less (2-4 chunks) under conditions with imposed constraints, b) a recognition process requires a second or so, c) the reaction time for simple tasks can be measured in tens or hundreds of milliseconds, and d) without rehearsal, individuals may lose almost all the contents of working memory within 20 seconds or so (Cowan, 2000; Miller, 1956; Peterson & Peterson, 1959; Simon, 1990). Therefore, in instructional design and delivery, whether or not an electronic format is used, it is essential to take those features and limitations of information processing into account.

However, long-term memory provides "a major way to relax the limits" (Simon, 1990, p. 7). Research has demonstrated that long-term memory participates actively in information processes, and the ultimate gains from effective learning should be indicated by changes in long-term memory. The evidence is found in the pioneering research of chess playing by de Groot (1965), Chase and Simon (1973), and Chi, Glaser, and Farr (1988). Compared with novices, expert chess players were better able to recognize and reproduce meaningful board configurations that were drawn from real games but did not respond better if random, nonsense board configurations were displayed. This result provided evidence that knowledgeable individuals can effectively activate and use their extensive experience and skill-related information that is stored in long-term memory for the execution of expertise-matched tasks. Under such conditions, the capacity of working memory "can grow to vast size as individual acts of recognition access larger and richer stores of information in long-term memory" (Simon, 1990, p. 16). This useful mechanism, labelled as "long-term working memory" by Ericsson and Kintsch (1995), which enhances the features of working memory by bringing back previously well-structured and automated information from long-term memory, is an effective and indeed essential way for experienced learners to deal with familiar material. To enhance the effectiveness and efficiency of learning, whether or not digital format/electronic device is used, we must consider learners' prior knowledge and previous experience (i.e., the massive relevant information stored in their long-term working memory) as a crucial factor in the equation of instructional design and delivery.

Cognitive load theory uses the cognitive architecture described above to generate instructional design principles. By testing instructional design principles in controlled experiments, the findings in turn verify the features of the relevant cogni-

tive structures and their interactions. The main objective of cognitive load theory is to optimize the acquisition of new knowledge/skills and to facilitate the cognitive process by which the obtained information is organized and stored in long-term memory. In essence, cognitive load theory proposes to use limited working memory in an effective and efficient way during teaching and learning, seeks to eliminate the violations of instructional principles based on human cognitive architecture, and to aid learners in their schema acquisition according to their expertise and other characteristics (see Low, Jin, & Sweller, 2011; or Sweller, Ayres, & Kalyuga, 2011, for a more detailed discussion regarding the relations between working memory characteristics and cognitive load theory).

More recently, Sweller and Sweller (2006) have elaborated some fundamental cognitive principles from the perspective of evolutionary psychology and linked those principles with cognitive load theory (Sweller, 2011; Sweller, Ayres, & Kalyuga, 2011). This evolutionary framework of human cognitive architecture is summarized as follows:

As pointed out by Geary (2002, 2005, 2007, 2008), there are two categories of knowledge: biologically primary and biologically secondary. Biologically primary knowledge is the knowledge that we have evolved to acquire over many thousands of generations, such as the knowledge to listen and speak one's mother tongue, which is essential for humans as a species. This long-term evolution enables us to acquire these skills simply by being immersed in a natural community. In contrast, biologically secondary knowledge, such as literature, mathematics, and science, has only recently been required as cultural knowledge. Therefore, although we may be able to acquire this type of knowledge that has been accumulated during the relatively short period of civilizations, we have not explicitly evolved to acquire such knowledge. Biologically secondary knowledge is typically taught in educational institutions or by experts; at least some assistance and considerable personal effort are needed to explicitly acquire a certain aspect of biologically secondary knowledge. It is this category of knowledge to which cognitive load theory applies.

There are five basic principles that can be used to describe the human information processing system from the perspective of evolution by natural selection (Sweller, et al., 2011; Sweller & Sweller, 2006). 1) The information store principle states that long-term memory contains a very large store of information governing most human cognitive activity consisting of the building blocks of knowledge known as schemata that can be used automatically or under conscious control. 2) The borrowing and reorganizing principle states that the bulk of information in long-term memory is obtained by borrowing information from other individuals with biologically secondary knowledge mainly combined with personal prior knowledge via this process. 3) The randomness as genesis principle states that although most of the information in long-term memory is borrowed from others, creativity occurs when a learner randomly generates a problem-solving move and tests its effectiveness. 4) The narrow limits of change principle states that large-scale, dramatic random changes could cause traumatic effects on the functionality of long-term memory and thus the limited capacity of working memory ensures small, incremental changes in long-term memory to maintain relative stability of the cognitive system. 5) The environmental linking and organizing principle states that whereas the amount of information from sensory memory that can be processed by working memory is limited, the amount of information from long-term memory organized as schemata that can be processed by working memory has no known limits. In discussing the application of these five principles to the use of the Internet by the elderly, we will examine the impact of aging on cognitive functions and then assess elderly people's available mental resources for using the Internet and relevant digital means in the following sections.

COGNITIVE FUNCTIONING AS INFLUENCED BY AGING

Aging is a natural, complex, life-long process that is accompanied by multifaceted biopsychosocial changes. Hence, aging is not a synonym of illness or ill-health. Fundamentally, aging individuals can accomplish most of the physiological as well as psychological functions of their youth, and a proportion of them even reach their peak of creativity and productivity in various domains, although they may take a longer time, need greater motivation, and require additional aids. A wide range of theories have been proposed to explain the aging process based on the evidence obtained from scientific observations and experiments at molecular, cellular, anatomical, systemic, cognitive, emotional, and behavioural levels. By and large, these theories form two basic perspectives: intrinsic (development-genetic) theories assuming that changes associated with aging are largely due to genetic influences, or extrinsic (stochastic) theories proposing that changes associated with aging are a consequence of a cumulative effect of random events or damage from environmental agents.

There are several ways to classify older adults into different groups: the chronological age (e.g., 65-74 as young-old, 74-84 as middle-old, and 85 and plus as old-old), biological age (according to biological markers such as forced expiratory volume at one second, systolic blood pressure, diastolic blood pressure, grip strength, and vision), and cognitive age (in terms of cognitive functions such as working memory, attention, processing speed, reasoning, and behavioural symptoms associated with dementia). As pointed out by Eastman and Iyer (2005), as far as Internet usage is concerned, seniors cannot be defined simply by their chronological age and it is meaningful to assess their technology-related activities by their cognitive age. Statistical analysis suggests that 1) seniors with a younger cognitive age use the Internet more than those seniors with an older cognitive age, and 2) seniors with a younger cognitive age actually have more social contact offline than those seniors with an older cognitive age.

According to Joshi and Morley (2006), we need to differentiate normal cognitive aging from non-normal (or accelerated) cognitive aging. During normal cognitive aging, the most obvious factor is the degeneration of sensory functioning (especially vision impairment and hearing loss) that constrains effective input of information/signals to the central nervous system (McCoy, Tun, Cox, Colangelo, Stewart, & Wingfield, 2005; Piccinin, Muniz, Sparks, & Bontempo, 2011). Older adults also may experience an inability to inhibit extraneous input or control irrelevant information in their cognitive processing (e.g., Conway, Tuholski, Shisler, & Engle, 1999; De Beni & Palladino, 2004; Lustig, Hasher, & Tonev, 2006). Therefore, the elderly are often faced with attention problems characterized by distractibility, a lack of attention focus, and anxiety of overwhelming demands. However, short-term memory is typically preserved unless there is a high demand imposed on mental processing (Joshi & Morley, 2006). As to long-term memory, during normal aging, individuals tend to have a generalized decrease in the efficiency by which information is processed and retrieved. This is evident when seniors are tested in free recall of stories and word lists. However, if structure is provided by the use of recognition testing or cueing, the gap between healthy older adults and young adults is reduced (Hess, 2005). The findings suggest that there is an association between normal cognitive aging and noticeable impairment of retrieval processes and that the cognitive capabilities of encoding and/or retention are almost intact.

There are basically two different paths for the memory of past events to be activated: 1) recollection, in which the activation of long-term memory about past events is based on retrieval accompanied by the recovery of specific contextual details, or 2) familiarity, in which the activation of long-term memory relies on the feeling that an event is old or new without the recovery of contextual details (Dodson, Bawa, & Krueger, 2007). According to research in neuropsychology, recollection is more dependent on the hippocampus, whereas familiarity is more dependent on the rhinal cortex. In addition, healthy aging leads to impairing effects on recollection rather than on familiarity. During normal aging, there appears to be a decreased functional connectivity within a hippocampal-retrosplenial-parietotemporal network but enhanced connectivity within a rhinal-frontal network, indicating that cognitively healthy seniors may compensate for hippocampal deficits by relying on the enhanced activities via the rhinal cortex (Craik, Byrd, & Swanson, 1987; Craik & Grady, 2002).

However, in comparison with younger subjects, normal seniors find it increasingly hard to manipulate the information that is being held in the working memory in experiments using cognitive tasks such as arranging digits in order or repeating a string of digits back in reverse order (Cowan, 2000; Miller, 1956). The life-span changes in working memory are characterized by an inverted U-curve, indicating that children and older adults experience a generalized lower level of performance in working memory in comparison with relatively young adults. As pointed out by Swanson (1999), working memory capacity peaks at approximately age 45 and begins to decline after age 50, in line with the pace of normal aging.

Previous studies, on the whole, confirm that healthy seniors show a decline in comparison with young adults across a variety of learning tasks and memory tests. This is largely due to a slow progressive decline in working memory and episodic memory over the lifespan. When the chunks in working memory become smaller and fewer, the elderly, even when they are healthy, may find it increasingly hard to maintain essential information while processing other tasks or dealing with distractors (Gilchrist, Cowan, & Naveh-Benjamin, 2008). Meanwhile, the diminished capabilities of storage of information in long-term memory and retrieval of information from long-term memory can add more difficulties for older adults to complete complex cognitive activities. In addition, seniors may have some obstacles in their prospective memory, which is the capacity to remember to take actions that need to be executed after a variable delay (Huppert & Beardsall, 1993; Huppert, Johnson, & Nickson, 2000; Rendell & Craik, 2000; Simons, Schölvinck, Gilbert, Frith, & Burgess, 2006; Smith, Della Sala, Logie, & Maylor, 2000). Notwithstanding, normal seniors only experience minor negative impact on their semantic memory (i.e., the retrieval of concepts) and implicit memory (i.e., the unconscious effects of memory), which are continuously available and can be effectively used (Joshi & Morley, 2006).

Neuropsychological tests that are sensitive to activities in the frontal and temporal regions of the brain reveal age-related differences in right and left prefrontal and parietal reactions (Whitman, 2011). As shown in a positron emission tomography study by Cabeza et al. (1997), in young adults the retrieval process basically results in high levels of activities in right-hemisphere networks, whereas in older adults both hemispheres are engaged during retrieval. This probably reflects a compensation effect, in that the elderly are able to recruit additional resources of right-hemisphere networks in response to the normal cognitive decline due to aging. This is in line with the two significant principles of learning and memory proposed by influential neuropsychologist Karl S. Lashley (1929, 1947, 1950): 1) the principle of "mass action," which states that the cerebral cortex as a whole maps sensory input in an orderly topographic fashion in many types of learning; and 2) the principle of "equipotentiality," which states that if certain parts of the brain are damaged, neighbouring regions may adapt to accomplish the lost function. For normally aged individuals, their cognitive potentiality is considerably useful.

As to non-normative cognitive decline in a proportion of the elderly, the symptoms are particularly represented as the development of dementia, which results from disorders that lead to severe, and often irreversible, damage in the critical association regions of the cerebral hemispheres or subcortical areas that subserve memory and learning. The typical indicators of non-normative cognitive decline reflect the permanent impairment of working memory and long-term memory (Huppert & Beardsall, 1993; Huppert, et al., 2000; Joshi & Morley, 2006; Piccinin, Muniz, Matthews, & Johansson, 2011; Piccinin, Muniz, Sparks, & Bontempo, 2011). This type of impairment is linked with handicaps in abstract thinking, reasonable judgment, capability of effective planning/organizing and other higher-order cortical functions, and such impairment is possibly conducive to undesirable changes in daily behaviours and personality. Consequently, this disturbance can be severe enough to affect personal activities in the workplace or familial/social settings. Older adults having accelerated cognitive aging need special care, and they may find that some digital devices, with or without on-line connections, useful to facilitate their cognitive processes and to maintain their routine activities.

COMPATIBILITY BETWEEN ELDERLY PEOPLE'S AVAILABLE MENTAL RESOURCES AND DIGITAL MEANS

To assess the compatibility between elderly people's available mental resources and digital means, it is useful to evaluate their cognitive functioning in term of the five general principles raised by Sweller and Sweller (2006).

The first principle on the information store emphasizes the crucial role of long-term memory in governing most cognitive activity and human's natural capacity to store a vast amount of information in the brain as long-term memory. This principle explicitly indicates that the ultimate indicator of learning is the alteration in the learner's long-term memory. As mentioned in the previous section, healthy older adults' long-term memory is largely retained. For them, learning how to use the Internet may not be effortless since the procedures are within the category of biologically secondary knowledge, but it is likely that their long-term memory can be altered in regard to the basic skills of Internet surfing if the facilitator provides adequate instruction and the aged learners put in considerable effort.

The second principle on borrowing and reorganizing clearly pointed out that the acquisition of biologically secondary knowledge, whether in formal education/training settings or in a home-based environment, usually occurs by learning from others and reforming corresponding schemata in long-term memory. If the learner possesses a certain degree of prior knowledge in the targeted aspect, the process of reorganizing often manifests a combination of existing and new schemata. Since the Internet has only been popularized during the last twenty years, most users learn this new skill from IT experts and their more experienced peers. Likewise, this is the main way for the elderly to learn IT skill. There is a disadvantage, however, that when the elderly were of school age decades ago; they had no exposure to the Internet and relevant digital technologies. In other words, older adults have less IT-related schemata in their long-term memory than younger adults who already possess abundant experiences in using the Internet and related technology. Therefore, older adults may need specific instruction at elementary and post-basic levels to "borrow" IT-related information from the long-term memory of their instructors and/or informal helpers.

The third principle on randomness as genesis refers to an important human cognitive function by which an individual can randomly generate a move and check the outcome of this new move for effectiveness. There has been no evidence to indicate that normal older adults lose their ability to engage in random exploration, taking initiatives, creative thoughts, and curiosity. However, one of the trends associated with aging is that the elderly in general have declining vision, hear-

ing, and speed of information processing, which may negatively affect their confidence in using the Internet and related IT technologies. Their anxiety associated with new digital environments and fear of failure in using IT products could add extra load to their working memory, push them to adopt a performance avoidance (learned helplessness) orientation, and prevent them from generating random moves (Elliott, Hufton, Willis, & Illushin, 2005; Hawi, 2010) when working by themselves without assistance. Of course, as is the case for everyone, learning is more rapid using the borrowing and reorganizing principle than the randomness as genesis principle that only should be used when assistance is unavailable.

The fourth principle on narrow limits of change highlights the limited capacity of working memory from an evolutionary, systemic perspective. One of the problems encountered by older adults is that the already limited capacity of working memory declines. The number of chunks held in working memory tends to drop, the size of chunks is decreased, the ability to inhibit distraction is lowered, and the speed of cognitive processing is reduced. In these aspects, older adults are relatively vulnerable in comparison with younger adults. Research using cognitive load theory provides an array of evidence-based strategies to use mental resources effectively and efficiently, which may be modified and tried in the context of on-line learning for the elderly.

The fifth principle, the environmental linking and organizing principle, underlines an important mechanism in cognitive activity: a large amount of organized relevant information stored as schemata in long-term memory can be retrieved as a single unit to working memory. The implication is that in line with the development of a learner's expertise the specific schemata activated and uploaded to working memory can significantly relax the constraints on working memory. For older learners of digital technologies, at first they need to build basic relevant schemata in long-term memory for using IT. Secondly, Internet program developers should take into account the increasing difficulty faced by the elderly in retrieving and selecting their relevant long-term memory, and thus step-by-step instructional procedures need to be designed and implemented to foster their use of the Internet and other IT facilities.

In sum, whereas healthy seniors retain the most essential functions in cognition, the normal aging process inevitably leads to a certain degree of cognitive impairment. On the whole, there is no compelling evidence to demonstrate that the elderly are not capable of using the Internet and associated means or contents. Rather, in order to facilitate the use of on-line or wireless digital technologies, it is time for policy makers, researchers, and IT-related practitioners to pay special attention to older adults' needs for compatible IT services and address the physiological, psychological, and social problems that prevent them from taking full advantages of digital technologies.

INSTRUCTIONAL DESIGN AND DELIVERY GUIDELINES FOR THE AGED SUBPOPULATION

According to cognitive load theory, in order to optimize learning, researchers and practitioners in the field of instructional design should seek to help learners 1) maximize working memory, 2) to minimize irrelevant information and/or operations, and 3) to build and use relevant schemata in long-term memory. Controlled experiments have been conducted to test the usefulness of those strategies derived from cognitive load theory. It should be noted that the data obtained in either traditional classroom settings or digital environments have in general endorsed the applications that are in line with human cognitive architecture (for an overview, see Low, et al., 2011; Low, Jin, & Sweller, 2012; Sweller, 1994, 2011; Sweller, et al., 2011).

As to elderly people's cognitive limitations due to normal aging, there are mainly four age-related declines. First, there is a decline in sensory functions, related perceptions, and psychomotor coordination among many of the elderly. Second, there is a decline in the capacity of working memory, meaning that seniors may manipulate and store a smaller amount of information for a shorter period than young adults. Third, there is a decline in the speed at which information is activated, sorted, and processed, resulting in decreased capability to simultaneously handle mutually dependent elements of information. Fourth, there is a decline in the ability to inhibit information flow that is irrelevant to or redundant for the central theme, thus increasing seniors' vulnerability to distractions when undertaking complex or novel tasks. For a large proportion of seniors, using Internet and related tools is a novel and often complex task. Such digital environments require: adequate visual, auditory, and tactile-pressure sensory inputs; integrated perceptions from such sensory inputs; functional psychomotor coordination (such as manoeuvring a mouse or activating multiple windows); available working memory to hold and manipulate information elements that appear from the multifaceted website; appropriate information processing to ensure that the activation of one element will not dissipate before other relevant information elements being activated to a certain threshold; and proper personal skills or built-in instructional procedures to counter the negative effects of distractors. These are but the tip of the iceberg concerning challenging issues for instructors and on-line educational program developers who are responsible for assisting older adults in using the Internet for life-long learning, daily maintenance issues (e.g., paying bills through the net-banking system, comparing prices on the website, on-line booking tickets and shopping, and seeking health/welfare information via the Internet), and pastimes (playing *go* or bridge with partners or virtual players via the Internet). Below we present some strategies that have been supported by empirical studies on elder people's usage of computers and on-line services.

Expand the Capacity of Working Memory

Theorists (e.g., Baddeley, 1992, 2003; Paivio, 1986) on working memory have proposed a dual-channel model, which divides working memory mainly into two mode-specific parts: 1) a visual-spatial sketch pad that processes visually based information, and 2) a phonological loop that processes auditory information. Learning occurs when a person draws his or her attention to incoming information, organizes obtained information into internalized mental representations, and integrates such mental representations with prior knowledge. Theoretically, it may be feasible to enhance working memory capacity by presenting information in mixed visual and auditory channels rather than a single mode. If effective working memory can be increased by using proper dual-modality presentation techniques, then improved information processing can result from this modality effect and thus learning can be facilitated. As pointed out by Van Gerven, Pass, Van Merriënboer, Hendriks, and Schmidt (2003), "the modality effect was first demonstrated by Mousavi, Low, and Sweller (1995) with high school students in the domain of geometry" (p. 492). In a series of experiments, Mousavi et al. demonstrated that a visually presented diagram and an auditorily presented textual explanation could expand effective working memory and thus resulted in better learning outcomes than conditions under which visual working memory alone must be used to process all the relevant information. Subsequently, this procedure has been adopted and further verified by a number of studies conducted in both conventional classrooms and computerized environments (Kalyuga, Chandler, & Sweller, 1999, 2000; Mayer, Bove, Bryman, Mars, & Tapangco, 1996; Mayer & Moreno, 1998; Moreno & Mayer, 1999; Tindall-Ford, Chandler, & Sweller, 1997).

The modality effect occurs when information presented in a mixed mode containing partly visual and partly auditory supplementary information is more effective than when the same information is presented in a single mode, either visually or in auditory form alone (see Low & Sweller, 2005, for an overview). In their experimental studies on multimedia learning, Mayer and Moreno (2002) have also noticed a relevant phenomenon called the temporal contiguity effect, which refers to the effectiveness of synchronization of mutually supportive information via pictorial and auditory forms. In an attempt to provide an effective computerized life-learning instruction for the elderly, Van Gerven et al. (2003) combined the principles of the modality effect and the contiguity effect in the design of a multimedia training program of problem solving. Similar to 60 secondary school students (mean age = 15.98 years, SD = 0.77), a total of 60 elderly participants (mean age = 64.48 years, SD = 4.92) reported less cognitive load and better performance in a narrated animation (multimedia) learning environment than a visual presentation only (unimodal) learning environment. Multimedia instructions guided by the principles of the modality and contiguity effects appear promising for older adults for their life-long learning with digital aids. A further study using two age groups (university students versus older adults) confirmed this significant modality effect (Van Gerven, Paas, Van Merriënboer, & Schmidt, 2006).

In designing instructions in a multimedia format, we need to take some age differences into account. For instance, in a study by Constantinidou and Baker (2002), relative to younger cohorts, older adults ranging in age from 50 to 77 appeared to rely more on visual input than auditory signals. This probably reflects the phenomenon that the quality of communication of many seniors with others is often negatively affected by a gradual, sometimes undetected hearing degeneration. To facilitate seniors' access to the Internet, informative pictures can be used to aid recall and provide additional support. The instructors can also help enhance older learners' information retrieval by designing menu-driven or pop-out computer programs with eye-catching icons related to specific tasks. In addition, to encourage seniors to use their auditory component of working memory, easy volume adjustment, hearing aids, and convenient replay functions (e.g., providing a virtual scroll bar) can be tested and established in the IT system.

Minimize Unnecessary Operations and Irrelevant Information

Research in the area of instructional design has developed a series of principles that can be used in both traditional classroom settings and digital contexts (Low, et al., 2011; Mayer, 2005; Sweller, 2011; Sweller, et al., 2011). Avoiding split-attention is one of those well-established principles. Split-attention occurs when learners are required to integrate multiple sources of essential information that are physically or temporally separate from each other. In order to understand and synthesize those separated elements, the learner needs to initially check one of those elements, hold the information obtained from this element, turn to the next element, and so forth until all pieces of essential information are gathered for processing. Such a high working memory load to mentally integrate disparate sources of information may interfere with learning. The classic study on split-attention was conducted by Tarmizi and Sweller (1988), who found in geometry problem solving that the conventional problem structure in the textbook was ineffective for learning because diagrams and statements (which were essential for understanding) were physically separate. In subsequent experiments, the researchers introduced a new method, in which statements were physically integrated with the diagram. This approach resulted in better learning outcomes than a conventional problem solving strategy. The integrated format alleviated the extraneous cognitive load imposed by the conventional condition in which attention was split between diagrams and text, thus freeing scarce working memory resources to attend

to information processes necessary for learning. Following Tarmizi and Sweller's (1988) work, a number of studies have extended the split attention effect to different domains, including learning of mathematics, science, technology, and languages (Chandler & Sweller, 1996; Sweller & Chandler, 1991; Sweller & Chandler, 1994; Sweller, Chandler, Tierney, & Cooper, 1990; Ward & Sweller, 1990; Yeung, Jin, & Sweller, 1997). Mayer and colleagues have demonstrated that split-attention could also occur with temporal separation, which may impose an unnecessary, extraneous load (Mayer & Anderson, 1991, 1992; Mayer & Sims, 1994; Moreno & Mayer, 1999).

The split attention effect has implications for instructional design in an Internet context. Internet pages often are heavily congested with various sources of information. Decades of educational psychology research suggest that multiple sources of information should be integrated into an optimal format to minimize extraneous cognitive load, and that those sources of information must be complementary to each other rather than merely repetition of the same information. On the one hand, an integrated format can be effective when the learning material has highly interactive elements. Since the intrinsic cognitive load under such conditions is relatively high, using an integrated method can reduce extraneous cognitive load and thus facilitate learning. On the other hand, if the elements in the learning material have little interaction and thus can be processed individually without affecting comprehension, there is a low level of intrinsic cognitive load. In this case, using an integrated format is unlikely to result in significantly beneficial effects on learning outcomes. Research also indicates that a crucial factor to be taken into account when integrating different sources of information is the learner's expertise that interacts with material characteristics (Kalyuga, Chandler, & Sweller, 1998; Yeung, et al., 1997). Material that is not intelligible in isolation and is high in element interactivity for low knowledge learners may be intelligible and low in element interactivity for learners with more knowledge and skills in a domain. In consideration of the reality that seniors have a much lower proportion of versatile users of the Internet and related technologies than younger subpopulations, guidelines should be provided for seniors to choose optimal paths.

Another important way to improve the efficiency of information processing is the application of the principle of eliminating redundant presentations in instructional design. The redundancy effect refers to the phenomenon in instruction where learning is less productive when additional information is presented to learners compared to the presentation of less information. For instance, when identical information is given to the learner in two or more forms such as pictures and words or text in both written and audio form, one of these forms may be redundant in the sense that it unnecessarily occupies limited working memory space. Therefore, this redundant information should be eliminated from the instructional presentation in order to enhance learning.

Although experimental evidence for the redundancy effect has a long history (see Sweller, 2005, for a discussion of early research), it first emerged as a cognitive load effect with an experiment on students' learning of cardiovascular functioning reported by Chandler and Sweller (1991). It was found that when a diagram was intelligible on its own, the text was redundant as it merely repeated the same information in a different form. Since Chandler and Sweller's (1991) work, the redundancy effect has been demonstrated in a number of controlled experiments such as computer courses (Chandler & Sweller, 1996; Sweller & Chandler, 1994), multimedia learning (Kalyuga, Chandler, & Sweller, 2004; Mayer, et al., 1996), and language learning (Diao & Sweller, 2007; Yeung, et al., 1997). The studies suggest that whether or not additional material is redundant can be determined by considering the cognitive load implications of that material in the context of learner expertise. Information that is intelligible for more expert learners may not make sense to novices who may require additional explanatory material, and vice versa. In short, the redundancy effect provides a useful guideline. Instructors should eliminate any redundant material or activity that may encourage learners to process the redundant information.

On the Internet, it is not uncommon for a Web-based program designer to intuitively consider providing the same information in different forms or presenting additional "bells and whistles," colourful decorations, moving logos, commercial messages, background music, uninvited comments, and pop-out agents constantly sending advice. However, since working memory is extremely limited in terms of its capacity and duration, the learner's cognitive process can be inhibited by being exposed to material on the Internet that includes the same information in multiple forms or some unnecessary or irrelevant details. Due to cognitive aging, older adults' ability to inhibit unnecessary information flows on their already reduced working memory may be particularly harmful. Such a forced input of redundant information can negatively affect the learning process.

Efficiently Build and Use Relevant Schemata for Complex Tasks

Experts can use complex, sophisticated schemata from long-term memory and bring it to working memory. In contrast, novices hold much simpler schemata in long-term memory. Because experts can organize interacting elements in a schema that acts as a single element in working memory, a task with high element interactivity may not result in a high cognitive load for them. Hence, the intrinsic cognitive load of a task varies with the level of expertise. It has been noted that age-related performance differences become larger as the task becomes more complex (Mayr & Kliegl, 1993; Mayr, Kliegl, & Krampe, 1996; Oberauer & Kliegl, 2001; Salthouse, 1992). In other words, because of the decline of cognitive functionality, especially the reduced capacity of working memory, lowered cognitive speed and decreased controllability of distracting information, the elderly may have greater difficulty in dealing with task complexity than young adults. Consequently, whereas surfing the Internet may be a routine "ride" for many senior secondary school students or university students, even a fairly simple application via the Internet can be a challenging task for inexperienced elderly people. For many seniors, as novices of IT, using the Internet requires complex processes such as task selection, searching, screening, switching, coordination, integration, and decision-making. One way to assist novices to gradually build relevant schemata is by using a worked example, which comprises the statement of a problem, showing solution steps, and providing the solution (Anderson, Fincham, & Douglass, 1997; Pass & van Gog, 2006; Renkl, 2005).

Studying worked examples provides the learner with step-by-step solutions to problems as a substitute for solving equivalent problems (Kirschner, Sweller, & Clark, 2006). In a conventional problem solving approach, searching for a solution may impose heavy demands on working memory. In contrast, by eliminating problem-solving search, a worked example can reduce extraneous cognitive load and thereby facilitate learning. Specifically, using worked examples can focus the learner's attention on problem states and operators, and thus efficiently foster the step-by-step construction of domain-related schemata. In this process, those initially established simple schemata can be transformed into more comprehensive ones, without overloading working memory. A number of experiments have demonstrated this beneficial worked example effect in young adults and children (e.g., Darabi, Nelson, & Palanki, 2007; Pass & van Gog, 2006; Paas & Van Merriënboer, 1994; Renkl, 2005; Sweller & Cooper, 1985; Ward & Sweller, 1990).

This strategy has been successfully applied to older adults' computerized learning. For example,

Van Gerven, Paas, Van Merriënboer, and Schmidt (2002) found worked examples to be a feasible and efficient training method for elderly learners in terms of invested mental effort and learning outcomes. In this experiment, senior participants ranging in age from 61 to 76 years (median = 66 years) used worked examples instead of conventional problems in the computer-aided training sessions of complex skills for solving problems. They experienced less cognitive load, required a shorter training time, and gained higher scores in the worked example condition than the conventional problem condition. Results indicate that worked examples were at least as beneficial for older as for younger adults when learning how to complete complex tasks.

For a large proportion of seniors who are novices when using the Internet and associated procedures, initially the learning tasks can be perceived as quite complex. Instructors may use a worked example strategy to help inexperienced seniors build up their computer proficiency. For example, instructors can develop several protocols for the design of worked examples. Below are some elementary protocols that may be used for seniors. Each can be transformed into a worked example by an appropriate series of diagrams depicting each action.

Anti-Virus Updating

1. Turn on the computer
2. Navigate the mouse, tablet pen or a finger (if the computer has a touch-screen function) on the screen
3. Reach the icon of "Symantec Endpoint Protection"
4. Click on the icon
5. Click on the box of "LiveUpdate"
6. Click on the button of "X" at the upper-right corner
7. Turn off the computer

Document Making

1. Turn on the computer
2. Navigate the mouse, tablet pen or a finger (if the computer has a touch-screen function) on the screen
3. Open the Microsoft Word program
4. Type the given sentence correctly
5. Print this document
6. Save this document
7. Close the Microsoft Word program
8. Reopen the document
9. Delete the document
10. Retrieve the document from the recycle bin
11. Turn off the computer

Internet Access

1. Turn on the computer
2. Navigate the mouse, tablet pen or a finger (if the computer has a touch-screen function) on the screen
3. Open an Internet browser
4. Go to the desired Web site using the Web site address
5. Click on the "ABOUT US" link
6. Turn off the computer

Using e-Mail

1. Turn on the computer
2. Navigate the mouse, tablet pen or a finger (if the computer has a touch-screen function) on the screen
3. Open an e-mail program
4. Open an e-mail in the inbox
5. Reply to an e-mail (using the "Reply" button)
6. Forward an e-mail using the address book
7. Forward an e-mail using the new e-mail address
8. Send a new e-mail using the address book
9. Send a new e-mail using the new e-mail address
10. Block an unwanted e-mail
11. Delete an e-mail
12. Turn off the computer

As discussed above, research has shown that it is effective to use worked examples in the initial stages of knowledge acquisition. At later learning stages that are characterized by increased learner expertise, guidance fading can be introduced to the learner. Guidance fading may be described as a three-stage instructional procedure: presenting full worked examples → gradually introducing incomplete worked examples → providing problems to be solved without worked examples. In essence, guidance fading is part of the dynamic worked-example-based instructional procedure that takes into account learners' accumulated knowledge and associated skills. The rationale for guidance fading is that, after a period of studying worked examples, a learner's enriched knowledge in long-term memory may become sufficient to act as a knowledge-based central executive to incrementally replace the detailed instructions given initially. For instance, Atkinson, Renkl, and Merrill (2003) reported that gradually fading out some multimedia elaborations is beneficial for the learning of probability principles. In digital environments, if elderly people are initially given intensive worked examples as part of their instruction on using the Internet, a guidance fading technique can be used. Once instructions appear to have some redundant elements no longer suitable for the aged learners at an advanced level, the instructional designer should consider omitting those elements (e.g., too many demonstrations and suggestions of basic steps) that interfere with learning at a higher level.

Special Supportive Measures for Cognitively Impaired Elders' Access to the Internet and Related Technologies

In addition to the issues discussed in the previous sections, we should bear in mind that a significant proportion of seniors need special support and this proportion is increasing due to increased life spans. In this regard, we will focus on three prominent issues that many seniors encounter: 1) decline of sensory and psychomotor functions, 2) progressive memory loss, and 3) anxiety associated with using the Internet and related IT technologies.

To assist hearing impaired, visually impaired, or psychomotor impaired seniors to access the Internet and related technologies, special aids and software can be adopted. Seniors having hearing loss can be equipped with hearing aids prescribed by an audiologist, adjust on-screen bars to increase volume or replay, or use read-aloud programs. Those with vision impairment can wear suitable eyeglasses and a screen prescribed by an optometrist, adopt larger fonts and icons, and use an on-screen magnifier. Those with psychomotor retardation may try a tablet pen, touch screen, or voice-driven software.

To assist seniors with memory loss to access the Internet and related technologies, special devices can be supplied and memory compensation strategies can be introduced. The devices designed for cognitively impaired elderly individuals range from handheld Personal Digital Assistants (PDAs) to integrated sensory cueing memory aids (Caprani, Greaney, & Porter, 2006). In general, data indicate that to a certain extent, electronic memory aids have the potential to support memory, especially prospective memory, in older individuals. Apart from providing external memory aids, instructors can train older adults to use memory compensation strategies, such as increasing recall-related effort, applying internal mnemonic techniques, investing extra time, and enhancing human collaborative assistance (de

Frias, Dixon, & Bäckman, 2003). Those strategies may be used by IT trainers for seniors with memory declines.

To assist seniors with high levels of computer anxiety to access the Internet and related technologies, instructors can organize training sessions for anxious seniors to learn coping strategies. As highlighted by a number of researchers (e.g., Dempsey, Haynes, Lucassen, & Casey, 2002; Jin, 2010; Low, 2010), and in line with the randomness as genesis principle of cognitive load theory, trial-and-error activities have been reported as the most frustrating experience by computer users, and anxiety has a detrimental impact on not only self-efficacy but also effective working memory for information processing (Hess, Hinson, & Statham, 2004). There are, in general, two types of coping strategies: emotion-focused and problem-focused (Smith, Jin, & Low, 2011). By learning emotion-focused coping strategies such as relaxation techniques, older adults can ameliorate the over reaction of the sympathetic system. IT professionals can also work with seniors to identity problems and obstacles that affect their access to the Internet. For example, educational technologists can provide demonstrations and clickable tips embedded in a bottleneck (i.e., a difficult process) to reduce senior users' anxiety. Under some circumstances, a professional is required to provide one-to-one assistance for the anxious, cognitively impaired seniors to use IT technologies.

CONCLUSION

In our rapidly progressing digital era with the occurrence of increased life spans, the gap between the elderly and younger generations in their use of computer-based technology is significantly wide. Researchers in behavioural and social sciences along with educators, welfare workers, and policy makers have expressed concern. Multi-disciplinary research, including psychology, neurology, and endocrinology, has demonstrated that cognitive aging is evident in reduced capacity of working memory, lowered information processing speed, and decreased resilience to distractions. However, for individuals with normal aging, many essential cognitive functions are well preserved. Based on the evidence accumulated in decades of experimental studies on human cognitive architecture, we have provided a series of recommendations in order to assist older adults in their activities associated with the Internet and other information technologies. These recommendations include expanding the capacity of working memory, minimizing unnecessary operations and irrelevant information, efficiently building and using relevant schemata for complex tasks, and providing special supporting measures for cognitively impaired elderly people's access to the Internet and related technologies. Research and applications in this direction appear to be promising.

REFERENCES

Anderson, J. R., Fincham, J. M., & Douglass, S. (1997). The role of examples and rules in the acquisition of a cognitive skill. *Journal of Experimental Psychology. Learning, Memory, and Cognition, 23*, 932–945. doi:10.1037/0278-7393.23.4.932

Atkinson, R. K., Renkl, A., & Merrill, M. M. (2003). Transitioning from studying examples to solving problems: Combining fading with prompting fosters learning. *Journal of Educational Psychology, 95*, 774–783. doi:10.1037/0022-0663.95.4.774

Atkinson, R. K., & Shiffrin, R. (1968). Human memory: A proposed system and its control processes. In Spence, K., & Spence, J. (Eds.), *The Psychology of Learning and Motivation* (*Vol. 2*, pp. 89–95). New York, NY: Academic Press. doi:10.1016/S0079-7421(08)60422-3

Baddeley, A. D. (1992). Working memory. *Science, 255*, 556–559. doi:10.1126/science.1736359

Baddeley, A. D. (2003). Working memory: Looking back and looking forward. *Nature Reviews. Neuroscience, 4*, 829–839. doi:10.1038/nrn1201

Cabeza, R., Grady, C. L., Nyberg, L., McIntosh, A. R., Tulving, E., & Kapur, S. (1997). Age-related differences in neural activity during memory encoding and retrieval: A position emission tomography study. *The Journal of Neuroscience, 17*, 391–400.

Caprani, N., Greaney, J., & Porter, N. (2006). A review of memory aid devices for an ageing population. *PsychNology, 4*(3), 205–243.

Chandler, P., & Sweller, J. (1991). Cognitive load theory and the format of instruction. *Cognition and Instruction, 8*, 293–332. doi:10.1207/s1532690xci0804_2

Chandler, P., & Sweller, J. (1996). Cognitive load while learning to use a computer program. *Applied Cognitive Psychology, 10*, 151–170. doi:10.1002/(SICI)1099-0720(199604)10:2<151::AID-ACP380>3.0.CO;2-U

Chase, W. G., & Simon, H. A. (1973). Perception in chess. *Cognitive Psychology, 4*, 55–81. doi:10.1016/0010-0285(73)90004-2

Chi, M. T. H., Glaser, R., & Farr, M. (Eds.). (1988). *The nature of expertise*. Hillsdale, NJ: Erlbaum.

Constantinidou, F., & Baker, S. (2002). Stimulus modality and verbal learning performance in normal aging. *Brain and Language, 82*, 296–311. doi:10.1016/S0093-934X(02)00018-4

Conway, A. R. A., Tuholski, S. W., Shisler, R. J., & Engle, R. W. (1999). The effect of memory load on negative priming: An individual differences investigation. *Memory & Cognition, 27*(6), 1042–1050. doi:10.3758/BF03201233

Cowan, N. (2000). The magical number 4 in short-term memory: A reconsideration of mental storage capacity. *The Behavioral and Brain Sciences*, *24*, 87–185. doi:10.1017/S0140525X01003922

Craik, F. I. M., Byrd, M., & Swanson, J. M. (1987). Patterns of memory loss in three elderly samples. *Psychology and Aging*, *2*, 79–86. doi:10.1037/0882-7974.2.1.79

Craik, F. I. M., & Grady, C. L. (2002). Aging, memory, and frontal lobes functioning. In Stuss, D. T., & Knight, R. T. (Eds.), *Principles of Frontally Lobe Function* (pp. 528–540). Oxford, UK: Oxford University Press. doi:10.1093/acprof:oso/9780195134971.003.0031

Crimmins, E. M., Kim, J. K., Langa, K. M., & Weir, D. R. (2011). Assessment of cognition using surveys and neuropsychological assessment: The health and retirement study and the aging, demographics, and memory study. *The Journals of Gerontology. Series B, Psychological Sciences and Social Sciences*, *66B*(S1), i162–i171. doi:10.1093/geronb/gbr048

Darabi, A. A., Nelson, D. W., & Palanki, S. (2007). Acquisition of troubleshooting skills in a computer simulation: Worked example vs. conventional problem solving instructional strategies. *Computers in Human Behavior*, *23*(4), 1809–1819. doi:10.1016/j.chb.2005.11.001

De Beni, R., & Palladino, P. (2004). Decline in working memory updating through ageing: Intrusion error analyses. *Memory (Hove, England)*, *12*, 75–89. doi:10.1080/09658210244000568

de Frias, C. M., Dixon, R. A., & Bäckman, L. (2003). Use of memory compensation strategies is related to psychosocial and health indicators. *The Journals of Gerontology. Series B, Psychological Sciences and Social Sciences*, *55B*(1), 12–p22. doi:10.1093/geronb/58.1.P12

de Groot, A. (1965). *Thought and choice in chess*. The Hague, The Netherlands: Mouton.

Dempsey, J. V., Haynes, L. L., Lucassen, B. A., & Casey, M. (2002). Forty simple computer games and what they could mean to educators. *Simulation & Gaming*, *33*, 157–168. doi:10.1177/1046878102332003

Diao, Y., & Sweller, J. (2007). Redundancy in foreign language reading comprehension instruction: Concurrent written and spoken presentations. *Learning and Instruction*, *17*, 78–88. doi:10.1016/j.learninstruc.2006.11.007

Dodson, C. S., Bawa, S., & Krueger, L. E. (2007). Aging, metamemory, and high-confidence errors: A misrecollection account. *Psychology and Aging*, *22*(1), 122–133. doi:10.1037/0882-7974.22.1.122

Eastman, J. K., & Iyer, R. (2005). The impact of cognitive age on internet use of the elderly: An introduction to the public policy implications. *International Journal of Consumer Studies*, *29*(2), 125–136. doi:10.1111/j.1470 6431.2004.00424.x

Elliott, J. G., Hufton, N. R., Willis, W., & Illushin, L. (2005). *Motivation, engagement, and educational performance: International perspectives on the contexts for learning*. New York, NY: Palgrave Macmillan. doi:10.1057/9780230509795

Ericsson, K. A., & Kintsch, W. (1995). Long-term working memory. *Psychological Review*, *102*, 211–245. doi:10.1037/0033-295X.102.2.211

Geary, D. (2002). Principles of evolutionary educational psychology. *Learning and Individual Differences*, *12*, 317–345. doi:10.1016/S1041-6080(02)00046-8

Geary, D. (2005). *The origin of mind: Evolution of brain, cognition, and general intelligence*. Washington, DC: American Psychological Association. doi:10.1037/10871-000

Geary, D. (2007). Educating the evolved mind: Conceptual foundations for an evolutionary educational psychology. In Carlson, J. S., & Levin, J. R. (Eds.), *Psychological Perspectives on Contemporary Educational Issues* (pp. 1–99). Greenwich, CT: Information Age Publishing.

Geary, D. (2008). An evolutionarily informed education science. *Educational Psychologist, 43*, 179–195. doi:10.1080/00461520802392133

Gilchrist, A. L., Cowan, N., & Naveh-Benjamin, M. (2008). Working memory capacity for spoken sentences decreases with adult ageing: Recall of fewer but not smaller chunks in older adults. *Memory (Hove, England), 16*(7), 773–787. doi:10.1080/09658210802261124

Hawi, N. (2010). Causal attributions of success and failure made by undergraduate students in an introductory-level computer programming course. *Computers & Education, 54*, 1127–1136. doi:10.1016/j.compedu.2009.10.020

Henke, M. (1999). Promoting independence in older persons through the Internet. *Cyberpsychology & Behavior, 2*(6), 521–527. doi:10.1089/cpb.1999.2.521

Hess, T. M. (2005). Memory and aging in context. *Psychological Bulletin, 131*(3), 383–406. doi:10.1037/0033-2909.131.3.383

Hess, T. M., Hinson, J. T., & Statham, J. A. (2004). Explicit and implicit stereotype activation effects on memory: Do age and awareness moderate the impact of priming? *Psychology and Aging, 19*(3), 495–505. doi:10.1037/0882-7974.19.3.495

Huppert, F. A., & Beardsall, L. (1993). Prospective memory impairment as an early indicator of dementia. *Journal of Clinical and Experimental Neuropsychology, 15*, 805–821. doi:10.1080/01688639308402597

Huppert, F. A., Johnson, T., & Nickson, J. (2000). High prevalence of prospective memory impairment in the elderly and in early-stage dementia: Findings from a population-based study. *Applied Cognitive Psychology, 14*, S63–S81. doi:10.1002/acp.771

Jin, P. (2010). Methodological considerations in educational research using serious games. In Van Eck, R. (Ed.), *Interdisciplinary Models and Tools for Serious Games: Emerging Concepts and Future Directions* (pp. 147–176). Hershey, PA: IGI Global. doi:10.4018/978-1-61520-719-0.ch007

Jin, P., & Low, R. (2011). Implications of game use for explicit instruction. In Tobias, S., & Fletcher, J. D. (Eds.), *Computer Games and Instruction* (pp. 395–416). Charlotte, NC: Information Age Publishers.

Joshi, S., & Morley, J. E. (2006). Cognitive impairment. *The Medical Clinics of North America, 90*, 769–787. doi:10.1016/j.mcna.2006.05.014

Kalyuga, S., Chandler, P., & Sweller, J. (1998). Levels of expertise and instructional design. *Human Factors, 40*, 1–17. doi:10.1518/001872098779480587

Kalyuga, S., Chandler, P., & Sweller, J. (1999). Managing split attention and redundancy in multimedia instruction. *Applied Cognitive Psychology, 13*, 351–371. doi:10.1002/(SICI)1099-0720(199908)13:4<351::AID-ACP589>3.0.CO;2-6

Kalyuga, S., Chandler, P., & Sweller, J. (2000). Incorporating learner experience into the design of multimedia instruction. *Journal of Educational Psychology, 92*, 126–136. doi:10.1037/0022-0663.92.1.126

Kalyuga, S., Chandler, P., & Sweller, J. (2004). When redundant on-screen text in multimedia technical instruction can interfere with learning. *Human Factors, 46*, 567–581. doi:10.1518/hfes.46.3.567.50405

Kaye, J. A., Maxwell, S. A., Mattek, N., Hayes, T. L., Dodge, H., & Pavel, M. (2011). Intelligent systems for assessing aging changes: Home-based, unobtrusive, and continuous assessment of aging. *The Journals of Gerontology. Series B, Psychological Sciences and Social Sciences, 66B*(S1), i180–i190. doi:10.1093/geronb/gbq095

Kirschner, P. A., Sweller, J., & Clark, R. E. (2006). Why minimal guidance during instruction does not work: An analysis of the failure of constructivist, discovery, problem-based, experiential, and inquiry-based teaching. *Educational Psychologist, 41*, 75–86. doi:10.1207/s15326985ep4102_1

Lashley, K. S. (1929). *Brain mechanisms and intelligence: A quantitative study of injuries to the brain.* Chicago, IL: University of Chicago Press. doi:10.1037/10017-000

Lashley, K. S. (1947). Structural variation in the nervous system in relation to behavior. *Psychological Review, 54*, 325–334. doi:10.1037/h0063654

Lashley, K. S. (1950). In search of the engram. *Society of Experimental Biology Symposium, 4*, 454–482.

Low, R. (2010). Examining motivational factors in serious educational games. In Van Eck, R. (Ed.), *Interdisciplinary Models and Tools for Serious Games: Emerging Concepts and Future Directions* (pp. 103–124). Hershey, PA: IGI Global. doi:10.4018/978-1-61520-719-0.ch005

Low, R., Jin, P., & Sweller, J. (2011). Cognitive load theory, attentional processes and optimized learning outcomes in a digital environment. In Roda, C. (Ed.), *Human Attention in Digital Environments* (pp. 93–113). Cambridge, UK: Cambridge University Press. doi:10.1017/CBO9780511974519.004

Low, R., Jin, P., & Sweller, J. (2012). Digital assessment of the acquisition and utility of biologically secondary knowledge: Perspectives based on human cognitive architecture. In Mayrath, M., Clarke-Midura, J., & Robinson, D. (Eds.), *Technology-Based Assessments for 21st Century Skills: Theoretical and Practical Implications from Modern Research.* New York, NY: Springer-Verlag.

Low, R., & Sweller, J. (2005). The modality principle in multimedia learning. In Mayer, R. E. (Ed.), *The Cambridge Handbook of Multimedia Learning* (pp. 147–158). Cambridge, UK: Cambridge University Press.

Lustig, C., Hasher, L., & Tonev, S. T. (2006). Distraction as a determinant of processing speed. *Psychonomic Bulletin & Review, 13*, 619–625. doi:10.3758/BF03193972

Mayer, R. E. (2005). Cognitive theory of multimedia learning. In Mayer, R. E. (Ed.), *The Cambridge Handbook of Multimedia Learning* (pp. 31–48). Cambridge, UK: Cambridge University Press.

Mayer, R. E., & Anderson, R. (1991). Animations need narrations: An experimental test of a dual-coding hypothesis. *Journal of Educational Psychology, 83*, 484–490. doi:10.1037/0022-0663.83.4.484

Mayer, R. E., & Anderson, R. (1992). The instructive animation: Helping students build connections between words and pictures in multimedia learning. *Journal of Educational Psychology, 84*, 444–452. doi:10.1037/0022-0663.84.4.444

Mayer, R. E., Bove, W., Bryman, A., Mars, R., & Tapangco, L. (1996). When less is more: Meaningful learning from visual and verbal summaries of science textbook lessons. *Journal of Educational Psychology, 88*, 64–73. doi:10.1037/0022-0663.88.1.64

Mayer, R. E., & Moreno, R. (1998). A split-attention effect in multimedia learning: Evidence for dual processing systems in working memory. *Journal of Educational Psychology, 90,* 312–320. doi:10.1037/0022-0663.90.2.312

Mayer, R. E., & Moreno, R. (2002). Aids to computer-based multimedia learning. *Learning and Instruction, 12,* 107–119. doi:10.1016/S0959-4752(01)00018-4

Mayer, R. E., & Sims, V. K. (1994). For whom is a picture worth a thousand words? Extensions of a dual-coding theory of multimedia learning. *Journal of Educational Psychology, 86,* 389–401. doi:10.1037/0022-0663.86.3.389

Mayr, U., & Kliegl, R. (1993). Sequential and coordinative complexity: Age-based processing limitations in figural transformations. *Journal of Experimental Psychology. Learning, Memory, and Cognition, 19,* 1297–1320. doi:10.1037/0278-7393.19.6.1297

Mayr, U., Kliegl, R., & Krampe, R. T. (1996). Sequential and coordinative processing dynamics in figural transformations across the life span. *Cognition, 59,* 61–90. doi:10.1016/0010-0277(95)00689-3

McCoy, S. L., Tun, P. A., Cox, L. C., Colangelo, M., Stewart, R. A., & Wingfield, A. (2005). Hearing loss and perceptual effort: Downstream effects on older adults' memory for speech. *The Quarterly Journal of Experimental Psychology Section A, 58*(1), 22–33. doi:10.1080/02724980443000151

Miller, G. A. (1956). The magical number seven, plus or minus two: Some limits on our capacity for processing information. *Psychological Review, 63,* 81–97. doi:10.1037/h0043158

Moreno, R., & Mayer, R. E. (1999). Cognitive principles of multimedia learning: The role of modality and contiguity. *Journal of Educational Psychology, 91,* 358–368. doi:10.1037/0022-0663.91.2.358

Mousavi, S. Y., Low, R., & Sweller, J. (1995). Reducing cognitive load by mixing auditory and visual presentation modes. *Journal of Educational Psychology, 87,* 319–334. doi:10.1037/0022-0663.87.2.319

Oberauer, K., & Kliegl, R. (2001). Beyond resources: Formal models of complexity effects and age differences in working memory. *The European Journal of Cognitive Psychology, 13,* 187–215. doi:10.1080/09541440042000278

Oerlemans, W. G. M., Bakker, A. B., & Veenhoven, R. (2011). Finding the key to happy aging: a day reconstruction study of happiness. *The Journals of Gerontology. Series B, Psychological Sciences and Social Sciences, 66*(6), 665–674. doi:10.1093/geronb/gbr040

Opalinski, L. (2001). Older adults and the digital divide: Assessing results of a web-based survey. *Journal of Technology in Human Services, 18*(3-4), 203–221. doi:10.1300/J017v18n03_13

Paas, F., & van Gog, T. (2006). Optimising worked example instruction: Different ways to increase germane cognitive lead. *Learning and Instruction, 16,* 87–91. doi:10.1016/j.learninstruc.2006.02.004

Paas, F., & Van Merriënboer, J. J. G. (1994). Variability of worked examples and transfer of geometrical problem-solving skills: A cognitive-load approach. *Journal of Educational Psychology, 86,* 122–133. doi:10.1037/0022-0663.86.1.122

Paivio, A. (1986). *Mental representations: A dual coding approach.* Oxford, UK: Oxford University Press.

Payette, H., Gueye, N. D. R., Gaudreau, P., Morais, J. A., Shatenstein, B., & Gray-Donald, K. (2011). Trajectories of physical function decline and psychological functioning: The Québec longitudinal study on nutrition and successful aging (NuAge). *The Journals of Gerontology. Series B, Psychological Sciences and Social Sciences, 66B*(S1), i82–i90. doi:10.1093/geronb/gbq085

Peterson, L., & Peterson, M. J. (1959). Short-term retention of individual verbal items. *Journal of Experimental Psychology*, *58*, 193–198. doi:10.1037/h0049234

Piccinin, A. M., Muniz, G., Matthews, F. E., & Johansson, B. (2011). Terminal decline from within- and between-person perspectives, accounting for incident dementia. *The Journals of Gerontology. Series B, Psychological Sciences and Social Sciences*, *66B*(4), 391–401. doi:10.1093/geronb/gbr010

Piccinin, A. M., Muniz, G., Sparks, C., & Bontempo, D. E. (2011). An evaluation of analytical approaches for understanding change in cognition in the context of aging and health. *The Journals of Gerontology. Series B, Psychological Sciences and Social Sciences*, *66B*(S1), i36–i49. doi:10.1093/geronb/gbr038

Reisenwitz, T., Iyer, R., Kuhlmeier, D. B., & Eastman, J. K. (2007). The elderly's Internet usage: An updated look. *Journal of Consumer Marketing*, *24*(7), 406–418. doi:10.1108/07363760710834825

Rendell, P. G., & Craik, F. I. M. (2000). Virtual week and actual week: Age-related differences in prospective memory. *Applied Cognitive Psychology*, *14*, S43–S62. doi:10.1002/acp.770

Renkl, A. (2005). The worked-out examples principle in multimedia learning. In Mayer, R. E. (Ed.), *The Cambridge Handbook of Multimedia Learning* (pp. 229–245). Cambridge, UK: Cambridge University Press.

Salthouse, T. A. (1992). Why do adult age differences increase with task complexity? *Developmental Psychology*, *28*, 905–918. doi:10.1037/0012-1649.28.5.905

Seeman, T. E., Miller-Martinez, D. M., Stein Merkin, S., Lachman, M. E., Tun, P. A., & Karlamangla, A. S. (2011). Histories of social engagement and adult cognition: Midlife in the US study. *The Journals of Gerontology. Series B, Psychological Sciences and Social Sciences*, *66B*(S1), i141–i152. doi:10.1093/geronb/gbq091

Simon, H. A. (1990). Invariants of human behavior. *Annual Review of Psychology*, *41*, 1–19. doi:10.1146/annurev.ps.41.020190.000245

Simons, J. S., Schölvinck, M. L., Gilbert, S. J., Frith, C. D., & Burgess, P. W. (2006). Differential components of prospective memory? Evidence from fMRI. *Neuropsychologia*, *44*, 1388–1397. doi:10.1016/j.neuropsychologia.2006.01.005

Smith, G., Della Sala, S., Logie, R. H., & Maylor, E. A. (2000). Prospective and retrospective memory in normal ageing and dementia: A questionnaire study. *Memory (Hove, England)*, *8*, 311–321. doi:10.1080/09658210050117735

Smith, J., Jin, P., & Low, R. (2011). *Managing stress in various contexts*. Sydney, Australia: Pearson Education.

Swanson, H. L. (1999). What develops in working memory? A life span perspective. *Developmental Psychology*, *35*, 986–1000. doi:10.1037/0012-1649.35.4.986

Sweller, J. (1994). Cognitive load theory, learning difficulty, and instructional design. *Learning and Instruction*, *4*, 295–312. doi:10.1016/0959-4752(94)90003-5

Sweller, J. (2011). Cognitive load theory. In Mestre, J., & Ross, B. (Eds.), *The Psychology of Learning and Motivation: Cognition in Education* (*Vol. 55*, pp. 37–76). Oxford, UK: Academic Press.

Sweller, J., Ayres, P., & Kalyuga, S. (2011). *Cognitive load theory*. New York, NY: Springer. doi:10.1007/978-1-4419-8126-4

Sweller, J., & Chandler, P. (1991). Evidence for cognitive load theory. *Cognition and Instruction, 8,* 351–362. doi:10.1207/s1532690xci0804_5

Sweller, J., & Chandler, P. (1994). Why some material is difficult to learn. *Cognition and Instruction, 12,* 185–233. doi:10.1207/s1532690xci1203_1

Sweller, J., Chandler, P., Tierney, P., & Cooper, M. (1990). Cognitive load as a factor in the structuring of technical material. *Journal of Experimental Psychology. General, 119,* 176–192. doi:10.1037/0096-3445.119.2.176

Sweller, J., & Cooper, G. (1985). The use of worked examples as a substitute for problem solving in learning algebra. *Cognition and Instruction, 2,* 59–89. doi:10.1207/s1532690xci0201_3

Sweller, J., & Sweller, S. (2006). Natural information processing systems. *Evolutionary Psychology, 4,* 434–458.

Tarmizi, R., & Sweller, J. (1988). Guidance during mathematical problem solving. *Journal of Educational Psychology, 80,* 424–436. doi:10.1037/0022-0663.80.4.424

Tindall-Ford, S., Chandler, P., & Sweller, J. (1997). When two sensory modes are better than one. *Journal of Experimental Psychology. Applied, 3,* 257–287. doi:10.1037/1076-898X.3.4.257

Van Gerven, P. W. M., Paas, F., Van Merriënboer, J. J. G., Hendriks, M., & Schmidt, H. G. (2003). The efficiency of multimedia learning into old age. *The British Journal of Educational Psychology, 73,* 489–505. doi:10.1348/000709903322591208

Van Gerven, P. W. M., Paas, F., Van Merriënboer, J. J. G., & Schmidt, H. G. (2000). Cognitive load theory and the acquisition of complex cognitive skills in the elderly: Towards an integrative framework. *Educational Gerontology, 26,* 503–521. doi:10.1080/03601270050133874

Van Gerven, P. W. M., Paas, F., Van Merriënboer, J. J. G., & Schmidt, H. G. (2002). Cognitive load theory and aging: Effects of worked examples on training efficiency. *Learning and Instruction, 12,* 87–105. doi:10.1016/S0959-4752(01)00017-2

Van Gerven, P. W. M., Paas, F., Van Merriënboer, J. J. G., & Schmidt, H. G. (2006). Modality and variability as factors in training the elderly. *Applied Cognitive Psychology, 20,* 311–320. doi:10.1002/acp.1247

Van Merriënboer, J. J. G., & Sweller, J. (2005). Cognitive load theory and complex learning: Recent developments and future directions. *Educational Psychology Review, 17,* 147–177. doi:10.1007/s10648-005-3951-0

Ward, M., & Sweller, J. (1990). Structuring effective worked examples. *Cognition and Instruction, 7,* 1–39. doi:10.1207/s1532690xci0701_1

Whitman, D. (2011). *Cognition.* Hoboken, NJ: John Wiley.

Yeung, A., Jin, P., & Sweller, J. (1997). Cognitive load and learner expertise: Split-attention and redundancy effects in reading with explanatory notes. *Contemporary Educational Psychology, 23,* 1–21. doi:10.1006/ceps.1997.0951

Zaphiris, P., & Rifaht, S. (2006). Trends, similarities, and differences in the usage of teen and senior public online Newsgroups. *ACM Transactions on Computer-Human Interaction, 13*(3), 403–422. doi:10.1145/1183456.1183461

ADDITIONAL READING

Atkinson, R. K., & Shiffrin, R. (1968). Human memory: A proposed system and its control processes. In Spence, K., & Spence, J. (Eds.), *The Psychology of Learning and Motivation* (Vol. 2, pp. 89–1195). New York, NY: Academic Press. doi:10.1016/S0079-7421(08)60422-3

Baddeley, A. D. (2003). Working memory: Looking back and looking forward. *Nature Reviews. Neuroscience, 4,* 829–839. doi:10.1038/nrn1201

Cabeza, R., Grady, C. L., Nyberg, L., McIntosh, A. R., Tulving, E., & Kapur, S. (1997). Age-related differences in neural activity during memory encoding and retrieval: A position emission tomography study. *The Journal of Neuroscience, 17,* 391–400.

Caprani, N., Greaney, J., & Porter, N. (2006). A review of memory aid devices for an ageing population. *PsychNology, 4*(3), 205–243.

Gilchrist, A. L., Cowan, N., & Naveh-Benjamin, M. (2008). Working memory capacity for spoken sentences decreases with adult ageing: Recall of fewer but not smaller chunks in older adults. *Memory (Hove, England), 16*(7), 773–787. doi:10.1080/09658210802261124

Henke, M. (1999). Promoting independence in older persons through the Internet. *Cyberpsychology & Behavior, 2*(6), 521–527. doi:10.1089/cpb.1999.2.521

Hess, T. M. (2005). Memory and aging in context. *Psychological Bulletin, 131*(3), 383–406. doi:10.1037/0033-2909.131.3.383

Low, R., & Sweller, J. (2005). The modality principle in multimedia learning. In Mayer, R. E. (Ed.), *The Cambridge Handbook of Multimedia Learning* (pp. 147–158). Cambridge, UK: Cambridge University Press.

Mayer, R. E. (2005). Cognitive theory of multimedia learning. In Mayer, R. E. (Ed.), *The Cambridge Handbook of Multimedia Learning* (pp. 31–48). Cambridge, UK: Cambridge University Press.

Simon, H. A. (1990). Invariants of human behavior. *Annual Review of Psychology, 41,* 1–19. doi:10.1146/annurev.ps.41.020190.000245

Smith, J., Jin, P., & Low, R. (2011). *Managing stress in various contexts*. Sydney, Australia: Pearson Education.

Swanson, H. L. (1999). What develops in working memory? A life span perspective. *Developmental Psychology, 35,* 986–1000. doi:10.1037/0012-1649.35.4.986

Sweller, J., Ayres, P., & Kalyuga, S. (2011). *Cognitive load theory*. New York, NY: Springer. doi:10.1007/978-1-4419-8126-4

Van Gerven, P. W. M., Paas, F., Van Merriënboer, J. J. G., Hendriks, M., & Schmidt, H. G. (2003). The efficiency of multimedia learning into old age. *The British Journal of Educational Psychology, 73,* 489–505. doi:10.1348/000709903322591208

Zaphiris, P., & Rifaht, S. (2006). Trends, similarities, and differences in the usage of teen and senior public online newsgroups. *ACM Transactions on Computer-Human Interaction, 13*(3), 403–422. doi:10.1145/1183456.1183461

KEY TERMS AND DEFINITIONS

Cognitive Load Theory: An instructional design theory based on our knowledge of human cognitive architecture.

Dual-Modality Presentation: The use of both auditory and visual information under split-attention conditions. Can be contrasted with single modality presentation, normally in visual only mode.

Human Cognitive Architecture: The manner in which structures and functions required for human cognitive processes are organized.

Long-Term Memory: The store holding all knowledge acquired during the processes of learning.

Schema: As cognitive structure that we use to organize information for storage in long-term memory. When brought into working memory from long-term memory, a schema allows us to treat multiple elements of information as a single integrated element.

Split-Attention Instructions: Instructions in which multiple sources of information are not physically integrated so that working memory resources need to be used for mental integration.

Worked-Example: Comprises the statement of a problem, the solution steps, and the final solution.

Working Memory: The structure that processes information coming from either the environment or long-term memory and that transfers learned information for storage in long-term memory.

Chapter 6
Design for Aging:
Enhancing Everyday Technology Use

Marita A. O'Brien
University of Alabama in Huntsville, USA

Wendy A. Rogers
Georgia Institute of Technology, USA

ABSTRACT

Modern technology incorporates a wide range of digital technologies, including those created specifically for everyday tasks typically operated in stand-alone mode. Yet, innovations in mobile technologies and the Internet influence design and adoption of these everyday technologies by introducing new interaction techniques and by providing access to information and people that facilitate effective use. This chapter describes best practices and challenges for enabling older adults to adopt everyday technologies transformed by technology innovations. First, the authors define everyday technologies and known factors influencing successful use including environmental support and context of use. Then, they discuss issues and challenges of design for everyday technologies and summarize the factors that influence everyday technology use in a conceptual diagram. The authors also present recommendations for specific constituents that may improve technology adoption by older adults. Lastly, they discuss future opportunities for enhancing everyday technology use with good design, useful support, and appropriate innovations.

INTRODUCTION

Modern technology incorporates a wide range of digital products that are used by older adults to satisfy many needs and wants. We have found that older adults use technologies that vary in levels of technological sophistication and ease of use (O'Brien, 2010; Olson, O'Brien, Rogers, & Charness, 2011). Some products are well designed to facilitate first-time use with little effort; others require significant effort, prior knowledge, and environmental support to achieve a goal. As we assessed the basis for successful use among older adults, we noted that older adults frequently apply

DOI: 10.4018/978-1-4666-1966-1.ch006

their lifetime of experience completing everyday tasks and resolving problems to their use of modern technologies. Thus, older adults can usually function well in technologically enabled communities in spite of generally lower experience with modern technologies compared to younger adults.

Researchers interested in helping older adults adopt new technologies can learn effective design practices from the successes and problems older adults encounter with everyday technologies for which some prior knowledge of the task goal or procedure is typically available. Although many modern technologies are used for everyday tasks, this chapter will focus on technologies other than Internet and Communications Technologies (ICT). We opted for this approach because other technologies are more likely to have been used in familiar contexts such as the home in which older adults initially learned specific tasks and general everyday problem-solving skills. In these familiar contexts, older adults often learned relevant strategies, domain knowledge, environmental cues, and sources of support that facilitate success across a range of tasks. Older adults combine their prior knowledge of these components and relevant technologies to the use of new everyday technologies.

In this chapter, we first present an overview of everyday technology use by older adults and factors that affect successful use. Then, we discuss challenges for designing everyday technologies with a focus on prior knowledge issues because the diversity of prior knowledge among older adults is particularly problematic for everyday technology design. This focus is highlighted in a conceptual diagram of factors influencing everyday technology use with prior knowledge at the center. We then propose solutions for different constituent groups to increase everyday technology adoption. Lastly, we discuss future research needs and opportunities for improving the design of everyday technologies and related instructional support.

BACKGROUND

Everyday technologies are characterized by the tasks they enable and the way in which they are first used. Everyday tasks occur in naturalistic environments during the ordinary activities of a target population, even if they are not conducted every day (Sinnott & Cook, 1989). For older adults, these everyday tasks have been generally specified as Activities of Daily Living (e.g., bathing, eating; Katz, Ford, Moskovitz, Jackson, & Jaffe, 1963); Instrumental Activities of Daily Living (e.g., managing medication, preparing meals; Lawton, 1990), and Enhanced Activities of Daily Living (e.g., communicating with family and friends, hobbies; Rogers, Meyer, Walker, & Fisk, 1998). Everyday technologies are typically used with little formal training or instruction.

The International Standards Organization (2006) recommended several practices for designers to follow in developing effective everyday technologies in the ISO 20282-1 standard, entitled "Ease of Operation of Everyday Products." In this section, we review research about these factors pertinent to older adults by describing potential sources of knowledge for using new technologies and contextual factors of use.

Everyday Technology Repertoire

ISO 20282-1 (International Standards Organization, 2006) prescribed that designers understand the "knowledge of comparable machines" for target users as a baseline for new technologies. No template for determining this knowledge was given. We examined several common approaches to estimate this repertoire of everyday technologies for a "typical" older adult. One method for estimating knowledge is large-scale surveys of representative users about their experience with technologies such as those developed by the Pew Research Center (e.g., Zickuhr, 2011). This approach is limited to describing a population's technology usage at a high-level, typically by reporting the percentage using specific technologies.

Frequency and recency of use influences the accessibility of knowledge (Reason, 1980), making more fine-grained information necessary. We therefore assessed breadth and depth of technology experience across functional domains (Olson, et al., 2011) by surveying 430 younger adults (18-28) and 251 older adults (65-90) in the southeastern U.S. We found a greater breadth of technologies used by younger adults overall, but older adults used more technologies such as microwave ovens and answering machines that have been available for several decades. Older adults were also more likely to complete functions with a person on the telephone than younger adults. Overall, though, older adults did not seem to avoid using technologies in general or any technology specifically, but their preferences and intensity of use differed from younger adults.

Survey results are limited to identifying technologies of interest to the researcher. We conducted a diary study that freed participants to provide more information. We also explored preference and ability effects for older adults with different levels of general technology experience by examining technology repertoires in two groups of older adults in the top (high) and bottom (low) thirds of technology experience for their cohort (O'Brien, 2010). Ten high-tech and ten low-tech older adults tracked their use of all products requiring electricity or batteries in handwritten diaries for ten consecutive days. A bottom-up process was used to group these technologies into categories based on user-mentioned similarities. Participants across levels of technology experience described diverse uses for technologies based on needs and preferences. This diversity suggests that older adults are flexible in using everyday technologies according to their functional need, though this may differ from the designer's intended use. Such functional knowledge in a population may not be obvious from survey data.

Table 1 shows the categorized count of everyday technologies listed by participants in each group during our diary study (O'Brien, 2010). Note that although high-tech older adults used significantly more technologies, low-tech older adults also used many technologies. We found that low-tech older adults used significantly fewer shopping technologies, with participant comments indicating a preference for in-person transactions. We also found that low-tech older adults individually used fewer features on their telephone and communication technologies. On the other hand, high-tech older adults reported trying new features on their cell phones and configuring programmable devices such as thermostats.

These different interests in technologies also surfaced when examining the depth of technology use (O'Brien, 2010). The percentage of technologies used at least once per week was nearly 75% for each group. For low-tech older adults the remainder were primarily infrequent such as when no in-person option for completing a transaction was available. For high-tech older adults nearly 10% of their technologies were completely new or new features of known technologies. Infrequent listings included features of known technologies such as customization or system maintenance. Thus, knowledge of given technologies may be unevenly distributed among available functions and features for a given individual.

In summary, our review of the everyday technology repertoires of older adults suggested that "knowledge of comparable machines" is difficult to assess, particularly with surveys. Even if the majority of a target population uses a specific technology, knowledge of a specific function may not be readily accessible for a particular task. Nonetheless, it is true that both age and overall technology experience implied some user preferences for how technology is used. We also identified the importance of the function or task goal for guiding technology use. Therefore, we outline a conceptual approach to evaluating po-

Table 1. Everyday technologies[1] used over a 10-day period by high-tech and low-tech older adults (O'Brien, 2010)

Category	Exemplars	High-Tech[2] Older Adults (n=10)	Low-Tech[2] Older Adults (n=10)
Entertainment & leisure	Digital camera, MP3 player, sewing machine, TiVo, TV	29	19
Home health care	Blood glucose monitor, CPAP, dial-a-dose insulin delivery	7	5
Kitchen	Blender, dishwasher, electric carving knife, stove, waffle iron	58	39
Non-PC office	Calculator, copier, fax machine, paper shredder	13	10
Other home	Alarm clock, fan, home security system, vacuum cleaner, washing machine	58	53
Personal care & fitness	Digital scale, electric toothbrush, hand dryer, heating pad, treadmill	21	13
Shopping & purchase	ATM, public transport ticket purchase, self-service checkout, vending machine	28	15
Telephone & communication	Answering machine, my cell phone, push-button automated response system, set ring profile	24	13
Transportation	Cruise control, escalator, GPS, public transport card swipe, sibling's car	28	18
Totals		**266**	**185**

Notes:

[1]As described in the introduction, we have excluded PC and Internet technologies from this list to focus on non-ICT technologies.

[2]Participants were categorized as high-tech (top third) or low-tech (bottom third) based on the breadth and depth of their everyday technology use, Internet use, and PC use as compared to 110 community-dwelling older adults (aged 65-75).

tential sources of knowledge that may influence everyday technology use.

Sources of Knowledge

In his book, *The Design of Everyday Things*, Norman (2002) recommended that designers understand two potential sources of information for correct use of their device. First, users may access information external to themselves, called Knowledge in the World (KiW). Second, users may access information from their own memory, called prior knowledge or Knowledge in the Head (KiH). Norman proposed that when KiW matches the existing KiH, users are satisfied with their device use. We collected data about sources of

information actually used for everyday technology encounters in our diary study (O'Brien, 2010).

KiW has also been called environmental support (e.g., Morrow & Rogers, 2008), specifically to highlight that information in the world reduces the user's need for memory retrieval. When we reviewed external sources of support in interview transcripts, two categories of KiW emerged (O'Brien, Weger, DeFour, & Reeves, 2011). First, participants used manuals, videos, and guidance specifically prepared as instructions. Instructions were accessed in paper form as well as through email and the Internet. Second, participants used information directly available on the technology such as labels, affordances, and on-screen guidance. This technology information included both feedback (i.e., response to user action) and feedforward (i.e., what to do next).

Participant descriptions of KiH were more varied than KiW descriptions. In some cases participants provided specific knowledge descriptions such as a similar technology ("a stud finder is pretty much like a metal detector"), feature from another technology ("the time buttons are like the plus and minus on my Cuisinart"), manual version of the technology ("the electric grill's just like my coal one"), or interaction techniques ("I know how to swipe a card"). In other cases, descriptions were quite broad such as a mental model ("all vending machines are the same"). Participants also mentioned knowledge of task goals and intermediate steps. More generally, some participants merely said, "I've used it before."

Participants also described encounters in which they used both KiW and KiH sources. As proposed by Norman (2002), this combination may be the dominant strategy even if participants attribute success or problems to either KiW or KiH alone. For example, ATM users may have experience with multiple ATMs so they feel knowledgeable about ATMs; however, using a specific ATM typically requires guidance on the device (KiW) about card insertion approach, question order, etc. Some participants described a successful guessing strategy (Polson & Lewis, 1990) with many everyday technologies in which they selected controls and options using their KiH about what task success looked like. Participants called this strategy trial and error even though they seemed to expend minimal effort explicitly defining expected results for selecting a particular option that may facilitate error identification. If users could not identify options that seemed related to their task goal, however, they typically reported use of systematic trial and error that required attention and effort (i.e., try one thing, assess the outcome, if not successful try the next option). Overall, participants attributed problem resolution to a combination strategy more than KiH or KiW alone.

Context of Use

By definition, everyday technologies are used for typical tasks within users' natural environments. Predicting successful use of everyday technologies thus requires an understanding of the contextual factors surrounding these encounters. The first important contextual factor is the task goal(s). When using many everyday technologies participants have an objective goal to accomplish a task, not learn the technology (Mitzner, et al., 2010). In our interviews with older adults about technologies reported in their diaries (O'Brien, 2010), some participants reported that they were successful because they knew the expected result (e.g., "the cake was done"; "the paper was printed"). Generally, participants needed minimal effort or attention for these successful encounters. When the expected result was not achieved, the goal was still helpful in identifying that there was a problem and for assessing alternate methods to achieve the goal.

For everyday technologies used in recreation such as video players and electronic games, user goals may be emotional and subjectively evaluated. Thus, the goal may be less relevant to increased adoption of these technologies than the user's experience (Reed & Monk, 2004). Technologies designed for experience may facilitate continued use by eliciting feelings of enjoyment and familiarity that can lead to novel behavior and perseverance when difficulties are encountered. The aesthetics of a technology may be implicitly used to determine whether task goals or subjective experiences should guide the interaction.

Another contextual factor is the location of use, which may provide environmental cues about correct use. Among adults over age 70, 80% of their activities were performed at home (Horgan, Wilms, & Baltes, 1998). This proportion is generally supported by the categorized list of technologies in Table 1, though the list also includes everyday technologies only used in public places such as stores. In such environments, factors such as light, noise, and crowds may also influence whether participants can easily perceive relevant KiW.

A third contextual factor is the presence of other people who can explicitly or implicitly provide support for technology use. Older adults are likely to be alone in their daily lives when they are interacting with everyday technologies (Horgan, et al., 1998). They may, however, initially use technologies in the presence of other people who can help them learn to use new technologies effectively. For example, home health caregivers frequently teach patients and their families to use medical devices (McBride, Beer, Mitzner, & Rogers, 2011). Family members may also occasionally help older users (O'Brien, 2010). Sometimes this help was ad hoc during regular visits, but some children have developed an infrastructure for supporting their parents with parallel technology configurations. Several older adults noted that they preferred other means because they did not like to bother their children.

During normal everyday activities, both facilitation and impairment effects of social support have been reported. For example, passengers can help older adults continue to drive safely and effectively as they age (Vrkljan & Miller Polgar, 2007). In this collaborative cognition, passengers provide encouragement, feedback, and assistance to the driver. This type of collaboration was also reported in our diary study (O'Brien, 2010) for participants navigating public transportation and completing complex repairs. Some supportive social information was provided intentionally by employees, bystanders and other users such as telling them how to insert a mass transit card. Participants also reported watching other users to learn how to interact with novel systems. On the other hand, several participants reported that other people interfered with successful task completion. One participant actually banished her husband from the kitchen when she was cooking after one burned meal.

The participant's mood and stress level during technology use can also be considered a context factor. In one study, a computer assistant was designed to provide advice to older diabetic patients about their diet and exercise (Blanson Henkemans, Rogers, Fisk, Neerincx, Lindenberg, & van der Mast, 2008). When a highly stressful situation was simulated (e.g. imagine glucose levels are elevated and a decision must be made quickly), the older adults made fewer errors with an assistant that provided specific guidance about what they should do. The comparison assistant was one that was more cooperative in nature, requiring the user to make choices. These data show that technology designers must understand the contexts of use that might influence a user's available cognitive capacity and consider adaptive designs that accommodate changes in circumstances, such as stress.

CHALLENGES AND SOLUTIONS FOR EVERYDAY TECHNOLOGIES

As described above, many factors that influence everyday technology use are understood such as the role of manuals, task goals, social support, and user mood. However, the specific influence of prior knowledge and the interaction of different types of prior knowledge are not well understood. Yet, research suggests that technology experience, a common estimate for prior knowledge, influences successful performance more than age alone (Blackler, Popovic, & Mahar, 2003; Czaja, et al., 2006; Freudenthal, 1998; Kang & Yoon, 2008; Langdon, Lewis, & Clarkson, 2007; O'Brien, 2010). Thus, the primary challenge is to understand prior knowledge and its use more accurately. In this section, we describe four issues about prior knowledge requiring further investigation. All of these issues have broad applicability and an age-specific component. A diagram incorporating relevant factors is then shown to illustrate an overall framework for systematically investigating their use in everyday technology interactions. We

Table 2. Proposed knowledge taxonomies for technology design

Blackler, Popovic, & Mahar (2003)	Hurtienne & Langdon (2009)	Serrano Baquero & Rogers (2010)
body reflector	innate	interface family
population stereotype	sensorimotor	specific displays
familiar feature from same domain	culture	specific controls
familiar feature from other domain	expertise	specific procedures
metaphor from other domain		contextual
		equipment

also present recommendations for three constituent groups to facilitate everyday technology adoption by older adults given the current state of research.

Issues, Controversies, Problems

Measuring Prior Knowledge

One major challenge for everyday technology designers is measurement of prior knowledge, which is often discussed rather vaguely as noted above. Yet, we also described different types of prior knowledge (KiH) to which users attributed technology success. Thus, one challenge is developing a framework that can guide assessment of users' KiH. Several research groups (Blackler, et al., 2003; Hurtienne & Langdon, 2009; Serrano Baquero & Rogers, 2010) have developed taxonomies of knowledge sources that can inform technology design. Table 2 shows that these taxonomies differ in their categorization approaches, though together they suggest that several knowledge bases (technology, task domain, and cultural) are accessed. Each taxonomy has been tested for specific projects, but none has yet been tested broadly.

Besides knowing the types of relevant knowledge that might be identified through a taxonomy, designers must also know the depth and fluency of this knowledge. This fluency has been estimated by frequency of technology experience, but some researchers have questioned whether prior experience effectively reflects technology knowledge, especially if the experience required little effort. Therefore, researchers have developed approaches that measure not only users' prior exposure to relevant technologies but also their competence with these technologies (e.g., Hurtienne, Horn, & Langdon, 2010). Competence has been evaluated through multiple-choice tests of declarative and procedural knowledge of the relevant technologies as well as behavioral tests completed on PCs and the Internet (Arning & Ziefle, 2008; Sengpiel & Wandke, 2010). These tests have shown some predictive value for new computer and Internet applications, but their predictive capabilities for other technologies are not yet known.

Similarly, competency tests may be useful for estimating relevant domain knowledge. For example, the Test of Functional Health Literacy in Adults is commonly used to evaluate oral literacy, print literacy, numeracy, and conceptual health knowledge of individuals and to predict their proficiency for using resources in the health care system (Baker, 2006). Health literacy was one success factor in effective use of a technology designed to improve medication adherence (Ownby, 2006), suggesting that users' domain knowledge and technical knowledge must be evaluated for design of effective technologies and related instructional support.

Metacognition

Knowledge of specific technical components and domain procedures is likely to be needed for success with particular products based on their proposed design and target task. However, our research also suggests that understanding users' metacognitive knowledge about technology is crucial for enhancing technology adoption. Metacognitive knowledge refers to a user's knowledge and beliefs about three types of variables that interact to influence success with specific cognitive tasks (Flavell, 1979). First are beliefs about oneself and others with respect to task processing, such as one's computer self-efficacy. Second is task information that can be used during the task such as familiarity with the interaction techniques for a particular technology. Third is knowledge of strategies that are effective for achieving task goals such as knowing that manuals are helpful for performing maintenance tasks.

Many studies have confirmed that lower computer self-efficacy is associated with lower technology adoption (e.g., Czaja, et al., 2006; Yi & Hwang, 2003), but limited research has examined metacognitive task and strategy variables for successful technology use. In our diary study (O'Brien, 2010) we observed that participants described more specific task knowledge when problems were resolved. For example, a participant trying to replace a toner cartridge on her printer examined the alignment of the existing cartridge carefully before removing it. She also remembered having heard an audible click when the new cartridge was seated properly. In contrast, participants described strategy knowledge very clearly for successes and problems. Several low-tech older adults reported that they select times and places when they will not be interrupted to complete tasks. Several high-tech older adults described the importance of following manuals exactly, especially for maintenance tasks. More research is needed to identify metacognitive knowledge that facilitates successful encounters.

As this knowledge is identified, recommendations for everyday technology design can be developed to facilitate metacognitive planning, monitoring, and evaluation based on Kirsh's (2004) proposal for improving elearning systems. Specifically, Kirsh recommended that visual layouts and workflow be organized to lead users to interact with a system in the most cognitively efficient manner, particularly by setting users' expectations and guiding attention to feedback and next steps. Because users interact with many everyday technologies such as cars and kitchen tools through the other senses, research must also investigate design elements that guide effective metacognition for auditory, olfactory, and tactile interactions.

Age Differences in Basic Technical Knowledge

Several studies (O'Brien, 2010; Zickuhr, 2011) have identified older adults who use recent technologies at similar rates to younger adults. However, usage frequency may not translate into similar levels of technical knowledge. For example, differences in the age at which a technology was first used and the number of predecessor technologies may cultivate different association networks and knowledge fluency.

Docampo Rama's (2001) studies on the technology-general procedural knowledge of adults across the lifespan suggested that age cohorts form 'technology generations' based on technologies available during their formative years. For example, she identified an "electromechanical generation" of older adults (born before 1940) who had primarily interacted with devices featuring 1-1 interaction between a button (or rotary dial selection) and a single function during their formative years. She also identified a "layered menu" generation cohort (born after 1970) who had primarily interacted with menu-based software populated with visual elements for navigation during their formative years. Within each generation, she proposed that the defining interface would be the broadest and most accessible even if users learned new interface styles. Monk (2009) highlighted the challenge in defining interface styles for a specific technology generation when he described technology knowledge changes based on when individuals live (i.e., the succession of functions, controls, and feedback for relevant technologies) compared to the simpler approach of merely noting how long they have lived.

Although Docampo Rama's (2001) research focused on age-related differences for interfaces and procedural knowledge, age cohorts may exist at the functional level as well (Stone, 2010). This functional knowledge may not only inform users about possible task goals and domain vocabulary, but also alternative methods for accomplishing tasks if technologies fail. For example, college students who have always conducted literature reviews using the Internet may find it difficult to conduct research in university libraries. Thus, older adults may actually have an advantage over younger adults because of the variety of technologies used over their life span to perform a task.

To illustrate possible effects of experience with predecessor technologies, we reviewed technologies that an American adult born in 1933 could have used for listening to music. At least ten devices were identified including a record player, radio, jukebox, cassette player, 8-track player, walkman, CD player, Internet radio, MP3 player, and smartphone. Users would have learned typical functions such as volume, play, and skip on one music technology that could be transferred to a new one (Reed & Monk, 2004).

Research has not, however, clearly identified how users learn completely new functions on novel technologies that did not exist on predecessor technologies. Younger users may have the advantage for learning these features because their lower experience with the function makes them less confident of their approach to the function and more dependent on information on the technology itself. With this strategy, a user may iterate access

of KiH (e.g., prior knowledge that the function is typically available for this task) and KiW (e.g., labels on the device) in a trial and error fashion until feedback (e.g., music playing) indicates that the goal has been accomplished. Attention to information on the technology may be particularly helpful for technologies undergoing a rapid pace of change such as mobile devices.

Interference from Prior Knowledge

Knowledge of predecessor technologies may be helpful in learning to use new technologies, but this knowledge may also interfere with correct use. For example, one high-tech older adult in our diary study (O'Brien, 2010) reported difficulty using several functions on the new email interface updated by his Internet provider because they were not the same as he had learned to use very successfully on the previous email version. Another high-tech older adult was hesitant at upgrading software because she had heard that the new interface was quite different to use. These reports of actual or expected interference are not new to technology interactions as Willis, Dolan, and Bertrand (1999) reported that 22% of errors in everyday problem-solving could be attributed to incorrect reliance on prior knowledge. These reports are troubling, though, because designers may not know in advance which prior knowledge is helpful and which is interfering. No design recommendations exist with guidance on how to elicit helpful prior knowledge and inhibit interfering prior knowledge. Thus, research is needed to identify design factors that manage multiple sources of prior knowledge effectively.

Identifying ways to mitigate interference may be particularly important for the design of technologies for older adults because of typical age-related declines that affect technology use (Rogers, O'Brien, & Fisk, 2012). For example, perceptual declines may obscure differences between features on the old and new technologies. Functional field of view, which allows users to

Figure 1. Conceptual framework of factors that influence everyday technology interactions

find possible items with a single glance, is also typically smaller, so older adults may have to intentionally look around the device more to identify feedback and feedforward information. Understanding older adults' use of metacognition in everyday technology encounters may provide clues about task and strategy knowledge that can be managed through design to reduce the need for prior knowledge use.

Solutions and Recommendations

Everyday Technology Framework

Figure 1 illustrates the factors that influence everyday technology interactions as discussed in this chapter. Note first that the user's prior knowledge (KiH) is at the core of the interaction, providing information from four different knowledge bases. The user's current disposition, including mood,

stress levels, attitude, and motivation, will also influence the interaction by influencing attentional capacity and direction. The user's task goal (or subjective experience) will also influence the interaction, potentially by shaping the user's current disposition and by prescribing the metacognitive knowledge that should be used. Lastly, information from the environment (KiW) can influence the interaction by cuing relevant KiH and filling in KiH gaps. This framework may be helpful for examining representative user interactions to identify relevant components that can be influenced by design.

Product and Instructional Designers

The most important factor for design of everyday technologies is including representative users in the development process from the beginning. Early in the process, designers should gather data about the technical and functional knowledge of older adults for the target product. Because context can provide users with important cues about how to use everyday technologies, designers should also collect data about older adults' activities in the target domain. Observations and interviews will be helpful techniques for gathering such information. In addition, storytelling techniques can elicit information about where, when, why, and how technologies are used (Gausepohl, Winchester, Arthur, & Smith-Jackson, 2011). During iterative design phases, older adults should participate in usability tests of the technologies to confirm that the task knowledge provided on the technology fits with prior knowledge and current goals (see Fisk, Rogers, Charness, Czaja, & Sharit, 2009, for guidelines about including older adults in the design process).

Design guidelines must accommodate typical age-related declines. For example, research on programming digital thermostats suggested that designers provide task knowledge on the device that guides older users through an optimal path rather than exposing all features simultaneously and giving the user complete freedom (Freudenthal & Mook, 2003). This procedural approach may be particularly important for older adults because it reduces the load on working memory by reminding users of the task goal to ensure they are selecting options toward that path and can recognize if they have been diverted. Usability test scripts should be developed to evaluate this task knowledge for both successful and unsuccessful selections. For specific guidelines for technology in general see Fisk et al. (2009); for display design see Pak and McLaughlin (2010); and for telehealth technologies see Charness, Demiris, and Krupinski (2011).

In addition to conducting usability testing of everyday technologies with older adults, usability testing of instructional support should also be conducted (Mykityshyn, Fisk, & Rogers, 2002). Although older adults reportedly use manuals

(Mitzner, et al., 2008; Tsai, Lee, & Rogers, 2012), they have also complained that instructions can be insufficient and confusing (O'Brien, 2010). Czaja and Lee (2003) summarized best practices for instructional design including good organization and use of language familiar to older adults for the target tasks.

Trainers

Users typically do not learn to use everyday technologies through formal training programs, but recommendations for training older adults can be helpful in developing instructional support materials such as demonstration videos used for everyday technologies such as medical devices (Mykityshyn, et al., 2002). For example, Mitzner et al. (2010) suggested that trainers emphasize the benefits of a technology during training to increase adoption. Listed benefits can also frame the training content because they specify typical procedures and task goals that users need to learn. Fisk et al. (2009) also suggested that trainers provide practice tasks and consider environmental support during training. They also emphasized that users be allowed to experience making and recovering from mistakes to gain confidence in their ability to use the technologies on their own.

These recommendations also apply to informal training, which is a large part of everyday technology use (O'Brien, 2010). From a consumer perspective, people who typically dispense technologies to older adults such as medical personnel and car salespeople could increase technology effectiveness and constituent satisfaction with specific techniques that guide older adults in using their technologies correctly. Family and friends may also be less frustrated trying to help older adults if they can learn specifically how typical declines affect technology use and ways to mitigate the effects of these declines during "helping" sessions. Both audiences may benefit from their own instructional videos or guidelines demonstrating effective techniques.

Older Adult Users

In our diary study (O'Brien, 2010) we identified several recommendations from older adults that may enhance adoption of everyday technologies by other older adults. First, older adults discussed strategies for managing their environment to reduce distractions, especially from other people. High-tech older adults mentioned this strategy when they were using a new technology or completing a complex task such as maintenance. Low-tech older adults used this strategy even for frequent technologies such as washing machines, but they may have adopted this strategy to avoid problems because their lower level of experience made recovery generally more difficult. Indeed, several reported problems ensued because older adults tried to use new or infrequent technologies and functions in busy environments without adequate support. Therefore, self-enforcement of this recommended strategy to prepare for new and complex encounters may increase efficiency and effectiveness.

Second, older adults reported helping each other to use everyday technologies successfully. Sometimes this help occurred in an organized manner with one high-tech older adult assisting a low-tech older adult as might be expected. Sometimes, though, this help occurred on an ad hoc basis such as in a community center when trying to watch a DVD or navigating a new public transportation environment. Typically, this peer-to-peer help was successful for providing encouragement and "another set of eyes and ears" in using an everyday technology for which knowledge was fairly similar among the users. Thus, even beyond functional or technical expertise, social support itself may be an effective way to mitigate some typically age-related declines.

FUTURE DIRECTIONS

Technological innovations are changing the way people complete many everyday tasks through redesigned interfaces, more widespread broadband Internet access, and increased mobile computing capabilities. For older adults to continue benefitting from these innovations, designers of technologies and instructional support should continue to monitor research findings and trends in three areas. First, design practices should evolve to help older adults to complete everyday tasks successfully with appropriate metacognitive guidance. Second, environmental and contextual support should be provided that effectively assist older adults who have varied preferences and levels of technology experience. Third, applications should be selected and customized to add value for older adults by improving how current activities are performed, integrating them into existing routines and environments, and newly enabling relevant tasks.

Good Design through Metacognition

Many design guidelines focus on trying to make technologies easy to use, often by leveraging users' familiarity with other technologies and by providing useful feedback. As discussed in this chapter, though, both techniques are challenging to implement because they rely on understanding users' prior knowledge, even though that prior knowledge may interfere with correct usage. Researchers should develop approaches for designers to better describe and manage prior knowledge, but designers can also improve user interactions by providing appropriate metacognitive guidance. This guidance may be specific task knowledge that unobtrusively steers users to efficient interactions. Guidance may also be strategic knowledge that advises users that effort or external support are needed for specific tasks. Both approaches emphasize interaction effectiveness, even at the expense of ease of use, to increase users' implicit knowledge and to build users' technology self-efficacy and potentially lead to higher long-term adoption.

Useful Support

The Internet is already changing the way people use other technologies by enabling access to recent support information, but more information is not necessarily better. For example, older adults use the Internet to find technical support from manufacturer sites and unofficial support sites updated by user groups (O'Brien, 2010). Participants were pleased that they could find general information and specific answers to their questions through a combination of these resources. Yet, participants also reported frustration when they could not find specific information or when using the resources required more extensive technical backgrounds than they had. More research is needed to understand how to provide support information on the Internet that can be easily accessed by target users (Czaja, Sharit, Hernandez, Nair, & Loewenstein, 2010).

Alternative methods of support must be identified as well for older adults who prefer in-person transactions or have limited PC capabilities. Individuals who prefer in-person transactions such as the low-technology older adults in our diary study (O'Brien, 2010) were also less likely to describe technology details clearly in their descriptions of everyday technology problems. Yet, these same individuals were quite open and verbose at describing the context of their encounters to the experimenter. This suggests two success factors for supporting these individuals' technology problems. First, the helper must have direct access to the technology with which they are providing assistance, either in person or through remote access. Second, the helper should provide the social cues expected in human-human interaction. Future technologies may enable this kind of support, but informal communities of peer support may be equally effective.

Innovative Applications

As technology advancement continues, there will be a broader array of products and systems that can be used to augment the ability of older adults to perform everyday tasks. We provide a couple of illustrative examples here.

Consider a technology coach. Older adults often have to (or want to) learn to interact with new devices and systems, as evidenced in our diary study (O'Brien, 2010). How might technology be harnessed to aid in the learning process? Rogers, Essa, and Fisk (2007) developed a computer vision system that monitored a user's interaction with a medical device in the home and provided feedback if an error was made. This system enabled users to make fewer errors as they learned how to use the device.

Robotics is also a rapidly advancing field that has much potential to support the needs of older adults. For example, robots are currently being designed to support many everyday activities of older adults (Smarr, Fausset, & Rogers, 2011). Importantly, older individuals seem to be quite receptive to the idea of having robots in their home to support a range of activities, especially chores (Ezer, Fisk, & Rogers, 2009a, 2009b).

The same design issues exist for these innovative applications as for other technologies discussed in this chapter. How does the user interact with the (coach, robot, etc.)? How should information be provided to support goal achievement? How can a user's prior knowledge or expectation enhance or impede the interaction? Involving older adults early in the design process will yield considerable payoffs for ultimate design success.

CONCLUSION

Modern technology continues to advance and evolve. Older adults will want or need to use new technologies to complete their everyday activities. The goal of designers is to ensure successful, efficient, safe, and enjoyable interactions. Our goal in the present chapter was to provide insights into factors that must be considered in design for aging.

Older adults have a wealth of knowledge that will transfer to their interactions with new products or systems; sometimes the transfer will be positive and ease use but other times it may be negative and hinder use. This prior knowledge represents a challenging concept for designers to harness successfully to improve interactions. Therefore, knowledge must also be provided externally, in the design itself, either to provide direction about what to do (feedforward) or information about what one just did (feedback). Moreover, instructional design has a critical role to play even beyond formal training development.

Future technologies may be the medium for performing tasks, but they may also be the method for providing instruction, guidance, and feedback. However, we must remain vigilant in designing the future so as to ensure that all segments of the population can benefit from technologies' potential.

REFERENCES

Arning, K., & Ziefle, M. (2008). Development and validation of a computer expertise questionnaire for older adults. *Behaviour & Information Technology*, *27*, 89–93. doi:10.1080/01449290701760633

Baker, D. W. (2006). The meaning and the measure of health literacy. *Journal of General Internal Medicine*, *21*, 878–883. doi:10.1111/j.1525-1497.2006.00540.x

Blackler, A., Popovic, V., & Mahar, D. (2003). The nature of intuitive use of products: An experimental approach. *Design Studies*, *24*, 491–506. doi:10.1016/S0142-694X(03)00038-3

Blanson Henkemans, O. A., Rogers, W. A., Fisk, A. D., Neerincx, M. A., Lindenberg, J., & van der Mast, C. A. P. G. (2008). Usability of an adaptive computer assistant that improves self-care and health literacy of older adults. *Methods of Information in Medicine*, *47*, 82–88.

Charness, N., Demiris, G., & Krupinski, E. (2011). *Designing telehealth for an aging population: A human factors perspective*. Boca Raton, FL: CRC Press.

Czaja, S. J., Charness, N., Fisk, A. D., Hertzog, C., Nair, S. N., Rogers, W. A., & Sharit, J. (2006). Factors predicting the use of technology: Findings from the center for research and education on aging and technology enhancement (CREATE). *Psychology and Aging*, *21*, 333–352. doi:10.1037/0882-7974.21.2.333

Czaja, S. J., & Lee, C. D. (2003). Designing computer systems for older adults. In Jacko, J. A., & Sears, A. (Eds.), *The Human-Computer Interaction Handbook: Fundamentals, Evolving Technologies, and Emerging Applications* (pp. 413–427). Mahwah, NJ: Erlbaum.

Czaja, S. J., Sharit, J., Hernandez, M. A., Nair, S. N., & Loewenstein, D. (2010). Variability among older adults in Internet health information-seeking performance. *Gerontechnology (Valkenswaard)*, *9*, 46–55. doi:10.4017/gt.2010.09.01.004.00

Docampo Rama, M. (2001). *Technology generations: Handling complex user interfaces*. Unpublished Dissertation. Eindhoven, The Netherlands: Technical University of Eindhoven.

Ezer, N., Fisk, A. D., & Rogers, W. A. (2009a). Attitudinal and intentional acceptance of domestic robots by younger and older adults. *Lecture Notes in Computer Science*, *5615*, 39–48. doi:10.1007/978-3-642-02710-9_5

Ezer, N., Fisk, A. D., & Rogers, W. A. (2009b). More than a servant: Self-reported willingness of younger and older adults to having a robot perform interactive and critical tasks in the home. In *Proceedings of the Human Factors and Ergonomics Society 53rd Annual Meeting,* (pp. 136-140). Santa Monica, CA: Human Factors and Ergonomics Society.

Fisk, A. D., Rogers, W. A., Charness, N., Czaja, S. J., & Sharit, J. (2009). *Designing for older adults: Principles and creative human factors approaches* (2nd ed.). Boca Raton, FL: CRC Press.

Flavell, J. H. (1979). Metacognitive and cognitive monitoring: A new area of cognitive developmental inquiry. *The American Psychologist, 34,* 906–911. doi:10.1037/0003-066X.34.10.906

Freudenthal, A., & Mook, H. J. (2003). The evaluation of an innovative intelligent thermostat interface: Universal usability and age differences. *Cognition Technology and Work, 5,* 55–66.

Freudenthal, T. D. (1998). *Learning to use interactive devices: Age differences in the reasoning process.* Unpublished Dissertation. Eindhoven, The Netherlands: Eindhoven University of Technology.

Gausepohl, K., Winchester, W. W., Arthur, J. D., & Smith-Jackson, T. (2011). Using storytelling to elicit design guidance for medical devices. *Ergonomics in Design, 19,* 19–24. doi:10.1177/1064804611408017

Horgan, A. L., Wilms, H.-U., & Baltes, M. M. (1998). Daily life in very old age: Everyday activities as expression of successful living. *The Gerontologist, 38,* 556–568. doi:10.1093/geront/38.5.556

Hurtienne, J. Horn, & Langdon, P. (2010). Facets of prior experience and their impact on product usability for older users. In P. M. Langdon, P. J. Clarkson, & P. Robinson (Eds.), *Designing Inclusive Interactions,* (pp. 123-132). London, UK: Springer.

Hurtienne, J., & Langdon, P. (2009). *Prior knowledge in inclusive design: The older, the more intuitive?* Paper presented at the 23rd British Computer Society Human Computer Interaction Workshop and Conference (HCI 2009). Cambridge, UK.

International Standards Organization. (2006). *Ease of operation of everyday products – Part 1: Design requirements for context of use and user characteristics.* ISO Standard 20282-1:2006(E). Geneva, Switzerland: International Standards Organization.

Kang, N. W., & Yoon, W. C. (2008). Age- and experience related user behavior differences in the use of complicated electronic devices. *International Journal of Human-Computer Studies, 66,* 425–437. doi:10.1016/j.ijhcs.2007.12.003

Katz, S., Ford, A. B., Moskovitz, R. W., Jackson, B. A., & Jaffe, M. W. (1963). Studies of illness in the aged: The index of ADL: A standardized measure of biological and psychosocial function. *Journal of the American Medical Association, 185*(12), 914–919. doi:10.1001/jama.1963.03060120024016

Kirsh, D. (2005). Metacognition, distributed cognition, and visual design. In Gardinfors, P., & Johansson, P. (Eds.), *Cognition, Education and Communication Technology* (pp. 147–180). New York, NY: Routledge.

Langdon, P., Lewis, T., & Clarkson, J. (2007). The effects of prior experience on the use of consumer products. *Universal Access in the Information Society, 6,* 179–191. doi:10.1007/s10209-007-0082-z

Lawton, M. P. (1990). Aging and performance on home tasks. *Human Factors, 32,* 527–536.

McBride, S. E., Beer, J. M., Mitzner, T. L., & Rogers, W. A. (2011). Challenges for home health care providers: A needs assessment. *Physical & Occupational Therapy in Geriatrics, 29*, 5–22. doi:10.3109/02703181.2011.552170

Mitzner, T. L., Boron, J. B., Fausset, C. B., Adams, A. E., Charness, N., & Czaja, S. J. (2010). Older adults talk technology: Their usage and attitudes. *Computers in Human Behavior, 26*, 1710–1721. doi:10.1016/j.chb.2010.06.020

Mitzner, T. L., Fausset, C. B., Boron, J. B., Adams, A. E., Dijkstra, K., Lee, C. C., & Fisk, A. D. (2008). Older adults' training preferences for learning to use technology. In *Proceedings of the Human Factors and Ergonomics Society 52nd Annual Meeting,* (pp. 2047-2051). Santa Monica, CA: Human Factors and Ergonomics Society.

Monk, A. (2009). *Why do the older old have problems with new domestic technologies?* Paper presented at Towards a Truly Inclusive Digital Economy. London, UK. Retrieved from http://www.computing.dundee.ac.uk/projects/iden/londonevent.asp

Morrow, D. G., & Rogers, W. A. (2008). Environmental support: An integrative framework. *Human Factors, 50*, 589–613. doi:10.1518/001872008X312251

Mykityshyn, A. L., Fisk, A. D., & Rogers, W. A. (2002). Learning to use a home medical device: Mediating age-related differences with training. *Human Factors, 44*, 354–364. doi:10.1518/0018720024497727

Norman, D. A. (2002). *The design of everyday things.* New York, NY: Basic Books.

O'Brien, M. A. (2010). *Understanding human-technology interactions: The role of prior experience and age.* Unpublished Doctoral Dissertation. Atlanta, GA: Georgia Institute of Technology.

O'Brien, M. A., Weger, K., DeFour, M. E., & Reeves, S. M. (2011). Examining the role of age and experience on use of knowledge in the world for everyday technology interactions. In *Proceedings of the Human Factors and Ergonomics Society 55th Annual Meeting,* (pp 177-181). Santa Monica, CA: Human Factors and Ergonomics Society.

Olson, K. E., O'Brien, M. A., Rogers, W. A., & Charness, N. (2011). Diffusion of technology for younger and older adults. *Ageing International, 36*(1), 123–145. doi:10.1007/s12126-010-9077-9

Ownby, R. (2006). Medication adherence and cognition: Medical, personal and economic factors influence level of adherence in older adults. *Geriatrics, 61*(2), 30–35.

Pak, R., & McLaughlin, A. C. (2010). *Designing displays for older adults.* Boca Raton, FL: CRC Press.

Polson, P. G., & Lewis, C. H. (1990). Theory-based design for easily learned interfaces. *Human-Computer Interaction, 5*, 191–220. doi:10.1207/s15327051hci0502&3_3

Reason, J. T. (1990). *Human error.* Cambridge, UK: Cambridge University Press.

Reed, D. J., & Monk, A. (2004). Using familiar technologies in unfamiliar ways and learning from the old about the new. *Universal Access in the Information Society, 3*, 114–121. doi:10.1007/s10209-004-0090-1

Rogers, W. A., Essa, I. A., & Fisk, A. D. (2007). Designing a technology coach. *Ergonomics in Design, 15*, 17–23. doi:10.1177/106480460701500303

Rogers, W. A., Meyer, B., Walker, N., & Fisk, A. D. (1998). Functional limitations to daily living tasks in the aged: A focus group analysis. *Human Factors, 40*, 111–125. doi:10.1518/001872098779480613

Rogers, W. A., O'Brien, M. A., & Fisk, A. D. (2013). Cognitive engineering to support successful aging. In Lee, J. D., & Kirlik, A. (Eds.), *Oxford Handbook of Cognitive Engineering*. Oxford, UK: Oxford University Press.

Sengpiel, M., & Wandke, H. (2010). Compensating the effects of age differences in computer literacy on the use of ticket vending machines through minimal video instruction. *Occupational Ergonomics, 9*(2), 87–98.

Serrano Baquero, D., & Rogers, W. A. (2010). *Knowledge and intuitive interface design: Developing a knowledge taxonomy*. Atlanta, GA: Georgia Institute of Technology.

Sinnott, J. D., & Clark, J. (1989). An overview – if not a taxonomy – of "everyday problems" used in research. In Sinnott, J. D. (Ed.), *Everyday Problem Solving: Theory and Applications* (pp. 40–54). New York, NY: Praeger.

Smarr, C. A., Fausset, C. B., & Rogers, W. A. (2011). *Understanding the potential for robot assistance for older adults in the home environment*. Atlanta, GA: Georgia Institute of Technology.

Stone, B. (2010). Old fogies by their 20s. *The New York Times*. Retrieved from http://www.nytimes.com

Tsai, W. C., Lee, C. F., & Rogers, W. A. (in press). Older adults' motivations, patterns, and improvised strategies of using product manuals. *International Journal of Design*.

Vrkljan, B., & Miller Polgar, J. (2007). *Driving safely in later life: exploring the older driver-passenger relationship*. Paper presented at TRANSED 2007 Conference. Montreal, Canada.

Willis, S. L., Dolan, M. M., & Bertrand, R. M. (1999). Problem-solving on health-related tasks of everyday living. In Park, D. C., Morrell, R. W., & Shifren, K. (Eds.), *Processing of Medical Information in Aging Patients* (pp. 199–219). Mahwah, NJ: Lawrence Erlbaum Associates.

Yi, M. Y., & Hwang, Y. (2003). Predicting the use of web-based information systems: Self-efficacy, enjoyment, learning goal orientation, and the technology acceptance model. *International Journal of Human-Computer Studies, 59*, 431–449. doi:10.1016/S1071-5819(03)00114-9

Zickuhr, K. (2011, February 3). *Generations and their gadgets*. Retrieved from http://www.pewinternet.org/Reports/2011/Generations-and-gadgets.aspx

ADDITIONAL READING

Boot, W., Nichols, T. A., Rogers, W. A., & Fisk, A. D. (2012). Design for aging. In Salvendy, G. (Ed.), *Handbook of Human Factors and Ergonomics* (4th ed.). Hoboken, NJ: John Wiley & Sons. doi:10.1002/9781118131350.ch52

Caine, K. E., Fisk, A. D., & Rogers, W. A. (2006). Benefits and privacy concerns of a home equipped with a visual sensing system: A perspective from older adults. In *Proceedings of the Human Factors and Ergonomics Society 50th Annual Meeting*, (pp. 180-184). Santa Monica, CA: Human Factors and Ergonomics Society.

Davis, F. D. (1989). Perceived usefulness, perceived ease of use and user acceptance of information technology. *Management Information Systems Quarterly, 13*, 319–339. doi:10.2307/249008

Dickinson, A., Arnott, J., & Prior, S. (2007). Methods for human-computer interaction research with older people. *Behaviour & Information Technology, 26*, 343–352. doi:10.1080/01449290601176948

Gorard, S., & Selwyn, N. (2008). The myth of the silver surfer. *Adults Learning, 19*(5), 28–30.

Hickman, J. M., Rogers, W. A., & Fisk, A. D. (2007). Training older adults to use new technology. *The Journals of Gerontology. Series B, Psychological Sciences and Social Sciences, 62B*, 77–84. doi:10.1093/geronb/62.special_issue_1.77

Mayhorn, C. B., Stronge, A. J., McLaughlin, A. C., & Rogers, W. A. (2004). Older adults, computer training, and the systems approach: A formula for success. *Educational Gerontology*, *30*, 185–203. doi:10.1080/03601270490272124

Mitzner, T. L., Smarr, C. A., Rogers, W. A., & Fisk, A. D. (2012). Aging, perception, and interface design. In Hoffman, R., & Szalma, J. (Eds.), *Handbook of Applied Perception Research*. Cambridge, UK: Cambridge University Press.

Mynatt, E. D., Melenhorst, A. S., Fisk, A. D., & Rogers, W. A. (2004). Aware technologies for aging in place: Understanding user needs and attitudes. *IEEE Pervasive Computing / IEEE Computer Society and IEEE Communications Society*, *3*, 36–41. doi:10.1109/MPRV.2004.1316816

Newell, A., Arnott, J., Carmichael, A., & Morgan, M. (2007). Methodologies for involving older adults in the design process: In *Proceedings of the 4th International Conference on Universal Access in Human Computer Interaction: Coping with Diversity*. Berlin, Germany: Springer-Verlag.

Rogers, W. A., & Fisk, A. D. (2010). Toward a psychological science of advanced technology design for older adults. *The Journals of Gerontology. Series B, Psychological Sciences and Social Sciences*, *65B*, 645–653. doi:10.1093/geronb/gbq065

Sanchez, J., Fisk, A. D., & Rogers, W. A. (2004). Reliability and age-related effects on trust and reliance of a decision-support aid. In *Proceedings of the Human Factors and Ergonomics Society 48th Annual Meeting*, (pp. 586-589). Santa Monica, CA: Human Factors & Ergonomics Society.

Selwyn, N. (2004). The information aged: A qualitative study of older adults' use of information and communications technology. *Journal of Aging Studies*, *18*, 369–384. doi:10.1016/j.jaging.2004.06.008

Wahl, H.-W., Oswald, F., & Zimprich, D. (1999). Everyday competence in visually impaired older adults: A case for person-environment perspectives. *The Gerontologist*, *39*, 140–149. doi:10.1093/geront/39.2.140

Wu, P., Preece, J., Shneiderman, B., Jaeger, P., & Qu, Y. (2007). Community response grids for older adults: Motivations, usability, and sociability. In *Proceedings of the 13th Americas Conference on Information Systems*. AMCIS.

KEY TERMS AND DEFINITIONS

Environmental Support: Environmental support is the information external to a user that assists in successful task completion. Environmental support includes instructions such as manuals, on-line information, and videos as well as on-device guidance such as labels and affordances. Another term that references similar information is Knowledge in the World.

Everyday Technology: Everyday technologies are technologies for the typical, ordinary activities of a particular population in their naturalistic environments, even if they are not used every day. They are usually used with little formal training or instruction.

Metacognition: Metacognition refers to a user's knowledge and beliefs that influence how they complete cognitive tasks. This knowledge includes beliefs about themselves and other people relevant to the task at hand, task-specific information, and information about possible strategies and selection criteria for these strategies.

Prior Knowledge: Prior knowledge is the information from a person's memory that assists in successful task completion. Prior knowledge includes both declarative and procedural memory and encompasses technical, domain, cultural, and metacognitive knowledge. Another term that references similar information is Knowledge in the Head.

Social Support: Social support refers to the individuals or groups of individuals who assist a user in performing tasks. The individuals may provide information and/or physical assistance. Social support may be accessed in several ways: explicitly or implicitly, synchronously or asynchronously, electronically or in-person.

Technology Generation: Technology generations are cohorts of similarly-aged individuals who used technologies with a common interface style during their formative years. This early experience makes the common interface style more easily accessible for fluent usage throughout their life even if an individual subsequently learns other interface styles.

Trial and Error: The trial and error strategy used in everyday technology interactions is an iterative approach by which the user guesses which action to take next by comparing available options to their understanding of the task goal or intermediate milestone. Little cognitive effort or attention is typically expended during this strategy, leading to little explicit knowledge of the task or technology.

Chapter 7
Internet Use among Older Adults:
Constraints and Opportunities

Yiwei Chen
Bowling Green State University, USA

Bob D. Lee
Bowling Green State University, USA

Robert M. Kirk
Bowling Green State University, USA

ABSTRACT

Older adults (65 and above) are the fastest growing population to use computers and the Internet in their everyday lives. The primary purpose of this chapter is to use a Lifespan Developmental Perspective to examine both the constraints and the opportunities of Internet use among older adults. Given age-related changes in physical, cognitive, and socio-emotional processes, older adults may encounter different constraints in Internet use from younger adults. The Selective Optimization with Compensation model is used to explore opportunities for older adults in using the Internet to improve quality of life. Future product designs and training programs should take into account older adults' physical and cognitive limitations, as well as their socio-emotional needs. It is also recommended that social policies should help older adults overcome these constraints in order to reduce age-related digital divide and promote quality of life for older adults.

DOI: 10.4018/978-1-4666-1966-1.ch007

INTRODUCTION

People around the world expect to live longer in the new millennium. Advances in medicine and health technologies have made significant contributions in extending longevity. Data from the Centers for Disease Control and Prevention estimate the average life expectancies of men and women in the U.S. at 75.7 and 80.6 years respectively (Kochanek, Xu, Murphy, Minino, & Kung, 2011). It is projected that by the year 2030, one in five, or 70 million people in the United States will be age 65 or older (U.S. Census Bureau, 2000). As the oldest members of the Baby Boomer generation reach age 65 in 2011, we face a rapidly aging society not only in the U.S., but all across the globe as well.

The new millennium has also witnessed tremendous growth in computer-based information technology. The influence of information technology has been profound, particularly with regard to the Internet. It is estimated that 2.09 billion people, or 30.2% of the global population, are current Internet users; this figure has exploded from 360 million in December of 2000, resulting in a 480.6% increase of Internet users over the past decade (Internet World Stats, 2011). Much like aging populations around the world, the rate of growth for Internet use is staggering. For better or worse, the Internet has changed the way many people live their lives, but what happens when a rapidly aging society collides with rapidly increasing computer-based information technology?

Older adults (65 years old and above) are the fastest growing population who use computers and the Internet in their everyday lives (Hart, Chaparro, & Halcomb, 2008). In the year 1996, only 2% of Americans aged 65 and older went online, whereas in the year 2004, about 22% of Americans over 65 reported using the Internet (Fox, 2004). Older adults do all sorts of activities on the Internet: from email to playing online games, from information searching (e.g., health, travel, leisure, etc.) to using government and community services, and

from shopping to banking (Lee, Chen, & Hewitt, 2011). There seems to be great benefits for older adults using the Internet. For example, older Internet users reported positive experiences such as reduced feelings of loneliness and depression, and enhanced feelings of connection, competence, and psychological well-being (Chen & Persson, 2002; Gatto & Tak, 2008). At the same time, however, a digital divide has been reported in "developed" countries such as the United States and some European countries (Gilleard & Higgs, 2008). Compared to younger adults, older adults seem to be reluctant to adopt new digital technology such as the Internet (Charness & Boot, 2009). According to the Pew Tracking Survey in 2007 (http://www.pewinternet.org), there were 39% of older Americans between 65-74 years old who used the Internet, compared to 85% in the age range of 18-24, 25-34, and 35-44 years old. What factors may contribute to the new digital divide? What kinds of constraints and opportunities would older adults have in Internet use?

The primary purpose of this chapter is to use the Lifespan Developmental Perspective (Baltes, 1987) to examine both the constraints and the opportunities older adults may encounter in using the Internet. The Lifespan Developmental Perspective proposes many important theoretical concepts in understanding the lifespan development of human behavior, such as intelligence. When it comes to new technologies, people often assume the stereotype that "you can't teach an old dog new tricks." Contradicting this assumption, the Lifespan Developmental Perspective suggests that development is a life-long process and understanding the dynamics between gains and losses is crucial for supporting older adults in their learning and use of information technologies.

More specifically, the chapter will be organized as follows: First, we will introduce the theoretical framework of the Lifespan Developmental Perspective and review age-related changes in physical, cognitive, and socio-emotional processes. Second, we will use our own study to illustrate how to use the Lifespan Developmental Perspective to identify constraints of Internet use among older adults. Third, we will apply the Selective Optimization with Compensation model (Baltes & Baltes, 1990) to explore opportunities of Internet use among older adults. Implications in product designs and training programs will also be discussed. Finally, we will present our conclusion and point out future directions.

THE LIFESPAN DEVELOPMENTAL PERSPECTIVE AND PSYCHOLOGICAL CHANGES IN LATER ADULTHOOD

The Lifespan Developmental Perspective (Baltes, 1987) studies constancy and change in behavior throughout the life course from conception to death. It has several major propositions and we will use it as a theoretical framework to discuss age-related changes in physical, cognitive, and socio-emotional processes, as they are relevant to Internet use among older adults.

First, the Lifespan Developmental Perspective states that ontogenetic development is a life-long process. No age period holds supremacy in regulating the nature of development. With respect to learning and using information technology, younger adults may be quicker to adopt new technology, but there is no reason for accepting the digital divide in Internet use in later life, especially when there is a plethora of literature documenting computer learning and usage among older adults (Kim, 2008). According to Baltes (1987), the notion of life-long development implies two aspects: 1) development extends over the entire life span; and 2) life-long development may involve processes of change that do not originate at birth but lie in later periods of the life span.

Baltes (1987) describes lifespan development as *multidimensional* and *multidirectional* in that, some psychological processes may show age-related increases whereas others may exhibit

stability or decreases in functioning. He used the psychometric theory of fluid-crystallized intelligence proposed by Cattell (1971) and Horn (1982) as an example. Intelligence consists of several major components. Fluid intelligence refers to one's mental abilities on how quickly one's brain processes a signal and how well information is organized (e.g. attention, working memory, processing speed, etc.); crystallized intelligence represents one's mental abilities that depend on life experiences and education (e.g., vocabulary, world knowledge, wisdom, etc.). Whereas fluid intelligence typically shows decline in later adulthood, crystallized intelligence usually exhibits stability or even increase throughout adulthood (Schaie, 1996).

In the area of adult development and aging, there is still much debate about when exactly is the turning point for fluid intelligence. Aartsen, Smith, van Tilburg, Knopscheer, and Degg (2002) suggested that cognitive decline may begin after midlife, but most often occurs at higher ages (70 or higher). Meanwhile, Ronnlund, Nyberg, Backman, and Nilsson (2005) reported little or no drop in performance before age 55. Salthouse (2009), on the other hand, demonstrated that certain cognitive abilities began to experience declines as early as young adulthood, in their 20s. Although there are some inconsistencies in the literature as to when these changes begin to occur, there seems to be a common agreement that fluid intelligence shows various degrees of decline in older adults.

When we examine Internet use among older adults, age-related changes in the following cognitive abilities may be especially relevant. Sensory register is one of the abilities in which we start to see these decreases with aging (Anstey, 2008). As Schneider and Pichora-Fuller (2000) point out, sensory variables have a unique effect on cognition because they influence perception. Vision and audition are both known to play an important role in this relationship. One study showed, however, that whereas auditory acuity predicted changes in memory performance, visual acuity was found to be a stronger predictor of memory decline (Valentijn, et. al., 2005). Such sensory register deficits can also make it difficult for older adults to navigate details of stimuli and/or perform multiple tasks at the same time in everyday life. For instance, making conversation while driving, browsing websites with multiple pull-down menus and pop-ups on a computer screen, etc. This is not to say that many older adults cannot perform these tasks. On the contrary, of course they can, but they may require some assistance in doing so. Corrective lenses, hearing aids, medical procedures (e.g., Lasik surgery and cochlear implants), and "senior friendly" web designs can all help offset these deficits.

Research has consistently shown a negative relationship between age and working memory (Old & Naveh-Benjamin, 2008; Bopp & Verhaeghen, 2005). Working memory is generally defined as "the preservation of information while simultaneously processing the same or other information" (Salthouse & Babcock, 1991). It is distinguished from short-term memory in that, short-term memory only requires maintenance, but working memory requires both maintenance and processing. Park et al. (2002) examined age differences for both short-term and working memory in young and older adults. They found that, whereas all measures of short-term and working memory decreased with age, these differences were significantly larger for working memory. In addition, the age-related differences they found became even more salient as the level of processing became more demanding. These findings supported the conclusion that younger adults were more adept than older adults at working memory tasks. For information seeking on the Internet, working memory is an important cognitive ability that influences search performance (Czaja, et al., 2006). In a simulated telecommuting task, Sharit et al. (2004) found that attention, memory span, and perceptual speed strongly predicted older adults' search performance.

In addition, processing speed has been shown to slow down throughout adulthood, with some research pointing to gradual and almost unnoticeable decreases at first, followed by pronouncedly more rapid decline as we continue into later adulthood (Salthouse, 2009). Another study found processing speed to be a leading indicator on age-related changes in memory and spatial ability (Finkel, McArdle, Reynolds, & Pedersen, 2007). Slower psychomotor speed and information processing speed may pose challenges for older adults to learn and use information technology. For example, Czaja et al. (2006) found that fluid intelligence (including measures of processing speed) was the strongest predictor of technology use.

However, it should be noted that there are a wide range of abilities encompassed by cognition; therefore, some areas may see deficits earlier on while others do not exhibit losses until considerably later. Baltes (1987) pointed out that much intraindividual *plasticity* (or within-person variability) has been demonstrated in life-long development. Plasticity refers to the potential that each individual has for different forms of behavior and development, which is modified by health behavior habits and psychosocial factors such as personality processes and social context (Aldwin, Spiro, & Park, 2006). The key developmental agenda, according to Baltes (1987), is searching for individual plasticity's range and its age-related changes and limits. Cognitive training research with the elderly has provided strong evidence that older adults are able to learn and improve their cognitive performance in a variety of cognitive tasks (Willis & Schaie, 1986). For example, after a brief cognitive training program, many older adults between 60 and 80 years old exhibited levels of performance comparable with untrained young adults.

Further, *development as gain/loss* refers to the "joint occurrence" of growth and decline. Baltes (1987) suggests that the process of development is not merely a process of incremental growth; rather, throughout life, development always consists of the joint occurrences of gains and losses. While the developmental trends of aging seem to portray a negative image from a fluid intelligence standpoint, crystallized intelligence shows stability and, in some cases, steady increase until very late in life (Schaie, 1996). For instance, it may take longer for older adults to learn successful website navigation due to age-related declines, yet they are simultaneously building their crystallized intelligence by acquiring these skills. Therefore, while an overall slowing down of processing speed is taking place, they are still gaining domain or task-specific knowledge. In addition, the socio-emotional changes associated with getting older illustrate a far more complimentary picture. One of the ways in which research has shown significant differences between younger and older individuals is in their positive versus negative emotional experiences (Carstensen, Mikels, & Mather, 2006). In a recent longitudinal study, Carstensen et al. (2011) found that older adults were more likely than younger adults to have a positive emotional status and less likely to dwell in a negative emotional state. Carstensen and colleagues (Carstensen, et al., 2006) proposed a positivity effect as "a developmental pattern in which a disproportionate preference for negative material in youth shifts across adulthood to a disproportionate preference for positive information in later life." Congruent with the positivity effect, it has been shown that older adults typically regulate their emotions more frequently, consistently, and effectively than younger adults (Lang & Carstensen, 2002; Gross, et al., 1997). Thus, although older adults have a smaller social network, they are just as satisfied as, if not more than, younger adults with the quality of their social network. The Internet provides a way for communication over physical distance and disability. Older adults were found more likely than young adults to use information technology to strengthen family relationships and gain positive emotional feedback from their close social support network (Chen & Persson, 2002).

In light of the developmental dynamics between growth and decline, Baltes and Blates (1990) proposed the Selective Optimization with Compensation model as a prototypical change mechanism of "successful aging." The process of selective optimization with compensation has three basic features. First, continual evolution of specialized forms of adaptation is a general feature of lifespan development. With increasing age, there is an age-related increase in selection of motivational and cognitive resources and skills. Second, adaptation refers to the conditions of biological and socio-cultural aging with its increasing limitation of plasticity. The reserve capacity for peak performance in fluid intelligence is reduced; on the other hand, some procedural and declarative knowledge systems continue to evolve and function at peak levels. Third, older adults strive to compensate declined functions for the purpose of life mastery and successful aging. When the limits of declined capacity are exceeded in an older adult, she or he could either increase selection or develop compensatory and substitute mechanisms for the declined functions.

Finally, Baltes (1987) proposed *historical contextualism* as paradigm for lifespan development. The biology and cultural architecture of human development is incomplete and subject to continuous change with biological and cultural conditions modifying each other. Thus, ontogenetic development varies greatly by historical-cultural conditions. Any particular course of individual development can be understood as the outcome of the interactions among three systems of developmental influence: normative age-graded, normative history-graded, and nonnormative (idiosyncratic). Normative age-graded influences refer to those biological and environmental determinants that have a fairly strong relation with chronological age and are therefore predictable in their temporal sequence. They are also similar in their developmental direction among individuals. Biological maturation and age-graded socialization events are examples of age-graded influences.

History-graded influences also involve biological and environmental determinants. However, they are typically associated with a specific historical time. When it comes to the digital divide in Internet use, we not only need to examine age-graded influences in physical, cognitive, and socio-emotional processes, but also need to take into consideration of "societal marginality" of older adults during the present historical time (Peacock & Kunemund, 2007). Older adults are much more likely than younger adults to have relative poverty, lower education, and greater disability. Older adults also experienced growing up in a different historical context than younger generations and were exposed to differential diffusion of domestic information and communication technologies (Gilleard & Higgs, 2008).

CONSTRAINTS OF INTERNET USE AMONG OLDER ADULTS

Using the Lifespan Developmental Perspective, we set out to identify constraints encountered by older adults in their learning and using the Internet (Lee, et al., 2011). Constraint here refers to various forms of restrictions for an older adult to access computer-based information technologies. It may implicate physical, psychological, cognitive, and social barriers. First of all, we acknowledge that development is a lifelong process. Thus, older adults are capable of learning computer-based information technology even at a very advanced age. Two-hundred and forty-three older adults participated in the current study, with a relatively large age range from 50 to 93 years old.

Another unique feature of this study was to analyze patterns of constraints related to Internet use for older adults at different age stages. In the past, old age was viewed by many as a single life stage. However, based on age-related changes in physical, cognitive, and socio-emotional processes, it was argued by Schaie and Willis (2002) that older adults should be divided into three age

stages: the young-old who are 65 to 74 years old, the old-old who are 75 to 85 years old, and the oldest-old who are 85 years old and beyond. Some researchers further suggested classification of 50 to 64 years old as pre-seniors to differentiate them from seniors 65 years and older (Whitford, 1998). Depending on the context of various studies on Internet use among older adults, older Internet users have been defined differently. For example, research in the workplace usually refers to those above 50 years old as older Internet users. Thus, we also included the pre-senior age group in the current study. Subsequently, participants in the current study were categorized into three age groups: pre-seniors (50-64 years old), young-old (65-74 years old), and older-old adults (75 years old and beyond).

Older adults reported the following seventeen constraints they encountered in using the Internet in the present study: Too old to learn; It is useless; Computer is too complex; Do not like it; Cannot control it; Never used it before; Fear of breaking it; Memory function decline; Logic reasoning decline; Spatial orientation decline; No one teaches me how; Have nobody to ask a question; Nobody to send email to; Nowhere to go to use a computer; Cost too much to own; Cost too much to purchase Internet access; and Cost too much to learn.

Similar barriers have been discovered in other studies as well (Adams, Stubbs, & Woods, 2005; Campbell, 2004; Carpenter & Buday, 2007; Charness & Boot, 2009; Czaja, Sharit, Ownby, Roth, & Nair, 2001; Gatto & Tak, 2008; Githens, 2007; Rosenthal, 2008). For example, Adams and colleagues (Adams, et al., 2005) examined what they called "psychological barriers" to Internet use among older adults in the United Kingdom. Among these were: Perceived usefulness, Perceived ease of use, Internet efficacy, Perceived complexity of navigation, and Perceived complexity of terminology. They found that those who had a more positive view of usefulness, ease of use, and efficacy were likely to use the Internet more often.

Experience with the Internet was also related to decreased perceptions of complexity in navigation. Rosenthal (2008) found that anxiety and lack of self-confidence were two main obstacles for older women to learn and use the Internet. In addition, Charness and Boot (2009) pointed out some cognitive constraints of information technology use among older adults: general slowing of cognitive processes, decreased memory capacity, declined attention control, and difficulty in goal maintenance. Finally, Gatto and Tak (2008) summarized the following barriers to computer and Internet use among older adults: 1) Frustration with learning and using the Internet including lack of lessons as well as spam, pop-ups, advertisements, unwanted e-mails, and pornography; 2) Physical and mental limitations prevented older adults from using the Internet more often and for longer periods of time; 3) Privacy and trustworthiness were also concerns of older adults; and 4) Many older adults felt that they did not have enough time to seek information or get support through the Internet. Cost of the computer-mediated information technology is yet another theme that affects older adults' Internet use (Carpenter & Buday, 2007; Saunders, 2004).

In the current study (Lee, et al., 2011), exploratory factor analysis (with principal components method of extraction and varimax rotation) was used to discover whether there were any underlying patterns of these seventeen constraints. Four factors were extracted that accounted for 72.44% of the total variance: intrapersonal (i.e., Too old to learn; It is useless; Computer is too complex; Do not like it; Cannot control it; Never used it before; and Fear to break it), interpersonal (i.e., No one teaches me how; Have nobody to ask a question; and Nobody to send email to), structural (i.e., Nowhere to go to use a computer; Cost too much to own; Cost too much to purchase Internet access; and Cost too much to learn), and functional factors (i.e., Memory function decline; Logic reasoning decline; and Spatial orientation decline).

More importantly, age differences among older adults were found for three out of the four factors: intrapersonal, interpersonal, and functional factors. Pre-seniors were at the lowest level, reporting fewer perceived constraints than the young-old and the older-old in these three dimensions. According to the Lifespan Developmental Perspective, this may be due to more pronounced physical and cognitive decline among older age groups. Schaie and Willis (2002) suggested that intellectual abilities such as memory, logical reasoning, and spatial abilities typically would not show significant decline until after age 65. In addition, older adults who are above 65 years old are often retired and face a diminishing social network (McPherson, Smith-Lovin, & Brachears, 2006; Schnittker, 2007). Thus, it was not very surprising that the two older age groups were more likely than the pre-seniors to report having no one to turn to when experiencing problems using the Internet, or even having no one to send an email to in the first place. Socio-emotional constraints were frequently ignored by past research, but older adults needed social support to learn and enjoy information technology (Chen & Persson, 2002; Clark, 2002). Carstensen (1991) suggested that older adults were more likely than younger adults to emphasize emotional goals. This may partially explain why some older Internet users reported that their feelings had been hurt when they were not noticed in a chat room (Clark, 2002).

The structural constraint seemed to be similar across all three age groups in our study (i.e., the pre-seniors, the young-old, and the older-old). This suggested that the lower rates of access to and the use of the Internet by older adults may be due to the same structural inequalities of our society. As Peacock and Kunemund (2007) suggested, this reflects the crystallization of existing socioeconomic inequalities within the older population. Older adults are, in general, poorer, have lower education, greater proportions of disability, and are less likely to learn about information technology from the workplace than younger adults (Cresci, Yarandi, & Morrell, 2010; Greenburg, 2009; Mann, Belchior, Tomita, & Kemp, 2005; Wagner,

Hassanein, & Head, 2010; US Department of Health and Human Services, 2001). Buse (2009) also argued that older adults' reluctance to learn computer technology might be due to their distinctive perception of the technology from younger adults. Whereas young adults may perceive the computer as a device for more leisure opportunities, older adults are more likely to perceive the computer as a work-related device.

Alternatively, Gilleard and Higgs (2008) proposed a technology diffusion perspective to explain the digital divide *within* the current over 50-year-old population in Europe and North America. Using the English Longitudinal Study of Ageing, they found that age/cohort differences in Internet use persisted after controlling for income, education, employment, and health status. However, age/cohort effects declined after taking into account engagement with domestic information and communication technology and cultural activities. In other words, they argued that the younger post-World War II cohorts were more likely than the older pre-World War II cohorts to pick up on domestic information and communication technology due to its introduction into the workplace and the increased prevalence of PCs and exposure to various types of electronic entertainment amongst younger generations.

According to the Lifespan Developmental Perspective (Baltes, 1987), lifespan development occurs within a historical context. Internet use is no exception to this rule. Martin and Robinson (2007) reported a rise in Internet use among older Americans between the years of 1997 and 2003. However, the narrowing of the age gap in Internet use was less marked outside North America. The geographic variations in the extent of the digital divide seem to suggest that socio-cultural factors play an important part in the digital divide of the older population (Peacock & Kunemund, 2007). Gilleard and Higgs' (2008) technology diffusion perspective is another example of how historical context can influence older adults' attitudes and experiences of the Internet.

OPPORTUNITIES OF INTERNET USE AMONG OLDER ADULTS

Given the constraints that older adults may encounter in Internet use, what can we do to increase Internet use among older adults and improve their experiences with such technology? Baltes and Baltes (1990) proposed a Selective Optimization with Compensation (SOC) model in older adults' adaptive capacity. They conceptualized development as inherently a process of selection and selective adaptation. Selection is due to biological, psychological, cultural, and environmental factors. Developmental advances are due to processes of optimization. With age-related declines in physical, cognitive, and socio-emotional processes, compensation is also part of the developmental agenda. The SOC model recommended that older adults need to invest their limited resources selectively (i.e., selection), optimize their behavior in the domains they selected (i.e., optimization), and use creative ways to compensate for their declined abilities (i.e., compensation). Internet use has created many opportunities for older adults to access information selectively, stay connected to meaningful relationships, optimize their emotional experiences, and compensate for their declined physical and cognitive abilities (Chen & Persson, 2002; Gatto & Tak, 2008). Professionals should provide supportive environments to facilitate older adults' computer-based learning and usage of the Internet (Hart, et al., 2008; Xie & Bugg, 2009).

First of all, why do older adults use the Internet? Answers to this question are important for us to understand their s*election.* The Pew Internet and American Life Project surveyed older adults in 2004 and found that older adults spent between 3 to 10 more hours online every week. The top reasons for older adults to use the Internet are (Fox, 2004; Gatto & Tak, 2008; Lee, et al., 2011; Mann, et al., 2005; Wagner, Hassanein, & Head, 2010): Using email and engaging in online groups; Searching information about travel, leisure, and health-related matters; Purchasing and paying bills online; and

Having fun such as playing online games. Thus, we could say that older adults definitely selected the Internet, but would the Internet benefit their everyday lives? In other words, is their selection a good one?

Past research has found both positive and negative impacts of Internet use on health and well-being. The negative impacts include increased feelings of loneliness, depression, sleep disorders, and social isolation, and decreased family communication, physical activities, and exercise, especially among younger adults (Bakken, Wenzel, Gotestam, Johansson, & Oren, 2009; Kraut, et al., 1998). In contrast, older Internet users usually report positive impacts such as reduced feelings of loneliness and depression, and enhanced feelings of connectedness, competence, utility, positive learning experience, and psychological well-being (Chen & Persson, 2002; Gatto & Tak, 2008; Thayer & Ray, 2006; Wagner, et al., 2010).

So why does the Internet have differential impacts on younger and older adults? The first reason may lie in the time spent on the Internet. In a stratified probability sample of Norwegian adult Internet users (16-74 years old), Bakken et al. (2009) found that Internet addiction and at-risk Internet use were strongly dependent on gender and age, with the highest prevalence among young males. Being male, young, having a university-level education, and an unsatisfactory financial situation were factors positively associated with "problematic Internet use." Time spent on the Internet was positively associated with a prevalence of self-reported sleep disorders, depression, and other psychological impairments. Problematic Internet use clearly affected the lives of many people, especially males who possessed these demographic variables.

The second reason may be due to the kinds of activities they do on the Internet. Older adults often use the Internet for the same activities as younger adults but do different activities to different degrees. For example, Thayer and Ray (2006) discovered age differences in a U.S. adult sample in online communication and relationship preferences: young adults indicated their higher preferences for online communication with friends and unknown individuals than middle-aged and older adults. Clark (2002) found that older adults usually felt online communication was limited because responses had to be typed and thus posed limits on long and detailed conversation. As a consequence, older Internet users usually did not take time away from face-to-face interactions with others. Instead, they decreased use of television and radio time and saw the Internet as a replacement for the library (Moody, 2001).

Last but certainly not least, the most important reason that has been largely ignored by past literature may be age-related changes in socio-emotional processes. According to the Socioemotional Selectivity Theory (Carstensen, et al., 2006), older adults perceive limited future time perspective and thus may prioritize their emotion goals over cognitive goals. Older adults of course use the Internet for information seeking, but they are more likely to use it for communication and social support (Clark, 2002; Gatto & Tak, 2008). Fox (2004) reported that 94% of older Internet users have sent and received email compared to 91% of Internet users of all ages. Older adults have greater disability and mobility issues and the Internet can help them to decrease their sense of isolation (Bradley & Poppen, 2003). Sum, Mattews, Hughes, and Campbell (2008) revealed that for senior Internet users, greater use of the Internet as a communication tool was associated with a lower level of social loneliness; in contrast, greater use of the Internet to find new people was associated with a higher level of emotional loneliness. Hogeboom, McDermott, Perrin, Osman, and Bell-Ellison (2010) used a large sample from the 2004 wave of the Health and Retirement Survey to study Internet use and social networking among middle-aged and older adults. They found that frequency of contact with friends and family had a significant positive association with Internet use for adults over 50 years old. The study joined a number of others (e.g., Katz & Rice, 2002) suggesting that Internet use could strengthen social networks for older adults. Overall, existing research seems to support the notion that Internet use provides great opportunities for older adults. Thus, it is fair to say that older adults made a good *selection* in using the Internet.

According to the SOC model (Baltes & Baltes, 1990), both *optimization* and *compensation* need to take into account age-related changes in physical, cognitive, and socio-emotional processes. When it comes to optimizing older adults' computer and Internet use, Fisk, Rogers, Charness, Czaja, and Sharit (2009) urged technology designers to consider these age-related changes in perceptual (e.g., vision and hearing), motor, and cognitive systems when designing technology for older adults. For example, Charness and Boot (2009) suggested that web designers should avoid backgrounds that create low contrast for the text, use large fonts, minimize scrolling, and provide navigation aids and instructional support. The National Institute on Aging (NIA) and the National Library of Medicine (NLM) have developed "senior friendly" guidelines that are specific to older Internet users, consisting of 25 empirically based guidelines for websites targeting users age 60 and older (NIA & NLM, 2001). These guidelines included three areas: Designing readable text; Increasing memory and comprehension of web content; and Increasing the ease of navigation. Becker (2004) examined the adherence of 125 news and health-related websites to the NIA/NLM guidelines. Results indicated low levels of compliance for the majority of the websites. Specifically, a mere 7% of websites were using the appropriate font size (12-point font). It is likely that smaller font sizes contributed to readability problems for older Internet users. In addition, about 24% of the websites used pull-down menus that required precise mouse control to navigate. Seventy-two

percent of websites in the newspaper category required excessive scrolling. Finally, only half of the websites provided access to help information. These are problems that can easily be avoided by "senior friendly" web designs, which should be in the primary concern of all Internet sites geared toward older populations.

In addition, Hart and colleagues (2008) proposed to use both the guidelines and usability testing when designing websites for older adults. They first evaluated 40 websites designed for older adults based on their adherence to the NIA/NLM guidelines. While seven guidelines were scored as either "frequently" or "always" present in 97% of the websites, four guidelines were only followed by 6% or fewer of the websites. The four guidelines were color (e.g., avoids using yellow, blue, and green in proximity; display understandable in black and white), animation, video, and audio (e.g., uses short segments to reduce download time), physical spacing (e.g., uses double-spacing in body text), and back/forward navigation (e.g., uses buttons such as "previous" and "next" for reviewing text). Then, they selected three websites with most, medium, and least compliance and conducted a usability test with older adults. Results indicated that the website most compliant with the "senior friendly" guidelines resulted in higher task success, but did not result in significantly better efficiency, satisfaction, and preference than the other two websites. It was concluded that "consideration must also be given to the goals and tasks the target users are likely to have when using a particular site (p. 198)."

Finally, it should be noted that one proposition of the Lifespan Developmental Perspective (Baltes, 1987) is plasticity or intraindividual variability in cognitive processes. Even though age-related declines in physical and cognitive capacities may pose constraints to older adults' learning and using the Internet, it does not mean that they cannot fully enjoy cognitive enrichment offered by information technology. Xie and Bugg (2009) conducted public library computer training for older adults to access high-quality Internet health information (i.e., http://nihseniorhealth.gov and http://medlineplus.gov). They found that older adults had overwhelmingly positive perceptions of the training program. Their computer anxiety significantly decreased while computer interest and efficacy significantly increased from pre- to post-training. After the study, older participants not only started to use these reliable online resources to find high quality health and medical information, but also used the information to guide their decision-making regarding their own health and medical matters.

Another recent study by Schmiedek, Bauer, Lovden, Brose, and Lindenberger (2010) used web-based training programs to help older adults maintain and improve their cognitive functioning. The rationale is based on the evidence that lifestyles with a high level of cognitive activity are usually associated with smaller cognitive declines in old age (Hertzog, Kramer, Wilson, & Lindenberger, 2009). Past research using computer games and software packages to improve older adults' cognitive abilities is inconclusive. While performance on specific trained tasks did show some improvement, there was little transfer to untrained tasks (Ackerman, Kanfer, & Calderwood, 2010). Schmiedek et al. (2010) argued for the advantages of developing Internet-based cognitive training: allowing new tasks to be introduced in a continuous fashion without the need to install new versions of the program and creating web communities that can exchange information of training experience. Older participants reported enjoyment of the study and positive training effects on their mental fitness. Remarkably, throughout the 6-month web-based training programs, the dropout rate was very low: 6.8% (15 out of 219). This suggested that older participants had strong intrinsic interests in cognitive practice. The study

also demonstrated that the Internet could provide older adults with community benefits for their learning experience.

CONCLUSION AND FUTURE DIRECTIONS

In conclusion, the Internet has been, and is continuing to become, a regular part of life for billions of people all around the world. Older adults (65 years old and above) are the fastest growing age group among Internet users. So what happens when a rapidly aging society collides with rapidly increasing computer-based information technology? As both developed and developing countries around the world march into an aging society, we can anticipate increasing numbers of older Internet users who learned how to use these technologies in their earlier years to continue using the Internet in their later lives. Rapid diffusion of computer-based information technologies is reshaping the way older adults live. At the same time, older adults are challenged by age-related changes in physical and cognitive processes that may pose unique constraints for older adults to access and use the Internet (Lee, et al., 2011). According to the Lifespan Developmental Perspective (Baltes, 1987), development is a lifelong process that is both multidimensional and multidirectional. Accumulated crystallized intelligence and improved socio-emotional processes may give older adults an edge in using the Internet to promote social networking. The SOC model (Baltes & Baltes, 1990) suggests that Internet use could provide important opportunities for older Internet users, such as positive learning experience, social support, and psychological well-being. Older adults made a good *selection* in using the Internet to improve the quality of their lives. Implementing the principles of SOC for the beneficial uses of the Internet among older adults, we recommend that older users preserve their attention and focus their interest in fewer selected domains. For example, they could narrow down the number of websites they frequently visit, instead of expanding their horizons by surfing the Internet. This may help them to increase their familiarity with the websites and optimize their visiting experience in order to compensate for age-related declines in attention span and working memory.

Both *optimization* and *compensation* need to take into account not only age-related changes in physical, cognitive, and socio-emotional processes, but also the financial status of older adults as well. Future research on Internet use among older adults should not only understand the constraints they face in using the Internet, but also the need to effectively overcome these constraints in an economically feasible manner. For example, product designers may have taken into consideration older adults' physical and cognitive limitations, specifically in spatial orientation, working memory, sensory loss, and processing speed, in creating user-friendly human/computer interfaces for older adults. In other words, they have assisted in *compensating* for certain losses. However, the cost of such technology is significantly higher, sometimes double or more, than that of the average human/computer interface. Those who market "senior friendly" products to the elderly need to consider their limited financial resources. Many seniors live on a fixed income and may not be able to afford expensive equipment based on a modest retirement plan. The discrepancy in cost for these technologies poses yet another limitation for some older adults, one that should be addressed in order to help bridge the digital divide. How do we make these products in a more cost-effective manner so that they are more accessible to older adults? This is a concern that computer science and information technology may want to focus on in the future to assist older adults in *optimizing* their *selection* of the Internet.

Furthermore, educators and specialists who interact with older populations need to consider the motivational and emotional shifts of older adults in maintaining social networks and seeking out positive emotional experiences. Creating collaborative learning environments and offering group-training sessions may help older adults counteract cognitive and affective constraints, thereby decreasing anxiety and increasing their positive learning experience in communal settings. This could ultimately enhance computer-based learning and Internet use among older adults. Instruction-based materials are available online to individuals, organizations, and communities looking to foster these learning environments. The National Institute of Aging, for example, has created pedagogical guidelines for making Internet training conducive to the needs of older adults (http://nihseniorhealth.gov/toolkit/toolkit-files/pdf/QuickTips.pdf). Utilizing resources of this nature offers valuable support to groups and organizations dedicated to helping older adults become proficient Internet users.

Finally, the benefits of Internet use among older adults rely on joint efforts of the individual, the community, and the society. The lower rates of access to and use of the Internet by older adults may be due to the structural inequalities of our society. Older adults are, in general, poorer, have lower education, greater proportions of disability, and are less likely to learn information technology from the workplace. It is recommended (Han & Braun, 2011) that social policies should help older adults overcome these structural constraints in order to reduce age-related digital divide and improve the quality of life for older adults. Reducing the costs of computers and Internet access for older adults, providing more free training classes in public libraries and community organizations, and reinforcing "senior friendly" guidelines are just among a few of the ways to increase Internet use among older adults.

REFERENCES

Aartsen, M. J., Smiths, C. H. M., van Tilburg, T., Knopscheer, K. C. P. M., & Deeg, D. J. H. (2002). Activity in older adults: Cause or consequence of cognitive functioning? A longitudinal study on everyday activities and cognitive performance in older adults. *The Journals of Gerontology. Series B, Psychological Sciences and Social Sciences*, *57B*, 153–162. doi:10.1093/geronb/57.2.P153

Ackerman, P. L., Kanfer, R., & Calderwood, C. (2010). Use it or lose it? Wii brain exercise practice and reading for domain knowledge. *Psychology and Aging*, *25*, 753–766. doi:10.1037/a0019277

Adams, N. J., Stubbs, D., & Woods, V. (2005). Psychological barriers to internet usage among older adults in the UK. *Informatics for Health & Social Care*, *30*, 3–17. doi:10.1080/14639230500066876

Aldwin, C. M., Spiro, A. III, & Park, C. L. (2006). Health, behavior, and optimal aging: A lifespan developmental perspective. In Birren, J., & Schaie, K. W. (Eds.), *Handbook of the Psychology of Aging* (pp. 85–104). Amsterdam, The Netherlands: Elsevier. doi:10.1016/B978-012101264-9/50008-2

Anstey, K. (2008). Cognitive aging and functional biomarkers: What do we know, and where to from here? In Hofer, S. M., & Alwin, D. F. (Eds.), *Handbook of Cognitive Aging: Interdisciplinary Perspectives* (pp. 327–339). Los Angeles, CA: Sage Publications. doi:10.4135/9781412976589.n20

Bakken, I. J., Wenzel, H. G., Gotestam, K. G., Johansson, A., & Oren, A. (2009). Internet addiction among Norwegian adults: A stratified probability sample study. *Scandinavian Journal of Psychology*, *50*, 121–127. doi:10.1111/j.1467-9450.2008.00685.x

Baltes, P. B. (1987). Theoretical propositions of life-span developmental psychology: On the dynamics between growth and decline. *Developmental Psychology*, *23*, 611–626. doi:10.1037/0012-1649.23.5.611

Baltes, P. B., & Baltes, M. M. (1990). Psychological perspectives on successful aging: The model of selective optimization with compensation. In Baltes, P. B., & Baltes, M. M. (Eds.), *Successful Aging: Perspectives from the Behavioral Sciences* (pp. 1–34). Cambridge, UK: Cambridge University Press. doi:10.1017/CBO9780511665684.003

Becker, S. A. (2004). A study of web usability for older adults seeking online health resources. *ACM Transactions on Computer-Human Interaction*, *11*, 387–406. doi:10.1145/1035575.1035578

Bopp, K. L., & Verhaeghen, P. (2005). Aging and verbal memory span: A meta-analysis. *The Journals of Gerontology. Series B, Psychological Sciences and Social Sciences*, *60B*, 223–233. doi:10.1093/geronb/60.5.P223

Bradley, N., & Poppen, W. (2003). Assertive technology, computers, and internet may decrease sense of isolation for homebound elderly and disabled persons. *Technology and Disability*, *15*, 19–25.

Buse, C. E. (2009). When you retire, does everything become leisure? Information and communication technology use and the work/leisure boundary in retirement. *New Media & Society*, *11*(7), 1143–1161. doi:10.1177/1461444809342052

Campbell, R. (2004). Older women and the internet. *Journal of Women & Aging*, *16*, 161–174. doi:10.1300/J074v16n01_11

Carpenter, B. D., & Buday, S. (2007). Computer use among older adults in a naturally occurring retirement community. *Computers in Human Behavior*, *23*, 3012–3024. doi:10.1016/j.chb.2006.08.015

Carstensen, L. L. (1991). Social and emotional patterns in adulthood: Support for the socioemotional selectivity theory. *Psychology and Aging*, *7*, 331–338. doi:10.1037/0882-7974.7.3.331

Carstensen, L. L., Mikels, J. A., & Mather, M. (2006). Aging and the intersection of cognition, motivation, and emotion. In Birren, J., & Schaie, K. W. (Eds.), *Handbook of the Psychology of Aging* (pp. 343–362). Amsterdam, The Netherlands: Elsevier. doi:10.1016/B978-012101264-9/50018-5

Carstensen, L. L., Turan, B., Scheibe, S., Ram, N., & Ersner-Hershfield, H. (2011). Emotional experience improves with age: Evidence based on over 10 years of experience sampling. *Psychology and Aging*, *26*, 21–33. doi:10.1037/a0021285

Cattell, R. B. (1971). *Abilities: Their structure, growth and action*. Boston, MA: Houghton Mifflin.

Charness, N., & Boot, W. R. (2009). Aging and information technology use: Potential and barriers. *Current Directions in Psychological Science*, *18*(5), 253–258. doi:10.1111/j.1467-8721.2009.01647.x

Chen, Y., & Persson, A. (2002). Internet use among young and older adults: Relation to psychological well-being. *Educational Gerontology*, *28*, 731–744. doi:10.1080/03601270290099921

Clark, D. J. (2002). Older adults living through and with their computers. *Computers, Informatics, Nursing*, *20*(3), 117–124. doi:10.1097/00024665-200205000-00012

Cresci, M. K., Yarandi, H. N., & Morrell, R. W. (2010). Pro-nets versus no-nets: Differences in urban older adults' predilections for internet use. *Educational Gerontology*, *36*(6), 500–520. doi:10.1080/03601270903212476

Czaja, S. J., Charness, N., Fisk, A. D., Hertzog, C., Nair, S. N., & Rogers, W. A. (2006). Factors predicting the use of technology: Findings from the center for research and education on aging and technology enhancement (CREATE). *Psychology and Aging*, *21*, 333–352. doi:10.1037/0882-7974.21.2.333

Czaja, S. J., Sharit, J., Ownby, R., Roth, D. L., & Nair, S. (2001). Examining age differences in performance of a complex information search and retrieval task. *Psychology and Aging*, *16*, 564–579. doi:10.1037/0882-7974.16.4.564

Finkel, D., McArdle, J. J., Reynolds, C. A., & Pedersen, N. L. (2007). Age changes in processing speed as a leading indicator of cognitive aging. *Psychology and Aging*, *22*, 558–568. doi:10.1037/0882-7974.22.3.558

Fisk, A. D., Rogers, W. A., Charness, N., Czaja, S. J., & Sharit, J. (2009). *Designing for older adults: Principles and creative human factors approaches* (2nd ed.). Boca Raton, FL: CRC Press.

Fox, S. (2004). Older Americans and the internet. *Pew Internet and American Life Project*. Retrieved July 22, 2011 from http://www.pewinternet.org

Gatto, S. L., & Tak, S. H. (2008). Computer, internet, and email use among older adults: Benefits and barriers. *Educational Gerontology*, *34*, 800–811. doi:10.1080/03601270802243697

Gilleard, C., & Higgs, P. (2008). Internet use and the digital divide in the English longitudinal study of ageing. *European Journal of Ageing*, *5*, 233–239. doi:10.1007/s10433-008-0083-7

Githens, R. P. (2007). Understanding interpersonal interaction in an online professional development course. *Human Development Quarterly*, *18*(2), 253–274. doi:10.1002/hrdq.1202

Greenburg. (2009). *A profile of older Americans*. Washington, DC: Administration on Aging.

Gross, J. J., Carstensen, L. L., Pasupathi, M., Skorpen, C. G., Tsai, J., & Hsu, A. Y. C. (1997). Emotion and aging: Experience, expression, and control. *Psychology and Aging*, *12*, 590–599. doi:10.1037/0882-7974.12.4.590

Han, D., & Braun, K. L. (2011). Promoting active ageing through technology training in Korea. In Soar, J., Swindell, R., & Tsang, P. (Eds.), *Intelligent Technologies for Bridging the Grey Digital Divide* (pp. 141–158). Hershey, PA: IGI Global. doi:10.4018/978-1-61520-825-8.ch010

Hart, T. A., Chaparro, B. S., & Halcomb, C. G. (2008). Evaluating websites for older adults: Adherence to "senior-friendly" guidelines and end-user performance. *Behaviour & Information Technology*, *27*, 191–199. doi:10.1080/01449290600802031

Hertzog, C., Kramer, A. F., Wilson, R. S., & Lindenberger, U. (2009). Regarding methods for studying human development. *Research in Human Development*, *7*, 1–8. doi:10.1080/15427600903578110

Hogeboom, D. L., McDermott, R. J., Perrin, K. M., Osman, H., & Bell-Ellison, B. A. (2010). Internet use and social networking among middle aged and older adults. *Educational Gerontology*, *36*, 93–111. doi:10.1080/03601270903058507

Horn, J. L. (1982). The theory of fluid and crystallized intelligence in relation to concepts of cognitive psychology and aging in adulthood. In Craik, F. I. M., & Trehub, S. E. (Eds.), *Aging and Cognitive Processes* (pp. 237–278). New York, NY: Plenum Press.

Internet World Stats. (2011). *Internet users in the world: Distribution by world regions*. Retrieved July, 3, 2011 from http://www.internetworldstats.com

Katz, J. E., & Rice, R. E. (2002). *Social consequences of internet use: Access, involvement, and interaction*. Cambridge, MA: MIT Press.

Kim, Y. S. (2008). Reviewing and critiquing computer learning and usage among older adults. *Educational Gerontology*, *34*, 709–735. doi:10.1080/03601270802000576

Kochanek, K., Xu, J., Murphy, S., Miniño, A. M., & Kung, C.-H. (2011). Deaths: Preliminary data for 2009. *National Vital Statistics Reports*, *59*(4), 1–51. Retrieved July 3, 2011 from http://www.cdc.gov/nchs/fastats/lifexpec.htm

Kraut, R., Patterson, M., Lundmark, V., Kiesler, S., Mukopadhyay, T., & Scherlis, W. (1998). A social technology that reduces social involvement and psychological well-being? *The American Psychologist*, *53*(9), 1017–1031. doi:10.1037/0003-066X.53.9.1017

Lang, F. R., & Carstensen, L. L. (2002). Time counts: Future time perspective, goals, and social relationships. *Psychology and Aging*, *17*, 125–139. doi:10.1037/0882-7974.17.1.125

Lee, B., Chen, Y., & Hewitt, L. (2011). Age differences in constraints encountered by seniors in their use of computers and the internet. *Computers in Human Behavior*, *27*, 1231–1237. doi:10.1016/j.chb.2011.01.003

Mann, W. C., Belchior, P., Tomita, M. R., & Kemp, B. J. (2005). Computer use by middle-aged and older adults with disabilities. *Technology and Disability*, *17*, 1–9.

Martin, S. P., & Robinson, J. P. (2007). The income digital divide: Trends and predictions for levels of internet use. *Social Problems*, *54*, 1–22. doi:10.1525/sp.2007.54.1.1

McPherson, M., Smith-Lovin, L., & Brachears, M. (2006). Social isolation in America: Changes in core discussion networks over two decades. *American Sociological Review*, *71*, 353–375. doi:10.1177/000312240607100301

Moody, E. J. (2001). Internet use and its relationship to loneliness. *Cyberpsychology & Behavior*, *4*, 393–401. doi:10.1089/109493101300210303

National Institute on Aging. (2007). *Quick tips for a senior friendly computer classroom*. Washington, DC: US Government Printing Office.

National Institute on Aging and National Library of Medicine. (2001). *Making your web site senior friendly: A checklist*. Washington, DC: US Government Printing Office.

Old, S. R., & Naveh-Benjamin, M. (2008). Age-related changes in memory: Experimental approaches. In Hofer, S. M., & Alwin, D. F. (Eds.), *Handbook of Cognitive Aging: Interdisciplinary Perspectives* (pp. 151–167). Los Angeles, CA: Sage Publications. doi:10.4135/9781412976589. n9

Park, D. C., Lautenschlager, G., Hedden, T., Davidson, N. S., Smith, A. D., & Smith, P. K. (2002). Models of visuospatial and verbal memory across the adult life span. *Psychology and Aging*, *17*, 299–320. doi:10.1037/0882-7974.17.2.299

Peacock, S. E., & Kunemund, H. (2007). Senior citizens and internet technology: Reasons and correlates of access versus non-access in a European comparative perspective. *European Journal of Ageing*, *4*, 191–200. doi:10.1007/s10433-007-0067-z

Ronnlund, M., Nyberg, L., Backman, L., & Nilsson, L. G. (2005). Stability, growth, and decline in adult life span development of declarative memory: Cross-sectional and longitudinal data from a population-based study. *Psychology and Aging*, *20*, 3–18. doi:10.1037/0882-7974.20.1.3

Rosenthal, R. (2008). Older computer-literate women: Their motivations, obstacles, and paths to success. *Educational Gerontology*, *34*, 610–626. doi:10.1080/03601270801949427

Salthouse, T. A. (2009). When does age-related cognitive decline begin? *Neurobiology of Aging*, *30*, 507–514. doi:10.1016/j.neurobiolaging.2008.09.023

Salthouse, T. A., & Babcock, R. L. (1991). Decomposing adult age differences in working memory. *Developmental Psychology*, *27*, 763–776. doi:10.1037/0012-1649.27.5.763

Saunders, E. J. (2004). Maximizing computer use among the elderly in rural senior centers. *Educational Gerontology*, *30*, 573–585. doi:10.1080/03601270490466967

Schaie, K. W. (1996). *Intellectual development in adulthood: The Seattle longitudinal study*. Cambridge, UK: Cambridge University Press.

Schaie, K. W., & Willis, S. L. (2002). *Adult development and aging* (5th ed.). New York, NY: Prentice-Hall.

Schmiedek, F., Bauer, C., Lovden, M., Brose, A., & Lindenberger, U. (2010). Cognitive enrichment in old age: Web-based training programs. *GeroPsych: The Journal of Gerontopsychology and Geriatric Psychiatry*, *23*(2), 59–67. doi:10.1024/1662-9647/a000013

Schneider, B., & Pichora-Fuller, M. (2000). Implications of perceptual deterioration for cognitive ageing research. In Craik, F. I. M., & Salthouse, T. A. (Eds.), *The Handbook of Aging and Cognition* (pp. 155–219). Mahwah, NJ: Lawrence Erlbaum.

Schnittker, J. (2007). Look at all the lonely people: Age and social psychology of social support. *Journal of Aging and Health*, *19*, 659–682. doi:10.1177/0898264307301178

Sharit, J., Czaja, S. J., Hernandez, M., Yang, Y., Perdomo, D., & Lewis, J. (2004). The evaluation of performance by older persons on a simulated telecommuting task. *Journal of Gerontology*, *59B*, 305–316.

Sum, S., Mathews, R. M., Hughes, I., & Campbell, A. (2008). Internet use and loneliness in older adults. *Cyberpsychology & Behavior*, *11*, 208–211. doi:10.1089/cpb.2007.0010

Thayer, S. E., & Ray, S. (2006). Online communication preferences across age, gender, and duration of internet use. *Cyberpsychology & Behavior*, *9*, 432–440. doi:10.1089/cpb.2006.9.432

US Census Bureau. (2000). *Profile of general demographic characteristics: 2000 census of population and housing*. Washington, DC: United State Census Bureau.

US Department of Health and Human Services. (2001). *A profile of older Americans*. Washington, DC: Administration on Aging.

Valentijn, S. A., van Boxtel, M. P., van Hooren, S. A., Bosma, H., Beckers, H. J., & Ponds, R. W. (2005). Change in sensory functioning predicts change in cognitive functioning: Results from a 6-year follow-up in the Maastricht aging study. *Journal of the American Geriatrics Society*, *53*, 374–380. doi:10.1111/j.1532-5415.2005.53152.x

Wagner, N., Hassanein, K., & Head, M. (2010). Computer use by older adults: A multidisciplinary review. *Computers in Human Behavior*, *26*, 870–882. doi:10.1016/j.chb.2010.03.029

Whitford, M. (1998). Market in motion. *Hotel and Motel Management*, *4*, 41–43.

Willis, S. L., & Schaie, K. W. (1986). Training the elderly on ability factors of spatial orientation and inductive reasoning. *Psychology and Aging*, *1*, 239–247. doi:10.1037/0882-7974.1.3.239

Xie, B., & Bugg, J. M. (2009). Public library computer training for older adults to access high-quality internet health information. *Library & Information Science Research*, *31*, 155–162. doi:10.1016/j.lisr.2009.03.004

ADDITIONAL READING

Birren, J. E., & Schaie, K. W. (2006). *Handbook of the psychology of aging*. Amsterdam, The Netherlands: Elsevier Academic Press.

Czaja, S. J., & Lee, C. C. (2007). Information technology and older adults. In Jacko, J. A., & Sears, A. (Eds.), *The Human-Computer Interaction Handbook* (2nd ed., pp. 777–792). New York, NY: Erlbaum. doi:10.1201/9781410615862.ch39

Dahlin, E., Nyberg, L., Backman, L., & Neely, A. S. (2008). Plasticity of executive functioning in young and older adults: Immediate training gains, transfer, and long-term maintenance. *Psychology and Aging*, *23*, 720–730. doi:10.1037/a0014296

Echt, K. V., & Backscheider-Burridge, A. (2011). Predictors of reported internet use in older adults with high and low health literacy: The role of sociodemographics and visual and cognitive function. *Physical & Occupational Therapy in Geriatrics*, *29*, 23–43. doi:10.3109/02703181.2010.547657

Fukuda, R. (2011). Affective technology for older adults: Does fun technology affect older adults and change their lives? *Lecture Notes in Computer Science*, *6766*, 140–148. doi:10.1007/978-3-642-21663-3_15

Heo, J., Kim, J., & Won, Y.-S. (2010). Exploring the relationship between internet use and leisure satisfaction among older adults. *Activities, Adaptation and Aging*, *35*, 43–54. doi:10.1080/01924788.2010.545975

Hofer, S. M., & Alwin, D. F. (2008). *Handbook of cognitive aging: Interdisciplinary perspectives*. Los Angeles, CA: Sage Publications.

Holzinger, A., Searle, G., Kleinberger, T., Seffah, A., & Javahery, H. (2008). Investigating usability metrics for the design and development of applications for the elderly. *Lecture Notes in Computer Science*, *5105*, 98–105. doi:10.1007/978-3-540-70540-6_13

Jones, S., & Fox, S. (2009). *Generations online in 2009*. Retrieved from http://www.pewinternet.org/Reports/2009/Generations-Online-in-2009.aspx

Ordonez, T. N., Yassuda, M. S., & Cachioni, M. (2011). Elderly online: Effects of a digital inclusion program in cognitive performance. *Archives of Gerontology and Geriatrics, 53*, 216–219. doi:10.1016/j.archger.2010.11.007

Slegers, K., van Boxtel, M. P. J., & Jolles, J. (2008). Effects of computer training and internet usage on the well-being and quality of life of older adults: A randomized, controlled study. *Journal of Gerontology, 63B*, 176–184.

Smith, A. (2010). *Mobile access 2010*. Retrieved from http://www.pewinternet.org/Reports/2010/Mobile-Access-2010.aspx

Soar, J., Swindell, R., & Tsang, P. (2011). *Intelligent technologies for bridging the grey digital divide*. Hershey, PA: IGI Global.

Tun, P. A., & Lachman, M. E. (2010). The association between computer use and cognition across adulthood: Use it so you won't lose it? *Psychology and Aging, 25*, 560–568. doi:10.1037/a0019543

Ybarra, M., & Suman, M. (2008). Reasons, assessments and actions taken: Sex and age differences in uses of internet health information. *Human Education Research, 23*, 512–521. doi:10.1093/her/cyl062

KEY TERMS AND DEFINITIONS

Community-Based Internet Training: Community-based Internet training refers to computer workshops and seminars offered by various service sectors at local community organizations, such as county libraries, senior centers, or park and recreation services.

Computer-Based Technology: Computer-based technology refers to computer hardware, software, networks, and other relevant technologies that enable transmission, processing, storage, and retrieval of information.

Constraints: Constraints refer to any factors that may restrict an older adult from accessing and using information technologies.

Digital Divide: The digital divide refers to inequality between those who have versus those who do not have access to digitized information technologies. Older adults, along with other underrepresented groups, often lack the resources to access information technologies.

Older Adults: Older adults refer to individuals who are 65 years old and above.

Opportunities: Opportunities refer to potential benefits an older adult may obtain from use of the Internet and computer-based technology.

Social Networking: Social networking is a structure of interpersonal relations that tie individuals together.

Chapter 8
Effective Online Learning for Older People:
A Heuristic Design Approach

Robert Z. Zheng
University of Utah, USA

ABSTRACT

This chapter examines the cognitive constraints related to older people in learning, particularly in e-learning, and proposes a new design approach that: (1) assists the instructional designer and Web development in identifying issues related to older people's involvement in e-learning; (2) helps reduce the mental load in designing and developing e-learning for older people; and (3) uses heuristics to systematically support the designers in making decisions about meeting the needs of older people in their learning and searching for information online.

INTRODUCTION

The aging process is associated with gradual declines in cognitive functioning, which include reduced working memory capacity, processing speed, and physical and mental coordination (Gardner & Hill, 2012; Rhodes & Kelley, 2005). Because of the decline in cognitive functioning, older adults face increasing challenges when learning new materials, especially learning new materials via the Word Wild Web. Research shows that the extent to which how well older people learn is dependent on the amount of cognitive load imposed on the learner during the learning process (Hawthorn, 2007; Low, Jin, & Sweller, 2012; Ouwehand, van Gog, & Paas, 2012; van Gerven, Paas, van Merrienboer, & Schmidt, 2002). In an early study, Sweller and Chandler (1994)

DOI: 10.4018/978-1-4666-1966-1.ch008

identified the relationship between the level of element interactivity and the challenges associated with learning. They noted that high-level element interactivity could impose high cognitive load, which makes the learning process difficult. It is thus agreed that reducing cognitive load by reducing the level of element interactivity in complex learning can significantly improve the effectiveness and efficiency in learning (Zheng & Cook, 2011; Low, et al., 2012; Ouwenhand, et al., 2012; Tindall-Ford, Chandler, & Sweller, 1997). Previous research has established that cognitive strategies such as worked examples, integrative instructional format, cueing, gesturing and signaling can significantly alleviate the cognitive load that the learner experiences in learning (Kirschner, Sweller, & Clark, 2006; Ouwenhand, et al., 2012; Sweller, 2010).

Along the same line researchers investigated ways to apply heuristics to E-learning design in an effort to reduce cognitive load in learning (Darabi, Arrastia, & Nelson, 2011; Hwang, Kuo, & Yin, 2010; Sweet & Ellaway, 2010). Hwang et al. (2010) employed a heuristic algorithm to guide the learning activities in a natural science course. The researchers found that students' learning behaviors had significantly improved through a heuristic design that aimed at personalizing the support for learners. Sweet and Ellaway (2010) argued that heuristic design, compared to conventional instructional design, results in heightened levels of critical thinking and sensitivity to learners' cognitive needs. They further pointed out that heuristics which use simple, experience based rules to guide instructional design not only serve as an effective tool for diagnosing the usability issues related to the physical design of the e-Learning but also function as a cognitive walk-through which identifies malpractices in e-Learning that often cause cognitive dysfunction and misunderstanding in learning. Lee and Reigeluth (2009) pointed out the benefits of applying heuristics to

the design of e-learning. They demonstrated that heuristic task analysis, a method developed for eliciting, analyzing, and representing expertise in complex cognitive tasks, provides a clear path for effective learning.

Nonetheless, research on cognitive load reduction via heuristic design is far and few between. There are some challenges associated with the use of heuristics in e-Learning design. One challenge is the alignment of heuristics with specific content in e-learning. As Lee and Reigeluth (2009) pointed out, due to the myriad contextual factors that arise in each individual work setting, it becomes extremely challenging to apply heuristics as a universal design rule for e-Learning. The other challenge is to identify what Simon (1990) called the "rules of thumb" so that the instructional designers and other professionals can follow those rules as they design and develop e-Learning for older adults who will not be cognitively overload as they surf the Web for personal, entertainment, health, and social needs. The current chapter offers a discussion of the above challenges in heuristics design by (a) examining the limitation of human cognitive architectures in general and older adults in particular, and (b) identifying ways that employ heuristics to effectively integrate instructional strategies (e.g., worked examples, instructional format, etc.) to develop e-Learning for older people. Specifically, the chapter focuses on:

1. literature in human cognitive architecture and how it affects learning,
2. instructional design, especially online design for older people,
3. heuristics as a design strategy for E-Learning for older people.

Finally, the chapter proposes some heuristic guidelines for designing effective online learning for older adults.

HUMAN COGNITIVE ARCHITECTURE AND LEARNING

Working Memory and Information Processing

In his seminal article, George Miller (1956) found that human's capacity to hold information in a short term was limited. He demonstrated that the store of short-term memory was 7 ± 2 items. Miller's work significantly contributed to late scientific queries, which explored the functional role of working memory in information processing (e.g., Atkinson & Shiffrin, 1968; Baddeley, 1997; Mayer, 2001; Sweller, 1988). The following sections offer an overview of theories related to human memory, especially working memory and how they influence human information processing in general and older people in particular.

Atkinson and Shiffrin's Memory Model

Atkinson and Shiffrin (1968) studied the structure of memory and proposed a psychological model of memory called multi-store model, also known as Atkinson and Shiffrin's memory model. Atkinson and Shiffrin asserted that human memory involved a sequence of stages when processing incoming information. These three stages include sensory memory, short-term memory and long-term memory. Each memory is defined as a storage for holding information, hence the multi-store memory model.

Humans see, hear, and feel numerous things each day, but only a small number are remembered. According to Atkinson and Shiffrin, human sense organs are quite limited in capacity in terms of storing the information accessed by our senses. The visual system possesses iconic memory for visual stimuli such as diagram, shape, size, color, and so forth. The hearing system has echoic memory for auditory stimuli. The information stored in the sensory memory has little connection with its associative meaning. That is, the information from

perceiving a shape of a triangle is only conveyed as something with three lines connected to each other. It does not relay the geometric definition of triangle. In other words, sensory memory is related to the unique physical characteristics of the object, but not its associative meaning. Both iconic and echoic memories can be very short, often eliminated within several hundred milliseconds. Since sensory memory is primarily considered on a "run time" basis for physical or psychosomatic reference, it is detached from either short-term memory or long-term memory in Atkinson and Shiffrin's model. However, in a later revision Atkinson and Shiffrin removed the sensory memory from their memory model and focused on the short-term and long-term memories by examining the functional role of rehearsal and its contribution to transferring information to long-term memory.

The short-term memory in Atkinson and Shiffrin's model is defined as information that is retained acoustically and visually in a temporary storage. Different from the information of the sensory memory, the information in short-term memory is long enough to use it. For example, when people dine at the restaurant, they often look up in the menu to find out what they want, remember it, and then tell the waiter/waitress what they like to order. Research suggests that information in short-term memory usually lasts between 15 and 30 seconds (Locke, 1971). Miller (1956) defined the limit of short-term memory, which holds about 7 ± 2 chunks of information. Another important nature of short-term memory is that it appears to mostly encode memory acoustically in terms of sound but can also retain visuospatial images (See Baddeley, 1996; Baddeley, Sala, & Baddeley, 1996). In addition to acoustic and visual encoding, the short-term memory also serves as a buffer that separates the environment from the memory system. Rather than paying attention to moment-to-moment occurrences in the environment to account for all the environmental changes, the short-term memory acts as buffer zone that detaches the environment from its memory system. This enables the short-term memory to focus on things at the moment without being distracted. However, such manipulation is usually temporary. For example, a person can focus on the phone number he/she is looking for and remember it momentarily but cannot last very long without being further distracted. Thus, in order to have the critical information encoded into long-term memory, the rehearsal of information becomes essential to prevent the information from decay.

The long-term memory in Atkinson and Shiffrin's model provides lasting retention of information, from minutes to lifetime. The long-term memory mostly preserves meaning related information, i.e., semantic memory as well as procedural skills and imageries. It is believed that long-term memory has an unlimited capacity to retain information. As it was mentioned above, for information to be encoded permanently into long-term memory, techniques such as rehearsal have been used in memory training, particularly for older people (Gardner & Hill, 2012; Kilb & Naveh-Benjamin, 2011; Opitz, 2010). For example, Gardner and Hill (2012) used the rehearsal technique to help older people memorize personal pin numbers. They found that repeated practice of entering one's personal pin numbers can lead to knowledge automaticity which reduces the load associated with the memorization, thus improves older people's performance in memorizing their pin numbers.

Baddeley's Model of Working Memory

Questioning the traditional definition of "short-term memory" which was only associated with its receptive nature when storing information, Baddeley and his colleagues (see Baddeley, 1997; Baddeley, et al., 1996; Baddeley & Hitch, 1974) pointed out that the term "short-term memory" did not reflect the manipulative nature in information encoding. They therefore proposed the term

Working Memory (WM) be used to capture the manipulative aspect of short-term memory.

Differing from Atkinson and Shiffrin's multi-store memory model, Baddeley proposed a multicomponent working memory model. Baddeley's working memory model contains three key components: a central executive, the phonological loop, and visuo-spatial sketchpad. The central executive is responsible for the supervision of information integration and for coordinating the information from phonological loop and visuo-spatial sketchpad, both of which he called *slave systems*. The phonological loop is mainly responsible for encoding phonological information such as sound. One way of preventing the phonological information from decay is to continuously articulate its contents, thereby refreshing the information in a rehearsal loop – a technique that has been widely used in memory training. The visuo-spatial sketchpad stores visual and spatial information. This memory component mainly functions as constructing the mental representation of spatial and visual images. The visuo-spatial sketchpad can be further broken down into two subsystems: visual system and spatial subsystem. The visual system mainly deals with shape, color, and texture, whereas the spatial subsystem deals with location. The information from both subsystems is coordinated and regulated by the central executive system which involves directing attention to relevant information, suppressing irrelevant information and inappropriate actions, and coordinating cognitive processes when more than one task must be done at the same time (e.g., multi-tasking) (see also Watson, Lambert, Cooper, Boyle, & Strayer, 2012).

Baddeley's working memory model is significant in terms of its contribution to the understanding of the relationship between sound and images, and the relationship between visuals and spatiality. His model helps explain why visuals can sometimes interfere with text in learning and vice versa (see Mayer, 2001; Mayer & Anderson, 1991; Mayer & Moreno, 2003; Mayer & Sims,

1994). For example, Mayer (2001) proposes a cognitive theory of multimedia learning based on Baddeley's working memory model. Mayer's theory explicates the relationships between working memory and multimedia design. His principles of multimedia design in particular elucidate the impact of modality on information processing in learning.

ONLINE INSTRUCTIONAL DESIGN FOR OLDER PEOPLE

As it was discussed above, the limitation of human working memory may result in significant cognitive consequences in learning as well as in the design of instructions for learning. In this section, my discussion will be focused on the cognitive consequences of limited working memory in instructional design from the perspective of John Sweller's cognitive load theory, followed by a discussion on Mayer's cognitive theory of multimedia learning and principles of multimedia design. Finally, an extensive discussion is made pertaining to the online instructional design for older people.

Cognitive Consequences of Limited Working Memory

One of the consequences of WM limitation is information overload in learning—a phenomenon which John Sweller (1988) described as cognitive overload. According to Sweller and Chandler (1994), "A heavy cognitive load imposed by a combination of high intrinsic element interactivity and … high extraneous element interactivity may be overwhelming" (p. 194). The Cognitive Load Theory (CLT) posits that learning can be adversely affected by two types of cognitive load: intrinsic and extraneous cognitive loads (Sweller, 1988; Sweller & Chandler, 1994; van Merrienboer & Sweller, 2005). The intrinsic cognitive load is induced by the structure and complexity of the

instructional material. Usually, the instructor or instructional designer can do little to influence the intrinsic cognitive load. An example of intrinsic cognitive cognitive load can be found in language acquisition. For instance, cognitive load associated with learning some vocabulary can be low because the elements of the content to be learned do not interact with each other. People can learn a single word without having to associate with or depend on other words. In other words, learning vocabulary can be accomplished in an isolated manner with minimum or no interaction with other vocabulary. On the other hand, acquiring a language at a syntax level would impose significantly high cognitive load on the learner due to a higher level of element interaction. It is well understood that the syntax of a language cannot be acquired in isolation. In learning the syntax the learner must put in perspective the syntactic and semantic relations of each word to every other word. Each element must be learned in conjunction with other words in order to generate meaningful understanding of the syntax. Evidently, learning a language at a syntax level can induce a higher level of cognitive load than merely learning the words. The cognitive load associated with syntax acquisition is defined by a high level of element interaction, which is an innate characteristic of the content and cannot be influenced or altered by the instructor or the instructional designer, hence the intrinsic cognitive load. For a detail of intrinsic cognitive load in language acquisition, please refer to Sweller and Chandler's (1994) article on the relations between complex material and difficulty of learning. The second type of cognitive load that may adversely affect the learner's learning is the extraneous cognitive load. The extraneous cognitive load refers to the cognitive load caused by the format and manner in which information is presented. For example, instructors may unwittingly increase learners' extraneous cognitive load by presenting materials that 'require students to mentally integrate mutually referring, disparate sources of information'

Figure 1. An example of instruction that may induce high extraneous cognitive load

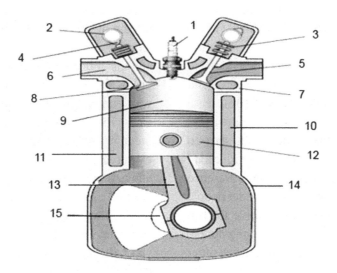

1. spark plug   2. camshaft   3. valve spring   4. cam
5. exhaust valve   6. mixture in   7. cylinder head
8. intake value   9. combustion chamber   10. cooling water
11. cylinder block   12. piston   13. connecting rod
14. crankcase   15. crankshaft

(Sweller & Chandler, 1991, p. 353). Consider the task presented in Figure 1. The learner would have to expend extra cognitive resources coordinating the information between the text and the image, which may overtax the working memory resources allocated to the processing of visual information. Instruction like that would be likely to induce a high level of extraneous cognitive load.

Research on Aging and Optimal Use of Cognitive Resources

As it was mentioned elsewhere in this chapter, cognitive aging is associated with gradual declines in cognitive functioning including a reduction in working memory. Older adults can be easily distracted or lack of attentional control when processing critical information (van Gerven, Paas, & Schmidt, 2000; Watson, et al., 2012). Research has demonstrated that older people often have a difficult time in repressing irrelevant information

when processing or learning new content which is due largely to the decline in working memory function especially the executive functioning in working memory (van Gerven, et al., 2000, 2002; Waston, et al., 2012). To minimize the irrelevant information and maximize the older adults' ability in complex cognitive skills acquisition, van Gerven and his colleagues (2000) proposed a framework based on cognitive load theory. The framework focuses on the construction of cognitive schemata for older adults by reducing extraneous cognitive load in learning. To achieve the above goal, the authors proposed a series of CLT-based instructional formats, which include goal-free problems, worked examples, avoiding split attention, distributing information over different modalities, and leaving out redundant information. In a follow-up study, van Gerven et al. (2006) tested the hypothesis of modality as a way to reduce extraneous cognitive load in training the elderly. They compared the college students (*n* = 40, mean age = 23.3) with older adults (n = 40, mean age = 65.1) in the performance of problem solving. The problem was a computerized version of Luchins' (1942) water-jug problem. There were two presentation modes pertaining to the problems: unimodal and bimodal. The cognitive load measures involved Paas's Subjective Cognitive-Load (SCL) measure and a secondary task using response time as an indicator of cognitive load. The results showed that bimodal training leads to lower cognitive load than unimodal training. A significant difference was found for modality in which the older people reported to experience lower cognitive load in bimodal than unimodal. Although young people showed the similar trend, it appears the older people were benefited more from the bimodal presentation than their counterparts.

In additional to testing the modality hypothesis, Paas et al. (2001) studied the goal specificity pertaining to older adults' abilities in problem solving. Based on cognitive load theory, the authors hypothesized that the presence or absence of a specific goal would disproportionately compromise or enhance older people's performance. To test the hypothesis, the authors recruited young and older participants to solve a maze problem by varying the problem solving approaches: goal specific and non-goal specific. Participants had to navigate through a computerized training-maze task. The finish point of the maze could be presented either as a specific location or in more general terms. After solving the maze problem, the participants were asked to start again, either by moving from start to finish or backward from finish to start. The results show that the older people benefited far more from goal free problem solving approach (M = 48.1 time in seconds) than goal specific problem solving approach (M = 90.3 time in seconds). The authors thus concluded that the use of goal-free format can compensate for the age-related cognitive declines and that "goal-free problems prevent the use of means-ends analysis, thereby saving cognitive resources that can be used for processes relevant for learning" (p. 185).

Another area of interest in the research of aging and cognitive load theory is to examine the effects of the worked examples in training the elderly (van Gerven, et al., 2002). van Gerven and his colleagues asserted that cognitive aging brings about several declines of working memory, which impede the acquisition of complex cognitive skills. To overcome the barriers caused by working memory declines, van Gerven and his colleagues explored the use of worked examples in older adults training based on the assumptions that the worked examples would enable an optimal use of the remaining cognitive resources, which can subsequently enhance older people's learning. It was believed that older people may suffer from a decline in fluid intelligence/reasoning (Gf) which is related to the capacity to think logically and solve problems in novel situations, independent of acquired knowledge, but they may still maintain a strong crystalized intelligence/reasoning (Gc) which is described as the ability to use skills, knowledge, and experience (Cattell, 1963, 1971). According to van Gerven et al. (2002), "it is true that, compared to young people, the elderly have a much richer and more integrated body of general and, depending on their professional background, specific knowledge at their disposal" (p. 88). If it is true, wouldn't it be beneficial to train the elderly by utilizing their existing knowledge base as a way to optimize the remaining cognitive resources of the older people? With that question in mind, van Gerven and his colleagues conducted a study that used worked examples to facilitate older people's learning. That is, the worked examples were used to facilitate their crystalized reasoning (Gc) by activating existing knowledge base while problem solving. Fifty-four participants were recruited with 30 college students (median 19.50 years old) and 24 elderly participants (median 66 years old). Two conditions were set up: one was the conventional problems condition and the other was the worked examples condition. Transfer tests were given at the end of the problem solving (water-jug problems). The results showed that the elderly group had a substantial lower cognitive load in worked examples condition than in the conventional problems condition. Performance wise, the elderly group displayed a substantial efficiency gain in the worked examples condition relative to the conventional problems condition. Regarding processing time, the elderly group showed a significant reduction in the use of time in the worked examples group. Interestingly, the young group overall did not benefit from the worked examples in this study. The authors concluded that the worked examples format helped elderly people to make a more efficient use of the available working-memory capacity than conventional problems.

The above research once again has demonstrated that appropriate format of instruction can be instrumental in improving the elderly people's information processing and knowledge acquisition. It should be noted that within this field of research, the emphasis on the design of the instruction based on cognitive load theory constitutes the core that guides the practices of learning optimization for the elderly people. In a 2003 article commenting on the efficiency of multimedia learning for the older people, van Gerven and his colleagues asserted that "the multimedia condition imposes significantly less cognitive load on the learner than the conventional condition" (p. 502). This view was echoed by Mayer and Moreno (2003) who took from a design perspective identified nine ways to reduce cognitive load in multimedia learning. Mayer's work on multimedia design and multimedia learning is substantial in terms of its influence on the research and practices of multimedia-based learning. The following section thus focuses on the design principles proposed by Mayer (2001) and their implications for the design of learning and training for the older people.

Theory of Multimedia Learning and Principles of Multimedia Design

Mayer and his colleagues studied the multimedia learning from a cognitive perspective. Drawn from theories related to human information processing which include the theories of working memory (Baddeley, 1997), dual coding theory (Paivio, 1986), theories related to individual differences and others, Mayer (2001) proposed a framework for multimedia design. It is believed that humans process incoming information differently. The auditory information (e.g., sound) is encoded differently from the visual information (e.g., text, images). According to dual coding theory (Paivio, 1986), the auditory information is registered in the auditory channel and the visual information is registered in the visual channel, both of which represent important characteristics in the working memory. Mayer (2001) claimed that incoming information from both visual and auditory channels are interacted in the working memory to form a mental representation of the external object. For example, the concept of "car" is represented both by the sound "car" and the word "car." The learner connects the sound of "k-är" with the letters "c-a-r" to form a mental representation of an external object that is "a motor vehicle with four wheels; usually propelled by an internal combustion engine" (Longman Group Ltd, 1978, p. 150). The information in the working memory stays only for a brief time. Some enter into the long term memory, others are filtered out. Therefore, it is critical that the working memory does not get overloaded with unrelated information in the process of schema construction, that is, relevant information that adds to the long term memory. In other words, the design of learning should be such that it only uses the precious cognitive resources in the working memory for learning that contributes to schema construction or meaningful, deep learning. To that extent, Mayer's theory of multimedia learning provides a unique perspective to understanding the relationship between multimedia and learning optimization. Mayer's theory of multimedia learning includes seven principles. They are multimedia principle, spatial contiguity principle, temporal contiguity principle, coherence principle, modality principle, redundancy principle, and individual differences principle.

Multimedia principle. The multimedia principle states that learners learn better from words and pictures than from words alone. Mayer and his colleagues studied the effects of multimedia on learning (Mayer & Anderson, 1991; Mayer & Sims, 1994). They found that when multimedia was used for learning, the learners showed better performance in problem solving compared to a single medium as measured by retention and knowledge transfer. Mayer (2001) thus concluded that "multimedia … adding illustrations to text or adding animation to narration can help students to better understand the presented explanation. We refer to this result as a *multimedia effect*" (p. 78).

Spatial contiguity principle. This principles states that learners learn better when corresponding words and pictures are presented near rather far from each other on the page or screen. Mayer and his colleagues examined the conditions in which learning contents were presented differently through spatial manipulation. In the first condition, the pictures and related texts are separated from each other by placing the pictures far from the text. In the second condition, the pictures and related text are integrated with the pictures close to the text or the text being embedded in the pictures. The results showed that the spatially integrated presentation (i.e., spatial contiguity) facilitated learners' learning as measured by retention and knowledge transfer. The authors claimed that by following the special contiguity principle, learning becomes more efficient and prevents *split attention* from occurring. As it was mentioned above, split attention can impair learning since the learner must mentally integrate disparate sources of information, which can impose a high extraneous cognitive load on the learner (Chandler & Sweller, 1992).

Temporal contiguity principle. This principle stipulates that learning becomes efficient when corresponding words and pictures are presented simultaneously rather than successively. The difference between the temporal contiguity principle and the spatial contiguity principle is that the former focuses on presenting corresponding words and pictures close to each other in time, whereas the latter deals with placing corresponding words and pictures close to each other on the page. Mayer and his colleagues researched the temporal effects on learning and found that simultaneous presentation of the words and pictures increased learners' retention and knowledge transfer as compared to successive presentation of the learning materials (Mayer & Anderson, 1992; Moreno & Mayer, 1999).

Coherence principle. The coherence principle states that learners learn better when extraneous material is excluded rather than included. Mayer and his colleagues (Moreno & Mayer, 2000) examined the effects of coherence principle on learning and concluded that (1) the learner's learning is hurt when interesting but irrelevant words and pictures are added to multimedia presentation, (2) the learner's learning is hurt when interesting but irrelevant sounds and music are added to multimedia presentation, and (3) the learner's learning is improved when unneeded words are eliminated from a multimedia presentation.

Modality principle. The modality principle states that learners learn better from animation and narration than from animation and on-screen text, that is, learners learn better when words in a multimedia message are presented as spoken text rather than printed text. In a series of studies conducted by Mayer and his colleagues (Mayer & Moreno, 1998, 1999), the authors examined the modality effects on cognitive learning. They found that when animation was used with narration, there was a general learning gain in both retention and knowledge transfer as opposed to combining animation with text. They thus concluded that the mode of presentation when appropriately designed such as animation with narration can significantly improve working memory in learning.

Redundancy principle. The redundancy principle refers to situations in which a redundant and unnecessary mode of presentation is present, which increases the working memory load in the information process. For example, when animation is combined with narration, the learner's learning improves (see the modality principle discussed above). However, if the presentation mode includes *animation*, *narration*, and *text*, learning becomes hampered. This is because when pictures and words are both presented visually (i.e., as animation and texts), the visual channel can become overloaded. Mayer, Heiser, and Lonn (2001) compared two mode conditions, one was animation + narration, the other was animation + narration + text. The results showed that animation with narration group outperformed their counterparts in both retention and transfer tests.

Individual differences principle. This principle identifies the individual differences in relation to multimedia presentation. For example, low-knowledge learners seemed to be more benefited from multimedia learning than high-knowledge learners. Another example of individual differences in multimedia learning is the spatial ability. Since multimedia involves visual presentation, spatial ability can be a critical factor in influencing learners' learning. Studies by Mayer and Sims (1994) revealed that high-spatial learners possess the cognitive capacity to mentally integrate visual and verbal representations from effective multimedia presentations; in contrast, low-spatial learners must devote so much cognitive capacity to holding the presented images in memory that they are less likely to have sufficient capacity left over to mentally integrate visual and verbal representations. This principle helps raise the awareness of individual differences among the designers as they design and develop multimedia learning.

Overall, Mayer's cognitive theory of multimedia learning and his principles of multimedia design contribute to the understanding of the functionality of the multimedia in terms of reducing the working memory load in the learning process. His principles of multimedia design complements Sweller's cognitive load theory in that his principles delineate instructional situations in which multimedia can be optimally designed to alleviate working memory load and in which learning is significantly improved by taking into consideration the cognitive functionality of multimedia in learning. Although research concerning the application of Mayer's multimedia theory and principles to the design of learning material for older people is far and few between, many of his theory and principles of multimedia design are relevant and can be very helpful for the design of learning material, especially Internet-based learning material for older people. Commenting on designing computerized instruction for older adults, van Gerven, Paas, and Tabbers (2006) pointed out that Sweller's cognitive load theory and Richard Mayer's cognitive theory of multimedia learning can be "used to accommodate the needs of elderly learners … It is argued that these instructional theories bear important benefits for older learners because they support an efficient use of available cognitive resources" (p. 141). Although the above theories are significant in providing theoretical framework for the design and development of instruction, it is unclear how to systematically integrate the above theories into instructional design, i.e., taking a systematic approach in prescribing design procedures for the instruction of elderly learners. Heuristics is deemed to be one of the approaches that hold promise for the future of practice and research in this direction (Lee & Reigeluth, 2009). The next section focuses on the heuristics as a design strategy for E-Learning for older people.

HEURISTICS AS A DESIGN STRATEGY FOR E-LEARNING FOR OLDER PEOPLE

Heuristics is related to decision-making processes for eliciting, analyzing, and representing expertise in complex cognitive tasks (Lee & Reigeluth, 2009). Simon (1990), the father of modern heuristics research, stated that heuristics are "methods for arriving at satisfactory solutions with modest amounts of computation" (p. 11). Lee and Reigeluth (2009) point out that heuristics can be instrumental in the process of instructional design in that they capture the most important aspects pertaining to both learners and the processes associated with learning. For heuristics to be effective and applicable to instructional design especially instructional design for E-learning for older adults, it is important to consider the framework proposed by Shah and Oppenheimer (2008) who identified principles for heuristic analysis.

Shah and Oppenheimer's Framework for Effort-Reduction for Heuristics

Shah and Oppenheimer (2008) proposed a framework that contains five principles guiding the design and development of heuristics related to various human activities. The five principles include: examining few cues; reducing the difficulty associated with retrieving and storing cue values; simplifying the weighing principles for cues; integrating less information; and examining fewer alternatives.

Examining fewer cues. The decision maker focuses on the most important cues. Although other alternative cues are available, the decision maker focuses only on one cue at a time, which helps reduce the amount of information that must be kept in working memory.

Reducing the difficulty associated with retrieving and storing cue values. Provide information that is easy to access and retrieve. For example, in comparing the fuel efficiency of a Mini Cooper and Hummer, use indicators with clear and simple comparison such as "greater than," "better than," "efficient than," etc. rather than actual difference in miles.

Simplifying the weighing principles for cues. Using nonvalidity based cue selection, the decision maker simplifies the cue weighing principles because they do not have to judge the predictive accuracy of each cue. The decision maker assigns equal weight to each cue and retains the alternative that is superior on the majority of cues when comparing two alternatives at a time. Without weights for each cue, the decision maker reduces cognitive effort in heuristic analysis.

Integrating less information. The decision maker integrates less information by setting cutoff levels for each cue and then selecting the first alternative in his/her search that surpasses the cutoff for each cue. Since each cue is evaluated independently, there is no need to integrate information across cues or form an overall impression of an alternative before it is eliminated. The noncompensatory nature of the heuristics thus reduces the mental effort of the decision maker.

Examining fewer alternatives. The decision maker may benefit from examining fewer alternatives in the heuristic analysis. Goal of examining fewer alternatives can be accomplished by (a) limiting the number of alternatives that are compared simultaneously. According to Shah and Oppenheimer (2008), reducing the number of alternatives that must be kept in working memory at once will reduce the demand on cognitive resources. Another way to accomplish this goal is gradually paring down the number of alternatives in the set. It is believed that heuristics that examine fewer alternatives can reduce effort by immediately eliminating some alternatives from the overall set of available alternatives.

Shah and Oppenheimer's framework highlights the importance of effort reduction in the application of heuristics to the work under study. According to Shah and Oppenheimer, the five principles are qualitatively different from one another and are therefore separate from each other. However, this does not exclude the possibility of combining one or two principles in the heuristic analysis. For example, a heuristic might not noticeably reduce the number of cues used but might instead use numerous easy-to-access cues. Under a different circumstance, the decision maker may use easy-to-access cues and meanwhile take the approach of reducing the number of alternatives. In that regard, the framework is robustly resilient and flexible enough to enable the designer or decision maker to conduct an efficient heuristic analysis that provides the insights to the content under the study. The next section offers a discussion on applying Shah and Oppenheimer's framework of heuristics to the design of instruction for elderly learning/training.

Instruction for Elderly Learning/ Training: A Heuristic Approach

In this section, I will propose a heuristic design approach to the design of instruction for elderly learning and training. The approach takes in perspective cognitive load theory and principles of multimedia learning when designing and developing learning content for older people. As it was discussed previously, older people experience a gradual decline of cognitive functioning including working memory, motor skills, information processing speed and so forth. Thus, designers should be particularly aware of the barriers that would lower the learning abilities of older people. For example, the content that causes extraneous load (e.g., split attention) can be particularly detrimental to older people's learning. On the other hand, learning materials that impose a high intrinsic load can be frustrating to senior adults. Appropriate support (e.g., worked examples, pre-training, etc.) must be provided to alleviate the level of their frustration.

Along the notion of extraneous load, multimedia that are inappropriately designed can lead to low performance cognitively and affectively. For example, redundancy in multimedia learning can cause distraction, thus lower older adults' overall performance. In a similar vein, inappropriately designed multimedia such as combining animation/image with text and narration will tax the decline working memory of older people, causing learning to be less efficient. Other issues such as spatial contiguity, coherence, and modality are equally important in the design of instruction for elderly people's training and learning. To put above issues in perspective when designing and developing multimedia /Web-based content for older people, a systematic design approach is proposed based on Shah and Oppenheimer's framework (Figure 2).

The proposed heuristics for the design of instruction for elderly training/learning incorporates Shah and Oppenheimer's framework of heuristics by focusing on the principles of *examining few cues, integrating less information,* and *examining fewer alternatives.* There are several advantages using this framework. First, by focusing on the most important cues and one cue at a time, the instructional designer is able to reduce the amount of information that must be kept in working memory. Second, the instructional designer integrates less information by evaluating each cue independently such as modality, spatial contiguity, and so forth. There is no need to integrate information across cues (modality, spatial contiguity, redundancy, etc.). In fact, the noncompensatory nature of the heuristics helps reduce the mental effort of the instructional designer. Finally, the instructional designer examines fewer alternatives. By limiting the number of alternatives that are compared simultaneously, the instructional designer is able to utilize the cognitive resources available to focus on the heuristic analysis of the instruction.

Another characteristics of the proposed heuristics is that it aligns cognitive load theory with multimedia design principles in a systematic manner in that the analysis of cognitive load is meshed with the principles of multimedia learning.

Figure 2. *Heuristics for instructional design for elderly training/learning*

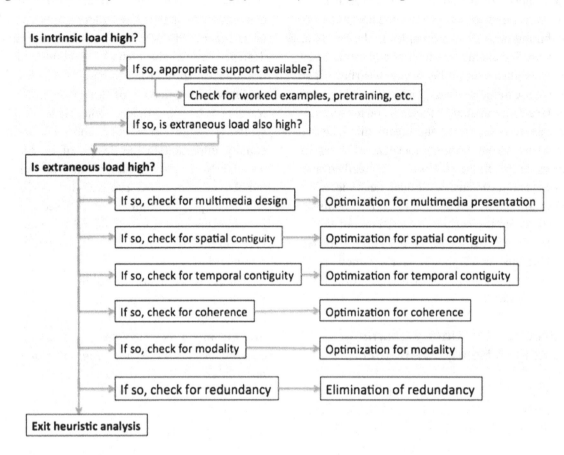

For example, the proposed heuristics starts with the analysis of intrinsic cognitive load. Two sub-questions follow with the last question serving as a linkage between intrinsic and extraneous cognitive load. The question presents important relationship between intrinsic and extraneous cognitive load: if the intrinsic cognitive load is high, the extraneous cognitive load must be low; however, if the intrinsic cognitive load is low, it does not matter whether the extraneous cognitive load is high or low. This is because with high intrinsic and extraneous cognitive loads, there will be few cognitive resources left in the working memory, hence the failure of learning (Sweller, 2010). The proposed heuristics identifies ways to manage the extraneous cognitive load so that it becomes low when the intrinsic cognitive load is high by

checking for the design of multimedia materials using Mayer's multimedia design principles.

DISCUSSION

The proposed heuristics suggests a new perspective in regard to the design and development of instruction for elderly training and learning. Different from the conventional design approaches, the proposed heuristics are grounded in cognitive learning theories on multimedia and human information processes as well as based on established principles of heuristic design. As a new instructional design approach, the proposed heuristics are specifically designed to reduce cognitive demands associated with the decision-making in instructional design. There are a few unique characteristics related to the proposed heuristics. Firstly, the proposed heuristics aim at reducing mental effort in the course of instructional design by adapting proven heuristic design principles. Secondly, the proposed heuristics take a systematic approach by integrating two cognitive learning theories related to multimedia learning. Specifically, the two constructs of cognitive load theory (i.e., intrinsic and extraneous cognitive loads) are used as the framework for the heuristics while Mayer's multimedia design principles and other proven methods for cognitive load reduction are filled in to provide operational definitions for the framework.

FUTURE TRENDS

As with other instructional design models and approaches, the proposed heuristics need to be empirically tested to verify their underlying theoretical principles and assumptions. Future research is needed to examine the functionality of the heuristics in terms of effort reduction for the instructional designer. Further exploration should be conducted to find out whether the proposed heuristics would effectively identify instructional problems associated with e-learning for older people, thus to design and develop instructional materials that would result in effective and efficient learning performance.

Research in future should focus on the measurement scheme that clearly identifies the performance and outcomes relating to the use of the proposed heuristics. Such measurement scheme should clearly explain the relationship between proposed functions of the heuristics and the expected outcomes, that is, older people's use of the instructional materials.

CONCLUSION

The growth of aging population globally demands that more support, both cognitively and affectively, should be provided to meet their personal, entertainment, health, and social needs. Internet has become increasingly a venue through which they access various information to meet their aforementioned needs. The challenge associated with this new form of information access is that few websites are designed by considering the needs of older people. In other words, the Web developers and instructional designers seldom take into consideration the cognitive factors of older people often seen as reduced working memory capacity, slow processing speed, and decline in physical and mental coordination. As a result, searching for the information from the Internet can sometimes become a challenge to many older adults. This chapter examined the cognitive constraints related to older people in learning, particularly in e-learning and proposed a new design approach, which (1) assists instructional designer and Web development in identifying issues related to older people's involvement in e-learning; (2) helps reduce the mental load in designing and developing e-learning for older people; and (3) uses heuristics to systematically support the designers in making decisions about meeting the needs of the older people in their learning and searching for information online.

It should be pointed out that the proposed approach should not be interpreted as the only design approach for e-learning design for the older people. Instead, it provides an alternative view to mainstream instructional design and calls for the need of studying the dynamic relationship between intrinsic and extraneous cognitive loads and between cognitive load theory and multimedia design principles.

155

REFERENCES

Atkinson, R. C., & Shiffrin, R. M. (1968). Human memory: A proposed system and its control processes. In Spence, K. W., & Spence, J. T. (Eds.), *The Psychology of Learning and Motivation: Advances in Research and Theory* (*Vol. 2*, pp. 89–195). New York, NY: Academic Press. doi:10.1016/S0079-7421(08)60422-3

Baddeley, A., Sala, S. D., & Baddeley, R. (1996). Working memory and executive control. *Philosophical Transactions of the Royal Society of London. Series B, Biological Sciences, 351*(1346), 1397–1404. doi:10.1098/rstb.1996.0123

Baddeley, A. D., & Hitch. (1974). Working memory, In G. A. Bower (Ed.), *The Psychology of Learning and Motivation: Advances in Research and Theory,* (Vol. 8), (pp. 47–89). New York, NY: Academic Press.

Baddeley, A. D. (1997). *Human memory: Theory and practice*. Hove, UK: Psychology Press.

Cattell, R. B. (1963). Theory of fluid and crystallized intelligence: A critical experiment. *Journal of Educational Psychology, 54*, 1–22. doi:10.1037/h0046743

Cattell, R. B. (1971). *Abilities: Their structure, growth, and action*. New York, NY: Houghton Mifflin.

Chandler, P., & Sweller, J. (1992). The split-attention effect as a factor in the design of instruction. *The British Journal of Educational Psychology, 62*, 233–246. doi:10.1111/j.2044-8279.1992.tb01017.x

Darabi, A., Arrastia, M. C., & Nelson, D. W. (2011). Cognitive presence in asynchronous online learning: A comparison of four discussion strategies. *Journal of Computer Assisted Learning, 27*(3), 216–227. doi:10.1111/j.1365-2729.2010.00392.x

Gardner, M., & Hill, R. (2012). Training older adults to improve their episodic memory: Three different approaches to enhancing numeric memory. In Zheng, R., Hill, R., & Gardner, M. (Eds.), *Engaging Older Adults with Modern Technology: Internet Use and Information*. Hershey, PA: IGI Global.

Hawthorn, D. (2007). Interface design and engagement with older people. *Behaviour & Information Technology, 26*(4), 333–341. doi:10.1080/01449290601176930

Hwang, G. J., Kuo, F. R., & Yin, P. Y. (2010). A heuristic algorithm for planning personalized learning paths for context-aware ubiquitous learning. *Computers & Education, 54*(2), 404–415. doi:10.1016/j.compedu.2009.08.024

Kilb, A., & Naveh-Benjamin, M. (2011). The effects of pure pair repetition on younger and older adults' associative memory. *Journal of Experimental Psychology. Learning, Memory, and Cognition, 37*(3), 706–719. doi:10.1037/a0022525

Kirschner, P. A., Sweller, J., & Clark, R. E. (2006). Why minimal guidance during instruction does not work: An analysis of the failure of constructivist, discovery, problem-based, experiential, and inquiry-based teaching. *Educational Psychologist, 41*, 75–86. doi:10.1207/s15326985ep4102_1

Lee, J. Y., & Reigeluth, C. M. (2009). Heuristic task analysis on e-learning course development: A formative research study. *Asia Pacific Education Review, 10*(2), 169–181. doi:10.1007/s12564-009-9016-1

Locke, D. (1971). *Memory*. Garden City, NY: Anchor Books.

Longman Group Ltd. (1978). *Longman dictionary of contemporary English*. Bath, UK: Pitman Press.

Mayer, R. E. (2001). *Multimedia learning*. Cambridge, UK: Cambridge University Press.

Mayer, R. E., & Anderson, R. B. (1991). Animations need narrations: An experimental test of a dual-coding hypothesis. *Journal of Educational Psychology, 83,* 484–490. doi:10.1037/0022-0663.83.4.484

Mayer, R. E., Heiser, J., & Lonn, S. (2001). Cognitive constraints on multimedia learning: When presenting more material results in less understanding. *Journal of Educational Psychology, 93*(1), 187–198. doi:10.1037/0022-0663.93.1.187

Mayer, R. E., & Moreno, R. (1998). A split-attention effect in multimedia learning: Evidence for dual processing systems in working memory. *Journal of Educational Psychology, 90,* 312–320. doi:10.1037/0022-0663.90.2.312

Mayer, R. E., & Moreno, R. (2003). Nine ways to reduce cognitive load in multimedia learning. *Educational Psychologist, 38*(1), 43–52. doi:10.1207/S15326985EP3801_6

Mayer, R. E., & Sims, V. K. (1994). For whom is a picture worth a thousand words? Extensions of a dual-coding theory of multimedia learning. *Journal of Educational Psychology, 86*(3), 389–401. doi:10.1037/0022-0663.86.3.389

Miller, G. A. (1956). The magical number seven, plus or minus two: Some limits on our capacity for processing information. *Psychological Review, 63,* 81–97. doi:10.1037/h0043158

Moreno, R., & Mayer, R. (1999). Cognitive principles of multimedia learning: The role of modality and contiguity. *Journal of Educational Psychology, 91,* 358–368. doi:10.1037/0022-0663.91.2.358

Moreno, R., & Mayer, R. (2000). A coherence effect in multimedia learning: The case for minimizing irrelevant sounds in the design of multimedia messages. *Journal of Educational Psychology, 92,* 117–125. doi:10.1037/0022-0663.92.1.117

Opitz, B. (2010). Context-dependent repetition effects on recognition memory. *Brain and Cognition, 73*(2), 110–118. doi:10.1016/j.bandc.2010.04.003

Ouwehand, K., van Gog, T., & Paas, F. (2012). The use of gesturing to facilitate older adults' learning from computer-based dynamic visualizations. In Zheng, R., Hill, R., & Gardner, M. (Eds.), *Engaging Older Adults with Modern Technology: Internet Use and Information.* Hershey, PA: IGI Global.

Paas, F., Camp, G., & Rikers, R. (2001). Instructional compensation for age-related cognitive declines: Effects of goal specificity in maze learning. *Journal of Educational Psychology, 93,* 181–186. doi:10.1037/0022-0663.93.1.181

Paivio, A. (1986). *Mental representations: A dual coding approach.* Oxford, UK: Oxford University Press.

Rhodes, M. G., & Kelley, C. M. (2005). Executive processes, memory accuracy, and memory monitoring: An aging and individual difference analysis. *Journal of Memory and Language, 52*(4), 578–594. doi:10.1016/j.jml.2005.01.014

Shah, A. K., & Oppenheimer, D. M. (2008). Heuristics made easy: An effort-reduction framework. *Psychological Bulletin, 134*(2), 207–222. doi:10.1037/0033-2909.134.2.207

Simon, H. A. (1990). Invariants of human behavior. *Annual Review of Psychology, 41,* 1–19. doi:10.1146/annurev.ps.41.020190.000245

Sweet, J., & Ellaway, R. (2010). Reuse as heuristic: From transmission to nurture in learning activity design. *Innovations in Education and Teaching International, 47*(2), 215–222. doi:10.1080/14703291003718943

Sweller, J. (1988). Cognitive load during problem solving: Effects on learning. *Cognitive Science, 12,* 257–285. doi:10.1207/s15516709cog1202_4

Sweller, J. (2010). Element interactivity and intrinsic, extraneous, and germane cognitive load. *Educational Psychology Review, 22,* 123–138. doi:10.1007/s10648-010-9128-5

Sweller, J., & Chandler, P. (1991). Evidence for cognitive load theory. *Cognition and Instruction, 8*(4), 351–362. doi:10.1207/s1532690xci0804_5

Sweller, J., & Chandler, P. (1994). Why some material is difficult to learn. *Cognition and Instruction, 12*(3), 185–233. doi:10.1207/s1532690xci1203_1

Tindall-Ford, S., Chandler, P., & Sweller, J. (1997). When two sensory modes are better than one. *Journal of Experimental Psychology. Applied, 3,* 257–287. doi:10.1037/1076-898X.3.4.257

van Gerven, P., Paas, F., & Schmidt, H. (2000). Cognitive load theory and the acquisition of complex cognitive skills in the elderly: Towards and integrative framework. *Educational Gerontology, 26,* 503–521. doi:10.1080/03601270050133874

van Gerven, P., Paas, F., & Tabbers, H. K. (2006). Cognitive aging and computer-based instructional design: Where do we go from here? *Educational Psychology Review, 18*(2), 141–157. doi:10.1007/s10648-006-9005-4

van Gerven, P., Paas, F., van Merrienboer, J. J. G., Hendriks, M., & Schmidt, H. (2003). The efficiency of multimedia learning into old age. *The British Journal of Educational Psychology, 73,* 489–505. doi:10.1348/000709903322591208

van Gerven, P., Paas, F., van Merrienboer, J. J. G., & Schmidt, H. (2002). Cognitive load theory and aging: Effects of worked examples on training efficiency. *Learning and Instruction, 12,* 87–105. doi:10.1016/S0959-4752(01)00017-2

van Gerven, P., Paas, F., van Merrienboer, J. J. G., & Schmidt, H. (2006). Modality and variability as factors in training the elderly. *Applied Cognitive Psychology, 20,* 311–320. doi:10.1002/acp.1247

van Merrienboer, J. J. G., & Sweller, J. (2005). Cognitive load theory and complex learning: Recent developments and future directions. *Educational Psychology Review, 17,* 147–177. doi:10.1007/s10648-005-3951-0

Watson, J. M., Lambert, A. E., Cooper, J. M., Boyle, I. V., & Strayer, D. L. (2012). On attentional control and the aging driver. In Zheng, R., Hill, R., & Gardner, M. (Eds.), *Engaging Older Adults with Modern Technology: Internet Use and Information.* Hershey, PA: IGI Global.

Zheng, R., & Cook, A. (2011). Solving complex problems: A convergent approach to cognitive load measurement. *British Journal of Educational Technology, 43*(2).

ADDITIONAL READING

Basak, C., Boot, W. R., Voss, M. W., & Kramer, A. F. (2008). Can training in a real-time strategy video game attenuate cognitive decline in older adults? *Psychology and Aging, 23,* 765–777. doi:10.1037/a0013494

Cattell, R. B. (1987). *Intelligence: Its structure, growth, and action.* New York, NY: Elsevier Science Pub. Co.

Cavanaugh, J. C., & Blanchard-Fields, F. (2006). *Adult development and aging* (5th ed.). Belmont, CA: Wadsworth Publishing/Thomson Learning.

Curran, K., Walters, N., & Robinson, D. (2007). Investigating the problems faced by older adults and people with disabilities in online environments. *Behaviour & Information Technology, 26,* 447–453. doi:10.1080/01449290600740868

Czaja, S. J., Charness, N., Fisk, A. D., Hertzog, C., Nair, S. N., Rogers, W. A., & Sharit, J. (2006). Factors predicting the use of technology: Findings from the center for research and education on aging and technology (CREATE). *Psychology and Aging*, *21*, 333–352. doi:10.1037/0882-7974.21.2.333

Czaja, S. J., Sharit, J., Ownby, R., & Roth, D. L. (2001). Examining age differences in performance of a complex information search and retrieval task. *Psychology and Aging*, *16*, 564–579. doi:10.1037/0882-7974.16.4.564

Germine, L. T., Duchaine, B., & Nakayama, K. (2011). Where cognitive development and aging meet: Face learning ability peaks after age 30. *Cognition*, *118*(2), 201–210. doi:10.1016/j.cognition.2010.11.002

Hogeboom, D. L., McDermott, R. J., Perrin, K. M., Osman, II., & Bell-Ellison, B. A. (2010). Internet use and social networking among middle aged and older adults. *Educational Gerontology*, *36*, 93–111. doi:10.1080/03601270903058507

Roelands, M., van Oost, P., Depoorter, A., & Buysse, A. (2002). A social-cognitive model to predict the use of assistive devices for mobility and self-care in elderly people. *The Gerontologist*, *42*, 39–50. doi:10.1093/geront/42.1.39

Saunders, E. J. (2004). Maximizing computer use among the elderly in rural senior centers. *Educational Gerontology*, *30*, 573–585. doi:10.1080/03601270490466967

Seals, C. D., Clanton, K., Agarwal, R., Doswell, F., & Thomas, C. M. (2008). Lifelong learning: Becoming computer savvy at a later age. *Educational Gerontology*, *34*, 1055–1069. doi:10.1080/03601270802290185

KEY TERMS AND DEFINITIONS

The Central Executive: The central executive is responsible for the supervision of information integration and for coordinating the information from phonological loop and visuo-spatial sketch pad, both of which he called *slave systems*.

Extraneous Cognitive Load: The extraneous cognitive load refers to the cognitive load caused by the format and manner in which information is presented. For example, instructors may unwittingly increase learners' extraneous cognitive load by presenting materials that 'require students to mentally integrate mutually referring, disparate sources of information' (Sweller & Chandler, 1991, p. 353).

Heuristics: Heuristics is related to decision-making processes for eliciting, analyzing, and representing expertise in complex cognitive tasks. Heuristics are "methods to for arriving at satisfactory solutions with modest amounts of computation" (Simon, 1990, p. 11).

Intrinsic Cognitive Load: The intrinsic cognitive load is induced by the structure and complexity of the instructional material. Usually, the instructor or instructional designer can do little to influence the intrinsic cognitive load.

Section 3
Practical Application of Technology for Older Adults

Chapter 9
Actual use of Computers and the Internet by Older Adults:
Potential Benefits and Risks

Karin Slegers
University of Leuven, Belgium & IBBT, Belgium

Martin P. van Boxtel
Maastricht University, The Netherlands

ABSTRACT

Improving autonomy and quality of life for older adults has become an increasingly important aim of gerontological research. Computer and Internet applications hold great promise to maintain autonomy and increase quality of life. This chapter focuses on the impact of computer and Internet use on several aspects of quality of life and autonomy of older adults. It is based on an intervention program that included concise computer training and the use of a computer and the Internet for twelve months. The results of this randomized, controlled study showed no effects, neither positive nor negative, of computer and Internet use on cognitive functioning, autonomy, well-being and social network, the use of everyday technological devices, and subjective physical functioning. Overall, it was concluded that computer and Internet usage by healthy older adults is a safe activity, albeit with no robust advantage for cognitive capacity in healthy older adults.

DOI: 10.4018/978-1-4666-1966-1.ch009

INTRODUCTION

Older adults are at a disadvantage in dealing with computer technology. Many individuals aged 65 or older have not learned to use computers at school or in the workplace. As a result, older adults experience more problems when they are faced with computer technology than younger adults do (Charness, Bosman, Kelley, & Mottram, 1996; Czaja & Sharit, 1993; Kelley & Charness, 1995). It has been shown in several studies, for instance, that older adults need more time to learn to use a computer system, make more errors and require more help (e.g. Kelley & Charness, 1995). As a consequence, older adults experience more problems with everyday activities that are increasingly computer-based and therefore their ability to maintain autonomous functioning may be jeopardized.

While adaptation to computer technology to perform everyday activities is posing problems for older adults, it seems obvious that older adults could benefit from (computer) technological innovations. Many technologies and products may help older adults with some of their age-related problems and thereby assist them in maintaining their autonomy. For instance, telemedicine applications enable communication with health care providers from home, hand-held computers can support individuals suffering from forgetfulness by providing contextual cues, and warning systems in the home may be used to monitor the health and safety of older adults without interfering with their daily life routines.

One of the computer-related developments that already helps older adults to deal with age-related changes and which may have impact on their quality of life is the Internet. For instance, the Internet facilitates autonomy with respect to many of the everyday activities that older adults may be restricted in doing, such as banking and shopping (Bouchard, Ryan, & Heaven, 1986; Czaja, Guerrier, Nair, & Landauer, 1993; Rogers & Fisk, 2000). Also, the Internet provides people with access to many sources of information (Cody, Dunn, Hoppin, & Wendt, 1999; Czaja & Lee, 2003; White, et al., 2002). This may be practical information, such as public transportation timetables and opening hours, and also information that can be used for entertainment, such as book reviews, online courses and games. Additional information is related to personal health. For instance, the Internet may improve access to health information as well as to health services and care givers (Czaja, 1996; Czaja & Lee, 2001; Morrell, et al., 2000; Rogers & Fisk, 2000; Stronge, Walker, & Rogers, 2001) and facilitate health care management (Czaja, 1997; Kelley & Charness, 1995).

Besides the facilitation of autonomy in everyday routines, the Internet also provides a way to maintain and improve one's social network and communication. Many researchers expect that the Internet and services such as e-mail, instant messaging and newsgroups facilitate social interaction and communication (Czaja & Lee, 2001; Mead, Batsakes, Fisk, & Mykityshyn, 1999; Morrell, Mayhorn, & Bennett, 2000; Rogers & Fisk, 2000), and also create opportunities for meeting new people (Czaja, 1996; White, et al., 2002). As a result, it has been argued that computer use can decrease feelings of being left out of modern society (Jones & Bayen, 1998; Lawhon, Ennis, & Lawhon, 1996) and improve self-esteem and satisfaction with life (Jones & Bayen, 1998; Lawhon, et al., 1996; Mead, et al., 1999; Sherer, 1996). On a more general level, computers and the Internet could potentially improve general wellbeing and the quality of life. For example, it has been proposed that the Internet provides mental stimulation and challenge to older adults (Jones & Bayen, 1998; McConatha, McConatha, & Dermigny, 1994; Mead, et al., 1999).

Finally, as older adults have little experience with using computers and Internet facilities, learning such a new skill is a cognitive challenging endeavor. Moreover, cognitive functions known to decline with age, such as memory, speed of information processing and selective attention, are involved in many computer and Internet-related activities. Therefore, by encouraging older adults to use computers and the Internet, their cognitive abilities, their engagement in interpersonal relations and productive activity, and their autonomy in performing everyday tasks may be stimulated. In addition, the skills older adults need to acquire in order to learn to use computers and the Internet may be useful in operating other everyday technology as well (e.g. train ticket vending machines or ATM's).

Besides the promising positive effects mentioned above, Internet use also may involve some risks. Possible risks associated to the use of computers and the Internet commonly are described in relation to excessive use of the Internet. In this respect, terms such as Internet addiction, pathological Internet use and problematic Internet use have been introduced (Yellowlees & Marks, 2007). Although excessive use of the Internet may not immediately be expected in novice elderly computer users, some associated risks are important to everyday autonomy in later life. Such risks include decreased interaction with family members at home and a smaller social circle (e.g. Kraut, Patterson, Lundmark, Kiesler, Mukopadhyay, & Scherlis, 1998), increased loneliness (e.g. Nalwa & Anand, 2003) and increased depression (Whang, Lee, & Chang, 2004). However, these risks may be outweighed by the positive effects that the Internet provides by offering means of maintaining and improve social interaction and communication. Besides the behavioral risks, intensive computer use has been related to physical functioning, more specifically to a complex of complaints related to the hand, arm and shoulder (Helliwell & Taylor, 2004).

The research described in this chapter is aimed at studying the impact, both positive and negative, of acquiring computer skills, and of using a computer and Internet facilities on several aspects of autonomy in later life. In order to achieve this objective, an intervention study was performed to investigate the impact of computer and In-

ternet use on four separate domains: cognitive functioning, wellbeing, quality of life and social network, the use of everyday technology, and physical functioning. The results of this research will be discussed in the light of recent developments regarding benefits and risks of computer and Internet use for older adults.

COGNITIVE RESERVE AND "USE IT OR LOSE IT": RATIONALE AND HYPOTHESES

The theoretical framework of the studies described in the present chapter was built from the perspective of successful aging, which has been defined as a threefold process of a) low probability of disease and disability, b) high cognitive and physical function capacity, and c) active engagement with life (Rowe & Kahn, 1997). The focus of the studies was to increase knowledge about how successful cognitive aging can be accomplished and to explore the efficacy of a new intervention strategy to stimulate successful aging.

More specifically, the concepts of 'cognitive reserve' and the 'use it or lose it' principle were essential notions in the research. The concept of reserve capacity, or the ability to compensate for (age-related) brain damage or disease (e.g. Stern, 2002), was introduced to explain individual differences in the onset of clinical symptoms after brain damage (Stern, 2002). For example, Katzman et al. (1989) described older women who showed neuropathological evidence of advanced Alzheimer's Disease (AD) at autopsy but who had been healthy and functioning normally until the moment of death. In a review, which has led to a renewed interest in the topic, Satz (1993) described a number of studies that showed differences in symptom onset in both Parkinson's disease and AD between individuals with comparable amounts of tissue damage or neuronal loss. Satz suggested that a reserve capacity might alter the threshold of symptom onset, such that individuals may have different degrees of brain damage before symptoms become clinically apparent. In other words, higher reserve capacity may result in later onset of symptoms of Parkinson's disease and AD.

Because there is no direct measure of reserve capacity, investigators often use indirect measures, such as intelligence, education, and brain volume (e.g. Prencipe, et al., 1996; Schmand, Smit, Geerlings, & Lindeboom, 1997; Tisserand, Bosma, van Boxtel, & Jolles, 2001). Next to this lack of a direct measure of reserve capacity, there is also no consensus on the true nature of this concept, and hence an unambiguous definition of the concept has not yet been formulated. More recently, reserve capacity has been defined more specifically in terms of passive and active brain reserve (Staff, Murray, Deary, & Whalley, 2004; Stern, 2002), where passive models of reserve assume a threshold of damage beyond which clinical manifestations of brain damage will occur (Satz, 1993; Staff, et al., 2004), while active models assume that brain functions actively compensate for the damage.

With this active, functional view of reserve capacity in mind, cognitive reserve has been operationally defined in terms of psychosocial variables, such as intelligence, education, or occupational attainment (e.g., Stern, 2002). This implies that individuals with high levels of intellectual, educational, or occupational attainment can sustain more brain damage before compensation mechanisms fail, and structural brain damage leads to clinical manifestations. Besides studies showing that factors established in early life, such as education, are indeed associated with (for instance) the prevalence of Alzheimer's disease (e.g. Barnes, 2011; Prencipe, et al., 1996; Schmand, et al., 1997), factors that are dynamic over the course of a lifetime have also been described in relation to cognitive reserve. Mostly, such factors are referred to as 'intellectually engaging activities,' or 'cognitive activities,' and are negatively related to cognitive decline (e.g. Hultsch, et al.,

1999; Wilson, et al., 2002) or the risk of developing dementia (e.g. Verghese, et al., 2003).

The notion that continued mental activity may protect against cognitive decline is in line with the 'use it or lose it' principle (Swaab, 1991; Swaab, et al., 2002). From a neurobiological perspective, this notion states that the use of neurons and neuronal networks prolongs the efficiency of Central Nervous System (CNS) activity during life. According to Swaab, activation of neuronal circuits may slow down the aging process. Candidate factors to stimulate the CNS may originate from within the organism itself, but also from the environment.

Translation of the 'use it or lose it' notion to cognitive functions implies that mental stimulation may have a protective effect against a decline in higher brain functions, especially in later life. This hypothesis is supported by several animal studies, which have shown that enriched environments, providing a stimulating and challenging habitat, are beneficial to the cognitive functioning of laboratory animals (e.g. Warren, Zerweck, & Anthony, 1982; Frick & Fernandez, 2003). A study by Milgram (2003) is especially interesting with regard to cognitive aging. Milgram investigated the effect of a behavioral enrichment program on old Beagle dogs. This program included housing with mates, regular exercise, and environmental enrichment by adding toys and regular experience with neuropsychological tests. After 2 years in this program, the behaviorally enriched group performed better than the control group on a discrimination and reversal task, suggesting that a prolonged period of cognitive enrichment helped to reverse or delay age-related cognitive decline. Thus, stimulating cognitive functions seems beneficial to cognitive functioning in later life.

Also in human subjects, several examples of interventions that target cognitive capacities have been described in literature. Many of these examples involve studies of memory training in older adults and generally show positive effects on memory performance (e.g. Brooks, Friedman,

Pearman, Gray, & Yesavage, 1999; Cavallini, Pagnin, & Vecchi, 2003; Moore, Sandman, Mc-Grady, & Kesslak, 2001; Stigsdotter & Backman, 1995). Other kinds of cognitive training programs, educational interventions for example (see Schaie, 1994), have been tested for efficacy as well. A reasoning or spatial orientation training program was shown to reverse cognitive decline in older adults over a 14-year period (Schaie & Willis, 1986). Later, the same authors showed that these interventions actually trained the ability underlying the test, rather than merely test performance (Schaie, Willis, Hertzog, & Schulenberg, 1987). Moreover, the improvement was sustained for 7 years (Kramer & Willis, 2002; Schaie, 1994). In addition, correlations were found between the trained abilities and measures of practical intelligence (Willis & Schaie, 1986) and objective measures of performance on instrumental tasks of daily living (Willis, Jay, Diehl, & Marsiske, 1992), which suggests a transfer of these abilities to daily activities. Ball et al. (2002) designed three types of intervention training: memory training, reasoning training, and speed-of-processing training that were all found to improve the cognitive abilities that were targeted. However, no type of training did affect everyday functioning.

In conclusion, it is assumed that the use of cognitive abilities in later life may support cognitive reserve and thereby slow the process of cognitive aging. Moreover, at least theoretically, it may be possible to boost cognitive reserve by promoting the participation in cognitively challenging activities. The intervention research described above suggests that it is possible to improve specific cognitive abilities of older adults with dedicated interventions. However, everyday functioning draws on multiple cognitive functions. For instance, a daily activity such as grocery shopping involves planning (how to reach the grocery store), memory (which items to buy), information processing (which of the items in the store are relevant), etcetera. Thus, multifactorial interventions (McDougall, 1999;

Stigsdotter & Backman, 1995) may be needed in order to sustain or improve autonomy in later life. A potential activity that may qualify for such a multifactorial intervention, and which could be incorporated into the lives of older adults quite smoothly, is the use of computers and the Internet.

It can be argued that several cognitive abilities are mobilized when using the Internet. For instance, long-term (procedural) memory is necessary for remembering the appropriate procedure to launch a browser. Short-term memory is essential to keep track of already attended information and already performed actions. One will need executive functions to structure the necessary actions into the correct order. Visual search is done to find relevant information cues on a Web page. Information processing is required to evaluate which information on a Web page is relevant, and to focus on those relevant cues and to ignore irrelevant cues, one needs attention skills.

In addition to the basic cognitive activities mentioned above, more complex processes have also been mentioned to play a role in finding information on the Web, such as problem solving and concept formation (Stronge, Walker, & Rogers, 2001). Problem solving is defined as a process of assembling an appropriate sequence of component procedures (or operators) to accomplish a goal (Carlson & Yaure, 1990), and is related to the structuring of actions mentioned above. Concept formation is needed when one deals with computer and Internet-related concepts, which are used as metaphors to facilitate interface mastery (e.g. 'desktop,' 'folder,' 'drag-and-drop'). Holt and Morrell (2002) mentioned the concept of processing speed in the context of presentation speed in Internet training. They suggested that information on the Internet should be presented in a self-paced fashion to allow the user to modify speed of processing. Finally, spatial orientation is also important. Spatial memory and spatial ability tend to decline in humans with advancing age (Kelley & Charness, 1995). Because of the hypertext-based nature of Websites, especially older users may have difficulties in keeping track of where they are in cyberspace (Lin, 2003). Web surfing thus will specifically stimulate skills related to spatial orientation and source monitoring and will thereby provide a cognitive challenge for older users.

In order to study the effectiveness of a multifactorial intervention consisting of acquiring computer skills and of using a computer and Internet facilities, we conducted a large-scale intervention study. This intervention targeted four main domains of everyday functioning in later life: cognitive functioning, autonomy, wellbeing and social network, the use of everyday technology, and subjective physical functioning. The results are discussed in this chapter for each domain separately. In addition, we will focus both on potential benefits and on potential risks of computer and Internet use by older adults.

DESIGN OF THE INTERVENTION STUDY

The intervention on which our study was based, consisted of a brief training and subsequent use of a computer with an Internet connection at home for a twelve-month period. Participants who were interested in learning to use a computer and the Internet were randomly assigned to the Intervention Group, the Training/No intervention Group, or the No training/No intervention Group. A fourth group consisted of participants with no interest in computer use.

Participants

A group of 236 older adults participated in the study. These participants were aged between 64 and 75, considered themselves to be healthy, and were sufficiently mobile to travel independently to the research center. Exclusion criteria were general mental functioning in a range suspect of a cognitive disorder (score below 24 on the Mini-

Mental State Examination [Folstein, Folstein, & McHugh, 1975]) and prior active computer experience. In addition, participants had to be willing to sign a form stating that they would refrain from any self-initiated computer use or computer lessons in case they were assigned to one of the non-intervention groups for the duration of this study. Each participant signed an informed consent form. The Medical Ethics Committee of Maastricht University Hospital approved the study.

Procedure

In 2002, invitation flyers were randomly sent to older adults from the Maastricht city register (The Netherlands). Individuals who were interested in participation called the research center for a screening interview by telephone. Persons who were found to be eligible for the study were included with respect to stratification to age, sex, and level of education.

All participants were scheduled for two baseline administrations of a cognitive test battery including tests of verbal memory, psychomotor speed, speed of processing general information, cognitive flexibility, selective attention, and subjective cognitive functioning. This dual baseline administration of the tests (with one to two weeks in between) was applied to familiarize the participants with the test procedures and to minimize procedural learning of the tests during the study period. For this reason, cognitive data from the first baseline measurement were discarded. The test battery was administered again after four and twelve months, using parallel test versions. In addition, a questionnaire was administered at all test occasions covering several domains of wellbeing, autonomous functioning, and the use of everyday technology.

After the baseline test administrations, participants with interest in learning to use computers and the Internet were randomly assigned to three groups in a two-phased randomization procedure (for a schematic overview of the recruitment and

Figure 1. Flowchart of the recruitment and two-phase randomization procedure showing the number of participants in each condition as well as the number of participants who dropped out during the process

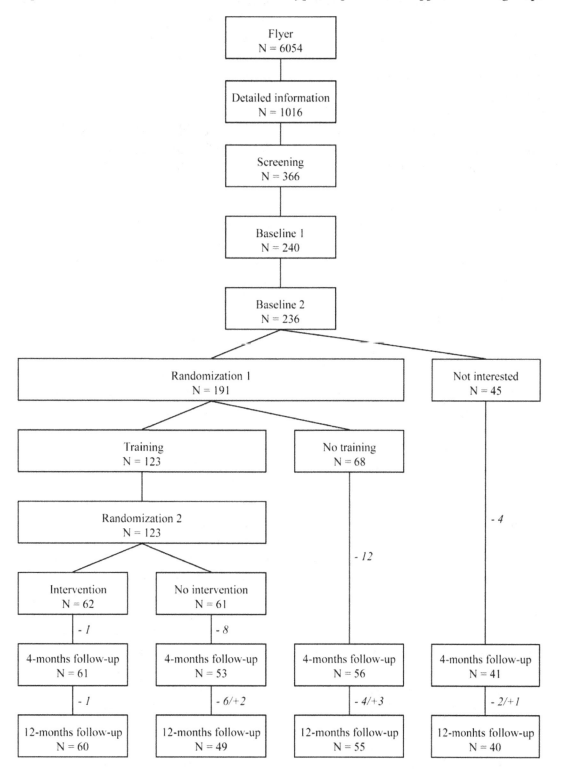

randomization procedures, see Figure 1). First, two thirds of these participants were selected for a three-session training course in general computer and Internet skills. The remaining participants did not receive this training and were assigned to the No training/No intervention Group.

The participants in the training condition were scheduled for three four-hour training sessions during a period of two weeks. In these sessions, participants were introduced to and could practice with a personal computer (Apple Macintosh) and its operating system (MacOS 9), customary software applications (for instance a word processor), and several Internet applications (i.e. an Internet browser and an e-mail program). Under supervision of an experienced teacher, participants received general information and were instructed about how to perform basic computer and Internet assignments from a custom-made course book. After this training, participants were randomly assigned to the Traning/Intervention Group and the Training/No intervention Group.

Participants in the Intervention Group were equipped with an up-to-date personal computer (Apple iMac) with high-speed Internet access (cable) in their homes for a twelve-month period. They received no specific instructions but were stimulated to use the computer in accordance with their personal needs. Internet-related assignments through e-mail (once every two weeks in the first four months, once every month in the remaining period of the study) were given to promote continuous use of the computer facilities and to track down participants who made insufficient progress with respect to their computer skills. These assignments were of increasing difficulty. Examples of early assignments are to reply to an e-mail message or to find easily accessible information on a specified Website. An example of a more difficult assignment is finding information about a book in an unspecified online library catalogue. A helpdesk with remote support facilities ('remote desktop') was available for all questions related to computers and Internet use during the project.

Participants in all no-intervention groups were to refrain from computer use during the intervention interval of twelve months, as they agreed to by signing the form mentioned above. Compliance to this agreement was again confirmed by signing a statement at the end of the study.

EFFECTS OF COMPUTER AND INTERNET USE ON EVERYDAY FUNCTIONING IN LATER LIFE

In this section, we discuss the impact of computer and Internet use of older adults with respect to each of four domains of everyday functioning: cognitive functioning, autonomy, wellbeing, and social network, the use of everyday technology, and subjective physical functioning.

Cognitive Functioning

Cognitive abilities tend to decline with age (for an extensive overview, see Craik & Salthouse, 2000). Several studies have suggested that engagement in cognitively challenging activities is associated with maintenance or even improvement of cognitive skills and seems to protect against age-related cognitive decline. For instance, Hultsch, Herzog, Small, and Dixon (1999) found a positive relationship between changes in participation in intellectually engaging activities and changes in cognitive functioning in middle-aged and older adults. Comparable observations were made by Wilson et al. (2002), who found that the rate of cognitive decline of people aged 65 and older in 4.5 years decreased for each additional cognitive activity they were engaged in. Also, participants in the Bronx Aging Study, aged 75 and older, who engaged more often in activities such as reading and playing games demonstrated a lower risk of developing dementia (Verghese, et al., 2003). In other studies, more general measures of activity, such as participation in everyday mental, social or physical activities, were found to be associated with protection from cognitive decline (e.g. Bosma, et al., 2002; Christensen, et al., 1996). These studies all suggest that intellectual and cognitively challenging activities are related to the preservation of cognitive capacity.

Besides studies showing associations between cognitive activities and maintenance of cognitive functions, several examples are available of interventions that specifically target cognitive capacities of older adults. Such studies involved memory training (e.g. Stigsdotter & Backman, 1995; Valentijn, et al., 2005) or mnemonic techniques (Ball, et al., 2002; Verhaeghen, Marcoen, & Goossens, 1992), all of which had positive effects on memory performance to a variable extent. Apart from memory, other cognitive abilities, such as reasoning, spatial orientation and speed of processing (Ball, et al., 2002; Schaie & Willis, 1986) have been taught successfully and shown to improve in older adults.

The studies cited above suggest that it is possible to improve cognitive functions of older adults with specific, dedicated interventions. However, in order to function independently in everyday life, multiple cognitive functions are drawn upon. As was argued in the section on the rationale and hypotheses of the studies presented in this chapter, the use of the Internet may qualify as a candidate activity in such a multifactorial intervention.

Methods

To test this hypothesis, six measures of cognitive functions known to decline with age were included in the test battery of the intervention study (Slegers, van Boxtel, & Jolles, 2009). Verbal memory (immediate recall, delayed recall and verbal learning) was measured with the Visual Verbal Learning Test (VVLT) (van der Elst, van Boxtel, van Breukelen, & Jolles, 2005). Psychomotor speed (response selection and inhibition of a prepotent response) was measured with the Motor Choice Reaction Time test (MCRT) (Houx & Jolles, 1993). The Letter-Digit Substitution Test

(LDST) (van der Elst, van Boxtel, van Breukelen, & Jolles, 2006a) was used to measure the speed of processing general information, an indication of general cognitive speed. Cognitive flexibility was tested with the Concept Shifting Test (CST) (van der Elst, van Boxtel, van Breukelen, & Jolles, 2006b) that measures slowing due to the shifting between two concepts. The Stroop Color Word Test (SCWT) (Houx, Jolles, & Vreeling, 1993) was used as a measure of selective attention and susceptibility to interference. Finally, subjective cognitive functioning was measured with the Cognitive Failure Questionnaire (CFQ) (Broadbent, Cooper, FitzGerald, & Parkes, 1982).

Results and Discussion

No effect of the intervention was found on almost all measures of cognitive functioning. A difference in change over time between the groups was found in regard to only one cognitive measure, the learning variable of the VVLT. However, this interaction effect between group and time was quite random and did not appear to be caused by the intervention. There were also some main effects of group membership, but since no interactions with time were found, these effects could not be attributed to the intervention.

We did find some interaction effects when the Intervention group was split into 'light' and 'heavy' computer users. Participants with better verbal memory and better capacities to inhibit a habitual response (which is an attentional process) used their computers more extensively (eight hours per week or more). On the other hand, participants who used their computers less than eight hours per week showed better verbal learning scores. This may be explained by the fact that these participants remembered fewer words in the first trial of the VVLT and could thus improve more in the following trials compared with the heavy computer users. These results suggest that there is a relationship between actual computer use and cognitive abilities of older adults. However, as the differences between light and heavy computer users remained stable over time, the intervention did not have an impact on these cognitive abilities. Rather, older adults with better cognitive abilities tended to use a computer more extensively. This relationship between computer use and cognitive abilities was also reflected in the baseline comparison between participants who were interested in learning to use a personal computer and the Internet and participants with no such interest. Interested participants reported significantly fewer cognitive failures in the CFQ compared with participants who were not interested.

Our findings differed from findings in earlier studies showing that computer-based interventions similar to ours to some extent yielded positive effects on several psychosocial (Cody, et al., 1999; Danowski & Sacks, 1980; McConatha, et al., 1994; McConatha, et al., 1995; Sherer, 1996; White, et al., 2002) and cognitive measures (McConatha, et al., 1994; McConatha, et al., 1995). There are a number of differences between these studies and ours that may explain these differences in findings. The first major difference is the study population. The aforementioned studies included residents of care facilities, i.e. these individuals were not older adults living independently, whereas the participants in our study were younger and more independent. It may be that our community dwelling participants had less to gain from the intervention as their level of cognitive functioning was quite high to begin with, and they might not have been able to benefit much from any kind of cognitive invervention.

A second major difference concerns the used measures of cognitive ability. Most of the aforementioned studies used a rather general measure of cognitive ability. For instance, McConatha et al. (1994, 1995) used the MMSE. In our study, more specific measures of cognitive functions were included. Because of these measures, we were able to study the impact of our intervention on many more aspects of cognitive functioning compared with the general measures used in previous research. Not only did these objective measures of cognitive abilities not change as a result of the intervention, we also did not find any effect of intervention on reported cognitive failures, which is a more subjective measure of cognitive functioning.

In conclusion, we could not demonstrate any impact of learning to use computers and the Internet on a broad range of cognitive ability measures in a healthy group of older adults with no prior computer experience. The results of this study do not support the notion that stimulating the cognitive skills of older, community dwelling adults actually increases their cognitive abilities. However, the question of whether persons with more outspoken cognitive impairments have more to gain from such interventions if they are able to master the routines that are necessary for successful computer use remained unresolved. Finally, another question that remains interesting for future research is whether older adults who have received training to use computers and Internet services earlier in life remain independent longer when functional limitations start to emerge.

AUTONOMY, WELLBEING, AND SOCIAL NETWORK

As was elaborated on in the introduction, computers and the Internet offer several benefits that may improve the quality of life of older adults. Although this seems obvious, only a few, mostly small experimental studies have been done to substantiate these claims. Moreover, these studies all involved interventions in care facilities, and many studies suffered from high attrition rates. Nevertheless, the findings of these studies are promising as they suggest that introducing older adults to the Internet may result in facilitation of communication with others (Danowski & Sacks, 1980), decreased depression ratings, increased Activities of Daily Living (ADL) scores and improved cognitive function (Mini-Mental State

Examination, MMSE) (McConatha, McConatha, & Dermigny, 1994; McConatha, McConatha, Deaner, & Dermigny, 1995), improved levels of self-esteem and life satisfaction (Sherer, 1996), and decreased levels of loneliness (White, et al., 1999). However, the latter effect of decreased levels of loneliness disappeared after five months of computer use, and a larger replication of this study showed no effect at all of computer use with respect to several aspects of quality of life (White, et al., 2002).

Thus, the studies on the impact of computer use on the lives of older adults described above showed mixed results. In fact, these studies were not entirely suitable for answering questions about the impact of the Internet on the lives of healthy older adults because most of them used small groups recruited in nursing homes or other care facilities. To provide a methodologically more sound and powerful test of the hypothesis that learning to use computers and the Internet is beneficial to the quality of life of older adults, we included several measures related to autonomy, wellbeing, and social network in our intervention study (Slegers, van Boxtel, & Jolles, 2008).

Methods

Several measures were included in our intervention study's test battery to evaluate the effect of our intervention in terms of autonomy, wellbeing and social network. The first set of measures was used to assess autonomy. This set included an Instrumental Activities of Daily Living (IADL) scale, and the physical and mental component of the SF-36, a questionnaire on general health and quality of life (Ware, Snow, Kosinski, & Gandek, 1993). The second set of measures aimed at assessing wellbeing and included the Loneliness Questionnaire (LQ) (De Jong-Gierveld & Kamphuis, 1986), the Satisfaction With Life Scale (SWLS) (Pavot, Diener, Colvin, & Sandvik, 1991), the depression, anxiety, and sleep complaints subscales of the Symptom Check List (SCL) (Arrindell &

Ettema, 1986), a Belief in External Control scale (Andriessen, 1972) that was used to measure locus of control (internal or external), and the Mastery scale (Pearlin & Schooler, 1978) that was used to ask participants about their perceived level of control over life. The final set of measures included four items to assess the nature and frequency of participants' social networks. The first item concerned the number of people participants know they can rely on for help with whom they share private matters (Stevens, Kaplan, Ponds, Diederiks, & Jolles, 1999). The second item concerned the number of people participants knew they can rely on for help, but with whom they did not discuss private matters. Both questions were followed by an indication of the frequency participants contacted one of these people.

Results and Discussion

No clear-cut effect of intervention was found for the majority of the measures of autonomy, wellbeing, and social network. The differences that were found were quite random and did not appear to be caused by the intervention. The only exception is the fact that participants in the Intervention Group indicated to spend more time on learning new things, which was to be expected as these participants learned to use a computer and the Internet during the study.

We did find some differences in changes over time between participants in the Intervention Group who used their computers 8 hours per week or more ('heavy' computer use) and participants who used their computers less than 8 hours per week ('light' computer use). Heavy users showed an increase in mastery, while light computer users did not. That is to say, participants who used their computers more often felt more in control of their lives as a result of their frequent computer use. We also found that heavy computer users in the Intervention Group gradually reported spending more time on their hobbies during the study, which is probably due to the fact that they considered using a computer as one of their hobbies. Both heavy and light computer users reported spending more time on acquiring new skills at the four-month follow-up than at baseline. As was anticipated, after the four-month follow-up the time spent on new skills dropped to baseline level for participants who did not use their computers very often, while this time dropped only slightly for the participants who used their computers more frequently. A final variable in which we found a change over time was the frequency with which participants reported contacting people with whom they discussed private matters. For the heavy computer users this frequency was stable during the study, for light computer users the frequency temporarily increased at the time of the four-month follow-up. These differences between heavy and light computer users appear rather unsystematic and may be a chance finding.

As was the case with the results of our study concerning cognitive functioning, our findings were not fully consistent with the findings of other intervention studies, which did find effects of computer and/or Internet use on measures of quality of life. Again, some differences between these studies and our own study might explain this. The first and most important difference concerns methodology used. Almost without exception, the earlier studies used far fewer participants, less systematic designs (e.g. no control groups), and a number of them reported quite dramatic attrition numbers. Also, unlike in our study, in most studies no special care was taken to control for social contact (e.g. with other participants or with the researchers) in the Intervention Group as a result of training or the use of a personal computer in a shared environment (McConatha, et al., 1995). This social contact may have caused contamination of the intervention effect in some studies. In our study, this effect was accounted for by including the Training/No intervention Group, who received the same training as the Intervention Group did.

Second, as was mentioned in the previous section, the current study was primarily focused on healthy older adults who live independently, while in most of the aforementioned intervention studies participants were recruited from residents in care facilities. Our study population may have been a particularly fit group of older adults who are not, or at least not yet, limited in their physical, mental and social capabilities. The lack of effect of this intervention could therefore be due to a restricted range in functional limitation in this group, with only limited gain to be expected from the intervention. Possibly, as was the case in the studies that did find an effect of intervention, the intervention in this study might be more effective when presented to older adults with functional limitations, such as nursing home residents. As was explained in the section on cognitive functioning, our group of community-dwelling participants may have had such a high level of functional limitation, that no gain could have been expected from any kind of intervention.

Summing up, in spite of scanty reports of a positive influence in earlier studies, we did not find consistent evidence for an impact, either positive or negative, of learning to use computers and the Internet on the everyday functioning, wellbeing, mood, social network, and personality or activity levels of healthy older adults. That is, in order to improve the quality of life of healthy older adults, no benefits of computer and Internet-related activities for personal have been found. Still, future research efforts could be aimed at identifying populations that may be more sensitive to Internet-based intervention. The question again remains as to whether older adults who have received timely training to use computers and Internet services for a while are able to profit from this skill sat the moment they are faced with functional limitations.

THE USE OF EVERYDAY TECHNOLOGY

Being able to use modern everyday technology has become increasingly important for the autonomy of older adults. Besides this necessity to use technological applications, everyday technological devices may also provide opportunities to increase the autonomy of older adults (McCreadie & Tinker, 2005; Zimmer & Chappell, 1999). Devices such as microwave ovens and microcomputers providing medication reminders can assist older adults in their everyday lives and allow them to live independently, even when they are in need of assistance.

As was discussed in the introduction, the use of technology by older adults is not always straightforward. Several attempts have been made to train older adults in the use of specific technological applications, such as the Internet (Cody, Dunn, Hoppin, & Wendt, 1999), the use of a word processor (Charness, Bosman, Kelley, & Mottram, 1996), or an automatic teller machine (Rogers, Fisk, Mead, Walker, & Cabrera, 1996). In order to improve technological skills on a more general level, ideally, the training of a specific technological skill should generalize to skills needed under different technological demands. This use of previous experience to devise a solution for a new problem or task has been described as 'problem-solving transfer' (Mayer & Wittrock, 1996).Not only may newly acquired technological skills be transferred to the use of other technological devices, individuals who master some technological skills may also feel more confident in using technology in general. As a result, they start using other technological applications as well and might experience fewer problems in doing so. In research into computer anxiety for instance, where it has been suggested that computer anxiety prevents individuals from using computers (Harrington, McElroy, & Morrow, 1990; Rosen & Weil, 1995), it has been shown that positive experiences with computers

may lead to decreases in anxiety (Chu & Spires, 1991). Thus, acquiring general technological skills should result in lower levels of perceived difficulties with and in a higher frequency of the use of everyday technological devices. Therefore, teaching older adults general technological skills may be an effective strategy in improving their use of everyday technology.

The present intervention study provided a first opportunity to experimentally test whether older adults are able to transfer newly acquired computer skills to the execution of everyday technological tasks. In order to measure the effect of computer and Internet skills on the execution of everyday technological tasks, a new test was developed, the Technological Transfer Test (TTT) (Slegers, van Boxtel, & Jolles, 2007).

Methods

The TTT was administered twice during the intervention study, once at baseline and once after twelve months. At both occasions, participants were instructed to successfully operate four technological devices that are commonly used in daily life. At baseline, these devices included a CD-player, a phone, an automatic teller machine (simulated on a touch screen) and a train ticket vending machine (simulated on a touch screen). The twelve-month follow-up test included a microwave oven, an alarm clock, a smartcard charger (simulated on a touch screen) and a telephone voice menu (simulated on a touch screen). The simulated devices were developed so that the procedures and interfaces exactly matched the original interfaces.

The performance time of each task and the number of errors participants made before completing the task (for the simulated devices only, because a log file including such information of the participant's actions was available for these devices) were used to measure the efficiency of operating the devices. Finally, for both administrations, an overall performance time score of the four devices was computed on each test occasion. As the tasks were quite different with respect to the time it took to perform the assignments, standardized scores (z-scores) were used for individual scores, to allow for better comparison. These scores were added up to the overall scores.

To measure the use of everyday technology, participants were asked to indicate the frequency with which they performed 17 specific techno-logical tasks (e.g. sending a fax, programming a video recorder or buying a parking ticket) and the difficulty they experienced when performing these tasks. Frequency was measured using a five-point scale ranging from "never" to "at least once a week." Difficulty was also rated on a five-point scale, ranging from "very easy" to "very difficult."

Two general measures of technology use were calculated. First, as a general measure of the frequency of using everyday technology, the mean frequency of regularly performed tasks was used. Second, the mean difficulty participants experience with performing these tasks was calculated. These measures were corrected for the number of tasks participants stated they perform.

Results and Discussion

The results did not support the hypothesis that older adults who mastered personal computer skills transfer those skills to other everyday technological tasks. No effect of the intervention was found in the efficiency of using everyday technological devices, both computer-based and other types of devices. Hence, transfer of newly acquired computer skills did not occur.

Some group differences were found with respect to performance of the TTT tasks that were administered after the intervention, while at baseline no differences were found. For both the alarm clock task and the voice menu task it was found that the Intervention group outperformed the Training/No intervention group, but not the No Training/No Intervention group and the Not Interested group. This difference can therefore

not be considered a direct effect of computer use, as the two latter groups did not use computers.

In line with the aforementioned results, no effect of intervention was found on either the frequency of or the difficulty with performing everyday technological tasks. In other words, older adults who had mastered personal computer skills and gained computer experience for twelve months did not show higher frequencies or fewer difficulties in the use of everyday technological devices.

In conclusion, the mere acquisition of computer and Internet skills is not a successful strategy for obtaining transfer of technological skills essential to everyday independent functioning in later life. Research in this area is very scarce, and because the present study in a large group of participants did not yield any evidence to suggest that transfer of technological skills actually occurs, we feel that more research should be done to develop efficient methods to improve technological efficiency. In addition, it may be worthwhile to outline possible conditions under which transfer of technological skills in older adults does occur. For instance, future research may focus on more generic technological skills that underlie many technological tasks and on the psychological barriers that might lie beneath problems with technology. In addition, the question of whether older individuals recognize analogous aspects of technological problems, which is essential to the transfer of skills and rules acquired in earlier problems, should be considered more specifically in such studies.

SUBJECTIVE PHYSICAL FUNCTIONING

Everyday computer activities are generally characterized by repetitive upper limb movements and a relatively fixed bodily position (Anonymous, 2004). Intensive interaction with a computer terminal interface, using a standard keyboard and a mouse, has been related to a complex of complaints related to the hand, arm and shoulder, often referred to as 'Repetitive Strain Injury' (RSI), or sometimes as 'cumulative trauma disorder,' 'non-specific work-related upper limb disorder' or 'repetitive strain disorder' (Helliwell & Taylor, 2004). This pain syndrome of the upper limb consists of protracted complaints of the hand, arm or shoulder, leading to functional impairment that is difficult to treat (Bongers, et al., 2002). While individuals over 65 are adapting fast to the societal trend towards extensive use of computer-based technologies and services, it is unclear whether the potential benefit of leisure-time computer usage by older adults may be limited due to the risk of RSI. Intervention programs aimed at familiarization of older persons with computer-based technologies may produce upper limb impairment as an unwanted side effect.

Exact prevalence figures of RSI are unavailable, in part due to a lack of valid working definitions of RSI as a diagnostic entity (Gezondheidsraad, 2000), but in a Dutch population survey RSI complaints were reported by 20–40 percent of the working population. Complaints are more prevalent in females and older workers (Gezondheidsraad, 2000), but dedicated information about non-working older computer users is lacking. Furthermore, all studies done in this area so far have been observational in nature. No systematic prospective studies of computer users have been done to study RSI in a controlled fashion.

Within the framework of the present intervention study we investigated if older computer users actually developed complaints and functional limitations of the upper limb. Apart from the use of a specific RSI-questionnaire, measures of general health were included in this study because upper limb bodily pain may be related to a reduction in overall health status in both younger and older individuals (Daffner, et al., 2003).

Methods

The scales for general health, physical functioning, mental health and bodily pain of the Short Form-36 (SF-36) scale (McHorney, et al., 1993) was used both at baseline and at the 12-month follow-up to assess the general wellbeing of the participants. All scores refer to health complaints that were experienced in the four weeks preceding the testing. Scores on the SF-36 scales range between 100 (optimal) and 0 (worst).

Complaints about and functional impairment of the upper limb were measured with the symptom and Functional Status Scale (SFS), a well-validated instrument that was originally developed for the assessment of upper limb pain, specifically the carpal tunnel syndrome (Levine, et al., 1993). It consists of eleven symptom items and eight functional impairment items, measured on five-point scales, with reference to the two weeks prior to testing. Domain scores for symptom severity and functional status were computed by taking the average of the items in each category. Thus the range of scores was between 1 (no complaint / impairment) to 5 (maximum severity of complaint / impairment).

Results and Discussion

A significant trend towards a poorer health status was apparent in both groups on the SF-36 subscales, including the bodily pain subscale. However, no indication was found that participants in the Intervention group were at greater risk as regards the development of health complaints or functional impairment of the upper limb than participants in the control group. It was remarkable that three out of four SF-36 measures showed a decrease over twelve months, which was unrelated to group membership. The SF-36 is a reliable instrument, known to be sensitive to even small age cohort differences (Van der Zee & Sanderman, 1993), but it remains rather unclear why the increase in reported bodily pain, in particular, occurred in this relatively short interval.

The absence of differences between the groups in reported health complaints may be a reflection of the lack of sufficient risk factors relating to developing RSI-like symptoms. Firstly, although the participants were well-motivated computer users, the mean time spent on computer related activities in the Intervention group was limited to 8.3 hours. This is, of course, much lower than the exposure of professional workers who use computers on a daily basis (Smulders & van den Bossche, 2004) but is still comparable to the average use in this age group of 7.7 hours (2002-2004) reported in a Dutch survey (CBS, 2005). Secondly, it has been found that adverse psychological factors, including work-related stress, may add to the effect of repetitive movements of the arms and wrists in the etiology of upper limb complaints (Macfarlane, et al., 2000). Since our participants used the computer mainly for personal goals, often related to leisure-time activities, this is another reason why the study group may have had a lower risk of RSI-like complaints than those who are professionally active computer users. Thirdly, unfavorable ergonomic conditions, such as prolonged fixed body postures, which are common in working environments in the presence of time pressure, are also less likely to occur in a home situation. Still, the question remains as to whether older users who engage more intensively in computer-related activities, or who continue such activities for a longer period of time, may develop upper limb complaints at a later stage.

In summary, older users of a standard computer interface with no prior computer experience were not at greater risk than older non-users of a poorer general health or of more symptoms or functional impairment of the upper extremity after a twelve-month episode of average, self-paced use. We therefore conclude that during the execution of community programs aimed at engaging older persons in activities that include computer-based

technology, in general no special precautions are necessary to prevent upper limb complaints.

GENERAL DISCUSSION

The primary aim of the research presented in this chapter was to study the effects of computer training and the subsequent use of a personal computer and the Internet on the autonomy of older adults. The focus of the longitudinal intervention study that was designed for this purpose was on four separate domains: cognitive functioning, autonomy, wellbeing and social network, the use of everyday technology, and subjective physical functioning. It was found that the intervention produced no effect in any of these domains. That is to say, older adults who mastered computer skills and engaged in using a personal computer and Internet facilities for twelve months, and thus acquired a new complex cognitive skill, showed neither improvement nor deterioration with respect to several domains of autonomous functioning.

The fact that we found no effect of our intervention on cognitive abilities seriously disputes the validity of the notions of (cognitive) reserve capacity and use-it-or-lose-it with respect to the prevention or reversibility of age-related functional decline in a relatively healthy, community-dwelling population of older adults. Studies that are put forward to support these notions (e.g. Stigsdotter & Backman, 1995; Schaie & Willis, 1986; Willis, Jay, Diehl, & Marsiske, 1992; Ball, et al., 2002) usually only provide observational and retrospective data. The present study however, used a randomized, controlled design, which is a much more valid approach for testing these hypotheses. Therefore, the findings of the present research seriously challenge the idea that it is possible to protect healthy older adults from age-related cognitive decline by stimulating them to engage in cognitive activities. The same holds for the commonly accepted belief that using computers and the Internet has benefits for older adults in terms of autonomy, wellbeing, and social network. No evidence for this belief was found in our studies. On a more positive note, no evidence was found for a causal relationship between computer and Internet use on the one hand and complaints to hand, arm and shoulder on the other hand.

Another theoretical approach that has been studied in the research described in this chapter was the concept of transfer in problem solving ability, assuming that previous experience may be used to devise a solution for a new problem or task (Mayer & Wittrock, 1996). According to this idea, individuals who have acquired computer skills may use these skills to solve problems in other technological domains as well. Regarding this question, we again did not find supporting evidence. Therefore, we conclude that no transfer of technological problem solving skills is to be expected as a result of mastering new computer skills by older adults.

After we finished our study, only a limited number of other studies have been conducted testing similar hypotheses. Most of these studies, however, again have the same limitations as the previous studies discussed in this chapter (e.g. small numbers of participants, mostly involving older adults living in a care facilities, high attrition rates). Shapira, Barak, and Gal (2007), for instance, found that after an Internet training, a group of 22 older adults who went to day-care centers or lived in nursing homes significantly improved in terms of life satisfaction, depression, loneliness and self control whereas a control group showed deterioration in these measures. Ordonez, Yassuda, and Cachioni (2011) found that a relatively small group of older adults of 60 years and older showed a significant improvement in their scores on a brief cognitive test battery in comparison to a control group after 15 computer lessons. Mellor, Firth, and Moore (2008) found rather similar results as we did, although their study involved a rather small sample of residents of a retirement village and suffered from attrition. This study showed no

quantifiable effects of Internet use on self-esteem, positive effect, personal well-being, optimism, and social connectedness. Finally, Hage (2008) found no differences in measures of cognition, social functioning, depression or perceived health in a fairly small group of long-term care residents after a self-paced computer training.

In conclusion, the intervention study presented in this chapter is, to date, the largest, methodologically most sound study of the impact of computer and Internet use on the autonomy of healthy older adults. Based on this study and the mixed results provided by related studies, it is highly questionable that computer and Internet use is an efficient strategy to prevent or slow down age-related decline of cognitive functions. On a positive note, we found no reason to assume that special precautions should be taken to prevent older novice computer users from computer-related risks, such as developing upper limb complaints due to computer-based leisure-time activities.

FUTURE TRENDS

In this section, we highlight a number of future trends that are relevant for the topic of this chapter. This section is organized around three main themes. First, we discuss some issues that future intervention programs may want to consider. Next, we briefly discuss a number of recommendations for older adults themselves. Finally, we discuss some more recent technological trends, such as social networks and mobile computing.

Implications for the Future Application of Interventions

The main conclusion of the research presented in this chapter is that no evidence was found to suggest that it is effective to stimulate healthy older adults to use computer and Internet facilities to boost their cognitive reserve. Therefore, we do not consider large-scale computer-based interventions developed for this purpose to be very useful. However, there may be some issues in this context that that need to be addressed in future research that may make technology-mediated interventions an interesting approach in improving quality of life for older adults.

To start with, organizers of future intervention programs for older adults might want to consider the specific needs of their target groups before designing their programs. The intervention discussed in this chapter was very broad: providing an Internet connection and introducing all thinkable computer and Internet services to healthy older adults. Perhaps interventions targeting very specific needs of the participants may be highly successful in improving the quality of life of the participants. For instance, the lives of older adults with particular medical needs may become much simpler when using appropriate services. Fulfilling such basic needs of older adults may be an important motivation for participation and persistence.

Besides addressing specific needs of older adults in interventions, it may be useful for future to consider whether older adults with specific background characteristics might benefit from interventions using a broad approach to improve mental stimulation from which healthy older adults did not benefit. For instance, it is possible that individuals with functional limitations, such as Mild Cognitive Impairment (MCI) (Petersen, et al., 1997) or low levels of acquired brain damage, may improve as a result of learning to use computers and the Internet. This was actually suggested by results of similar, but smaller, intervention studies using computers and the Internet (Cody, Dunn, Hoppin, & Wendt, 1999; McConatha, McConatha, & Dermigny, 1994; McConatha, McConatha, Deaner, & Dermigny, 1995). The participants in these studies were not community dwelling healthy older adults, but residents of nursing homes or other care facilities. It may be hypothesized that when older adults have more to gain in terms of both cognitive abilities and aspects of wellbeing

and quality of life (i.e. those older adults with less than optimal levels of cognitive ability, wellbeing, and quality of life), computers and Internet-based interventions are more effective. An issue one has to bear in mind, though, is that teaching complex skills, such as operating a personal computer and surfing the Internet, may be quite hard to accomplish in individuals with cognitive limitations. In any case, such studies should be pursued using a randomized controlled design, particularly to control for bias in the training phase, as was done in our study.

A more practical suggestion for future intervention programs concerns the intervention period. In the current study, the intervention period was twelve months, which may have been too short in order to detect prospective group differences. On the other hand, other cognitive intervention studies, although not exactly similar to the present study with respect to size and target group (e.g. Ball, et al., 2002; Kliegl, Smith, & Baltes, 1989; Schaie & Willis, 1986; Stigsdotter & Backman, 1995), with even shorter follow-up durations, provided support for the idea that one year should be long enough to detect differential improvement as a result of an intervention like the one used in the present study. On the other hand, older adults who have already mastered computer skills may not show observable benefits from this experience until they have to cope with more substantial age-related cognitive challenges at later stages in their lives. For instance, the ability to use computers and the Internet may provide them with more supportive strategies to deal with these limitations. Since none of the participants showed such limitations in the present study sample, this possibility should be investigated more thoroughly. However, studying this option implies much longer intervention periods. This in turn may be hard to accomplish with an adequately controlled design because of the decreasing population of older adults without computer experience, the ethical issue of refraining participants from computer use for such a long period, and the risk of selective attrition.

In addition, some other practical consequences and suggestions for further research should be noted. First of all, we found no evidence suggesting that teaching general technological computer skills to older adults generalized to their use of everyday technological devices. Therefore, we suggest that future research should focus on identifying and developing other strategies to improve older adults' execution of everyday tasks. Potential approaches in this context may be training methods aimed at specific actions or devices, design solutions, a focus on generational differences in technological abilities, or a dedicated type of psycho-education to remove psychological barriers older adults might have in the use of technological applications. Another suggestion concerns the exploration of possible conditions under which transfer of technological skills in older adults does occur. One possible cause of the lack of this transfer may be the fact that the older adults in this study were not able to recognize the similarities between computer use and the use of other everyday technologies. Finding ways to help individuals recognize analogies between familiar and novel tasks may be an effective strategy for improving technological abilities.

A final recommendation based on the present intervention study is that when stimulating older adults to use computers, e.g. because of the practical benefits computers and the Internet have to offer, older adults who are not inclined to start using computers on their own preferably should be the target population. Among older adults, women, individuals who are older, individuals who have lower levels of education, and individuals who feel lonely might be interesting to target.

Implications for the Target Group: Recommendations for Older Adults

Although no effects of using computer and Internet facilities were found, we feel that older adults should still be stimulated to (start to) use computers. Even though no quantifiable positive effects

of computer use are to be expected on cognitive abilities and several measures of wellbeing and quality of life, the practical benefits that computer and Internet facilities have to offer make using these facilities very worthwhile for older adults. Examples of these benefits that can be of particular interest in regard to older adults are services that facilitate life-long learning (such as online courses), entertainment (games, chatting etc.), and practicing one's hobbies. Therefore, we still recommend that older individuals should be motivated to engage in computer-based activities, not in order to objectively improve their autonomous functioning and wellbeing, but in order to allow them to profit from the numerous practical and entertaining features of both computers and the Internet.

RECENT TECHNOLOGICAL TRENDS: OPPORTUNITIES

Besides everyday use of computers and the Internet as they were covered by our intervention study in 2002 and 2003, there are a few more recent trends that might be worthwhile in terms of increasing autonomy and quality of life for older adults. Three of such trends will be discussed here: advances in computer hardware and mobile computing, the use of social networking sites and gaming.

Computer Hardware and Mobile Computing

In recent years, computer platforms have evolved from bulky pieces of technology that required extensive knowledge of the operator towards compact mobile devices, of which the user interface better accommodates the logic and workflow of the average user. Mobile platforms such as smartphones or tablet computers like the iPad have paved the way for a new generation of versatile applications that support us in our daily routines. Touch-based tablet devices seem to be adapted much faster by older adults, in part due to a more practical implementation of metaphors of relevant daily actions or activities that stay close to the real world experience, such as the agenda, notebook, ebook-reader, or the photo album. Thus, mobile technology is radically changing the ways we interact with our environment: staying connected and in touch with the world has become the norm (see next paragraph). Studies in patient groups already have shown the benefits of mobile devices as assistive technology for behavior planning and memory support (de Joode, van Heugten, Verhey, & van Boxtel, 2010). Systematic studies on how this new technology affects our basic functional capacities are still lacking, but it seems unlikely that this impact on daily routines, and ultimately, on the autonomy and wellbeing of older persons is overestimated in such studies.

Social Networking Sites

Facilitation of social interaction and communication is generally considered one of the most important benefits of the Internet for older adults (Czaja & Lee, 2001; Mead, et al., 1999; Morrell, et al., 2000; Rogers & Fisk, 2000). In this line of reasoning, the use of Social Networking Sites (SNS) might be especially beneficial for older adults. This is supported by the fact that the fastest growing group of users of social networking sites at this moment is the group of Internet users who are 74 and older. The proportion of SNS users in this group has quadrupled between 2008 and 2010, from 4% to 16% (Zickuhr, 2010).

Thus far, research on the impact of SNS usage has mostly focused on younger users. Most research has shown positive effects on psychological well-being (Ellison, Steinfeld, & Lampe, 2007, 2008) and life satisfaction (Valenzuele, Park, & Kee, 2009). Research regarding the impact of SNS on the quality of life of older adults, to our knowledge, hardly exists. An exception is a very recent study of Shyam Sundar, Oeldorf-Hirsch, Nussbaum, and Behr (2011) who did a survey amongst 168 adults aged 55 and older measuring quality of life. The results of this study show that quality of life was not related to the use of a social networking site (Facebook), which may have been caused by the fact that the participants of the survey only reported small amounts of time spent on Facebook and already had high levels of quality of life.

In conclusion, although, clear evidence is still lacking, especially with respect to older users. it seems that using social networking sites may have beneficial effects in terms of social network, loneliness, and other aspects of well-being. Therefore, we suggest that future research should focus on clarifying the impact of the use of social networking sites on the quality of life of older adults and on specific ways in which such sites may help to increase quality of life.

Games

Playing digital games has become increasingly popular amongst older adults in the last decade. Although research into gaming in later life is increasing as well, especially within the domain of interaction design research (e.g. IJsselstijn, Nap, de Kort & Poels, 2007), gerontological research is still quite scarce (De Schutter, 2011). Although research is ongoing with respect to games that are especially designed for cognitive training and rehabilitation (such as ACTIVE [Jobe, et al., 2001] and ELDERGAMES [Gamberini, Alcaniz, Barresi, Fabregat, Ibanez, & Prontu, 2006]), within the framework of this chapter especially the use of casual computer games by older adults is interesting. Particularly since the majority of older digital game players are classified as casual gamers: De Schutter (2011) found that 80% of elderly gamers preferred casual games, while only 20% preferred other games such as shooting games, action games or racing games. Elderly casual gamers seemed to especially prefer puzzle games and digital adaptations of traditional games. Unfortunately, available research on the impact of playing such casual games in later life is very scarce. Intervention studies such as the one described in this chapter focusing on the causal relationship between such casual games and cognitive or emotional wellbeing might be particularly interesting.

In the early days of video games, a few studies showed that playing video games may have a positive effect on autonomous functioning in later life, for example on reaction time tasks (Dustman, et al., 1984; Clark, Lamphear, & Riddick, 1987) and on self-esteem (Drew & Waters, 1986). More recently, Goldstein, Cajko, Oosterbroek, Michielsen, van Houten, and Salverda (1997) found that non-institutionalized older adults who played Super Tetris for five hours a week, for five weeks, significantly improved with respect to a reaction time task and to an increase in self-reported wellbeing. Torres (2008) showed in a small randomized trial that the use of casual videogames resulted in improvements in cognitive functioning (although measured on a rather crude scale) and to maintenance of the self-concept and quality of life in a group of adults aged 65 years and older.

In sum, there appears to be some preliminary evidence suggesting that engaging in digital games may have advantageous effects on certain aspects of cognitive functioning and well-being of older adults. This fits the notions of cognitive reserve and the use-it-or-lose-it hypothesis very well, but should be investigated further in more detail.

CONCLUSION

The findings presented in this chapter provide knowledge about possible strategies to promote successful (cognitive) aging. In conclusion, it was found that teaching older adults computer skills and stimulating them to use the Internet for twelve months—an attempt to improve both the level of cognitive functioning and the level of active engagement with life—was not an effective method to help older adults age more successfully. This

finding is not in accordance with the often-stated assumption that older adults should benefit from using computers and the Internet with respect to domains such as autonomy, social network, and psychological wellbeing. This contrast shows the importance of evidence-based research methods to test commonly accepted beliefs. By conducting a randomized controlled trial in this case, it was possible to examine an idea that has great societal potential, but which would not be very cost efficient when implemented on a large scale. In sum, by conducting thorough and systematic research, we were able to test and reject the generally believed assumption of a beneficial effect of using computers and the Internet on several aspects of autonomy of healthy older adults. Although the outcome gave us a less optimistic outlook on the use of computer technology by older adults, it contributes to our existing knowledge on strategies to promote successful cognitive aging.

REFERENCES

Andriessen, J. H. T. H. (1972). Interne of externe beheersing [Internal or external control]. *Nederlands Tijdschrift voor de Psychologie en Haar Grensgebieden, 27*, 173–178.

Anonymous,. (2004). *Arbobalans 2004: Arbeidsrisico's, effecten en maatregelen in Nederland* [Arbo balance 2004: Occupational risks, effects and measures in the Netherlands]. Den Haag, The Netherlands: Ministerie van Sociale Zaken en Werkgelegenheid.

Arrindell, W. A., & Ettema, J. H. M. (1986). *SCL-90: Een multidimensionele psychopathologie indicator* [The SCL-90: A multidimensional instrument for the assessment of psychopathology]. Lisse, The Netherlands: Swets & Zeitlinger.

Ball, K., Berch, D. B., Helmers, K. F., Jobe, J. B., Leveck, M. D., & Marsiske, M. (2002). Effects of cognitive training interventions with older adults: A randomized controlled trial. *Journal of the American Medical Association, 288*(18), 2271–2281. doi:10.1001/jama.288.18.2271

Barnes, D. E., & Yaffe, K. (2011). The projected effect of risk factor reduction on Alzheimer's disease prevalence. *The Lancet Neurology, 10*(9), 819–828. doi:10.1016/S1474-4422(11)70072-2

Bongers, P. M., de Vet, H. C., & Blatter, B. M. (2002). RSI: Vóórkomen, ontstaan, therapie en preventive. [Repetitive strain injury (RSI): occurrence, etiology, therapy and prevention]. *Nederlands Tijdschrift voor Geneeskunde, 146*(42), 1971–1976.

Bosma, H., van Boxtel, M. P., Ponds, R. W., Jelicic, M., Houx, P., & Metsemakers, J. (2002). Engaged lifestyle and cognitive function in middle and old-aged, non-demented persons: A reciprocal association? *Zeitschrift für Gerontologie und Geriatrie, 35*(6), 575–581. doi:10.1007/s00391-002-0080-y

Bouchard Ryan, E., & Heaven, R. K. B. (1986). Promoting vitality among older adults with computers. *Activities, Adaptation and Aging, 8*(1), 15–30. doi:10.1300/J016v08n01_03

Broadbent, D. E., Cooper, P. F., FitzGerald, P., & Parkes, K. R. (1982). The cognitive failure questionnaire (CFQ) and its correlates. *The British Journal of Clinical Psychology, 21*, 1–16. doi:10.1111/j.2044-8260.1982.tb01421.x

Brooks, J. O., Friedman, L., Pearman, A. M., Gray, C., & Yesavage, J. A. (1999). Mnemonic training in older adults: Effects of age, lenght of training, and type of cognitive pretraining. *International Psychogeriatrics, 11*(1), 75–84. doi:10.1017/S1041610299005608

Carlson, R. A., & Yaure, R. G. (1990). Practice schedules and the use of component skills in problem solving. *Journal of Experimental Psychology. Learning, Memory, and Cognition, 16*, 484–496. doi:10.1037/0278-7393.16.3.484

Cavallini, E., Pagnin, A., & Vecchi, T. (2003). Aging and everyday memory: The beneficial effect of memory training. *Archives of Gerontology and Geriatrics, 37*, 241–257. doi:10.1016/S0167-4943(03)00063-3

Charness, N., Bosman, E., Kelley, C., & Mottram, M. (1996). Cognitive theory and word processing training: When prediction fails. In Rogers, W. A., Fisk, A. D., & Walker, N. (Eds.), *Aging and Skilled Performance: Advances in Theory and Applications*. Mahwah, NJ: Lawrence Erlbaum Associates.

Christensen, H., Korten, A., Jorm, A. F., Henderson, A. S., Scott, R., & Mackinnon, A. J. (1996). Activity levels and cognitive functioning in an elderly community sample. *Age and Ageing, 25*(1), 72–80. doi:10.1093/ageing/25.1.72

Chu, P. C., & Spires, E. E. (1991). Validating the computer anxiety ratin scale: Effects of cognitive style and computer courses on computer anxiety. *Computers in Human Behavior, 7*, 7–21. doi:10.1016/0747-5632(91)90025-V

Clark, J., Lamphear, A., & Riddick, C. (1987). The effects of video game playing on the response selection processing of elderly adults. *Journal of Gerontology, 42*, 82–85.

Cody, M. J., Dunn, D., Hoppin, S., & Wendt, P. (1999). Silver surfers: Training and evaluating internet use among older adult learners. *Communication Education, 48*, 269–286. doi:10.1080/03634529909379178

Craik, F. I. M., & Salthouse, T. A. (2000). *The handbook of aging and cognition* (2nd ed.). Mahwah, NJ: Erlbaum.

Czaja, S. J. (1996). Aging and the acquisition of computer skills. In Rogers, W. A., Fisk, A. D., & Walker, N. (Eds.), *Aging and Skilled Performance: Advances in Theory and Applications* (pp. 201–220). Mahwah, NJ: Lawrence Erlbaum Associates.

Czaja, S. J. (1997). Computer technology and the older adult. In Helander, M., Landauer, T. K., & Prabhu, P. (Eds.), *Handbook of Human-Computer Interaction* (pp. 797–812). Amsterdam, The Netherlands: Elsevier Science.

Czaja, S. J., Guerrier, J. H., Nair, S. N., & Landauer, T. K. (1993). Computer communication as an aid to independence for older adults. *Behaviour & Information Technology*, *12*(4), 197–207. doi:10.1080/01449299308924382

Czaja, S. J., & Lee, C. C. (2001). The internet and older adults: Design challenges and opportunities. In Charness, N., Parks, D. C., & Sabel, B. A. (Eds.), *Communication, Technology and Aging* (pp. 60–78). New York, NY: Springer.

Czaja, S. J., & Lee, C. C. (2003). Designing computer systems for older adults. In Jacko, J., & Sears, A. (Eds.), *The Human-Computer Interaction Handbook* (pp. 413–427). Mahwah, NJ: Lawrence Erlbaum Associates.

Czaja, S. J., & Sharit, J. (1993). Age differences in the performance of computer-based work. *Psychology and Aging*, *8*(1), 59–67. doi:10.1037/0882-7974.8.1.59

Daffner, S. D., Hilibrand, A. S., Hanscom, B. S., Brislin, B. T., Vaccaro, A. R., & Albert, T. J. (2003). Impact of neck and arm pain on overall health status. *Spine*, *28*(17), 2030–2035. doi:10.1097/01.BRS.0000083325.27357.39

Danowski, J. A., & Sacks, W. (1980). Computer communication and the elderly. *Experimental Aging Research*, *6*(2), 125–135. doi:10.1080/03610738008258350

De Jong-Gierveld, J., & Kamphuis, F. H. (1986). The development of a rash-type loneliness scale. *Applied Psychological Measurement*, *9*, 289–299. doi:10.1177/014662168500900307

De Joode, E., van Heugten, C., Verhey, F., & van Boxtel, M. (2010). Efficacy and usability of assistive technology for patients with cognitive deficits: A systematic review. *Clinical Rehabilitation*, *24*(8), 701–714. doi:10.1177/0269215510367551

De Schutter, B. (2011). Never too old to play: The appeal of digital games to an older audience. *Games and Culture*, *6*(2), 155–170. doi:10.1177/1555412010364978

Drew, B., & Waters, J. (1986). Video games: Utilization of a novel strategy to improve perceptual motor skills and cognitive functioning in the non-institutionalized elderly. *Cognitive Rehabilitation*, *4*(2), 26–31.

Dustman, R., Emmerson, R., Ruhling, R., Shearer, D., Steinhaus, L., & Johnson, S. (1984). Aerobic exercise training and improved neuropsychological function of older individuals. *Neurobiology of Aging*, *5*, 35–42. doi:10.1016/0197-4580(84)90083-6

Ellison, N. B., Steinfield, C., & Lampe, C. (2007). The benefits of Facebook "friends": Social capital and college students' use of online social network sites. *Journal of Computer-Mediated Communication*, *12*, 11431168. doi:10.1111/j.1083-6101.2007.00367.x

Folstein, M. F., Folstein, S. E., & McHugh, P. R. (1975). Mini-mental state: A practical method for grading the cognitive state of patients for the clinician. *Journal of Psychiatric Research*, *12*, 189–198. doi:10.1016/0022-3956(75)90026-6

Frick, K. M., & Fernandez, S. M. (2003). Enrichment enhances spatial memory and increases synaptophysin levels in aged female mice. *Neurobiology of Aging*, *24*(4), 615–626. doi:10.1016/S0197-4580(02)00138-0

Gamberini, L., Alcaniz, M., Barresi, G., Fabregat, M., Ibanez, F., & Prontu, L. (2006). Cognition, technology and games for the elderly: An introduction to the ELDERGAMES project. *PsychNology Journal*, *4*(3), 285–308.

Goldstein, J., Cajko, L., Oosterbroek, M., Michielsen, M., van Houten, O., & Salverda, F. (1997). Video games and the elderly. *Social Behavior and Personality*, *25*(4), 345–352. doi:10.2224/sbp.1997.25.4.345

Hage, B. (2008). *Bridging the digital divide: The impact of computer training, internet and e-mail use on levels of cognition, depression and social functioning in older adults*. Paper presented at The 6th International Conference of the International Society for Gerontechnology. Pisa, Italy.

Harrington, K. V., McElroy, J. C., & Morrow, P. C. (1990). Computer anxiety and compuer-based training: A laboratory experiment. *Journal of Educational Computing Research*, *6*(3), 343–358. doi:10.2190/34Q7-0HHF-8JDL-DR09

Helliwell, P. S., & Taylor, W. J. (2004). Repetitive strain injury. *Postgraduate Medical Journal*, *80*(946), 438–443. doi:10.1136/pgmj.2003.012591

Holt, B. J., & Morrell, R. W. (2002). Guidelines for web site design for older adults: The ultimate influence of cognitive factors. In Morrell, R. W. (Ed.), *Older Adults, Health Information and the World Wide Web*. Mahwah, NJ: Erlbaum.

Houx, P. J., & Jolles, J. (1993). Age-related decline of psychomotor speed: Effects of age, brain health, sex, and education. *Perceptual and Motor Skills*, *76*, 195–211. doi:10.2466/pms.1993.76.1.195

Hultsch, D. F., Herzog, C., Small, B. J., & Dixon, R. A. (1999). Use it or lose is: Engaged lifestyle as a buffer of cognitive decline in aging? *Psychology and Aging*, *14*(2), 245–263. doi:10.1037/0882-7974.14.2.245

IJsselstijn, W., Nap, H. H., de Kort, Y., & Poels, K. (2007). Digital game design for elderly users. In *Proceedings of the 2007 Conference on Future Play*, (pp. 17-22). Future Play.

Jobe, J. B., Smith, D. M., Ball, K., Tennstedt, S. L., Marsiske, M., & Willis, S. L. (2001). ACTIVE: A cognitive intervention trial to promote independence in older adults. *Controlled Clinical Trials*, *22*(4), 453–479. doi:10.1016/S0197-2456(01)00139-8

Jones, B. D., & Bayen, U. J. (1998). Teaching older adults to use computers: Recommendations based on cognitive aging research. *Educational Gerontology*, *24*(7), 675–689. doi:10.1080/0360127980240705

Katzman, R., Aronson, M., Fuld, P., Kawas, C., Brown, T., & Morgenstern, H. (1989). Development of dementing illnesses in an 80-year old volunteer cohort. *Annals of Neurology*, *25*, 317–324. doi:10.1002/ana.410250402

Kelley, C. L., & Charness, N. (1995). Issues in training older adults to use computers. *Behaviour & Information Technology*, *14*(2), 107–120. doi:10.1080/01449299508914630

Kliegl, R., Smith, J., & Baltes, P. B. (1989). Testing-the-limits and the study of adults age differences in cognitive plasticity of a mnemonic skill. *Developmental Psychology*, *25*(2), 247–256. doi:10.1037/0012-1649.25.2.247

Kramer, A. F., & Willis, S. L. (2002). Enhancing the cognitive vitality of older adults. *Current Directions in Psychological Science*, *11*(5), 173–177. doi:10.1111/1467-8721.00194

Kraut, R., Patterson, M., Lundmark, V., Kiesler, S., Mukopadhyay, T., & Scherlis, W. (1998). Internet paradox: A social technology that reduces social involvement and psychological well-being? *The American Psychologist*, *53*(9), 1017–1031. doi:10.1037/0003-066X.53.9.1017

Lawhon, T., Ennis, D., & Lawhon, D. C. (1996). Senior adults and computers in the 1990s. *Educational Gerontology*, *22*(2), 193–201. doi:10.1080/0360127960220205

Levine, D. W., Simmons, B. P., Koris, M. J., Daltroy, L. H., Hohl, G. G., & Fossel, A. H. (1993). A self-administered questionnaire for the assessment of severity of symptoms and functional status in carpal tunnel syndrome. *Journal of Bone and Joint Surgery*, *75*(11), 1585–1592.

Lin, D.-Y. M. (2003). Hyptertext for the aged: Effects of text topologies. *Computers in Human Behavior*, *19*, 201–209. doi:10.1016/S0747-5632(02)00045-6

Macfarlane, G. J., Hunt, I. M., & Silman, A. J. (2000). Role of mechanical and psychosocial factors in the onset of forearm pain: Prospective population based study. *British Medical Journal*, *321*(7262), 676–679. doi:10.1136/bmj.321.7262.676

Mayer, R. E., & Wittrock, M. C. (1996). Problem-solving transfer. In Berliner, D. C. (Ed.), *Handbook of Educational Psychology* (pp. 47–62). New York, NY: Macmillan Library Reference.

McConatha, D., McConatha, J. T., & Dermigny, R. (1994). The use of computer services to enhance the quality of life for long-term care residents. *The Gerontologist*, *34*(4), 553–556. doi:10.1093/geront/34.4.553

McConatha, J. T., McConatha, D., Deaner, S. L., & Dermigny, R. (1995). A computer-based intervention for the education and therapy of institutionalized older adults. *Educational Gerontology*, *21*, 129–138. doi:10.1080/0360127950210202

McCreadie, C., & Tinker, A. (2005). The acceptability of assistive technology to older people. *Ageing and Society*, *25*, 91–110. doi:10.1017/S0144686X0400248X

McDougall, G. J. (1999). Cognitive interventions among older adults. In Fitzpatrick, J. J. (Ed.), *Annual Review of Nursing Research* (*Vol. 17*, pp. 219–240). New York, NY: Springer.

McHorney, C. A., Ware, J. J. E., & Raczek, A. E. (1993). The MOS 36-item short-form health survey (SF-36): II: Psychometric and clinical tests of validity in measuring physical and mental health constructs. *Medical Care*, *31*(3), 247–263. doi:10.1097/00005650-199303000-00006

Mead, S. E., Batsakes, P., Fisk, A. D., & Mykityshyn, A. (1999). Application of cognitive theory to training and design solutions for age-related computer use. *International Journal of Behavioral Development*, *23*(3), 553–573. doi:10.1080/016502599383694

Mellor, D., Firth, L., & Moore, K. (2008). Can the internet improve the well-being of the elderly? *Ageing International*, *32*(1), 25–42. doi:10.1007/s12126-008-9006-3

Milgram, N. W. (2003). Cognitive experience and its effect on age-dependent cognitive decline in beagle dogs. *Neurochemical Research*, *28*(11), 1677–1682. doi:10.1023/A:1026009005108

Moore, S., Sandman, C. A., & McGrady, K., & Kesslak. (2001). Memory training improves cognitive ability in patients with dementia. *Neuropsychological Rehabilitation*, *11*(3/4), 245–261. doi:10.1080/09602010042000222

Morrell, R. W., Mayhorn, C. B., & Bennett, J. (2000). A survey of world wide web use in middle-aged older adults. *Human Factors*, *42*(2), 175–182. doi:10.1518/001872000779656444

Nalwa, K., & Anand, A. P. (2003). Internet addiction in students: A cause of concern. *Cyberpsychology & Behavior*, *6*(6), 653–656. doi:10.1089/109493103322725441

Ordonez, T. N., Yassuda, M. S., & Cachioni, M. (2011). Elderly online: Effects of a digital inclusion program in cognitive performance. *Archives of Gerontology and Geriatrics*, *53*(2), 216–219. doi:10.1016/j.archger.2010.11.007

Pavot, W., Diener, E., Randall Colvin, C. R., & Sandvik, E. (1991). Further validation of the satisfaction with life scale: Evidence for the cross-method convergence of well-being measures. *Journal of Personality Assessment*, *57*(149), 167–176.

Pearlin, L. I., & Schooler, C. (1978). The structure of coping. *Journal of Health and Social Behavior*, *19*(1), 2–21. doi:10.2307/2136319

Petersen, R. C., Smith, G. E., Waring, S. C., Ivnik, R. J., Kokmen, E., & Tangelos, E. G. (1997). Aging, memory, and mild cognitive impairment. *International Psychogeriatrics*, *9*(1), 65–69. doi:10.1017/S1041610297004717

Prencipe, M., Casini, A. R., Ferretti, C., & Lattanzio, M. T. (1996). Prevalence of dementia in an elderly rural population: Effects of age, sex, and education. *Journal of Neurology, Neurosurgery, and Psychiatry*, *60*(6), 628–633. doi:10.1136/jnnp.60.6.628

Rogers, W. A., & Fisk, A. D. (2000). Human factors, applied cognition and aging. In Craik, F. I. M., & Salthouse, T. A. (Eds.), *The Handbook of Aging and Cognition* (pp. 559–591). Mahwah, NJ: Erlbaum.

Rogers, W. A., Fisk, A. D., Mead, S. E., Walker, N., & Cabrera, E. F. (1996). Training older adults to use automatic teller machines. *Human Factors*, *38*, 425–433. doi:10.1518/001872096778701935

Rosen, L. D., & Weil, M. M. (1995). Computer availability, computer experience and technophobia among public school teachers. *Computers in Human Behavior*, *11*(1), 9–31. doi:10.1016/0747-5632(94)00018-D

Rowe, J. W., & Kahn, R. L. (1997). Successful aging. *The Gerontologist*, *37*(4), 433–440. doi:10.1093/geront/37.4.433

Satz, P. (1993). Brain reserve capacity on symptom onset after brain injury: A formulation and review of evidence for threshold theory. *Neuropsychology*, *7*(3), 273–295. doi:10.1037/0894-4105.7.3.273

Schaie, K. W. (1994). The course of adult intellectual development. *The American Psychologist*, *49*(4), 304–313. doi:10.1037/0003-066X.49.4.304

Schaie, K. W., & Willis, S. L. (1986). Can decline in adult intellectual functioning be reversed? *Developmental Psychobiology*, *22*(2), 223–232.

Schaie, K. W., Willis, S. L., Hertzog, C., & Schulenberg, J. E. (1987). Effects of cognitive training on primary mental ability structure. *Psychology and Aging*, *2*(3), 233–242. doi:10.1037/0882-7974.2.3.233

Schmand, B., Smit, J. H., Geerlings, M. I., & Lindeboom, J. (1997b). The effects of intelligence and education on the development of dementia: A test of the brain reserve hypothesis. *Psychological Medicine*, *27*, 1337–1344. doi:10.1017/S0033291797005461

Sherer, M. (1996). The impact of using personal computers on the lives of nursing home residents. *Physical & Occupational Therapy in Geriatrics*, *14*(2), 13–31. doi:10.1080/J148v14n02_02

Shyham Sundar, S., Oeldorf-Hirsch, A., Nussbaum, J. F., & Behr, R. A. (2011). *Retirees on Facebook: Can online social networking enhance their health and wellness?* Paper presented at CHI 2011. Vancouver, Canada.

Slegers, K., van Boxtel, M. P. J., & Jolles, J. (2007). The effects of computer training and internet usage on the use of everyday technology by older adults: A randomized controlled study. *Educational Gerontology*, *33*(2), 91–110. doi:10.1080/03601270600846733

Slegers, K., van Boxtel, M. P. J., & Jolles, J. (2008). The effects of computer training and internet usage on wellbeing and quality of life of older adults: A randomized controlled study. *The Journals of Gerontology. Series B, Psychological Sciences and Social Sciences, 63*, 176–P184. doi:10.1093/geronb/63.3.P176

Slegers, K., van Boxtel, M. P. J., & Jolles, J. (2009). The effects of computer training and internet usage on cognitive abilities of older adults: A randomised controlled study. *Aging Clinical and Experimental Research, 21*(1), 43–54.

Smulders, P., & van den Bossche, S. (2004). *TNO Arbeid – Eerste resultaten nationale enquête arbeidsomstandigheden* [TNO Work and Employment - First results of the National Survey Occupational Conditions]. Hoofddorp, the Netherlands: TNO Arbeid.

Staff, R. T., Murray, A. D., Deary, I. J., & Whalley, L. J. (2004). What provides cerebral reserve? *Brain, 127*(5), 1191–1199. doi:10.1093/brain/awh144

Steinfield, C., Ellison, N. B., & Lampe, C. (2008). Social capital, self-esteem, and the use of online social network sites: A longitudinal analysis. *Journal of Applied Developmental Psychology, 29*, 434–445. doi:10.1016/j.appdev.2008.07.002

Stern, Y. (2002). What is cognitive reserve? Theory and research application of the reserve concept. *Journal of the International Neuropsychological Society, 8*, 448–460. doi:10.1017/S1355617702813248

Stevens, F. C. J., Kaplan, C. D., Ponds, R. W. H. M., Diederiks, J. P. M., & Jolles, J. (1999). How ageing and social factors affect memory. *Age and Ageing, 28*, 379–384. doi:10.1093/ageing/28.4.379

Stigsdotter, A., & Backman, L. (1995). Effects of multifactorial memory training in old age: Generalizability across tasks and individuals. *Journal of Gerontology, 50B*(3), 134–P140.

Stronge, A. J., Walker, N., & Rogers, W. A. (2001). Searching the world wide web: Can older adults get what they need? In Rogers, W. A., & Fisk, A. D. (Eds.), *Human Factors Interventions for the Health Care of Older Adults* (pp. 255–269). Mahwah, NJ: Erlbaum.

Swaab, D. F. (1991). Brain aging and Alzheimer's disease, "wear and tear" versus "use it or lose it". *Neurobiology of Aging, 12*(4), 317–324. doi:10.1016/0197-4580(91)90008-8

Swaab, D. F., Dubelaar, E. J., Hofman, M. A., Scherder, E. J., van Someren, E. J., & Verwer, R. W. (2002). Brain aging and alzheimer's disease; use it or lose it. *Progress in Brain Research, 138*, 343–373. doi:10.1016/S0079-6123(02)38086-5

Tisserand, D. J., Bosma, H., van Boxtel, M. P. J., & Jolles, J. (2001). Head size and cognitive ability in nondemented older adults are related. *Neurology, 56*(7), 969–971. doi:10.1212/WNL.56.7.969

Torres, A. (2008, November). *Cognitive effects of videogames on older people.* Paper presented at ZON Digital Games 2008, Porto, Portugal.

Valentijn, S. A. M., van Hooren, S. A. H., Bosma, H., Touw, D. M., Jolles, J., & van Boxtel, M. P. J. (2005). The effect of two types of memory training on subjective and objective memory performance in healthy individuals aged 55 years and older: A randomized controlled trial. *Patient Education and Counseling, 57*, 106–114. doi:10.1016/j.pec.2004.05.002

Valenzuela, S., Park, N., & Kee, K. F. (2009). Is there social capital in a social networking site? Facebook use and college students' life satisfaction, trust, and participation. *Journal of Computer-Mediated Communication, 14*, 875–890. doi:10.1111/j.1083-6101.2009.01474.x

Van Boxtel, M. P. J., Slegers, K., Jolles, J., & Ruijgrok, J. M. (2007). Risk of upper limb complaints due to computer use in older persons: A randomized study. *BMC Geriatrics, 7*(21).

Van der Elst, W., van Boxtel, M. P., van Breukelen, G. J., & Jolles, J. (2006c). The Stroop color-word test: Influence of age, sex, and education; and normative data for a large sample across the adult age range. *Assessment, 13*(1), 62–79. doi:10.1177/1073191105283427

Van der Elst, W., van Boxtel, M. P. J., van Breukelen, G., & Jolles, J. (2006b). The concept shifting test: Adult normative data. *Psychological Assessment, 18*(4), 424–432. doi:10.1037/1040-3590.18.4.424

Van der Elst, W., van Boxtel, M. P. J., van Breukelen, G. J. P., & Jolles, J. (2006a). The letter digit substitution test: Normative data for 1,858 healthy participants aged 24-81 from the Maastricht aging study (MAAS): Influence of age, education, and sex. *Journal of Clinical and Experimental Neuropsychology, 28*, 998–1009. doi:10.1080/13803390591004428

Van der Elst, W., van Boxtel, M. P. J., van Breukelen, G. P. J., & Jolles, J. (2005). Rey's verbal learning test: Normative data for 1855 healthy participants aged 24-81 years and the influence of sex, education, and model of presentation. *Journal of the International Neuropsychological Society, 11*, 290–302. doi:10.1017/S1355617705050344

Van der Zee, K. I., & Sanderman, R. (1993). *Het meten van de algemene gezondheidstoestand met de RAND-36: Een handleiding* [Measurement of general health with the RAND-36: A manual]. Groningen, The Netherlands: Noordelijk Centrum voor Gezondheidsvraagstukken NCG.

Verghese, J., Lipton, R. B., Katz, M. J., Hall, C. B., Derby, C. A., & Kuslansky, G. (2003). Leisure activities and the risk of dementia in the elderly. *The New England Journal of Medicine, 348*(25), 2508–2516. doi:10.1056/NEJMoa022252

Verhaeghen, P., Marcoen, A., & Goossens, L. (1992). Improving memory performance in the aged through mnemonic training: A meta-analytic study. *Psychology and Aging, 7*(2), 242–251. doi:10.1037/0882-7974.7.2.242

Ware, J. J. E., Snow, K. K., Kosinski, M., & Gandek, B. (1993). *Sf-36 health survey manual and interpretation guide*. Boston, MA: New England Medical Center.

Warren, J. M., Zerweck, C., & Anthony, A. (1982). Effects of environmental enrichment on old mice. *Developmental Psychobiology, 15*(1), 13–18. doi:10.1002/dev.420150104

Whang, L. S., Lee, S., & Chang, G. (2003). Internet over-users' psychological profiles: A behavior sampling analysis on internet addiction. *Cyberpsychology & Behavior, 6*(2), 143–150. doi:10.1089/109493103321640338

White, H., McConnell, E., Clipp, E., Branch, L., Sloane, R., & Pieper, C. (2002). A randomized controlled trial of the psychosocial impact of providing internet training and access to older adults. *Aging & Mental Health, 6*(3), 213–221. doi:10.1080/13607860220142422

White, H., McConnell, E., Clipp, E., Bynum, L., Teague, C., & Navas, L. (1999). Surfing the net in later life: A review of the literature and pilot study computer use and quality of life. *Journal of Applied Gerontology, 18*(3), 358–378. doi:10.1177/073346489901800306

Willis, S. L., Jay, G. M., Diehl, M., & Marsiske, M. (1992). Longitudinal change and prediction of everyday task competence in the elderly. *Research on Aging, 14*, 68–91. doi:10.1177/0164027592141004

Wilson, R. S., Mendes de Leon, C. F., Barnes, L. L., Schneider, J. A., Bienias, J. L., & Evans, D. A. (2002). Participation in cognitively stimulating activities and risk of incident Alzheimer disease. *Journal of the American Medical Association, 287*, 742–748. doi:10.1001/jama.287.6.742

Yellowlees, P. M., & Marks, S. (2007). Problematic internet use or internet addicton? *Computers in Human Behavior*, *23*(3), 1447–1453. doi:10.1016/j.chb.2005.05.004

Zickuhr, K. (2010). *Generations (San Francisco, Calif.)*, Washington, DC: Pew Internet.

Zimmer, Z., & Chappell, N. L. (1999). Receptivity to new technology among older adults. *Disability and Rehabilitation*, *21*(5/6), 222–230.

ADDITIONAL READING

Charness, N., & Boot, W. R. (2009). Aging and information technology use: Potential and barriers. *Current Directions in Psychological Science*, *18*, 253–258. doi:10.1111/j.1467-8721.2009.01647.x

Charness, N., Demiris, G., & Krupinski, E. (2011). *Designing telehealth for an aging population: A human factors perspective*. Boca Raton, FL: CRC Press.

Charness, N., Fox, M. C., & Mitchum, A. L. (2011). Life-span cognition and information technology. In Fingerman, K. L., Berg, C. A., Smith, J., & Antonucci, T. C. (Eds.), *Handbook of Life-Span Development* (pp. 331–361). New York, NY: Springer.

Czaja, S. J., Nair, S. N., Lee, C. C., & Sharit, J. (2008). Older adults and technology adoption. In *Proceedings of the Human Factors and Ergonomics Society 52nd Annual Meeting*, (pp. 139-143). New York, NY: Human Factors and Ergonomics Society.

Czaja, S. J., & Sharit, J. (2009). *Aging and work: Issues and implications in a changing landscape*. Baltimore, MD: Johns Hopkins University Press.

Fisk, A. D., Rogers, W., Charness, N., Czaja, S. J., & Sharit, J. (2009). *Designing for older adults: Principles and creative human factors approach* (2nd ed.). London, UK: CRC Associates.

Greenwood, P. M., & Parasuraman, R. (2010). Neuronal and cognitive plasticity: A neurocognitive framework for ameliorating cognitive aging. *Frontiers in Aging Neuroscience*, *2*, 1–14. doi:10.3389/fnagi.2010.00150

Herzog, C., Kramer, A. F., Wilson, R. S., & Lindenberger, U. (2009). Enrichment effects on adult cognitive development: Can the functional capacity of older adults be preserved and enhanced? *Psychological Science in the Public Interest*, *9*(9), 1–65.

Jeste, D. V., & Depp, C. A. (2009). *Handbook of successful cognitive and emotional aging*. Washington, DC: American Psychiatric Publishing.

Lesnoff-Caravaglia, G. (2007). *Gerontechnology: Growing old in a technological society*. New York, NY: Charles C. Thomas Pub. Ltd.

Mann, W. C. (2005). *Smart technology for aging, disability, and independence*. Hoboken, NJ: John Wiley and Sons. doi:10.1002/0471743941

Pew, R. W., & Van Hemel, S. B. (2004). *Technology for adaptive aging*. Washington, DC: The National Academies Press.

Shultz, K. S., & Adams, G. A. (2007). *Aging and work in the 21st century*. Mahwah, NJ: Erlbaum.

Stern, Y. (Ed.). (2007). *Cognitive reserve: Theory and applications*. New York, NY: Taylor & Francis.

KEY TERMS AND DEFINITIONS

Autonomy: Autonomy refers to the ability to carry out everyday tasks without any help of others. Tasks that are often referred to in the context of ageing include so-called instrumental tasks of daily living, such as getting dressed, cooking, household tasks, etc.

Cognitive Ageing: Cognitive ageing refers to the decline of most human cognitive functions as a result of a normal ageing process.

Cognitive Reserve: Cognitive reserve refers to the ability to compensate for (age-related) brain damage or disease. The term was introduced to explain individual differences in the onset of clinical symptoms after brain damage. A reserve capacity might alter the threshold of symptom onset, such that individuals may have different degrees of brain damage before symptoms become clinically apparent.

Randomized Controlled Trial: A randomized controlled trial is a specific type of design for a scientific experiment that involves random allocation of participants to the conditions of the experiment including one or more control groups.

Repetitive Strain Injury: Repetitive strain injury is a term that is often referred to in the context of a complex of complaints related to the hand, arm and shoulder that has been related to intensive interaction with a computer terminal interface, using a standard keyboard and a mouse. It is also referred to as 'cumulative trauma disorder,' 'non-specific work-related upper limb disorder' or 'repetitive strain disorder.'

Skill Transfer: Skill transfer is the use of a skill from previous experience to devise a solution for a new problem or task.

Use-It-or-Lose-It: The notion of Use-it-or-lose-it refers to the assumption that continued mental activity protects against cognitive decline. This principle states that mental stimulation may have a protective effect against a decline in higher brain functions, especially in later life.

Chapter 10
Training Older Adults to Improve their Episodic Memory:
Three Different Approaches to Enhancing Numeric Memory

Michael K. Gardner
University of Utah, USA

Robert D. Hill
University of Utah, USA

ABSTRACT

This chapter reviews the episodic memory difficulties typically encountered by older adults. It presents data that demonstrates that mnemonic interventions can improve episodic memory in the elderly, though such improvements often do not transfer broadly and do not result in improvements in the area of subjective memory assessment. It then presents three approaches to improving episodic memory for numeric information, each based upon a different approach. These approaches demonstrate: (a) that a mnemonic targeted at numeric information can improve number recall; (b) that self-generated strategies can improve recall at nearly the same level as a targeted mnemonic; and (c) that episodic memory can be converted into procedural memory, though this approach did not demonstrate improved episodic memory performance. Future directions for memory remediation are discussed, based upon research findings to date.

DOI: 10.4018/978-1-4666-1966-1.ch010

INTRODUCTION

Memory complaints are common among older adults (Blazer, Hays, Fillenbaum, & Gold, 1997; Cutler & Grams, 1988; Verhaeghen, Geraerts, & Marcoen, 2000). In part, this is due to the fear of developing Alzheimer's disease, but it is also due to the very real fact that aging is associated with increased forgetting in everyday situations (Bäckman, Small, & Wahlin, 2001; Hultsch & Dixon, 1990; Poon, 1985; Smith, 1996). Examples of commonly reported memory difficulties include: (a) remembering names; (b) remembering where things (such as keys) were placed; (c) remembering telephone numbers that have just been looked up; (d) remembering words; (e) knowing whether you have already told someone something; and (f) remembering things people tell you. Each of these events (from the Metamemory Questionnaire [Zelinski, Gilewsky, & Thompson, 1980]) were reported as memory problems by 49% or more of a sample of adults (age range: 39 to 89, $M = 62$) in a study by Bolla, Lindgren, Bonaccorsy, and Bleecker (1991), and age was related to frequency of forgetting.

The types of forgetting outlined above are examples of episodic memory (Tulving, 1972). Episodic memory includes tasks such as free recall (remembering a grocery list), recognition (deciding which of a group of people you have previously met), and paired-associate recall (learning the foreign language equivalents for a set of words you know in your native language). Each of these tasks requires that an individual consciously decides whether particular items are part of the person's previous experience. This kind of memory can be contrasted with several other memory types including: (a) semantic memory (one's knowledge of the world, as well the meanings of words and the relationships among such meanings); (b) priming (the facilitation in performance due to previous exposure to the same item or a related item); and (c) procedural memory (knowledge of how to do something, such as riding a bicycle, that does not

require calling information into conscious awareness but involves accessing tacit or implicit steps that are part of a previously rehearsed routine. In general, these non-episodic forms of memory show much less impairment with aging than does episodic memory. For example, with regard to semantic memory, the organizational structure of the internal lexicon has been found to remain relatively stable throughout adulthood (Bäckman, Small, & Wahlin, 2001; Laver & Burke, 1993). Priming studies have shown that aging has little to no effect on the degree of facilitation due to the presentation of a prime (Bäckman, Small, & Wahlin, 2001; LaVoie & Light, 1994; Light & Albertson, 1989; Light, Singh, & Capps, 1986; Mitchell, 1989). Evidence with regard to procedural memory is mixed (Bäckman, Small, & Wahlin, 2001), with some researchers finding no deterioration with aging in the ability to reproduce routines or procedures (e.g., Schugens, Daum, Spindler, & Birbaumer, 1997) while other studies have found reduced performance with increasing age (e.g., Hashtoudi, Chrosniak, & Schwartz, 1991; Moscovitch, Winocur, McLachlan, 1986; Wright & Payne, 1985). Bäckman, Small, and Wahlin (2001) note that some of these discrepancies in research findings may due to the fact that some of the tasks used to measure procedural memory required strategies requiring episodic memory, and that when this confound exists it is difficult to disentangle deficits in procedural memory from deficits in episodic memory.

Episodic memory does appear to decline with age (e.g., Verhaeghen & Marcoen, 1993), though the degree of measured decline differs depending upon the study's methodology. Cross-sectional studies of episodic memory have indicated a steady decline that begins as early as the 20s or 30s, reaches one standard deviation below peak performance by the 60s, and continues to approximately two standard deviations by the 80s (Nilsson, et al., 1997; Schaie, 1994; Park, et al., 2002; Verhaeghen & Salthouse, 1997). The problem with cross sectional studies is that they confound age effects with cohort effects (effects due to the era in which an individual was born, including education availability, access to information via media, nutritional differences, etc.). Longitudinal studies can assess age effects independent of cohort effects. However, pure longitudinal studies require extremely long time frames and suffer from internal validity threats such as drop out effects.

Rönnlund, Nyberg, Bäckman, and Nilsson (2005) present an interesting analysis of episodic memory data that combines cross sectional analysis and longitudinal analysis. They studied the five year changes in memory performance for 10 age cohorts from 35 to 80 years of age (total $N = 829$). They also adjusted their measures for practice effects (given that the participants were tested at two points in time). Their findings revealed that episodic memory remains relatively stable between ages 35 and 60, followed by a steady decline past age 60, in contrast to the steady, linear decline found in purely cross sectional studies. Interestingly, they also analyzed semantic memory performance and found improvements between ages 35 and 60, with smaller decrements in semantic memory (as compared to episodic memory) between ages 60 and 85.

BACKGROUND

Mnemonic interventions to improve episodic memory. Given the demonstrated decline in episodic memory, what can be done to assist otherwise healthy elderly individuals improve their memory performance? Most researchers interested in enhancing episodic memory in the elderly have focused on the use of mnemonics. A mnemonic is a technique that matches an encoding method with a retrieval method, usually focused on a particular type of memory task (say list learning or number learning). The encoding method supports the retrieval method, so as to enhance it. An example of an often used mnemonic is the

method of loci (e.g., Yesavage & Rose, 1984). In the method of loci, the learner is taught to remember visual images of several places along an imaginary walk (often a place already familiar to the learner). Then, during encoding, the first item on the to-be-remembered list is visualized, and an interactive image is formed of the first item and the first location along the walk. For maximum effectiveness, this interacting image should be as distinctive as possible. Each successive list item is visually associated with each successive image of a place along the imaginary walk. At retrieval, the learner follows the walk and retrieves interacting images, allowing the learner both to better remember the list (through the use of distinctive images) and its serial order (by following the cueing images from the walk). As you can see, encoding and retrieval are intimately linked in the method of loci, as they are in most mnemonic methods. The retrieval cues provided overlap with the encoding of the to-be-remembered items, which allows retrieval to benefit from the encoding specificity principle (Tulving & Thomson, 1973).

There is an existing literature which has employed advanced technology for delivering mnemonic techniques to older adults who are aging normally and who are concerned about episodic memory deficits (Mahncke, et al., 2006), as well as for attenuating deficits and possibly preserving memory capabilities. The basis of this growing body of technology, however, presumes that such techniques are effectives in reducing memory deficits in older adults.

How effective are mnemonic strategies in improving episodic memory among the elderly? The answer is that they are very effective. Verhaeghen, Marcoen, and Goossens (1992) performed a meta-analysis of 31 research articles, containing a total of 33 studies, using mnemonic training to facilitate memory in the elderly. Verhaeghen et al. found effect size of 0.7 standard deviations of improvement in memory performance for groups undergoing mnemonic training. They also found that target memory tasks, for which the mnemonic had been specifically designed, improved more than non-target tasks (i.e., transfer tasks, for which the mnemonic had not been specifically designed). This points out one important limitation of traditional mnemonic training: it does not transfer broadly to new or different episodic memory tasks (Kliegl, Smith, & Baltes, 1989; Mohs, et al., 1998; Oswald, Ruppreccht, Gunzelmann, & Tritt, 1996; Rebok, Carlson, & Langbaum, 2007; Yesavage, 1985). Other findings from Verhaeghen et al.'s (1992) meta-analysis included: (a) elderly participants who were younger performed better than older participants; (b) mnemonic interventions that used shorter training sessions performed better than those that used longer training sessions (perhaps due to limitations of attention among the elderly); and (c) the use of pretraining (e.g., relaxation training, training in the formation of visual images, and teaching of judgments of things such as pleasantness of visual images, or a combination of these) resulted in better performance than the absence of pretraining. Finally, there appeared to be no differences in memory facilitation as a function of the particular mnemonic techniques taught (e.g., the method of loci produced just as much gain as did, say, the pegword method). Although in this meta-analysis many of the studies reviewed presented information regarding the benefits (or lack thereof) of training interventions, the protocols across almost all of these studies were paper-and-pencil and, for the most part, not informed or benefitted by advanced computer training interface techniques, new technologies for information delivery, or Web-based instructional tools.

Pretraining prior to mnemonic interventions. Pretraining prior to actual mnemonic training was pioneered Yesavage and colleagues (Hill, Sheikh, & Yesavage, 1988; Shiehk, Hill, & Yesavage, 1986; Yesavage, 1984, 1985; Yesavage & Jacobs, 1984). The idea behind pretraining is as follows: learning complex mnemonic systems can be confusing, complicated, and anxiety

producing; pretraining aims at mitigating these problems (Yesavage, Lapp, & Sheikh, 1989). Hill, Sheikh, and Yesavage (1988) demonstrated that pretraining in visual imagery, semantic judgment, and relaxation training prior to actual mnemonic training improved memory performance over control conditions of either being retested or hearing lectures on memory and aging. Visual imagery and semantic judgment pretraining are thought to work by enhancing encoding skills critical to mnemonic training, and by facilitating deep processing of to-be-remembered material (Craik & Lockhart, 1972; Stigsdotter Neely, 2000; Yesavage, 1983; Yesavage, Rose, & Bower, 1983). Relaxation pretraining is thought to work by reducing anxiety and allowing older adults to focus on learning the complex mnemonic (Hill, Sheikh, & Yesavage, 1988; Stigsdotter Neely, 2000; Shiehk, Hill, & Yesavage, 1986). Indeed, reducing anxiety is particularly important for older adults with high levels of anxiety (Yesavage, Sheikh, Decker Tanke, & Hill, 1988).

Subjective memory assessment and non-cognitive factors. Several non-cognitive factors are thought to affect perceptions of memory, though not necessarily memory ability, in the elderly. Several researchers have found evidence that memory complaints may be related to depression (Bolla, Lindgren, Bonaccorsy, & Bleecker, 1991; Kahn, Zarit, Hilbert, & Niederehe, 1975; Niederehe & Yoder, 1989). In particular, Bolla et al. (1991) found a stronger relationship between memory complaints and depression than between memory complaints and actual memory performance. Others have related memory complaints to anxiety and stress (e.g., Broadbent, Cooper, Fitzgerald, & Parkes, 1982; Larrabee & Levin, 1986). Again, Larrabee and Levin (1986) found that memory complaints loaded on a factor that included depression, while memory performance loaded on a separate factor.

The dissociations between memory performance and complaints of memory impairment have led some researchers to investigate how subjective memory ratings change after older adults receive a mnemonic training intervention. Floyd and Scogin (1997) performed a meta-analysis of 25 research papers containing a total of 27 studies. Only 10 of these studies overlapped with the 31 research papers meta-analyzed earlier by Verhaeghen, Marcoen, and Goossens (1992). Floyd and Scogin (1997) found that the impact of mnemonic memory training on subjective measures of memory performance was approximately 0.2 standard deviations, considerably smaller than the 0.7 standard deviations found by Verhaeghen et al. (1992) on objective measures of performance. The smaller impact on subject measures was due, in part, to the inclusion of measures of depression and mental health, which were not responsive to mnemonic training. Floyd and Scogin (1997) also found that pretraining was related to improved memory performance, that the greatest improvements in subjective memory assessment occurred in programs that combined mnemonic training (which improved objective memory performance) with expectancy modification (developing more positive attitudes toward memory performance, which directly improved subjective memory assessment).

In conclusion, depression, anxiety, and mood states appear to be related to memory complaints. However, changing memory performance (through mnemonic training) does not appear to directly improve these mood states. Pretraining appears to help improve memory performance, but subjective assessments of overall memory performance in the elderly do not appear to change quickly or easily. This may be due to the lack of broad applicability of the mnemonics taught, or it may be due to the fact that memory expectations are built over years and decades of real world experience. Finally, from the vantage point of the 21st century, which has introduced a number of avenues through which technology-assisted training might occur, this research has to date not examined the added benefits of incorporating advanced technologies either in pre-training or training for facilitating

memory function in older adults. In fact this issue has been a motivating force for the emergence of scientific publication outlets such as *Gerotechnology* (http://www.gerontechnology.info/Journal/) devoted to the study of the application of advanced technologies for a range of issues facing older adults, including age-related cognitive decline. Early trends in scientific publication outlets are suggestive of a shift towards the delivery of memory training interventions through Web-based or computer-aided mechanisms. Whether there is added value in computer, technology, or Web mediated procedures is an important area of future research.

THREE DIFFERENT INTERVENTIONS TO IMPROVE EPISODIC MEMORY FOR NUMERIC INFORMATION

In the next section, we present in greater detail three different approaches to episodic memory training. All three of these interventions focus on memory for numeric information. We focus on memory for numeric information for two reasons. First, number recall and technology usage are tightly intertwined. This is evident, for example, in the fact that many computer passwords consist of number strings. Therefore, efficient technology usage in later life may depend on number memory facility. Memory for numeric information is not confined to recalling computer passwords. Personal identification numbers, or PINs, are used to control access to banking (Engley, 1995) and credit card accounts. Many government services are accessed via "smart cards," which likewise require PINs to uniquely identify users (Bulkeley, 1995; Sampson, Dover, Mandell, Pant, & Blanchard, 2007). Because creating a single PIN that can be used to access all of one's personal information is not a wise security strategy, the typical American adult must remember PINs for at least three different credit and/or debit card accounts (Harrow, 1995).

Further, the number of accounts an individual has is likely to grow with age.

Second, numbers are typically difficult memory stimuli. The primary reason for this is that, unlike nouns or verbal labels, they are abstract. They do not easily lend themselves to visually based mnemonics, such as the method of loci (e.g., Yesavage & Rose, 1984) or the pegword method (e.g., Wood & Pratt, 1987). It is difficult to generate a concrete visual image for an abstract concept such as a number. Thus, many traditional mnemonic interventions are poorly suited to helping older adults remember the passwords they need to access technologically based information or security protected services. Without access to such information (e.g., retirement brokerage accounts, health insurance accounts, and government services accounts), the ease of engaging in day-to-day activities will be more difficult, and the quality of life of older individuals is likely to suffer. Thus, a strong case can be made for the need to discover robust and easy-to-use strategies to facilitate number recall in old age.

The three mnemonic interventions presented next differ in their approach. The first is closest to the traditional mnemonic intervention, though it is not imagery-based. The second compares the first mnemonic approach to self-generated strategy training, in which participants practice and refine their own internally generated encoding and retrieval cues. The third leverages procedural processes to boost episodic memory. With each approach there are lessons to be learned about how the instructional process impacts number learning and recall in older adults.

The traditional mnemonic. Hill, Campbell, Foxley, and Lindsay (1997) attempted to teach a group of older adults to remember numeric information using a modification of the number-consonant mnemonic (Higbee, 1988). This mnemonic involves four separate steps:

1. The first step requires the individual to learn a series of digit-to-letter transformations. The transformations used by Hill et al. (1997) were: 1=L, 2=n, 3=m, 4=r, 5=f or v, 6=b or d, 7=s or soft c, 8=t, 9=p or z, and 0=z. The transformations must be overlearned for the mnemonic to be effective. The particular transformations were chosen so that either a physical characteristic or a sound was common to both the letter and the number. For instance, both 1 and L involve a single downward stroke.

2. The second step is word generation. After the individual has transformed the numbers into consonant letters using the transformations in step one (e.g., 7532 yields SVMN), placeholder vowels are inserted between the consonants to produce a small number of words (e.g., SVMN could be transformed into SaVe MoNey).

3. The third step involves committing to memory the words created in step two. In the Hill et al. (1997) study, participants were trained to create words of concrete objects that could be easily visualized and connected to the original cue for the numbers. This is the only point in the number-consonant mnemonic that involves visualization, and the visualization relates to the concrete nouns created, not the original numbers. SaVe MoNey might involve an image of dollar bills being deposited into an ATM machine.

4. The fourth step involves decoding the remembered words, reversing the processes of steps one through three, and using the number-consonant associations to reproduce the original numbers.

Hill et al. (1997) recruited older volunteers through radio and newspaper advertisements. Participants were screened for mental status issues and for depression. Thirty-six older adults (age: M=67.39, SD=5.14) passed the screening and were randomly assigned to either the number-consonant mnemonic condition (N=17) or a placebo training condition (N=19).

Mnemonic training involved groups of five to seven persons. Group training was face-to-face and was not mediated by technology. Training involved three sessions over a two week interval. In session one, participants attended a one hour class where an instructor introduced them to the number-consonant mnemonic. They were provided with a 15 page take home manual that covered the four steps involved in the procedure and provided homework assignments. Completing the manual and homework required about two hours (or less). In session two, participants completed one and one half hours of classroom training covering the four steps of the mnemonic along with practicing its application to number string memory. Again, participants received homework to complete before the final training session. In session three, participants received approximately 45 minutes of individualized instruction that varied with the current skill level of each participant.

Placebo training was designed to equate the two groups with regard face-to-face exposure, while providing no active memory skills. Trainers provided instruction designed to improve map reading skills. The training followed a manualized format, and was conducted by the same individuals who provided the mnemonic instruction. Although participants were not taught the number-consonant mnemonic, they did receive practice in learning number strings that were part of street addresses (which were related to places on the map).

At the conclusion of training, both groups received a posttest. This consisted of attempting to remember four lock combinations each comprising three two-digit numbers. The combinations were created by randomly combining digits (e.g., bike lock: 46 82 79). Testing was done individually and face-to-face using paper-and-pencil measures. In order to provide as clear a distinction between the two conditions as possible, participants in the placebo group were told not to use any memory procedure, but rather to repeat the numbers as fast as possible during the study time (a procedure that would approximate rehearsal).

The mnemonic group was told to use the number-consonant mnemonic they had been taught, and they were provided with space for writing down the number-to-letter transformations they used, as well as for writing down the words they had transformed the letters into. Participants were given 10 minutes to study the four combinations, and were then provided with 30 minutes worth of distractor tasks. Finally, they were provided with the names of the four locks whose combinations they were to remember, along with three spaces in which they were to write the correct two-digit numbers. Five minutes were provided to write down the combinations.

Participants returned three days later and were again asked to remember the four lock combinations. This was a surprise test, as participants only thought they were returning to be paid and debriefed. Finally, seven days after the original posttest, participants were contacted by telephone, and asked to remember the four lock combinations. Again, this was a surprise test.

Results found no difference between the number-consonant mnemonic and placebo conditions at immediate posttest. However, the differences between the groups increased over time. At three day recall, the difference between the groups approached significance (p=.055), and by seven days, the difference was significant (p<.001). Thus, while both groups displayed forgetting over time, the group trained with the number-consonant mnemonic displayed significantly less forgetting than the placebo group.

The authors interpreted the findings as supporting the usefulness of the number-consonant mnemonic in diminishing the rate of forgetting in those older persons who received training. However, some criticisms of the study can be made. First, although the study equated groups with regard to amount of time spent in training, the groups were not equated with regard to initial level of learning of the material at posttest. This raises questions about the interpretation that the placebo group forgot the combinations more quickly. It is possible that they never learned the combination initially as well as the mnemonic group. In fairness, it is extremely difficult to equate on both amount of training and amount of learning simultaneously. Second, the number-consonant mnemonic group received prompting during the posttest to use the trained mnemonic; such prompting would not occur in real world situations. Likewise, the placebo group was instructed not use mnemonics (other than rehearsal), a move which likely magnified the differences between the groups. In spite of these criticisms, the Hill et al. (1997) study demonstrates that the use of a mnemonic tailored to the particular requirements of number memory can result in improved memory performance by older adults.

In the mid-1990s, when this study was conducted, face-to-face procedures were typically used when training interventions were involved. This is noteworthy because given the sophistication of interactive technology that exists in the 21st century it would be possible to redesign this study using technology-mediated techniques that could address most of the above criticisms. For example, a computer tutorial could be programmed to provide individual feedback and ongoing assessment to guarantee equivalent training time in both groups. In the mnemonic group, manualized training could be interactive, with feedback provided to learners to ameliorate issues that occur during the learning process. This would ensure that by the end of the intervention participants could employ the mnemonic to encode numbers. Testing for both groups could also occur in simulated real-world contexts (e.g., the presentation of virtual locks that could be opened with the correct number sequences). This would not only add realism to the training and assessment, but more closely mirror the kinds of demands placed on an individual at the point of recalling a security number sequence (i.e., the numbers must be manipulated to disengage the lock). It is quite possible the small advantage of the mnemonic for minimizing forgetting found in this study might be magnified, due to the bet-

ter controls allowed by a technologically-based training procedure.

Comparison of a traditional mnemonic with self-generated strategy training. The number-consonant mnemonic has been shown to boost memory for numeric information (e.g., Hill, Campbell, Foxley, & Lindsay, 1997), however it requires considerable cognitive resources to master and apply the number-consonant mnemonic. Participants must overlearn the four steps of the mnemonic, and must be able to apply the steps to stimuli on the fly. Derwinger, Stigsdotter Neely, Persson, Hill, and Bäckman (2003) tested the possibility that an equal amount of time spent training older adults to use self-generated strategies might also result in improved memory performance: perhaps, performance equal to that of the number-consonant mnemonic.

Derwinger et al. (2003) compared the performance of the three groups of 30 elderly participants using the number-consonant mnemonic (age: M=71.1, SD=6.7), self-generated strategy training (age: M=70.3, SD=5.5), or a control condition receiving no training (age: M=71.2. SD=6.5). The three groups were equated for years of education, vocabulary, and level of depression (those with clinical depression were excluded).

In this case, the number-consonant mnemonic group received four one-hour sessions aimed at teaching them how to use the mnemonic (i.e., the four steps involved that were outlined in an earlier section of this chapter). The other two groups did not receive specific pretraining. Both the number-consonant mnemonic group and the self-generated strategy group received ten one-hour training sessions devoted to acquiring skill in the particular technique they were being taught. For the number-consonant mnemonic group, this involved using the number-consonant mnemonic to: (a) translate numbers into consonants, (b) create words from the consonant using placeholder vowels, (c) remembering the words via imagery and association, and (d) reversing the process to reproduce the original numbers. For the self-generated strategy group, this involved: (a) having participants explore their own memory processes, (b) generating and practicing strategies (such as the use of important dates like 1776) for memorization, (c) rejecting inefficient strategies, and (d) developing "key statements" that might later cue them to the correct number sequence (e.g., Declaration of Independence). The control group did not receive any training.

Recall was assessed at several points in time, and in several different ways. Each recall test involved three trials using the Buschke selective reminding procedure (Buschke, 1973; Stigsdotter Neely & Bäckman, 1993a, 1993b, 1995). This procedure involves presenting all memory items on the first trial, and on subsequent trials presenting only those items that were not recalled on the previous trial. The items to be remembered were 10 four-digit numbers presented for 45 seconds. Recall was assessed for all groups at pretest, at posttest without cognitive support, and at posttest with cognitive support. The cognitive support involved: (a) for the number-consonant mnemonic group, inputting the number-letter transformation and the words derived from the consonants; and (b) for the self-generated strategy group, inputting the key statement that described processing during encoding. Recall was also assessed for the two intervention groups during training on sessions four, six, and eight. Finally, transfer was assessed by comparing recall of 16 concrete words and 16 abstract words at pretest and posttest.

Both the number-consonant mnemonic group and the self-generated strategy group displayed similar patterns of improvement across training sessions. Overall recall comparisons at pretest, posttest without cognitive support, and posttest with cognitive support showed that the groups were indistinguishable at pretest and posttest without support; however, both of the intervention groups performed significantly better at posttest with cognitive support. When each condition's performance was compared over testing occasions, the number-consonant mnemonic group displayed

significant improvement from pretest to posttest without support, and from posttest without support to posttest with support. The self-generated strategy group showed a non-significant trend toward improvement from pretest to posttest without support, and a significant improvement from posttest without support to posttest with support. The control group showed no improvement across all three conditions.

The authors interpreted their results as demonstrating that training in the use of self-generated strategies could be as effective as an elaborate mnemonic (such as the number-consonant mnemonic), at least when cognitive support was allowed as part of the recall procedure. They point out that each approach has advantages and drawbacks. Self-generated strategies do not require an elaborate overlearning "pretraining" phase, may be less cognitively taxing, and may be more likely to be engaged in during everyday memory tasks. Mnemonics, such as the number-consonant mnemonic, are more adaptable to widely varying stimuli (say, numbers that do not easily correspond to a known date) and guarantee cues that will yield one and only one number during retrieval.

Data from the transfer test indicated all three groups improved from pretest to posttest, but neither of the intervention groups outperformed the control at each testing time. Thus, memory gains from both the number-consonant mnemonic and self-generated strategies did not transfer to non-numeric materials. This finding is consistent with other memory training research that has found little to no transfer beyond the task trained (e.g., Scogin & Bienas, 1988; Scogin, Storandt, & Lott, 1985; Stigsdotter Neely & Bäckman, 1989, 1993a, 1995).

In considering these results, we note that both intervention groups received extensive training (i.e., 10 hours) in their techniques. This level of training almost never occurs in the real world, so these results represent an optimum level of performance. The number-consonant mnemonic group slightly outperformed the self-generated strategy group, but they also received an additional four hours of training in the steps of the mnemonic. This makes it difficult to determine whether the two intervention groups would have differed at all had it not been for the additional time spent by the number-consonant mnemonic group in learning the mnemonic. It is encouraging, however, that self-generated strategies can result in performance that is similar to that attained by training in a mnemonic that has been tailored to the memory task at hand.

Once again, the weaknesses of this study could be addressed by employing contemporary technology-mediated tools for training and assessment. In this study, practice was approximated and exposure time was controlled. Whether participants were actually engaged in the learning process during the training and practice is unknown, but the extensive time in training and practice was likely overkill for most of the subjects to learn the technique. With more sophisticated technologically-driven tools, accurate monitoring of time spent on-task during training is possible. It is probably the case that maximum learning for some persons occurred in four hours versus 10 hours for others. Individual differences in exposure to and practice with the mnemonic could be achieved using contemporary technology. In this study, the transfer task was verbal material. Once again, it is now possible to design a transfer task that mirrors the real-world operation of numbers, perhaps by altering the keypad press requirements from an ATM to a telephone keypad. This would make the transfer task more meaningful in understanding whether this approach to number learning could facilitate recall under different conditions.

Use of procedural memory. Gardner, Hill, and Was (2011) tested a novel intervention designed to improve memory for numbers by converting declarative knowledge into procedural knowledge. They noted that when people attempt to remember numbers, such as the PINs used to access account information, they typically treat the to-be-remembered numbers as pieces of declarative

knowledge: information that needs to be called into conscious awareness. However, as we have already noted, numbers are poor memory stimuli due to their abstractness and lack of distinctiveness. Furthermore, episodic memory deteriorates with advancing age. However, it usually is not necessary to call a PIN into conscious awareness; all that is required is the ability to produce the PIN at a keypad when needed to access the account. This amounts to treating the PIN as a piece of procedural knowledge: a set of keystrokes that can be produced as needed. As we stated in our earlier review, procedural knowledge may be less susceptible to deterioration with aging than episodic (i.e., declarative) memory (Bäckman, Small, & Wahlin, 2001), and may be controlled by different neural systems (Squire, 1986, 1987). It should be noted that in this study advanced technology was employed in both the training of the technique and the outcome assessment. Further, strategy training was embedded in real-world scenarios; that it, participants were required to enter the target number stimuli into a keypad to access dollars from an ATM or services from a bank, etc. Thus, by using advanced computer-mediated technology, it was hoped that the training would have direct application to real-world number demands.

Gardner et al. (2011) recruited 55 older adults (ages 61 to 92) and 37 younger adults (ages 18 to 40), who were randomly assigned to either a procedural, motor skill learning condition (older group, N=29, age: M=72.34, SD=7.97; younger group, N=22, age: M=22.14, SD=3.30) or a control condition (older group, N=26, age: M=71.31, SD=7.64; younger group, N=15, age: M=24.67, SD=4.92). Participants were screened for overall cognitive impairment using the Short Portable Mental Status Exam (Pfeiffer, 1975) and for depression using the Geriatric Depression Scale (Short Form; Sheikh & Yesavage, 1986).

The task in this study was to learn 4 four-digit PINs, each of which was for use in a different location (i.e., bank, telephone, grocery, and computer). Both conditions received three training sessions consisting of 12 blocks of 12 trials each (on Monday, Wednesday, and Friday of the first week of the study). Three posttests were conducted: (a) immediately following training; (b) four days after training was completed; and (c) seven days after training was completed. During posttests, participants were presented with the location for using the PIN and had to recall the four digits of the PIN in the correct serial order by entering them into a keypad attached to a computer. Dependent variables were error rate, latency to response, and speed of correct responding (a composite measure that combined latency and error rate).

The procedural, motor skill training was designed using two basic principles: (a) the method of vanishing cues, and (b) errorless learning. Glisky and her colleagues (Glisky & Delaney, 1996; Glisky & Schacter, 1987, 1988a, 1988b; Glisky, Schacter, & Tulving, 1986a, 1986b) developed the method of vanishing cues to teach information to amnesic individuals. The procedure involved presenting participants with sufficient "cueing information" (part of the correct response) so that they could respond correctly to a set of memory items. The cueing information was then reduced over subsequent trials. By the end of training, participants could respond correctly with only minimal cueing. This technique is similar to the behavioral principle of "fading" (Alberto & Troutman, 2003).

It should be noted that the group of participants in this study were aging normally and were screened for cognitive or mental health issues. Thus, a substantial question was whether this technique, which was previously designed for memory rehabilitation in impaired persons, could be of benefit to older adults who were, for the most part, unimpaired. Further, this study made use of an applied context (e.g., entering numbers on a computer keypad). This provided ecological validity: participants had the sense of performing a simulation of a real world task, rather than performing a laboratory study in which the numbers were essentially meaningless digit strings to be remembered. It was hoped that this would both motivate participants, and increase the likelihood that the results would generalize to real world numeric memory problems.

Another essential component of the training curriculum was the minimization of errors during training. Baddeley and his colleagues (Wilson, Baddeley, Evans, & Shiel, 1994) demonstrated the importance of errorless learning, especially with regard to learning in amnesiacs. Wilson et al. found that performance on a memory task in a condition that required amnesiacs to produce guesses (which were usually errors) was poorer than in a condition that prevented guessing. Presumably, this finding occurs because the incorrect guesses become incorporated into the mental representation of the knowledge, which results in more errors in the future.

On a given trial during procedural, motor skill training, the name of one of the four locations appeared for one second (i.e., bank, grocery, telephone, or computer). The screen then changed to one containing pictures of the four locations. The participant next had to respond by pressing one of four arrows (up, down, left, or right) that indicated the location of the picture that matched the location presented earlier. If the response was wrong, the word "Incorrect" was presented over computer speakers, and the same trial was re-initiated. Next, cueing information was presented. This was some portion of the PIN number, and the amount of cueing information was varied over blocks (see below). The participant then entered the entire four-digit PIN into a separate keypad attached to the computer. This separate keypad simulated the experience of entering a PIN into a detached keypad in the real world. If the response was wrong, the word "Incorrect" was presented over computer speakers and the correct PIN was presented as feedback. Following this, the same trial was re-initiated. If the response was correct, participants proceeded to the next trial. Thus, participants in the procedural, motor skill condition were: (a) encouraged to associate each PIN with its correct context of usage; (b) were supported in their procedural learning via the method of vanishing cues; and (c) were forced to enter the correct response before proceeding to the next trial.

Procedural, motor skill training occurred over three sessions (on separate days), and consisted of 12 blocks of training of 12 trials each (that is, each block presented each of the four PINs three times in random order). During blocks one and two of each session, all four digits of the PIN served as cueing information. During blocks three and four, the first three digits of the PIN served as cueing information. During blocks five and six, the first two digits of the PIN served as cueing condition. During blocks seven and eight, the first digit of the PIN served as cueing information. During blocks nine through twelve, only a blank screen served as cueing information. Thus, consistent with the method of vanishing cues, cueing support was faded over blocks of trials.

The control condition was designed to be parallel to the procedural, motor skill condition, but participants made no responses on a keypad, and therefore could not develop a procedural skill for entering the PIN. Each trial started with the name of one of the four locations for using a PIN (i.e., bank, grocery, telephone, or computer) presented for one second. The next screen presented the four pictures, with a visual arrow on the screen indicating the correct picture, which remained until the participant pressed the spacebar (a 10 second time limit was enforced). The full four-digit PIN was then presented and remained until the participant pressed the spacebar to continue (a 10 second time limit was enforced). Thus, in the control condition participants saw the full PINs an equal number of times, but could enter no information on the computer other than spacebar presses.

When individuals learn a skill, their latencies usually display a power function, sometimes referred to as the "power law of learning" (Newell & Rosenbloom, 1981). Both conditions' training latencies were fit to a power function. The results found both conditions were well fit by a power function during the first training session; however, the procedural, motor skills condition continued to be fit by a power function during training sessions two and three. We interpreted this by assuming that both groups were learning the skill of participating in the study during session one. However, only the procedural, motor skill group was acquiring the skill of entering the PINs into the keypad. This skill continued to be acquired during training sessions two and three.

Posttest recall data (error rate, latency, and speed of correct responding) was compared using mixed model ANOVAs (procedural, motor skill condition versus control condition [between subjects factor], old versus young [between subjects factor], and immediate, four day, and seven day testing time [within subjects factor]). There was a clear main effect for age, with younger participants being more accurate, faster, and producing more correct responses per unit time than older participants. Unfortunately, there was no significant difference between the procedural, motor skill condition and the control condition.

This study demonstrates a novel approach to episodic memory enhancement and it provides a strong feasibility test for applying computer-mediated technology to train older adults to recall number strings. There were several advantages associated with our computer-mediated technology:

- Training procedures were adjusted for individual differences in performance capability.
- Testing was associated with a real-world application; that is, participants were required to enter PINs via a keypad for several real world contexts: a bank account, a telephone calling card, a grocery debit card, or a computer password.
- We were able to measure a number of parameters of training that in the previous two studies were not possible. For example, we measured the latency of responding, which is a strong indirect indicator of memory

consolidation. We also measured errors during training, which can help gauge how well an individual is acquiring the stimuli (i.e., the PINs).

- The computer-mediated training also could have allowed us to train PINs for other contexts, such as a doctor's office or the front door security code. All that would have been needed were different words and pictures to associate PINs with these contexts.

- The computerized nature of training also would have allowed us to train longer number sequences, or even number and letter sequences. If letters were used, the keypad would have required letter labeling, such as is found on telephones.

The findings from this study provide strong evidence of an overall training effect associated with practice. We, of course, found that older persons were less able to acquire the number strings than younger persons; that is, younger persons reached a training asymptote sooner than older persons. We did not, however, find that the vanishing cues approach was better than rote rehearsal. This was unexpected; however, the study almost certainly suffered from ceiling effects. Younger participants' percentage of correct responses, averaged over training conditions, was over 95% at each of the three testing times. Older participants' percentage of correct responses ranged from 87% to 92%. A better test may have involved less training (say, one session) or a larger number of PINs (say 8 or 16). Future research will need to examine the parameters of training with the goal of determining, at least for motor based procedures, what is an optimum training intervention for a healthy person (for a given number of PINs), and whether that training interval is appreciably different for younger versus older persons.

CONCLUSION

In this chapter, we have reviewed findings concerning episodic memory in older adults, and approaches to improving episodic memory for numeric information in particular. Episodic memory declines with age, especially after the age of 60. This stands in contrast to other forms of memory, such as semantic memory, priming memory, and procedural memory, which show little or no decline with advancing age. Mnemonic interventions, which match a set of encoding procedures to a later retrieval process, can be quite effective in improving episodic memory performance. One factor that has been shown to enhance mnemonic memory training programs is "pretraining": training in things such as visual imagery, semantic judgments, or relaxation. These factors are thought to enhance either encoding skills necessary for mnemonic training, or attentional processes necessary for learning complex skills.

Complaints about episodic memory tend be related to non-cognitive factors such as depression, anxiety, and impaired mood, rather than actual memory performance. Likewise, mnemonics that improve objective memory performance have a much smaller effect on subjective memory assessment. Subjective memory assessment may change over time, but improvements on one memory task targeted by an intervention are insufficient to move the needle.

As our society becomes more reliant on technology, memory for numeric information, such as PINs, has become more important. Numbers are difficult memory stimuli, because they are abstract and lack distinctiveness. We reviewed three approaches to improving episodic memory for numeric information in the elderly. The first used a mnemonic technique, the number-consonant mnemonic, to facilitate number memory. Data showed that the number-consonant mnemonic is effective in enhancing number memory, though it requires lengthy training in the technique. The second approach compared self-generated numeric memory strategies with the number-consonant mnemonic. Data from this study demonstrated that, with enough training, self-generated strategies can produce gains on a par with the number-consonant mnemonic. In both of these approaches, the procedures relied on paper-and-pencil training methods and assessments, which we view as substantially constraining. Clearly, people differ in the amount of training they need to acquire and use a mnemonic procedure. We discussed how introducing more flexible training and assessment procedures through computer-aided tools represents an important area for further exploration of memory training and rehabilitation.

The third approach attempted to convert the episodic memory of number strings into a procedural skill of entering the numbers into a keypad. In this study, the format was entirely adapted to computer-mediated tools. Participants, for example, entered PIN numbers through a keypad versus wrote them down on a piece of paper. The multiple advantages of this format were highlighted not only for future research, but also for developing next generation training protocols for memory facilitation in older adults.

With respect to the third study, given that procedural memory is less impacted by aging than episodic memory, this approach seemed promising. Data supported general trends in aging: that is, younger persons were faster at acquiring the number strings and made fewer errors along the way. There were no differences between rote rehearsal and the motor skill training techniques, but this suggests that it may be important to search for procedural strategies that are tailored to older persons who are not impaired.

Future attempts to improve numeric memory in the elderly must take into account several factors. First, although structured mnemonics (i.e., the number-consonant mnemonic) can improve episodic memory for numbers, it requires extensive training and places extensive cognitive demands on the learner while acquiring the mnemonic.

This is not an ideal state of affairs. Many older adults resist the training necessary to become proficient in a mnemonic. Indeed, even memory experts like cognitive psychologists do not rely on mnemonics in everyday life (Park, Smith, & Cavanaugh, 1990; Stigsdotter Neely, 2000). It could be, however, that introducing computer-mediated strategies for memory improvement might be one way to change perceptions and motivations around memory maintenance interventions. The is one of the advantages of one such intervention (i.e., the Brain Fitness Program, Posit Science, San Francisco, AG) designed to improve memory through structured practice on tasks that train skills underlying fundamental memory processes (http://www.positscience.com/). Early trials with this kind of computer-mediated feedback intensive strategy training format has been very positive, especially for older adults who are experiencing significant cognitive impairment (Smith, et al., 2009; Delahunt, et al., 2009).

Training research must face up to the lack of transfer found for most episodic memory mnemonic training programs (both for numeric information and for verbal information). One reason we have presented programs based upon self-generated strategies and procedural memory is that they offer the potential for greater transfer. Most individuals would employ different self-generated strategies for numbers versus abstract words. Whether these individually generated strategies would be equally efficient in both cases is difficult to say. Likewise, many tasks can be proceduralized, including programming a digital video recorder, refilling a prescription, and utilizing mass transit. Thus, these later approaches are, at least in principle, more general, as they do not require an entirely different mnemonic to approach each new task. The issue of training transfer will certainly be aided by making the training protocol fit as closely as possible the demands that the individual will experience at the point of recall. This is where advanced technology may play a role. In fact, we argue that it is as important to design training for transfer to the real world context where the memory skill will be used as it is to provide pretraining to ensure that essential features for learning are in place for optimal training to occur. The investigation of strategies of training for transfer, and employing advanced technologically-based techniques to enable this to occur, is a promising direction for future research.

We are confident that the future will involve many new approaches to enhancing episodic memory in general, and episodic memory for numeric information in particular. The world's aging population will greatly benefit from these approaches, because the ability to function in a technologically-based society will require the recall of random number strings to access accounts and services. Enhancing memory for numeric information is not just an academic problem; for the elderly, it is a quality of life problem as well.

REFERENCES

Alberto, P. A., & Troutman, A. C. (2003). *Applied behavior analysis for teachers* (6th ed.). Upper Saddle River, NJ: Pearson Education.

Bäckman, L., Small, B. J., & Wahlin, Å. (2001). Aging and memory: Cognitive and biological perspectives. In Birren, J. E., & Schaie, K. W. (Eds.), *Handbook of the Psychology of Aging* (5th ed., pp. 349–377). San Diego, CA: Academic Press.

Blazer, D. G., Hays, J. C., Fillenbaum, G. G., & Gold, D. T. (1997). Memory complaint as a predictor of cognitive decline: A comparison of African American and White elders. *Journal of Aging and Health*, *9*(2), 171–184. doi:10.1177/089826439700900202

Bolla, K. I., Lindgren, K. N., Bonaccorsy, C., & Bleecker, M. L. (1991). Memory complaints in older adults: Fact or fiction? *Archives of Neurology*, *48*(1), 61–64. doi:10.1001/archneur.1991.00530130069022

Broadbent, D. E., Cooper, P. F., Fitzgerald, P., & Parkes, K. R. (1982). The cognitive failures questionnaire (CFQ) and its correlates. *The British Journal of Clinical Psychology*, *21*(1), 1–16. doi:10.1111/j.2044-8260.1982.tb01421.x

Buckley, W. M. (1995, April 19). To read this, give us the password…Ooops! Try it again. *The Wall Street Journal*, pp. A1, A8.

Buschke, H. (1973). Selective reminding for analysis of memory and learning. *Journal of Verbal Learning and Verbal Behavior*, *12*(5), 543–550. doi:10.1016/S0022-5371(73)80034-9

Craik, F. I. M., & Lockhart, R. S. (1972). Levels of processing: A framework for memory research. *Journal of Verbal Learning and Verbal Behavior*, *11*(6), 671–684. doi:10.1016/S0022-5371(72)80001-X

Cutler, S. J., & Grams, A. E. (1988). Correlates of self-reported everyday memory problems. *Journal of Gerontology*, *43*(3), S82–S90.

Delahunt, P. B., Ball, K. K., Roenker, D. L., Hardy, J. L., Mahncke, H. W., & Merzenich, M. M. (2009). Computer-based cognitive training to facilitate neural plasticity. *Gerontechnology (Valkenswaard)*, *8*(1), 52–53. doi:10.4017/gt.2009.08.01.005.00

Derwinger, A., Stigsdotter Neely, S., Persson, M., Hill, R. D., & Bäckman, L. (2003). Remembering numbers in old age: Mnemonic training versus self-generated strategy training. *Neuropsychology, Development, and Cognition. Section B, Aging, Neuropsychology and Cognition*, *10*(3), 202–214. doi:10.1076/anec.10.3.202.16452

Engley, H. L. (1995, October 2). ATM turns 30: What did we do without it? *Salt Lake Tribune*, p. C2.

Floyd, M., & Scogin, F. (1997). Effects of memory training on the subjective memory functioning and mental health of older adults: A meta-analysis. *Psychology and Aging, 12*(1), 150–161. doi:10.1037/0882-7974.12.1.150

Gardner, M. K., Hill, R. D., & Was, C. A. (2011). A procedural approach to remembering personal identification numbers. *PLoS ONE, 6*(10), e25428. doi:10.1371/journal.pone.0025428

Glisky, E. L., & Delaney, S. M. (1996). Implicit memory and new semantic learning in posttraumatic amnesia. *The Journal of Head Trauma Rehabilitation, 11*(2), 31–42. doi:10.1097/00001199-199604000-00004

Glisky, E. L., & Schacter, D. L. (1987). Acquisition of domain-specific knowledge in organic amnesia: Training for computer-related work. *Neuropsychologia, 25*(6), 893–906. doi:10.1016/0028-3932(87)90094-7

Glisky, E. L., & Schacter, D. L. (1988a). Acquisition of domain-specific knowledge in patients with organic memory disorders. *Journal of Learning Disabilities, 21*(6), 333–339, 351. doi:10.1177/002221948802100604

Glisky, E. L., & Schacter, D. L. (1988b). Long-term retention of computer learning by patients with memory disorders. *Neuropsychologia, 26*(1), 173–178. doi:10.1016/0028-3932(88)90041-3

Glisky, E. L., Schacter, D. L., & Tulving, E. (1986a). Computer learning by memory-impaired patients: Acquisition and retention of complex knowledge. *Neuropsychologia, 24*(3), 313–328. doi:10.1016/0028-3932(86)90017-5

Glisky, E. L., Schacter, D. L., & Tulving, E. (1986b). Learning and retention of computer-related vocabulary in memory-impaired patients: Method of vanishing cues. *Journal of Clinical and Experimental Neuropsychology, 8*(3), 292–312. doi:10.1080/01688638608401320

Harrow, R. O. (1995, November 17). You must remember this: Passwords are easy to forget. *Salt Lake Tribune*, p. A1.

Hashtroudi, S., Chrosniak, L. D., & Schwartz, B. L. (1991). Effects of aging on priming and skill acquisition. *Psychology and Aging, 6*(4), 605–615. doi:10.1037/0882-7974.6.4.605

Higbee, K. (1988). *Your memory: How it works and how to improve it*. New York, NY: Paragon House.

Hill, R. D., Campbell, B. W., Foxley, D., & Lindsay, S. (1997). Effectiveness of the number-consonant mnemonic for retention of numeric material in community-dwelling older adults. *Experimental Aging Research, 23*(3), 275–286. doi:10.1080/03610739708254284

Hill, R. D., Sheikh, J. I., & Yesavage, J. A. (1988). Pretraining enhances mnemonic training in elderly adults. *Experimental Aging Research, 14*(4), 207–211. doi:10.1080/03610738808259749

Hultsch, D. F., & Dixon, R. A. (1990). Learning and memory in aging. In Birren, J. E., & Schaie, K. W. (Eds.), *Handbook of the Psychology of Aging* (3rd ed., pp. 258–274). San Diego, CA: Academic Press.

Kahn, R. L., Zarit, S. H., Hilbert, N. M., & Niederehe, G. (1975). Memory complaint and impairment in the aged: The effect of depression and altered brain function. *Archives of General Psychiatry, 32*(12), 1569–1573. doi:10.1001/archpsyc.1975.01760300107009

Kliegl, R. K., Smith, J., & Baltes, P. B. (1989). Testing the limits and the study of adult age differences in cognitive plasticity of a mnemonic skill. *Developmental Psychology, 26*(2), 894–904.

Larrabee, G. J., & Levin, H. S. (1986). Memory self-ratings and objective test performance in a normal elderly sample. *Journal of Clinical and Experimental Neuropsychology, 8*(3), 275–284. doi:10.1080/01688638608401318

Laver, G. D., & Burke, D. M. (1993). Why do semantic priming effects increase in old age: A meta-analysis. *Psychology and Aging, 8*(1), 34–43. doi:10.1037/0882-7974.8.1.34

LaVoie, D., & Light, L. L. (1994). Adult age differences in repetition priming: A meta-analysis. *Psychology and Aging, 9*(4), 539–553. doi:10.1037/0882-7974.9.4.539

Light, L. L., & Albertson, S. A. (1989). Direct and indirect tests of memory for category exemplars in young and older adults. *Psychology and Aging, 4*(4), 487–492. doi:10.1037/0882-7974.4.4.487

Light, L. L., Singh, A., & Capps, J. L. (1996). Dissociation of memory and awareness in young and older adults. *Journal of Clinical and Experimental Neuropsychology, 8*(1), 62–74. doi:10.1080/01688638608401297

Mahncke, H. W., Connor, B. B., Appelman, J., Ahsanuddin, O. N., Hardy, J. L., & Wood, R. A. … Merzenich, M. M. (2006). *Proceedings of the National Academy of Sciences USA, 103*(33), 12523-12528.

Mitchell, D. B. (1989). How many memory systems? Evidence from aging. *Journal of Experimental Psychology. Learning, Memory, and Cognition, 15*(1), 31–49. doi:10.1037/0278-7393.15.1.31

Mohs, R. C., Ashman, T. A., Jantzen, K., Albert, M., Brandt, J., & Gordon, B. (1998). A study of the efficacy of a comprehensive memory enhancement program in healthy elderly persons. *Psychiatry Research, 77*(3), 183–195. doi:10.1016/S0165-1781(98)00003-1

Moscovitch, M., Winocur, G., & McLachlan, D. (1986). Memory as assessed by recognition and reading time in normal and memory-impaired people with Alzheimer's disease and other neurological disorders. *Journal of Experimental Psychology. General, 115*(4), 331–347. doi:10.1037/0096-3445.115.4.331

Newell, A., & Rosenbloom, P. S. (1981). Mechanisms of skill acquisition and the law of practice. In Anderson, J. R. (Ed.), *Cognitive Skills and Their Acquisition* (pp. 1–55). Hillsdale, NJ: Erlbaum.

Niederehe, G., & Yoder, C. (1989). Metamemory perceptions in depressions of young and older adults. *The Journal of Nervous and Mental Disease, 177*(1), 4–14. doi:10.1097/00005053-198901000-00002

Nilsson, L.-G., Bäckman, L., Erngrund, K., Nyberg, L., Adolfsson, R., & Bucht, G. (1997). The Betula prospective cohort study: Memory, health, and aging. *Neuropsychology, Development, and Cognition. Section B, Aging, Neuropsychology and Cognition, 4*(1), 1–32. doi:10.1080/13825589708256633

Oswald, W. D., Rupprecht, R., Gunzelmann, T., & Tritt, K. (1996). The SIMA-project: Effects of 1 year cognitive and psychomotor training on cognitive abilities of the elderly. *Behavioural Brain Research, 78*(1), 67–72. doi:10.1016/0166-4328(95)00219-7

Park, D. C., Lautenschlager, G., Hedden, T., Davison, N., Smith, A. D., & Smith, P. K. (2002). Models of visuospatial and verbal memory across the adult life span. *Psychology and Aging, 17*(2), 299–320. doi:10.1037/0882-7974.17.2.299

Park, D. C., Smith, A. D., & Cavanaugh, J. C. (1990). Metamemories of memory researchers. *Memory & Cognition, 18*(3), 321–327. doi:10.3758/BF03213885

Pfeiffer, E. (1975). A short portable mental status questionnaire for the assessment of organic brain deficit in elderly patients. *Journal of the American Geriatrics Society*, *23*(10), 433–441.

Poon, L. W. (1985). Differences in human memory with aging: Nature, causes, and clinical interpretations. In Birren, J. E., & Schaie, K. W. (Eds.), *Handbook of the Psychology of Aging* (2nd ed., pp. 427–462). New York, NY: Van Nostrand Reinhold.

Rebok, G. W., Carlson, M. C., & Langbaum, J. B. S. (2007). Training and maintaining memory abilities in healthy older adults: Traditional and novel approaches. *Journals of Gerontology: Series B*, *62B*, 53–61. doi:10.1093/geronb/62. special_issue_1.53

Rönnlund, M., Nyberg, L., Bäckman, L., & Nilsson, L.-G. (2005). Stability, growth, and decline in adult life span development of declarative memory: Cross-sectional and longitudinal data from a population-based study. *Psychology and Aging*, *20*(1), 3–18. doi:10.1037/0882-7974.20.1.3

Sampson, E. L., Dover, D., Mandell, M., Pant, A., & Blanchard, M. R. (2007). Personal identification (PIN) numbers: A new cause of financial exclusion in older people. *International Journal of Geriatric Psychiatry*, *22*(5), 492–493. doi:10.1002/gps.1708

Schaie, K. W. (1994). The course of adult intellectual development. *The American Psychologist*, *49*(4), 304–313. doi:10.1037/0003-066X.49.4.304

Schugens, M. M., Daum, I., Spindler, M., & Birbaumer, N. (1997). Differential effects of aging on explicit and implicit memory. *Neuropsychology, Development, and Cognition. Section B, Aging, Neuropsychology and Cognition*, *4*(1), 33–44. doi:10.1080/13825589708256634

Scogin, F., & Bienias, J. L. (1988). A three year follow-up of older adult participants in a memory-skills training program. *Psychology and Aging*, *3*(4), 334–337. doi:10.1037/0882-7974.3.4.334

Scogin, F., Storandt, M., & Lott, L. (1985). Memory-skills training, memory complaints, and depression in older age. *Journal of Gerontology*, *40*(5), 562–568.

Sheikh, J. I., Hill, R. D., & Yesavage, J. A. (1986). Long-term efficacy of cognitive training for age-associated memory impairment: A six-month follow-up study. *Developmental Neuropsychology*, *2*(4), 413–421. doi:10.1080/87565648609540358

Sheikh, J. K., & Yesavage, J. A. (1986). Geriatric depression scale (GDS): Recent evidence and development of a shorter version. In Brink, T. L. (Ed.), *Clinical Gerontology: A Guide to Assessment and Intervention* (pp. 165–173). New York, NY: Haworth Press.

Smith, A. D. (1996). Memory. In Birren, J. E., & Schaie, K. W. (Eds.), *Handbook of the Psychology of Aging* (4th ed., pp. 236–250). San Diego, CA: Academic Press.

Smith, G. E., Housen, P., Yaffe, K., Ruff, R., Kennison, R. F., Mahncke, H. W., & Zlinski, E. E. (2009). A cognitive training program based on principles of brain plasticity: Results from the improvement in memory with plactiticy-based adaptive cognitive training (IMPACT) study. *Journal of the American Geriatrics Association*, *57*(4), 594–603. doi:10.1111/j.1532-5415.2008.02167.x

Squire, L. R. (1986). Mechanisms of memory. *Science*, *232*, 1612–1619. doi:10.1126/science.3086978

Squire, L. R. (1987). *Memory and brain*. Oxford, UK: Oxford University Press.

Stigsdotter Neely, A. (2000). Multifactorial memory training in normal aging: In search of memory improvement beyond the ordinary. In Hill, R. D., Bäckman, L., & Stigsdotter Neely, A. (Eds.), *Cognitive Rehabilitation in Old Age* (pp. 63–80). Oxford, UK: Oxford University Press.

Stigsdotter Neely, S., & Bäckman, L. (1989). Multifactorial memory training with older adults: How to foster maintenance of improved performance. *Gerontology, 35*(5-6), 260–267. doi:10.1159/000213035

Stigsdotter Neely, S., & Bäckman, L. (1993a). Maintenance of gains following multifactorial and unifactorial memory training in late adulthood. *Educational Gerontology, 19*(2), 105–117. doi:10.1080/0360127930190202

Stigsdotter Neely, S., & Bäckman, L. (1993b). Long-term maintenance of gains from memory training in older adults: Two 3½-year follow-up studies. *Journal of Gerontology, 48*(5), 233–P237.

Stigsdotter Neely, S., & Bäckman, L. (1995). Effects of multifactorial training in old age: Generalizability across tasks and individuals. *Journals of Gerontolgoy: Series B: Psychological Sciences, 50B*(3), 134–P140. doi:10.1093/geronb/50B.3.P134

Tulving, E. (1972). Episodic and semantic memory. In E. Tulving & W. Donaldson (Eds.), *Organization of Memory,* (pp. 381-403). New York, NY: Academic Press.

Tulving, E., & Thomson, D. M. (1973). Encoding specificity and retrieval processes in episodic memory. *Psychological Review, 80*(5), 352–373. doi:10.1037/h0020071

Verhaeghen, P., Geraerts, N., & Marcoen, A. (2000). Memory complaints, coping, and well-being in old age: A systemic approach. *The Gerontologist, 40*(5), 540–548. doi:10.1093/geront/40.5.540

Verhaeghen, P., & Marcoen, A. (1993). More of less the same? A memorability analysis on episodic memory tasks in young and old adults. *Journal of Gerontology, 48*(4), 172–178.

Verhaeghen, P., Marcoen, A., & Goossens, L. (1992). Improving memory performance in the aged through mnemonic training: A meta-analytic study. *Psychology and Aging, 7*(2), 242–251. doi:10.1037/0882-7974.7.2.242

Verhaeghen, P., & Salthouse, T. (1997). Meta-analyses of age-cognition relations in adulthood: Estimates of linear and nonlinear age effects and structural models. *Psychological Bulletin, 122*(3), 231–249. doi:10.1037/0033-2909.122.3.231

Wood, L. E., & Pratt, J. D. (1987). Pegword mnemonic as an aid to memory in the elderly: A comparison of four age groups. *Educational Gerontology, 13*(4), 325–339. doi:10.1080/0360127870130404

Wright, B. M., & Payne, R. B. (1985). Effects of aging on sex differences in psychomotor reminiscence and tracking proficiency. *Journal of Gerontology, 40*(2), 179–184.

Yesavage, J. A. (1983). Imagery pretraining and memory training in the elderly. *Gerontology, 29*(4), 271–275. doi:10.1159/000213126

Yesavage, J. A. (1984). Relaxation and memory training in 39 elderly patients. *The American Journal of Psychiatry, 141*(6), 778–781.

Yesavage, J. A. (1985). Nonpharmacologic treatments for memory losses with normal aging. *The American Journal of Psychology, 142*(5), 600–605.

Yesavage, J. A., & Jacobs, R. (1984). Effects of relaxation and mnemonics on memory, attention and anxiety in the elderly. *Experimental Aging Research, 10*, 211–214. doi:10.1080/03610738408258467

Yesavage, J. A., Lapp, D., & Sheikh, J. I. (1989). Mnemonics as modified for use by the elderly. In Poon, L. W., Rubin, D. C., & Wilson, B. A. (Eds.), *Everyday Cognition in Adulthood and Late Life* (pp. 598–611). Cambridge, UK: Cambridge University Press.

Yesavage, J. A., & Rose, T. L. (1984). Semantic elaboration and the method of loci: A new trip for older learners. *Experimental Aging Research, 10*(3), 155–159. doi:10.1080/03610738408258560

Yesavage, J. A., Rose, T. L., & Bower, G. H. (1983). Interactive imagery and affective judgments improve face-name learning in the elderly. *Journal of Gerontology, 38*(2), 197–203.

Yesavage, J. A., Sheikh, J. I., Decker Tanke, E. D., & Hill, R. D. (1988). Response to memory training and individual differences in verbal intelligence and state anxiety. *The American Journal of Psychiatry, 145*(5), 636–639.

Zelinski, E. M., Gilewski, M. J., & Thompson, L. W. (1980). Do laboratory tests relate to self-assessment of memory ability in the young and old? In Poon, L. W., Toyard, J. L., Cermack, L. S., & Arenberg, D. (Eds.), *New Directions in Memory and Aging* (pp. 519–544). Hillsdale, NJ: Lawrence Erlbaum Associates.

ADDITIONAL READING

Bäckman, L., Small, B. J., & Wahlin, Å. (2001). Aging and memory: Cognitive and biological perspectives. In Birren, J. E., & Schaie, K. W. (Eds.), *Handbook of the Psychology of Aging* (5th ed., pp. 349–377). San Diego, CA: Academic Press.

Derwinger, A., Stigsdotter Neely, S., Persson, M., Hill, R. D., & Bäckman, L. (2003). Remembering numbers in old age: Mnemonic training versus self-generated strategy training. *Neuropsychology, Development, and Cognition. Section B, Aging, Neuropsychology and Cognition, 10*(3), 202–214. doi:10.1076/anec.10.3.202.16452

Gardner, M. K., Hill, R. D., & Was, C. A. (2011). A procedural approach to remembering personal identification numbers. *PLoS ONE, 6*(10), e25428. doi:10.1371/journal.pone.0025428

Hill, R. D., Campbell, B. W., Foxley, D., & Lindsay, S. (1997). Effectiveness of the number-consonant mnemonic for retention of numeric material in community-dwelling older adults. *Experimental Aging Research, 23*(3), 275–286. doi:10.1080/03610739708254284

Hultsch, D. F., & Dixon, R. A. (1990). Learning and memory in aging. In Birren, J. E., & Schaie, K. W. (Eds.), *Handbook of the Psychology of Aging* (3rd ed., pp. 258–274). San Diego, CA: Academic Press.

Verhaeghen, P., Marcoen, A., & Goossens, L. (1992). Improving memory performance in the aged through mnemonic training: A meta-analytic study. *Psychology and Aging, 7*(2), 242–251. doi:10.1037/0882-7974.7.2.242

KEY TERMS AND DEFINITIONS

Episodic Memory: Memory for events that have been previously experienced by an individual. Examples of tasks that involve episodic memory include free recall, recognition, and paired-associate recall.

Mnemonics: Memory enhancement techniques that typically involve an encoding strategy (e.g., "associate each item to be remembered with a place along a familiar walk") that is matched with a corresponding retrieval strategy (e.g., "proceed along the walk, retrieving each item from each of the familiar places you used during the learning phase"). Many mnemonic strategies have been shown to be effective in boosting recall, though they often take considerable time to learn.

Pretraining: Techniques sometimes taught prior to learning a mnemonic. These techniques are designed to make the mnemonic easier to learn or easier to use. Examples include relaxation training, the formation of visual images, or the ability to make semantic judgments such as pleasantness.

Priming: The facilitation in performance that results from having been exposed to something previously. For example, if you had decided that "nurse" is a noun, you would be faster to make that same decision about "nurse" soon afterwards.

Procedural Memory: Memory for skills that are typically demonstrated, rather than consciously recalled. Individuals have a procedural memory for how to ride a bicycle or play a musical instrument.

Semantic Memory: Memory concerning relationships in the world, including the meanings of words and the relationships among words (e.g., spoon is a tool used for eating liquids; sparrows are a type of bird).

Chapter 11
The Internet and Older Adults:
Initial Adoption and Experience of Use

Eulàlia Hernández Encuentra
Universitat Oberta de Catalunya, Spain

Modesta Pousada Fernández
Universitat Oberta de Catalunya, Spain

Beni Gómez-Zúñiga
Universitat Oberta de Catalunya, Spain

ABSTRACT

This chapter examines older adults' adoption and experience of using Information and Communication Technologies (ICT), in particular the Internet. The main arguments are based on the experiences of a group of older people, all already users of ICT, in a collaborative, relaxed, and self-managing environment—the virtual campus of the Universitat Oberta de Catalunya (an online university). Older adults adopt ICT with a personal project, sometimes as a tool to for achievement; therefore, ICT use has to be done on their own initiative, with a positive attitude, and under their control. Based on the Selective Optimization and Compensation (SOC) theory of adaptation processes, the authors believe that introducing ICT through selection and optimization strategies can be a successful means of assuring effective adoption of these technologies.

INTRODUCTION

"I considered the Internet as being within an evolutionary process, it is an evolution, and I accepted it. It's not about seeing it as a change, but as a normal evolution. I think this is the secret" Joan Casals *(73 years old).*

The relationship between older adults and ICT, including the Internet itself, has been explored mainly as a matter of how to connect these two different worlds, focusing on the difficulties in bringing them together. On the contrary, this chapter aims to focus on their points of confluence by exploring in-depth the meaning ICT adoption has for older adults, and also on the affective dimension

DOI: 10.4018/978-1-4666-1966-1.ch011

derived from it, in particular by looking at personal projects as the keystone of ICT adoption. From a psychological point of view, SOC theory will serve as a guide for examining how they commit to ICT in their adaptation processes during their lifespan trajectories.

BACKGROUND

In recent years, the literature on the possibilities opened up to the elderly through use of ICT is growing significantly. Authors in this field emphasize the personal and professional benefits linked to the use of online services, such as banking, shopping, health management, communication, or recreation (Wagner, Hassanein, & Head, 2010).

Faced with the reality of an aging society (in the coming decades the growth of the older population in relation to other age groups will be substantially higher), both public authorities and certain professional sectors see technology as a useful tool for support, care and independent living during this period of life.

Most of the empirical studies that have looked at these potential benefits have been conducted with elderly people who were not habitual users of ICT. Although Internet users older than 65 years of age are still in a minority (Rainie, Purcell, & Smith, 2011; Eurostat European Commission, 2011; INE, 2011; Idescat, 2011), they now make up the fastest growing consumer segment among Internet users (Hart, Chaparro, & Halcomb, 2008; cited in Wagner, Hassanein, & Head, 2010). Furthermore, an analysis of how they first started using ICT, what they are using the Internet for, and how they feel about this experience can provide revealing data and, in turn, be useful for obtaining ideas on how to facilitate the introduction of these technologies in the lives of older non-users.

In this context, in 2004 Blit-Cohen and Litwin conducted a study to understand how older people viewed the cyber-revolution and what impact it has had on their lives. They interviewed 10 elder users and 10 non-users about their reasons for using or resisting computer usage, and found some interesting themes emerging from the interviews. One of them was related to the different conception of time in old age: while cyber-participants (as they call ICT users) tended to look ahead in time and face new challenges in an active mood, non-participants (that means, non-users) tended to look back and to dwell upon the past. They also found that, compared with non-users, Internet users clearly agreed with the idea that elderly people are able to learn new skills, especially computer-related ones.

In the same way, Melenhorst, Rogers, and Bouwhuis (2006) designed and analyzed 18 focus groups of ICT users and non-users in order to examine older adults' motivation to adopt technological innovation. They concluded that, although cost can be an obstacle for older adults in selecting an activity, the key factor was related to its perceived benefits. So, rather than effort, lack of skills, or expenses, the main factor that explains the adoption or non-adoption of innovation is the perception of clear benefits.

Although there are some other studies analyzing older ICT users (see Wagner, et al., 2010, for a multi-disciplinary review), these have mainly focused on this population's activities or behaviors. As we concluded in a previous work (Hernández-Encuentra, Pousada, & Gómez-Zúñiga, 2009), the affective and emotional dimensions of the use of technology are of particular importance in the case of the elderly. Psychological variables such as attitudes, satisfaction, stress or self-efficacy, among others, may explain the elderly's orientation towards ICT, but have often been neglected in the study of ICT adoption.

In that previous work, we have taken as a reference point the SOC Model (Baltes & Baltes, 1993), a model that is widely known in the field of developmental psychology and that is applicable to different stages and areas of people's lives. In accordance with this theoretical approach, individuals take an active role throughout their lives, whereby they not only respond to the changes that occur in relation to age (biological, social, etc.) but also generate changes in an attempt to bring conditions into line with their preferences, needs or desires. Therefore, development throughout one's life is understood, firstly, as a *selection* process – selecting from possibilities, aims, or certain domains, and disregarding others. Secondly, having chosen certain paths or domains, individuals then seek to *optimize* them, using the means and resources at their disposal to make them more effective. Third, when these means or resources are not present or are diminished, they use the *compensation* mechanism, acquiring new means or reconstructing the old ones to achieve the proposed goals, or replacing them with new accessible goals using the means available (Baltes, Lindenberger, & Staudinger, 1998).

The integration of these three mechanisms enables people, throughout their lives, to grow, maintain their levels of functioning, and also regulate their losses. Taken together, all this should promote successful aging.

We are convinced that ICT can be understood as a means or as instruments that form part of the processes and mechanisms of selection, optimization, and compensation in the context of successful aging. We understand, then, that ICT may not only be useful tools for minimizing the losses that might be experienced by the elderly, but also, and fundamentally, as tools to help them develop in areas where they already have a certain level of competence and performance.

Based again on this theoretical framework, in this chapter we present some information about the affective and emotional dimension of the use of the Internet, exploring how attitudes, self-efficacy, and satisfaction are related to this use in the case of the elderly. We also explore if the adoption of technology under the mechanisms of selection and optimization allays the elderly's fear of delegating functions and control to technological devices and, above all, we explore how the use of the Internet

is connected to meaningful experiences of use and, in the end, with personal objectives.

WHAT USERS SAY FROM A PSYCHOLOGICAL PERSPECTIVE

In order to provide new and reveling data about the experiences of older people who use ICT in their daily lives, we sent a questionnaire to 87 elderly people (Appendix 1; Schwarzer & Jerusalem, 1995; Bäßler & Schwarzer, 1996) and conducted 10 (5 women and 5 men) in-depth interviews (Appendix 2). As in our previous study (Hernández-Encuentra, et al., 2009), we used a "critical case" as our basic source of information (Turner, Turner, & Van de Valle, 2007). A critical case can be defined as a person/group/situation having strategic importance in relation to the general problem (Flyvbjerg, 2011). It aims to produce knowledge not only as a mere instrument of exploration, but also to test and to build theory.

The elderly subjects we worked with were students of the Universitat Oberta de Catalunya (UOC) and, in addition to being older than 65 years of age, they met the following criteria: a) were ICT users for everyday and pleasure activities (such as studying); b) had done an introductory course on computers and had been practicing for a minimum of 6 months; and c) were attending online courses with adults and younger classmates. These characteristics put them on the same standing, regarding Internet use, as the population that uses the Internet regularly in our country (INE, 2011; Idescat, 2011).

Overview of Our Users

A rate response of almost 50% of the elder students at UOC (48.27%, 42 out of 87 contacted) was obtained. They were mostly men (73%), their average age was 68.1 years (max 82; min 63), and 80% of them were between 65 and 74 years old. That means the participants were young elderly men, most of them living the first period after their retirement.

Most of the participants used a desktop and a laptop computer, usually in combination. The main uses were searching for information on the Internet (90%), followed by e-mail (88%) and their studies (88%), and lowest for online shopping (76%) and administrative procedures (57%). These uses of the Internet are in line with the Internet behaviors identified by previous studies (McMellon & Schiffman, 2002; Wagner, et al., 2010).

We also found that 57% of those who answered the questionnaire initially started to make use of the Internet for accessing information, expanding knowledge, keeping in touch and connecting to the world. Forty-five percent initially started for work, and it was later when they started to study on-line.

All but three of the participants felt comfortable using the Internet, although 30% responded that they would feel better if the Internet were more secure. In line with this feeling of being comfortable on the Internet, only one of the interviewees stated that it was a source of stress. Everyone else said it was a help and a way to stay active, at the same time being a good tool for communication.

Lastly, 90.5% of respondents recommended using the Internet to other people, and their arguments revolved around the following (in this order): access to information and access to communication that has a direct link to the use they themselves make of the Internet. Also, but less important for them, they made the recommendation because these days it is considered necessary, it is of help, and it keeps one up to date.

The majority of the those participants perceived themselves as having a high level of quality of life (92%; 21% very high – 71% high), a high satisfaction with their health (88%; 24% very high – 64% high) and felt they had high rates of general self-efficacy (average 33/40). Moreover, as students at a university offering non-obligatory education and courses that are not free of taxes, we

can assume their socioeconomic status as being medium-high. Therefore, according to previous studies (Eastin & LaRose, 2000; Gracia & Herrero, 2009) this population would be expected to show high levels of self-efficacy and ICT use beyond the digital divide.

To sum up, the description of our sample is similar to the one used in other articles on the same topic (Wagner, et al., 2010); i.e. people with higher levels of cognitive abilities, computer interests, computer self-efficacy, higher education, better health and wellbeing and higher incomes.

Users' Experience in their Own Words

A few themes emerged when analyzing the interviews previously transcribed verbatim. By using an inductive procedure, the majority of the themes that emerged were related to using ICT as a tool for living one's own life and for active aging. Let us look at these themes and some illustrative examples for each of them.

How did it start?
What does it mean in their lives?
    A challenge
    A way to live life
    After retirement
What are their attitudes towards Internet?
    General attitudes
    Keeping control
    Critical thinking
    Going forward

When they were asked about the first time they heard of the existence of the Internet or saw someone using it, some of our interviewees did not clearly remember that moment. The Internet has become such an everyday tool, that some of them have almost forgotten when and how they had their first contact with it.

"(...) it's a tool that because it is used every day it, draws you into using it" (interviewee 1)

With continued questioning, most of them said their first contact with ICT was the context of their job. They explained how the introduction of personal computers happened in their workplace, and how they began to use software related to their tasks or to internal networks or mail systems in the organizations they worked for. Therefore, they were really talking about how they started using ICT rather than about the Internet itself.

Initially, starting to use the Internet for professional motives could be considered a good beginning, in the sense that people do not have to take the decision themselves; rather it is taken for them. Someone else decides that it is necessary and they just have to adapt to it.

"(...) being inside the world of business (...) the introduction of electronic things was taken for granted..." (interviewee 8)

In contrast, it would be more difficult to start using ICT and the Internet without first having those experiences in the work place and having to depend only on yourself, that might prove daunting considering the effort that might be needed.

We do not think that this situation is particularly associated with age, nor that older people are more socially pressured than younger people to adopt ICT, as stated in a previous study (Chung, Park, Wang, Fulk, & McLauglhin, 2010). Instead, we think that adoption is something related to the context of the activity itself that, in some circumstances, allows the person to avoid the decision process and forces her into adopting IT, whether she likes it or not.

Additionally, we have observed that the presence of a young person in the home environment, usually a son or a daughter, has a decisive role in the adoption of ICT, particularly of the Internet. This young person is usually the first user of the Internet at home and this becomes an incentive

for older family members; he or she also becomes an information source and a trainer during their first forays online.

"I have a daughter who works in IT, she bought a computer and connected it to the Internet; she said "you see, Mama?" This would be great for you, you could communicate with your brothers and sisters-(...) She had already opened an (e-mail) account for me, she explained to me over the phone everything I needed to do and...then I was connected to the Internet!" (interviewee 6)

Therefore, the combination of having a younger family member that already used the Internet, combined with pressure at work to adopt some ICT tools, seemed to be the perfect mix to make our interviewees good candidates for becoming new Internet users. And, even more so, having ongoing support while the person is adopting ICT tools appears as an important factor in them becoming a regular user (as in Magnusson, Hanson, Birto, Berthold, Chambers, & Daly, 2002; Shewan, Tetley, Clarke, & Hanson, 2000; Aula, 2005; Hernández-Encuentra, et al., 2009). These ideas are related to the Action Planned Theory (Ajzen & Fishbein, 1980). According to this theory, social pressure, regardless of age, is one of the most important aspects tied to the adoption of new behaviors.

Besides the context where adoption initially first takes place, our interviewees explained that when this step is taken, and they have become an ICT user, it is easier for them to move on to other tools, including the Internet. This is perhaps because of: attitude (a kind of threshold is crossed); skills and habits (in relation to the concept of crystallized intelligence, according to which a new use is easier when associated with previous experiences); or because of the similarity to a previously-used device (in line with Lepa & Tatnall, 2006; Chung, et al., 2010).

What is the Aim of These New Users when They Start Adopting the Internet?

Something very clear is that all of them have a concrete goal to achieve. This means that they do not initially start using the Internet just to try something new or to know how it works; instead, they start in order to solve a concrete problem. It may be a professional issue (like dealing with banks, establishing a better communication system with partners, and so on), or a personal affair (like entering in a virtual university campus or looking for relevant personal information). However, in all cases, they have a clear objective in mind.

As we will see below, this trend is something that still characterizes the approach of our interviewees towards the Internet and the way they use ICT tools.

What Does It Mean in Their Lives?

A Challenge

Initially, for our participants, dealing with the Internet seems like as a challenge to be overcome. It is a social requirement to which they are aware that must adapt themselves, even though not all of them might not be open to doing so. This adaptation requires an initial effort but, when achieved, brings them a great satisfaction.

Somehow, according to previous studies (Hanson, Gibson, Coleman, Bobrowicz, & McKay, 2010; Mitzner, et al., 2010), Internet users seem to emphasize the benefits over the costs that they perceive.

"...it is an effort, but I do not find it an effort because I like it and it is an incentive, it is a pleasure...." (interviewee 10)

"It gives me a lot." (interviewee 10)

After the initial challenge, and even though they seem to be *keen users* (Juznic, Blazic, Mercun, & Plestenjak, 2006), the Internet was not integrated in an uncritical or widespread manner into the lives of our interviewees, but was always linked to concrete objectives (Selwyn, Gorard, Furlong, & Madden, 2003). They only use the Internet for what they consider essential, only to address specific ends. Therefore, they do not surf; they use the Internet to solve their problems; to meet their needs. They are able to use and using it gives them satisfaction.

"The important thing is thinking about what you can use it for. Not so much to go online and look for this and that, but to think deliberately to do this or that and then it (the Internet) gives you many possibilities." (interviewee 7)

"...I consider it an absolutely essential tool ... I would not know what to do without it, I suppose I could, but I do not see how." (interviewee 8)

Therefore, elderly people use the Internet because it is useful; it helps. According to the previous literature, perceived usefulness seems to be the cornerstone of Internet use (Melenhorst, et al., 2006; Mitzner, et al., 2010; Selwyn, et al., 2003), more than perceived ease of use (Chung, et al., 2010). Consequently, focusing only on the usability of websites and ICT devices will not assure the involvement of the elder person unless its usefulness is perceived. In other words, they get something positive because it fulfills their own objectives, it is a positive reward in terms of the basic mechanisms of cognitive-behavioral theory that provides a pleasant and satisfactory experience (Lorca & Jadad, 2006).

A Way to Live Life

Although the Internet in a general sense seems to have a positive impact on older people (McMellon & Schiffman, 2002), our participants clearly stated that despite having noticed some impact, their lives weren't changed by using the Internet, at least in terms of basic life goals.

"No, it does not change my life, nor do I think it has to. I think the Internet has a great cultural impact. One thing is that it change certain habits of yours, another thing is that it changes your life." (interviewee 9)

And while some of them said that the Internet had completely changed some routines in their lives, when asked for examples of more details, even when asked if they recommended the use of Internet to people around them and what were their arguments in doing so, recommendations were not backed up in any significant way by arguments. In fact, it ended up changing the way of doing some things, but not their meaning nor their life in any substantial way.

Thus, the Internet becomes an extension of the means available (e.g. to call a friend by phone to let them know they have sent them a file by email, or check/complement information from the press/ radio), that ends up being a tool of control applied to everyday situations.

"I go from the electronic press to the news and then I read the newspaper. Or vice versa, and I can seek further information, for example, where was the epicenter of the earthquake that I heard about on six o'clock news on the radio." (interviewee 8)

Moreover, the Internet is a tool that helps them realize their dreams and achieve their goals, in some cases delayed from youth. In a certain way, the Internet becomes a mechanism of adaptation (assimilation according to Brandstädter & Rothermund, 2002) to reduce the distance between their objectives in life and their current situation; thus, it becomes a tool for well-being.

"It's my attitude, it's my way of being. I have another set of motivations that I can still take advantage of... get more out of life." (interviewee 1)

Keeping some objectives in mind and making some efforts to reach them seems to be an important factor in the wellbeing of the elderly. That is why, introducing the Internet for specific selected objectives and optimizing the tools for reaching them, would be the best way to guide the adoption of ICT (in line with Baltes & Baltes, 1993; Burnett-Wolle & Godbey, 2007).

After Retirement

The elderly in our sample were not retirees who accessed the Internet because they had spare time, but for the most part were already familiar with or were previous users of the Internet and ICT in general. However, just after retirement when there was no longer pressure from some of the basic elements that had structured their lives thus far (i.e. timetables, social relationships, tasks, routines). Internet use seems to play the role of a trigger in this life transition. We found the same idea of the Internet being a useful tool in the transition to retirement in the study of Salovaara, Lehmuskallio, Hedman, Valkinen, and Näsänen (2010). Thus, the Internet enables them to fill their free time with new activities, to continue a habit of having a daily structure and keeping their minds active. Somehow, it even creates new objectives related to learning and mastering new devices and the Internet itself.

As expected, our interviewees alluded at some point to the years they have left to live, and some even believed that they had arrived too late to integrate technology across the board in their lives (in line with Turner, et al., 2007). Either way, the Internet allows them to free up time, it gives them time and, therefore, enables them to enjoy more of it, thus increasing their quality of life.

"…I think it has left me with time for other things, that otherwise…" (interviewee 9)

"…in ten minutes you have done what you needed to do, before it would have taken you the whole morning or you did not do it all." (interviewee 9)

Moreover, just after retirement, the Internet makes them feel more secure, despite being aware of some of its risks (i.e. becoming dependent on it). The Internet is for them, now more than ever, a convenience.

"It's a tool that makes life easier for me without making me feel a slave to it, this I think is fundamental." (interviewee 8)

"Using it gives you freedom without having to leave home." (interviewee 1)

What are Their Attitudes towards Internet?

General Attitudes

Our participants were receptive to the Internet, and ICT in general. In addition, they had this attitude right from the beginning, from the moment they started using it.

"I always bet on new technologies from the outset." (interviewee 9)

The involvement of users with everything new denotes an open and receptive attitude.

"It seems good to me. Anything that is innovative and creates convenience and enables us to do new things; well, for me that's good." (interviewee 3)

In addition, they highly valued the Internet, because it is a very good tool, in all senses.

"I think the Internet, on overall balance, is absolutely, radically positive." (interviewee 9)

However, it is important to note here that, although it is very valued, the issue of data privacy, including intrusion or violation of privacy, is of particular concern to older people, and makes them cautious in their use of the Internet.

"Because, first, regulation of the Internet is impossible due to its lop-sidedness, here now it's a crime to exploit a database, but perhaps not so in China, Japan, or the Philippines. So if some data is stolen from you here and are sent to China, and from there this data are distributed, then, really, what coercive powers are there to stop such things happening? None." (interviewee 5)

"Well, I have made the odd purchase, but neither do I find it very attractive for reasons of confidentiality and privacy, and overall because there is money at issue and you have to use the credit card, etc." (interviewee 7)

Nevertheless, the Internet is not a source of stress, because they usually get what they are searching for on the Web. Perceived self-efficacy is high, and therefore, they do not face the task with stress. As we have said, elderly people began using the Internet as a challenge, but it ceased to be so because they ended up dominating it and, then, it is seen as helpful. High levels of perceived self-efficacy and willingness to take on this challenge seem to go together. The Internet makes them feel they can do more; it gives them strength and confidence to cope with everyday life. As well as their perceived high self-efficacy, they feel more empowered by using the Internet.

These personal resources have also been identified as being relevant by previous research (Hobfoll, 2002; Berg, Hassing, McClearn, & Johansson, 2006; Blit-Cohen & Litwin, 2004; Wagner, et al., 2010; Gilhooly, Gilhooly, & Jones, 2008). According to them, self-efficacy and confidence, together with higher health rates and social support, appear to be some of the important elements of wellbeing for the elderly. These reduce stress, reduce feelings of loneliness, and improve quality of life. Even though it is not entirely clear what are the mechanisms by which the Internet affects the quality of life, as Dickinson and Gregor (2007) pointed out, it does seem to increase the wellbeing and quality of life of elderly people, such as in the subjects of our study.

Keeping Control

According to the literature (Chaffin & Harlow, 2005; Beisgen & Kraitchman, 2003; Selwyn, 2004), people have a deep need to be self-directed all throughout their lifespan, and this is especially so for the elderly. These are the years when life trajectory becomes meaningful as a whole and when the loss of some abilities becomes more common due to the changes related to aging. In line with that, our participants showed a deep need to be self-directed and in this context, they expressed that the Internet has to be under the control of the person, not vice versa.

"... listen, using technology in full power and knowing how to use it to help me..." (interviewee 1)

Autonomy and sense of control are related to self-efficacy, and high levels of self-efficacy have effects on perceived ease of use and, therefore, on Internet use (as described in Eastin & Larose, 2000; Chung, et al., 2010; Lam & Lee, 2006). As we have mentioned before, our participants had high rates of self-efficacy. In addition, they had previous experience with Internet use for specific purposes, so they had incorporated the Internet into their lives and used it almost every day. This appears to result in a positive experience and to reinforce the use and also autonomy itself.

Our participants clearly associated this situation with personal autonomy, despite the fact that they were not able to explain this relationship

easily. In this sense, older people's feelings about the Internet are mixed. It is important to them but they fear the dependence it can give rise to: addiction versus use, but usefulness prevails. The question is, then, are older people on the Internet because they are independent, or can being on the Internet make them more autonomous than they already are?

"...you are independent and use the Internet, or you use the Internet and you become independent because you do not have any other choice." (interviewee 10)

Even though the Internet has to be used under personal control, people accepted that ICT, and the Internet as an specific example, can be a technological aid in their future life, as they get older and need help because of handicaps associated with age or disease.

"If you're too old and cannot leave the house, you can do the shopping online and they deliver it to your home, I don't need it yet. For the next 10 years I do not think I'll need it." (interviewee 6)

Compensation of losses is not the primary use of the Internet according to the elderly (contrary to other studies, McMellon & Schiffman, 2002; Ambrosi-Randic & Plavsic, 2011). It is not the key for their adoption of the technology. Instead, the Internet is a tool for their own projects. It is a tool for life.

Critical Thinking

The Internet also allowed our participants to go beyond their given circumstances, not to settle for just what they have, but for example, to seek more information from a critical perspective, or to organize a trip according to their own preferences, etc.

In fact, one of the concerns that constantly appeared was the amount of information that can be found on the Internet. Perhaps this is the reason why they felt the need to emphasize a critical perspective, particularly in order to select the information that is relevant to them.

"You have to filter all that information and know what is right and what is not right. Because obviously, there is a lot (misinformation). (...) You can't swallow the first thing that comes your way (...) you have to evaluate it and contrast it, as with everything." (interviewee 1)

Going Forward

Consistent with what has been said so far, for our interviewees the Internet is a means of not getting stuck where you are. It is a means of keeping up, a way to continue feeling active, and also a way for going forward, because if a person is not online, she is left behind.

"...no, but also, finally, I believe that the Internet allows me to keep one thing that for me is precious: mental agility. It forces me to think and continue criticizing and ... this is no less than a mental exercise." (interviewee 8)

"I said: Ah! Well, a new technology! Bring it on!" (interviewee 2)

In this sense, the Internet becomes a window to the world and gives them many possibilities.

"... For example, [with the Internet] I feel like I have an enormous library at home." (interviewee 10)

"Maybe years ago when at a certain age you were left a little cornered ... technology and the computer and the Internet and all of this has opened this world to older people and given them freedom to be a little up to date with everything." (interviewee 3)

Nevertheless, it is not only a matter of using the Internet as a tool in order to be more involved in society (somehow like social capital, as presented by Blit-Cohen & Litwin, 2010; Selwyn, 2004), but also a matter of using it because of being previously more active and committed to society (as in Sum, Mathews, Hughes, & Campbell, 2008). That means adopting a perspective that goes from the person to the technology; something in which we strongly believe.

FUTURE TRENDS

Following on from the SOC Model (Baltes & Baltes, 1993), we would expect that if a person decides to use ICT and the Internet through a mechanism of selection or optimization, it would be easier to ensure the adoption of this technology, and to guarantee an enjoyable experience of its use. From this model, the Internet should be considered as a tool for personal development, and not as a tool to replace what has been lost (Hernández-Encuentra, et al., 2009).

What our interviewees told us fits perfectly with this perspective, because they started using the Internet to solve a concrete problem, to achieve a specific goal. Moreover, most of them had their first contact with ICT due to professional reasons, at the same time as someone close to the family, usually a son or daughter, encouraged and helped them in their adoption process of the new technologies.

Accordingly, if we want to promote the use of technology among those who are still reluctant, firstly it would be useful to find a clear necessity they really want to fill and show them how technology can be an answer to this. If they perceive the concrete benefits that using technology can bring them in a specific context, then they will move closer to adopting it. All along this process, it would be a guarantee of success having being sure to have the support and help of someone with more experience.

We also have to keep in mind that, in this period of life, facing challenges means keeping control over one's life, and therefore being independent. In this sense, using the Internet is for our interviewees one more way of practicing their autonomy, and, at the same time, it reinforces their perception of independence and self-efficacy. They began to use the Internet as a challenge, but it ceased to be so because they ended up managing to use it with a certain degree of expertise. This is the reason why they say the Internet makes them feel they can do more: it gives them strength and confidence to cope with everyday life.

In consequence, the object of an intervention aimed at promoting active aging means creating opportunities so the older person formulates their own activities and life projects. This would be the basis for the voluntary adoption of technology and the Internet as a tool at the service of these projects, and not the contrary.

Looking at the scientific research outlined in this study, we would say that further work is necessary on this topic in order to overcome some methodological limitations. Firstly, the qualitative nature of our study can give interesting insights into technology adoption and experience of use in the case of the elderly, but it does not examine the cause-and-effect relationships of the variables we have observed. Consequently, we will probably need studies specifically addressed to some of the variables we have identified as important, in order to have a clear account of them. For instance: what aspects need support in order to promote the adoption of ICT? How is users' general self-efficacy related to adoption? Are those who have already used ICT for pleasure activities more inclined to also use them as assistive technologies?

Finally, making generalizations based on our findings is limited due to the fact that we have no absolute guarantee that the participants in our study represent a case that is clearly likely to either confirm or falsify our propositions. Thus, other samples would be needed in order to generalize our observations.

CONCLUSION

Overall, the elderly in our study use the Internet to look for information and communicate with their family and friends, and this use enables them to be up to date with what is going on, connected to the world and active. They value the Internet very highly, and the challenge they assumed in the beginning ended up being a motive for satisfaction and well-being.

Adopting use of the Internet constitutes a significant support in the improvement of their daily lives. It helps them to make the most out of life. It opens for them a window to the world.

In the scientific literature, having positive attitudes to the new seems to be a common characteristic of older technology users, and we are convinced that this attitude, not only in old age, but also throughout the lives of our interviewees, can be considered as a personality trait that is linked with the experience of their use, with their satisfaction.

We should highlight, nevertheless, that this experience of using the Internet is mediated by a high perception of self-efficacy and satisfaction with their health, fundamental factors when evaluating the adoption of technology and enjoyment that can be taken from using the Internet.

REFERENCES

Ajzen, I., & Fishbein, M. (1980). *Understanding attitudes and predicting social behavior*. Englewood Cliffs, NJ: Prentice-Hall.

Ambrosi-Randic, N., & Plavsic, M. (2011). Strategies for goal-achievement in older people with different levels of well-being. *Studia Psychologica*, *53*(1), 97–106.

Aula, A. (2005). User study on older adults' use of the web and search engines. *University Access in the Information Society*, *4*(1), 67–81. doi:10.1007/s10209-004-0097-7

Baltes, P., Lindenberger, U., & Staudinger, U. (1998). Life-span theory in developmental psycholgoy. In Lerner, R. (Ed.), *Theoretical Models of Human Development* (*Vol. 1*, pp. 1039–1143). Handbook of Child Psychology New York, NY: Wiley.

Baltes, P. B., & Baltes, M. M. (1993). Psychological perspectives on successful aging: The model of selective optimization with compensation. In Baltes, P. B., & Baltes, M. M. (Eds.), *Successful Aging: Perspectives from the Behavioral Sciences* (pp. 1–34). Cambridge, UK: Cambridge University Press. doi:10.1017/CBO9780511665684.003

Bäßler, J., & Schwarzer, R. (1996). Evaluación de la autoeficacia: Adaptación española de la escala de autoeficacia general. [Measuring generalized self-beliefs: A Spanish adaptation of the general self-efficacy scale]. *Ansiedad y Estrés*, *2*(1), 1–8.

Beisgen, B., & Kraitchman, M. (2003). *Senior centers: Opportunities for successful aging*. New York, NY: Springer Publishing Company.

Berg, A. I., Hassing, L. B., McClearn, G. E., & Johansson, B. (2006). What matters for life satisfaction in the oldest-old? *Aging & Mental Health*, *10*, 257–264. doi:10.1080/13607860500409435

Blit-Cohen, E., & Litwin, H. (2004). Elder participation in cyberspace: a qualitative analysis of Israeli retirees. *Journal of Aging Studies*, *18*, 385–398. doi:10.1016/j.jaging.2004.06.007

Brandtstädter, J., & Rothermund, K. (2002). The life-course dynamics of goal pursuit and goal adjustment: A two-process framework. *Developmental Review*, *22*, 117–150. doi:10.1006/drev.2001.0539

Burnett-Wolle, S., & Godbey, G. (2007). Refining research on older adults' leisure: Implications of selection, optimization and compensation and socioemotional selectivity theories. *Journal of Leisure Research*, *39*(3), 498–513.

Chaffin, A., & Harlow, S. (2005). Cognitive learning applied to older adult learners and technology. *Educational Gerontology*, *31*(4), 301–329. doi:10.1080/03601270590916803

Chung, J. E., Park, N., Wang, H., Fulk, J., & McLaughlin, M. (2010). Age differences in perceptions of online community participation among non-users: An extension of the technology acceptance model. *Computers in Human Behavior*, *26*, 1674–1684. doi:10.1016/j.chb.2010.06.016

Dickinson, A., & Gregor, P. (2006). Computer use has no demonstrated impact on the wellbeing of older adults. *International Journal of Human-Computer Studies*, *64*, 744–753. doi:10.1016/j.ijhcs.2006.03.001

Eastin, M. S., & LaRose, R. (2000). Internet self-efficacy and the psychology of the digital divide. *Journal of Computer-Mediated Communication*, *6*(1). Retrieved on March, 26th, 2011, from http://www.ascusc.org/jcmc/

Eurostat European Commission. (2011). *Computers and the internet*. Retrieved June, 25th, 2011 from http://epp.eurostat.ec.europa.eu/portal/page/portal/information_society/data/database

Flyvbjerg, B. (2001). Case study. In Denzin, N. K., & Lincoln, Y. S. (Eds.), *The Sage Handbook of Qualitative Research* (4th ed., pp. 301–316). Thousand Oaks, CA: Sage.

Gilhooly, M. L., Gilhooly, K. J., & Jones, B. (2008). Quality of life: Conceptual challenges in exploring the role of ICT in active ageing. *Assistive Technology Research Series*, *23*, 1–27.

Gracia, E., & Herrero, J. (2009). Internet use and self-rated health among older people: A national survey. *Journal of Medical Internet Research*, *11*(4), e49. doi:10.2196/jmir.1311

Hanson, V. K., Gibson, L., Coleman, G. W., Bobrowicz, A., & McKay, A. (2010). *Engaging those who are disinterested: Access for digitally excluded older adults*. Paper presented at Conference on Human Factors in Computing Systems (CHI2010). Atlanta, GA.

Hernández-Encuentra, E., Pousada, M., & Gómez-Zúñiga, B. (2009). ICT and older people: Beyond usability. *Educational Gerontology, 35*, 226–245. doi:10.1080/03601270802466934

Hobfoll, S. F. (2002). Social and psychological resources and adaptation. *Review of General Psychology, 6*, 307–324. doi:10.1037/1089-2680.6.4.307

Idescat. (2011). *Ús de l'ordinador i d'Internet, 2010*. Barcelona, Spain: Institut Nacional d'Estadística. Retrieved June, 25th, 2011 from http://www.idescat.cat/pub/?id=aec&n=617

INE. (2011). *Resumen de datos de personas por sexo, características demográficas y tipo de uso de TIC, 2010*. Madrid, Spain: Instituto Nacional de Estadística. Retrieved June, 25th, 2011 from http://www.ine.es/jaxi/menu.do?type=pcaxis&path=/t25/p450&file=inebase

Juiznic, P., Blazic, M., Mercun, T., & Plestenjak, B. (2006). Who says that old dogs cannot learn new tricks? *New Library World, 107*(7-8), 332–345. doi:10.1108/03074800610677308

Lam, J. C., & Lee, M. K. (2006). Digital inclusiveness-Longitudinal study of internet adoption by older adults. *Journal of Management Information Systems, 22*(4), 177–206. doi:10.2753/MIS0742-1222220407

Lepa, J., & Tatnall, A. (2006). Using actor-network theory to understanding virtual community networks of older people using the Internet. *Journal of Business Systems. Governance and Ethics, 1*(4), 1–14.

Lorca, J., & Jadad, A. (2006). En busca del ebi-enestar: Una dimensión esencial de la esalud. [In search of e-well-being: An essential dimension of e-health]. *Revista Esalud, 2*(6), 1.

Magnusson, L., Hanson, E., Birto, L., Berthold, H., Chambers, M., & Daly, T. (2002). Supporting family careers through the use of information and communication technology—The EU project ACTION. *International Journal of Nursing Studies, 39*, 369–381. doi:10.1016/S0020-7489(01)00034-7

McMellon, C. A., & Schiffman, L. G. (2002). Cybersenior empowerment: How some older individuals are taking control of their lives. *Journal of Applied Gerontology, 21*(2), 157–175. doi:10.1177/07364802021002002

Melenhorst, A. S., Rogers, W. A., & Bouwhuis, D. G. (2006). Older adults' motivated choice for technological innovation: Evidence for benefit-driven selectivity. *Psychology and Aging, 21*(1), 190–195. doi:10.1037/0882-7974.21.1.190

Mitzner, T. L., Boron, J. B., Fausset, C. B., Adams, A. E., Charness, N., & Czaja, S. J. (2010). Older adults talk technology: Technology usage and attitudes. *Computers in Human Behavior, 26*(6), 1710–1721. doi:10.1016/j.chb.2010.06.020

Rainie, L., Purcell, K., & Smith, A. (2011). *Social side of the internet survey*. Retrieved June, 25th, 2011 from http://www.pewinternet.org/Shared-Content/Data-Sets/2010/December-2010--Social-Side-of-the-Internet.aspx

Salovaara, A., Lehmuskallio, A., Hedman, L., Valkonen, P., & Näsänen, J. (2010). Information technologies and transitions in the lives of 55-65-year-olds: The case of colliding life interests. *International Journal of Human-Computer Studies, 68*(11), 803–821. doi:10.1016/j.ijhcs.2010.06.007

Schwarzer, R., & Jerusalem, M. (1995). Generalized self-efficacy scale. In Weinman, J., Wright, S., & Johnston, M. (Eds.), *Measures in Health Psychology: A User's Portfolio: Causal and Control Beliefs* (pp. 35–37). Windsor, UK: NFER-NELSON.

Selwyn, N. (2004). The information aged: A qualitative study of older adult's use of information and communications technology. *Journal of Aging Studies*, *18*, 369–384. doi:10.1016/j.jaging.2004.06.008

Selwyn, N., Gorard, S., Furlong, J., & Madden, L. (2003). Older adults' use of information and communications technology in everyday life. *Ageing and Society*, *23*(5), 561–571. doi:10.1017/S0144686X03001302

Shewan, J., Tetley, J., Clarke, A., & Hanson, E. (2000). *Evaluation of the outcome of the project, the telematics applications and technical system in relation to user friendliness, user acceptance and quality and function of the technology which have been adapted, developed and used.* Unpublished EU Project Report DE3001. Brussels, Belgium: EU.

Sum, S., Mathews, R., Hughes, I., & Campbell, A. (2008). Internet use and loneliness in older adults. *Cyberpsychology & Behavior*, *11*(2), 2008–2011. doi:10.1089/cpb.2007.0010

Turner, P., Turner, S., & Van de Walle, G. (2007). How older people account for their experiences with interactive technology. *Behaviour & Information Technology*, *26*(4), 287–296. doi:10.1080/01449290601173499

Wagner, N., Hassanein, K., & Head, M. (2010). Computer use by older adults: A multidisciplinary review. *Computers in Human Behavior*, *26*(5), 870–882. doi:10.1016/j.chb.2010.03.029

ADDITIONAL READING

Ambrosi-Randic, N., & Plavsic, M. (2011). Strategies for goal-achievement in older people with different levels of well-being. *Studia Psychologica*, *53*(1), 97–106.

Baltes, P. B., & Baltes, M. M. (Eds.). (1993). *Successful aging: Perspectives from the behavioral sciences.* Cambridge, UK: Cambridge University Press.

Hernández-Encuentra, E., Pousada, M., & Gómez-Zúñiga, B. (2009). ICT and older people: Beyond usability. *Educational Gerontology*, *35*, 226–245. doi:10.1080/03601270802466934

Lorca, J., & Jadad, A. (2006). En busca del ebienestar: una dimensión esencial de la esalud. [In search of e-well-being: An essential dimension of e-health]. *Revista Esalud*, *2*(6), 1.

Schaie, K. W., & Willis, S. H. (2009). *Adult development and aging* (5th ed.). Upper Saddle River, NJ: Prentice-Hall.

Sun, H., & Zhang, P. (2005). The role of moderating factors in user technology acceptance. *International Journal of Human-Computer Studies*, *64*, 53–78. doi:10.1016/j.ijhcs.2005.04.013

Wagner, N., Hassanein, K., & Head, M. (2010). Computer use by older adults: A multi-disciplinary review. *Computers in Human Behavior*, *26*(5), 870–882. doi:10.1016/j.chb.2010.03.029

KEY TERMS AND DEFINITIONS

Adaptation: In models for successful aging, Adaptation is the dynamic process resulting from mechanisms of acting, evaluating and readjusting one person's behaviors, goals or targets to others more suitable to his/her present reality.

Compensation Mechanism (see SOC theory): In the SOC theory, Compensation is the mechanism whereby the person reconstructs, replaces or acquires new goals and means, as a reaction to biological, psychological or social losses.

Optimization Mechanism (see SOC theory): In the SOC theory, Optimization is the mechanism whereby the person maximizes the resources she or he has, and also looks for tools to help from the environment to be more effective.

Selective Optimization and Compensation (SOC) Theory: SOC is a theory widely known in the field of developmental psychology that explains the active role individuals, especially older people, take to adapt positively to changes that occur throughout their lives. This process of adaptation is made through three different mechanisms: selection, optimization and compensation.

Selection Mechanism (see SOC theory): In the SOC theory, Selection is the mechanism whereby the person reduces the repertoire of abilities, aims or domains he or she usually displays to prioritize the focus of his/her efforts.

Self-Efficacy: Self-efficacy is the self-perception about one's capabilities to behave effectively. It includes cognitive, motivational, affective, and behavioral components and therefore determines how the person thinks, motivates herself, feels and behaves.

Successful Aging: Successful aging is the attitude resulting from being physical and psychological healthy, active and socially engaged while aging. People who age successfully are satisfied with their lives and this enhances their quality of life.

APPENDIX 1

List of topics of the Questionnaire about Internet Uses

- Sex
- Age
- How would you describe your quality of life?

(From Excellent to Very Poor)

- Are you satisfied with your health?

  (From Extremely satisfied to Not at all satisfied)

- General Self-efficacy (we used the Spanish version of Schwarzer & Jerusalem, 1995; Bäßler & Schwarzer, 1996).
- What devices do you use to connect to the Internet?

  (list with some options)

- What do you use the Internet for?

  (list with some options)

- Why did you start using the Internet?
- How do you feel when using the Internet?
- For you, the Internet is......
  A tool
  A challenge
  A tool for doing new things
  A source of stress
  A tool to feel more active
  A tool to keep on doing my routines
  A tool to compensate my own losses
  A tool for security at home
- What arguments do you use when recommending the Internet to friends and acquaintances?

APPENDIX 2

Interview Guide

- Did you already use the Internet when you decided to study at UOC?
- Do you remember when and how you first learned of the Internet? Did you already know someone who was using it?
- In the beginning, did you think it could be useful or interesting?
- Did you want to start using it immediately; did you feel capable of doing so?
- Did it take a long time before you started using it on your own?
- What were your first experiences like using the Internet?
- Did you have someone to help/support you? Did you ask for this help/support?
- What did you use the Internet for the first few times?
- How do you feel being a regular user of IT?
- What do you do if there is something you don't know how to do?
- Has the Internet changed your way of living? In what way? Do you think this is a good or a bad thing?
- What is the Internet for you?
- Do you recommend using the Internet to your friends or acquaintances? If so, how?
- What would you like the Internet to be able to do for you?

Chapter 12
E-Health for Older Adults

Shane O'Hanlon
University of Limerick, Ireland

Alan Bourke
University of Limerick, Ireland

Valerie Power
University of Limerick, Ireland

ABSTRACT

e-Health has become a major focus for research in healthcare, with significant funding and political support at an international level. Older people stand to benefit more than others, as e-Health aims to facilitate provision of care at a distance and promote independent living for as long as possible. However, barriers remain including an immature evidence-base; questions about risk and safety; and variable rates of uptake in this population. This chapter explores these issues and reviews the literature on e-Health for older adults. Successful clinical trials are identified and the e-CAALYX project is described in detail as a case study. E-Health has presents many exciting opportunities but needs further development and guidance.

INTRODUCTION

This Chapter discusses recent developments in the area of e-Health, or electronic health, for older adults. As with traditional healthcare, e-health aims to promote independent living for as long as possible. Older adults are frequent users of healthcare resources, but unlike in younger groups there is a focus on keeping seniors out of hospital. Areas of e-Health such as telemedicine help to remotely monitor their health; consumer informatics promotes access to their own health information as well as furthering their health education, in particular through the Internet; and in healthcare institutions Electronic Health Records (EHRs) and Clinical Decision Support Systems (CDSS) are helping to improve patient safety. We begin by outlining the need for new models of healthcare provision for older people, then review how recent trends in e-Health are helping to accomplish this. We look at examples of e-Health interventions that are evidence-based, and also provide a case study of a recently developed e-Health home and mobile monitoring system. Finally, future research

DOI: 10.4018/978-1-4666-1966-1.ch012

opportunities are outlined and we conclude with a call for more funding and a strengthening of the evidence base in this area.

HEALTHCARE FOR OLDER ADULTS

As this section of the population is expanding rapidly, there is a pressing need to redesign service provision. In particular, physicians have recognised that there is a much greater role to be played by preventive medicine. Traditionally healthcare has been concerned with treatment of disease rather than prevention, but increasingly there is a need to focus on how we can promote greater periods of healthy active living. Figure 1 shows the most common disease trajectories. Where once seniors experienced a short period of accelerated decline in their health towards the end of their lives, it is now more common to see a slow deterioration in function over several years. The "compression of morbidity" scenario is now changing to a situation where better treatment options ensure that chronic disease has a less progressive course. Sometimes this is associated with intermittent episodes of reduced function for a short period of time, which may be reversible with brief hospitalisations or a period of rehabilitation in a multidisciplinary environment.

Healthcare is not without its risks: in terms of encounters for each fatality it is more hazardous than driving, using a scheduled airline, or nuclear power (Commission on Systemic Interoperability, 2005). Typically 10% of inpatients are the victims of medical error (Leape, 1994). Hospitals harbour many pathogens and hospital-acquired infections are more common in older people. The development of specialty training for the care of older people is not widespread, and many older patients are treated by physicians without relevant specialist qualifications. This can lead to inappropriate interventions, or indeed under-treatment. Contact with physicians may in itself result in more prescriptions, and even community dwelling

older adults take an average of 6 drugs (Barry, Gallagher, & Ryan, 2008). In short, healthcare does not always prioritise patient safety. It is this potential for adverse outcomes that has promoted the development of e-Health.

e-Health

Many may be familiar with the term 'e-Health' (electronic health) but a concise definition for this term remains elusive, with over 50 definitions in use. Eysenbach's (2001) appears to be the most accepted and states that:

"E-health is an emerging field in the intersection of medical informatics, public health and business, referring to health services and information delivered or enhanced through the Internet and related technologies. In a broader sense, the term characterizes not only a technical development, but also a state-of-mind, a way of thinking, an attitude, and a commitment for networked, global thinking, to improve health care locally, regionally, and worldwide by using information and communication technology" (p. E20).

Numerous other terms such as telehealth, telemedicine and m-health (mobile health) are often used interchangeably with e-health, and a range of definitions for each term exist. However, these are now recognised to be individual entities within the broader area of e-Health. The themes of health and technology and the interaction between these fields appear to be common links across all attempts to define such a broad construct (Oh, Rizo, Enkin & Jadad, 2005).

Classifying the components of e-health is challenging because of this variation in terms and definitions. Tulu, Chatterjee and Laxminarayan (2005) attempted to create a single taxonomy for telemedicine with the aim of clarifying its components and functions, which can be used to consider the broad definition of e-health referred to in this chapter. Their taxonomy included the following main dimensions:

Figure 1. Typical illness trajectories for people with progressive chronic illness. Adapted from Lynn and Adamson (2003). With permission from RAND Corporation, Santa Monica, California, USA.

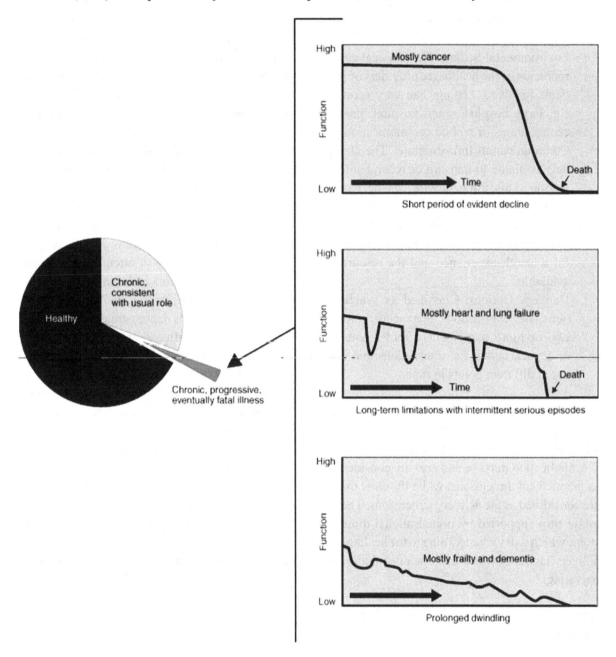

- Application Purpose: Which can be categorised as
  - Clinical – triage, diagnostic, surgical and non-surgical treatment, consultation, monitoring and supervision purposes, etc.
  - Non-clinical – administration, public health, research, patient education, professional, and medical education purposes
- Application Area: The medical domain(s) in which the application is intended for use

231

e.g. neurology, cardiology, ophthalmology, mental health. Various information formats—text, audio, video etc.—can be used.

- Environmental Setting: The physical environments of the healthcare providers or patients involved. Settings can vary greatly, e.g. large hospital, small hospital, health centre, home, or mobile communications.
- Communication Infrastructure: The channels available to transmit or receive information. This infrastructure can be based on a range of wired or wireless telecommunication technologies, depending on the requirements for creating a successful e-health experience and the resources available.
- Delivery Options: Classified as synchronous, i.e. transactions that occur among two or more participants simultaneously, or asynchronous, i.e. transactions that occur at different points in time.

The interactions of these dimensions determine the requirements and nature of any e-health or telemedicine solution, illustrated in Figure 2. The application purpose and area are considered as the medical dimensions, while the final three are considered as the delivery dimensions. These are in turn supported by organisational dimensions, which will vary according to the healthcare delivery model in which the e-health solution is operating.

Recent Trends in e-Health for Older Adults

As technology has become increasingly pervasive in modern life, e-health has developed and expanded rapidly for both younger and older people alike. While it is the case that younger adults engage with technology in greater numbers than older adults (Czaja, Charness, Fisk, Hertzog, Nair, Rogers, & Sharit, 2006), it is a common misconception that negative attitudes towards technology prevail among older people. Older adults have reported using technology in many forms, especially in the home, and have also reported predominantly positive attitudes towards its usage (Mitzner, et al., 2010). Despite this there is a proportion of older adults who are resistant to technology use. In one survey of 224 community-dwelling older adults, participants were asked "'*How willing and able do you feel about increasing your use of technologies, computers and the Internet?*' 57.1% were 'very' or 'reasonably willing' and 42.9% 'not keen'" (Squires, 2009). Willingness to use technologies was positively associated with educational attainment, perceived social support from friends, frequency of attendance at social meetings, voluntary work in the past year, MMSE (memory test) score, driving, mobile phone use and Internet use. This demonstrates that there are several factors that influence whether older people will take up technology in any area.

E-health is fast becoming an integral aspect of healthcare provision, and is expected to become ubiquitous as the current technology-driven younger generations age. It is of particular relevance to older people as healthcare consumers, since this group are more likely than younger adults to experience restricted mobility, chronic diseases, and multiple health conditions, including concomitant cognitive and mental health disorders. Such health conditions necessitate regular contact with healthcare providers, and often those experiencing these conditions require care and assistance, as evidenced by the increasing 'elderly dependency ratio' reported in many developed countries (Schäfer, 2008). A report by the American Association of Retired Persons (AARP) highlighted that older adults prefer to remain living independently in their own homes for as long as possible, even when additional support is required to achieve this (Barrett, 2008). Unfortunately, this independence may be threatened when the levels of care they require exceed the capacities of family and/or other care givers to provide it. This report

Figure 2. Telemedicine taxonomy (Tulu, et al. 2005, used with kind permission of the copyright holder, IEEE)

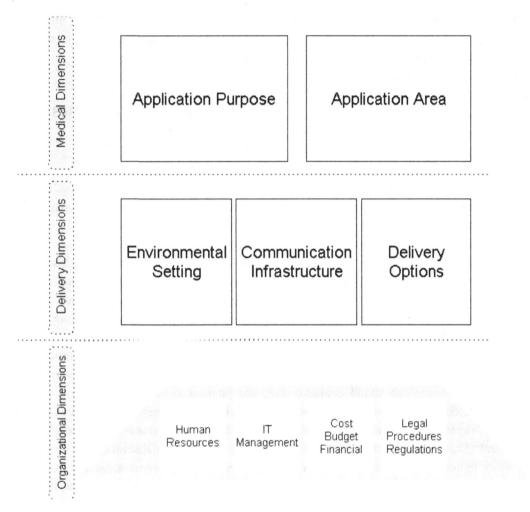

identified that older adults recognise the potential roles that e-health may play in helping to maintain their independence, citing a willingness to use a range of technologies "to maintain social contact, gather information, be safe at home, and promote their personal health and wellness."

Telemedicine—the use of Information and Communications Technology (ICT) as a substitute for face-to-face contact between healthcare providers and their clients (Bashshur, 1995)—is one aspect of e-health which has received considerable attention in the academic literature. Its potential to reduce healthcare costs, provide rapid access to care regardless of location, and to broaden access to specialist care are attractive features of telemedicine which are likely to have contributed to this focus. Evidence has shown that telemedicine can be clinically effective in managing a number of conditions that commonly affect older adults, including diabetes, heart failure, other cardiac diseases, and mental health (Bensink, Hailey, & Wooton, 2006). An example of the type of telemedicine services that may be useful for older adults can be seen in the Informatics for Diabetes Education and Telemedicine (IDEATel) project, in which participants were provided with a home telemedicine unit and a pedometer (Weinstock, et al., 2011). The unit provided videoconferencing capabilities, home blood glucose and blood pressure monitoring, messaging and Internet access, while the pedometer was used to monitor physical activity levels. The aims of the project were to promote improved monitoring of relevant health markers, provide frequent rapid feedback from healthcare providers, support from healthcare providers and peers to encourage health-related behaviours, and educational material to increase patients' understanding of their condition. Participants receiving this intervention experienced better health outcomes than those receiving usual primary care, in terms of improved diabetic control, blood pressure and cholesterol levels and reduced rates of decline in physical activity and physical function.

Despite the promise it shows, there is still a lot to be learned about telemedicine and its potential utility. Ekeland, Bowes, and Flottorp (2010) reviewed 80 systematic reviews of the effects and costs of telemedicine and found evidence to suggest that telemedicine may be effective, but that most evidence was incomplete and/or inconsistent. Their findings emphasised the need for more large-scale controlled studies of telemedicine interventions, increased collaboration in developing more complex telemedicine solutions and a greater focus on patients' perspectives. They also noted the need for more thorough economic evaluations of telemedicine. This has been echoed in a more recent review of the cost-effectiveness of telemedicine and telecare, which found that no conclusive evidence exists to show that telemedicine and telecare interventions are cost-effective compared to conventional health care (Mistry, 2011).

It is evident that the area of e-health, telemedicine, and telecare is a broad area of research and development in recent decades, intensifying recently with the advancement of technology form factor, processing power and affordability. Today this area is now an area of commercial interest and

investment as the proportion of people reaching retirement age increasing by 2 million per year in Europe. Greater emphasis will thus be put on technology to allow older adults to age safely in their own home for longer.

E-HEALTH INTERVENTIONS FOR OLDER PEOPLE: THE EVIDENCE BASE

In medicine there is a well-established requirement for evidence of efficacy to be demonstrated before any new medication is introduced. In the United States, the FDA (Food and Drug Administration) must provide approval and this depends on extensive development, testing and enrolment of participants in carefully monitored clinical trials. Phase 1 trials involve human testing to establish safety, Phase 2 assesses how well a drug works, Phase 3 is a randomised controlled multicentre trial (the gold standard for testing any intervention), and Phase 4 is the post marketing surveillance trial. If there is absence of evidence for the use of a medication then it is not approved. Similarly, if there is an unacceptable level of adverse outcomes it is not brought to market. Despite having similar characteristics to a pharmacological intervention, e-Health interventions do not as yet require such a demanding period of testing. Such a regimen has been proposed, in an effort to improve confidence in e-Health (Catwell & Sheikh, 2009). Clinicians' desire for evidence has also led to a drive towards the setting up of trials to determine whether e-Health interventions can be proven to have a beneficial effect. Ideally, it should be possible to demonstrate that such interventions reduce hospital admissions, morbidity, or mortality.

In a recent review of the literature on e-Health interventions for older people (O'Hanlon, 2010), a significant dearth of evidence was highlighted. Of 3,168 e-Health studies identified, only 57 demonstrated evidence of benefit. Telemedicine was the most common category of intervention (Figure

Figure 3. Categories of e-health intervention for older people with evidence of benefit

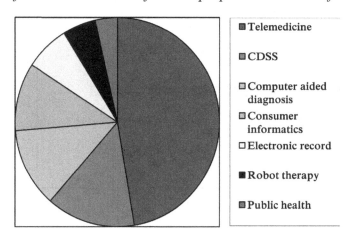

3). This is consistent with the drive to keep older people out of hospital while maintaining regular monitoring at a distance. The most common type of benefit seen was improved patient outcome (Table 1). While there is some proof that benefit is obtained using certain tools, many studies are poorly designed or seek user opinions rather than demonstrating any hard outcomes. A further problem is that most of the studies involved preliminary testing, rather than clinical trials at the frontline of the health service. Figure 4 displays the number of trials at each stage, corresponding with the FDA's research phases for pharmaceutical trials.

A broader search of the literature to see whether e-Health impacted on the quality and safety of healthcare was disappointing: the authors found a large gap between the postulated and demonstrated benefits of e-Health, noting that "techno-enthusiasts" were driving its implementation without much evidence (Black, et al., 2011). These reviews are limited by the fact that many overlapping terms exist in this area, and finding relevant research may be challenging. For example, even in 2012, the most widely used database of biomedical research, MEDLINE does not have an accepted search term for e-Health within its list of Medical Subject Headings (MeSH). As with all areas of scientific publication there is also a bias towards publication of positive results, with unsuccessful trials sometimes being suppressed.

Table 1. Types of benefit demonstrated in studies of e-health interventions for older people

Type of benefit	%
Improved patient outcome	39%
Improved diagnosis	11%
Better patient education	9%
Improved decision making	7%
Benefit for doctor	7%
Better prescribing	7%
Increased patient satisfaction	5%
Other	15%

Patient Safety and e-Health

Black et al.'s study also noted a lack of research on the risks of implementing these technologies. Though it seems unlikely there is still a risk involved for patients who use e-Health interventions. The safety of any technology needs to be established, as there have been case reports of detrimental outcomes. One website called "Bad health informatics can kill" [*iig.umit.at/efmi/badinformatics.htm*] maintains an unofficial list of examples. One of the most dramatic that has been reported in the medical literature was the finding that mortality increased from 2.8% to 6.57% after implementation of a commercially sold computerised physician order entry system

Figure 4. Number of trials in each phase of intervention testing

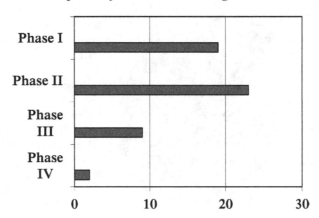

in a hospital (Han, et al., 2005). There is no doubt that adding technology to clinicians' practice can have unexpected sociotechnical effects. A simple reminder of this is the result of adding a computer to the consultation room, which has been found to negatively impact on body posture of the doctor, and the amount of information given by the doctor to the patient (Noordman, Verhaak, van Beljouw, & van Dulmen, 2010). Three considerations in particular need to be assessed when considering how mistakes can be made by introducing technology: errors in the process of entering and retrieving information, errors in the communication and coordination process, and latent errors (Ash, Berg, & Coiera, 2004). It is important the e-Health interventions are designed with patients and clinicians in mind, and that usability is tested before introduction (O'Hanlon, 2011). The idea of applying the FDA classification of research phases to this testing has been posited (Nguyen, Cuenco, Wolpin, Benditt, & Carrieri-Kohlman, 2007).

e-Health has strong political and industry support. The European Commission's 7th research framework programme involves an investment of more than 50 billion euro from 2007-2013, with prioritisation of e-Health. In the United States, the HITECH legislation envisaged up to $27 billion financial stimulus, with incentives for health information technology. President Obama emphasized that solutions must satisfy "meaningful use"

criteria, which ties funding to demonstration of effectiveness. A potential next step would be to ensure that funding only follows if interventions are fully tested through all phases and outcomes are published whether successful or not.

Examples of e-Health Interventions for Older People

In order to see where the evidence base lies, it is useful to review some of the areas where benefit has been shown from e-Health interventions for older people.

Example 1: Improved Patient Outcomes

Evaluating the Evidence Base for the Use of Home Telehealth Remote Monitoring in Elderly with Heart Failure

Dang, Dimmick, and Kelkar (2009) reviewed nine studies which demonstrated clear benefit for the monitoring of patients with heart failure—a debilitating and dangerous chronic illness. There was evidence for a reduction in admission to hospital, a reduction in mortality and a reduction in healthcare utilisation costs. There was a reduction in bed-days of care, in the number of Emergency Department visits and overall improvements in outcomes. The authors concluded that further study is needed to determine the exact population, which can benefit from telemonitoring and how technology can best be used to improve outcomes in a cost-effective way.

Example 2: Improved Prescribing

Improving Anticoagulation Control in Hospitalized Elderly Patients on Warfarin

Warfarin is a potentially dangerous medication that requires constant monitoring and can be difficult to dose in order to produce the optimum response. Gouin-Thibault, Levy, Pautas, Cambus, Drouet, Mahe, and Siguret (2010) assigned patients taking the drug in a care unit to a Computer-Generated Dosing Group (CGD) or the standard management group. The proportion of time that patients spent in the therapeutic range was significantly greater in the CGD group. Use of the computer was associated with less frequent overdosing and reduced dependency on regular blood monitoring tests. It was particularly useful that this was demonstrated in an older population (mean age 86 years), as this group is the most likely to be taking this drug and has the highest potential for adverse effects.

Example 3: Improved Decision Support

Video Decision Support Tool for Advance Care Planning in Dementia: Randomised Controlled Trial

Volandes, Paasche-Orlow, Barry, Gillick, Minaker, Chang, and Mitchell (2009) produced a video decision support tool for older people to explore the possible care options and their outcomes in the event of developing dementia. This was a randomised controlled trial comparing a verbal narrative with or without the video tool. Participants in the video group were more likely to prefer comfort care than those in the verbal group, which is consistent with most health providers' recommendations when advanced dementia develops.

Their preferences also remained more stable with time than the other group.

Example 4: Using Telerehabilitation to Assess Apraxia of Speech in Adults

Hill, Theodoros, Russell, and Ward (2009) assessed eleven participants with speech difficulties using a telerehabilitation system run by videoconference. The results were compared with face-to-face assessments. There were no significant differences between the subtest scores obtained in either group. There was moderate to very good agreement between the two environments for testing. Findings from the patient satisfaction survey were also positive.

As can be seen, there is significant variation in the types of study being conducted, the interventions used, and the location of study. Although there is well-established benefit in the area of telemedicine, there is a need to perform studies in many other clinical situations. It is vital that healthcare providers work with informaticians, information technologists, and software engineers to progress such developments. The clinical workforce needs to equip itself with health informatics knowledge to help drive this. This has been aided by the recent decision in the United States to make clinical informatics a board-certified medical specialty.

E-HEALTH SYSTEMS: A WORKED CASE STUDY

One e-Health system that is being developed to meet the challenges of promoting independent living is the eCAALYX project. Here we will detail some of the aspects developed by this system and the technological and ethical challenges it has faced in making such a system a reality.

eCAALYX

The eCAALYX project (*Enhanced Complete Ambient Assisted Living Experiment*) (06/2009-05/2012 – http://ecaalyx.org/) is a three-year project funded by the European Commission under the Ambient Assisted Living (AAL) Joint Programme (http://www.aal-europe.eu/). The project builds on the strengths of the infrastructure and functionality already developed in the CAALYX project (http://caalyx.eu/). The main objectives of the eCAALYX project are to provide a complete solution to improve the quality of life of older people suffering from co-morbidity by monitoring and assessing changes in their health and vital signs, and by proposing focused education on their lifestyle so that their independent living at home can be extended safely and their hospitalisation or admission to a nursing homes for dependent care can be postponed. The system aims to fulfil these functions both inside and outside the home.

In detail, the main objectives for the eCAALYX system are:

- Identify key symptoms and physical signs to promptly detect cardiac decompensation, and identify the habits, tasks, or activities that promote health and prevent diseases on the aged affected by multiple chronic conditions.
- Implement a robust and auto-configurable home health care system that: 1) is efficiently manageable at large scale and suitable for long-term monitoring; 2) is easily expandable, and thus adaptable to the changing condition(s) of patients suffering from comorbidity; and 3) integrates currently deployed equipment and standards, and in the end results in a commercially viable solution.
- Develop an intelligent device (ISS—Intelligent Sensor System), linked to the home based system, which integrates the most relevant sensors for monitoring of

common chronic conditions and implements algorithms to detect atrial fibrillation, risk of other Cardiovascular (CV) diseases, and the progression of Chronic Obstructive Pulmonary Disease (COPD).

- Produce a comfortable garment linked to a smart phone, embedding health, mobility and position sensors so that data for assessing the risk of cardiovascular diseases and for raising alerts are gathered and processed.
- Embed in the garment enhanced fall, balance and mobility sensing and reporting. Monitor for fall-risk by determining suitable fall risk criteria for fall prevention. Enable mobility qualified physiological signs based on energy expenditure. Extract mobility patterns through the integration of mobility sensing and location.
- Complete the implementation of a distributed, adaptable and scalable monitoring infrastructure (based upon Observation Patterns) to allow for the continuous acquisition of the users' sensors data by multiple entities simultaneously e.g. the user's doctors and carers. This infrastructure will be implemented by the home system; the mobile system and the caretaker site and integrate with doctor's monitoring applications and health/medical records.
- Implement a caretaker site/server able to process data collected from mobile and home sensors so as to generate, by using data-mining techniques, levels of risk, which would switch on preventive actions, provide education/training; serve as evidence for diagnosis and allow cooperation among several health professionals/specialists; with capabilities to work out a daily health agenda.
- Build a set of extensive test beds through iterative refinement and perform extensive trials, involving older adult users with comorbidity and their caretakers, and

Figure 5. The eCAALYX system

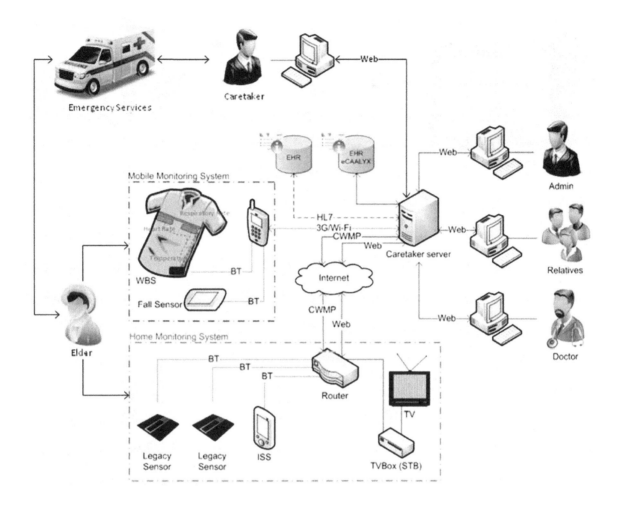

gather detailed feedback to advance the system specification, implementation, and exploitation.

- Achieve all of the above goals by providing a solution that is *commercially viable*, acceptable by all users/stakeholders, reliable, long-term, flexible, scalable, and virtually maintenance-free in a non-technical environment, thus providing a suitable e-Health system for real-world deployment.

The eCAALYX system is thus composed of three main subsystems namely; (1) the Home subsystem, the Mobile Subsystem and the Caretaker site (see Figure 5). (2) The Home Monitoring Subsystem, consists of: a Set-top-box (STB)/ interactive TV (to deliver health education and other functions) (see Figure 6), Router, ISS (Intelligent Sensor System) and home sensors (those sensors that are stationary and not continuously worn on the body such as the scales) (see Figure 7), all located at home. (3) The Mobile Subsystem, which includes a smart garment, with all sensors integrated into a wireless BAN Wearable Body Sensors (WBS), including a fall and activity monitoring sensor and a mobile phone to enable further propagation of information (see Figure 8), the Caretaker Site, which includes the Caretaker Server and the Auto-configuration Server (see Figure 9).

Figure 6. The TV and set-top-box

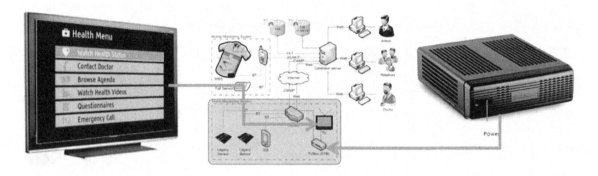

Figure 7. The scales and ISS

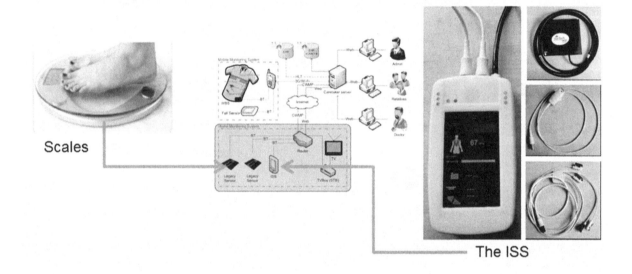

CHALLENGES IN CONVERTING FROM THEORY TO PRACTICE

When putting into practice an idea that works well on paper, there are some notable issues to address. Acceptability of monitoring technology is a potential barrier but appears to be a minor issue for most older people (Alwan, Dalal, Mack, Kell, Turner, Leachtenauer, & Felder, 2006). It is also important to ensure that the data that is gathered can be used for a clinical purpose, and that the quality if high enough to make clinical decisions.

One of the main feature objectives of the eCAALYX system was the detection of a cardiac decompensation. Chronic cardio-respiratory diseases are a major cause of death and admission to hospital among older people in Europe and are often concurrent with a number of other chronic conditions. During the course of such diseases, repeated cardiac decompensation episodes occur typically, which lead to frequent hospitalization of patients. Therefore, it was proposed to have a system capable of controlling a cardiac decompensation through improved clinical controls before hospitalization becomes necessary. The

Figure 8. The mobile monitoring subsystem

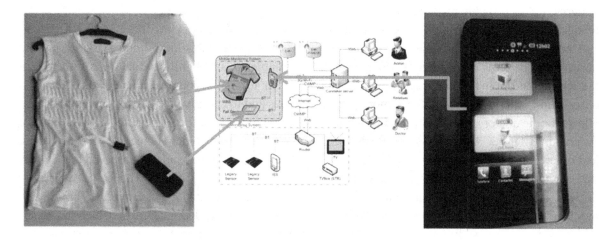

Figure 9. The caretaker server

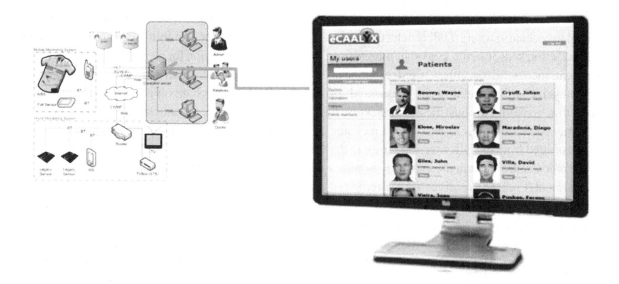

eCAALYX system provides a novel solution to this situation and is achieved in practice by monitoring the cardio-respiratory effort during regular activity using the integrated activity monitoring sensor, the heart rate monitor and respiratory chest bands in the vital sign monitoring garment. All these sensors combined allow the system to provide an assessment of the user's cardio-respiratory condition and allow for early detection of user decompensation.

A key requirement of a e-health monitoring system is its ability to monitor and raise alerts if a particular vital sign exceeds a certain threshold. However, since the main target audience is older users suffering from co-morbidity the range of vital signs across the user population would inevitably be different. Thus, it was essential that the system allow the physician to dynamically tailor a monitoring profile for each individual user. This was achieved at the interface level using

Observation Patterns. Using these Observation Patterns, it was possible for a physician to set a unique method of monitoring the user vital signs and activity from the caretaker portal. These observation patterns were then downloaded to the mobile and home monitoring systems. The observation pattern-based distributed monitoring allows for the doctors to tailor the monitoring infrastructure of the eCAALYX system (WBS, ISS, and other sensors) that can be deployed and set for each user's needs. Thus further allowing the doctors to collaboratively allocate and configure the elder's monitoring system. In this way, the user will have to return less frequently to the doctor for preventive medical check-ups.

Having reliable communication from end to end in both the home and mobile monitoring system is essential for a reliable e-Health system. Given the scenario where a fall is detected by the fall detection sensor in the vital sign monitoring garment, successful transmission and reception of this message at the caretaker site is essential. In order to achieve this, a robust messaging acknowledgement protocol was adopted. When a message is transmitted from the fall detection sensor to the Electronic Control Unit in the vital sign monitoring garment (Figure 8), received via a wired serial communication, the ECU further packages this message with a unique header, message start and stop bytes (Figure 10) and transmits this new message wirelessly via Bluetooth to the smart phone. When this message is received and processed by the phone an acknowledgement message is sent back from to the fall detection sensor via the ECU (Figure 11), if no acknowledgement message is received by the fall sensor the original message is resent. At the smart phone, the fall-event message is further propagated wirelessly over the Internet to caretaker site where it is processed and handled by a caretaker operator. This sequence of message acknowledgements ensures that if an emergency situation such as an injurious fall has been detected that the critical messages are propagated to the appropriate actor.

Data Gathering and Protection

During the development of the eCAALYX system, 3 sets of trials with older adults as volunteers were completed, and significant data was gathered. In order to take account of all relevant ethical issues and to comply with the fundamental ethical principles in the use of personal data, and in the involvement of older subjects in trial activities, the project partners closely observed the Charter of Fundamental Rights of The European Union, published in the *Official Journal of the European Communities* (2000/C 364/01), which has established general ethical principles as fundamental rights in Europe, such as protection of human dignity and human life, protection of personal data and privacy as well as the environment. In accordance with Community law and International conventions, the project also followed International and National regulation for medical purposes, such as Declaration of Helsinki and Ethical Principles for Medical Research involving Human Subjects by the World Medical Association, the International Code of Medical Ethics or Directive 2001/20/EC on Good Clinical Practice. The project followed the European Data Protection legislation (Directive 95/46/EC), the related legislation of the Member States of the partners involved in the project, and the EU Directive on Privacy and Electronic Communications (2002/58/EC) (issued in 2002 for implementation by October 31, 2003) and/or Federal Communications Commission Wireless Location Privacy regulations.

Since personal information is gathered, processed, transferred, and stored during the trials, close attention was paid to tools and algorithms so that user's right of privacy is not compromised. Of course, eCAALYX could not achieve its goals/benefit for older users without collecting and reasoning with their personal data, however this was done without forgetting the privacy issues pertaining to eCAALYX users. In order to guarantee privacy of the users of the system; encrypted communication channels, protected servers, PIN

Figure 10. The fall-event message transmission, reception, and acknowledgement protocol for the fall detection sensor, ECU, and smart phone

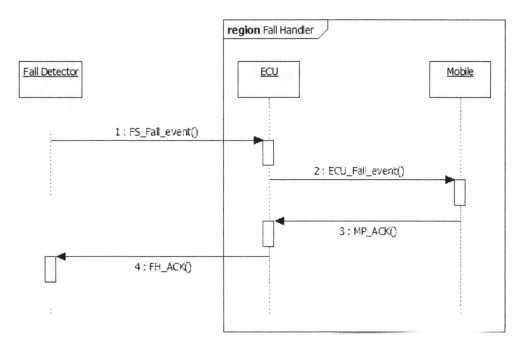

Figure 11. Fall sensor message packaging

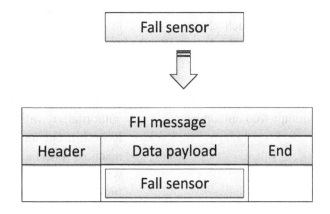

number to identify users, and certificates to identify end-user equipment was performed. Ethical Approval was sought at the local ethical committee so that research is accomplished respecting and guaranteeing individual rights.

The following is a list of specific actions and procedure put in place by specific partners to ensure privacy, anonymity, and dignity of the volunteers and their recorded information:

- The caretaker server was physically located in the Germany where the trials took place.
- The server was operated independently of the hospital's IT system.

- The different components of the eCAA-LYX system sent timestamp for when a message was transmitted along with a sequence number. A record was kept at the caretaker site of when this message arrived.
- Logs regarding data quality was also be stored.
- Only certain staff members of the trial partner hold the "key" to identify the system volunteers and the relevant patient number.
- Apart from the members of the trial partner, no other member from the 10 other partners were present at the trial site at the time of the trial thus further ensuring trial participant privacy.
- The partner responsible for the development of the caretaker server implemented a login/password mechanism for the caretaker operators and system administration to restrict access to private and sensitive health information about elders

As can be seen, such systems require extensive planning, design and testing at each phase of implementation. The above case study demonstrates the extent of work invested in just one single project. This attention to detail means that the project has a greater chance of success and in turn is more like to result in improved outcomes for older patients.

FUTURE RESEARCH

Despite more than 3,000 e-Health studies for older people listed by biomedical trial databases, there is clearly a need to strengthen the evidence base. From a medical and patient perspective, there are certain areas that clearly need such work:

- Electronic health records: health information remains quite difficult to access, with many separate databases in use depending on the healthcare provider and even within

providers. On admission to hospital, it is sometimes necessary for patients to give their demographic details to administrative staff, then nursing staff, medical staff, and again at x-ray departments. Such duplication of data is expensive and wasteful. In addition, despite recognition that patients have a right to access their health information there are few providers who permit patients to do so in a user-friendly fashion.
- Clinical decision support: Several guidelines exist which aim to help physicians adhere to evidence-based medicine. However it is difficult for physicians to access them, and they change over time. Integrating clinical decision support systems ought to produce better health outcomes, but there is as yet little evidence to prove this.
- Consumer informatics: There is a proliferation of health information on the Internet. Much of this is not quality controlled, and it is difficult to know who the target audience is. Medical journals tend to exclude healthcare consumers, and some of the best sources of information require payment to access. We need to enable patients to keep abreast of medical advancements and to educate themselves on the Internet in an authoritative, validated way.
- Robotics: The recent development of brain machine interfaces has heralded an era where "bionics" may become a part of limb replacement or rehabilitation after stroke. Despite some progress, it is necessary to improve the reliability and accuracy of such systems. There is potential for much functional improvement if this exciting technology can be harnessed.

CONCLUSION

In conclusion e-Health is an area with much development which requires more focus on producing solid evidence of benefit. There is significant financial investment in the area and this should be linked to outcomes. There is a strong argument for introducing an approval system for e-Health interventions and for post-implementation monitoring. A health informatics workforce needs to be trained, and patients and clinicians need to work with developers to ensure that such systems are usable and acceptable.

This chapter aimed to present an overview of recent trends in e-Health for older people as well as describing how developments have the potential to change patient care. Examples of areas where evidence exist were highlighted, and a case study of a developed e-Health system, the eCAALYX system was presented. In conclusion, e-Health systems to promote safer independent living for older people are becoming a reality. However, the long-term adoption of these systems is still to be analysed and it will be some time before the true financial and societal impact can be realised.

REFERENCES

Alwan, M., Dalal, S., Mack, D., Kell, S. W., Turner, B., Leachtenauer, J., & Felder, R. (2006). Impact of monitoring technology in assisted living: Outcome pilot. *IEEE Transactions on Information Technology in Biomedicine*, *10*(1), 192–198. doi:10.1109/TITB.2005.855552

Ash, J. S., Berg, M., & Coiera, E. (2004). Some unintended consequences of information technology in health care: The nature of patient care information system-related errors. *Journal of the American Medical Informatics Association*, *11*(2), 104–112. doi:10.1197/jamia.M1471

Barrett, L. L. (2008). *Healthy @ home*. Washington, DC: AARP Foundation.

Barry, P. J., Gallagher, P., & Ryan, C. (2008). Inappropriate prescribing in geriatric patients. *Current Psychiatry Reports*, *10*(1), 37–43. doi:10.1007/s11920-008-0008-3

Bashshur, R. L. (1995). On the definition and evaluation of telemedicine. *Telemedicine Journal*, *1*(1), 19–30. doi:10.1089/tmj.1.1995.1.19

Bensink, M., Hailey, D., & Wootton, R. (2006). A systematic review of successes and failures in home telehealth. *Journal of Telemedicine and Telecare*, *12*(S3), 8–16. doi:10.1258/135763306779380174

Black, A. D., Car, J., Pagliari, C., Anandan, C., & Cresswell, K., Bokun, & Sheikh, A. (2011). The impact of ehealth on the quality and safety of health care: A systematic overview. *PLoS Medicine*, *8*(1), e1000387. doi:10.1371/journal.pmed.1000387

Catwell, L., & Sheikh, A. (2009). Evaluating ehealth interventions: The need for continuous systemic evaluation. *PLoS Medicine*, *6*(8), e1000126. doi:10.1371/journal.pmed.1000126

Commission on Systemic Interoperability. (2005). *Ending the document game: Connecting and transforming your healthcare through information technology*. Washington, DC: US Government Printing Office (GPO).

Czaja, S. J., Charness, N., Fisk, A. D., Hertzog, C., Nair, S. N., Rogers, W. A., & Sharit, J. (2006). Factors predicting the use of technology: Findings from the center for research and education on aging and technology enhancement (CREATE). *Psychology and Aging*, *21*(2), 333–352. doi:10.1037/0882-7974.21.2.333

Dang, S., Dimmick, S., & Kelkar, G. (2009). Evaluating the evidence base for the use of home telehealth remote monitoring in elderly with heart failure. *Telemedicine Journal and e-Health*, *15*(8), 783–796. doi:10.1089/tmj.2009.0028

Ekeland, A. G., Bowes, A., & Flottorp, S. (2010). Effectiveness of telemedicine: A systematic review of reviews. *International Journal of Medical Informatics*, *79*(11), 736–771. doi:10.1016/j.ijmedinf.2010.08.006

Eysenbach, G. (2001). What is e-health? *Journal of Medical Internet Research*, *3*(2), E20. doi:10.2196/jmir.3.2.e20

Gouin-Thibault, I., Levy, C., Pautas, E., Cambus, J. P., Drouet, L., & Mahe, I. (2010). Improving anticoagulation control in hospitalized elderly patients on warfarin. *Journal of the American Geriatrics Society*, *58*(2), 242–247. doi:10.1111/j.1532-5415.2009.02675.x

Han, Y. Y., Carcillo, J. A., Venkataraman, S. T., Clark, R. S. B., Watson, R. S., & Nguyen, T. C. (2005). Unexpected increased mortality after implementation of a commercially sold computerized physician order entry system. *Pediatrics*, *116*(6), 1506–1512. doi:10.1542/peds.2005-1287

Hill, A. J., Theodoros, D., Russell, T., & Ward, E. (2009). Using telerehabilitation to assess apraxia of speech in adults. *International Journal of Language & Communication Disorders*, *44*(5), 731–747. doi:10.1080/13682820802350537

Leape, L. L. (1994). Error in medicine. *Journal of the American Medical Association*, *272*(23), 1851–1857. doi:10.1001/jama.1994.03520230061039

Lynn, J., & Adamson, D. M. (2003). *Living well at the end of life: Adapting health care to serious chronic illness in old age*. Washington, DC: Rand Health.

Mistry, H. (2012). Systematic review of studies of the cost-effectiveness of telemedicine and telecare: Changes in the economic evidence over twenty years. *Journal of Telemedicine and Telecare*, *18*(1), 1–6. doi:10.1258/jtt.2011.110505

Mitzner, T. L., Boron, J. B., Fausset, C. B., Adams, A. E., Charness, N., & Czaja, S. J. (2010). Older adults talk technology: Technology usage and attitudes. *Computers in Human Behavior*, *26*(6), 1710–1721. doi:10.1016/j.chb.2010.06.020

Nguyen, H. Q., Cuenco, D., Wolpin, S., Benditt, J., & Carrieri-Kohlman, V. (2007). Methodological considerations in evaluating ehealth interventions. *Canadian Journal of Nursing Research*, *39*(1), 116–134.

Noordman, J., Verhaak, P., van Beljouw, I., & van Dulmen, S. (2010). Consulting room computers and their effect on general practitioner-patient communication. *Family Practice*, *27*(6), 644–651. doi:10.1093/fampra/cmq058

O'Hanlon, S. (2010). *E-health interventions for older people*. Paper presented at the meeting of the European Union Geriatric Medicine Society. Dublin, Ireland.

O'Hanlon, S. (2011). *The dangers of e-health*. Paper presented at the meeting of HEALTHINF. Rome, Italy.

Oh, H., Rizo, C., Enkin, M., & Jadad, A. (2005). What is ehealth (3): A systematic review of published definitions. *Journal of Medical Internet Research*, *7*(1), e1. doi:10.2196/jmir.7.1.e1

Schäfer, G. (2008). *Europe in figures - Eurostat statistical yearbook 2008*. Luxembourg, Luxembourg: Eurostat.

Squires, S., Romero-Ortuno, R., & Wherton, J. (2008). *Technology rejection, perception and implications for tele-care technology amongst older Irish adults: A mixed method approach*. Paper presented at the meeting of the Irish Gerontological Society. Kilkenny, Ireland.

Tulu, B., Chatterjee, S., & Laxminarayan, S. (2005). A taxonomy of telemedicine efforts with respect to applications, infrastructure, delivery tools, type of setting and purpose. In *Proceedings of the Hawaii International Conference on System Sciences*, (p. 147b). IEEE Press.

Volandes, A. E., Paasche-Orlow, M. K., Barry, M. J., Gillick, M. R., Minaker, K. L., & Chang, Y. (2009). Video decision support tool for advance care planning in dementia: Randomised controlled trial. *British Medical Journal*, *28*(338), b2159. doi:10.1136/bmj.b2159

Weinstock, R. S., Brooks, G., Palmas, W., Morin, P. C., Teresi, J. A., & Eimicke, J. P. (2011). Lessened decline in physical activity and impairment of older adults with diabetes with telemedicine and pedometer use: Results from the IDEATel study. *Age and Ageing*, *40*(1), 98–105. doi:10.1093/ageing/afq147

ADDITIONAL READING

Aalbers, T., Baars, M. A., & Rikkert, M. G. (2011). Characteristics of effective internet-mediated interventions to change lifestyle in people aged 50 and older: A systematic review. *Ageing Research Reviews*, *10*(4), 487–497. doi:10.1016/j.arr.2011.05.001

Andreassen, H. K., Bujnowska-Fedak, M. M., Chronaki, C. E., Dumitru, R. C., Pudule, I., & Santana, S. (2007). European citizens' use of e-health services: A study of seven countries. *BMC Public Health*, *10*(7), 53. doi:10.1186/1471-2458-7-53

Black, A. D., Car, J., Pagliari, C., Anandan, C., Cresswell, K., & Bokun, T. (2011). The impact of ehealth on the quality and safety of health care: A systematic overview. *PLoS Medicine*, *8*(1), e1000387. doi:10.1371/journal.pmed.1000387

Botella, C., Etchemendy, E., Castilla, D., Baños, R. M., García-Palacios, A., & Quero, S. (2009). An e-health system for the elderly (butler project): A pilot study on acceptance and satisfaction. *Cyberpsychology & Behavior*, *12*(3), 255–262. doi:10.1089/cpb.2008.0325

Chaffin, A. J., & Maddux, C. D. (2007). Accessibility accommodations for older adults seeking e-health information. *Journal of Gerontological Nursing*, *33*(3), 6–12.

Eysenbach, G., Powell, J., Englesakis, M., Rizo, C., & Stern, A. (2004). Health related virtual communities and electronic support groups: Systematic review of the effects of online peer to peer interactions. *British Medical Journal*, *328*(7449), 1166. doi:10.1136/bmj.328.7449.1166

Jennett, P. A., Hall, L. A., Hailey, D., Ohinmaa, A., Anderson, C., & Thomas, R. (2003). The socioeconomic impact of telehealth: A systematic review. *Journal of Telemedicine and Telecare*, *9*(6), 311–320. doi:10.1258/135763303771005207

Kim, E., Stolyar, A., Lober, W. B., Herbaugh, A. L., Shinstrom, S. E., & Zierler, B. K. (2009). Challenges to using an electronic personal health record by a low-income elderly population. *Journal of Medical Internet Research*, *11*(4), e44. doi:10.2196/jmir.1256

Krishna, S., Boren, S. A., & Balas, E. A. (2009). Healthcare via cell phones: A systematic review. *Telemedicine and e-Health*, *15*(3), 231-240.

Macfarlane, A., Clerkin, P., Murray, E., Heaney, D. J., Wakeling, M., & Pesola, U. M. (2011). The e-health implementation toolkit: Qualitative evaluation across four European countries. *Implementation Science; IS*, *6*(1), 122. doi:10.1186/1748-5908-6-122

Neafsey, P. J., M'lan, C. E., Ge, M., Walsh, S. J., Lin, C. A., & Anderson, E. (2011). Reducing adverse self-medication behaviors in older adults with hypertension: Results of an e-health clinical efficacy trial. *Ageing International*, *36*(2), 159–191. doi:10.1007/s12126-010-9085-9

Norman, G. J., Zabinski, M. F., Adams, M. A., Rosenberg, D. E., Yaroch, A. L., & Atienza, A. A. (2007). A review of ehealth interventions for physical activity and dietary behavior change. *American Journal of Preventive Medicine*, *33*(4), 336–345. doi:10.1016/j.amepre.2007.05.007

Stroetmann, V. N., Hüsing, T., Kubitschke, L., & Stroetmann, K. A. (2002). The attitudes, expectations and needs of elderly people in relation to e-health applications: Results from a European survey. *Journal of Telemedicine and Telecare*, *8*(2), 82–84. doi:10.1258/135763302320302154

Tse, M. M., Choi, K. C., & Leung, R. S. (2008). E-health for older people: The use of technology in health promotion. *Cyberpsychology & Behavior*, *11*(4), 475–479. doi:10.1089/cpb.2007.0151

Wu, S., Chaudhry, B., Wang, J., Maglione, M., Mojica, W., & Roth, E. (2006). Systematic review: Impact of health information technology on quality, efficiency, and costs of medical care. *Annals of Internal Medicine*, *144*(10), 742–752.

KEY TERMS AND DEFINITIONS

Assisted Living: Prolonging independent living using technology.

Clinical Decision Support System: A system to aid health professionals make decisions regarding patient management.

e-Health: Information and communication technology for health.

Electronic Health Record: A digitised version of a patient's health and social care records, often with added functionality.

Patient Safety: A movement towards identifying and reducing risk for people receiving healthcare.

Telecare: Provision of care to patients at a distance.

Telemedicine: The practice of medicine at a distance.

Chapter 13
Remote Care Delivery Technologies:
An Applications Framework for Chronic Disease Management in Older Adults

Robert D. Hill
University of Utah, USA

ABSTRACT

This chapter presents a guided framework for describing Remote Care Delivery Technologies (RCDT) in the processes of healthcare management among older patients diagnosed with chronic disease. To date, a process framework for the application of RCDT for chronic health conditions has not been systematically described, although much of the literature in RCDT, including telemedicine and telehealth, has focused on intervening with issues that involve the monitoring of chronic disease symptoms and the coordination of ongoing care. To elucidate how this process framework operates in managing chronic health conditions examples are provided from the published literature to clarify and differentiate each of the steps of this framework. A final section describes guidelines informed by this framework for providing RCDT in the management of chronic disease.

DOI: 10.4018/978-1-4666-1966-1.ch013

INTRODUCTION

Remote Care Delivery Technologies: Strategies for Addressing Health Issues in Older Adults

Remote Care Delivery Technologies (RCDT), defined as the application of advanced technology for the delivery of healthcare, offers the promise of an accessible and cost-effective method to meet the ever increasing need for healthcare services in the United States. A current focus of RCDT is telehealthcare that has been characterized in the published literature as technology-driven personalized care delivery to patients in remote and rural regions (McLean, Protti, & Sheikh, 2011).

Through in-home RCDT it is possible to connect every American household linked through wire or the air waves to a medical provider. Industry advocates including telemedicine device manufacturers and national telemedicine organizations have for more than a decade championed various forms of telehealthcare as a best practices venue for patient-centered care. This latter point is underscored by the expanding number of medical specialties employing telemedicine delivery approaches.

The impact of RCDT in the form of simple telephone-mediated services through POTS (Plain Old Telephone Lines) or through more sophisticated devices and transmission infrastructure such as the Internet (Mead & Dunbar, 2004) has been documented to be at least as effective as traditionally delivered in-person face-to-face services especially for routine medical tasks such as monitoring health symptoms or diagnosing disease. Of the unique contributions that this technology affords is its reach to those in remote and underserved regions. In fact, the extent to which RCDT achieves its full impact will be in serving persons who, for various reasons, are unable to make use of standard facility-based medical care even though they may have the social and/or fiscal resources to receive such care.

A high proportion of persons living in rural and underserved regions are adults over the age of 60 years. Demographic studies suggest that older rural adults are less likely than their counterparts in urban settings to leave their homes when they have health issues or to seek out healthcare options outside of their immediate community even when the resources to treat their condition do not fully exist within their local community healthcare infrastructure. Further, older residents of rural communities may have less access to necessary services because in rural settings those services rely more heavily on private transportation than would be the case in more urban settings (Collelo, 2007). The interaction of older adult demographic characteristics and features of RCDT suggests that this approach could have some distinct advantages especially in linking expert medical care to patient health concerns. The barriers presented for older persons when contemplating the adoption of this technology, however, are sizeable and must be negotiated to actualize the full benefits of the RCDT.

On the positive side, an example of an area where the impact of RCDT on older adult patient health has already been recognized as having substantial value is in the coordination of services and information for older adults who are homebound with substantial chronic care needs (Luptak, et al., 2010). This is especially true when the care is for ongoing monitoring of chronic disease symptoms—an area where RCDT is already in wide use and where intervention requires multiple processes including patient education, the monitoring of that patient's ongoing health status, and ongoing follow-up (Karunanithi, 2007). The following case illustration highlights the challenges faced by persons with chronic illness:

Steve is a 75 year old Vietnam veteran. He lives in northeastern Nevada with a stepdaughter. For most of his life Steve has viewed himself as very independent and has managed to keep a roof over his head in spite of multiple challenging personal situations. As of late, however, Steve has started to experience problems with his health. He has a 55 year cigarette smoking history, and he was recently diagnosed with COPD. His doctor suggested that Steve quit smoking, but Steve feels like it would be too difficult to kick the habit. Recently, Steve began having trouble with his vision. His problems have worsened to the point where he cannot drive. Since he lives over 2 hours from Elko, his stepdaughter drove him into town, and he met with an optometrist who told Steve that Steve was suffering from Age-Related Macular Degeneration (ARMD) and that Steve would be blind (or nearly blind) before the end of the year. Steve is unable to drive, his stepdaughter is only intermittently helpful, but Steve does have a VA caseworker in Salt Lake City, Utah, who manages Steve's health issues including Steve's ongoing prescriptions from the regional Veterans Administration Medical Center (VAMC) located in Salt Lake City. Steve needs to get a full medical work-up and see a specialist for his vision problems, but Steve is unable to arrange for a trip to Salt Lake City. Even if Steve confirms his medical problems, his lifestyle behaviors and his progressive medical conditions will soon make it impossible for Steve to leave his home and receive continuing medical care.

- How will Steve negotiate the process of obtaining more information about his medical condition?
- How will his VA case manager help Steve to monitor and adjust his medication as Steve becomes more restricted as a result of Steve's progressive medical condition?

This vignette underscores the fact that older adults are among those persons who are at the highest risk for complications that result when advanced aging is confounded by chronic disease. In fact, recent estimates suggest that 80% of persons who are 65 years of age or older suffer from at least one chronic disease condition (Karmarow,

2007). The national fiscal outlay for chronic disease treatment for persons over the age of 65 years exceeds 70 billion dollars annually (Druss, et al., 2002). This data suggests, therefore, that chronic disease among older adults is a substantial public health concern that would benefit from innovative approaches for delivering care to ameliorate its negative consequences on the healthy longevity.

The most common forms of chronic diseases in old age are heart disease, cancer, osteoporosis, and diabetes. These are conditions that require ongoing disease symptom management. Among these conditions, heart disease is the most costly and at the same time it is also the most common cause of death in the United States. If progressive diseases of the brain—such as dementia—are included in this list then the number and the frequency of older persons who experience some form of chronic disease increases substantially. A further complicating factor for older persons is the co-occurrence of chronic diseases such as the four noted above and dementia. When two or more chronic diseases are present it makes healthcare delivery even more difficult to manage from a distance.

The effectiveness of any healthcare intervention for chronic disease depends on the context within which the intervention is employed. In this chapter, the context is defined as settings in which an older persons or the "geriatric patient" resides. It is well known that most older persons live in their homes and a growing number of older adults, due to their increased frailty in advanced age, are confined to their homes. Healthcare delivery to the old and to the very old, therefore, requires both in-home care along with the continuum of institutional services including hospital and nursing home care. It is important that any model of chronic disease treatment that focuses on the older patient is flexible enough to incorporate the demands that can come from multiple sources of impairment, including mobility problems, that are inherently part of growing old, but can be further complicated if a chronic disease condition is present. In the case of the vignette presented earlier, Steve's declining mobility due to his own aging is further complicated by ARMD, which precipitates progressive loss of vision. The interaction of his health conditions and his advancing aging put Steve at a high risk for becoming permanently homebound.

CHRONIC DISEASE MANAGEMENT FRAMEWORK

In 2004 the CBO published a process model of chronic disease management (Congressional Budget Office, 2004). This model is based on the idea that optimal management of chronic disease occurs when the patient is: (1) educated about his or her disease condition and understands the connections between manifest symptoms and disease course, (2) is able to actively monitor manifest symptoms, and (3) engages with the healthcare system to address manifest symptoms. In doing so, the patient is able to forestall or at least control the progression of chronic disease. The scope and cost of chronic disease in older persons underscores the need to operationalize this process as it relates to the implementation of healthcare delivery strategies.

The CBO (2004) report distinguishes between two types of chronic disease care: case management and disease management. The case management approach focuses on tailored treatment strategies for the individual "high risk" patient in response to specific patient health needs. Health needs result from an interaction of a chronic disease state (e.g., diabetes) with the patient's unique personal circumstances and/or characteristics (a low income female patient who is sedentary and overweight). In contrast, disease management focuses on the disease process itself and the predictable health issues that result as a chronic disease progresses. For example, as chronic obstructive pulmonary disease progresses lung function as measured by forced expiratory flow (FEV_1) will

decline, and an individual will experience more frequent and intense periods of shortness of breath and reduced stamina.

In disease management it is understood that as chronic disease progresses the risk of a catastrophic physical event increases. In the case of hypertension, with the passage of time, if untreated, high blood pressure increases the risk of the occurrence of heart attack. Disease management involves controlling disease progression with the aim of preventing risk of major or catastrophic events (e.g., controlling blood pressure over time lowers the risk of heart attack). Disease management, therefore, requires the implementation of standardized interventions that diminish the progressive nature of chronic disease.

The CBO chronic disease management model describes an approach to chronic disease treatment based on a graded 4-step approach. These steps are:

1. Implementation of a health curriculum
2. Obtaining process outcomes from the health curriculum
3. Intermediate health outcomes monitoring
4. Tracking disease incident factors.

RCDT can play an important role at each of these four steps of chronic disease treatment in addressing issues specific to each step. To highlight how RCDT may be useful within a comprehensive treatment paradigm the following example is instructive. At the curriculum implementation step, this might be the delivery of educational material such as the presentation—using an electronic device—of diabetes education information. At the process outcome step, this would be to engage the patient in a curriculum of care, and then assess process changes that result from such engagement. For example, if the curriculum involved the monitoring of blood pressure, RCDT procedures could be established to make this monitoring possible. This might involve the installation of a blood pressure cuff to an RCDT device that the patient can use to monitor his or her blood pressure over time. The "process outcome," or the ability to monitor, would be the evaluation of how regularly the patient uses the cuff to take her or his blood pressure readings, if the patient uses the cuff correctly, and if the patient is able to record correctly the information that is displayed on the RCDT blood pressure monitoring device.

For immediate health outcomes, RCDT could be involved in the assessment of health variables (blood pressure) and, ostensibly, any change in those variables as a consequence of the intervention (recall that in the 2nd step there is the assurance that the patient is providing accurate blood pressure data from the device). Immediate health outcomes monitoring might consist of gauging patient self-reported symptomatology and as a therapeutic intervention is introduced noting whether the self-reported symptoms of the patient decline. The fourth step, disease incident factors, is the addressing of disease consequences (or complications) that result from a chronic health condition. This might consist, for cardiovascular disease, of risk for a heart attack or stroke.

Consider the hypothetical case of an 80 year old patient with a long-term diagnosis of chronic obstructive pulmonary disease. RCDT disease management based on the above presented scheme would be: (1) the optimal delivery of a tailored smoking cessation curriculum, (2) the monitoring of its adherence with the goal of cessation of cigarette smoking, (3) assessing change in expired carbon monoxide (CO) and improvement FEV_1 in response to the smoking cessation protocol, (4) the documenting of lowered incidence of acute anoxic episodes as a result of slowing the progression of COPD. It is assumed that disease management through this framework would yield improved quality of life (which is the 5th step of the CBO chronic disease management model). The sections that follow review the role of RCDT within each of these four stages of disease management with a focus on the older adult with chronic disease.

Implementation of a Health Curriculum

RCDT has been an invaluable resource for delivering healthcare information through educational programming. Diabetes management is one of the more challenging health education curriculum protocols to administer among patients. Not only is it important in diabetes education to manage one's diet and physical exercise, but pharmacological therapy is often required for controlling manifest disease symptoms and optimizing blood glucose control. Older patients, in particular, may require extra educational support to become proficient in understanding how to use these devices and how to follow correct procedures for self-monitoring of blood glucose. Although there can be stand-alone RCDT systems that are able to deliver a diabetes health education curriculum to an older clientele, it is more common that RCDT is integrated in a setting where there is also face-to-face health provider and patient contact.

Older adults face added challenges when the management curriculum is complex. In this case they need to learn how to manage their health problems and at the same time acquire the skills to negotiate this learning experience through a computer or telemedicine interface. The literature suggests that among older adults whose resources are extended due to the effects of a chronic disease and this is compounded by complex demands for behavior change (such as diet and exercise) to control symptoms the likelihood of adherence declines (West, et al., 2010).

One example of how such an RCDT-mediated delivery system might operate has been described as part of the Promotora Telemedicine Project that is underway in Santa Clara County, CA (Higgins, et al., 2003). In this program, a typical telemedicine session is mediated by face-to-face assistance. Particularly for older adult patients, it was felt that without face-to-face support the older patients would not be able to acquire the computer-delivered curricular skills via the Web.

Thus, to maximize program success, at a local community center, the Promotora Program would establish a residential presence, and patients would be recruited to come to this local treatment center (versus a more removed outpatient medical clinic) for their diabetes education and care. At this community center a health aid would obtain the patient's weight and vital signs and then assist the patient in logging on to a computer (which connects the patient to a healthcare team). It is at this computer workstation where the essential health education curriculum is initiated. Thus, at an appointed time, a healthcare provider logs on and a two-way videoconferencing system interacts with the patient. The treatment plan to the patient is tailored via an RCDT protocol, including detailed instructions regarding medications, diet and exercise. When necessary, through this medium it is possible to demonstrate techniques for home glucose testing, insulin injection, as well as instructing the patient in diet, exercise, and other features of the intervention. Tailored devices allow patients to practice, ask questions, and receive feedback until a minimum level of understanding and competency is achieved. The patient then returns home and engages in the intervention but then returns to the center at regular intervals to receive ongoing remote feedback and instructions. This kind of system would be representative of a best-practices approach to RCDT health education delivery.

Process Outcomes

Is the Patient Following (or Adhering) to the Health Education Curriculum?

This is a critical question that is at the crux of why a treatment intervention for any health issue succeeds or fails. The issue of understanding and doing what is expected as part of the educational curriculum, adherence to the protocol, making adjustments when needed to address individual needs, is challenging. Addressing process issues

in the delivery of a curriculum however, is critical to the success of the curriculum in terms of outcomes from the training. This is particularly true when behavior change is involved such as in weight control, diet, cessation of smoking, the taking of medications and many other activities for promoting health. Weight control and diet, for example, are required topics in almost every diabetes education program, and they are also key behavioral components in the control of adult hypertension. The management of weight always involves dieting, and dieting always involves the controlling of eating habits. Whether an intervention for diabetes or hypertension control works (or not) depends in large measure on how well the patient follows the prescribed educational regimen. Monitoring and assessing process outcomes from a health education curriculum, therefore, is of importance in any RCDT intervention. Process outcomes for chronic disease management are often overlooked in program development. If a patient fails to follow a prescribed protocol, the target symptoms will not diminish and manifestations of disease symptoms will continue to be present. Further, even if monitoring of a symptom (e.g., blood pressure) is effective, if the individual is not taking his or her prescribed medication appropriately, or if the individual is not attending to his or her eating habits, or fails to follow an exercise regimen, this could represent the "weak link" where an intervention fails.

RCDT has played a significant role in this area including a wide range of devices that have proliferated to measure eating habits. These are often reported in the form of food intake diaries. A relatively recent RCDT device known as a "DAI system" allows for interaction between the patient and a healthcare provider through uniquely programmed cellphone software. The DAI works in the following way: At each meal prescribed foods are shown as pictures along with a listing of the suggested portions for each food type. Foods eaten (and proportions) are automatically recorded and the software calculates the respective nutritional value of each meal. The program also interfaces with self-report exercise software so that the amount of food intake can be adjusted depending upon the number of calories burned. The mobile phone device uploads data to the healthcare educator and it provides a method for quick contact with the educator should there be issues about following the diet/exercise protocol (Rossi, et al., 2010).

The goal of this device is to provide an integrated system (with one's cellphone) for easy access and quick information response about a treatment protocol. RCDT can be an asset in this regard since diary keeping is labor intensive and there are substantial issues with recalling food consumed, cigarettes smoked, and exercise engaged in after a period of time has elapsed. Thus, the more immediate and easy this kind of information can be recorded, the more responsive the educator can be to the needs of the patient.

Although not frequently seen as an RCDT intervention, the elimination of unhealthy behaviors that negatively impact chronic disease is an important area for further RCDT development. An example of this would be smoking cessation programming. It is without question that ongoing cigarette smoking adversely impacts almost any chronic disease, yet there has been very little attention in developing a process outcome scheme for evaluating adherence to smoking cessation programming. There is great social press for helping patients with chronic disease who are elderly quit smoking. For example, recent Medicare legislation has created coverage for smoking cessation services provided by video conferencing (see http://securetelehealth.com/for-smoking-cessation-programs.html).

What currently exists in the published literature linking RCDT to smoking cessations paradigms are treatments that have employed telephone call prompts as support for maintaining cessation. In one study where cigarette smokers were divided between those receiving smoking cessation materials through face-to-face programming versus

the same programming offered through an online modality, quit rates did not differ and long-term follow-up data suggested that mode of cessation method did not impact sustained quitting. Although this study did not highlight the unique benefits of RCDT for the treatment of cigarette smoking it did indicate that it was possible to deliver a cigarette smoking health education intervention and assess process outcomes over the internet (Carlson, et al., 2012).

Intermediate Health Outcomes Monitoring

RCDT as a strategy for monitoring intermediate outcomes from an intervention is most widely documented for blood pressure control. For older adults blood pressure assessment often occurs in the home. There are multiple devices and strategies for collecting in-home blood pressure remotely. For example, the tele-HEART program (Gellis, et al., 2012) is a multidimensional telehealth treatment for blood pressure control in frail homebound older adults. Features of the tele-HEART intervention for monitoring blood pressure include: (a) in-home setup of the telehealth monitoring device; (b) computerized management and tracking tool; and (c) integration with the electronic medical record. The features of the tele-HEART device are straight-forward, requiring the wearing of a cuff and an automatic method for cuff inflation. Phone lines are the point of information transfer. It should be noted that the larger tele-Heart protocol involved substantial support from face-to-face healthcare staff as well as remote staff who were accessible through the phone. The goal was that through accurate monitoring of blood pressure in the home that the effects (or outcome) of the intervention could be documented.

The monitoring of symptoms through self-report, physiological means, or from clinical expert observation is a strength of RCDT. Otherwise, this information can only be obtained if the patient travels to the healthcare facility. This is both costly and, for many older persons who are confined to home, difficult. There are also issues about getting accurate measurements or self-reports in a hospital or outpatient treatment facility. With the development of RCDT it is feasible to obtain ongoing assessment of symptoms in the more natural home environment, thus enhancing the capacity to obtain accurate process outcomes from medical interventions.

An area critical for chronic disease care is the management of psychological or emotional concerns. The traditional model of psychotherapy for the treatment of depression and/or anxiety secondary to a chronic condition is problematic for many reasons. Foremost among these is the challenge experienced by the patient to return to a facility-based office weekly for treatment. Given that in chronic disease emotional issues often fluctuate with the disease state, the act of getting out of one's house and traveling a distance for an hour-long talk therapy session could create emotional trauma just from the stress of traveling and negotiating such weekly meetings. Alternatively, a growing body of research has suggested that RCDT delivered psychological care can be as effective as face-to-face care for the treatment of depression and anxiety in chronically ill persons (Kroenke, 2010). The application of RCDT for addressing the psychological concerns of chronically ill older adults is appealing for a number of reasons: (1) such a strategy makes it possible to provide treatment sessions as needed versus the standard once or twice weekly intervals; (2) the time duration for a session can be modified to fit with the learning capabilities and the emotional and physical stamina of the patient. Too often, an hour long session can be difficult for a person who is struggling with a long-term health problem to negotiate. Shorter sessions that are more frequent have the advantage of providing high levels of continuity while at the same time providing more opportunities for learning and feedback as the client acquires skills to deal with her or his emotional conditions; and (3) there are more opportunities

for follow-up with an older client who may need additional support especially if a chronic condition is impacting emotional symptomatology.

Disease Incident Factors

Approaches for the management of incident factors associated with chronic disease are strategies that target the onset of predictable consequences or health complications that occur due to chronic disease. Examples of complications include amputations due to diabetes, anoxic episodes due to COPD or emphysema, heart attacks, and even death. In this area RCDT has not developed much beyond providing support or warning when a complication occurs. This kind of advanced warning device provides information to emergency providers, but it has little benefit for chronic disease management. Another challenge surrounding the development of devices that can identify and/or monitor physical complications that are a result of chronic disease is that more invasive procedures (e.g., direct hear monitoring) must be in place for accurate assessment to occur. Most of the infrastructure and equipment for these kinds of assessment exists primarily within the medical clinic.

Development of these kinds of devices is currently underway primarily in the area of cardiovascular treatment. For example, there are second- or third-generation telemedical systems that are mostly noninvasive but that can measure remotely variables such as pulmonary artery pressure, left atrial pressure, impedance, and the detection of life-threatening arrhythmias in addition to atrial fibrillation or ventricular tachycardia. One example of this type of device is the COMPASS-HF (Chronicle Offers Management to Patients with Advanced Signs and Symptoms of Heart Failure). As an RCDT device, the COMPASS-HF measures remotely (and on an ongoing basis) absolute right ventricular pressures and estimates pulmonary artery diastolic pressures which are highly related to incident of heart attack. The system consists of

3 components: 1) a programmable device similar in appearance and implantation technique to a pacemaker; 2) a transvenous lead that is implanted in the right ventricular artery; and 3) a small external device carried by the patient. To install this device requires significant medical intervention and whether such a device can accurately anticipate heart attack is yet to be definitively determined. However, the COMPASS-HF is an example of the kinds of technological developments that are moving forward to address this fourth domain of chronic disease management.

A disease incident factor issue heavily invested in RCDT is telestroke management. For the most part telestroke involves employing RCDT to facilitate communication between neurological experts with remote and rural centers to provide treatment that wouldn't otherwise be available at such a local center. Several studies have found that remote-expert guided procedures including drug delivery are as effective through RCDT as in-person stroke care at comprehensive care facilities (Switzer, et al., 2009).

SPECIALIZED RCDT GUIDELINES FOR MANAGING CHRONIC HEALTH CONDITIONS IN GERIATRIC PATIENTS

The previous sections of this chapter have elucidated the four steps of chronic disease management and the employment of RCDT in the management process in an older clientele. These sections highlighted the complexity of this process as well as the fact that RCDT alone is probably not sufficient to fully manage chronic health conditions, particularly in a population of adults who do not have familiarity with 21st Century technology. Below is a short listing of guidelines that are worth keeping in mind as one develops new and innovative technology geared to the treatment of older adults who are diagnosed with chronic health conditions. These guidelines represent ideas

distilled from the existing literature and could represent areas of future research in the domain of RCDT interface design.

1. Design RCDT interface to shift dynamically in response to sensory needs of the older person. Fonts do not necessarily need to be larger unless there is an expressed need by the individual for a larger font. If there is a need for font change, an easy method for the user to change the font size should exist. Screen lighting or coloring can change to optimize sensory input. Again, in this case, the changing of screen parameters should be easily accessed by the user; probably existing on the screen itself without any addition steps needed to get to the buttons or devices for screen/font change. There are several sites that currently employ accessible and easy interface adjustments (see http://alzonline.com). Learning materials should be made as dynamic as possible to adjust to the needs of the older learner.

2. Break the components of the healthcare curriculum down into manageable steps or learning modules that can be complete in a short period of time. Moving through modules that are quickly completed can reinforce persons who are challenged with working and short-term memory deficits. Benefits from segmented information are also accrued by persons (due to age or a chronic disease or both) who may not have the stamina to persist through longer learning exercises.

3. Support RCDT with in-person assistance. This was highlighted in several of the case examples in this chapter. Even if the goal is to develop a stand-alone system, person-to-person contact to initially learn (or receive training) in the curriculum is critical.

4. Feedback from users of the RCDT is essential. Involvement of patients in the development of RCDT for a specific health condition provides feedback as to how best design and

structure tasks, what issues to emphasize in greater detail, and areas where attention to detail may be less needed. It is too often the case that health education information is driven by the content of the information and its relationship to the health condition (dieting to reduce symptoms of diabetes). Although there are many standardized approaches to this kind of education it is essential to involve the intended audience for your RCDT to determine how the RCDT interface, the unique features of your audience, and the type of learning material interact in the flow of information presentation.

5. Support written instructions with visual (or auditory) design augmentation (Mayer, 2009). For older adults, research points to the need to involve multiple sensory inputs. Once again, this should be tempered by giving the learner the choice to employ multiple modalities because not all older persons benefit from the general idea that "more input is better." But, where deficits exist in one modality (visual) these deficits can often be offset by supporting information that comes through a second modality (auditory).

In summary, the added value of RCDT is elucidated by tailored health outcomes that are linked to specific stages of the disease management process. These stages were labeled as steps in a disease management model; namely: (1) implementation of a health curriculum, (2) facilitating process outcomes, (3) intermediate health outcomes monitoring, (4) lowering risk for disease incident events. For example, it is well-known that ongoing monitoring either of a specific disease management intervention, symptomatic change, or disease consequences is a common benefit of RCDT. Monitoring may be improved by RCDT, but monitoring itself is not a unique (or added) value of RCDT. Added value comes when the RCDT introduces an innovative and more effi-

cacious dimension to care, as would be the case in devices that actually deliver a medication and providing incentives for taking the medication on a tightly circumscribed time table.

Future Research

In spite of its efficiency and reach, the real test of RCDT is to determine whether patient health is benefitted from this tool and in what form those benefits are realized. Several questions arise that are important for future research:

- What components of a medical intervention are enhanced by RCDT?
- What, if any, added benefits to the patient are a direct result from RCDT?

Although patient health gains from medical interventions that have employed RCDT have been documented, what is not known is the extent to which RCDT can have a direct impact on those gains. In other words, whether RCDT makes a unique contribution to a traditional medical intervention and; if so, what role does RCDT play in the realization of such gains. To date, it is unknown, apart from the medical intervention itself, whether RCDT makes its own contribution to healthcare beyond its role as a delivery tool. This problem was noted in the negative findings of a recent Cochran Group review of 17 telemedicine studies (Currell, Urquhart, Wainwright, & Lewis, 2000). After contrasting comparable studies that employed or did not employ RCDT in care delivery, the authors concluded:

"The findings of the review have demonstrated the feasibility of establishing systems using telecommunications technologies for patient care, but provide very little evidence of clinical benefits (p. 11)".

It is certainly the case that RCDT is supportive of traditional medical interventions. However, the extent to which it makes its own contribution to patient care and whether this contribution is efficacious is relatively unknown. It could be the case that in the drug regimen study highlight above that RCDT was effective in facilitating adherence to the administered pharmacological aid, but that the drug itself was ineffective. In this case, RCDT was effective although the intervention was not; therefore, RCDT was ultimately judged as ineffective when it actually delivered the drug in an efficacious manner. Without the ability to disentangle the unique contribution of RCDT from other components of a treatment to an overall healthcare intervention one could only conclude, as did the Cochrane Group, that RCDT is not, by itself, associated with clinical benefits. Given this state of affairs, an area of critical importance for future research would be the development of tailored assessment instruments that can gauge whether RCDT is associated with positive healthcare outcomes irrespective of other components of an intervention.

The second question relates somewhat to the first in that it is currently unknown if RCDT can provide added value to a medical intervention. In the case of blood pressure assessment, such a procedure could be accomplished in a physician's office or at home with an RCDT device. Intuitively, it would seem that in either case there would be no added value of the RCDT monitoring beyond the provision of adding convenience for the patient to receive blood pressure assessments at home. This could be a reason to employ RCDT, but it could be argued that the accuracy of the blood pressure assessment was not better (or worse) in either setting. Thus, whether the RCDT technology simply supported or facilitated a medical intervention (as noted in this blood pressure assessment example) or if RCDT was intervention itself, which then added value to the treatment, is unknown.

Are there instances when RCDT would add unique value as a medical intervention?

Some proponents of RCDT would argue that there is. Take, for example, the situation in which a telemedicine device provide a pattern of continuous blood pressure monitoring over the period of a week versus the monitoring of a patient during a weekly medication visit. In this case where the optimum dosage of a hypertensive medication is desired the RCDT device should be more effective at determining the optimum dose in relation to blood pressure fluctuations over a week period versus a single blood pressure measure taken in a physician's office. In this instance RCDT could provide added value in establishing the appropriate dosage level of a well-established efficacious drug. In this case, developing a method along with appropriate metrics to assess for this effect would be an important research direction and could yield significant public health benefits for drug dosing of all types.

These are just two areas where future research is needed in the evolution of this technology. Other areas of research that are currently underway focus on the design of telemedicine devices to make them more users friendly and more likely to improve adherence rates in older patients (Joseph, 2006).

REFERENCES

Anderson, G., & Horvath, J. (2004). The growing burden of chronic disease in America. *Public Health Reports*, *119*, 263–270. doi:10.1016/j.phr.2004.04.005

Bourge, R. C., Abraham, W. T., Adamson, P. B., Aaron, M. F., Aranda, J. M., & Magalski, A. (2008). Randomized controlled trial of an implantable continuous hemodynamic monitor in patients with advanced heart failure: The COMPASS-HF study. *Journal of the American College of Cardiology*, *51*, 1073–1079. doi:10.1016/j.jacc.2007.10.061

Bregnell, M., Wootton, R., & Gray, L. (2007). The application of telemedicine to geriatric medicine. *Age and Ageing*, *36*, 369–374. doi:10.1093/ageing/afm045

Carlson, L. E., Lounsberry, J. J., Maciejewski, O., Wright, K., Collacutt, V., & Taenzer, P. (2012). Telehealth-delivered group smoking cessation for rural and urban participants: Feasibility and cessation rates. *Addictive Behaviors, 31*, 108–114. doi:10.1016/j.addbeh.2011.09.011

Colello, K. J. (2007). *Where do older adults live? Geographic distribution of the older population.* Washington, DC: Congressional Research Services.

Congressional Budget Office. (2004). *An analysis of the literature on disease management programs.* Washington, DC: Government Printing Office.

Currell, R., Urquhart, C., Wainwright, P., & Lewis, R. (2000). Telemedicine versus face to face patient care: Effects on professional practice and health care outcome. *Cochrane Database of Systematic Reviews, 2*, 1–35.

Dellifraine, J. L., & Dansky, K. H. J. (2008). Home-based telehealth: A review and meta analysis. *Telemed Telecare, 14*, 62–65. doi:10.1258/jtt.2007.070709

Dorra, D., Bonnerb, L. M., Cohenc, A. N., Shoaic, R. S., Perrind, R., Chaneyb, E., & Young, A. S. (2007). Informatics systems to promote improved care for chronic illness: A literature review. *Journal of the American Medical Informatics Association, 14*, 156–163. doi:10.1197/jamia.M2255

Druss, B. G., Marcus, S. C., Olfson, M., & Pincus, H. A. (2002). The most expensive medical conditions in America. *Health Affairs, 21*, 105–111. doi:10.1377/hlthaff.21.4.105

Gellis, Z. D., Kenaley, B., & McGinty, J., Bardelli, Davitt, J., & Have, T. T. (2012). Outcomes of a telehealth intervention for homebound older adults with heart or chronic respiratory failure: A randomized controlled trial. *The Gerontologist, 34*, 1–15.

Goodman, C. S. (1998). Healthcare technology assessment: Methods, framework, and role in policy making. *The American Journal of Managed Care, 4*, 200–214.

Joseph, A. M. (2006). Care coordination and telehealth technology in promoting self-management among chronically ill patients. *Telemedicine Journal and e-Health, 12*, 156–159. doi:10.1089/tmj.2006.12.156

Karunanithi, M. (2007). Monitoring technology for the elderly patient. *Expert Review of Medical Devices, 4*, 267–277. doi:10.1586/17434440.4.2.267

Kramarow, E., Lubitz, J., Lentzner, H., & Gorina, Y. (2007). Trends in the health of older americans, 1970-2005. *Health Affairs, 26*, 1417–1425. doi:10.1377/hlthaff.26.5.1417

Kroenke, K. (2010). Effect of telecare management on pain and depression in patients with cancer: A randomized trial. *Journal of the American Medical Association, 304*, 163–171. doi:10.1001/jama.2010.944

Luptak, M., Dailey, N., Juretic, M., Rupper, R., Hill, R., Hicken, B., & Bair, B. (2010). The care coordination home telehealth (CCHT) rural demonstration project: An innovative health care delivery approach for older veterans in remote geographical settings. *Rural and Remote Health, 10*, 1375.

Mayer, R. E. (2009). *Multimedia learning* (2nd ed.). New York, NY: Cambridge University Press.

Mead, B. J., & Dunbar, J. A. (2004). A virtural clinic: Assessment and monitoring for rural and remote areas. *Rural and Remote Health, 4*, 1–6.

Norris, S. L. (2002). The effectiveness of disease and case management for people with diabetes: A systematic review. *American Journal of Preventive Medicine, 22*, 15–38. doi:10.1016/S0749-3797(02)00423-3

Rossi, M. C., Perozzi, C., Consorti, C., Almonti, K. T., Foglini, K. P., & Giostra, N. (2010). An interactive diary for diet management (DAI): A new telemedicine system able to promote body weight reduction, nutritional education, and consumption of fresh local produce. *Diabetes Technology & Therapeutics, 12*, 641–647. doi:10.1089/dia.2010.0025

Switzer, J. A., Hall, C., Harmut, G., Waller, J., Nichols, F. T., & Wang, S. (2009). A web-based telestroke system facilitates rapid treatment of acute ischemic stroke patients in rural emergency departments. *The Journal of Emergency Medicine, 36*, 16–18. doi:10.1016/j.jemermed.2007.06.041

West, S. P., Lagua, C., Trief, P. M., Izquierdo, R., & Weinstock, R. S. (2010). Goal setting using telemedicine in rural underserved older adults with diabetes: Experiences from the informatics for diabetes education and telemedicine project. *Telemedicine Journal and e-Health, 16*, 405–416. doi:10.1089/tmj.2009.0136

Whitten, P., & Mickus, M. (2007). Home telecare for COPD/CHF patients: Outcomes and perceptions. *Journal of Telemedicine and Telecare, 13*, 69–73. doi:10.1258/135763307780096249

ADDITIONAL READING

American Telemedicine Association. (2009). *Telemental health standard and guidelines working group: Evidence-based practice for telemental health*. Washington, DC: American Telemedicine Association.

ATA. (2006). *Federal policy recommendations for home telehealth and remote monitoring*. Retrieved from http://www.americantelemed.org/i4a/pages/index.cfm?pageID=3335

Bensink, M., Haliey, D., & Wootton, R. (2006). A systematic review of successes and failures in home telehealth. *Journal of Telemedicine and Telecare, 12*, 8–16. doi:10.1258/135763306779380174

Heinzelmann, P. J., Williams, C. M., Lugn, N. E., & Kvedar, J. C. (2005). Clinical outcomes associated with telemedicine/telehealth. *Telemedicine and e-Health, 11*, 329-347.

Hill, R. D., Luptak, M. K., & Rupper, R. W. (2011). Review of veterans health administration telemedicine interventions. *The American Journal of Managed Care, 16*, 303–310.

Jones, B. N. III. (2001). Telepsychiatry and geriatric care. *Current Psychiatry Reports, 3*, 29–36. doi:10.1007/s11920-001-0068-0

McIntosh, E., & Cairns, J. (1997). A framework for the economic evaluation of telemedicine. *Journal of Telemedicine and Telecare, 3*, 132–139. doi:10.1258/1357633971931039

McLean, S., Protti, D., & Sheikh, A. (2011). Telehelthcare for long term conditions. *British Medical Journal, 342*, d120. doi:10.1136/bmj.d120

Mort, M., Finch, T., & May, C. (2009). Making and unmaking telepatients: Identity and governance in new health technologies. *Science, Technology & Human Values, 34*, 9–33. doi:10.1177/0162243907311274

Pare, G., Jaana, M., & Sicotte, C. (2007). A systematic review of home telemonitoring for chronic diseases: The evidence base. *Journal of the Merican Medical Information Assocaition, 14*, 269–277. doi:10.1197/jamia.M2270

Pulier, M. L. (2007). Technology, geriatric practice, and the future of psychiatry. *Journal of Psychiatric Practice, 13*, 269–272. doi:10.1097/01.pra.0000281489.19570.b1

Saligari, J., Flicker, L., Loh, P. K., Maher, S., Ramesh, P., & Goldswain, P. (2002). The clinical achievements of a geriatric telehealth project in its first year. *Journal of Telemedicine and Telecare*, *8*, 53–55. doi:10.1258/13576330260440862

Seidman, D. A., Westmaas, L. J., Goldband, S., Rabius, S., Katkin, E. S., & Pike, K. J. (2010). Randomized controlled trial of an interactive internet smoking cessation program with long term follow-up. *Annals of Behavioral*, *39*, 48–60. doi:10.1007/s12160-010-9167-7

Sood, S., Mbarika, V., Jugoo, S., Dookhy, R., Doarn, C. R., & Prakash, N. (2007). What is telemedicine? A collection of 104 peer-reviewed perspectives and theoretical underpinnings. *Telemedicine Journal and e-Health*, *13*, 573–590. doi:10.1089/tmj.2006.0073

Thomas, E. J., Lucke, J. F., Wueste, L., Weavind, L., & Patel, B. (2009). Association of telemedicine for remote monitoring of intensive care patients with mortality, complications, and length of stay. *Journal of the American Medical Association*, *302*, 2671–2678. doi:10.1001/jama.2009.1902

KEY TERMS AND DEFINITIONS

Chronic Disease: Disease of long-term duration that is progressive and is associated with a unique symptom complex. The end state of chronic disease is death usually from those organ systems most affected by the chronic disease state.

Geriatrics: A field of medicine relating to the aged or to characteristics of the aging process.

Plain Old Telephone Lines (POTS): Formal term to describe standard telephone lines to deliver personalized medicine to rural and remote areas or areas where Web-based infrastructure through broadband access is not available.

Remote Care Delivery Technology (RCDT): Care that is delivered remotely through technology.

Telemedicine: Personalized medicine delivered through electronic means either over the Internet or by telephone line.

Videoconferencing: Conducting a conference between two or more participants at different sites by using computer networks to transmit audio and video data. For example, a point-to-point (two-person) video conferencing system works much like a video telephone.

Chapter 14
Using Technology to Reach Caregivers of Veterans with Dementia

Candice M. Daniel
VA Salt Lake City Health Care System, USA

Bret Hicken
VA Salt Lake City Health Care System, USA & University of Utah, USA

Marilyn Luptak
University of Utah, USA

Marren Grant
VA Salt Lake City Health Care System, USA

Randall Rupper
*VA Salt Lake City Geriatric Research, Education, and Clinical Center, USA
& University of Utah, USA*

ABSTRACT

Caregivers of persons with dementia experience higher levels of anxiety, depressive symptoms, and other mental health problems, as well as increased rates of hypertension, cardiovascular disease, and premature mortality compared to their non-caregiving peers. They also face significant challenges in accessing support from local, state, and VA resources. Several empirically supported treatments have been developed to assist these caregivers. However, accessing these interventions can be difficult given the extent and demand of their caregiving duties. To address this problem, the authors developed a psycho-educational caregiver intervention for use with in-home digital technology that is currently underway at three Veteran's Health Affairs (VA) health care centers. The chapter provides: 1) a brief summary of the background and rationale for intervention development; 2) an overview of the project; and 3) the issues and lessons learned from developing interventions using digital technology for use with older adults.

DOI: 10.4018/978-1-4666-1966-1.ch014

INTRODUCTION

Nearly 4 million older adults in the U.S. are currently living with dementia (Plassman, et al., 2007) and this number is expected to increase to more than 7 million people by 2030 (Alzheimer's Association, 2010). Dementia is characterized by impairment in multiple areas of cognition, including memory, resulting in functional impairment that affects daily life. Alzheimer's disease, the most common form of dementia, is a progressive and degenerative disease that involves gradual loss in functioning. Vascular dementia, the second most frequent type of dementia, commonly results in abrupt, stepwise changes in functional abilities. Language and motor impairment are common, in addition to impairment in memory, executive skills, and visuospatial abilities. These functional declines due to Alzheimer's and vascular dementia result in increased need for support and daily care.

Most older adults with dementia reside in their homes and are cared for by nearly 11 million unpaid caregivers (Alzheimer's Association, 2010). Informal caregivers of older adults with dementia are commonly spouses and children. Spouses are frequently older adults themselves, often facing their own chronic illnesses and health declines. Adult children typically have additional responsibilities, such as caring for their own children and working outside the home. As a result, informal caregivers have multiple responsibilities and demands on their time, in addition to their caregiving duties.

Caregivers manage a range of multiple issues related to basic and more complex instrumental activities of daily living for the individual with dementia (i.e., "care recipient"). Basic activities of daily living include basic self-care behaviors, such as eating, bathing, dressing, toileting, and transferring. For the caregiver, assisting with self-care behaviors may involve managing incontinence or assistance with dressing. Instrumental activities of daily living are more complex behaviors that involve the skills needed to function independently in the community, such as managing finances and medication, driving or utilizing other transportation, and housework. Caregivers often take over these instrumental activities of daily living during the early stages of dementia. In addition to behaviors associated with daily living, caregivers cope with mood changes that the person with dementia may experience, including frustration, irritability, and agitation. Finally, caregivers manage behavioral problems common to dementia, such as wandering and aggression.

Given the extent of caregiving responsibilities identified above, caregiving requires large amounts of time committed to providing care. When compared to their non-dementia caregiving peers, caregivers of people with dementia spend more hours per week providing care (Ory, et al., 1999). The care of a person with dementia can require 24-hour involvement or supervision, while the amount of formal and informal care increases proportionately with the severity of dementia (Wimo, von Strauss, Nordberg, Sassi, & Johansson, 2002). Informal, or non-paid care, is often very time-intensive, measuring four times the amount of formal caregiving that patients with dementia receive (Wimo, et al., 2002). Given these diverse, challenging, and time-intensive caregiving responsibilities, caregivers often face increased stress, depression, and burden associated with caregiving (Ory, Hoffman, Yee, Tennstedt, & Schulz, 1999).

Compared to their non-caregiving peers, caregivers experience higher levels of depressive symptoms and other mental health problems (Schulz, O'Brien, Bookwala, & Fleissner, 1995). Caregiving can also take a toll on physical health. The health costs of caregiving include unintentional injuries related to caregiving duties; poorer self-reported health; and compromised immune systems. Increased rates of hypertension, cardiovascular disease (Monin, Schulz, Martire, Jennings, Lingler, & Greenberg, 2010; von Kanel, et al., 2008), and premature mortality (Schulz & Beach, 1999) have also been observed among those that endorse "caregiving stress" or increased stress related to their caregiving duties. In some instances, poor health may hinder a caregiver's ability to address the care recipient's needs potentially increasing the need for institutionalization or long-term nursing home placement.

Interventions designed to address caregivers' needs typically involve improving the caregiver's knowledge about dementia and its progression, teaching skills for coping with problem behaviors common to dementia, and promoting the overall mental and physical health of the caregiver. These multi-component interventions have demonstrated good efficacy for improving depressive symptoms and reducing stress, both statistically and clinically (Goy, Freeman, & Kansagara, 2010). They have also shown improvement in overall caregiver well-being (Gitlin, Winter, Dennis, Hodgson, & Hauck, 2010). For example, participation in a caregiver intervention was associated with a clinically significant reduction in depressive symptoms for the caregiver (Schulz, et al., 2002). Caregivers who endorsed depressive symptoms placing them "at risk" for clinical depression prior to participation, reported depressive symptoms at a level considered "normative" in the general population, following their participation in the intervention.

Caregiver interventions may also reduce the health care costs associated with dementia. Reducing or delaying nursing home placement and health care utilization rates of the person with dementia has been an important goal in caregiver intervention research for several reasons (Brodaty, Green, & Koschera, 2003; Shulz, et al., 2002). Persons with dementia often prefer to stay at home. A routine and a familiar environment can maximize the capabilities of a person with dementia. The high costs associated with nursing home placement are often a significant financial burden to the family and, more broadly, society. Problem behaviors, such as wandering and incontinence, are often behaviors that lead to institutionalization of the person with dementia. Improving caregiver knowledge and skill for managing problem be-

haviors common to dementia is thought to result in reduced rates and delayed nursing home placement. Caregiver interventions have been shown to delay nursing home placement up to 1 ½ years (Mittelman, Haley, Clay, & Rosh, 2006; Shulz, et al., 2002).

Although these interventions are very promising, the most compelling evidence for efficacy has been demonstrated by individually-tailored, multicomponent, resource- and time-intensive interventions that address several issues simultaneously (Goy, et al., 2010; Shulz, et al., 2002). The feasibility of disseminating complex, individualized, and multi-component interventions is unclear given the number of barriers to implementing them. Barriers exist at the system-level (i.e., cost and limited resource availability), and, most notably, at the individual- or caregiver-level. Caregiver participation in these types of interventions can be difficult for several reasons. First, physical and emotional isolation is common among caregivers (Tebb & Jivanjee, 2000). Lack of community resources or knowledge of how to access community resources contributes to isolation among caregivers. Caregivers may also spend less time with their personal social network because of the extent of caregiving duties. Second, travel time and time away from the care-recipient is often limited. As dementia progresses, care recipients require 24-hour supervision, providing caregivers with little opportunity for time away from their caregiving duties. It can be very challenging for caregivers to take time for self-care, or even manage simple errands, such as grocery shopping. Third, participation in caregiver interventions can incur indirect costs for the caregiver, such as money for gas to travel to the intervention site or clinic or time away from work. Caregivers, commonly older adults with fixed incomes, may have limited financial resources and access to transportation. Consequently, addressing the needs of caregivers is difficult.

Telephone-based interventions to support caregivers have produced mixed results (Glueckauf, et al., 2007; Mahoney, Tarlow, & Jones, 2003; Tremont, et al., 2008; Wray, Shulan, Toseland, Freeman, Vasquez, & Gao, 2010). Participants have found the support valuable and have reported improvement in their caregiving skills (Wray, et al., 2010). However, clinically meaningful outcomes, for the caregiver and care recipient, have been inconsistent. Caregiver stress was not improved among participants participating in a 1-year automated telephone support program (Mahoney, et al., 2003). On the other hand, Wray et al. (2010) investigated the dementia care recipients' VA health care costs among caregivers who participated in telephone education and support groups over 10 weeks. Caregiver participation in the intervention resulted in a decrease in cost of care for the veteran during and following intervention participation (approximately 6 months). Unfortunately, these cost decreases were not maintained 6 months after completing the intervention. Additionally, telephone technology has a number of limitations. Traditional telephone lines limit the types of information that can be disseminated to verbal delivery or exchanges. For telephone support groups, simply scheduling a time that works for each individual may be difficult. Telephone support provided by a clinician or support groups is often preplanned and inflexible.

Interventions utilizing digital technology, such as the Internet, are beginning to emerge in order to address these problems and meet the needs of dementia caregivers (Finkle, Czaja, Schulz, Martinovich, Harris, & Pezzuto, 2007; Glueckauf, Ketterson, Loomis, & Dages, 2004; Lewis, Hobday, & Hepburn, 2010; Schulz, Lustig, Handler, & Martire, 2002). Initial research suggests the acceptability and feasibility of Internet-based psychoeducational programs for dementia caregivers is excellent (Lewis, et al., 2010) and the efficacy of caregiver interventions delivered via technology is promising (Finkel, et al., 2007). Digital technology, such as the Internet and in-home telehealth technology, has many advantages over in-person and telephone-based support. First, this technology can be used to access isolated populations. The Internet has been used to improve health behaviors among geographically and socially or emotionally isolated persons (Griffiths, Lindenmeyer, Powell, Lowe, & Thorogood, 2006; Bowen, Horvath, & Williams, 2007). Given the frequency of isolation among caregivers of persons with dementia, digital technology is a particularly useful tool for reaching this population. Second, technology can be tailored to meet caregivers' demanding schedule. Caregivers can access the content at their convenience and in the privacy of their own home. Furthermore, the educational content can be paced to meet the caregiver's own unique learning needs. Technology-based caregiver interventions may also be time saving and cost-effective, eliminating need for the caregiver travel to the clinic or intervention site (Finkel, et al., 2007). The use of digital technology to reach older adult caregivers remains a new and innovative approach. Sample sizes are small and studies utilizing comparison groups or randomized controlled trial methods are limited (Schulz, Lustig, Handler, & Martire, 2002). Clearly, much more research and program development is needed.

We developed the Supporting Caregivers of Rural Veterans Electronically (SCORE) Project to address obstacles unique to dementia caregivers. The intervention is a multi-component, individually tailored, technology-based intervention for older adult caregivers who are providing care for veterans with dementia. We are currently in the data collection phase of the project. This chapter will provide a case example of the development and application of an innovative technology-based intervention for this unique population of older adults.

SCORE PROJECT OVERVIEW

The SCORE Project is a multi-site randomized controlled trial currently underway at three Veteran's Health Administration (VA) health care centers in Salt Lake City, Loma Linda, and North Florida/South Georgia. This project was funded through the VA Office of Rural Health and VA Geriatrics and Extended Care (GEC). The Institutional Review Boards and VA Research and Development Committees at each individual site approved all study procedures.

Recruiting Caregivers. Caregivers of veterans with dementia were recruited between May 2010 and March 2012 through medical provider referrals, advertisements, and VA electronic medical claims data. Medical providers referred potential caregivers using multiple methods, the telephone, electronic medical record notification, and referral forms. Advertisements individually tailored to target caregivers were placed around medical centers providing a brief overview of the project and study contact information. Additional advertisements, tailored to providers, were placed in employee common areas to facilitate referrals. Study staff also provided brief presentations at various staff meetings. Potential caregivers recruited through electronic medical records were initially identified by submitting a request to VA Information Resource Management to determine Veterans 1) with a previous dementia or Alzheimer's disease diagnosis in his or her medical chart or 2) who were prescribed an anti-dementia medication, such as cholinesterase inhibiters or NMDA receptor antagonists. We sent potentially eligible Veterans and their caregivers a letter describing the program and indicating that they would receive a telephone call from a project staff member. The letter also included an "opt out" form and a stamped envelope to return to us if they preferred not to receive a follow-up phone call. Potential participants received a phone call to assess interest and eligibility.

Intervention Design. Interested and enrolled participants are assigned a Care Manager, a Licensed Clinical Social Worker, whose role is to provide telephone support, assist with delivery of the educational content, and address any questions or concerns over the course of the study.

Participants may contact their care manager at any point during their participation in the study. Participants are then randomized into one of two groups: 1) telephone support, which serves as an "attention control group," or 2) intervention. Study participation lasts approximately 26 weeks.

In the telephone support arm, participants receive printed educational material about dementia and caregiving and monthly telephone contact from their Care Manager. The purpose of the monthly telephone contact is to assess participants' overall well-being and answer any questions they may have. The telephone group acts as an "attention-control group," providing minimal support to potentially burdened and stressed caregivers. We elected to provide minimal support, rather than traditional or "wait-list" control groups, because we wanted all participants to experience some increased level of clinical service.

Participants randomized to the intervention group, receive information via in-home technology, in addition to printed educational materials about dementia. Participants receive intervention material through one of two in-home technology platforms: 1) the Internet for older adults who already use and have access to the Internet; or 2) a simple in-home telehealth device that utilizes a telephone line to receive and transmit digital information. The intervention content transmitted through both devices is identical. Participants access the intervention content three days per week for approximately 10 to 15 minutes. The intervention material disseminated through the devices consists of: 1) video vignettes portraying the progression of dementia and caregiving skills (once per week); 2) text about health topics and caregiving skills (2-3 times per week); 3) brief assessments of health and well-being (2-3 times per week). Individuals in both groups also participate in regular telephone discussion with their Care Manager about the educational content and their answers to the assessment questions. For example, if a participant endorses severe stress on an assessment question, then a Care Manager may contact the participant to further assess stress and offer additional stress reduction techniques. Participants were able to request, through the Internet and telehealth machine, that the care manager contact them by telephone for additional support. The Internet and home-telehealth technology allows Care Managers to efficiently monitor participants' intervention progress and assessment responses remotely and triage responses according to greatest need.

Participants who did not have access to or feel comfortable using the Internet were provided with an in-home telehealth device to receive the intervention content. Participants in this group accessed the intervention content using a very simple touch screen on the telehealth device that guided them through the educational content. The telehealth device also provided reminders, with the use of beeping and flashing light, when new content was available.

Content Overview. Given the statistical and clinical improvements seen with individually-tailored, multi-component interventions, we designed caregiver support content with the following in mind: 1) disseminating educational information using the Internet or a home telehealth device, printed materials, and video content, 2) technique and skill training to improve interaction and outcomes with the cognitively impaired person, 3) mood management and self-care strategies, and 4) telephone support and assistance with VA and community resource access in the form of a licensed clinical social worker. The educational curriculum addressed several topics that are common in dementia caregiving, such as communicating with medical providers, information about common legal issues (i.e., health care power of attorney), and the importance of home safety.

Technique and skill training involves developing strategies to manage common behaviors associated with dementia, such as preventing wandering or addressing repeated questions. Caregivers are provided with an overview of the behavior, including common examples, and

multiple methods to address the behavior are discussed. Mood management and self-care strategies provide cognitive and behavioral-based techniques aimed at alleviating depressive symptoms and stress associated with caregiving. We introduce relaxation techniques and positive activity scheduling focused on the caregiver. Improving VA and community resource access, such as respite services, provides caregivers with the knowledge and skills to access and obtain much needed services now or in the future.

Given this multi-component framework, we are able to address the complex issues that are common to dementia and dementia caregiving. Furthermore, each section is followed by questions related to the topic allowing for interactive learning of the educational content.

PRELIMINARY QUALITATIVE DATA

We are currently in the final stages of data collection. Preliminary qualitative results are very promising. Caregivers enrolled in our program are likely to be older (mean 75.97, standard deviation 10.51) wives of patients with dementia. Among our current sample, 84% of caregivers are spouses, 11% are daughters, and 5% are sons. Caregivers are likely to be isolated. Many live in hard to reach or less frequently accessed places, such as rural (34%) or highly rural (17%) areas. We believe it is particularly important to include this population as these areas have fewer VA and community resources than urban communities.

Feedback about the intervention has generally been positive. Our attrition rate is very low (7%), particularly for a 6-month randomized controlled trial intervention study. Initial qualitative data that was collected post-intervention suggests good likability and acceptability among this unique population. Both groups reported satisfaction with the use of technology to tailor their intervention participation to their personal schedule. One participant reported, "I could do it in spurts" when it worked for her schedule. Many caregivers appreciated the educational information. One caregiver said, "I really felt like a sponge. It was a great learning experience." Another reported greater insight into dementia and the care recipient's abilities, "I understand him more, his memory is not really good. He's easily frustrated and angered." A veteran's wife and caregiver has learned new methods to interact with her husband, "I have softened my tone of voice and he is sweeter to me." Many caregivers report a better understanding of dementia and its progression. One caregiver indicated that the program "Opened my eyes to what to expect." Several caregivers feel better equipped to cope with dementia, "The program gave me perspective of what I might be facing,"and "I don't feel terror, I feel more prepared as things progress." Caregivers frequently cited the care manager support as most useful, reporting, "I loved the support program." Telephone support often addressed feelings of isolation, "I appreciated the support. It was comforting to know I wasn't alone."

Participants in the Internet group identified the convenience of Internet use for intervention content access as a strength of our program. Participants who regularly used the Internet appreciated the ease of accessing educational information. Participants in the in-home telehealth group discussed: 1) initial intimidation associated with new technology use; 2) ease of use of the telehealth device once it was set up; and 3) cited the helpfulness of the reminder to complete intervention content. Many participants who received the telehealth device were initially anxious about the idea of using technology to access information. In fact, several participants even described themselves as "technophobic." Once project staff walked these participants through connecting and setting up the machine, we found participants were able to easily use the device and even "loved" the straightforwardness of it. Several participants reported the telehealth device was "very easy to use." Participants appreciated that the devices

"reminded" them when new content was available. One participant described the effectiveness of the reminder in detail, "When the light went off I went right to it and did it."

UNIQUE ADAPTATIONS OF SCORE

The SCORE Project adapted two new digital technology platforms as methods of intervention and adapted content for a new population with distinct needs, older adults. During intervention development, we considered several perceptual and cognitive changes common to aging. First, sensory and perception declines with age, mainly due to vision and hearing changes. Given the sensory changes associated with normal aging, we felt it was important to adapt technology to accommodate these changes. Initial problems hearing or seeing the content will result in insufficient learning and retention of new information. We adapted the educational content with these vision and hearing changes in mind. The Internet webpage and telehealth device needed to be sufficiently large to ensure older caregivers would be able to read the text without added effort or strain. We also ensured good sound quality and adjustable volume when creating the video vignettes to make certain caregivers could hear the educational content clearly and easily. The video vignettes included subtitles to accommodate caregivers with hearing impairment.

Second, the efficiency of dividing or switching attention between tasks declines with age (Riddle, 2007). In other words, tracking multiple sources of information or switching between content can be difficult for people as they get older. For example, a video vignette embedded within a webpage that contains other text information can be distracting and overwhelming for many older adults. As a result, we kept the written materials, which were presented digitally (Internet webpage and telehealth device screen) or in printed form, simple and free from potentially distracting information. The video vignettes were introduced individually, separate from other content, to avoid distraction. Finally, each component of the intervention is brief, lasting 10 minutes to 15 minutes. The modules are self-paced and flexible allowing for the time limitations associated with the nature of caregiving, as well as adapting to the learning needs of older adult learners.

Third and finally, adapting technology for use with older adults who describe themselves as "technophobic" was essential for reaching this subgroup of older adults. We discovered our selection of the digital technology device was particularly important. We selected a telehealth device that used a straightforward touch screen. We limited the number of steps involved in setting up the machine by connecting most of the hook-ups prior to sending it out. Participants followed three steps to set up the telehealth machine. We also preprogrammed each machine with intervention material that automatically opened upon start up. Participants did not have to complete any preliminary steps before accessing the intervention material. Although many older adults were initially resistant to the idea of using technology to access information, they found the in-home telehealth device simple and easy to use.

It is important to note that at the very early stages of this research project, we piloted the use of a device that provides Internet access through the use of an adapter that connected to a television. The few participants who piloted these devices found them cumbersome and overwhelming due to complicated set-up and access to intervention material. These devices required the use of multiple cords (audio/video cable, phone line splitter, phone line, and AC power adapter), a keyboard, and remote control. Participants needed to complete several preliminary steps before they were able to access intervention content, including dial-in access and setting up and using another account simply for Internet access. Participants also had a separate account to access intervention content, further complicating access to the intervention.

Given the difficulty our pilot participants had with these machines, we are not surprised these devices quickly became obsolete.

LESSONS LEARNED AND FUTURE TRENDS

Overall, our preliminary results suggest adapting empirically established caregiver interventions for in-home dissemination through the use of digital technology is useful and feasible. We were able to address the specific learning needs of a hard to reach population. Digital technology was successful in addressing the needs for Internet-savvy older adults, as well as Internet-naïve, and even those older adults who considered themselves "technology phobic." It is important to note, technology cannot completely replace the human component or regular contact with the Care Manager. Care Manager support to guide, advocate, direct, and encourage caregivers was valued immensely by our participants. Nevertheless, technology allows easy dissemination and tailoring of educational material.

We have several recommendations for working with this population and future research in area of digital technology. First, we recommend future researchers create even more adaptive interventions that adjust to the caregiver's unique needs, particularly as technology continues to advance. Rather than progressive learning modules, we recommend disseminating information to coincide with the caregiver's immediate need and employ contextual learning strategies. For example, a caregiver whose care recipient is having problems with incontinence would be able to access that learning module immediately. Second, we recommend researchers employ creative methods to use digital technology when working with "Internet naïve" older adults. We found, though older adults were initially intimidated by the use of the telehealth device, they grew to love it. Finally, we recommend using a multi-method approach (e.g., video content, telephone support from a Care Manager, and educational content accessed via Internet) to address the unique needs of this population.

CONCLUSION

The largest generation yet will be facing dementia and dementia caregiving as the baby boomers continue to age. Addressing their needs will soon be a public health concern. Digital technology and remote support is an excellent method to reach this unique and often isolated population. This relatively new and innovative approach has the potential to reach a large number of people who face multiple barriers to accessing services. Digital technology can be used to tailor educational information and adjust to busy schedules and time limitations. Furthermore, incorporating digital technology into interventions aimed at older adults will be essential as generations accustomed to technology continue to age and technology is embedded into our everyday lives.

REFERENCES

Alzheimer's Association. (2010). Alzheimer's disease facts and figures. *Alzheimer's & Dementia, 6.*

Bowen, A. M., Horvath, K., & Williams, M. L. (2007). A randomized control trial of internet-delivered HIV prevention targeting rural MSM. *Health Education Research, 22*(1), 120–127. doi:10.1093/her/cyl057

Brodaty, H., Green, A., & Koschera, A. (2003). Meta-analysis of psychosocial interventions for caregivers of people with dementia. *Journal of the American Geriatrics Society, 51,* 657–664. doi:10.1034/j.1600-0579.2003.00210.x

Finkle, S., Czaja, Schulz, R., Martinovich, Z., Harris, C., & Pezzuto, D. (2007). E-care: A telecommunications technology intervention for family caregivers of dementia patients. *The American Journal of Geriatric Psychiatry, 15*(5), 443–447. doi:10.1097/JGP.0b013e3180437d87

Gitlin, L. N., Belle, S. H., Burgio, L. D., Czaja, S. J., Mahoney, D., & Gallagher-Thompson, D. (2003). Effect of multicomponent interventions on caregiver burden and depression: The REACH multisite initiative at 6-month follow-up. *Psychology and Aging, 18,* 361–374. doi:10.1037/0882-7974.18.3.361

Gitlin, L. N., Winter, L., Dennis, M. P., Hodgson, N., & Hauck, W. W. (2010). A biobehavioral home-based intervention and the well-being of patients with dementia and their caregivers: the COPE randomized trial. *Journal of the American Medical Association, 304*(9), 983–991. doi:10.1001/jama.2010.1253

Glueckauf, R. L., Jeffers, S. B., Sharma, D., Massey, A. J., Davis, W. S., & Wesley, L. M. (2007). Telephone-based cognitive-behavioral intervention for distressed rural dementia caregivers. *Clinical Gerontologist, 31*(1), 21–41. doi:10.1300/J018v31n01_03

Glueckauf, R. L., Ketterson, T. U., Loomis, J. S., & Dages, P. (2004). Online support and education for dementia caregivers: Overview, utilization, and initial program evaluation. *Telemedicine Journal and e-Health, 10*(2), 223–232. doi:10.1089/tmj.2004.10.223

Goy, E., Freeman, M., & Kansagara, D. (2010). *A systematic evidence review of interventions for nonprofessional caregivers of individuals with dementia.* VA-ESP Project #05-225. Washington, DC: Veterans Affairs.

Griffiths, F., Lindenmeyer, A., Powell, J., Lowe, P., & Thorogood, M. (2006). Why are health care interventions delivered over the Internet? A systematic review of the published literature. *Journal of Medical Internet Research, 8*(2), e.10.

Lewis, M. L., Hobday, J. V., & Hepburn, K. W. (2010). Internet-based program for dementia caregivers. *American Journal of Alzheimer's Disease and Other Dementias, 25*(8), 674–679. doi:10.1177/1533317510385812

Mittelman, M. S., Haley, W. E., Clay, O. J., & Rosh, D. L. (2006). Improving caregiver well-being delays nursing home placement of patients with Alzheimer disease. *Neurology, 67*, 1592–1599. doi:10.1212/01.wnl.0000242727.81172.91

Monin, J. K., Schulz, R., Martire, L. M., Jennings, J. R., Lingler, J. H., & Greenberg, M. S. (2010). Spouses' cardiovascular reactivity to their partners' suffering. *The Journals of Gerontology. Series B, Psychological Sciences and Social Sciences, 65B*(2), 195–201. doi:10.1093/geronb/gbp133

Ory, M. G., Hoffman, R. R., Yee, J. L., Tennstedt, S., & Schulz, R. (1999). Prevalence and impact of caregiving: A detailed comparison between dementia and non-dementia caregivers. *The Gerontologist, 39*, 177–185. doi:10.1093/geront/39.2.177

Riddle, D. R. (Ed.). (2007). *Brain aging: Models, methods, and mechanisms*. Boca Raton, FL: CRC Press.

Schulz, R., Lustig, A., Handler, S., & Martire, L. M. (2002). Technology-based caregiver intervention research: Current status and future directions. *Gerontechnology (Valkenswaard), 2*(1), 15–47. doi:10.4017/gt.2002.02.01.003.00

Schulz, R., O'Brien, A., Czaja, S., Ory, M., Norris, R., & Martire, L. M. (2002). Dementia caregiver intervention research: In search of clinical significance. *The Gerontologist, 42*, 589–602. doi:10.1093/geront/42.5.589

Schulz, R., O'Brien, A. T., Bookwala, J., & Fleissner, K. (1995). Psychiatric and physical morbidity effects of Alzheimer's disease caregiving: Prevalence, correlates, and causes. *The Gerontologist, 35*, 771–791. doi:10.1093/geront/35.6.771

Talley, R. C., & Crews, J. E. (2007). Framing the public health of caregiving. *American Journal of Public Health, 97*(2), 224–228. doi:10.2105/AJPH.2004.059337

Tebb, S., & Jivanjee, P. (2000). Caregiver isolation. *Journal of Gerontological Social Work, 34*(2), 51–72. doi:10.1300/J083v34n02_06

Tremont, G., Davis, J. D., Bishop, D. S., & Fortinsky, R. H. (2008). Telephone-delivered psychosocial intervention reduces burden in dementia caregivers. *Dementia (London), 7*, 503. doi:10.1177/1471301208096632

Von Kanel, R., Mausbach, B. T., Patterson, T. L., Dimsdale, J. E., Aschbacher, K., & Mills, P. J. (2008). Increased Framingham coronary heart disease risk score in dementia caregivers relative to non-caregiving controls. *Gerontology, 54*, 131–137. doi:10.1159/000113649

Wimo, A., von Strauss, E., Nordberg, G., Sassi, F., & Johansson, L. (2002). Time spent on informal and formal care giving for persons with dementia in Sweden. *Health Policy (Amsterdam), 61*, 255–268. doi:10.1016/S0168-8510(02)00010-6

Wray, L. W., Shulan, M. D., Toseland, R. W., Freeman, K. E., Vásquez, B. E., & Gao, J. (2010). The effect of telephone support groups on costs of care for veterans with dementia. *The Gerontologist, 50*(5), 623–631. doi:10.1093/geront/gnq040

ADDITIONAL READING

Centers for Disease Control and Prevention. (2009). *Improving health literacy for older adults: Expert panel report 2009.* Atlanta, GA: US Department of Health and Human Services.

Czaja, S., Charness, N., Fisk, A. D., Hertzog, C., Nair, S. N., Rogers, W., & Sharit, J. (2006). Factors predicting the use of technology: Findings from the center for research and education on aging and technology (CREATE). *Psychology and Aging, 21*(2), 333–352. doi:10.1037/0882-7974.21.2.333

Daniel, C. M., Hill, R., Luptak, M., Hicken, B., Zheng, R., Turner, C., & Rupper, R. (2011). Reaching out to caregivers of veterans with dementia. *Federal Practitioner, 28*(11), 43–47.

Hernandez-Encuentra, E., Pousada, M., & Gomez-Zuniga, B. (2009). ICT and older people: Beyond usability. *Educational Gerontology, 35,* 226–245. doi:10.1080/03601270802466934

Hill, R., Luptak, M., Rupper, R., Peterson, C., Dailey, N., Bair, B., & Hicken, B. (2010). A review of veterans health administration telemedicine interventions. *The American Journal of Managed Care, 16*(12), e302–e310.

Juretic, M., Hill, R., Luptak, M., Rupper, R., Bair, B., & Floyd, J. (2010). Reaching out to older veterans in need: The Elko clinic demonstration project. *The Journal of Rural Health, 26*(4), 325–332. doi:10.1111/j.1748-0361.2010.00302.x

Luptak, M., Dailey, N., Juretic, M., Rupper, R., Hill, R., Hicken, B., & Bair, B. (2010). The care coordination home telehealth (CCHT) rural demonstration project: An innovative health care delivery approach for older veterans in remote geographical settings. *Rural and Remote Health, 10,* 1375. Retrieved from http://www.rrh.org.au

Roelands, M., van Oost, P., & Depoorter, A. M. (2002). A social-cognitive model to predict the use of assistive devices for mobility and self-care in elderly people. *The Gerontologist, 42*(1), 39–50. doi:10.1093/geront/42.1.39

Rupper, R., Dailey, N., Hill, B., Luptak, M., Hicken, B., & Noyes, B. (2008). Reaching out to aging veterans in rural areas: Innovative use of telehealth and care coordination. *The Federal Practitioner, 25*(5), 21–24.

Rupper, R., Hill, R., Hicken, B., Luptak, M., Dailey, N., & Bair, B. (2010). *Review of selected published VA telehealth case-controlled studies.* Washington, DC: Department of Veterans Affairs.

Saunders, E. (2004). Maximizing computer use among the elderly in rural senior centers. *Educational Gerontology, 30,* 573–585. doi:10.1080/03601270490466967

KEY TERMS AND DEFINITIONS

Activities of Daily Living (ADL): Basic self-care behaviors, such as eating, bathing, dressing, toileting, and transferring.

Caregiver: A person who provides care or support to another individual.

Caregiving: The act of providing, often unpaid, assistance or support.

Dementia: Dementia is characterized by impairment in multiple areas of cognition, including memory, resulting in functional impairment that affects daily life.

Instrumental Activities of Daily Living (IADL): Complex behaviors that involve the skills needed to function independently, such as managing finances and medication, driving or utilizing other transportation, and housework.

Compilation of References

Aartsen, M. J., Smiths, C. H. M., van Tilburg, T., Knopscheer, K. C. P. M., & Deeg, D. J. H. (2002). Activity in older adults: Cause or consequence of cognitive functioning? A longitudinal study on everyday activities and cognitive performance in older adults. *The Journals of Gerontology. Series B, Psychological Sciences and Social Sciences, 57B*, 153–162. doi:10.1093/geronb/57.2.P153

Achtman, R. L., Green, C. S., & Bavelier, D. (2008). Video games as a tool to train visual skills. *Restorative Neurology and Neuroscience, 26*(4-5), 435–446.

Ackerman, P. L., Kanfer, R., & Calderwood, C. (2010). Use it or lose it? Wii brain exercise practice and reading for domain knowledge. *Psychology and Aging, 25*, 753–766. doi:10.1037/a0019277

Adams, N. J., Stubbs, D., & Woods, V. (2005). Psychological barriers to internet usage among older adults in the UK. *Informatics for Health & Social Care, 30*, 3–17. doi:10.1080/14639230500066876

AHIMA. (2009). *How to choose a PHR supplier.* Retrieved on January 26, 2009, from http://myphr.com/resources/phr_search.asp

Ajzen, I., & Fishbein, M. (1980). *Understanding attitudes and predicting social behavior.* Englewood Cliffs, NJ: Prentice-Hall.

Alberto, P. A., & Troutman, A. C. (2003). *Applied behavior analysis for teachers* (6th ed.). Upper Saddle River, NJ: Pearson Education.

Aldwin, C. M., Spiro, A. III, & Park, C. L. (2006). Health, behavior, and optimal aging: A lifespan developmental perspective. In Birren, J., & Schaie, K. W. (Eds.), *Handbook of the Psychology of Aging* (pp. 85–104). Amsterdam, The Netherlands: Elsevier. doi:10.1016/B978-012101264-9/50008-2

Allianz. (2006). *Who causes car accidents: Percent of at-fault accidents on all accidents with injuries.* Retrieved from http://knowledge.allianz.com/mobility/?807/Who-Causes-Car-Accidents

Alpay, L., Verhoef, J., Xie, B., Te'eni, D., & Zwetsloot-Schonk, J. H. M. (2009). Current challenge in consumer health informatics: Bridging the gap between access to information and information understanding. *Biomedical Informatics Insights, 2*, 1–10.

Alwan, M., Dalal, S., Mack, D., Kell, S. W., Turner, B., Leachtenauer, J., & Felder, R. (2006). Impact of monitoring technology in assisted living: Outcome pilot. *IEEE Transactions on Information Technology in Biomedicine, 10*(1), 192–198. doi:10.1109/TITB.2005.855552

Alzheimer's Association. (2010). Alzheimer's disease facts and figures. *Alzheimer's & Dementia, 6*.

Amadieu, F., Mariné, C., & Laimay, C. (2011). The attention-guiding effect and cognitive load in the comprehension of animations. *Computers in Human Behavior, 27*, 36–40. doi:10.1016/j.chb.2010.05.009

Ambrosi-Randic, N., & Plavsic, M. (2011). Strategies for goal-achievement in older people with different levels of well-being. *Studia Psychologica, 53*(1), 97–106.

Anderson, G., & Horvath, J. (2004). The growing burden of chronic disease in America. *Public Health Reports, 119*, 263–270. doi:10.1016/j.phr.2004.04.005

Anderson, J. R. (1982). Acquisition of cognitive skill. *Psychological Review, 89*(4), 396–406. doi:10.1037/0033-295X.89.4.369

Anderson, J. R., Fincham, J. M., & Douglass, S. (1997). The role of examples and rules in the acquisition of a cognitive skill. *Journal of Experimental Psychology. Learning, Memory, and Cognition, 23*, 932–945. doi:10.1037/0278-7393.23.4.932

Anderson, N. D., & Craik, F. I. M. (2006). The mnemonic mechanisms of errorless learning. *Neuropsychologica, 44*, 2806–2813. doi:10.1016/j.neuropsychologia.2006.05.026

Andriessen, J. H. T. H. (1972). Interne of externe beheersing. [Internal or external control]. *Nederlands Tijdschrift voor de Psychologie en Haar Grensgebieden, 27*, 173–178.

Anonymous,. (2004). *Arbobalans 2004: Arbeidsrisico's, effecten en maatregelen in Nederland* [Arbo balance 2004: Occupational risks, effects and measures in the Netherlands]. Den Haag, The Netherlands: Ministerie van Sociale Zaken en Werkgelegenheid.

Anstey, K. (2008). Cognitive aging and functional biomarkers: What do we know, and where to from here? In Hofer, S. M., & Alwin, D. F. (Eds.), *Handbook of Cognitive Aging: Interdisciplinary Perspectives* (pp. 327–339). Los Angeles, CA: Sage Publications. doi:10.4135/9781412976589.n20

Arning, K., & Ziefle, M. (2008). Development and validation of a computer expertise questionnaire for older adults. *Behaviour & Information Technology, 27*, 89–93. doi:10.1080/01449290701760633

Arrindell, W. A., & Ettema, J. H. M. (1986). *SCL-90: Een multidimensionele psychopathologie indicator* [The SCL-90: A multidimensional instrument for the assessment of psychopathology]. Lisse, The Netherlands: Swets & Zeitlinger.

Ash, J. S., Berg, M., & Coiera, E. (2004). Some unintended consequences of information technology in health care: The nature of patient care information system-related errors. *Journal of the American Medical Informatics Association, 11*(2), 104–112. doi:10.1197/jamia.M1471

Aspden, P. Wolcott. J. A., Bootman, J. L., & Croenwett. L. R. (2007). *Preventing medication errors.* Washington, DC: The National Academies Press.

Atkinson, R. C., & Shiffrin, R. M. (1968). Human memory: A proposed system and its control processes. In Spence, K. W., & Spence, J. T. (Eds.), *The Psychology of Learning and Motivation: Advances in Research and Theory* (*Vol. 2*, pp. 89–195). New York, NY: Academic Press. doi:10.1016/S0079-7421(08)60422-3

Atkinson, R. K., Derry, S. J., Renkl, A., & Wortham, D. (2000). Learning from examples: Instructional principles from the worked examples research. *Review of Educational Research, 70*, 181–214.

Atkinson, R. K., Renkl, A., & Merrill, M. M. (2003). Transitioning from studying examples to solving problems: Combining fading with prompting fosters learning. *Journal of Educational Psychology, 95*, 774–783. doi:10.1037/0022-0663.95.4.774

Atkinson, R. K., & Shiffrin, R. (1968). Human memory: A proposed system and its control processes. In Spence, K., & Spence, J. (Eds.), *The Psychology of Learning and Motivation* (*Vol. 2*, pp. 89–95). New York, NY: Academic Press. doi:10.1016/S0079-7421(08)60422-3

Aula, A. (2005). User study on older adults' use of the web and search engines. *University Access in the Information Society, 4*(1), 67–81. doi:10.1007/s10209-004-0097-7

Ayres, P., & Sweller, J. (2005). The split-attention principle in multimedia learning. In Mayer, R. E. (Ed.), *The Cambridge Handbook of Multimedia Learning* (pp. 135–146). Cambridge, UK: Cambridge University Press.

Bäckman, L., Small, B. J., & Wahlin, Å. (2001). Aging and memory: Cognitive and biological perspectives. In Birren, J. E., & Schaie, K. W. (Eds.), *Handbook of the Psychology of Aging* (5th ed., pp. 349–377). San Diego, CA: Academic Press.

Baddeley, A. D., & Hitch. (1974). Working memory, In G. A. Bower (Ed.), *The Psychology of Learning and Motivation: Advances in Research and Theory,* (Vol. 8), (pp. 47–89). New York, NY: Academic Press.

Baddeley, A. (1993). Working memory or working attention? In Baddeley, A., & Weiskrantz, L. (Eds.), *Attention: Selection, Awareness, and Control: A Tribute to Donald Broadbent* (pp. 152–170). Oxford, UK: Clarendon Press.

Baddeley, A. D. (1992). Working memory. *Science, 255*, 556–559. doi:10.1126/science.1736359

Baddeley, A. D. (1997). *Human memory: Theory and practice*. Hove, UK: Psychology Press.

Baddeley, A. D. (2003). Working memory: Looking back and looking forward. *Nature Reviews. Neuroscience*, *4*, 829–839. doi:10.1038/nrn1201

Baddeley, A., Sala, S. D., & Baddeley, R. (1996). Working memory and executive control. *Philosophical Transactions of the Royal Society of London. Series B, Biological Sciences*, *351*(1346), 1397–1404. doi:10.1098/rstb.1996.0123

Baddeley, A., & Wilson, B. A. (1994). When implicit learning fails: Amnesia and the problem of error elimination. *Neuropsychologia*, *32*(1), 53–68. doi:10.1016/0028-3932(94)90068-X

Baker, D. W. (2006). The meaning and the measure of health literacy. *Journal of General Internal Medicine*, *21*, 878–883. doi:10.1111/j.1525-1497.2006.00540.x

Bakken, I. J., Wenzel, H. G., Gotestam, K. G., Johansson, A., & Oren, A. (2009). Internet addiction among Norwegian adults: A stratified probability sample study. *Scandinavian Journal of Psychology*, *50*, 121–127. doi:10.1111/j.1467-9450.2008.00685.x

Ball, K., Berch, D. B., Helmers, K. F., Jobe, J. B., Leveck, M. D., & Marsiske, M. (2002). Effects of cognitive training interventions with older adults: A randomized controlled trial. *Journal of the American Medical Association*, *288*(18), 2271–2281. doi:10.1001/jama.288.18.2271

Ball, K., Owsley, C., Sloane, M. D., Roenker, D. L., & Bruni, J. R. (1993). Visual attention problems as a predictor of vehicle accidents in older drivers. *Investigative Ophthalmology & Visual Science*, *34*, 3110–3123.

Ball, M., Smith, C., & Bakalar, R. (2007). Personal health records: Empowering consumers. *Journal of Healthcare Information Management*, *21*, 76–86.

Baltes, P. B. (1987). Theoretical propositions of life-span developmental psychology: On the dynamics between growth and decline. *Developmental Psychology*, *23*, 611–626. doi:10.1037/0012-1649.23.5.611

Baltes, P. B., & Baltes, M. M. (1990). Psychological perspectives on successful aging: The model of selective optimization with compensation. In Baltes, P. B., & Baltes, M. M. (Eds.), *Successful Aging: Perspectives from the Behavioral Sciences* (pp. 1–34). Cambridge, UK: Cambridge University Press. doi:10.1017/CBO9780511665684.003

Baltes, P. B., & Lindenberger, U. (1997). Emergence of a powerful connection between sensory and cognitive function across the adult life span: A new window to the study of cognitive aging? *Psychology and Aging*, *12*, 12–21. doi:10.1037/0882-7974.12.1.12

Baltes, P., Lindenberger, U., & Staudinger, U. (1998). Life-span theory in developmental psycholgoy. In Lerner, R. (Ed.), *Theoretical Models of Human Development* (*Vol. 1*, pp. 1039–1143). Handbook of Child Psychology New York, NY: Wiley.

Barnes, D. E., & Yaffe, K. (2011). The projected effect of risk factor reduction on Alzheimer's disease prevalence. *The Lancet Neurology*, *10*(9), 819–828. doi:10.1016/S1474-4422(11)70072-2

Barrett, L. L. (2008). *Healthy @ home*. Washington, DC: AARP Foundation.

Barry, P. J., Gallagher, P., & Ryan, C. (2008). Inappropriate prescribing in geriatric patients. *Current Psychiatry Reports*, *10*(1), 37–43. doi:10.1007/s11920-008-0008-3

Basak, C., Boot, W. R., Voss, M. V., & Kramer, A. F. (2008). Can training in a real-time strategy video game attenuate cognitive decline in older adults? *Psychology and Aging*, *23*(4), 765–777. doi:10.1037/a0013494

Bashshur, R. L. (1995). On the definition and evaluation of telemedicine. *Telemedicine Journal*, *1*(1), 19–30. doi:10.1089/tmj.1.1995.1.19

Bäßler, J., & Schwarzer, R. (1996). Evaluación de la autoeficacia: Adaptación española de la escala de autoeficacia general. [Measuring generalized self-beliefs: A Spanish adaptation of the general self-efficacy scale]. *Ansiedad y Estrés*, *2*(1), 1–8.

Bass, S. B. (2003). How will internet use affect the patient? A review of computer network and closed internet-based system studies and the implications in understanding how the use of the internet affects patient populations. *Journal of Health Psychology, 8,* 25–38. doi:10.1177/1359105303008001427

Bastin, C., & Van der Linden, M. (2006). The effects of aging on the recognition of different types of associations. *Experimental Aging Research, 32,* 61–77. doi:10.1080/03610730500326291

Beauchamp, M. S., Argall, B. D., Bodurka, J., Duyn, J. H., & Martin, A. (2004). Unraveling multisensory integration: Patchy organisation within human STS multisensory cortex. *Nature Neuroscience, 7,* 1190–1192. doi:10.1038/nn1333

Beauchamp, M. S., Lee, K. E., Argall, B. D., & Martin, A. (2004). Integration of auditory and visual information about objects in superior temporal sulcus. *Neuron, 41,* 809–823. doi:10.1016/S0896-6273(04)00070-4

Becker, S. A. (2004). A study of web usability for older adults seeking online health resources. *ACM Transactions on Computer-Human Interaction, 11,* 387–406. doi:10.1145/1035575.1035578

Beier, M. E., & Ackerman, P. L. (2005). Age, ability and the role of prior knowledge on the acquisition of new domain knowledge. *Psychology and Aging, 20,* 341–355. doi:10.1037/0882-7974.20.2.341

Beilock, S. L., & Goldin-Meadow, S. (2010). Gesture changes thought by grounding it in action. *Psychological Science, 21,* 1605–1610. doi:10.1177/0956797610385353

Beisgen, B., & Kraitchman, M. (2003). *Senior centers: Opportunities for successful aging.* New York, NY: Springer Publishing Company.

Bensink, M., Hailey, D., & Wootton, R. (2006). A systematic review of successes and failures in home telehealth. *Journal of Telemedicine and Telecare, 12*(S3), 8–16. doi:10.1258/135763306779380174

Berg, A. I., Hassing, L. B., McClearn, G. E., & Johansson, B. (2006). What matters for life satisfaction in the oldest-old? *Aging & Mental Health, 10,* 257–264. doi:10.1080/13607860500409435

Black, A. D., Car, J., Pagliari, C., Anandan, C., & Cresswell, K., Bokun, & Sheikh, A. (2011). The impact of ehealth on the quality and safety of health care: A systematic overview. *PLoS Medicine, 8*(1), e1000387. doi:10.1371/journal.pmed.1000387

Blackler, A., Popovic, V., & Mahar, D. (2003). The nature of intuitive use of products: An experimental approach. *Design Studies, 24,* 491–506. doi:10.1016/S0142-694X(03)00038-3

Blanson Henkemans, O. A., Rogers, W. A., Fisk, A. D., Neerincx, M. A., Lindenberg, J., & van der Mast, C. A. P. G. (2008). Usability of an adaptive computer assistant that improves self-care and health literacy of older adults. *Methods of Information in Medicine, 47,* 82–88.

Blazer, D. G., Hays, J. C., Fillenbaum, G. G., & Gold, D. T. (1997). Memory complaint as a predictor of cognitive decline: A comparison of African American and White elders. *Journal of Aging and Health, 9*(2), 171–184. doi:10.1177/089826439700900202

Blit-Cohen, E., & Litwin, H. (2004). Elder participation in cyberspace: a qualitative analysis of Israeli retirees. *Journal of Aging Studies, 18,* 385–398. doi:10.1016/j.jaging.2004.06.007

Bodenheimer, T., Lorig, K., Holman, H., & Grumbach, K. (2002). Patient self-management of chronic illness in primary care. *Journal of the American Medical Association, 288,* 2469–2475. doi:10.1001/jama.288.19.2469

Bolla, K. I., Lindgren, K. N., Bonaccorsy, C., & Bleecker, M. L. (1991). Memory complaints in older adults: Fact or fiction? *Archives of Neurology, 48*(1), 61–64. doi:10.1001/archneur.1991.00530130069022

Bongers, P. M., de Vet, H. C., & Blatter, B. M. (2002). RSI: Vóórkomen, ontstaan, therapie en preventive. [Repetitive strain injury (RSI): occurrence, etiology, therapy and prevention]. *Nederlands Tijdschrift voor Geneeskunde, 146*(42), 1971–1976.

Boot, W. R., Basak, C., Erickson, K. I., Neider, M., Simons, D. J., & Fabiani, M. (2010). Transfer of skill engendered by complex task training under conditions of variable priority. *Acta Psychologica, 135*(3), 349–357. doi:10.1016/j.actpsy.2010.09.005

Bopp, K. L., & Verhaeghen, P. (2005). Aging and verbal memory span: A meta-analysis. *The Journals of Gerontology. Series B, Psychological Sciences and Social Sciences*, *60*, 223–233. doi:10.1093/geronb/60.5.P223

Boroditsky, L. (2000). Metaphoric structuring: Understanding time through spatial metaphors. *Cognition*, *75*, 1–28. doi:10.1016/S0010-0277(99)00073-6

Boroditsky, L. (2001). Does language shape thought? Mandarin and English speakers' conceptions of time. *Cognitive Psychology*, *43*, 1–22. doi:10.1006/cogp.2001.0748

Bosma, H., van Boxtel, M. P., Ponds, R. W., Jelicic, M., Houx, P., & Metsemakers, J. (2002). Engaged lifestyle and cognitive function in middle and old-aged, non-demented persons: A reciprocal association? *Zeitschrift für Gerontologie und Geriatrie*, *35*(6), 575–581. doi:10.1007/s00391-002-0080-y

Bouchard Ryan, E., & Heaven, R. K. B. (1986). Promoting vitality among older adults with computers. *Activities, Adaptation and Aging*, *8*(1), 15–30. doi:10.1300/J016v08n01_03

Bourge, R. C., Abraham, W. T., Adamson, P. B., Aaron, M. F., Aranda, J. M., & Magalski, A. (2008). Randomized controlled trial of an implantable continuous hemodynamic monitor in patients with advanced heart failure: The COMPASS-HF study. *Journal of the American College of Cardiology*, *51*, 1073–1079. doi:10.1016/j.jacc.2007.10.061

Bowen, A. M., Horvath, K., & Williams, M. L. (2007). A randomized control trial of internet-delivered HIV prevention targeting rural MSM. *Health Education Research*, *22*(1), 120–127. doi:10.1093/her/cyl057

Bradley, N., & Poppen, W. (2003). Assertive technology, computers, and internet may decrease sense of isolation for homebound elderly and disabled persons. *Technology and Disability*, *15*, 19–25.

Brainerd, C. J., & Reyna, V. F. (1993). Memory independence and memory interference in cognitive development. *Psychological Review*, *100*, 42–67. doi:10.1037/0033-295X.100.1.42

Brandtstädter, J., & Rothermund, K. (2002). The life-course dynamics of goal pursuit and goal adjustment: A two-process framework. *Developmental Review*, *22*, 117–150. doi:10.1006/drev.2001.0539

Brault, L. M., Gilbert, J. R., Lansing, C. R., McCarley, J. S., & Kramer, A. F. (2010). Bimodal stimulus presentation and expanded auditory bandwidth improve older adults' speech perception. *Human Factors*, *52*, 479–491. doi:10.1177/0018720810380404

Bregnell, M., Wootton, R., & Gray, L. (2007). The application of telemedicine to geriatric medicine. *Age and Ageing*, *36*, 369–374. doi:10.1093/ageing/afm045

Broadbent, D. E., Cooper, P. F., Fitzgerald, P., & Parkes, K. R. (1982). The cognitive failures questionnaire (CFQ) and its correlates. *The British Journal of Clinical Psychology*, *21*(1), 1–16. doi:10.1111/j.2044-8260.1982.tb01421.x

Brodaty, H., Green, A., & Koschera, A. (2003). Meta-analysis of psychosocial interventions for caregivers of people with dementia. *Journal of the American Geriatrics Society*, *51*, 657–664. doi:10.1034/j.1600-0579.2003.00210.x

Brooks, J. O., Friedman, L., Pearman, A. M., Gray, C., & Yesavage, J. A. (1999). Mnemonic training in older adults: Effects of age, lenght of training, and type of cognitive pretraining. *International Psychogeriatrics*, *11*(1), 75–84. doi:10.1017/S1041610299005608

Brown, T. L., Lee, J. D., & McGehee, D. V. (2001). Human performance models and rear-end collision avoidance algorithms. *Human Factors*, *43*, 462–482. doi:10.1518/001872001775898250

Brunken, R., Plass, J. L., & Leutner, D. (2003). Direct measurement of cognitive load in multimedia learning. *Educational Psychologist*, *38*, 53–61. doi:10.1207/S15326985EP3801_7

Bub, D. N., Masson, M. E. J., & Lalonde, C. E. (2006). Cognitive control in children: Stroop interference and suppression of word reading. *Psychological Science*, *17*, 351–357. doi:10.1111/j.1467-9280.2006.01710.x

Buckley, W. M. (1995, April 19). To read this, give us the password…Ooops! Try it again. *The Wall Street Journal*, pp. A1, A8.

Buisine, S., & Martin, J. C. (2007). The effects of speech–gesture cooperation in animated agents' behavior in multimedia presentations. *Interacting with Computers, 19*, 484–493. doi:10.1016/j.intcom.2007.04.002

Burnett-Wolle, S., & Godbey, G. (2007). Refining research on older adults' leisure: Implications of selection, optimization and compensation and socioemotional selectivity theories. *Journal of Leisure Research, 39*(3), 498–513.

Buschke, H. (1973). Selective reminding for analysis of memory and learning. *Journal of Verbal Learning and Verbal Behavior, 12*(5), 543–550. doi:10.1016/S0022-5371(73)80034-9

Buse, C. E. (2009). When you retire, does everything become leisure? Information and communication technology use and the work/leisure boundary in retirement. *New Media & Society, 11*(7), 1143–1161. doi:10.1177/1461444809342052

Cabeza, R., Grady, C. L., Nyberg, L., McIntosh, A. R., Tulving, E., & Kapur, S. (1997). Age-related differences in neural activity during memory encoding and retrieval: A position emission tomography study. *The Journal of Neuroscience, 17*, 391–400.

Campbell, R. (2004). Older women and the internet. *Journal of Women & Aging, 16*, 161–174. doi:10.1300/J074v16n01_11

Cansino, S., Guzzon, D., Martinelli, M., Barollo, M., & Casco, C. (2011). *Memory and cognition*. Advance online publication. doi:10.3758/s13421-011-0109-9

Caprani, N., Greaney, J., & Porter, N. (2006). A review of memory aid devices for an ageing population. *PsychNology, 4*(3), 205–243.

Carlson, L. E., Lounsberry, J. J., Maciejewski, O., Wright, K., Collacutt, V., & Taenzer, P. (2012). Telehealth-delivered group smoking cessation for rural and urban participants: Feasibility and cessation rates. *Addictive Behaviors, 31*, 108–114. doi:10.1016/j.addbeh.2011.09.011

Carlson, R. A., & Yaure, R. G. (1990). Practice schedules and the use of component skills in problem solving. *Journal of Experimental Psychology. Learning, Memory, and Cognition, 16*, 484–496. doi:10.1037/0278-7393.16.3.484

Carpenter, B. D., & Buday, S. (2007). Computer use among older adults in a naturally occurring retirement community. *Computers in Human Behavior, 23*, 3012–3024. doi:10.1016/j.chb.2006.08.015

Carr, D. B., Duchek, J. M., Meuser, T. M., & Morris, J. C. (2006). Older adult drivers with cognitive impairment. *American Family Physician, 73*, 1029–1034.

Carstensen, L. L. (1991). Social and emotional patterns in adulthood: Support for the socioemotional selectivity theory. *Psychology and Aging, 7*, 331–338. doi:10.1037/0882-7974.7.3.331

Carstensen, L. L., Mikels, J. A., & Mather, M. (2006). Aging and the intersection of cognition, motivation, and emotion. In Birren, J., & Schaie, K. W. (Eds.), *Handbook of the Psychology of Aging* (pp. 343–362). Amsterdam, The Netherlands: Elsevier. doi:10.1016/B978-012101264-9/50018-5

Carstensen, L. L., Turan, B., Scheibe, S., Ram, N., & Ersner-Hershfield, H. (2011). Emotional experience improves with age: Evidence based on over 10 years of experience sampling. *Psychology and Aging, 26*, 21–33. doi:10.1037/a0021285

Casasanto, D. (2008). Similarity and proximity: When does close in space mean close in mind? *Memory & Cognition, 36*, 1047–1056. doi:10.3758/MC.36.6.1047

Casasanto, D. (2009). Embodiment of abstract concepts: Good and bad in right- and left-handers. *Journal of Experimental Psychology. General, 138*, 351–367. doi:10.1037/a0015854

Casasanto, D., & Boroditsky, L. (2008). Time in the mind: Using space to think about time. *Cognition, 106*, 579–593. doi:10.1016/j.cognition.2007.03.004

Castel, A. D., & Craik, F. I. M. (2003). The effects of aging and divided attention on memory for item and associative information. *Psychology and Aging, 18*(4), 873–885. doi:10.1037/0882-7974.18.4.873

Cattell, R. B. (1963). Theory of fluid and crystallized intelligence: A critical experiment. *Journal of Educational Psychology, 54*, 1–22. doi:10.1037/h0046743

Cattell, R. B. (1971). *Abilities: Their structure, growth and action*. Boston, MA: Houghton Mifflin.

Catwell, L., & Sheikh, A. (2009). Evaluating ehealth interventions: The need for continuous systemic evaluation. *PLoS Medicine*, *6*(8), e1000126. doi:10.1371/journal.pmed.1000126

Cavallini, E., Pagnin, A., & Vecchi, T. (2003). Aging and everyday memory: The beneficial effect of memory training. *Archives of Gerontology and Geriatrics*, *37*, 241–257. doi:10.1016/S0167-4943(03)00063-3

Celnik, P., Stefan, K., Hummel, F., Duque, J., Classen, J., & Cogen, L. G. (2005). Encoding a motor memory in the older adult by action observation. *NeuroImage*, *29*, 677–684. doi:10.1016/j.neuroimage.2005.07.039

Chaffin, A., & Harlow, S. (2005). Cognitive learning applied to older adult learners and technology. *Educational Gerontology*, *31*(4), 301–329. doi:10.1080/03601270590916803

Chalfonte, B. L., & Johnson, M. K. (1996). Feature memory and binding in young and older adults. *Memory & Cognition*, *24*, 403–416. doi:10.3758/BF03200930

Chandler, P., & Sweller, J. (1991). Cognitive load theory and the format of instruction. *Cognition and Instruction*, *8*, 293–332. doi:10.1207/s1532690xci0804_2

Chandler, P., & Sweller, J. (1992). The split-attention effect as a factor in the design of instruction. *The British Journal of Educational Psychology*, *62*, 233–246. doi:10.1111/j.2044-8279.1992.tb01017.x

Chandler, P., & Sweller, J. (1994). Why some material is difficult to learn. *Cognition and Instruction*, *12*, 185–233. doi:10.1207/s1532690xci1203_1

Chandler, P., & Sweller, J. (1996). Cognitive load while learning to use a computer program. *Applied Cognitive Psychology*, *10*, 151–170. doi:10.1002/(SICI)1099-0720(199604)10:2<151::AID-ACP380>3.0.CO;2-U

Chan, J. C. K., & McDermott, K. B. (2007). Effects of frontal lobe functioning and age on veridical and false recall. *Psychonomic Bulletin & Review*, *14*(4), 606–611. doi:10.3758/BF03196809

Charness, N., & Boot, W. R. (2009). Aging and information technology use: Potential and barriers. *Current Directions in Psychological Science*, *18*(5), 253–258. doi:10.1111/j.1467-8721.2009.01647.x

Charness, N., Bosman, E., Kelley, C., & Mottram, M. (1996). Cognitive theory and word processing training: When prediction fails. In Rogers, W. A., Fisk, A. D., & Walker, N. (Eds.), *Aging and Skilled Performance: Advances in Theory and Applications*. Mahwah, NJ: Lawrence Erlbaum Associates.

Charness, N., Demiris, G., & Krupinski, E. (2011). *Designing telehealth for an aging population: A human factors perspective*. Boca Raton, FL: CRC Press.

Chase, W. G., & Simon, H. A. (1973). Perception in chess. *Cognitive Psychology*, *4*, 55–81. doi:10.1016/0010-0285(73)90004-2

Chen, Y., & Persson, A. (2002). Internet use among young and older adults: Relation to psychological well-being. *Educational Gerontology*, *28*, 731–744. doi:10.1080/03601270290099921

Cherry, K. E., & Stadler, M. A. (1995). Implicit learning of a nonverbal sequence in younger and older adults. *Psychology and Aging*, *10*(3), 379–394. doi:10.1037/0882-7974.10.3.379

Chi, M. T. H., Glaser, R., & Farr, M. (Eds.). (1988). *The nature of expertise*. Hillsdale, NJ: Erlbaum.

Chin, J., D'Andrea, L., Morrow, D. G., Stine-Morrow, E. A. L., Conner-Gercia, T., Graumlich, J. F., & Murray, M. D. (2009a). Cognition and illness experience are associated with illness knowledge among older adults with hypertension. In *Proceedings of the 53rd Annual Meeting of the Human Factors and Ergonomics Society 2009*. Santa Monica, CA: Human Factors and Ergonomics Society.

Chin, J., Fu, W.-T., & Kannampallil, T. (2009b). Adaptive information search: Age-dependent interactions between cognitive profiles and strategies. In *Proceedings of the 27th ACM Conference on Human Factors in Computing Systems CHI 2009*. Boston, MA: ACM Press.

Chin, J., Morrow, D., Stine-Morrow, E. A. L., Conner-Garcia, T., Graumlich, J. F., & Murray, M. D. (2011). The process-knowledge model of health literacy: Evidence from a componential analysis of two commonly used measures. *Journal of Health Communication*, *16*, 222–241. doi:10.1080/10810730.2011.604702

Chong, T. T.-J., Cunnington, R., Williams, M. A., & Mattingley, J. B. (2009). The role of selective attention in matching observed and executed actions. *Neuropsychologia*, *47*, 786–795. doi:10.1016/j.neuropsychologia.2008.12.008

Christensen, H., Korten, A., Jorm, A. F., Henderson, A. S., Scott, R., & Mackinnon, A. J. (1996). Activity levels and cognitive functioning in an elderly community sample. *Age and Ageing*, *25*(1), 72–80. doi:10.1093/ageing/25.1.72

Chu, M., & Kita, S. (2011). The nature of gestures' beneficial role in spatial problem solving. *Journal of Experimental Psychology. General*, *140*, 102–116. doi:10.1037/a0021790

Chung, J. E., Park, N., Wang, H., Fulk, J., & McLaughlin, M. (2010). Age differences in perceptions of online community participation among non-users: An extension of the technology acceptance model. *Computers in Human Behavior*, *26*, 1674–1684. doi:10.1016/j.chb.2010.06.016

Chu, P. C., & Spires, E. E. (1991). Validating the computer anxiety ratin scale: Effects of cognitive style and computer courses on computer anxiety. *Computers in Human Behavior*, *7*, 7–21. doi:10.1016/0747-5632(91)90025-V

Clare, L., & Jones, R. S. P. (2008). Errorless learning in the rehabilitation of memory impairment: A critical review. *Neuropsychology Review*, *18*, 1–23. doi:10.1007/s11065-008-9051-4

Clark, D. J. (2002). Older adults living through and with their computers. *Computers, Informatics, Nursing*, *20*(3), 117–124. doi:10.1097/00024665-200205000-00012

Clark, H. H. (1996). *Using language*. Cambridge, UK: Cambridge University Press.

Clark, H. H., & Brennan, S. E. (1991). Grounding in communication. In Resnick, L. B., Levine, J., & Teasley, S. D. (Eds.), *Perspectives on Socially Shared Cognition* (pp. 127–149). Washington, DC: American Psychological Association. doi:10.1037/10096-006

Clark, J. M., & Paivio, A. (1991). Dual coding and education. *Educational Psychology Review*, *3*, 149–210. doi:10.1007/BF01320076

Clark, J., Lamphear, A., & Riddick, C. (1987). The effects of video game playing on the response selection processing of elderly adults. *Journal of Gerontology*, *42*, 82–85.

Cody, M. J., Dunn, D., Hoppin, S., & Wendt, P. (1999). Silver surfers: Training and evaluating internet use among older adult learners. *Communication Education*, *48*, 269–286. doi:10.1080/03634529909379178

Cohn, N. B., Dustman, R. E., & Bradford, D. C. (1984). Age-related decrements in Stroop color test performance. *Journal of Clinical Psychology*, *40*, 1244–1250. doi:10.1002/1097-4679(198409)40:5<1244::AID-JCLP2270400521>3.0.CO;2-D

Colello, K. J. (2007). *Where do older adults live? Geographic distribution of the older population*. Washington, DC: Congressional Research Services.

Commission on Systemic Interoperability. (2005). *Ending the document game: Connecting and transforming your healthcare through information technology*. Washington, DC: US Government Printing Office (GPO).

Congressional Budget Office. (2004). *An analysis of the literature on disease management programs*. Washington, DC: Government Printing Office.

Constantinidou, F., & Baker, S. (2002). Stimulus modality and verbal learning performance in normal aging. *Brain and Language*, *82*, 296–311. doi:10.1016/S0093-934X(02)00018-4

Conway, A. R. A., Kane, M. J., Bunting, M. F., Hambrick, D. Z., Wilhelm, O., & Engle, R. W. (2005). Working memory span tasks: A methodological review and user's guide. *Psychonomic Bulletin & Review*, *12*, 769–786. doi:10.3758/BF03196772

Conway, A. R. A., Tuholski, S. W., Shisler, R. J., & Engle, R. W. (1999). The effect of memory load on negative priming: An individual differences investigation. *Memory & Cognition*, *27*(6), 1042–1050. doi:10.3758/BF03201233

Cowan, N. (2000). The magical number 4 in short-term memory: A reconsideration of mental storage capacity. *The Behavioral and Brain Sciences*, *24*, 87–185. doi:10.1017/S0140525X01003922

Craig, S. D., Gholson, B., & Driscoll, D. M. (2002). Animated pedagogical agents in multimedia educational environments: Effects of agent properties, picture features and redundancy. *Journal of Educational Psychology*, *94*, 428–434. doi:10.1037/0022-0663.94.2.428

Craik, F. I. M., & Bosman, E. A. (1992). Age-related changes in memory and learning. In Berman, H., & Graafmans, J. A. M. (Eds.), *Gerontechnology* (pp. 79–92). Burke, VA: IOS Press.

Craik, F. I. M., Byrd, M., & Swanson, J. M. (1987). Patterns of memory loss in three elderly samples. *Psychology and Aging, 2*, 79–86. doi:10.1037/0882-7974.2.1.79

Craik, F. I. M., Govoni, R., Naveh-Benjamin, M., & Anderson, N. D. (1996). The effects of divided attention on encoding and retrieval processes in human memory. *Journal of Experimental Psychology. General, 125*(2), 159–180. doi:10.1037/0096-3445.125.2.159

Craik, F. I. M., & Grady, C. L. (2002). Aging, memory, and frontal lobes functioning. In Stuss, D. T., & Knight, R. T. (Eds.), *Principles of Frontally Lobe Function* (pp. 528–540). Oxford, UK: Oxford University Press. doi:10.1093/acprof:oso/9780195134971.003.0031

Craik, F. I. M., & Lockhart, R. S. (1972). Levels of processing: A framework for memory research. *Journal of Verbal Learning and Verbal Behavior, 11*(6), 671–684. doi:10.1016/S0022-5371(72)80001-X

Craik, F. I. M., & Salthouse, T. A. (2000). *The handbook of aging and cognition* (2nd ed.). Mahwah, NJ: Erlbaum.

Cresci, M. K., Yarandi, H. N., & Morrell, R. W. (2010). Pro-nets versus no-nets: Differences in urban older adults' predilections for internet use. *Educational Gerontology, 36*(6), 500–520. doi:10.1080/03601270903212476

Crimmins, E. M., Kim, J. K., Langa, K. M., & Weir, D. R. (2011). Assessment of cognition using surveys and neuropsychological assessment: The health and retirement study and the aging, demographics, and memory study. *The Journals of Gerontology. Series B, Psychological Sciences and Social Sciences, 66B*(S1), i162–i171. doi:10.1093/geronb/gbr048

Currell, R., Urquhart, C., Wainwright, P., & Lewis, R. (2000). Telemedicine versus face to face patient care: Effects on professional practice and health care outcome. *Cochrane Database of Systematic Reviews, 2*, 1–35.

Cutler, S. J., & Grams, A. E. (1988). Correlates of self-reported everyday memory problems. *Journal of Gerontology, 43*(3), S82–S90.

Czaja, S. J. (1996). Aging and the acquisition of computer skills. In Rogers, W. A., Fisk, A. D., & Walker, N. (Eds.), *Aging and Skilled Performance: Advances in Theory and Applications* (pp. 201–220). Mahwah, NJ: Lawrence Erlbaum Associates.

Czaja, S. J. (1997). Computer technology and the older adult. In Helander, M., Landauer, T. K., & Prabhu, P. (Eds.), *Handbook of Human-Computer Interaction* (pp. 797–812). Amsterdam, The Netherlands: Elsevier Science.

Czaja, S. J., Charness, N., Fisk, A. D., Hertzog, C., Nair, S. N., Rogers, W. A., & Sharit, J. (2006). Factors predicting the use of technology: Findings from the center for research and education on aging and technology enhancement (CREATE). *Psychology and Aging, 21*(2), 333–352. doi:10.1037/0882-7974.21.2.333

Czaja, S. J., Guerrier, J. H., Nair, S. N., & Landauer, T. K. (1993). Computer communication as an aid to independence for older adults. *Behaviour & Information Technology, 12*(4), 197–207. doi:10.1080/01449299308924382

Czaja, S. J., & Lee, C. C. (2001). The internet and older adults: Design challenges and opportunities. In Charness, N., Parks, D. C., & Sabel, B. A. (Eds.), *Communication, Technology and Aging* (pp. 60–78). New York, NY: Springer.

Czaja, S. J., & Lee, C. D. (2003). Designing computer systems for older adults. In Jacko, J. A., & Sears, A. (Eds.), *The Human-Computer Interaction Handbook: Fundamentals, Evolving Technologies, and Emerging Applications* (pp. 413–427). Mahwah, NJ: Erlbaum.

Czaja, S. J., & Sharit, J. (1993). Age differences in the performance of computer-based work. *Psychology and Aging, 8*(1), 59–67. doi:10.1037/0882-7974.8.1.59

Czaja, S. J., Sharit, J., Hernandez, M. A., Nair, S. N., & Loewenstein, D. (2010). Variability among older adults in Internet health information-seeking performance. *Gerontechnology (Valkenswaard), 9*, 46–55. doi:10.4017/gt.2010.09.01.004.00

Czaja, S. J., Sharit, J., Ownby, R., Roth, D. L., & Nair, S. (2001). Examining age differences in performance of a complex information search and retrieval task. *Psychology and Aging, 16*, 564–579. doi:10.1037/0882-7974.16.4.564

Czaja, S. K. (1996). Aging and the acquisition of computer skills. In Rogers, W. A., Fisk, A. D., & Walker, N. (Eds.), *Aging and Skilled Performance: Advances in Theory and Applications* (pp. 201–220). Mahwah, NJ: Erlbaum.

Czaja, S. K. (2005). The impact of aging on access to technology. *Comput, 83*, 7–11.

Daffner, S. D., Hilibrand, A. S., Hanscom, B. S., Brislin, B. T., Vaccaro, A. R., & Albert, T. J. (2003). Impact of neck and arm pain on overall health status. *Spine, 28*(17), 2030–2035. doi:10.1097/01.BRS.0000083325.27357.39

Dang, S., Dimmick, S., & Kelkar, G. (2009). Evaluating the evidence base for the use of home telehealth remote monitoring in elderly with heart failure. *Telemedicine Journal and e-Health, 15*(8), 783–796. doi:10.1089/tmj.2009.0028

Danowski, J. A., & Sacks, W. (1980). Computer communication and the elderly. *Experimental Aging Research, 6*(2), 125–135. doi:10.1080/03610738008258350

Darabi, A. A., Nelson, D. W., & Palanki, S. (2007). Acquisition of troubleshooting skills in a computer simulation: Worked example vs. conventional problem solving instructional strategies. *Computers in Human Behavior, 23*(4), 1809–1819. doi:10.1016/j.chb.2005.11.001

Darabi, A., Arrastia, M. C., & Nelson, D. W. (2011). Cognitive presence in asynchronous online learning: A comparison of four discussion strategies. *Journal of Computer Assisted Learning, 27*(3), 216–227. doi:10.1111/j.1365-2729.2010.00392.x

De Beni, R., & Palladino, P. (2004). Decline in working memory updating through ageing: Intrusion error analyses. *Memory (Hove, England), 12*, 75–89. doi:10.1080/09658210244000568

de Frias, C. M., Dixon, R. A., & Bäckman, L. (2003). Use of memory compensation strategies is related to psychosocial and health indicators. *The Journals of Gerontology. Series B, Psychological Sciences and Social Sciences, 55B*(1), 12–p22. doi:10.1093/geronb/58.1.P12

de Groot, A. (1965). *Thought and choice in chess*. The Hague, The Netherlands: Mouton.

De Jong-Gierveld, J., & Kamphuis, F. H. (1986). The development of a rash-type loneliness scale. *Applied Psychological Measurement, 9*, 289–299. doi:10.1177/014662168500900307

De Joode, E., van Heugten, C., Verhey, F., & van Boxtel, M. (2010). Efficacy and usability of assistive technology for patients with cognitive deficits: A systematic review. *Clinical Rehabilitation, 24*(8), 701–714. doi:10.1177/0269215510367551

De Koning, B. B., Tabbers, H. K., Rikers, R. M. J. P., & Paas, F. (2007). Attention cueing as a means to enhance learning from an animation. *Applied Cognitive Psychology, 21*, 731–746. doi:10.1002/acp.1346

De Koning, B. B., Tabbers, H. K., Rikers, R. M. J. P., & Paas, F. (2009). Towards a framework for attention cueing in instructional animations: Guidelines for research and design. *Educational Psychology Review, 21*, 113–140. doi:10.1007/s10648-009-9098-7

De Schutter, B. (2011). Never too old to play: The appeal of digital games to an older audience. *Games and Culture, 6*(2), 155–170. doi:10.1177/1555412010364978

Dehaene, S., Bossini, S., & Giraux, P. (1993). The mental representation of parity and number magnitude. *Journal of Experimental Psychology. General, 122*, 371–396. doi:10.1037/0096-3445.122.3.371

Delahunt, P. B., Ball, K. K., Roenker, D. L., Hardy, J. L., Mahncke, H. W., & Merzenich, M. M. (2009). Computer-based cognitive training to facilitate neural plasticity. *Gerontechnology (Valkenswaard), 8*(1), 52–53. doi:10.4017/gt.2009.08.01.005.00

Dellifraine, J. L., & Dansky, K. H. J. (2008). Home-based telehealth: A review and meta analysis. *Telemed Telecare, 14*, 62–65. doi:10.1258/jtt.2007.070709

Dempsey, J. V., Haynes, L. L., Lucassen, B. A., & Casey, M. (2002). Forty simple computer games and what they could mean to educators. *Simulation & Gaming, 33*, 157–168. doi:10.1177/1046878102332003

Derwinger, A., Stigsdotter Neely, S., Persson, M., Hill, R. D., & Bäckman, L. (2003). Remembering numbers in old age: Mnemonic training versus self-generated strategy training. *Neuropsychology, Development, and Cognition. Section B, Aging, Neuropsychology and Cognition, 10*(3), 202–214. doi:10.1076/anec.10.3.202.16452

Detmer, D., Bloomrosen, M., Raymond, B., & Tang, P. (2008). Integrated personal health records: Transformative tools for consumer-centric care. *BMC Medical Informatics and Decision Making, 8*, 45. doi:10.1186/1472-6947-8-45

Detterman, D. K., & Sternberg, R. (1982). *How and how much can intelligence be increased.* New York, NY: Ablex Publishing.

Detterman, D. K., & Sternberg, R. J. (1993). *Transfer on trial: Intelligence, cognition, and instruction.* Westport, CT: Ablex Publishing.

Di Pellegrino, G., Fadiga, L., Fogassi, L., Gallese, V., & Rizzolatti, G. (1992). Understanding motor events: A neurophysiological study. *Experimental Brain Research, 91*, 176–180.

Diao, Y., & Sweller, J. (2007). Redundancy in foreign language reading comprehension instruction: Concurrent written and spoken presentations. *Learning and Instruction, 17*, 78–88. doi:10.1016/j.learninstruc.2006.11.007

Dickinson, A., & Gregor, P. (2006). Computer use has no demonstrated impact on the wellbeing of older adults. *International Journal of Human-Computer Studies, 64*, 744–753. doi:10.1016/j.ijhcs.2006.03.001

Docampo Rama, M. (2001). *Technology generations: Handling complex user interfaces.* Unpublished Dissertation. Eindhoven, The Netherlands: Technical University of Eindhoven.

Dodson, C. S., Bawa, S., & Krueger, L. E. (2007). Aging, metamemory, and high-confidence errors: A misrecollection account. *Psychology and Aging, 22*(1), 122–133. doi:10.1037/0882-7974.22.1.122

Donchin, E. (1995). Video games as research tools: The space fortress game. *Behavior Research Methods, Instruments, & Computers, 27*(2), 217–223. doi:10.3758/BF03204735

Dorra, D., Bonnerb, L. M., Cohenc, A. N., Shoaic, R. S., Perrind, R., Chaneyb, E., & Young, A. S. (2007). Informatics systems to promote improved care for chronic illness: A literature review. *Journal of the American Medical Informatics Association, 14*, 156–163. doi:10.1197/jamia.M2255

Drew, B., & Waters, J. (1986). Video games: Utilization of a novel strategy to improve perceptual motor skills and cognitive functioning in the non-institutionalized elderly. *Cognitive Rehabilitation, 4*(2), 26–31.

Druss, B. G., Marcus, S. C., Olfson, M., & Pincus, H. A. (2002). The most expensive medical conditions in America. *Health Affairs, 21*, 105–111. doi:10.1377/hlthaff.21.4.105

Dunsworth, Q., & Atkinson, R. K. (2007). Fostering multimedia learning of science: Exploring the role of an animated agent's image. *Computers & Education, 49*, 677–690. doi:10.1016/j.compedu.2005.11.010

Durso, F. T., Rawson, K. A., & Girotto, S. (2007). Comprehension and situation awareness. In F. T. Durso, R. S. Nickerson, S. T., Dumais, S. Lewandowsky, & T. J. Perfect (Eds.), *Handbook of Applied Cognition,* (pp. 163-194). Chichester, UK: Wiley.

Durston, S., Thomas, K. M., Yang, Y., Ulŭg, A. M., Zimmerman, R. D., & Casey, B. J. (2002). A neural basis for the development of inhibitory control. *Developmental Science, 5*, 9–16. doi:10.1111/1467-7687.00235

Dustman, R., Emmerson, R., Ruhling, R., Shearer, D., Steinhaus, L., & Johnson, S. (1984). Aerobic exercise training and improved neuropsychological function of older individuals. *Neurobiology of Aging, 5*, 35–42. doi:10.1016/0197-4580(84)90083-6

Dye, M. W. G., Green, C. S., & Bavelier, D. (2009a). The development of attention skills in action video game players. *Neuropsychologia, 47*(8-9), 1780–1789. doi:10.1016/j.neuropsychologia.2009.02.002

Dye, M. W. G., Green, S., & Bavelier, D. (2009b). Increasing speed of processing with action video games. *Current Directions in Psychological Science, 18*(6), 321–326. doi:10.1111/j.1467-8721.2009.01660.x

Eastin, M. S., & LaRose, R. (2000). Internet self-efficacy and the psychology of the digital divide. *Journal of Computer-Mediated Communication, 6*(1). Retrieved on March, 26th, 2011, from http://www.ascusc.org/jcmc/

Eastman, J. K., & Iyer, R. (2005). The impact of cognitive age on internet use of the elderly: An introduction to the public policy implications. *International Journal of Consumer Studies, 29*(2), 125–136. doi:10.1111/j.1470-6431.2004.00424.x

Ekeland, A. G., Bowes, A., & Flottorp, S. (2010). Effectiveness of telemedicine: A systematic review of reviews. *International Journal of Medical Informatics, 79*(11), 736–771. doi:10.1016/j.ijmedinf.2010.08.006

Elliott, J. G., Hufton, N. R., Willis, W., & Illushin, L. (2005). *Motivation, engagement, and educational performance: International perspectives on the contexts for learning.* New York, NY: Palgrave Macmillan. doi:10.1057/9780230509795

Ellison, N. B., Steinfield, C., & Lampe, C. (2007). The benefits of Facebook "friends": Social capital and college students' use of online social network sites. *Journal of Computer-Mediated Communication, 12*, 11431168. doi:10.1111/j.1083-6101.2007.00367.x

Engelkamp, J. (1998). *Memory for actions. Hove, UK.* UK: Psychology Press/Taylor & Francis.

Engelkamp, J. (2001a). Action memory: A systems-oriented approach. In Zimmer, H. D., Cohen, R. L., Guynn, M. J., Engelkamp, J., Kormi-Nouri, R., & Foley, M. A. (Eds.), *Memory for Action: A Distinct Form of Episodic Memory?* (pp. 49–96). Oxford, UK: Oxford University Press.

Engley, H. L. (1995, October 2). ATM turns 30: What did we do without it? *Salt Lake Tribune*, p. C2.

Ericsson, K. A., & Kintsch, W. (1995). Long-term working memory. *Psychological Review, 102*, 211–245. doi:10.1037/0033-295X.102.2.211

Estabrook, L., Witt, E., & Rainie, L. (2007). *Information searches that solve problems: How people use the internet, libraries, and government agencies when they need help.* Washington, DC: Pew Internet & American Life Project. Retrieved on August 10, 2008 from http://www.pewinternet.org/pdfs/Pew_UI_LibrariesReport.pdf

Eurostat European Commission. (2011). *Computers and the internet.* Retrieved June, 25th, 2011 from http://epp.eurostat.ec.europa.eu/portal/page/portal/information_society/data/database

Eysenbach, G. (2001). What is e-health? *Journal of Medical Internet Research, 3*(2), E20. doi:10.2196/jmir.3.2.e20

Eysenck, M. W. (2009). Prospective memory. In A. Baddeley, M. W. Eysenck, & M. C. Anderson (Eds.), *Memory,* (343-356). New York, NY: Psychology Press.

Ezer, N., Fisk, A. D., & Rogers, W. A. (2009b). More than a servant: Self-reported willingness of younger and older adults to having a robot perform interactive and critical tasks in the home. In *Proceedings of the Human Factors and Ergonomics Society 53rd Annual Meeting,* (pp. 136-140). Santa Monica, CA: Human Factors and Ergonomics Society.

Ezer, N., Fisk, A. D., & Rogers, W. A. (2009a). Attitudinal and intentional acceptance of domestic robots by younger and older adults. *Lecture Notes in Computer Science, 5615,* 39–48. doi:10.1007/978-3-642-02710-9_5

Feyereisen, P. (2009). Enactment effects and integration processes in younger and older adults' memory for actions. *Memory (Hove, England), 17*, 374–385. doi:10.1080/09658210902731851

Finkel, D., McArdle, J. J., Reynolds, C. A., & Pedersen, N. L. (2007). Age changes in processing speed as a leading indicator of cognitive aging. *Psychology and Aging, 22*, 558–568. doi:10.1037/0882-7974.22.3.558

Finkle, S., Czaja, Schulz, R., Martinovich, Z., Harris, C., & Pezzuto, D. (2007). E-care: A telecommunications technology intervention for family caregivers of dementia patients. *The American Journal of Geriatric Psychiatry, 15*(5), 443–447. doi:10.1097/JGP.0b013e3180437d87

Finucane, M. L., Mertz, C. K., Slovic, P., & Scholze Schmidt, E. S. (2005). Task complexity and older adults' decision-making competence. *Psychology and Aging, 20*, 71–84. doi:10.1037/0882-7974.20.1.71

Fisk, A. D., Rogers, W. A., Charness, N., Czaja, S. J., & Sharit, J. (2009). *Designing for older adults: Principles and creative human factors approaches* (2nd ed.). Boca Raton, FL: CRC Press.

Fisk, A. D., Rogers, W., Charness, N., Czaja, S. J., & Sharit, J. (2009). *Designing for older adults: Principles and creative human factors approach* (2nd ed.). London, UK: CRC Associates.

Fitts, P. M. (1947). *Psychological research on equipment design*. Washington, DC: US Government Printing Office.

Flavell, J. H. (1979). Metacognitive and cognitive monitoring: A new area of cognitive developmental inquiry. *The American Psychologist, 34*, 906–911. doi:10.1037/0003-066X.34.10.906

Floyd, M., & Scogin, F. (1997). Effects of memory training on the subjective memory functioning and mental health of older adults: A meta-analysis. *Psychology and Aging, 12*(1), 150–161. doi:10.1037/0882-7974.12.1.150

Flynn, K. E., Smith, M. A., & Freese, J. (2006). When do older adults turn to the Internet for health information? Findings from the Wisconsin longitudinal study. *Journal of General Internal Medicine, 21*, 1295–1301. doi:10.1111/j.1525-1497.2006.00622.x

Flyvbjerg, B. (2001). Case study. In Denzin, N. K., & Lincoln, Y. S. (Eds.), *The Sage Handbook of Qualitative Research* (4th ed., pp. 301–316). Thousand Oaks, CA: Sage.

Folstein, M. F., Folstein, S. E., & McHugh, P. R. (1975). Mini-mental state: A practical method for grading the cognitive state of patients for the clinician. *Journal of Psychiatric Research, 12*, 189–198. doi:10.1016/0022-3956(75)90026-6

Fox, S. (2004). Older Americans and the internet. *Pew Internet and American Life Project*. Retrieved July 22, 2011 from http://www.pewinternet.org

Fox, S. (2007). *E-patients with a disability or chronic disease*. Washington, DC: PEW Internet & American Life. Retrieved on August 20, 2009 from http://www.pewinternet.org/~/media//Files/Reports/2007/EPatients_Chronic_Conditions_2007.pdf

Freudenthal, T. D. (1998). *Learning to use interactive devices: Age differences in the reasoning process.* Unpublished Dissertation. Eindhoven, The Netherlands: Eindhoven University of Technology.

Freudenthal, A., & Mook, H. J. (2003). The evaluation of an innovative intelligent thermostat interface: Universal usability and age differences. *Cognition Technology and Work, 5*, 55–66.

Frick, K. M., & Fernandez, S. M. (2003). Enrichment enhances spatial memory and increases synaptophysin levels in aged female mice. *Neurobiology of Aging, 24*(4), 615–626. doi:10.1016/S0197-4580(02)00138-0

Friedman, D. B., Hoffman-Goetz, L., & Arocha, J. F. (2006). Health literacy and the world wide web: Comparing the readability of leading incident cancers on the internet. *Medical Informatics and the Internet in Medicine, 31*, 67–87. doi:10.1080/14639230600628427

Frost, J., & Massagli, M. (2009). PatientsLikeMe the case for a data-centered patient community and how ALS patients use the community to inform treatment decisions and manage pulmonary health. *Chronic Respiratory Disease, 6*, 225–229.

Gaillard, V., Destrebecqz, A., Michiels, S., & Cleeremans, A. (2009). Effects of age and practice in sequence learning: A graded account of aging, learning and control. *The European Journal of Cognitive Psychology, 21*, 255–282. doi:10.1080/09541440802257423

Gallese, V., Fadiga, L., Fogassi, L., & Rizzolatti, G. (1996). Action recognition in the premotor cortex. *Brain, 119*, 593–609. doi:10.1093/brain/119.2.593

Gamberini, L., Alcaniz, M., Barresi, G., Fabregat, M., Ibanez, F., & Prontu, L. (2006). Cognition, technology and games for the elderly: An introduction to the ELDER-GAMES project. *PsychNology Journal, 4*(3), 285–308.

Gamboz, N., Russo, R., & Fox, E. (2002). Age differences and the identity negative priming effect: An updated meta-analysis. *Psychology and Aging, 17*, 525–531. doi:10.1037/0882-7974.17.3.525

Gardner, M. K., Hill, R. D., & Was, C. A. (2011). A procedural approach to remembering personal identification numbers. *PLoS ONE, 6*(10), e25428. doi:10.1371/journal.pone.0025428

Gardner, M., & Hill, R. (2012). Training older adults to improve their episodic memory: Three different approaches to enhancing numeric memory. In Zheng, R., Hill, R., & Gardner, M. (Eds.), *Engaging Older Adults with Modern Technology: Internet Use and Information*. Hershey, PA: IGI Global.

Gatto, S. L., & Tak, S. H. (2008). Computer, internet, and email use among older adults: Benefits and barriers. *Educational Gerontology*, *34*, 800–811. doi:10.1080/03601270802243697

Gausepohl, K., Winchester, W. W., Arthur, J. D., & Smith-Jackson, T. (2011). Using storytelling to elicit design guidance for medical devices. *Ergonomics in Design*, *19*, 19–24. doi:10.1177/1064804611408017

Gazzola, V., & Keysers, C. (2008). The observation and execution of actions share motor and somatosensory voxels in all tested subjects: Single-subject analyses of unsmoothed fMRI data. *Cerebral Cortex*, *19*, 1239–1255. doi:10.1093/cercor/bhn181

Geary, D. (2002). Principles of evolutionary educational psychology. *Learning and Individual Differences*, *12*, 317–345. doi:10.1016/S1041-6080(02)00046-8

Geary, D. (2005). *The origin of mind: Evolution of brain, cognition, and general intelligence*. Washington, DC: American Psychological Association. doi:10.1037/10871-000

Geary, D. (2007). Educating the evolved mind: Conceptual foundations for an evolutionary educational psychology. In Carlson, J. S., & Levin, J. R. (Eds.), *Psychological Perspectives on Contemporary Educational Issues* (pp. 1–99). Greenwich, CT: Information Age Publishing.

Geary, D. (2008). An evolutionarily informed education science. *Educational Psychologist*, *43*, 179–195. doi:10.1080/00461520802392133

Gellis, Z. D., Kenaley, B., & McGinty, J., Bardelli, Davitt, J., & Have, T. T. (2012). Outcomes of a telehealth intervention for homebound older adults with heart or chronic respiratory failure: A randomized controlled trial. *The Gerontologist*, *34*, 1–15.

Gibbs, R. W. Jr. (2006). *Embodiment and cognitive science*. Cambridge, UK: Cambridge University Press.

Gilchrist, A. L., Cowan, N., & Naveh-Benjamin, M. (2008). Working memory capacity for spoken sentences decreases with adult ageing: Recall of fewer but not smaller chunks in older adults. *Memory (Hove, England)*, *16*(7), 773–787. doi:10.1080/09658210802261124

Gilhooly, M. L., Gilhooly, K. J., & Jones, B. (2008). Quality of life: Conceptual challenges in exploring the role of ICT in active ageing. *Assistive Technology Research Series*, *23*, 1–27.

Gilleard, C., & Higgs, P. (2008). Internet use and the digital divide in the English longitudinal study of ageing. *European Journal of Ageing*, *5*, 233–239. doi:10.1007/s10433-008-0083-7

Ginns, P. (2005). Meta-analysis of the modality effect. *Learning and Instruction*, *15*, 313–331. doi:10.1016/j.learninstruc.2005.07.001

Githens, R. P. (2007). Understanding interpersonal interaction in an online professional development course. *Human Development Quarterly*, *18*(2), 253–274. doi:10.1002/hrdq.1202

Gitlin, L. N., Belle, S. H., Burgio, L. D., Czaja, S. J., Mahoney, D., & Gallagher-Thompson, D. (2003). Effect of multicomponent interventions on caregiver burden and depression: The REACH multisite initiative at 6-month follow-up. *Psychology and Aging*, *18*, 361–374. doi:10.1037/0882-7974.18.3.361

Gitlin, L. N., Winter, L., Dennis, M. P., Hodgson, N., & Hauck, W. W. (2010). A biobehavioral home-based intervention and the well-being of patients with dementia and their caregivers: the COPE randomized trial. *Journal of the American Medical Association*, *304*(9), 983–991. doi:10.1001/jama.2010.1253

Glenberg, A. M., & Robertson, D. A. (2000). Symbol grounding and meaning: A comparison of high-dimensional and embodied theories of meaning. *Journal of Memory and Language*, *43*, 379–401. doi:10.1006/jmla.2000.2714

Glisky, E. L., & Delaney, S. M. (1996). Implicit memory and new semantic learning in posttraumatic amnesia. *The Journal of Head Trauma Rehabilitation*, *11*(2), 31–42. doi:10.1097/00001199-199604000-00004

Glisky, E. L., & Schacter, D. L. (1987). Acquisition of domain-specific knowledge in organic amnesia: Training for computer-related work. *Neuropsychologia, 25*(6), 893–906. doi:10.1016/0028-3932(87)90094-7

Glisky, E. L., & Schacter, D. L. (1988b). Long-term retention of computer learning by patients with memory disorders. *Neuropsychologia, 26*(1), 173–178. doi:10.1016/0028-3932(88)90041-3

Glisky, E. L., & Schacter, D. L. (1989). Extending the limits of complex learning in organic amnesia: Computer training in a vocational domain. *Neuropsychologia, 27*(1), 107–120. doi:10.1016/0028-3932(89)90093-6

Glisky, E. L., Schacter, D. L., & Tulving, E. (1986). Computer learning by memory-impaired patients: Acquisition and retention of complex knowledge. *Neuropsychologia, 24*(3), 313–328. doi:10.1016/0028-3932(86)90017-5

Glisky, E. L., Schacter, D. L., & Tulving, E. (1986b). Learning and retention of computer-related vocabulary in memory-impaired patients: Method of vanishing cues. *Journal of Clinical and Experimental Neuropsychology, 8*(3), 292–312. doi:10.1080/01688638608401320

Glueckauf, R. L., Jeffers, S. B., Sharma, D., Massey, A. J., Davis, W. S., & Wesley, L. M. (2007). Telephone-based cognitive-behavioral intervention for distressed rural dementia caregivers. *Clinical Gerontologist, 31*(1), 21–41. doi:10.1300/J018v31n01_03

Glueckauf, R. L., Ketterson, T. U., Loomis, J. S., & Dages, P. (2004). Online support and education for dementia caregivers: Overview, utilization, and initial program evaluation. *Telemedicine Journal and e-Health, 10*(2), 223–232. doi:10.1089/tmj.2004.10.223

Goel, M. S., Brown, T. L., Williams, A., Hasnain-Wynia, R., Thompson, J. A., & Baker, D. W. (2011). Disparities in enrollment and use of an electronic patient portal. *Journal of General Internal Medicine, 26*, 1112–1116. doi:10.1007/s11606-011-1728-3

Goldin-Meadow, S., Nusbaum, H., Kelly, S. D., & Wagner, S. (2001). Explaining math: Gesturing lightens the load. *Psychological Science, 12*, 516–522. doi:10.1111/1467-9280.00395

Goldstein, J., Cajko, L., Oosterbroek, M., Michielsen, M., Van Houten, O., & Salverda, F. (1997). Video games and the elderly. *Social Behavior and Personality: An International Journal, 25*(4), 345–352. doi:10.2224/sbp.1997.25.4.345

Goodman, C. S. (1998). Healthcare technology assessment: Methods, framework, and role in policy making. *The American Journal of Managed Care, 4*, 200–214.

Gopher, D., Weil, M., & Bareket, T. (1994). Transfer of skill from a computer game trainer to flight. *Human Factors, 36*(3), 387–405.

Gopher, D., Weil, M., & Siegel, D. (1989). Practice under changing priorities: An approach to the training of complex skills. *Acta Psychologica, 71*(1-3), 147–177. doi:10.1016/0001-6918(89)90007-3

Gouin-Thibault, I., Levy, C., Pautas, E., Cambus, J. P., Drouet, L., & Mahe, I. (2010). Improving anticoagulation control in hospitalized elderly patients on warfarin. *Journal of the American Geriatrics Society, 58*(2), 242–247. doi:10.1111/j.1532-5415.2009.02675.x

Goy, E., Freeman, M., & Kansagara, D. (2010). *A systematic evidence review of interventions for nonprofessional caregivers of individuals with dementia.* VA-ESP Project #05-225. Washington, DC: Veterans Affairs.

Gracia, E., & Herrero, J. (2009). Internet use and self-rated health among older people: A national survey. *Journal of Medical Internet Research, 11*(4), e49. doi:10.2196/jmir.1311

Grant, E. R., & Spivey, M. J. (2003). Eye movements and problem solving: Guiding attention guides thought. *Psychological Science, 14*, 462–466. doi:10.1111/1467-9280.02454

Grant, R. W., Wald, J. S., Poon, E. G., Schnipper, J. L., & Gandhi, T. K. (2006). Design and implementation of a web-based patient portal linked to an ambulatory care electronic health record: Patient gateway for diabetes collaborative care. *Diabetes Technology & Therapeutics, 8*, 576–586. doi:10.1089/dia.2006.8.576

Greenburg. (2009). *A profile of older Americans.* Washington, DC: Administration on Aging.

Green, C. S., & Bavelier, D. (2006). Effect of action video games on the spatial distribution of visuospatial attention. *Journal of Experimental Psychology. Human Perception and Performance, 32*(6), 1465–1478. doi:10.1037/0096-1523.32.6.1465

Green, C. S., & Bavelier, D. (2007). Action-video-game experience alters the spatial resolution of vision. *Psychological Science, 18*(1), 88–94. doi:10.1111/j.1467-9280.2007.01853.x

Greene, M. G., Adelman, R. D., Friedmann, E., & Charon, R. (1994). Older patient satisfaction with communication during an initial medical encounter. *Social Science & Medicine, 38*, 1279–1288. doi:10.1016/0277-9536(94)90191-0

Grèzes, J., & Decety, J. (2002). Does visual perception of object afford action? Evidence from a neuroimaging study. *Neuropsychologia, 40*, 212–222. doi:10.1016/S0028-3932(01)00089-6

Griffiths, F., Lindenmeyer, A., Powell, J., Lowe, P., & Thorogood, M. (2006). Why are health care interventions delivered over the Internet? A systematic review of the published literature. *Journal of Medical Internet Research, 8*(2), e.10.

Gross, J. J., Carstensen, L. L., Pasupathi, M., Skorpen, C. G., Tsai, J., & Hsu, A. Y. C. (1997). Emotion and aging: Experience, expression, and control. *Psychology and Aging, 12*, 590–599. doi:10.1037/0882-7974.12.4.590

Gustafson, D., Hawkins, R., Boberg, E., Pingree, S., Serlin, R., & Graziano, F. (1999). Impact of a patient-centered, computer-based health information/support system. *American Journal of Preventive Medicine, 16*, 1–9. doi:10.1016/S0749-3797(98)00108-1

Hage, B. (2008). *Bridging the digital divide: The impact of computer training, internet and e-mail use on levels of cognition, depression and social functioning in older adults.* Paper presented at The 6th International Conference of the International Society for Gerontechnology. Pisa, Italy.

Halamka, J. D., Mandl, K. D., & Tang, P. C. (2008). Early experiences with personal health records. *Journal of the American Medical Informatics Association, 15*, 1–7. doi:10.1197/jamia.M2562

Hall, C. B., Lipton, R. B., Sliwinski, M., Katz, M. J., Derby, C. A., & Vergese, J. (2009). Cognitive activities delay onset of memory decline in persons who develop dementia. *Neurology, 73*(5), 356–361. doi:10.1212/WNL.0b013e3181b04ae3

Hall, J. A., Roter, D. L., & Katz, N. R. (1988). Meta-analysis of correlates of provider behaviors in medical encounters. *Medical Care, 26*, 657–675. doi:10.1097/00005650-198807000-00002

Han, D., & Braun, K. L. (2011). Promoting active ageing through technology training in Korea. In Soar, J., Swindell, R., & Tsang, P. (Eds.), *Intelligent Technologies for Bridging the Grey Digital Divide* (pp. 141–158). Hershey, PA: IGI Global. doi:10.4018/978-1-61520-825-8.ch010

Hanson, V. K., Gibson, L., Coleman, G. W., Bobrowicz, A., & McKay, A. (2010). *Engaging those who are disinterested: Access for digitally excluded older adults.* Paper presented at Conference on Human Factors in Computing Systems (CHI2010). Atlanta, GA.

Han, Y. Y., Carcillo, J. A., Venkataraman, S. T., Clark, R. S. B., Watson, R. S., & Nguyen, T. C. (2005). Unexpected increased mortality after implementation of a commercially sold computerized physician order entry system. *Pediatrics, 116*(6), 1506–1512. doi:10.1542/peds.2005-1287

Harrington, K. V., McElroy, J. C., & Morrow, P. C. (1990). Computer anxiety and compuer-based training: A laboratory experiment. *Journal of Educational Computing Research, 6*(3), 343–358. doi:10.2190/34Q7-0HHF-8JDL-DR09

Harrow, R. O. (1995, November 17). You must remember this: Passwords are easy to forget. *Salt Lake Tribune*, p. A1.

Hartman, M., & Hasher, L. (1991). Aging and suppression: Memory for previously relevant information. *Psychology and Aging, 6*, 587–594. doi:10.1037/0882-7974.6.4.587

Hart, T. A., Chaparro, B. S., & Halcomb, C. G. (2008). Evaluating websites for older adults: Adherence to "senior-friendly" guidelines and end-user performance. *Behaviour & Information Technology, 27*, 191–199. doi:10.1080/01449290600802031

Hasher, L., Stoltzfus, E. R., Zacks, R. T., & Rypma, B. (1991). Age and inhibition. *Journal of Experimental Psychology. Learning, Memory, and Cognition, 17*, 163–169. doi:10.1037/0278-7393.17.1.163

Hashtroudi, S., Chrosniak, L. D., & Schwartz, B. L. (1991). Effects of aging on priming and skill acquisition. *Psychology and Aging, 6*(4), 605–615. doi:10.1037/0882-7974.6.4.605

Hassol, A., Walker, J. M., Kidder, D., Rokita, K., Young, D., & Pierdon, S. (2004). Patient experiences and attitudes about access to a patient electronic health care record and linked web messaging. *Journal of the American Medical Informatics Association, 11*, 505–513. doi:10.1197/jamia.M1593

Hauk, O., Johnsrude, I., & Pulvermüller, F. (2004). Somatotopic representation of action words in human motor and premotor cortex. *Neuron, 41*, 310–307. doi:10.1016/S0896-6273(03)00838-9

Hawi, N. (2010). Causal attributions of success and failure made by undergraduate students in an introductory-level computer programming course. *Computers & Education, 54*, 1127–1136. doi:10.1016/j.compedu.2009.10.020

Hawthorn, D. (2007). Interface design and engagement with older people. *Behaviour & Information Technology, 26*(4), 333–341. doi:10.1080/01449290601176930

Hay, J. F., & Jacoby, L. L. (1996). Separating habit and recollection: Memory slips, process dissociations, and probability matching. *Journal of Experimental Psychology. Learning, Memory, and Cognition, 22*(6), 1323–1335. doi:10.1037/0278-7393.22.6.1323

Hazlehurst, B., Gorman, P. N., & McMullen, C. K. (2008). Distributed cognition: an alternative model of cognition for medical informatics. *International Journal of Medical Informatics, 77*, 226–234. doi:10.1016/j.ijmedinf.2007.04.008

Healthit. (2011). *Federal health IT strategic plan*. Retrieved on June 27, 2011, from http://healthit.hhs.gov/portal/server.pt/document/954074/federal_hit_strategic_plan_public_comment_period

Hedden, T., & Gabrieli, J. D. (2004). Insights into the ageing mind: A view from cognitive neuroscience. *Nature Reviews. Neuroscience, 5*, 87–96. doi:10.1038/nrn1323

Helliwell, P. S., & Taylor, W. J. (2004). Repetitive strain injury. *Postgraduate Medical Journal, 80*(946), 438–443. doi:10.1136/pgmj.2003.012591

Henke, M. (1999). Promoting independence in older persons through the Internet. *Cyberpsychology & Behavior, 2*(6), 521–527. doi:10.1089/cpb.1999.2.521

Hernández-Encuentra, E., Pousada, M., & Gómez-Zúñiga, B. (2009). ICT and older people: Beyond usability. *Educational Gerontology, 35*, 226–245. doi:10.1080/03601270802466934

Hertzog, C., Kramer, A. F., Wilson, R. S., & Lindenberger, U. (2009). Regarding methods for studying human development. *Research in Human Development, 7*, 1–8. doi:10.1080/15427600903578110

Hess, R., Bryce, C. L., & McTigue, K. (2006). The diabetes patient portal: Patient perspectives on structure and delivery. *Diabetes Spectrum, 92*, 106–110. doi:10.2337/diaspect.19.2.106

Hess, T. M. (2005). Memory and aging in context. *Psychological Bulletin, 131*(3), 383–406. doi:10.1037/0033-2909.131.3.383

Hess, T. M., Hinson, J. T., & Statham, J. A. (2004). Explicit and implicit stereotype activation effects on memory: Do age and awareness moderate the impact of priming? *Psychology and Aging, 19*(3), 495–505. doi:10.1037/0882-7974.19.3.495

Higbee, K. (1988). *Your memory: How it works and how to improve it*. New York, NY: Paragon House.

Hill, A. J., Theodoros, D., Russell, T., & Ward, E. (2009). Using telerehabilitation to assess apraxia of speech in adults. *International Journal of Language & Communication Disorders, 44*(5), 731–747. doi:10.1080/13682820802350537

Hill, R. D., Campbell, B. W., Foxley, D., & Lindsay, S. (1997). Effectiveness of the number-consonant mnemonic for retention of numeric material in community-dwelling older adults. *Experimental Aging Research, 23*(3), 275–286. doi:10.1080/03610739708254284

Hill, R. D., Sheikh, J. I., & Yesavage, J. A. (1988). Pretraining enhances mnemonic training in elderly adults. *Experimental Aging Research, 14*(4), 207–211. doi:10.1080/03610738808259749

Hirst, S., & Graham, R. (1997). The format and presentation of collision warnings. In Noy, Y. I. (Ed.), *Ergonomics and Safety of Intelligent Driver Interfaces* (pp. 203–319). Hillsdale, NJ: Lawrence Erlbaum.

Hobfoll, S. F. (2002). Social and psychological resources and adaptation. *Review of General Psychology*, *6*, 307–324. doi:10.1037/1089-2680.6.4.307

Höffler, T. N., & Leutner, D. (2007). Instructional animation versus static pictures: A meta-analysis. *Learning and Instruction*, *17*, 722–738. doi:10.1016/j.learnistruc.2007.09.013

Hoffman, L., McDowd, J. M., Atchley, P., & Dubinsky, R. (2005). The role of visual attention in predicting driver impairment in older adults. *Psychology and Aging*, *20*, 610–622. doi:10.1037/0882-7974.20.4.610

Hogeboom, D. L., McDermott, R. J., Perrin, K. M., Osman, H., & Bell-Ellison, B. A. (2010). Internet use and social networking among middle aged and older adults. *Educational Gerontology*, *36*, 93–111. doi:10.1080/03601270903058507

Holt, B. J., & Morrell, R. W. (2002). Guidelines for web site design for older adults: The ultimate influence of cognitive factors. In Morrell, R. W. (Ed.), *Older Adults, Health Information and the World Wide Web*. Mahwah, NJ: Erlbaum.

Horgan, A. L., Wilms, H.-U., & Baltes, M. M. (1998). Daily life in very old age: Everyday activities as expression of successful living. *The Gerontologist*, *38*, 556–568. doi:10.1093/geront/38.5.556

Horn, J. L. (1982). The theory of fluid and crystallized intelligence in relation to concepts of cognitive psychology and aging in adulthood. In Craik, F. I. M., & Trehub, S. E. (Eds.), *Aging and Cognitive Processes* (pp. 237–278). New York, NY: Plenum Press.

Horrey, W. J., & Wickens, C. D. (2006). Examining the impact of cell phone conversations on driving using meta-analytic techniques. *Human Factors*, *48*, 196–205. doi:10.1518/001872006776412135

Hostetter, A. B., Alibali, M. W., & Kita, S. (2007). I see it in my hands' eye: Representational gestures reflect conceptual demands. *Language and Cognitive Processes*, *22*, 313–336. doi:10.1080/01690960600632812

Houx, P. J., & Jolles, J. (1993). Age-related decline of psychomotor speed: Effects of age, brain health, sex, and education. *Perceptual and Motor Skills*, *76*, 195–211. doi:10.2466/pms.1993.76.1.195

Houx, P. J., Jolles, J., & Vreeling, F. W. (1993). Stroop interference: Aging effects assessed with the Stroop color-word test. *Experimental Aging Research*, *19*, 209–224. doi:10.1080/03610739308253934

Howard, D. V., & Howard, J. H. (1989). Ages differences in learning serial patterns: Direct versus indirect measures. *Psychology and Aging*, *4*, 357–364. doi:10.1037/0882-7974.4.3.357

Howard, D. V., & Howard, J. H. (1992). Adult age differences in the rate of learning serial patterns: Evidence from direct and indirect tests. *Psychology and Aging*, *7*, 232–241. doi:10.1037/0882-7974.7.2.232

Hugenschmidt, C. E., Mozolic, J. L., & Laurienti, P. J. (2009). Suppression of multisensory integration by modality-specific attention in aging. *Neuroreport*, *20*, 349–353. doi:10.1097/WNR.0b013e328323ab07

Hultsch, D. F., & Dixon, R. A. (1990). Learning and memory in aging. In Birren, J. E., & Schaie, K. W. (Eds.), *Handbook of the Psychology of Aging* (3rd ed., pp. 258–274). San Diego, CA: Academic Press.

Hultsch, D. F., Herzog, C., Small, B. J., & Dixon, R. A. (1999). Use it or lose is: Engaged lifestyle as a buffer of cognitive decline in aging? *Psychology and Aging*, *14*(2), 245–263. doi:10.1037/0882-7974.14.2.245

Huppert, F. A., & Beardsall, L. (1993). Prospective memory impairment as an early indicator of dementia. *Journal of Clinical and Experimental Neuropsychology*, *15*, 805–821. doi:10.1080/01688639308402597

Huppert, F. A., Johnson, T., & Nickson, J. (2000). High prevalence of prospective memory impairment in the elderly and in early-stage dementia: Findings from a population-based study. *Applied Cognitive Psychology*, *14*, S63–S81. doi:10.1002/acp.771

Hurtienne, J. Horn, & Langdon, P. (2010). Facets of prior experience and their impact on product usability for older users. In P. M. Langdon, P. J. Clarkson, & P. Robinson (Eds.), *Designing Inclusive Interactions*, (pp. 123-132). London, UK: Springer.

Hurtienne, J., & Langdon, P. (2009). *Prior knowledge in inclusive design: The older, the more intuitive?* Paper presented at the 23rd British Computer Society Human Computer Interaction Workshop and Conference (HCI 2009). Cambridge, UK.

Hutchins, E. (1995). How a cockpit remembers its speeds. *Cognitive Science, 19*, 265–288. doi:10.1207/s15516709cog1903_1

Hwang, G. J., Kuo, F. R., & Yin, P. Y. (2010). A heuristic algorithm for planning personalized learning paths for context-aware ubiquitous learning. *Computers & Education, 54*(2), 404–415. doi:10.1016/j.compedu.2009.08.024

Idescat. (2011). *Ús de l'ordinador i d'Internet, 2010.* Barcelona, Spain: Institut Nacional d'Estadística. Retrieved June, 25th, 2011 from http://www.idescat.cat/pub/?id=aec&n=617

IJsselstijn, W., Nap, H. H., de Kort, Y., & Poels, K. (2007). Digital game design for elderly users. In *Proceedings of the 2007 Conference on Future Play,* (pp. 17-22). Future Play.

INE. (2011). *Resumen de datos de personas por sexo, características demográficas y tipo de uso de TIC, 2010.* Madrid, Spain: Instituto Nacional de Estadística. Retrieved June, 25th, 2011 from http://www.ine.es/jaxi/menu.do?type=pcaxis&path=/t25/p450&file=inebase

Institute of Medicine. (2003). *Key capabilities of an electronic health record system: Letter report.* Washington, DC: Institute of Medicine, Board on Health Care Services, Committee on Data Standards for Patient Safety.

International Standards Organization. (2006). *Ease of operation of everyday products – Part 1: Design requirements for context of use and user characteristics.* ISO Standard 20282-1:2006(E). Geneva, Switzerland: International Standards Organization.

Internet World Stats. (2011). *Internet users in the world: Distribution by world regions.* Retrieved July, 3, 2011 from http://www.internetworldstats.com

Isaacs, E., & Clark, H. H. (1987). References in conversation between experts and novices. *Journal of Experimental Psychology. General, 116*, 26–37. doi:10.1037/0096-3445.116.1.26

Iverson, J. M., & Goldin-Meadow, S. (2005). Gestures pave the way for language development. *Psychological Science, 16*, 367–371. doi:10.1111/j.0956-7976.2005.01542.x

Jacoby, L. (1991). A process dissociation framework: Separating automatic from intentional uses of memory. *Journal of Memory and Language, 30*, 513–541. doi:10.1016/0749-596X(91)90025-F

Jamet, E., Gavota, M., & Quaireau, C. (2008). Attention guiding in multimedia learning. *Learning and Instruction, 18*, 135–145. doi:10.1016/j.learninstruc.2007.01.011

Java, R. I., & Gardiner, J. M. (1991). Priming and aging: Further evidence of preserved memory function. *The American Journal of Psychology, 104*(1), 89–100. doi:10.2307/1422852

Jensen, A. R. (1969). How much can we boost IQ and scholastic achievement? *Harvard Educational Review, 39*(1), 1–123.

Jin, P. (2010). Methodological considerations in educational research using serious games. In Van Eck, R. (Ed.), *Interdisciplinary Models and Tools for Serious Games: Emerging Concepts and Future Directions* (pp. 147–176). Hershey, PA: IGI Global. doi:10.4018/978-1-61520-719-0.ch007

Jin, P., & Low, R. (2011). Implications of game use for explicit instruction. In Tobias, S., & Fletcher, J. D. (Eds.), *Computer Games and Instruction* (pp. 395–416). Charlotte, NC: Information Age Publishers.

Jobe, J. B., Smith, D. M., Ball, K., Tennstedt, S. L., Marsiske, M., & Willis, S. L. (2001). ACTIVE: A cognitive intervention trial to promote independence in older adults. *Controlled Clinical Trials, 22*(4), 453–479. doi:10.1016/S0197-2456(01)00139-8

Jones, B. D., & Bayen, U. J. (1998). Teaching older adults to use computers: Recommendations based on cognitive aging research. *Educational Gerontology, 24*(7), 675–689. doi:10.1080/0360127980240705

Joseph, A. M. (2006). Care coordination and telehealth technology in promoting self-management among chronically ill patients. *Telemedicine Journal and e-Health, 12*, 156–159. doi:10.1089/tmj.2006.12.156

Joshi, S., & Morley, J. E. (2006). Cognitive impairment. *The Medical Clinics of North America*, *90*, 769–787. doi:10.1016/j.mcna.2006.05.014

Juiznic, P., Blazic, M., Mercun, T., & Plestenjak, B. (2006). Who says that old dogs cannot learn new tricks? *New Library World*, *107*(7-8), 332–345. doi:10.1108/03074800610677308

Kaelber, D. C., Jha, A. K., Johnston, D., Middleton, B., & Bates, D. W. (2008). A research agenda for personal health records (PHRs). *Journal of the American Medical Informatics Association*, *15*, 729–736. doi:10.1197/jamia.M2547

Kahn, R. L., Zarit, S. H., Hilbert, N. M., & Niederehe, G. (1975). Memory complaint and impairment in the aged: The effect of depression and altered brain function. *Archives of General Psychiatry*, *32*(12), 1569–1573. doi:10.1001/archpsyc.1975.01760300107009

Kalyuga, S., Chandler, P., & Sweller, J. (1998). Levels of expertise and instructional design. *Human Factors*, *40*, 1–17. doi:10.1518/001872098779480587

Kalyuga, S., Chandler, P., & Sweller, J. (1999). Managing split attention and redundancy in multimedia instruction. *Applied Cognitive Psychology*, *13*, 351–371. doi:10.1002/(SICI)1099-0720(199908)13:4<351::AID-ACP589>3.0.CO;2-6

Kalyuga, S., Chandler, P., & Sweller, J. (2000). Incorporating learner experience into the design of multimedia instruction. *Journal of Educational Psychology*, *92*, 126–136. doi:10.1037/0022-0663.92.1.126

Kalyuga, S., Chandler, P., & Sweller, J. (2004). When redundant on-screen text in multimedia technical instruction can interfere with learning. *Human Factors*, *46*, 567–581. doi:10.1518/hfes.46.3.567.50405

Kane, M. J., & Engle, R. W. (2002). The role of prefrontal cortex in working-memory capacity, executive attention, and general fluid intelligence: An individual-differences perspective. *Psychonomic Bulletin & Review*, *9*, 637–671. doi:10.3758/BF03196323

Kang, N. W., & Yoon, W. C. (2008). Age- and experience-related user behavior differences in the use of complicated electronic devices. *International Journal of Human-Computer Studies*, *66*, 425–437. doi:10.1016/j.ijhcs.2007.12.003

Kannampallil, T., Waicekauskas, K., Morrow, D., Kopren, K., & Fu, W.-T. (2011). *Collaborative tools for a simulated patient-provider medication scheduling task*. Paper presented at the 54th Conference of the Human Factors and Ergonomics Society. San Francisco, CA.

Karunanithi, M. (2007). Monitoring technology for the elderly patient. *Expert Review of Medical Devices*, *4*, 267–277. doi:10.1586/17434440.4.2.267

Katz, J. E., & Rice, R. E. (2002). *Social consequences of internet use: Access, involvement, and interaction*. Cambridge, MA: MIT Press.

Katzman, R., Aronson, M., Fuld, P., Kawas, C., Brown, T., & Morgenstern, H. (1989). Development of dementing illnesses in an 80-year old volunteer cohort. *Annals of Neurology*, *25*, 317–324. doi:10.1002/ana.410250402

Katz, S., Ford, A. B., Moskovitz, R. W., Jackson, B. A., & Jaffe, M. W. (1963). Studies of illness in the aged: The index of ADL: A standardized measure of biological and psychosocial function. *Journal of the American Medical Association*, *185*(12), 914–919. doi:10.1001/jama.1963.03060120024016

Kaye, J. A., Maxwell, S. A., Mattek, N., Hayes, T. L., Dodge, H., & Pavel, M. (2011). Intelligent systems for assessing aging changes: Home-based, unobtrusive, and continuous assessment of aging. *The Journals of Gerontology. Series B, Psychological Sciences and Social Sciences*, *66B*(S1), i180–i190. doi:10.1093/geronb/gbq095

Kelley, C. L., & Charness, N. (1995). Issues in training older adults to use computers. *Behaviour & Information Technology*, *14*(2), 107–120. doi:10.1080/01449299508914630

Kelly, S. D., Creigh, P., & Bartolotti, J. (2009). Integrating speech and iconic gestures in a Stroop-like task: Evidence for automatic processing. *Journal of Cognitive Neuroscience*, *22*, 683–694. doi:10.1162/jocn.2009.21254

Keselman, A., Slaughter, L., Smith, C. A., Kim, H., Divita, G., Browne, A., et al. (2007). Towards consumer-friendly PHRs: Patients' experience with reviewing their health records. In *Proceedings of the AIMA 2007 Symposium,* (pp. 399-403). AIMA.

Kessels, R. P. C., Hobbel, D., & Postema, A. (2007). Ageing, context memory and binding: A comparison of "what, where and when" in young and older adults. *The International Journal of Neuroscience, 117,* 795–810. doi:10.1080/00207450600910218

Kieley, J. M., & Hartley, A. A. (1997). Age-related equivalence of identity suppression in the Stroop color-word task. *Psychology and Aging, 12,* 22–29. doi:10.1037/0882-7974.12.1.22

Kilb, A., & Naveh-Benjamin, M. (2011). The effects of pure pair repetition on younger and older adults' associative memory. *Journal of Experimental Psychology. Learning, Memory, and Cognition, 37*(3), 706–719. doi:10.1037/a0022525

Kim, Y. S. (2008). Reviewing and critiquing computer learning and usage among older adults. *Educational Gerontology, 34,* 709–735. doi:10.1080/03601270802000576

Kirschner, P. A., Sweller, J., & Clark, R. E. (2006). Why minimal guidance during instruction does not work: An analysis of the failure of constructivist, discovery, problem-based, experiential, and inquiry-based teaching. *Educational Psychologist, 41,* 75–86. doi:10.1207/s15326985ep4102_1

Kirsh, D. (2005). Metacognition, distributed cognition, and visual design. In Gardinfors, P., & Johansson, P. (Eds.), *Cognition, Education and Communication Technology* (pp. 147–180). New York, NY: Routledge.

Kliegl, R., Smith, J., & Baltes, P. B. (1989). Testing-the-limits and the study of adults age differences in cognitive plasticity of a mnemonic skill. *Developmental Psychology, 25*(2), 247–256. doi:10.1037/0012-1649.25.2.247

Knopman, D. S., & Nissen, M. J. (1987). Implicit learning in patients with probable Alzheimer's disease. *Neurology, 37*(5), 784–788. doi:10.1212/WNL.37.5.784

Kochanek, K., Xu, J., Murphy, S., Miniño, A. M., & Kung, C.-H. (2011). Deaths: Preliminary data for 2009. *National Vital Statistics Reports, 59*(4), 1–51. Retrieved July 3, 2011 from http://www.cdc.gov/nchs/fastats/lifexpec.htm

Kormi-Nouri, R., & Nilsson, L.-G. (2001). The motor component is not crucial! In Zimmer, H. D., Cohen, R. L., Guynn, M. J., Engelkamp, J., Kormi-Nouri, R., & Foley, M. A. (Eds.), *Memory for Action: A Distinct from Episodic Memory?* (pp. 97–111). Oxford, UK: Oxford University Press.

Kramarow, E., Lubitz, J., Lentzner, H., & Gorina, Y. (2007). Trends in the health of older americans, 1970-2005. *Health Affairs, 26,* 1417–1425. doi:10.1377/hlthaff.26.5.1417

Kramer, A. F., Larish, J. F., & Strayer, D. L. (1995). Training for attentional control in dual task settings: A comparison of young and old adults. *Journal of Experimental Psychology. Applied, 1*(1), 50–76. doi:10.1037/1076-898X.1.1.50

Kramer, A. F., & Willis, S. L. (2002). Enhancing the cognitive vitality of older adults. *Current Directions in Psychological Science, 11*(5), 173–177. doi:10.1111/1467-8721.00194

Kraut, R., Patterson, M., Lundmark, V., Kiesler, S., Mukopadhyay, T., & Scherlis, W. (1998). Internet paradox: A social technology that reduces social involvement and psychological well-being? *The American Psychologist, 53*(9), 1017–1031. doi:10.1037/0003-066X.53.9.1017

Kreider, A., & Haselton, N. (1997). *The systems challenge.* Chicago, IL: American Hospital Publishing.

Kroenke, K. (2010). Effect of telecare management on pain and depression in patients with cancer: A randomized trial. *Journal of the American Medical Association, 304,* 163–171. doi:10.1001/jama.2010.944

Lakoff, G., & Johnson, M. (1999). *Philosophy in the flesh.* New York, NY: Basic Books.

Lam, J. C., & Lee, M. K. (2006). Digital inclusiveness-Longitudinal study of internet adoption by older adults. *Journal of Management Information Systems, 22*(4), 177–206. doi:10.2753/MIS0742-1222220407

Langdon, P., Lewis, T., & Clarkson, J. (2007). The effects of prior experience on the use of consumer products. *Universal Access in the Information Society*, *6*, 179–191. doi:10.1007/s10209-007-0082-z

Lang, F. R., & Carstensen, L. L. (2002). Time counts: Future time perspective, goals, and social relationships. *Psychology and Aging*, *17*, 125–139. doi:10.1037/0882-7974.17.1.125

Larrabee, G. J., & Levin, H. S. (1986). Memory self-ratings and objective test performance in a normal elderly sample. *Journal of Clinical and Experimental Neuropsychology*, *8*(3), 275–284. doi:10.1080/01688638608401318

Lashley, K. S. (1950). In search of the engram. *Society of Experimental Biology Symposium*, *4*, 454–482.

Lashley, K. S. (1929). *Brain mechanisms and intelligence: A quantitative study of injuries to the brain*. Chicago, IL: University of Chicago Press. doi:10.1037/10017-000

Lashley, K. S. (1947). Structural variation in the nervous system in relation to behavior. *Psychological Review*, *54*, 325–334. doi:10.1037/h0063654

Laurenti, P. J., Burdette, J. H., Maldjian, J. A., & Wallace, M. T. (2006). Enhanced multisensory integration in older adults. *Neurobiology of Aging*, *27*, 1155–1163. doi:10.1016/j.neurobiolaging.2005.05.024

Laver, G. D., & Burke, D. M. (1993). Why do semantic priming effects increase in old age? A meta-analysis. *Psychology and Aging*, *8*, 34–43. doi:10.1037/0882-7974.8.1.34

LaVoie, D., & Light, L. L. (1994). Adult age differences in repetition priming: A meta-analysis. *Psychology and Aging*, *9*(4), 539–553. doi:10.1037/0882-7974.9.4.539

Lawhon, T., Ennis, D., & Lawhon, D. C. (1996). Senior adults and computers in the 1990s. *Educational Gerontology*, *22*(2), 193–201. doi:10.1080/0360127960220205

Lawton, M. P. (1990). Aging and performance on home tasks. *Human Factors*, *32*, 527–536.

Leape, L. L. (1994). Error in medicine. *Journal of the American Medical Association*, *272*(23), 1851–1857. doi:10.1001/jama.1994.03520230061039

Lee, B., Chen, Y., & Hewitt, L. (2011). Age differences in constraints encountered by seniors in their use of computers and the internet. *Computers in Human Behavior*, *27*, 1231–1237. doi:10.1016/j.chb.2011.01.003

Lee, J. Y., & Reigeluth, C. M. (2009). Heuristic task analysis on e-learning course development: A formative research study. *Asia Pacific Education Review*, *10*(2), 169–181. doi:10.1007/s12564-009-9016-1

Leonard, K. J. (2004). The role of patients in designing health information systems: The case of applying simulation techniques to design an electronic patient record (EPR) interface. *Health Care Management Science*, *7*, 275–284. doi:10.1007/s10729-004-7536-0

Lepa, J., & Tatnall, A. (2006). Using actor-network theory to understanding virtual community networks of older people using the Internet. *Journal of Business Systems. Governance and Ethics*, *1*(4), 1–14.

Levine, D. W., Simmons, B. P., Koris, M. J., Daltroy, L. H., Hohl, G. G., & Fossel, A. H. (1993). A self-administered questionnaire for the assessment of severity of symptoms and functional status in carpal tunnel syndrome. *Journal of Bone and Joint Surgery*, *75*(11), 1585–1592.

Lewis, M. L., Hobday, J. V., & Hepburn, K. W. (2010). Internet-based program for dementia caregivers. *American Journal of Alzheimer's Disease and Other Dementias*, *25*(8), 674–679. doi:10.1177/1533317510385812

Liao, Q., Chin, C., McKeever, S., Kopren, K., Morrow, D., & Davis, K. … Graumlich, J. (2011). Medtable: An EMR-based tool to support collaborative planning for medication use. In *Proceedings of the Human Factors and Ergonomics Society 55th Annual Meeting*. Santa Monica, CA: Human Factors & Ergonomics Society.

Light, L. L., & Albertson, S. A. (1989). Direct and indirect tests of memory for category exemplars in young and older adults. *Psychology and Aging*, *4*(4), 487–492. doi:10.1037/0882-7974.4.4.487

Light, L. L., Singh, A., & Capps, J. L. (1996). Dissociation of memory and awareness in young and older adults. *Journal of Clinical and Experimental Neuropsychology*, *8*(1), 62–74. doi:10.1080/01688638608401297

Lin, C., Wittevrongel, L., Moore, L., Beaty, B., & Ross, S. (2005). An internet-based patient-provider communication system: Randomized controlled trial. *Journal of Medical Internet Research, 7*(4), e47. doi:10.2196/jmir.7.4.e47

Lin, D.-Y. M. (2003). Hyptertext for the aged: Effects of text topologies. *Computers in Human Behavior, 19*, 201–209. doi:10.1016/S0747-5632(02)00045-6

Lober, W. B., Zierler, A., Herbaugh, S. E., Shinstrom, A., & Stolyar, E. H. Kim, et al. (2006). Barriers to the use of a personal health record by an elderly population. In *Proceedings of the American Medical Informatics Association Annual Meeting,* (pp. 514-518). Washington, DC: AMIA.

Locke, D. (1971). *Memory.* Garden City, NY: Anchor Books.

Longman Group Ltd. (1978). *Longman dictionary of contemporary English.* Bath, UK: Pitman Press.

Lorca, J., & Jadad, A. (2006). En busca del ebienestar: Una dimensión esencial de la esalud. [In search of e-well-being: An essential dimension of e-health]. *Revista Esalud, 2*(6), 1.

Low, R. (2010). Examining motivational factors in serious educational games. In Van Eck, R. (Ed.), *Interdisciplinary Models and Tools for Serious Games: Emerging Concepts and Future Directions* (pp. 103–124). Hershey, PA: IGI Global. doi:10.4018/978-1-61520-719-0.ch005

Low, R., Jin, P., & Sweller, J. (2011). Cognitive load theory, attentional processes and optimized learning outcomes in a digital environment. In Roda, C. (Ed.), *Human Attention in Digital Environments* (pp. 93–113). Cambridge, UK: Cambridge University Press. doi:10.1017/CBO9780511974519.004

Low, R., Jin, P., & Sweller, J. (2012). Digital assessment of the acquisition and utility of biologically secondary knowledge: Perspectives based on human cognitive architecture. In Mayrath, M., Clarke-Midura, J., & Robinson, D. (Eds.), *Technology-Based Assessments for 21st Century Skills: Theoretical and Practical Implications from Modern Research.* New York, NY: Springer-Verlag.

Low, R., & Sweller, J. (2005). The modality principle in multimedia learning. In Mayer, R. E. (Ed.), *The Cambridge Handbook of Multimedia Learning* (pp. 147–158). Cambridge, UK: Cambridge University Press.

Luchins, A. S. (1942). Mechanization in problem solving. *Psychological Monographs, 54.*

Luo, L., & Craik, F. I. M. (2008). Aging and memory: A cognitive approach. *Canadian Journal of Psychiatry, 53*(6), 346–353.

Luptak, M., Dailey, N., Juretic, M., Rupper, R., Hill, R., Hicken, B., & Bair, B. (2010). The care coordination home telehealth (CCHT) rural demonstration project: An innovative health care delivery approach for older veterans in remote geographical settings. *Rural and Remote Health, 10*, 1375.

Lusk, M. M., & Atkinson, R. K. (2007). Animated pedagogical agents: Does their degree of embodiment impact learning from static or animated worked examples? *Applied Cognitive Psychology, 21*, 747–764. doi:10.1002/acp.1347

Lustig, C., Hasher, L., & Tonev, S. T. (2006). Distraction as a determinant of processing speed. *Psychonomic Bulletin & Review, 13*, 619–625. doi:10.3758/BF03193972

Lynn, J., & Adamson, D. M. (2003). *Living well at the end of life: Adapting health care to serious chronic illness in old age.* Washington, DC: Rand Health.

Macfarlane, G. J., Hunt, I. M., & Silman, A. J. (2000). Role of mechanical and psychosocial factors in the onset of forearm pain: Prospective population based study. *British Medical Journal, 321*(7262), 676–679. doi:10.1136/bmj.321.7262.676

Machtinger, E., Wang, F., Chen, L., Rodríguez, M., Wu, S., & Schillinger, D. (2007). A visual medication schedule to improve anticoagulant care: A randomized controlled trial. *Joint Commission Journal on Quality and Patient Safety, 13*, 263–268.

Magnusson, L., Hanson, E., Birto, L., Berthold, H., Chambers, M., & Daly, T. (2002). Supporting family careers through the use of information and communication technology—The EU project ACTION. *International Journal of Nursing Studies, 39*, 369–381. doi:10.1016/S0020-7489(01)00034-7

Mahncke, H. W., Connor, B. B., Appelman, J., Ahsanuddin, O. N., Hardy, J. L., & Wood, R. A. … Merzenich, M. M. (2006). *Proceedings of the National Academy of Sciences USA, 103*(33), 12523-12528.

Makoul, G., Arntson, P., & Schofield, T. (1995). Health promotion in primary care: Physician-patient communication and decision making about prescription medications. *Social Science & Medicine, 41*, 1241–1254. doi:10.1016/0277-9536(95)00061-B

Mane, A. M., & Donchin, E. (1989). The space fortress game. *Acta Psychologica, 71*(1-3), 17–22. doi:10.1016/0001-6918(89)90003-6

Mangels, J. A., & Heinberg, A. (2006). Improved episodic integration through enactment: Implications for aging. *The Journal of General Psychology, 26*, 1170–1187.

Mann, W. C., Belchior, P., Tomita, M. R., & Kemp, B. J. (2005). Computer use by middle-aged and older adults with disabilities. *Technology and Disability, 17*, 1–9.

Martin, S. P., & Robinson, J. P. (2007). The income digital divide: Trends and predictions for levels of internet use. *Social Problems, 54*, 1–22. doi:10.1525/sp.2007.54.1.1

Mathis, A., Schunk, T., Erb, G., Namer, I. J., & Luthringer, R. (2009). The effect of aging on the inhibitory function in middle-aged subjects: A functional MRI study coupled with a color-matched Stroop task. *International Journal of Geriatric Psychiatry, 24*, 1062–1071. doi:10.1002/gps.2222

Mautone, P. D., & Mayer, R. E. (2001). Signaling as a cognitive guide in multimedia learning. *Journal of Educational Psychology, 93*, 377–389. doi:10.1037/0022-0663.93.2.377

Mayer, R. E. (2001). *Multimedia learning*. Cambridge, UK: Cambridge University Press.

Mayer, R. E. (2005). Cognitive theory of multimedia learning. In Mayer, R. E. (Ed.), *The Cambridge Handbook of Multimedia Learning* (pp. 31–48). Cambridge, UK: Cambridge University Press.

Mayer, R. E. (2009). *Multimedia learning* (2nd ed.). New York, NY: Cambridge University Press.

Mayer, R. E., & Anderson, R. (1992). The instructive animation: Helping students build connections between words and pictures in multimedia learning. *Journal of Educational Psychology, 84*, 444–452. doi:10.1037/0022-0663.84.4.444

Mayer, R. E., & Anderson, R. B. (1991). Animations need narrations: An experimental test of a dual-coding hypothesis. *Journal of Educational Psychology, 83*, 484–490. doi:10.1037/0022-0663.83.4.484

Mayer, R. E., Bove, W., Bryman, A., Mars, R., & Tapangco, L. (1996). When less is more: Meaningful learning from visual and verbal summaries of science textbook lessons. *Journal of Educational Psychology, 88*, 64–73. doi:10.1037/0022-0663.88.1.64

Mayer, R. E., Heiser, J., & Lonn, S. (2001). Cognitive constraints on multimedia learning: When presenting more material results in less understanding. *Journal of Educational Psychology, 93*(1), 187–198. doi:10.1037/0022-0663.93.1.187

Mayer, R. E., & Moreno, R. (1998). A split-attention effect in multimedia learning: Evidence for dual processing systems in working memory. *Journal of Educational Psychology, 90*, 312–320. doi:10.1037/0022-0663.90.2.312

Mayer, R. E., & Moreno, R. (2002). Aids to computer-based multimedia learning. *Learning and Instruction, 12*, 107–119. doi:10.1016/S0959-4752(01)00018-4

Mayer, R. E., & Moreno, R. (2003). Nine ways to reduce cognitive load in multimedia learning. *Educational Psychologist, 38*(1), 43–52. doi:10.1207/S15326985EP3801_6

Mayer, R. E., & Sims, V. K. (1994). For whom is a picture worth a thousand words? Extensions of a dual-coding theory of multimedia learning. *Journal of Educational Psychology, 86*, 389–401. doi:10.1037/0022-0663.86.3.389

Mayer, R. E., & Wittrock, M. C. (1996). Problem-solving transfer. In Berliner, D. C. (Ed.), *Handbook of Educational Psychology* (pp. 47–62). New York, NY: Macmillan Library Reference.

Mayr, U., & Kliegl, R. (1993). Sequential and coordinative complexity: Age-based processing limitations in figural transformations. *Journal of Experimental Psychology. Learning, Memory, and Cognition, 19,* 1297–1320. doi:10.1037/0278-7393.19.6.1297

Mayr, U., Kliegl, R., & Krampe, R. T. (1996). Sequential and coordinative processing dynamics in figural transformations across the life span. *Cognition, 59,* 61–90. doi:10.1016/0010-0277(95)00689-3

McBride, S. E., Beer, J. M., Mitzner, T. L., & Rogers, W. A. (2011). Challenges for home health care providers: A needs assessment. *Physical & Occupational Therapy in Geriatrics, 29,* 5–22. doi:10.3109/02703181.2011.552170

McConatha, D., McConatha, J. T., & Dermigny, R. (1994). The use of computer services to enhance the quality of life for long-term care residents. *The Gerontologist, 34*(4), 553–556. doi:10.1093/geront/34.4.553

McConatha, J. T., McConatha, D., Deaner, S. L., & Dermigny, R. (1995). A computer-based intervention for the education and therapy of institutionalized older adults. *Educational Gerontology, 21,* 129–138. doi:10.1080/0360127950210202

McCoy, S. L., Tun, P. A., Cox, L. C., Colangelo, M., Stewart, R. A., & Wingfield, A. (2005). Hearing loss and perceptual effort: Downstream effects on older adults' memory for speech. *The Quarterly Journal of Experimental Psychology Section A, 58*(1), 22–33. doi:10.1080/02724980443000151

McCreadie, C., & Tinker, A. (2005). The acceptability of assistive technology to older people. *Ageing and Society, 25,* 91–110. doi:10.1017/S0144686X0400248X

McDougall, G. J. (1999). Cognitive interventions among older adults. In Fitzpatrick, J. J. (Ed.), *Annual Review of Nursing Research* (*Vol. 17,* pp. 219–240). New York, NY: Springer.

McDowd, J. M., & Filion, D. L. (1995). Aging and negative priming in a location suppression task: The long and the short of it. *Psychology and Aging, 10,* 34–47. doi:10.1037/0882-7974.10.1.34

McDowd, J. M., & Oseas-Kreger, D. M. (1991). Aging, inhibitory processes, and negative priming. *The Journals of Gerontology. Series B, Psychological Sciences and Social Sciences, 46,* 340–345.

McHorney, C. A., Ware, J. J. E., & Raczek, A. E. (1993). The MOS 36-item short-form health survey (SF-36): II: Psychometric and clinical tests of validity in measuring physical and mental health constructs. *Medical Care, 31*(3), 247–263. doi:10.1097/00005650-199303000-00006

McLeod, C. M. (1991). Half a century of research on the Stroop effect: An integrative review. *Psychological Bulletin, 109,* 163–203. doi:10.1037/0033-2909.109.2.163

McMellon, C. A., & Schiffman, L. G. (2002). Cybersenior empowerment: How some older individuals are taking control of their lives. *Journal of Applied Gerontology, 21*(2), 157–175. doi:10.1177/07364802021002002

McNeill, N. M., Alibali, M. W., & Evans, J. L. (2000). The role of gesture in children's comprehension of spoken language: Now they need it, now they don't. *Journal of Nonverbal Behavior, 24,* 131–150. doi:10.1023/A:1006657929803

McNutt, R. A. (2004). Shared medical decision making: Problems, process, progress. *Journal of the American Medical Association, 292,* 2516–2518. doi:10.1001/jama.292.20.2516

McPherson, M., Smith-Lovin, L., & Brachears, M. (2006). Social isolation in America: Changes in core discussion networks over two decades. *American Sociological Review, 71,* 353–375. doi:10.1177/000312240607100301

Mead, B. J., & Dunbar, J. A. (2004). A virtual clinic: Assessment and monitoring for rural and remote areas. *Rural and Remote Health, 4,* 1–6.

Mead, S. E., Batsakes, P., Fisk, A. D., & Mykityshyn, A. (1999). Application of cognitive theory to training and design solutions for age-related computer use. *International Journal of Behavioral Development, 23*(3), 553–573. doi:10.1080/016502599383694

Mead, S., Lamson, N., & Rogers, W. A. (2002). Human factors guidelines for web site usability: Health-oriented websites for older adults. In Morrell, R. W. (Ed.), *Older Adults, Health Information, and the World Wide Web* (pp. 89–107). Hillsdale, NJ: Erlbaum.

Melenhorst, A. S., Rogers, W. A., & Bouwhuis, D. G. (2006). Older adults' motivated choice for technological innovation: Evidence for benefit-driven selectivity. *Psychology and Aging, 21*(1), 190–195. doi:10.1037/0882-7974.21.1.190

Melinger, A., & Kita, S. (2007). Conceptualisation load triggers gesture production. *Language and Cognitive Processes, 22*, 473–500. doi:10.1080/01690960600696916

Mellor, D., Firth, L., & Moore, K. (2008). Can the internet improve the well-being of the elderly? *Ageing International, 32*(1), 25–42. doi:10.1007/s12126-008-9006-3

Mikels, J. A., Löckenhoff, C. E., Maglio, S. J., Carstensen, L. L., Goldstein, M. K., & Garber, A. (2010). Following your heart or your head: Focusing on emotions versus information differentially influences the decisions of younger and older adults. *Journal of Experimental Psychology. Applied, 16*, 87–95. doi:10.1037/a0018500

Milgram, N. W. (2003). Cognitive experience and its effect on age-dependent cognitive decline in beagle dogs. *Neurochemical Research, 28*(11), 1677–1682. doi:10.1023/A:1026009005108

Miller, G. A. (1956). The magical number seven, plus or minus two: Some limits on our capacity for processing information. *Psychological Review, 63*, 81–97. doi:10.1037/h0043158

Miller, L. M. S., Stine-Morrow, E. A. L., Kirkorian, H. L., & Conroy, M. L. (2004). Adult age differences in knowledge-driven reading. *Journal of Educational Psychology, 96*(4), 811–821. doi:10.1037/0022-0663.96.4.811

Mistry, H. (2012). Systematic review of studies of the cost-effectiveness of telemedicine and telecare: Changes in the economic evidence over twenty years. *Journal of Telemedicine and Telecare, 18*(1), 1–6. doi:10.1258/jtt.2011.110505

Mitchell, B., & Begoray, D. (2010). Electronic personal health records that promote self-management in chronic illness. *Online Journal of Issues in Nursing, 15*(3).

Mitchell, D. B. (1989). How many memory systems? Evidence from aging. *Journal of Experimental Psychology. Learning, Memory, and Cognition, 15*(1), 31–49. doi:10.1037/0278-7393.15.1.31

Mitchell, D. B., Brown, A. S., & Murphy, D. R. (1990). Dissociations between procedural and episodic memory: Effects of time and aging. *Psychology and Aging, 5*(2), 264–276. doi:10.1037/0882-7974.5.2.264

Mittelman, M. S., Haley, W. E., Clay, O. J., & Rosh, D. L. (2006). Improving caregiver well-being delays nursing home placement of patients with Alzheimer disease. *Neurology, 67*, 1592–1599. doi:10.1212/01.wnl.0000242727.81172.91

Mitzner, T. L., Fausset, C. B., Boron, J. B., Adams, A. E., Dijkstra, K., Lee, C. C., & Fisk, A. D. (2008). Older adults' training preferences for learning to use technology. In *Proceedings of the Human Factors and Ergonomics Society 52nd Annual Meeting,* (pp. 2047-2051). Santa Monica, CA: Human Factors and Ergonomics Society.

Mitzner, T. L., Boron, J. B., Fausset, C. B., Adams, A. E., Charness, N., & Czaja, S. J. (2010). Older adults talk technology: Technology usage and attitudes. *Computers in Human Behavior, 26*(6), 1710–1721. doi:10.1016/j.chb.2010.06.020

Mohs, R. C., Ashman, T. A., Jantzen, K., Albert, M., Brandt, J., & Gordon, B. (1998). A study of the efficacy of a comprehensive memory enhancement program in healthy elderly persons. *Psychiatry Research, 77*(3), 183–195. doi:10.1016/S0165-1781(98)00003-1

Monin, J. K., Schulz, R., Martire, L. M., Jennings, J. R., Lingler, J. H., & Greenberg, M. S. (2010). Spouses' cardiovascular reactivity to their partners' suffering. *The Journals of Gerontology. Series B, Psychological Sciences and Social Sciences, 65B*(2), 195–201. doi:10.1093/geronb/gbp133

Monk, A. (2009). *Why do the older old have problems with new domestic technologies?* Paper presented at Towards a Truly Inclusive Digital Economy. London, UK. Retrieved from http://www.computing.dundee.ac.uk/projects/iden/londonevent.asp

Monk, A. F. (2009). Common ground in electronically mediated conversation. In Carroll, J. M. (Ed.), *Synthesis Lectures on Human-Centered Informatics* (pp. 1–50). New York, NY: Morgan & Claypool.

Moody, E. J. (2001). Internet use and its relationship to loneliness. *Cyberpsychology & Behavior*, *4*, 393–401. doi:10.1089/109493101300210303

Moon, Y. (1999). The effects of physical distance and response latency on persuasion in computer-mediated communication and human-computer communication. *Journal of Experimental Psychology. Applied*, *5*, 379–392. doi:10.1037/1076-898X.5.4.379

Moore, S., Sandman, C. A., & McGrady, K., & Kesslak. (2001). Memory training improves cognitive ability in patients with dementia. *Neuropsychological Rehabilitation*, *11*(3/4), 245–261. doi:10.1080/09602010042000222

Moreno, R., & Mayer, R. (1999). Cognitive principles of multimedia learning: The role of modality and contiguity. *Journal of Educational Psychology*, *91*, 358–368. doi:10.1037/0022-0663.91.2.358

Moreno, R., & Mayer, R. (2000). A coherence effect in multimedia learning: The case for minimizing irrelevant sounds in the design of multimedia messages. *Journal of Educational Psychology*, *92*, 117–125. doi:10.1037/0022-0663.92.1.117

Morrell, R. W., Mayhorn, C. B., & Bennett, J. (2000). A survey of world wide web use in middle-aged older adults. *Human Factors*, *42*(2), 175–182. doi:10.1518/001872000779656444

Morrow, D. G., & Durso, F. T. (2011). Patient safety research that works: Introduction to the special issue on human performance and health care. *Journal of Experimental Psychology. Applied*, *17*, 191–194. doi:10.1037/a0025244

Morrow, D. G., & Fischer, U. M. (2012). Communication in socio-technical systems. In Lee, J. D., & Kirlik, A. (Eds.), *Oxford Handbook of Cognitive Engineering*. Oxford, UK: Oxford University Press.

Morrow, D. G., & Leirer, V. (1999). Designing medication instructions for older adults. In Park, D., Morrell, R., & Shifren, K. (Eds.), *Aging Patients and Medical Treatment: An Information-Processing Perspective* (pp. 249–265). Mahwah, NJ: Erlbaum.

Morrow, D. G., Menard, W. E., Stine-Morrow, E. A. L., Teller, T., & Bryant, D. (2001). The influence of task factors and expertise on age differences in pilot communication. *Psychology and Aging*, *16*, 31–46. doi:10.1037/0882-7974.16.1.31

Morrow, D. G., & Rogers, W. A. (2008). Environmental support: An integrative framework. *Human Factors*, *50*, 589–613. doi:10.1518/001872008X312251

Morrow, D. G., & Wilson, E. A. H. (2010). Medication adherence among older adults: A systems perspective. In Cavanaugh, J. C., & Cavanaugh, C. K. (Eds.), *Aging in America: Psychological, Physical, and Social Issues* (*Vol. 2*). Westport, CT: Greenwood.

Moscovitch, M., Winocur, G., & McLachlan, D. (1986). Memory as assessed by recognition and reading time in normal and memory-impaired people with Alzheimer's disease and other neurological disorders. *Journal of Experimental Psychology. General*, *115*(4), 331–347. doi:10.1037/0096-3445.115.4.331

Mousavi, S. Y., Low, R., & Sweller, J. (1995). Reducing cognitive load by mixing auditory and visual presentation modes. *Journal of Educational Psychology*, *87*, 319–334. doi:10.1037/0022-0663.87.2.319

Mykityshyn, A. L., Fisk, A. D., & Rogers, W. A. (2002). Learning to use a home medical device: Mediating age-related differences with training. *Human Factors*, *44*, 354–364. doi:10.1518/0018720024497727

Nalwa, K., & Anand, A. P. (2003). Internet addiction in students: A cause of concern. *Cyberpsychology & Behavior*, *6*(6), 653–656. doi:10.1089/109493103322725441

National Highway and Traffic Safety Administration. (2007). *Traffic safety facts: Older population.* Retrieved from http://www.nhtsa.dot.gov/portal/site/nhtsa/menuitem.31176b9b03647a189ca8e410dba046a0/

National Highway and Traffic Safety Administration. (2009a). *Traffic safety facts: Identifying situations associated with older drivers' crashes.* Retrieved from http://www.nhtsa.gov/DOT/NHTSA/Communication%20&%20Consumer%20Information/Traffic%20Tech%20Publications/Associated%20Files/tt380.pdf

National Highway and Traffic Safety Administration. (2009b). *Traffic safety facts research note: Fatal crashes involving young drivers.* Retrieved from http://www-nrd.nhtsa.dot.gov/Pubs/811218.PDF

National Institute on Aging and National Library of Medicine. (2001). *Making your web site senior friendly: A checklist.* Washington, DC: US Government Printing Office.

National Institute on Aging. (2007). *Quick tips for a senior friendly computer classroom.* Washington, DC: US Government Printing Office.

Naveh- Benjamin, M. (2000). Adult age differences in memory performance: Tests of an associative deficit hypothesis. *Journal of Experimental Psychology. Learning, Memory, and Cognition, 25,* 1179–1187.

Naveh-Benjamin, M., Guez, J., Kilb, A., & Reedy, S. (2004). The associative memory deficit of older adults: Further support using face-name associations. *Psychology and Aging, 19,* 541–546. doi:10.1037/0882-7974.19.3.541

Naveh-Benjamin, M., Hussain, Z., Guez, J., & Bar-On, M. (2003). Adult age differences in episodic memory: Further support for an associative-deficit hypothesis. *Journal of Experimental Psychology. Learning, Memory, and Cognition, 29,* 826–837. doi:10.1037/0278-7393.29.5.826

Neuhauser, L., & Kreps, G. L. (2003). Rethinking communication in the e-health era. *Journal of Health Psychology, 8,* 7–23. doi:10.1177/1359105303008001426

Newell, A., & Rosenbloom, P. S. (1981). Mechanisms of skill acquisition and the law of practice. In Anderson, J. R. (Ed.), *Cognitive Skills and Their Acquisition* (pp. 1–55). Hillsdale, NJ: Erlbaum.

Nguyen, H. Q., Cuenco, D., Wolpin, S., Benditt, J., & Carrieri-Kohlman, V. (2007). Methodological considerations in evaluating ehealth interventions. *Canadian Journal of Nursing Research, 39*(1), 116–134.

Niederehe, G., & Yoder, C. (1989). Metamemory perceptions in depressions of young and older adults. *The Journal of Nervous and Mental Disease, 177*(1), 4–14. doi:10.1097/00005053-198901000-00002

Nielsen-Bohlman, L., Panzer, A. M., & Kindig, D. A. (2004). *Health literacy: A prescription to end confusion.* Washington, DC: The National Academies Press.

Nilsson, L. G. (2000). Remembering actions and words. In Tulving, E., & Craik, F. I. M. (Eds.), *The Oxford Handbook of Memory* (pp. 137–148). Oxford, UK: Oxford University Press.

Nilsson, L.-G., Bäckman, L., Erngrund, K., Nyberg, L., Adolfsson, R., & Bucht, G. (1997). The Betula prospective cohort study: Memory, health, and aging. *Neuropsychology, Development, and Cognition. Section B, Aging, Neuropsychology and Cognition, 4*(1), 1–32. doi:10.1080/13825589708256633

Nissen, M. J., & Bullemer, P. (1987). Attentional requirements of learning: Evidence from performance measures. *Cognitive Psychology, 19,* 1–32. doi:10.1016/0010-0285(87)90002-8

Nissen, M. J., Knopman, D. S., & Schacter, D. L. (1987). Neurochemical dissociation of memory systems. *Neurology, 37*(5), 789–784. doi:10.1212/WNL.37.5.789

Noordman, J., Verhaak, P., van Beljouw, I., & van Dulmen, S. (2010). Consulting room computers and their effect on general practitioner-patient communication. *Family Practice, 27*(6), 644–651. doi:10.1093/fampra/cmq058

Norman, D. A. (2002). *The design of everyday things.* New York, NY: Basic Books.

Norris, S. L. (2002). The effectiveness of disease and case management for people with diabetes: A systematic review. *American Journal of Preventive Medicine, 22,* 15–38. doi:10.1016/S0749-3797(02)00423-3

O'Brien, M. A. (2010). *Understanding human-technology interactions: The role of prior experience and age.* Unpublished Doctoral Dissertation. Atlanta, GA: Georgia Institute of Technology.

O'Brien, M. A., Weger, K., DeFour, M. E., & Reeves, S. M. (2011). Examining the role of age and experience on use of knowledge in the world for everyday technology interactions. In *Proceedings of the Human Factors and Ergonomics Society 55th Annual Meeting*, (pp 177-181). Santa Monica, CA: Human Factors and Ergonomics Society.

O'Connor, J., & Johanson, J. (2000). Use of the web for medical information by a gastroenterology clinic population. *Journal of the American Medical Association, 284*, 1962–1964. doi:10.1001/jama.284.15.1962

O'Hanlon, S. (2010). *E-health interventions for older people.* Paper presented at the meeting of the European Union Geriatric Medicine Society. Dublin, Ireland.

O'Hanlon, S. (2011). *The dangers of e-health.* Paper presented at the meeting of HEALTHINF. Rome, Italy.

Oberauer, K., & Kliegl, R. (2001). Beyond resources: Formal models of complexity effects and age differences in working memory. *The European Journal of Cognitive Psychology, 13*, 187–215. doi:10.1080/09541440042000278

Obermeier, C., Holle, H., & Gunter, T. C. (2011). What iconic gesture fragments reveal about gesture–speech integration: When synchrony is lost, memory can help. *Journal of Cognitive Neuroscience, 23*, 1648–1663. doi:10.1162/jocn.2010.21498

Oerlemans, W. G. M., Bakker, A. B., & Veenhoven, R. (2011). Finding the key to happy aging: a day reconstruction study of happiness. *The Journals of Gerontology. Series B, Psychological Sciences and Social Sciences, 66*(6), 665–674. doi:10.1093/geronb/gbr040

Oh, H., Rizo, C., Enkin, M., & Jadad, A. (2005). What is ehealth (3): A systematic review of published definitions. *Journal of Medical Internet Research, 7*(1), e1. doi:10.2196/jmir.7.1.e1

Old, S. R., & Naveh-Benjamin, M. (2008). Age-related changes in memory: Experimental approaches. In Hofer, S. M., & Alwin, D. F. (Eds.), *Handbook of Cognitive Aging: Interdisciplinary Perspectives* (pp. 151–167). Los Angeles, CA: Sage Publications. doi:10.4135/9781412976589.n9

Old, S. R., & Naveh-Benjamin, M. (2008). Differential effects of age on item and associative measures of memory: A meta-analysis. *Psychology and Aging, 23*, 104–118. doi:10.1037/0882-7974.23.1.104

Olson, G. M., & Olson, J. S. (2008). Computer-support cooperative work. In Durso, F. T., Nickerson, R. S., Dumais, S. T., Lewandowsky, S., & Perfect, T. J. (Eds.), *Handbook of Applied Cognition* (pp. 497–526). Chichester, UK: Wiley.

Olson, K. E., O'Brien, M. A., Rogers, W. A., & Charness, N. (2011). Diffusion of technology for younger and older adults. *Ageing International, 36*(1), 123–145. doi:10.1007/s12126-010-9077-9

Opalinski, L. (2001). Older adults and the digital divide: Assessing results of a web-based survey. *Journal of Technology in Human Services, 18*(3-4), 203–221. doi:10.1300/J017v18n03_13

Opitz, B. (2010). Context-dependent repetition effects on recognition memory. *Brain and Cognition, 73*(2), 110–118. doi:10.1016/j.bandc.2010.04.003

Or, C. K. L., Karsh, B.-T., Severtson, D. J., Burke, L. J., Brown, R. L., & Brennan, P. F. (2010). Factors affecting home care pateints' acceptance of a web-based interactive self-management technology. *Journal of the American Medical Informatics Association, 18*, 51–59. doi:10.1136/jamia.2010.007336

Ordonez, T. N., Yassuda, M. S., & Cachioni, M. (2011). Elderly online: Effects of a digital inclusion program in cognitive performance. *Archives of Gerontology and Geriatrics, 53*(2), 216–219. doi:10.1016/j.archger.2010.11.007

Ory, M. G., Hoffman, R. R., Yee, J. L., Tennstedt, S., & Schulz, R. (1999). Prevalence and impact of caregiving: A detailed comparison between dementia and non-dementia caregivers. *The Gerontologist, 39*, 177–185. doi:10.1093/geront/39.2.177

Oswald, W. D., Ruppreccht, R., Gunzelmann, T., & Tritt, K. (1996). The SIMA-project: Effects of 1 year cognitive and psychomotor training on cognitive abilities of the elderly. *Behavioural Brain Research, 78*(1), 67–72. doi:10.1016/0166-4328(95)00219-7

Ouwehand, K., van Gog, T., & Paas, F. (2012). The use of gesturing to facilitate older adults' learning from computer-based dynamic visualizations. In Zheng, R., Hill, R., & Gardner, M. (Eds.), *Engaging Older Adults with Modern Technology: Internet Use and Information.* Hershey, PA: IGI Global.

Ownby, R. (2006). Medication adherence and cognition: Medical, personal and economic factors influence level of adherence in older adults. *Geriatrics, 61*(2), 30–35.

Owsley, C., Ball, K. K., Sloane, M. E., Roenker, D. L., & Bruni, J. R. (1991). Visual/cognitive correlates of vehicle accidents in older drivers. *Psychology and Aging, 6*, 403–415. doi:10.1037/0882-7974.6.3.403

Paasche-Orlow, M. K., Schillinger, D., Greene, S. M., & Wagner, E. H. (2006). How health care systems can begin to address the challenge of limited literacy. *Journal of General Internal Medicine, 21*, 884–887. doi:10.1111/j.1525-1497.2006.00544.x

Paas, F., Camp, G., & Rikers, R. (2001). Instructional compensation for age-related cognitive declines: Effects of goal specificity in maze learning. *Journal of Educational Psychology, 93*, 181–186. doi:10.1037/0022-0663.93.1.181

Paas, F., Renkl, A., & Sweller, J. (2003). Cognitive load theory and instructional design: Recent developments. *Educational Psychologist, 38*, 1–4. doi:10.1207/S15326985EP3801_1

Paas, F., & Sweller, J. (2011). An evolutionary upgrade of cognitive load theory: Using the human motor system and collaboration to support the learning of complex cognitive tasks. *Educational Psychology Review, 24*(1), 1–19.

Paas, F., & Van Gog, T. (2006). Optimizing worked example instruction: Different ways to increase germane cognitive load. *Learning and Instruction, 16*, 87–91. doi:10.1016/j.learninstruc.2006.02.004

Paas, F., & Van Merriënboer, J. J. G. (1994). Variability of worked examples and transfer of geometrical problem-solving skills: A cognitive-load approach. *Journal of Educational Psychology, 86*, 122–133. doi:10.1037/0022-0663.86.1.122

Paivio, A. (1963). Learning of adjective-noun paired associates as a function of adjective-noun order and noun abstractness. *Canadian Journal of Psychology, 17*, 370–379. doi:10.1037/h0083277

Paivio, A. (1965). Abstractness, imagery and meaningfulness in paired associate learning. *Journal of Verbal Learning and Verbal Behavior, 4*, 32–38. doi:10.1016/S0022-5371(65)80064-0

Paivio, A. (1986). *Mental representations: A dual coding approach.* Oxford, UK: Oxford University Press.

Pak, R., & McLaughlin, A. C. (2010). *Designing displays for older adults.* Boca Raton, FL: CRC Press.

Park, D. C., Lautenschlager, G., Hedden, T., Davidson, N. S., Smith, A. D., & Smith, P. K. (2002). Models of visuospatial and verbal memory across the adult life span. *Psychology and Aging, 17*, 299–320. doi:10.1037/0882-7974.17.2.299

Park, D. C., Lautenschlager, G., Hedden, T., Davison, N., Smith, A. D., & Smith, P. K. (2002). Models of visuospatial and verbal memory across the adult life span. *Psychology and Aging, 17*(2), 299–320. doi:10.1037/0882-7974.17.2.299

Park, D. C., Smith, A. D., & Cavanaugh, J. C. (1990). Metamemories of memory researchers. *Memory & Cognition, 18*(3), 321–327. doi:10.3758/BF03213885

Pavot, W., Diener, E., Randall Colvin, C. R., & Sandvik, E. (1991). Further validation of the satisfaction with life scale: Evidence for the cross-method convergence of well-being measures. *Journal of Personality Assessment, 57*(149), 167–176.

Payette, H., Gueye, N. D. R., Gaudreau, P., Morais, J. A., Shatenstein, B., & Gray-Donald, K. (2011). Trajectories of physical function decline and psychological functioning: The Québec longitudinal study on nutrition and successful aging (NuAge). *The Journals of Gerontology. Series B, Psychological Sciences and Social Sciences, 66B*(S1), i82–i90. doi:10.1093/geronb/gbq085

Peacock, S. E., & Kunemund, H. (2007). Senior citizens and internet technology: Reasons and correlates of access versus non-access in a European comparative perspective. *European Journal of Ageing, 4*, 191–200. doi:10.1007/s10433-007-0067-z

Pearlin, L. I., & Schooler, C. (1978). The structure of coping. *Journal of Health and Social Behavior, 19*(1), 2–21. doi:10.2307/2136319

Peters, K., Niebling, M., Green, T., Slimmer, C., & Schumacher, R. (2009). *Consumers compare online personal health record (PHR) applications.* Retrieved on August 10, 2010 from http://www.usercentric.com/publications/2009/02/02/google-health-vs-microsoft-healthvault-consumers-compare-online-personal-hea

Peters, E., Dieckmann, N. F., Västfjäll, D., Mertz, C. K., Slovic, P., & Hibbard, J. H. (2009). Bringing meaning to numbers: The impact of evaluative categories on decisions. *Journal of Experimental Psychology. Applied, 15*, 213–227. doi:10.1037/a0016978

Petersen, R. C., Smith, G. E., Waring, S. C., Ivnik, R. J., Kokmen, E., & Tangelos, E. G. (1997). Aging, memory, and mild cognitive impairment. *International Psychogeriatrics, 9*(1), 65–69. doi:10.1017/S1041610297004717

Peterson, L., & Peterson, M. J. (1959). Short-term retention of individual verbal items. *Journal of Experimental Psychology, 58*, 193–198. doi:10.1037/h0049234

Pew Internet and American Life Project. (2011). *Mind the gap: Peer-to-peer healthcare.* Retrieved on August 25, 2011 from http://pewinternet.org/Reports/2011/20-Mind-the-Gap.aspx

Pfeiffer, E. (1975). A short portable mental status questionnaire for the assessment of organic brain deficit in elderly patients. *Journal of the American Geriatrics Society, 23*(10), 433–441.

Piccinin, A. M., Muniz, G., Matthews, F. E., & Johansson, B. (2011). Terminal decline from within- and between-person perspectives, accounting for incident dementia. *The Journals of Gerontology. Series B, Psychological Sciences and Social Sciences, 66B*(4), 391–401. doi:10.1093/geronb/gbr010

Piccinin, A. M., Muniz, G., Sparks, C., & Bontempo, D. E. (2011). An evaluation of analytical approaches for understanding change in cognition in the context of aging and health. *The Journals of Gerontology. Series B, Psychological Sciences and Social Sciences, 66B*(S1), i36–i49. doi:10.1093/geronb/gbr038

Ping, R., & Goldin-Meadow, S. (2008). Hands in the air: Using ungrounded iconic gestures to teach children conservation of quantity. *Developmental Psychology, 44*, 1277–1287. doi:10.1037/0012-1649.44.5.1277

Ping, R., & Goldin-Meadow, S. (2010). Gesturing saves cognitive resources when talking about nonpresent objects. *Cognitive Science, 34*, 602–619. doi:10.1111/j.1551-6709.2010.01102.x

Polson, P. G., & Lewis, C. H. (1990). Theory-based design for easily learned interfaces. *Human-Computer Interaction, 5*, 191–220. doi:10.1207/s15327051hci0502&3_3

Poon, L. W. (1985). Differences in human memory with aging: Nature, causes, and clinical interpretations. In Birren, J. E., & Schaie, K. W. (Eds.), *Handbook of the Psychology of Aging* (2nd ed., pp. 427–462). New York, NY: Van Nostrand Reinhold.

Prencipe, M., Casini, A. R., Ferretti, C., & Lattanzio, M. T. (1996). Prevalence of dementia in an elderly rural population: Effects of age, sex, and education. *Journal of Neurology, Neurosurgery, and Psychiatry, 60*(6), 628–633. doi:10.1136/jnnp.60.6.628

Radvansky, G. A., & Dijkstra, K. (2007). Aging and situation model processing. *Psychonomic Bulletin & Review, 14*, 1027–1042. doi:10.3758/BF03193088

Rainie, L., Purcell, K., & Smith, A. (2011). *Social side of the internet survey.* Retrieved June, 25th, 2011 from http://www.pewinternet.org/Shared-Content/Data-Sets/2010/December-2010--Social-Side-of-the-Internet.aspx

Reason, J. T. (1990). *Human error.* Cambridge, UK: Cambridge University Press.

Rebok, G. W., Carlson, M. C., & Langbaum, J. B. S. (2007). Training and maintaining memory abilities in healthy older adults: Traditional and novel approaches. *Journals of Gerontology: Series B, 62B*, 53–61. doi:10.1093/geronb/62.special_issue_1.53

Reed, D. J., & Monk, A. (2004). Using familiar technologies in unfamiliar ways and learning from the old about the new. *Universal Access in the Information Society, 3*, 114–121. doi:10.1007/s10209-004-0090-1

Reisenwitz, T., Iyer, R., Kuhlmeier, D. B., & Eastman, J. K. (2007). The elderly's Internet usage: An updated look. *Journal of Consumer Marketing*, *24*(7), 406–418. doi:10.1108/07363760710834825

Rendell, P. G., & Craik, F. I. M. (2000). Virtual week and actual week: Age-related differences in prospective memory. *Applied Cognitive Psychology*, *14*, S43–S62. doi:10.1002/acp.770

Renkl, A. (2005). The worked-out examples principle in multimedia learning. In Mayer, R. E. (Ed.), *The Cambridge Handbook of Multimedia Learning* (pp. 229–245). Cambridge, UK: Cambridge University Press.

Rhodes, M. G., & Kelley, C. M. (2005). Executive processes, memory accuracy, and memory monitoring: An aging and individual difference analysis. *Journal of Memory and Language*, *52*(4), 578–594. doi:10.1016/j.jml.2005.01.014

Richardson, D. C., Dale, R., & Kirkham, N. Z. (2007). The art of conversation is coordination: Common ground and the coupling of eye movements during dialogue. *Psychological Science*, *18*(5), 407–413. doi:10.1111/j.1467-9280.2007.01914.x

Riddle, D. R. (Ed.). (2007). *Brain aging: Models, methods, and mechanisms*. Boca Raton, FL: CRC Press.

Rizolatti, G., Fadiga, L., Matelli, M., Bettinardi, V., Paulesu, E., & Perani, D. (1996). Localization of grasp representations in humans by PET: 1 observation versus execution. *Experimental Brain Research*, *111*, 246–252. doi:10.1007/BF00227301

Rockoff, M. L., Czaja, S., Kahn, J. S., Miller, N., & Szerencsy, A. (2010). Spanning the digital divide: Personal health records and patient portals for the underserved. In *Proceedings of the American Medical Informatics Association Annual Meeting,* (pp. 1400-1402). Washington, DC: AMIA.

Roediger, H. L., Rajaram, S., & Srinivas, K. (1990). Specifying criteria for postulating memory systems. *Annals of the New York Academy of Sciences*, *608*, 572–595. doi:10.1111/j.1749-6632.1990.tb48910.x

Rogers, W. A., Essa, I. A., & Fisk, A. D. (2007). Designing a technology coach. *Ergonomics in Design*, *15*, 17–23. doi:10.1177/106480460701500303

Rogers, W. A., & Fisk, A. D. (2000). Human factors, applied cognition and aging. In Craik, F. I. M., & Salthouse, T. A. (Eds.), *The Handbook of Aging and Cognition* (pp. 559–591). Mahwah, NJ: Erlbaum.

Rogers, W. A., Fisk, A. D., Mead, S. E., Walker, N., & Cabrera, E. F. (1996). Training older adults to use automatic teller machines. *Human Factors*, *38*, 425–433. doi:10.1518/001872096778701935

Rogers, W. A., Meyer, B., Walker, N., & Fisk, A. D. (1998). Functional limitations to daily living tasks in the aged: A focus group analysis. *Human Factors*, *40*, 111–125. doi:10.1518/001872098779480613

Rogers, W. A., O'Brien, M. A., & Fisk, A. D. (2012). Cognitive engineering to support successful aging. In Lee, J. D., & Kirlik, A. (Eds.), *Oxford Handbook of Cognitive Engineering*. Oxford, UK: Oxford University Press.

Rollins, G. (2003). Adverse drug events among elderly outpatients are common and preventable. *Report on Medical Guidelines & Outcomes Research, 14*, 6–7.

Rönnlund, M., Nyberg, L., Bäckman, L., & Nilsson, L.-G. (2005). Stability, growth, and decline in adult life span development of declarative memory: Cross-sectional and longitudinal data from a population-based study. *Psychology and Aging*, *20*(1), 3–18. doi:10.1037/0882-7974.20.1.3

Rosen, L. D., & Weil, M. M. (1995). Computer availability, computer experience and technophobia among public school teachers. *Computers in Human Behavior*, *11*(1), 9–31. doi:10.1016/0747-5632(94)00018-D

Rosenthal, R. (2008). Older computer-literate women: Their motivations, obstacles, and paths to success. *Educational Gerontology*, *34*, 610–626. doi:10.1080/03601270801949427

Rossi, M. C., Perozzi, C., Consorti, C., Almonti, K. T., Foglini, K. P., & Giostra, N. (2010). An interactive diary for diet management (DAI): A new telemedicine system able to promote body weight reduction, nutritional education, and consumption of fresh local produce. *Diabetes Technology & Therapeutics*, *12*, 641–647. doi:10.1089/dia.2010.0025

Roth, W. M. (2001). Gestures: Their role in teaching and learning. *Review of Educational Research, 71,* 365–392. doi:10.3102/00346543071003365

Rowe, J. W., & Kahn, R. L. (1997). Successful aging. *The Gerontologist, 37*(4), 433–440. doi:10.1093/geront/37.4.433

Salovaara, A., Lehmuskallio, A., Hedman, L., Valkonen, P., & Näsänen, J. (2010). Information technologies and transitions in the lives of 55-65-year-olds: The case of colliding life interests. *International Journal of Human-Computer Studies, 68*(11), 803–821. doi:10.1016/j.ijhcs.2010.06.007

Salthouse, T. A. (1991). Mediation of adult age differences in cognition by reductions in working memory and speed of processing. *Psychological Science, 2*(3), 179–183. doi:10.1111/j.1467-9280.1991.tb00127.x

Salthouse, T. A. (1992). Why do adult age differences increase with task complexity? *Developmental Psychology, 28,* 905–918. doi:10.1037/0012-1649.28.5.905

Salthouse, T. A. (1994). The aging of working memory. *Neuropsychology, 8,* 535–543. doi:10.1037/0894-4105.8.4.535

Salthouse, T. A. (1996). The processing-speed theory of adult age differences in cognition. *Psychological Review, 103,* 403–428. doi:10.1037/0033-295X.103.3.403

Salthouse, T. A. (2009). When does age-related cognitive decline begin? *Neurobiology of Aging, 30,* 507–514. doi:10.1016/j.neurobiolaging.2008.09.023

Salthouse, T. A., & Babcock, R. L. (1991). Decomposing adult age differences in working memory. *Developmental Psychology, 27,* 763–776. doi:10.1037/0012-1649.27.5.763

Sampson, E. L., Dover, D., Mandell, M., Pant, A., & Blanchard, M. R. (2007). Personal identification (PIN) numbers: A new cause of financial exclusion in older people. *International Journal of Geriatric Psychiatry, 22*(5), 492–493. doi:10.1002/gps.1708

Sarkar, U., Karter, A. J., Liu, J. Y., Adler, N. E., Nguyen, R., López, A., & Schillinger, D. (2010). The literacy divide: Health literacy and the use of an internet-based patient portal in an integrated health system—Results from the diabetes study of Northern California (DISTANCE). *Journal of Health Communication, 15*(2), 183–196. doi:10.1080/10810730.2010.499988

Sarkar, U., Karter, A. J., Liu, J. Y., Adler, N. E., Nguyen, R., López, A., & Schillinger, D. (2011). Social disparities in internet patient portal use in diabetes: Evidence that the digital divide extends beyond access. *Journal of the American Informatics Association, 18,* 318–321. doi:10.1136/jamia.2010.006015

Satz, P. (1993). Brain reserve capacity on symptom onset after brain injury: A formulation and review of evidence for threshold theory. *Neuropsychology, 7*(3), 273–295. doi:10.1037/0894-4105.7.3.273

Saunders, E. J. (2004). Maximizing computer use among the elderly in rural senior centers. *Educational Gerontology, 30,* 573–585. doi:10.1080/03601270490466967

Schäfer, G. (2008). *Europe in figures - Eurostat statistical yearbook 2008.* Luxembourg, Luxembourg: Eurostat.

Schaie, K. W. (1994). The course of adult intellectual development. *The American Psychologist, 49*(4), 304–313. doi:10.1037/0003-066X.49.4.304

Schaie, K. W. (1996). *Intellectual development in adulthood: The Seattle longitudinal study.* Cambridge, UK: Cambridge University Press.

Schaie, K. W., & Willis, S. L. (1986). Can decline in adult intellectual functioning be reversed? *Developmental Psychobiology, 22*(2), 223–232.

Schaie, K. W., & Willis, S. L. (2002). *Adult development and aging* (5th ed.). New York, NY: Prentice-Hall.

Schaie, K. W., Willis, S. L., Hertzog, C., & Schulenberg, J. E. (1987). Effects of cognitive training on primary mental ability structure. *Psychology and Aging, 2*(3), 233–242. doi:10.1037/0882-7974.2.3.233

Schmand, B., Smit, J. H., Geerlings, M. I., & Lindeboom, J. (1997b). The effects of intelligence and education on the development of dementia: A test of the brain reserve hypothesis. *Psychological Medicine, 27,* 1337–1344. doi:10.1017/S0033291797005461

Schmiedek, F., Bauer, C., Lovden, M., Brose, A., & Lindenberger, U. (2010). Cognitive enrichment in old age: Web-based training programs. *GeroPsych: The Journal of Gerontopsychology and Geriatric Psychiatry, 23*(2), 59–67. doi:10.1024/1662-9647/a000013

Schneider, B., & Pichora-Fuller, M. (2000). Implications of perceptual deterioration for cognitive ageing research. In Craik, F. I. M., & Salthouse, T. A. (Eds.), *The Handbook of Aging and Cognition* (pp. 155–219). Mahwah, NJ: Lawrence Erlbaum.

Schnittker, J. (2007). Look at all the lonely people: Age and social psychology of social support. *Journal of Aging and Health, 19*, 659–682. doi:10.1177/0898264307301178

Schroeter, M. L., Zysset, S., Wahl, M., & Von Cramon, D. Y. (2004). Prefrontal activation due to Stroop interference increases during development: An event-related fNIRS study. *NeuroImage, 23*, 1317–1325. doi:10.1016/j.neuroimage.2004.08.001

Schugens, M. M., Daum, I., Spindler, M., & Birbaumer, N. (1997). Differential effects of aging on explicit and implicit memory. *Neuropsychology, Development, and Cognition. Section B, Aging, Neuropsychology and Cognition, 4*(1), 33–44. doi:10.1080/13825589708256634

Schulz, R., Lustig, A., Handler, S., & Martire, L. M. (2002). Technology-based caregiver intervention research: Current status and future directions. *Gerontechnology (Valkenswaard), 2*(1), 15–47. doi:10.4017/gt.2002.02.01.003.00

Schulz, R., O'Brien, A. T., Bookwala, J., & Fleissner, K. (1995). Psychiatric and physical morbidity effects of Alzheimer's disease caregiving: Prevalence, correlates, and causes. *The Gerontologist, 35*, 771–791. doi:10.1093/geront/35.6.771

Schulz, R., O'Brien, A., Czaja, S., Ory, M., Norris, R., & Martire, L. M. (2002). Dementia caregiver intervention research: In search of clinical significance. *The Gerontologist, 42*, 589–602. doi:10.1093/geront/42.5.589

Schwarzer, R., & Jerusalem, M. (1995). Generalized self-efficacy scale. In Weinman, J., Wright, S., & Johnston, M. (Eds.), *Measures in Health Psychology: A User's Portfolio: Causal and Control Beliefs* (pp. 35–37). Windsor, UK: NFER-NELSON.

Scogin, F., & Bienias, J. L. (1988). A three year follow-up of older adult participants in a memory-skills training program. *Psychology and Aging, 3*(4), 334–337. doi:10.1037/0882-7974.3.4.334

Scogin, F., Storandt, M., & Lott, L. (1985). Memory-skills training, memory complaints, and depression in older age. *Journal of Gerontology, 40*(5), 562–568.

Seeman, T. E., Miller-Martinez, D. M., Stein Merkin, S., Lachman, M. E., Tun, P. A., & Karlamangla, A. S. (2011). Histories of social engagement and adult cognition: Midlife in the US study. *The Journals of Gerontology. Series B, Psychological Sciences and Social Sciences, 66B*(S1), i141–i152. doi:10.1093/geronb/gbq091

Selwyn, N. (2004). The information aged: A qualitative study of older adults' use of information and communications technology. *Journal of Aging Studies, 18*, 369–384. doi:10.1016/j.jaging.2004.06.008

Selwyn, N., Gorard, S., Furlong, J., & Madden, L. (2003). Older adults' use of information and communications technology in everyday life. *Ageing and Society, 23*(5), 561–571. doi:10.1017/S0144686X03001302

Sengpiel, M., & Wandke, H. (2010). Compensating the effects of age differences in computer literacy on the use of ticket vending machines through minimal video instruction. *Occupational Ergonomics, 9*(2), 87–98.

Serrano Baquero, D., & Rogers, W. A. (2010). *Knowledge and intuitive interface design: Developing a knowledge taxonomy.* Atlanta, GA: Georgia Institute of Technology.

Shah, A. K., & Oppenheimer, D. M. (2008). Heuristics made easy: An effort-reduction framework. *Psychological Bulletin, 134*(2), 207–222. doi:10.1037/0033-2909.134.2.207

Shapiro, L. (2007). The embodied cognition research programme. *Philosophy Compass, 2*, 338–346. doi:10.1111/j.1747-9991.2007.00064.x

Sharit, J., Czaja, S. J., Hernandez, M., Yang, Y., Perdomo, D., & Lewis, J. (2004). The evaluation of performance by older persons on a simulated telecommuting task. *Journal of Gerontology, 59B*, 305–316.

Sharit, J., Hernandez, M., Czaja, S. J., & Pirolli, P. (2008). Investigating the roles of knowledge and cognitive abilities in older adult information seeking on the web. *ACM Transactions on Computer-Human Interaction, 15*, 1–25. doi:10.1145/1352782.1352785

Sheikh, J. I., Hill, R. D., & Yesavage, J. A. (1986). Long-term efficacy of cognitive training for age-associated memory impairment: A six-month follow-up study. *Developmental Neuropsychology, 2*(4), 413–421. doi:10.1080/87565648609540358

Sheikh, J. K., & Yesavage, J. A. (1986). Geriatric depression scale (GDS): Recent evidence and development of a shorter version. In Brink, T. L. (Ed.), *Clinical Gerontology: A Guide to Assessment and Intervention* (pp. 165–173). New York, NY: Haworth Press.

Sherer, M. (1996). The impact of using personal computers on the lives of nursing home residents. *Physical & Occupational Therapy in Geriatrics, 14*(2), 13–31. doi:10.1080/J148v14n02_02

Shewan, J., Tetley, J., Clarke, A., & Hanson, E. (2000). *Evaluation of the outcome of the project, the telematics applications and technical system in relation to user friendliness, user acceptance and quality and function of the technology which have been adapted, developed and used*. Unpublished EU Project Report DE3001. Brussels, Belgium: EU.

Shyham Sundar, S., Oeldorf-Hirsch, A., Nussbaum, J. F., & Behr, R. A. (2011). *Retirees on Facebook: Can online social networking enhance their health and wellness?* Paper presented at CHI 2011. Vancouver, Canada.

Simon, H. A. (1990). Invariants of human behavior. *Annual Review of Psychology, 41*, 1–19. doi:10.1146/annurev.ps.41.020190.000245

Simons, J. S., Schölvinck, M. L., Gilbert, S. J., Frith, C. D., & Burgess, P. W. (2006). Differential components of prospective memory? Evidence from fMRI. *Neuropsychologia, 44*, 1388–1397. doi:10.1016/j.neuropsychologia.2006.01.005

Singley, M. K., & Anderson, J. R. (1985). The transfer of text-editing skill. *International Journal of Man-Machine Studies, 22*(4), 403–423. doi:10.1016/S0020-7373(85)80047-X

Singley, M. K., & Anderson, J. R. (1989). *The transfer of cognitive skill*. Cambridge, MA: Harvard University Press.

Sinnott, J. D., & Clark, J. (1989). An overview – if not a taxonomy – of "everyday problems" used in research. In Sinnott, J. D. (Ed.), *Everyday Problem Solving: Theory and Applications* (pp. 40–54). New York, NY: Praeger.

Slegers, K., van Boxtel, M. P. J., & Jolles, J. (2007). The effects of computer training and internet usage on the use of everyday technology by older adults: A randomized controlled study. *Educational Gerontology, 33*(2), 91–110. doi:10.1080/03601270600846733

Slegers, K., van Boxtel, M. P. J., & Jolles, J. (2008). The effects of computer training and internet usage on well-being and quality of life of older adults: A randomized controlled study. *The Journals of Gerontology. Series B, Psychological Sciences and Social Sciences, 63*, 176–P184. doi:10.1093/geronb/63.3.P176

Slegers, K., van Boxtel, M. P. J., & Jolles, J. (2009). The effects of computer training and internet usage on cognitive abilities of older adults: A randomised controlled study. *Aging Clinical and Experimental Research, 21*(1), 43–54.

Smarr, C. A., Fausset, C. B., & Rogers, W. A. (2011). *Understanding the potential for robot assistance for older adults in the home environment*. Atlanta, GA: Georgia Institute of Technology.

Smith, A. D. (1996). Memory. In Birren, J. E., & Schaie, K. W. (Eds.), *Handbook of the Psychology of Aging* (4th ed., pp. 236–250). San Diego, CA: Academic Press.

Smith, G. E., Housen, P., Yaffe, K., Ruff, R., Kennison, R. F., Mahncke, H. W., & Zlinski, E. E. (2009). A cognitive training program based on principles of brain plasticity: Results from the improvement in memory with plactiticy-based adaptive cognitive training (IMPACT) study. *Journal of the American Geriatrics Association, 57*(4), 594–603. doi:10.1111/j.1532-5415.2008.02167.x

Smith, G., Della Sala, S., Logie, R. H., & Maylor, E. A. (2000). Prospective and retrospective memory in normal ageing and dementia: A questionnaire study. *Memory (Hove, England), 8*, 311–321. doi:10.1080/09658210050117735

Smith, J., Jin, P., & Low, R. (2011). *Managing stress in various contexts*. Sydney, Australia: Pearson Education.

Smulders, P., & van den Bossche, S. (2004). *TNO Arbeid – Eerste resultaten nationale enquête arbeidsomstandigheden* [TNO Work and Employment - First results of the National Survey Occupational Conditions]. Hoofddorp, the Netherlands: TNO Arbeid.

Spencer, W. D., & Raz, N. (1995). Differential effects of aging on memory for content and context: A meta-analysis. *Psychology and Aging, 10*, 527–539. doi:10.1037/0882-7974.10.4.527

Spieler, D. H., Balota, D. A., & Faust, M. E. (1996). Stroop performance in healthy younger and older adults and in individuals with dementia of the Alzheimer's type. *Journal of Experimental Psychology. Human Perception and Performance, 22*(2), 461–479. doi:10.1037/0096-1523.22.2.461

Squire, L. R. (1986). Mechanisms of memory. *Science, 232*, 1612–1619. doi:10.1126/science.3086978

Squire, L. R. (1987). *Memory and brain.* Oxford, UK: Oxford University Press.

Squire, L. R., & Knowlton, B. J. (1994). The organization of memory. In Morowitz, H., & Singer, J. L. (Eds.), *The Mind, the Brain, and Complex Adaptive Systems* (pp. 63–97). Reading, MA: Addison Wesley/Addison Wesley Longman, Inc.

Squires, S., Romero-Ortuno, R., & Wherton, J. (2008). *Technology rejection, perception and implications for tele-care technology amongst older Irish adults: A mixed method approach.* Paper presented at the meeting of the Irish Gerontological Society. Kilkenny, Ireland.

Staff, R. T., Murray, A. D., Deary, I. J., & Whalley, L. J. (2004). What provides cerebral reserve? *Brain, 127*(5), 1191–1199. doi:10.1093/brain/awh144

Stanovich, K. E., West, R. F., & Harrison, M. R. (1995). Knowledge growth and maintenance across the life span: The role of print exposure. *Developmental Psychology, 31*, 811–826. doi:10.1037/0012-1649.31.5.811

Stead, W. W., & Linn, H. S. (2009). *Computational technology for effective health care: Immediate steps and strategic directions.* Washington, DC: National Academies Press.

Steinfield, C., Ellison, N. B., & Lampe, C. (2008). Social capital, self-esteem, and the use of online social network sites: A longitudinal analysis. *Journal of Applied Developmental Psychology, 29*, 434–445. doi:10.1016/j.appdev.2008.07.002

Stern, Y. (2002). What is cognitive reserve? Theory and research application of the reserve concept. *Journal of the International Neuropsychological Society, 8*, 448–460. doi:10.1017/S1355617702813248

Stevens, F. C. J., Kaplan, C. D., Ponds, R. W. H. M., Diederiks, J. P. M., & Jolles, J. (1999). How ageing and social factors affect memory. *Age and Ageing, 28*, 379–384. doi:10.1093/ageing/28.4.379

Stewart, M. (1995). Effective physician-patient communication and health outcomes: A review. *Journal of the Canadian Medical Association, 152*, 1423–1433.

Stigsdotter Neely, A. (2000). Multifactorial memory training in normal aging: In search of memory improvement beyond the ordinary. In Hill, R. D., Bäckman, L., & Stigsdotter Neely, A. (Eds.), *Cognitive Rehabilitation in Old Age* (pp. 63–80). Oxford, UK: Oxford University Press.

Stigsdotter Neely, S., & Bäckman, L. (1989). Multifactorial memory training with older adults: How to foster maintenance of improved performance. *Gerontology, 35*(5-6), 260–267. doi:10.1159/000213035

Stigsdotter Neely, S., & Bäckman, L. (1993a). Maintenance of gains following multifactorial and unifactorial memory training in late adulthood. *Educational Gerontology, 19*(2), 105–117. doi:10.1080/0360127930190202

Stigsdotter Neely, S., & Bäckman, L. (1993b). Long-term maintenance of gains from memory training in older adults: Two 3½-year follow-up studies. *Journal of Gerontology, 48*(5), 233–P237.

Stigsdotter Neely, S., & Bäckman, L. (1995). Effects of multifactorial training in old age: Generalizability across tasks and individuals. *Journals of Gerontolgoy: Series B: Psychological Sciences, 50B*(3), 134–P140. doi:10.1093/geronb/50B.3.P134

Stigsdotter, A., & Backman, L. (1995). Effects of multifactorial memory training in old age: Generalizability across tasks and individuals. *Journal of Gerontology, 50B*(3), 134–P140.

Stolzfus, E. R., Hasher, L., Zacks, R. T., Ulivi, S., & Goldstein, D. (1993). Investigations of inhibition and interference in younger and older adults. *The Journals of Gerontology. Series B, Psychological Sciences and Social Sciences, 48*, 179–188.

Stone, B. (2010). Old fogies by their 20s. *The New York Times.* Retrieved from http://www.nytimes.com

Straube, B., Green, A., Weis, S., Chatterjee, A., & Kircher, T. (2009). Memory effects of speech and gesture binding: cortical and hippocampal activation in relation to subsequent memory performance. *Journal of Cognitive Neuroscience, 21*, 821–836. doi:10.1162/jocn.2009.21053

Strayer, D. L., & Watson, J. M. (2012, March/April). Supertaskers and the multitasking brain. *Scientific American Mind.*

Strayer, D. L., & Drews, F. A. (2004). Profiles in driver distraction: Effects of cell phone conversations on younger and older drivers. *Human Factors, 46*, 640–649. doi:10.1518/hfes.46.4.640.56806

Strayer, D. L., Watson, J. M., & Drews, F. A. (2011). Cognitive distraction while multitasking in the automobile. In Ross, B. (Ed.), *The Psychology of Learning and Motivation* (Vol. 54, pp. 29–58). Burlington, VT: Academic Press. doi:10.1016/B978-0-12-385527-5.00002-4

Stronge, A. J., Walker, N., & Rogers, W. A. (2001). Searching the world wide web: Can older adults get what they need? In Rogers, W. A., & Fisk, A. D. (Eds.), *Human Factors Interventions for the Health Care of Older Adults* (pp. 255–269). Mahwah, NJ: Erlbaum.

Stroop, J. R. (1935). Studies of interference in serial verbal reactions. *Journal of Experimental Psychology, 18*, 643–662. doi:10.1037/h0054651

Sum, S., Mathews, R. M., Hughes, I., & Campbell, A. (2008). Internet use and loneliness in older adults. *Cyberpsychology & Behavior, 11*, 208–211. doi:10.1089/cpb.2007.0010

Sum, S., Mathews, R., Hughes, I., & Campbell, A. (2008). Internet use and loneliness in older adults. *Cyberpsychology & Behavior, 11*(2), 2008–2011. doi:10.1089/cpb.2007.0010

Swaab, D. F. (1991). Brain aging and Alzheimer's disease, "wear and tear" versus "use it or lose it". *Neurobiology of Aging, 12*(4), 317–324. doi:10.1016/0197-4580(91)90008-8

Swaab, D. F., Dubelaar, E. J., Hofman, M. A., Scherder, E. J., van Someren, E. J., & Verwer, R. W. (2002). Brain aging and alzheimer's disease; use it or lose it. *Progress in Brain Research, 138*, 343–373. doi:10.1016/S0079-6123(02)38086-5

Swanson, H. L. (1999). What develops in working memory? A life span perspective. *Developmental Psychology, 35*, 986–1000. doi:10.1037/0012-1649.35.4.986

Sweet, J., & Ellaway, R. (2010). Reuse as heuristic: From transmission to nurture in learning activity design. *Innovations in Education and Teaching International, 47*(2), 215–222. doi:10.1080/14703291003718943

Sweller, J. (1988). Cognitive load during problem solving: Effects on learning. *Cognitive Science, 12*, 257–285. doi:10.1207/s15516709cog1202_4

Sweller, J. (1994). Cognitive load theory, learning difficulty, and instructional design. *Learning and Instruction, 4*, 295–312. doi:10.1016/0959-4752(94)90003-5

Sweller, J. (2010). Element interactivity and intrinsic, extraneous, and germane cognitive load. *Educational Psychology Review, 22*, 123–138. doi:10.1007/s10648-010-9128-5

Sweller, J. (2011). Cognitive load theory. In Mestre, J., & Ross, B. (Eds.), *The Psychology of Learning and Motivation: Cognition in Education* (Vol. 55, pp. 37–76). Oxford, UK: Academic Press.

Sweller, J., Ayres, P., & Kalyuga, S. (2011). *Cognitive load theory.* New York, NY: Springer. doi:10.1007/978-1-4419-8126-4

Sweller, J., Ayres, P., & Kalyuga, S. (2011). The split-attention effect. In Sweller, J., Ayres, P., & Kalyuga, S. (Eds.), *Cognitive Load Theory* (pp. 111–128). Berlin, Germany: Springer. doi:10.1007/978-1-4419-8126-4_9

Sweller, J., & Chandler, P. (1991). Evidence for cognitive load theory. *Cognition and Instruction, 8*(4), 351–362. doi:10.1207/s1532690xci0804_5

Sweller, J., & Chandler, P. (1994). Why some material is difficult to learn. *Cognition and Instruction, 12*(3), 185–233. doi:10.1207/s1532690xci1203_1

Sweller, J., Chandler, P., Tierney, P., & Cooper, M. (1990). Cognitive load as a factor in the structuring of technical material. *Journal of Experimental Psychology. General, 119*, 176–192. doi:10.1037/0096-3445.119.2.176

Sweller, J., & Cooper, G. (1985). The use of worked examples as a substitute for problem solving in learning algebra. *Cognition and Instruction, 2*, 59–89. doi:10.1207/s1532690xci0201_3

Sweller, J., & Sweller, S. (2006). Natural information processing systems. *Evolutionary Psychology, 4*, 434–458.

Sweller, J., Van Merriënboer, J. J. G., & Paas, F. (1998). Cognitive architecture and instructional design. *Educational Psychology Review, 10*, 251–296. doi:10.1023/A:1022193728205

Switzer, J. A., Hall, C., Harmut, G., Waller, J., Nichols, F. T., & Wang, S. (2009). A web-based telestroke system facilitates rapid treatment of acute ischemic stroke patients in rural emergency departments. *The Journal of Emergency Medicine, 36*, 16–18. doi:10.1016/j.jemermed.2007.06.041

Tabbers, H. K., Martens, R. L., & Van Merriënboer, J. J. G. (2004). Multimedia instructions and cognitive load theory: Effects of modality and cueing. *The British Journal of Educational Psychology, 74*, 71–81. doi:10.1348/000709904322848824

Talley, R. C., & Crews, J. E. (2007). Framing the public health of caregiving. *American Journal of Public Health, 97*(2), 224–228. doi:10.2105/AJPH.2004.059337

Tang, P. C., Ash, J. S., Bates, D. W., Overhage, M., & Sands, D. Z. (2006). Personal health records: Definitions, benefits, and strategies for overcoming barriers to adoption. *Journal of the American Medical Informatics Association, 13*, 121–126. doi:10.1197/jamia.M2025

Tarmizi, R., & Sweller, J. (1988). Guidance during mathematical problem solving. *Journal of Educational Psychology, 80*, 424–436. doi:10.1037/0022-0663.80.4.424

Tebb, S., & Jivanjee, P. (2000). Caregiver isolation. *Journal of Gerontological Social Work, 34*(2), 51–72. doi:10.1300/J083v34n02_06

Tenforde, M., Jain, A., & Hickner, J. (2011). The value of personal health records for chronic disease management: What do we know? *Family Medicine, 43*, 351–354.

Thayer, S. E., & Ray, S. (2006). Online communication preferences across age, gender, and duration of internet use. *Cyberpsychology & Behavior, 9*, 432–440. doi:10.1089/cpb.2006.9.432

Thomas, L. E., & Lleras, A. (2007). Moving eyes and moving thought: On the spatial compatibility between eye movements and cognition. *Psychonomic Bulletin & Review, 14*, 663–668. doi:10.3758/BF03196818

Thompson, L. A., Aidinejad, M. R., & Ponte, J. (2001). Aging and the effects of facial and prosodic cues on emotional intensity ratings and memory reconstructions. *Journal of Nonverbal Behavior, 25*, 101–125. doi:10.1023/A:1010749711863

Thorndike, E. L., & Woodworth, R. S. (1901). The influence of improvement in one mental function upon the efficiency of other functions. *Psychological Review, 8*, 247–261. doi:10.1037/h0074898

Tindall-Ford, S., Chandler, P., & Sweller, J. (1997). When two sensory modes are better than one. *Journal of Experimental Psychology. Applied, 3*, 257–287. doi:10.1037/1076-898X.3.4.257

Tipper, S. P. (1985). The negative priming effect: Inhibitory priming by ignored objects. *Quarterly Journal of Experimental Psychology, 37*, 571–590. doi:10.1080/14640748508400920

Tisserand, D. J., Bosma, H., van Boxtel, M. P. J., & Jolles, J. (2001). Head size and cognitive ability in nondemented older adults are related. *Neurology, 56*(7), 969–971. doi:10.1212/WNL.56.7.969

Torres, A. (2008, November). *Cognitive effects of videogames on older people.* Paper presented at ZON Digital Games 2008, Porto, Portugal.

Tremont, G., Davis, J. D., Bishop, D. S., & Fortinsky, R. H. (2008). Telephone-delivered psychosocial intervention reduces burden in dementia caregivers. *Dementia (London), 7*, 503. doi:10.1177/1471301208096632

Tsai, W. C., Lee, C. F., & Rogers, W. A. (2012). (in press). Older adults' usage of and attitudes toward product manuals. *International Journal of Design.*

Tulu, B., Chatterjee, S., & Laxminarayan, S. (2005). A taxonomy of telemedicine efforts with respect to applications, infrastructure, delivery tools, type of setting and purpose. In *Proceedings of the Hawaii International Conference on System Sciences,* (p. 147b). IEEE Press.

Tulving, E. (1972). Episodic and semantic memory. In E. Tulving & W. Donaldson (Eds.), *Organization of Memory,* (pp. 381-403). New York, NY: Academic Press.

Tulving, E., & Thomson, D. M. (1973). Encoding specificity and retrieval processes in episodic memory. *Psychological Review*, *80*(5), 352–373. doi:10.1037/h0020071

Turner, P., Turner, S., & Van de Walle, G. (2007). How older people account for their experiences with interactive technology. *Behaviour & Information Technology*, *26*(4), 287–296. doi:10.1080/01449290601173499

Undem, T. (2010). *Consumers and health information technology: A national survey.* Retrieved on July 31, 2011, from http://www.chcf.org/publications/2010/04/consumers-and-health-information-technology-a-national-survey

US Census Bureau. (2000). *Profile of general demographic characteristics: 2000 census of population and housing.* Washington, DC: United State Census Bureau.

US Department of Health and Human Services. (2001). *A profile of older Americans.* Washington, DC: Administration on Aging.

Valentijn, S. A. M., van Hooren, S. A. H., Bosma, H., Touw, D. M., Jolles, J., & van Boxtel, M. P. J. (2005). The effect of two types of memory training on subjective and objective memory performance in healthy individuals aged 55 years and older: A randomized controlled trial. *Patient Education and Counseling, 57*, 106–114. doi:10.1016/j.pec.2004.05.002

Valentijn, S. A., van Boxtel, M. P., van Hooren, S. A., Bosma, H., Beckers, H. J., & Ponds, R. W. (2005). Change in sensory functioning predicts change in cognitive functioning: Results from a 6-year follow-up in the Maastricht aging study. *Journal of the American Geriatrics Society*, *53*, 374–380. doi:10.1111/j.1532-5415.2005.53152.x

Valenzeno, L., Alibali, M. W., & Klatzky, R. (2003). Teachers' gestures facilitate students' learning: A lesson in symmetry. *Contemporary Educational Psychology*, *28*, 187–204. doi:10.1016/S0361-476X(02)00007-3

Valenzuela, S., Park, N., & Kee, K. F. (2009). Is there social capital in a social networking site? Facebook use and college students' life satisfaction, trust, and participation. *Journal of Computer-Mediated Communication*, *14*, 875–890. doi:10.1111/j.1083-6101.2009.01474.x

Van Boxtel, M. P. J., Slegers, K., Jolles, J., & Ruijgrok, J. M. (2007). Risk of upper limb complaints due to computer use in older persons: A randomized study. *BMC Geriatrics*, *7*(21).

Van der Elst, W., van Boxtel, M. P. J., van Breukelen, G. J. P., & Jolles, J. (2006a). The letter digit substitution test: Normative data for 1,858 healthy participants aged 24-81 from the Maastricht aging study (MAAS): Influence of age, education, and sex. *Journal of Clinical and Experimental Neuropsychology*, *28*, 998–1009. doi:10.1080/13803390591004428

Van der Elst, W., van Boxtel, M. P. J., van Breukelen, G. P. J., & Jolles, J. (2005). Rey's verbal learning test: Normative data for 1855 healthy participants aged 24-81 years and the influence of sex, education, and model of presentation. *Journal of the International Neuropsychological Society*, *11*, 290–302. doi:10.1017/S1355617705050344

Van der Elst, W., van Boxtel, M. P. J., van Breukelen, G., & Jolles, J. (2006b). The concept shifting test: Adult normative data. *Psychological Assessment*, *18*(4), 424–432. doi:10.1037/1040-3590.18.4.424

Van der Elst, W., van Boxtel, M. P., van Breukelen, G. J., & Jolles, J. (2006c). The Stroop color-word test: Influence of age, sex, and education; and normative data for a large sample across the adult age range. *Assessment*, *13*(1), 62–79. doi:10.1177/1073191105283427

Van der Zee, K. I., & Sanderman, R. (1993). *Het meten van de algemene gezondheidstoestand met de RAND-36: Een handleiding* [Measurement of general health with the RAND-36: A manual]. Groningen, The Netherlands: Noordelijk Centrum voor Gezondheidsvraagstukken NCG.

Van Gerven, P. W. M., Paas, F., Van Merriënboer, J. J. G., Hendriks, M., & Schmidt, H. G. (2003). The efficiency of multimedia learning into old age. *The British Journal of Educational Psychology*, *73*, 489–505. doi:10.1348/000709903322591208

Van Gerven, P. W. M., Paas, F., Van Merriënboer, J. J. G., & Schmidt, H. G. (2000). Cognitive load theory and the acquisition of complex cognitive skills in the elderly: Towards an integrative framework. *Educational Gerontology*, *26*, 503–521. doi:10.1080/03601270050133874

Van Gerven, P. W. M., Paas, F., Van Merriënboer, J. J. G., & Schmidt, H. G. (2002). Cognitive load theory and aging: Effects of worked examples on training efficiency. *Learning and Instruction*, *12*, 87–105. doi:10.1016/S0959-4752(01)00017-2

Van Gerven, P. W. M., Paas, F., Van Merriënboer, J. J. G., & Schmidt, H. G. (2006). Modality and variability as factors in training the elderly. *Applied Cognitive Psychology*, *20*, 311–320. doi:10.1002/acp.1247

van Gerven, P., Paas, F., & Schmidt, H. (2000). Cognitive load theory and the acquisition of complex cognitive skills in the elderly: Towards and integrative framework. *Educational Gerontology*, *26*, 503–521. doi:10.1080/03601270050133874

van Gerven, P., Paas, F., & Tabbers, H. K. (2006). Cognitive aging and computer-based instructional design: Where do we go from here? *Educational Psychology Review*, *18*(2), 141–157. doi:10.1007/s10648-006-9005-4

Van Gog, T., Paas, F., Marcus, N., Ayres, P., & Sweller, J. (2009). The mirror neuron system and observational learning: Implications for the effectiveness of dynamic visualizations. *Educational Psychology Review*, *21*, 21–30. doi:10.1007/s10648-008-9094-3

Van Gog, T., & Rummel, N. (2010). Example-based learning: Integrating cognitive and social-cognitive research perspectives. *Educational Psychology Review*, *22*, 155–174. doi:10.1007/s10648-010-9134-7

Van Merriënboer, J. J. G., & Sweller, J. (2005). Cognitive load theory and complex learning: Recent developments and future directions. *Educational Psychology Review*, *17*, 147–177. doi:10.1007/s10648-005-3951-0

Vecchi, T., Richardson, J., & Cavallini, E. (2005). Passive storage versus active processing in working memory: Evidence from age-related variations in performance. *Journal of Cognitive Psychology*, *17*, 521–539. doi:10.1080/09541440440000140

Verghese, J., Lipton, R. B., Katz, M. J., Hall, C. B., Derby, C. A., & Kuslansky, G. (2003). Leisure activities and the risk of dementia in the elderly. *The New England Journal of Medicine*, *348*(25), 2508–2516. doi:10.1056/NEJMoa022252

Verhaeghen, P., & Cerella, J. (2002). Aging, executive control, and attention: a review of meta-analyses. *Neuroscience and Biobehavioral Reviews*, *26*, 849–857. doi:10.1016/S0149-7634(02)00071-4

Verhaeghen, P., & De Meersman, L. (1998). Aging and the Stroop effect: A meta-analysis. *Psychology and Aging*, *13*, 120–126. doi:10.1037/0882-7974.13.1.120

Verhaeghen, P., Geraerts, N., & Marcoen, A. (2000). Memory complaints, coping, and well-being in old age: A systemic approach. *The Gerontologist*, *40*(5), 540–548. doi:10.1093/geront/40.5.540

Verhaeghen, P., & Marcoen, A. (1993). More of less the same? A memorability analysis on episodic memory tasks in young and old adults. *Journal of Gerontology*, *48*(4), 172–178.

Verhaeghen, P., Marcoen, A., & Goossens, L. (1992). Improving memory performance in the aged through mnemonic training: A meta-analytic study. *Psychology and Aging*, *7*(2), 242–251. doi:10.1037/0882-7974.7.2.242

Verhaeghen, P., & Salthouse, T. (1997). Meta-analyses of age-cognition relations in adulthood: Estimates of linear and nonlinear age effects and structural models. *Psychological Bulletin*, *122*(3), 231–249. doi:10.1037/0033-2909.122.3.231

Volandes, A. E., Paasche-Orlow, M. K., Barry, M. J., Gillick, M. R., Minaker, K. L., & Chang, Y. (2009). Video decision support tool for advance care planning in dementia: Randomised controlled trial. *British Medical Journal*, *28*(338), b2159. doi:10.1136/bmj.b2159

Von Kanel, R., Mausbach, B. T., Patterson, T. L., Dimsdale, J. E., Aschbacher, K., & Mills, P. J. (2008). Increased Framingham coronary heart disease risk score in dementia caregivers relative to non-caregiving controls. *Gerontology*, *54*, 131–137. doi:10.1159/000113649

Vrkljan, B., & Miller Polgar, J. (2007). *Driving safely in later life: exploring the older driver-passenger relationship.* Paper presented at TRANSED 2007 Conference. Montreal, Canada.

Wagner, E. H., Bennett, S. M., Austin, B. T., Greene, S. M., Schaefer, J. K., & Vonkorff, M. (2005). Finding common ground: Patient-centeredness and evidence-based chronic illness care. *Journal of Alternative and Complementary Medicine (New York, N.Y.), 11,* S7–S15. doi:10.1089/acm.2005.11.s-7

Wagner, N., Hassanein, K., & Head, M. (2010). Computer use by older adults: A multidisciplinary review. *Computers in Human Behavior, 26*(5), 870–882. doi:10.1016/j.chb.2010.03.029

Wald, H. S., Dube, C. E., & Anthony, D. C. (2007). Untangling the web—The impact of internet use on health care and the physician-patient relationship. *Patient Education &. Counseling, 68,* 218–224.

Ward, M., & Sweller, J. (1990). Structuring effective worked examples. *Cognition and Instruction, 7,* 1–39. doi:10.1207/s1532690xci0701_1

Ware, J. J. E., Snow, K. K., Kosinski, M., & Gandek, B. (1993). *Sf-36 health survey manual and interpretation guide.* Boston, MA: New England Medical Center.

Warren, J. M., Zerweck, C., & Anthony, A. (1982). Effects of environmental enrichment on old mice. *Developmental Psychobiology, 15*(1), 13–18. doi:10.1002/dev.420150104

Watson, J. M., Lambert, A. E., Cooper, J. M., Boyle, I. V., & Strayer, D. L. (2012). On attentional control and the aging driver. In Zheng, R., Hill, R., & Gardner, M. (Eds.), *Engaging Older Adults with Modern Technology: Internet Use and Information.* Hershey, PA: IGI Global.

Watson, J. M., Lambert, A. E., Miller, A. E., & Strayer, D. L. (2011). The magical letters P, F, C, and sometimes U: The rise and fall of executive attention with the development of prefrontal cortex. In Fingerman, K., Berg, C., Antonucci, T., & Smith, J. (Eds.), *Handbook of Lifespan Psychology* (pp. 409–438). London, UK: Springer.

Watson, J. M., & Strayer, D. L. (2010). Supertaskers: Profiles in extraordinary multitasking ability. *Psychonomic Bulletin & Review, 17,* 479–485. doi:10.3758/PBR.17.4.479

Weingart, S. N., Rind, D., Tofias, Z., & Sands, D. Z. (2006). Who uses the patient portal internet? The PatientSite experience. *Journal of the American Medical Informatics Association, 13,* 91–95. doi:10.1197/jamia.M1833

Weinstock, R. S., Brooks, G., Palmas, W., Morin, P. C., Teresi, J. A., & Eimicke, J. P. (2011). Lessened decline in physical activity and impairment of older adults with diabetes with telemedicine and pedometer use: Results from the IDEATel study. *Age and Ageing, 40*(1), 98–105. doi:10.1093/ageing/afq147

West, R. (1996). An application of prefrontal cortex function theory to cognitive aging. *Psychological Bulletin, 120,* 272–292. doi:10.1037/0033-2909.120.2.272

West, R., & Alain, C. (2000). Age-related decline in inhibitory control contributes to the increased Stroop effect observed in older adults. *Psychophysiology, 37,* 179–189. doi:10.1111/1469-8986.3720179

West, S. P., Lagua, C., Trief, P. M., Izquierdo, R., & Weinstock, R. S. (2010). Goal setting using telemedicine in rural underserved older adults with diabetes: Experiences from the informatics for diabetes education and telemedicine project. *Telemedicine Journal and e-Health, 16,* 405–416. doi:10.1089/tmj.2009.0136

Whang, L. S., Lee, S., & Chang, G. (2003). Internet over-users' psychological profiles: A behavior sampling analysis on internet addiction. *Cyberpsychology & Behavior, 6*(2), 143–150. doi:10.1089/109493103321640338

Wheeler, M. A., Stuss, D. T., & Tulving, E. (1997). Toward a theory of episodic memory: The frontal lobes and autonoetic consciousness. *Psychological Bulletin, 121,* 331–354. doi:10.1037/0033-2909.121.3.331

White, H., McConnell, E., Clipp, E., Branch, L., Sloane, R., & Pieper, C. (2002). A randomized controlled trial of the psychosocial impact of providing internet training and access to older adults. *Aging & Mental Health, 6*(3), 213–221. doi:10.1080/13607860220142422

White, H., McConnell, E., Clipp, E., Bynum, L., Teague, C., & Navas, L. (1999). Surfing the net in later life: A review of the literature and pilot study computer use and quality of life. *Journal of Applied Gerontology, 18*(3), 358–378. doi:10.1177/073346489901800306

Whitford, M. (1998). Market in motion. *Hotel and Motel Management*, *4*, 41–43.

Whitman, D. (2011). *Cognition*. Hoboken, NJ: John Wiley.

Whitten, P., & Mickus, M. (2007). Home telecare for COPD/CHF patients: Outcomes and perceptions. *Journal of Telemedicine and Telecare*, *13*, 69–73. doi:10.1258/135763307780096249

Willis, S. L., Dolan, M. M., & Bertrand, R. M. (1999). Problem-solving on health-related tasks of everyday living. In Park, D. C., Morrell, R. W., & Shifren, K. (Eds.), *Processing of Medical Information in Aging Patients* (pp. 199–219). Mahwah, NJ: Lawrence Erlbaum Associates.

Willis, S. L., Jay, G. M., Diehl, M., & Marsiske, M. (1992). Longitudinal change and prediction of everyday task competence in the elderly. *Research on Aging*, *14*, 68–91. doi:10.1177/0164027592141004

Willis, S. L., & Schaie, K. W. (1986). Training the elderly on ability factors of spatial orientation and inductive reasoning. *Psychology and Aging*, *1*, 239–247. doi:10.1037/0882-7974.1.3.239

Wilson, R. S., Mendes de Leon, C. F., Barnes, L. L., Schneider, J. A., Bienias, J. L., & Evans, D. A. (2002). Participation in cognitively stimulating activities and risk of incident Alzheimer disease. *Journal of the American Medical Association*, *287*, 742–748. doi:10.1001/jama.287.6.742

Wimo, A., von Strauss, E., Nordberg, G., Sassi, F., & Johansson, L. (2002). Time spent on informal and formal care giving for persons with dementia in Sweden. *Health Policy (Amsterdam)*, *61*, 255–268. doi:10.1016/S0168-8510(02)00010-6

Wingfield, A., & Tun, P. A. (2007). Cognitive supports and cognitive constraints on comprehension of spoken language. *Journal of the American Academy of Audiology*, *18*, 548–558. doi:10.3766/jaaa.18.7.3

Wong, A., Marcus, N., Ayres, P., Smith, L., Cooper, G. A., Paas, F., & Sweller, J. (2009). Instructional animations can be superior to statics when learning human motor skills. *Computers in Human Behavior*, *25*, 339–347. doi:10.1016/j.chb.2008.12.012

Wood, L. E., & Pratt, J. D. (1987). Pegword mnemonic as an aid to memory in the elderly: A comparison of four age groups. *Educational Gerontology*, *13*(4), 325–339. doi:10.1080/0360127870130404

Woodrow, H. (1927). The effect of type of training upon transference. *Journal of Educational Psychology*, *18*, 159–172. doi:10.1037/h0071868

Wouters, P., Tabbers, H. K., & Paas, F. (2007). Interactivity in video-based models. *Educational Psychology Review*, *19*, 327–342. doi:10.1007/s10648-007-9045-4

Wray, L. W., Shulan, M. D., Toseland, R. W., Freeman, K. E., Vásquez, B. E., & Gao, J. (2010). The effect of telephone support groups on costs of care for veterans with dementia. *The Gerontologist*, *50*(5), 623–631. doi:10.1093/geront/gnq040

Wright, B. M., & Payne, R. B. (1985). Effects of aging on sex differences in psychomotor reminiscence and tracking proficiency. *Journal of Gerontology*, *40*(2), 179–184.

Xie, B. (2009). Older adults' health information wants in the internet age: Implications for patient-provider relationships. *Journal of Health Communication*, *14*(6), 510–524. doi:10.1080/10810730903089614

Xie, B., & Bugg, J. M. (2009). Public library computer training for older adults to access high-quality internet health information. *Library & Information Science Research*, *31*, 155–162. doi:10.1016/j.lisr.2009.03.004

Yellowlees, P. M., & Marks, S. (2007). Problematic internet use or internet addicton? *Computers in Human Behavior*, *23*(3), 1447–1453. doi:10.1016/j.chb.2005.05.004

Yesavage, J. A. (1983). Imagery pretraining and memory training in the elderly. *Gerontology*, *29*(4), 271–275. doi:10.1159/000213126

Yesavage, J. A. (1984). Relaxation and memory training in 39 elderly patients. *The American Journal of Psychiatry*, *141*(6), 778–781.

Yesavage, J. A. (1985). Nonpharmacologic treatments for memory losses with normal aging. *The American Journal of Psychology*, *142*(5), 600–605.

Yesavage, J. A., & Jacobs, R. (1984). Effects of relaxation and mnemonics on memory, attention and anxiety in the elderly. *Experimental Aging Research, 10*, 211–214. doi:10.1080/03610738408258467

Yesavage, J. A., Lapp, D., & Sheikh, J. I. (1989). Mnemonics as modified for use by the elderly. In Poon, L. W., Rubin, D. C., & Wilson, B. A. (Eds.), *Everyday Cognition in Adulthood and Late Life* (pp. 598–611). Cambridge, UK: Cambridge University Press.

Yesavage, J. A., & Rose, T. L. (1984). Semantic elaboration and the method of loci: A new trip for older learners. *Experimental Aging Research, 10*(3), 155–159. doi:10.1080/03610738408258560

Yesavage, J. A., Rose, T. L., & Bower, G. H. (1983). Interactive imagery and affective judgments improve face-name learning in the elderly. *Journal of Gerontology, 38*(2), 197–203.

Yesavage, J. A., Sheikh, J. I., Decker Tanke, E. D., & Hill, R. D. (1988). Response to memory training and individual differences in verbal intelligence and state anxiety. *The American Journal of Psychiatry, 145*(5), 636–639.

Yeung, A., Jin, P., & Sweller, J. (1997). Cognitive load and learner expertise: Split-attention and redundancy effects in reading with explanatory notes. *Contemporary Educational Psychology, 23*, 1–21. doi:10.1006/ceps.1997.0951

Yi, M. Y., & Hwang, Y. (2003). Predicting the use of web-based information systems: Self-efficacy, enjoyment, learning goal orientation, and the technology acceptance model. *International Journal of Human-Computer Studies, 59*, 431–449. doi:10.1016/S1071-5819(03)00114-9

Zaphiris, P., & Rifaht, S. (2006). Trends, similarities, and differences in the usage of teen and senior public online Newsgroups. *ACM Transactions on Computer-Human Interaction, 13*(3), 403–422. doi:10.1145/1183456.1183461

Zelinski, E. M., Gilewski, M. J., & Thompson, L. W. (1980). Do laboratory tests relate to self-assessment of memory ability in the young and old? In Poon, L. W., Toyard, J. L., Cermack, L. S., & Arenberg, D. (Eds.), *New Directions in Memory and Aging* (pp. 519–544). Hillsdale, NJ: Lawrence Erlbaum Associates.

Zheng, R., & Cook, A. (2011). Solving complex problems: A convergent approach to cognitive load measurement. *British Journal of Educational Technology, 43*(2).

Zhou, Y. Y., Kanter, M. H., & Wang, J. J. (2010). Improve quality at Kaiser Permanente through email between physicians and patients. *Health Affairs, 29*, 1370–1375. doi:10.1377/hlthaff.2010.0048

Zickmund, S. L., Hess, R., Bryce, C. L., McTigue, K., Olshansky, E., Fitzgerald, K., & Fischer, G. S. (2008). Interest in the use of computerized patient portals: Role of the provider–patient relationship. *Journal of General Internal Medicine, 23*(1), 20–26. doi:10.1007/s11606-007-0273-6

Zickuhr, K. (2011, February 3). *Generations and their gadgets*. Retrieved from http://www.pewinternet.org/Reports/2011/Generations-and-gadgets.aspx

Zickuhr, K. (2010). *Generations (San Francisco, Calif.)*, Washington, DC: Pew Internet.

Zimmer, H. D. (2001). Why do actions speak louder than words: Action memory as a variant of encoding manipulations or the result of a specific memory system? In Zimmer, H. D., & Cohen, R. L. (Eds.), *Memory for Action: A Distinct Form of Episodic Memory?* (pp. 151–198). Oxford, UK: Oxford University Press.

Zimmer, Z., & Chappell, N. L. (1999). Receptivity to new technology among older adults. *Disability and Rehabilitation, 21*(5/6), 222–230.

Zwaan, R. A., & Madden, C. J. (2005). Embodied sentence comprehension. In Pecher, D., & Zwaan, R. A. (Eds.), *Grounding Cognition: The Role of Perception and Action in Memory, Language, and Thinking* (pp. 224–246). Cambridge, UK: Cambridge University Press. doi:10.1017/CBO9780511499968.010

About the Contributors

Robert Z. Zheng is an Associate Professor of Educational Psychology at the University of Utah in Salt Lake City, Utah. His publications include edited books, book chapters, and journal papers covering the topics of online learning, multimedia, cognition, and educational technology for lifelong learning. He is the editor and co-editor of many books including *Understanding Online Instructional Modeling: Theories and Practices*, *Cognitive Effects of Multimedia Learning*, *Adolescent Online Social Communication, and Behavior: Relationship Formation on the Internet*, and *Engaging Older Adults with Modern Technology: Internet Use and Information Access Needs*. He is the current editor-in-chief of the *International Journal of Cyber Behavior, Psychology, and Learning*. His work appears in academic outlets such as *British Journal of Educational Technology*, *Journal of Educational Computing Research*, *Educational Technology Research & Development*, and *Journal of Technology, Instruction, Cognition, and Learning*.

Robert D. Hill is Professor of the Department of Educational Psychology at the University of Utah in Salt Lake City, Utah. Professor Hill received his Ph.D. in Counseling Psychology from Stanford University in 1987. He was a Fulbright Scholar in The Netherlands in 2003-2004 at the Brain and Behavior Institute, Maastricht University. In 1993-1994, Dr. Hill was in residence at the Karolinska Institute in Stockholm, Sweden, where he studied cognitive factors that distinguish normal aging from dementia. He is a licensed Psychologist in the State of Utah and a Diplomate in Counseling Psychology from the American Board of Professional Psychology (ABPP), as well as a Fellow of the American Psychological Association. Dr. Hill has conducted research on memory and memory rehabilitation in older adults for over two decades. His research also examines the efficacy of healthcare delivery systems to an aging clientele. He is currently a member of the "Supporting Caregivers of Older Veterans Electronically" (SCORE) research team at the Salt Lake City Veterans Administration Geriatric Research Education and Clinical Center (GRECC).

Michael K. Gardner is Professor and Associate Chair of the Department of Educational Psychology, University of Utah. Professor Gardner received a B.A. in Psychology from Stanford University, and an M.S., M.Phil., and Ph.D. in Psychology from Yale University, with a specialty in Cognitive Psychology. He has conducted research on memory and aging, analogical reasoning and human intelligence, cognitive skill acquisition, detection of deception using psychophysiological methods, and methodological issues in psychology. He has received over 1.1 million dollars in research funding from the US Department of Defense for his various research projects, and serves as a grant reviewer for the National Science Foundation.

* * *

Alan Bourke is a Postdoctoral Researcher working in the area of fall-detection and ambulatory monitoring of older adults using wearable MEMS-based kinematic sensors. He completed his PhD titled "Fall Detection using Kinematic Sensors" in 2007, before completing a postdoctoral research fellowship on the FP6 EU-funded project: CAALYX (Complete Ambient Assisted Living Experiment). This project aimed at promoting more independent living in the elderly population of Europe through ambient monitoring and tailored ICT for this population group. He is currently working on the AAL project, eCAALYX (Enhanced Complete Ambient Assisted Living Experiment), which aims at increasing the autonomy and self-confidence of older people who suffer from co-morbidity by developing a wearable body system capable of remotely measuring specific vital signs and monitoring activity, as well as accurately and reliably detecting falls.

Istenya V. Boyle earned her Bachelor of Science degree in Psychology from the University of Utah in May, 2011. The foundation of her undergraduate work was in Cognitive Neuroscience with a focus on Memory and Attention Studies. She assisted in Dr. Jason M. Watson's Cognitive Science Lab for two years. Currently, Istenya Boyle is employed with the Neuropsychiatric Institute as a Psychiatric Technician in the Mood Disorder Clinic. Istenya has always loved neuroscience, and enjoys leisure reads on neuroplasticity. Recently, she has been exploring ways to bring her research background into practical work with individuals. In her spare time, she enjoys art galleries, traveling to NY, and independent foreign film.

Yiwei Chen obtained his Ph.D. at the Georgia Institute of Technology in 1998 and is now an Associate Professor of Psychology at the Psychology Department of Bowling Green State University, OH. Dr. Chen is interested in how information technology may influence our everyday lives. Since her major was in adult development and aging, she studied the relationship between Internet use and psychological well-being among older adults. She also examined constraints older adults may encounter in using the Internet. Her other research interests include age-related differences in cognitive and socio-emotional processes, causal attribution, decision making and aging, and cross-cultural differences in subjective well-being. Dr. Chen has published more than 30 articles in peer-reviewed journals and book chapters. Her research has been funded by the National Institute on Aging. She is currently serving on the Editorial Board of *Psychology and Aging*.

Jessie Chin is a Ph.D. student in the Department of Educational Psychology and the Beckman Institute for Advanced Science and Technology. She earned her M.S. degree in Human Factors at the University of Illinois at Urbana Champaign. Jessie Chin's research focuses on age differences in the use of health information technology (particularly for Web information search) in terms of the relationships among cognitive ability, health literacy, and domain knowledge. She is working with Professors Dan Morrow, Elizabeth Stine-Morrow, and Wai-Tat Fu.

Joel Cooper is a Research Assistant Professor in the Center for the Prevention of Distracted Driving and the Owner of Precision Driving Research Inc. Joel received his Ph.D. in Cognitive Psychology from the University of Utah. Following, Joel worked at the Texas Transportation Institute in the Human Factors group where he led research on driver attention/distraction using instrumented research vehicles and driving simulation. Since 2002, Joel has assisted and lead numerous sponsored research studies looking at various human factors and driving issues including the effects of age, driving experience, driver training, cognitive distraction, visual distraction, and basic vehicle control mechanisms.

Candice Daniel, PhD, is a licensed Clinical Psychologist and VA Special Fellow in Advanced Geriatrics at the VA SLC HCS GRECC. She is currently the Project Manager for the Supporting Caregivers of Veterans Electronically (SCORE) Project. Her previous research focused on adherence among chronically ill and medically complex patients in rural areas. Currently, she is gaining specialized research and clinical training with dementia and geriatric populations.

Beni Gómez-Zúñiga (PhD in Psychology) is a Lecturer at the Open University of Catalunya since 2005 and Researcher for PSiNET. From 1994 to 2005, she worked at the University of Barcelona teaching the History of Psychology and the Basic Psychological Processes of Thought and Memory.

Marren Grant, MSW, LCSW, graduated from Weber State University and the University of Utah. She began her career working in mental health. She has worked with adolescents utilizing equine therapy. She has advocated for women to educate themselves. She assisted with development and promotion of the PEER Program at Weber State University advocating for awareness toward sexual assault. She has worked with both victims and perpetrators of sexual assault. Her most extensive work has been working with clients suffering from chronic mental illness. She frequently facilitates individual, family, and group therapy. She promotes stabilization with clients in crisis. Most recently, Marren has been involved in the VA SCORE Project (Supporting Caregivers of Rural Veterans Electronically). She is currently providing support and guidance to caregivers of Veterans suffering from cognitive decline. She has enthusiastically assumed the role of Caregiver Advocate, and she promotes active, healthy aging with her clients.

Eulàlia Hernández-Encuentra (PhD in Psychology) is a Lecturer at the Open University of Catalunya and Researcher for PSiNET. From 1992 to 2010, her work in the Universitat Autònoma of Barcelona and Universitat Ramon Llull was related to Developmental Psychology.

Bret Hicken has a Bachelor's degree in Psychology from the University of Utah and a PhD in Clinical Psychology and a Master's in Public Health from the University of Alabama at Birmingham. Dr. Hicken is a Research Scientist for the Veterans Rural Health Resource Center – Western Region and a Clinical Assistant Professor at the University of Utah. Dr. Hicken's research focuses on dementia care with emphasis on 1) evaluation of mental capacities and 2) support for caregivers of older adults with dementia, with particular emphasis on individuals with limited access to care (e.g., rural, homebound, etc.). Dr. Hicken is also a Clinical Supervisor for the Psychology Internship Program at the Salt Lake VA.

Putai Jin is Senior Lecturer at the University of New South Wales. His research interest is in educational psychology with special emphasis on learning, stress management, and quantitative research methods.

Robert Kirk is a Graduate Student in the PhD program for Developmental Psychology at Bowling Green State University (BGSU) in Bowling Green, OH. As an undergraduate at BGSU, Robert earned his Bachelor's degree in Psychology with a minor in Sociology. He then relocated to Cleveland, OH, where he earned a Master's degree, also in Psychology, from Cleveland State University (CSU). After finishing his graduate career at CSU, Robert moved to Toledo, OH, where he began teaching as an Adjunct Psychology Instructor at Owens Community College (OCC). It was during his 3-year stay at OCC that Robert applied and was accepted to the Doctoral Program at BGSU. He currently resides in Bowling Green once again, where he ardently works to finish his graduate training.

Ann E. Lambert recently completed her Doctorate in Cognitive Psychology at the University of Utah, where her research focused on how cognitive-developmental changes in controlled processing inform our understanding of behavior in applied settings. As a graduate student at the University of Utah, her dissertation examined how individual differences in executive attention moderate the impact of stereotype threat on senior driving performance. She is currently a Postdoctoral Fellow at the University of Virginia, investigating the roles of executive function and physical fitness in adolescent risk-taking behind the wheel.

Bob Lee is an Associate Professor in the Program of Tourism, Leisure, and Event Planning at Bowling Green State University, Ohio. His research interests include leisure and aging, information communication technology and older adults, and tourism marketing. He has written extensively on senior users' constraints to access information communication technology, family recreation, and tourism destination administration. Lee's publications have appeared in refereed journals, non-refereed journals, magazines, and as book chapters. He has also served as an Associated Editor for the *Annual of Therapeutic Recreation* and sat in the Steering Committee for the Northeast Recreation Research Symposium.

Renae Low is Senior Lecturer at the University of New South Wales. Her research interest is in educational psychology for learning and teaching.

Marilyn Luptak is an Assistant Professor and Belle S. Spafford Endowed Chair in Social Work in the University of Utah College of Social Work, where she also directs the Social Work in Aging Emphasis for Master's Students. Additionally, she is a J. A. Hartford Geriatric Social Work Faculty Scholar, which has enabled her to advocate for older adults at the state and national levels. She brings more than 25 years of experience to her work to improve the health and well-being of older adults and their families in rural and urban settings.

Dan Morrow is a Professor in the Department of Educational Psychology and the Beckman Institute of Advanced Science and Technology, University of Illinois at Urbana-Champaign. He received a PhD in Cognitive Psychology from the University of California Berkeley. He is Associate Editor of the *Journal of Experimental Psychology: Applied*, and Editor of the *Human Factors and Ergonomics Review*, Volume 8 (special issue on health care). He is President-Elect of Division 21 of the American Psychological Association (Applied Experimental and Engineering Psychology). His research interests include the impact of aging on cognition and communication in health care, aviation, and other complex domains in which people interact with technology.

Marita A. O'Brien is Assistant Professor of Psychology at the University of Alabama in Huntsville with a specialization in Engineering Psychology. Dr. O'Brien earned her Ph.D. in Engineering Psychology from the Georgia Institute of Technology with a minor in Cognitive Aging. She also holds an

M.S. in Telecommunications Engineering from the University of Colorado and an A.B. in Math from Duke University. Her current research focuses on investigating differences in everyday technology use based on variables such as age, general technology background, computer anxiety, and occupational background. She is a member of the Human Factors and Ergonomics Society (HFES), and she is serving as President of the Tennessee Valley HFES chapter. Prior to her academic career, she spent more than 10 years advising Fortune 500 clients on the design of customer interfaces at Deloitte Consulting and Morgan Stanley and Company.

Shane O'Hanlon teaches Health Informatics at the Graduate Entry Medical School, University of Limerick, Ireland. He graduated with a degree in Medicine in 2003. He also holds a Master's degree in Health Informatics and a Bachelor's degree in Law. He has presented papers on e-Health at national and international conferences. He currently works as a Clinician in Geriatric Medicine and Rehabilitation, and a Clinical Fellow in Medicine at University Hospital Limerick. His research interests include e-Health for older people, in particular consumer informatics and clinical decision support systems for diagnosis of cognitive impairment.

Kim Ouwehand is currently a PhD student at the Institute of Psychology at the Erasmus University Rotterdam in The Netherlands. She holds a Master degree in Cognitive Neuroscience from Leiden University (2010). In her PhD project, she focuses on the effect of coverbal gestures (gestures that accompany speech) in instructional design on learning.

Fred Paas works as a Full Professor of Educational Psychology at Erasmus University Rotterdam in The Netherlands, as Professorial Fellow at the University of Wollongong in Australia, and as Adjunct Professor at the University of New-South Wales, Sydney, Australia. His main research interest is in instructional control of cognitive load in lifelong learning of complex tasks. His six most influential publications have been cited over 4000 times. They are "Cognitive Load Theory and Instructional Design" (*Educational Psychologist*, 2003), "Cognitive Load Measurement as a Means to Advance Cognitive Load Theory" (*Educational Psychologist*, 2003), "Cognitive Architecture and Instructional Design" (*Educational Psychology Review*, 1998), "Variability of Worked Examples and Transfer of Geometrical Problem-Solving Skill" (*Journal of Educational Psychology*, 1994), "The Efficiency of Instructional Conditions" (*Human Factors*, 1993), and "Training Strategies for Attaining Transfer of Problem-Solving Skill in Statistics" (*Journal of Educational Psychology*, 1992).

Modesta Pousada (PhD in Psychology) is a Lecturer at the Open University of Catalunya since 2001 and Researcher for PSiNET. From 1991 to 2001, her work in the University of Barcelona was related to the history of psychology and the basic psychological processes of attention and memory.

Valerie Power is a Chartered Physiotherapist and is currently a PhD candidate at the University of Limerick, Ireland. Her PhD research involves the use of wireless sensor technology to investigate physical activity patterns and fall-risk factors in community-dwelling older adults, and to examine the effects which participation in a physiotherapy-led falls prevention programme has on these variables.

Wendy A. Rogers is Professor in the School of Psychology at the Georgia Institute of Technology. She received her B.A. from the University of Massachusetts – Dartmouth, and her M.S. (1989) and Ph.D. (1991) from the Georgia Institute of Technology. Her research interests include design for aging; human factors; cognitive aging; technology acceptance; aging-in-place; human-robot interaction; and skill acquisition and training. She is Co-Director of the Human Factors and Aging Laboratory (www. hfaging.org), funded in part by the National Institutes of Health (National Institute on Aging) through the Center for Research and Education on Aging and Technology Enhancement (CREATE; www.create-center.org). She is an active member of the Aware Home Research Initiative (http://awarehome.imtc. gatech.edu). Dr. Rogers is a Certified Human Factors Professional (BCPE Certificate #1539). She is a Fellow of the Human Factors and Ergonomics Society and the American Psychological Association. She is Editor of the *Journal of Experimental Psychology: Applied*.

Randall Rupper, MD, MPH, is a Geriatrician at the VA Salt Lake City Health Care Center and Assistant Professor in the Division of Geriatrics, Internal Medicine Department at the University of Utah's School of Medicine. He is the Principal Investigator of the Supporting Caregivers of Rural Veterans Electronically (SCORE) Project. Dr. Rupper's current research agenda involves improving access to care for aging rural individuals and their caregivers. His work involves the demonstration of new models of access, especially within Federal programs including Medicare and the Veterans Health Administration. Examples of outreach models include the use of Internet-based support for caregivers of dementia patients and the use of community navigators to improve chronic disease care.

Karin Slegers is a Cognitive Psychologist and works as Senior Researcher at the Centre for User Experience Research of the University of Leuven (KU Leuven) and at IBBT in Belgium. Her work is situated in the fields of human-computer interaction, user experience, and user-centred design. Her main research interests are participatory design methods, generative and creative user research methods, early user involvement in innovation processes, and involving users with disabilities. Karin has a Master's degree in Cognitive Psychology and specialized in Cognitive Ergonomics during her studies. She received a PhD from the University of Maastricht (The Netherlands) in the combined area of Cognitive Aging and Human Computer Interaction. After her PhD research, she worked as a Senior User Researcher for Vodafone Group R&D from 2006 until 2008, where she worked on generative user research in order to develop new, innovative mobile services.

David L. Strayer is a Professor in the Department of Psychology at the University of Utah. He received his Ph.D. from the University of Illinois at Urbana-Champaign. Professor Strayer's research focuses on attention and performance in natural environments. He has published several articles on driving and multitasking (available on-line at http://www.psych.utah.edu/lab/appliedcognition). In 2010, Professor Strayer received the University of Utah Distinguished Scholarly and Creative Research Award. He spends his free time hiking, canoeing, and rafting in southern Utah.

John Sweller is an Emeritus Professor of Education at the University of New South Wales. He joined the University as a Lecturer in 1974. His research is associated with cognitive load theory. The theory is a contributor to both research and debate on issues associated with human cognition, its links to evolution by natural selection, and the instructional design consequences that follow.

Martin van Boxtel is a Medical Doctor and an Associate Professor at the School for Mental Health and Neuroscience (MeHNS), Maastricht University, The Netherlands. He teaches at both the Faculty of Health, Medicine, and Life Sciences, and the Faculty of Psychology and Neuroscience of Maastricht University. After his training, he worked as Research Associate in Psychopharmacological Research. He did his PhD in Cognitive Development and Ageing, more specifically Health-Related Determinants of Cognitive Ageing. His research is for a large part embedded in the Maastricht Ageing Study (MAAS), a longitudinal study into adult cognitive development. Extensions of this research resulted in projects on interventions in cognitively normal individuals and in patients with brain damage, diabetes and cognition, biomarkers for cognitive decline, and the use of assistive technology by brain damaged patients or older persons.

Tamara van Gog is Associate Professor of Educational Psychology at the Institute of Psychology of the Erasmus University Rotterdam, The Netherlands. She holds a Master's degree in Developmental and Educational Psychology from Tilburg University (2001) and a PhD in Educational Technology from the Open University of The Netherlands (2006). Her research focuses mainly on instructional design for example-based learning and learning from dynamic visualizations (e.g., video, animations), on self-assessment and self-regulated learning, and on uncovering cognitive processes using verbal reports and eye tracking. Tamara is a member of the Young Academy of the Royal Netherlands Academy of Arts and Sciences.

Christopher Was is an Associate Professor of Educational Psychology at Kent State University. After receiving his Bachelor's degree in Psychology and Master of Science degree in Education, both awarded by Indiana University, he received his Ph.D. from the University of Utah in Educational Psychology, with an emphasis in learning, memory, and cognition. His research interests are models of working memory, implicit cognitive processes, and metacognition. More recently, his research has focused on implicit learning processes and their relationship to intelligence. His work in these areas has been published in outlets such as *Journal of Experimental Psychology: Learning Memory and Cognition, Journal of Memory and Language, Psychonomic Bulletin & Review,* and *Memory &Cognition.*

Jason M. Watson is an Assistant Professor in the Department of Psychology and an Assistant Investigator at The Brain Institute at The University of Utah. Prior to arriving at Utah, Professor Watson received a B.A. in Psychology from The University of Arkansas, and an M.A. and Ph.D. in Psychology from Washington University in St. Louis, with a specialty in experimental cognitive psychology. Professor Watson also received post-doctoral training at Washington University, where he used functional magnetic resonance imaging to examine neural correlates of various cognitive phenomena including language, memory, and attention. He has conducted and published research on illusions of memory, age-related changes in cognition, brain-behavior relations, individual differences in attentional control, and multitasking. Jason lives in Salt Lake City with his wife and two boys, where he enjoys jogging, an occasional family hike in the mountains, and coaching his kids' soccer teams in his spare time.

Dan Woltz is a Professor of Educational Psychology at the University of Utah. He received his PhD in Educational Psychology from Stanford University in 1986. Following his graduate work, he worked for five years conducting basic research on learning and memory at the Air Force Human Resources

(Armstrong) Laboratory. His primary areas of research are: 1) attention-driven, capacity-limited processes that underlie and constrain complex problem solving and 2) implicit memory processes that underlie various forms of automatic facilitation in learning and comprehension. His work in these areas has been published in outlets such as *Journal of Experimental Psychology: General, Journal of Experimental Psychology: Learning Memory and Cognition, Journal of Memory and Language,* and *Memory & Cognition.*

Index